A HISTORY
OF THE
CHRISTIAN CHURCH

By

LARS P. QUALBEN
St. Olaf College

Revised and Enlarged

THOMAS NELSON AND SONS   NEW YORK

1942

PREFACE TO FIRST EDITION

This volume, primarily intended as a textbook for college and seminary classes, has grown out of the author's own needs.

An attempt has been made to be fair to all parties by recording facts without distortion. The book should prove acceptable to all denominations. It gives a synoptic view in order that the reader may understand how the Church has been a chief factor in the development of civilization as we know it.

Four main divisions of Church history have been made clear, (1) the organic relation between Christianity and the Old Testament religion, (2) the formative period of the Early Church, (3) the underlying principles of the Reformation and the Counter Reformation, and (4) the development of American Christianity.

The author expresses his appreciation to President L. W. Boe of St. Olaf College, to Dr. Carl August Mellby of St. Olaf College, to Dr. O. M. Norlie of Luther College, and to Dr. George T. Fritschel of Wartburg Theological Seminary for valuable suggestions and criticism.

August 1, 1933. Lars P. Qualben

PREFACE TO SECOND EDITION

Critics, universities, theological seminaries, colleges and mission schools, received the text of the first edition cordially. The second edition should prove more useful because the section on the Middle Ages has been lengthened, and three chapters have been added, dealing with Churches in Canada, Christian Missions, and Church Unity respectively.

No apology is needed for the large space given to the history of Christianity in North America. The American student should know that portion of the Christian world of which he is a part, and have an intelligent understanding of what the various church bodies stand for, and what role they play in national and world affairs. The story of these religious bodies has been condensed to a relatively small compass.

Teachers of elementary courses, or of one semester courses, need not be frightened by the bulk of textual material. The text is uniformly divided into lesson units, and the teacher should find it comparatively easy to select those units which are particularly suited to the purpose of the course.

August 20, 1936. Lars P. Qualben

PREFACE TO FOURTH EDITION

In this edition only a few minor changes have been made, including bringing up-to-date the record of the union of American Methodism.

From the second edition of this book, the first twenty chapters have been translated into Chinese, for use in Chinese schools. Upon request from the translators, the author has condensed the remaining chapters of the book into a proportionate scope for Oriental use. Furthermore, a new section on *The Church in the Orient* is being prepared for this Chinese edition. The new section will include chapters on China, Japan, Chorea, Manchukuo, Mongolia, Tibet, India, Africa and Oceania.

This section will not appear in the American edition. If there should be a general demand, these chapters may be printed in a separate or companion volume.

However, the time may be ripe for a slight departure from the traditional treatment of church history. Ordinarily, it has traced the course of Christianity from Palestine through Asia into Southern and Western Europe, with a detour to Russia and Scandinavia, and then over to America. From a few lofty mountain peaks along this traditional route, the student has been able to get occasional glimpses of Africa, Australia, Oceania, India, China and Japan; but for additional information concerning Christianity in these lands, he has been obliged to turn to a history of missions.

With the rapid spread of Christianity in the 19th and 20th centuries, the development of modern means of communication, the rising tide of nationalism, and the formation of national Oriental churches, the time seems to be here when the history of Christianity in at least some of these countries should be treated in a general church history rather than in a book on missions.

January 15, 1942.   LARS P. QUALBEN

CONTENTS

THE ANCIENT PERIOD
From Jesus Christ to Gregory I (A.D. 1-590)

v

CONTENTS

THE MODERN PERIOD
From the Reformation to the Present

THE CHURCH IN THE "OLD WORLD"

THE CHURCH IN THE "NEW WORLD"

CONTENTS

DIAGRAMS AND MAPS

PART I

THE ANCIENT PERIOD

From Jesus Christ to Gregory the First (A.D. 1-590)

INTRODUCTION

1. Definition, Scope, and Divisions of Church History.— What is Church History? In the broadest sense it is the History of God's Kingdom upon earth. As such it naturally deals with the founding and the development of this Kingdom, with the fortunes of its citizens, the congregation of saints and true believers. These citizens include the Old Testament believers[1] as well as those of the New. Hence Church History proper extends from the Creation, as recorded in Genesis, down to the present.

The central event in this long record, as well as in universal history, is the coming of Jesus Christ as the Savior of the world. He is not merely the center of all history; he is the very keystone to the universe. "All things were made through him; and without him was not anything made that hath been made."[2] "In him were all things created, in the heavens and upon earth . . . all things have been created through him, and unto him; and he is before all things, and in him all things consist. And he is the head of the body, the church."[3]

With Jesus Christ the central figure, and his coming to earth the central event in history, it is natural to consider the history of mankind *before* his birth as essentially a period of preparation for his coming, and the history *after* his death, resurrection, and ascension as a record of the gradual development of the Kingdom of Heaven which he founded upon earth. The history of God's people may, therefore, be divided into a pre-Christian and a Christian world.

In the pre-Christian world God's people, the congregation of believers, are designated by two terms: "edhah" and "kahal," both meaning "assembly." In the Christian world this body of true believers is referred to as the "ecclesia" or as the Christian "church." The word ecclesia is from a Greek term meaning "those

---

[1] Matth. 8:11.   [2] John 1:3.   [3] Col. 1:16-18.

I

called together," or "those called out," or simply "assembly." The
word "church" is evidently from another Greek word "kyriakon,"
which means "the Lord's," and may refer to one of two things:
(1) the Lord's "body," or the congregation of believers; (2) the
Lord's "house," or the consecrated building. The word "Christian"
was coined in Antioch in Syria around 40 A.D.[4]

Attention is called to the organic connection between the religion
of the Old Testament and the religion of the Gospels—between the
Old and the New Testament Israel. This intimate relation is well
expressed by St. Augustine: "The New Testament is concealed in
the Old, and the Old is revealed in the New." The definition of
church history as given above rests, therefore, on a broad and solid
foundation.

But the term "church history" is now commonly used in a more
restricted sense, designating merely the *second* stage in the development of God's Kingdom upon earth. Church History in this sense
is synonymous with the History of the *Christian* Church. The pre-
Christian Israel is usually treated under some other title, such as
the History of Israel, or the History of the Old Testament, or
the History of the Jewish Church. In this narrower sense, Church
History may be defined as the History of God's Kingdom upon
earth from the time of Jesus Christ and the first Pentecost down
to the present. The subject-matter of the present text—with the
exception of the first chapter—is presented from this more limited
point of view.

The nature or character of the Christian Church is well described
in two of the Lord's parables. "The kingdom of heaven is like
unto a grain of mustard seed, which a man took, and sowed in his
field: which indeed is less than all seeds; but when it is grown, it is
greater than the herbs, and becometh a tree, so that the birds of
the heaven come and lodge in the branches thereof. Another parable
spake he unto them, the kingdom of heaven is like unto leaven,
which a woman took, and hid in three measures of meal, till it was
leavened."[5]

In these parables the Lord describes the small and slight beginnings, the gradual progress, and the marvelous increase of the
Christian Church. The history of Christianity in twenty centuries
is but a commentary on these two parables in their gradual fulfillment. The extensive territorial progress of Christianity from
land to land is described in the first parable; the intensive spiritual

power of Christianity to transform the hearts and minds of men, and to renovate society, is described in the second.

Christianity came to penetrate and to touch human life in all its phases. Hence Church History is concerned with the record of the influence of Christianity upon the religious, intellectual, social, cultural, economic, and political life of the people with whom it came in contact. It is concerned with Christian influence upon the world of art, letters, and science, as well as with the reaction of these upon the Church. The Church was to be *in* the world, but not *of* the world. Yet, at certain periods, the Church has been sadly secularized and paganized. In order to understand these influences, the student of Church History is frequently brought in contact with individuals and movements outside the Church.

From the parables of the grain of mustard seed and the leaven, it appears that the Kingdom of God upon earth is in principle and aim as comprehensive and extensive as humanity itself. Christ told his disciples to preach the Gospel unto all nations.[6] It is designed for the Jew as well as for the Gentile; for bond and free; for male and female;[7] for all classes and for all peoples until the end of time. But the aim of God's Kingdom on earth—to make disciples of all nations—is not yet fully realized. A large part of mankind has been, and is still, alienated from God.[8] Hence the Kingdom of God on earth is not identical with humanity, but includes the true believers only.[9] This fact naturally imposes a corresponding limitation upon scope of Church History. It is not identical with universal history; it is not even identical with the spiritual or religious history of mankind. It deals only with the life, the struggles, and the triumphs of the Christian Church.

Various aspects or branches of Church History may be distinguished, depending on whether the emphasis is upon practice, forms, thought, or opposition. Christianity as expressed in *practical life* naturally deals with the History of Home and Foreign Missions, and their subordinate activities such as charities, hospitals, and rescue missions. Special study of the *forms* of Christian life would lead to a History of Church Polity (organization and discipline), and a History of Christian Worship. Similar attention to Christian *thought* would lead to a History of Creeds and Confessions, and a History of Christian Theology or Learning. Special consideration of the *opposing forces* would lead to a History of Persecutions, or a History of Religious Liberty.

[6] Matth. 28:18.
[7] Gal. 3:28.
[8] Consult diagram on page 8.
[9] Matth. 25:31-46.

It is convenient to divide the History of the Christian Church into larger divisions or periods,[10] because these serve as landmarks along the route the student is to travel. The Ancient Period extends from the time of Jesus Christ to the age of Gregory the Great (590); the Medieval Period extends to the time of Martin Luther (1517); the Modern Period, taking its beginning with the Lutheran Reformation (1517), extends to the present.

During the Ancient Period the Christian Church was founded, and its influence was extended to all parts of the civilized world. Graeco-Roman civilization flourished until it perished in the Deluge of Barbarism caused by invading Barbaric tribes. These tribes overthrew the western Roman Empire in 476 A.D., which date terminates the ancient period in secular history. But in church

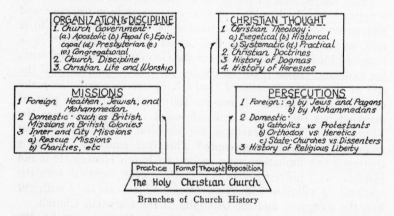

Branches of Church History

history the great divide between the ancient and medieval periods is the accession of Gregory the Great to the papal chair in 590 A.D. Gregory the Great stood on the confines between the old and the new order of things. He was the last Roman bishop and the first medieval pope.

The Medieval Period is so-called because of its chronological position between ancient and modern times. It was a transition period between the old Graeco-Roman and the new Teutonic-Latin civilization destined to control the future of the western world. The early part of the medieval period is frequently referred to as the Dark Ages because of the destruction, ignorance, lawlessness, and violence brought on by the Barbarian invasions. But the mingling of Christian, Graeco-Roman, and Teutonic elements

[10] See diagram on page 137.

gradually produced a new civilization which rose slowly on the ruins of the old. It took centuries for this new Teutonic-Latin civilization to arrive at the age of its maturity. The Latin spirit attained to its majority during the Renaissance, while the Teutonic spirit, conscious of its maturity, emancipated itself in the Reformation.

Graeco-Roman——————→Roman-Teutonic——————→Western
(Ancient)   (Medieval)   (Modern)

Just at the time this western civilization attained to its majority, the New World was re-discovered. Columbus came to America twenty-five years before Luther nailed his theses to the church door at Wittenberg. It is interesting to note that immigration of foreign peoples into the United States of America since 1840, was much more rapid than the movement of the Teutonic tribes into the old Roman Empire. It seems natural, therefore, to divide modern church history into two general sections: first, the Church in the Old World; second, the Church in the New World.

2. The Value of a Study of Church History.—

1. Church History brings the student in touch with his Spiritual ancestry. A patriotic citizen should know the history of his country, because such knowledge makes for better citizenship; a corresponding knowledge of Church History makes for better and more intelligent church membership.

2. A knowledge of church backgrounds broadens the perspective, and gives a more correct evaluation of Jesus Christ. He is the central figure in both universal and church history. In the pre-Christian systems of religion, philosophy, and government, mankind was prepared—positively and negatively—for his coming. The full significance of Christ for the Christian world is revealed, not merely in the New Testament, but also in the twenty centuries of Christian history. Church history helps to portray the fullness of the stature of Christ.

3. It promotes highmindedness and toleration. It reveals the comprehensiveness of the Kingdom of God upon earth. It leads to a study of Christianity in all its phases. The study of the great religious controversies of the past should cultivate proper respect for the opinions and convictions of others. A general and widely diffused knowledge of the Church is also a most powerful factor in eliminating disconnected, isolated group movements.

4. A knowledge of the Church of the past serves as a basis for understanding the present. History does not necessarily repeat itself; yet, the past has many parallels to the present. Adequate knowledge is the best preventive for the repetition of the mistakes of the past; it greatly helps in the solution of problems of the present.

5. It has a stabilizing influence. Christianity has a stabilizing influence upon society. But we live in an age of scepticism. The very foundations of Christianity are challenged and shaken. The older order of things must, as it seems, give room to new customs, modes, and ideas. Are these new things simply old errors exploded long ago, or are we witnessing the birthpangs of a new order? Shall we display the red signal at every attempt to change things? Will these changes lead to chaos and defeat, or to ultimate victory

for the Church? The records of the Church will shed much light on these problems, and Church History will furnish one of the strongest proofs of the continuous presence of the Lord with his people.

6. Many think it strange that the Christian Church is broken up into so many sects and denominations. Why the many doctrinal systems and variegated forms of organization, life, and worship? Church History will answer the *why*. It will reveal the larger unity which exists between these groups.

7. It has a special value of such study for church leaders. Church History is a veritable storehouse of information on successful religious leadership. Christian leaders cannot preserve the historic continuity of their groups without a knowledge of the past. Furthermore, this history presents a wealth of material that may be used in sermons and addresses.

8. Finally, it has intellectual, cultural, and stimulating values. The constant search for the relation between cause and effect develops the intellect. Furthermore, the Christian Church has always succeeded in establishing itself in the great centers of culture and civilization. Christianity and true culture go hand in hand. The influence of Christianity upon society has produced some of the choicest fruits of modern culture. Knowledge of Church History leads to a better appreciation of this culture. Lastly, the study of the noble lives and the great ideals of apostles, evangelists, martyrs, reformers, and other saints of God, is pregnant with inspiration and vitalizing enthusiasm.

1. REVIEW QUESTIONS

1. Is there any difference between Church History and a History of the Christian Church? Why?
2. What place has Jesus Christ in history? Why?
3. Why should the Old Testament believers be included in God's Kingdom upon earth?
4. Why do we not call the Old Testament believers Christians?
5. What is the twofold meaning of the word *church*?
6. What did the Lord say about the nature of the Church?
7. Is the Kingdom of God on earth identical with all of mankind?
8. How is Church History related to universal history, and to the religious history of mankind? Why?
9. Name the various branches of Church History.
10. Why is the history of the Church divided into larger and smaller divisions?
11. Discuss the values of a study of Church History.

TOPICS FOR SPECIAL STUDY

1. Discuss Luther's view of the Church. Consult his Catechisms and the Book of Concord. Is his view different from that of Roman Catholicism? Does he differ from the Reformed and the Anglican views?
2. Discuss the secular meaning of the Greek *ecclesia* and the Latin *curia*.
3. Compare the Graeco-Roman, the Latin-Teutonic, and the Modern civilizations.

CHAPTER I

THE WORLD INTO WHICH CHRISTIANITY CAME

I. **"The Fullness of Time."**—Attention has been called to the unique position of Jesus Christ in history. John the Baptist, whom God sent to prepare the *immediate* way for his coming, said in his message to the people: "The time is fulfilled, and the kingdom of God is at hand."[1] The apostle Paul, whom God used more than any other individual to *extend* this kingdom unto the nations, wrote these remarkable words: "When the fullness of time came, God sent forth his Son, born of a woman."[2] God did not send his Son until the world had been prepared for his coming. The essential part of this preparation was to disclose to the nations the world's need of a redemption and a Redeemer. That the people in general had become fairly conscious of this need is commonly admitted. There has perhaps never been a period in all history when mankind was more concerned with the problem of redemption than from 300 B.C. to 300 A.D.

Preparation for the redemption of mankind begins with the first human pair—after the fall. The first divine promise of a Redeemer is given in Gen. 3:15. But of the entire Old Testament, only the first eleven chapters are primarily concerned with the early history of the world, or of mankind in general. The remainder of the Old Testament is mainly a record of the founding and the development of the Theocratic People, Israel.

Abraham's obedience to God's call, with the subsequent development of Israel as God's chosen people, divided mankind into two large groups: Israel, or the Jewish world; and the pagan or non-Jewish world. Consequently, from Abraham until Christ the preparation of mankind for the redemption had a twofold aspect: in Israel, man developed under the influence of a direct, divine revelation; in paganism, man developed his native ability *apart* from the influence of a direct, divine revelation. For Israel it was essentially "an approach of God to Man;" for paganism it was "an approach of man to God." "In Judaism, the true religion is prepared for man; in heathenism, man is prepared for true religion."

[1] Mark 1:15.   [2] Gal. 4:4.

7

How these two groups, Israel and the non-Jewish world, united in Jesus Christ through his Gospel is disclosed in the record of the Christian Church, from Peter's vision and the subsequent visit to Cornelius,[3] down to our own time.

The nations most vitally concerned in the preparation for the coming of Christ were all represented by the superscription on the cross of Christ. This writing was in Hebrew, Latin, and Greek.[4] The Hebrews, the Greeks, and the Romans constituted the three great cornerstones of western civilization. It was in the Graeco-Roman world that Christianity first made its appearance.[5]

II. External Preparations in the Graeco-Roman World.— The birth of Christianity and the birth of the Roman Empire (31 B.C.) were not far apart in time. The Roman Empire was an important agency in paving the way for Christianity. Some

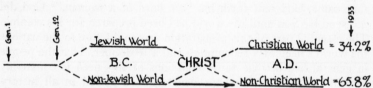

How the Jewish and the Pagan People Met and Separated in Christ

have even conceived it as the secular counterpart to the Christian Church. Geographically it extended from the Euphrates to the Atlantic, from the Danube, the Rhine, and the firths of Scotland to the African deserts. This vast territory was naturally divided into two general divisions: the Orient, or the East; and the Occident, or the West. The former included Egypt, Arabia, and Roman territory to the east of the Adriatic Sea. The latter included Roman territory to the west of Asia.

Unsuccessful attempts had previously been made in the ancient world to unite mankind in a political form, among them the empires of ancient Egypt, Babylonia, Assyria, Chaldea, Persia, and Macedonia. Each marked a necessary stage in the gradual advancement of civilization, in the preparation for Christianity. The universal Kingdom of God could not succeed properly in a world made up of a chaos of small, isolated, and warring states. Mankind needed to be brought together in peaceful intercourse. Each nation must cease to be strictly separated, and merely live and labor for itself. There had to be a certain unity of mankind in the secular sphere as a preparation for things spiritual. If the Kingdom of

[3] Acts, Chap. 10.   [4] John 19:20.   [5] Consult map on page 9.

Heaven be like a leaven, and humanity like a heap of meal,[6] that heap of meal had to be shaken together before it could take up the leaven. This shaking together was accomplished by the Roman Empire.

Ancient Egypt, Babylonia, Assyria, Chaldea, and Persia were despotisms. Under each, nations and tribes were welded together merely for tributary purposes. There was no approach to an organic union. Tributary tribes and nations were never assimilated in a uniform culture and civilization; the individual counted for little or nothing.

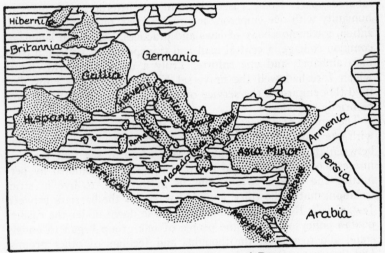

THE ROMAN EMPIRE, 100 A.D.

In the Macedonian Empire conditions were somewhat different. The Greeks did at least attribute a moral value to the individual. Through the conquests of Alexander the Great the sympathies of men, hitherto so narrow and local, were widened; the distinction between Greek and Barbarian was gradually obliterated. Greek civilization, with its matchless language, literature, art, philosophy, and science, spread over Egypt and Western Asia. The civilized world was given a universal language. The rediscovery of the sea route from India to Europe greatly stimulated trade and commerce. Several famous universities and libraries were founded.

Yet, the Macedonian Empire left little of political importance.

[6] Matth. 13:33.

This vast empire fell to pieces, and perished with its founder. Politically Macedonia could not hold what she had won. It was left for Rome to unite civilization into a political whole. But Macedonia had made possible the intellectual world conquest by the Greeks, a very important factor in preparation of mankind for Christianity.

In the course of five hundred years (31 B.C.-476 A.D.), the Roman Empire united with itself all the civilized nations of its time—an unique feature of this empire. The intellectual world conquest by the Greeks reached its culmination under the protection of Rome. Hitherto the nations of the world had lived and labored apart. Rome fused them into a heterogeneous mass of humanity with one emperor, one government, one military organization, a common body of laws and practices, a common language, common coinage, a central mail and transportation system, a common alphabet, and one culture. Truly a universal world empire which foreshadowed the universal Kingdom of God. How God used this empire in the service of his Kingdom on earth will now be briefly considered.

The union of tribes and peoples into one visible government, with one visible head, the emperor, revealed the desirable relation between the one and the many. Men came to see that the best interests of mankind could not be successfully promoted by permitting the nations to continue, as in the past, to live in strict isolation, mutual hostility, and civil wars. As the barriers between Jew, Greek, Roman, and Barbarian broke down under the cosmopolitan policy of Rome, the people of one group began to understand and to respect the thoughts and feelings of other groups. Did they not, after all, have many interests in common? One of the great object lessons was that above the nations and the peoples there is a higher unity, visibly demonstrated in a universal empire, with a universal emperor. From this concrete situation the people could easily turn to the abstract; and from the secular they could turn to the religious. The nations united in the Roman Empire could not help becoming conscious of the fact that above their own national gods, there must be a higher spiritual unity, a universal God.

As these external conditions promoted the idea of a supreme, universal God, so they also promoted the idea of a higher unity of mankind. The early Roman government formed the policy of tolerance, patience, conciliation, and assimilation. Rome treated her subjects as friends, not as conquered peoples. Subjects saw that their interests were identical with those of the Government. This was partly done by bestowing Roman citizenship upon the provincials and by permitting them to take part in the local government according to their own traditions, through their own governors and officials. Caesar Augustus initiated the policy of bestowing Roman citizenship upon a limited number of provincials. Succeeding emperors extended it until it included, in 212 A.D., all free-born inhabitants in all the Roman provinces. This ideal— a universal Roman citizenship for all free-born subjects—paved the way for a true appreciation of Christianity. In the Gospel of Jesus Christ there is no distinction of persons before God.[7] There is neither Jew nor Greek, neither bond nor free, but all are one in Christ.[8]

There was also the unifying influence of Roman jurisprudence. The Roman law was for the Roman citizen alone, and wherever there were citizens, this law was operative. As Roman citizenship gradually extended to all free-born subjects in the Empire, the sphere of Roman law correspondingly widened. A Roman citizen in Africa, or in the far East, or in the far North, received the same protection and justice as a Roman citizen in Italy. This common law for all citizens developed the idea of the universal worth of the individual; it naturally promoted a just appreciation of true Christian democracy.

Permitting a conquered people to take part in local government according to its own traditions and through its own officials fostered the ability to form independent organizations without weakening the world empire. This was not without significance for the Christian Church. There is nearly always, in any nation, a close relation between the political form of government and the form of church organization. The Roman Empire was no exception to this rule. Christian churches, each with an independent organization and with local officers, were established throughout the Empire. These local congregations strengthened the Church as a whole by recognizing their essential unity in Christ Jesus.[9]

Peace prevailed during the first Christian century. The many bloody conquests and the terrible civil wars had temporarily come to an end, offering marvelous opportunities for the spread of the Gospel of the Prince of Peace. Otherwise the extensive missionary work of Paul and other apostles and evangelists could never have been so successful.

[7] Rom. 2:11; James 2:1; 1 Peter 1:17.   [8] Gal. 3:28.   [9] Col. 1:18.

At the time of Christ Greek was the universal cultural language. The Empire was, of course, bilingual. Latin was the official language of the Roman courts and of the army, as well as the language generally used in the Roman dominions west of the Adriatic and in Africa. But Greek was not only the general language of the Roman provinces in the East; it was also the language of commerce and the vehicle of polite intercourse throughout the Empire. Greek was used and understood almost everywhere. For this reason practically all the New Testament Books were originally written in Greek. The Gospel of "peace and good will toward men" was to use as its first written medium of expression the most perfect instrument for the embodiment and conveyance of thought the world has ever known.

The Roman army was also a preparatory agency for Christianity. It was an important agent in disseminating Graeco-Roman culture to the more remote Roman provinces. The military stations in the distant regions recruited themselves to a large extent from the provinces. Furthermore, Rome never kept auxiliary troops in their native districts. Thus separated from their native soil, surrounded by strong Romanizing influences in the military stations, the stay of the soldiers was like attending a school of civilization. This civilizing process was surprisingly rapid. The army helped to shake the heap of meal[10] together into a more uniform body.

Certain cities became strategic centers for trade and commerce, culture and religion. Paul and other early missionaries made good use of these flourishing centers of humanity. Paul particularly established and developed Christian congregations in large cities. From these centers, Christianity spread easily to the surrounding territory.

A splendid highway system and well arranged sea routes afforded remarkable facilities for intercourse between the central and the more remote districts. In the forum at Rome, Caesar Augustus had erected a golden milestone. From there went out five main highways which with their many branches connected Rome with all parts of the Empire. Along these roads were stations where the traveller could secure lodging and change horses. Milestones along the roads informed the traveler of his progress, while maps indicated the distance from place to place. These highways were of great service, not only to the Government and to private enterprise, but also to the spread of the Gospel.

[10] Matth. 13:33.

Caesar Augustus established a postal system which provided transportation by land for government agents and officials, and also for official commodities. This system was soon copied by private citizens who provided similar means of travel for the public. The comparative ease, swiftness, and safety of travel gave a strong impetus to commercial intercourse and to travel in general, promoting a cosmopolitan atmosphere hitherto unknown. Nations came closer together. Sympathies and interests were broadened. The provincials became absorbed in the Roman race. Dress, manners, political and legal institutions, language, and religion became more and more uniform—a unity in diversity. The great mass of humanity was shaken together as a heap of meal,[11] in order that the leavening process of Christianity might be the more successful.

Of less general importance was the educational system. The youth had opportunity to attend the Ludus or Primary School from the age of 6 or 7 to 12; the School of the Grammaticus, or Secondary School from 12 to 16; the School of the Rhetor, or College from 16 to 18 or 19; and the University from 18 or 19 to 21 or 25. But the State did not require education of any one, nor was there any governmental supervision over these schools and their teachers. Practically every provincial town had its own Grammar School, but these schools reached only a small select group.

The lively commercial intercourse between various parts of the Empire brought enormous riches to the larger cities, while conditions were reversed in the rural districts. This situation was aggravated by an unfair system of taxation. The sturdy, self-supporting, and self-respecting farmer with a small farm faced an increasingly difficult situation. Taxes were heavy and prices were poor. Grain from Spain and Africa could be bought cheaper than he could raise it on his own soil. The reduced income was generally too small to pay his taxes and support his family. Many were forced to leave their farms, and the land was bought by rich land owners and used for cattle and sheep ranches. The farmers usually went to the cities to seek an honest living there, but what could they do? Slaves were used for almost every type of service. So many of these former country folks became soldiers, while not a few joined the rabble of the city.

A consequence of this uneven distribution of wealth was a general desire among the common people to seek protection against

[11] cf. Matth. 13:33.

the social and economic pressure in some fraternal order, secret society, or secret cult. These societies had their classical age during the three centuries immediately before and after Christ. All of these societies had a specific religious purpose, even those which were predominantly secular; practically all of them had the subordinate purpose of providing a burial place for and a decent burial of deceased members. These fraternities or secret orders supplied to their members a religion which was not the religion of the Christian Church, a rather disturbing element for the early Christians.

Outwardly, the Roman Empire enjoyed a Golden Age up to around 100 A.D., but this outward splendor failed to produce a corresponding strength and happiness in morals and religion.

2. REVIEW QUESTIONS

1. What is indicated by the expression "fullness of time"?
2. Why the Jewish and the non-Jewish world before Christ?
3. How did the Roman Empire differ from previous empires and kingdoms?
4. Why did the nations come to see that there must be a higher spiritual unity, a universal God?
5. How did the Roman Empire promote the Christian ideal of the universal worth of the individual?
6. Discuss the benefits to Christianity of universal peace, a universal language, the civilizing influence of the army, the flourishing Roman cities, the splendid highway and postal system, and the school system in the Roman Empire.
7. What were the general economic conditions within the Empire at the time of Christ?
8. Why did secret societies flourish during this period, and how did they affect the Christian Church?

TOPICS FOR SPECIAL STUDY

1. Superimpose the map of the Roman Empire on the map of the United States of America so as to show the relative size. What is your conclusion?
2. Study the history of the great Chinese Wall. Would such walls around the various peoples of the Graeco-Roman world have been conducive to the spread of the Gospel? Explain.

III. Internal Preparations through Religion and Philosophy.—The more significant preparations of mankind for "the fullness of time" were transformations in the world of thought and emotion. Attention is called to specific developments in the religion and in the philosophy of the Greeks, the Romans, and the Jews, because these groups constituted the cornerstone of the civilization of that period.

Although the Greeks, the Romans, and the Jews differed in their outlook on life, they also had certain things in common. The Mosaic Law was the most highly treasured common possession of the Jews. This Law prepared them rather *negatively* for the coming of the Messiah because it revealed to them that by the works of the Law, no man is justified in God's sight.[12] The Law became a tutor to bring Israel to Christ.[13] In the non-Jewish world the most treasured common possession was Greek philosophy. It was this very philosophy which dealt the death blow to pagan religions, and gradually emptied the Olympic heaven of its divinities. The religious void thus created made the pagan mind conscious of its own impotence for satisfying the religious cravings of the soul. In this sense, pagan philosophy became a tutor which prepared the pagan for Christ.

Again, the Jews enjoyed a more positive and subjective preparation in the Prophets. The revelation of God to man was received, preserved, and transmitted as "the Law and the Prophets." In the non-Jewish world, there was a corresponding positive, subjective preparation. Consider the imaginative, subjective, artistic, idealistic, philosophic, literary, and scientific contributions of the Greeks; and the concrete, practical, constructive contributions of the Romans in the form of law, order, government, dissemination of culture, and the constructive, practical undertakings, such as engineering projects, commercial processes, and the like.

a. *The Greeks*. The mythological divinities of the early Greeks were the spontaneous creations of the Greeks themselves. Their gods were the forces of nature personified and deified. These deities were like human beings—male and female—with greatly magnified powers, vices, and virtues. They were jealous of their superiority, and envied rather than loved man. Hence they denied man perfect happiness. Being enslaved by the same earthly passions as man, these Greek gods of the Olympic heaven could not raise their worshippers above the level of their own morality. There was no devil in the early religious system of the Greeks. Evil suggestions and evil doings were generally credited to the gods. And the Greeks had no true conception of sin. Their moral consciousness was identical with the sense of the beautiful. Hence beauty—and not holiness—was their supreme ideal. Sin was practically identified with ignorance.

There were three distinct stages in the development of Greek

[12] Rom. 3:20.   [13] Gal. 3:24.

philosophy and religion. 1. With the rise of rational inquiry and historical study (after 500 B.C.), philosophy emancipated itself from the traditional theology and morality. Man became the measure of all things. 2. With the fall of Athens (404 B.C.), and also during the Macedonian supremacy, philosophy and religion freed themselves from political or state interests. 3. In time philosophy and religion were also divorced from scientific interests, and from universal philosophy. A flood of narrow individualism resulted. Perhaps a very brief discussion of the three stages may be in order.

(1) The Sophists (fifth and fourth centuries B.C.) ushered in a new intellectualism. "Man is the measure of all things" was their dictum. Traditional authority was shaken off; and human reason, conscience, and experience became the main component parts of the new religious and philosophic fabric. This new intellectualism had a marked influence upon all phases of Greek life. Particularly noticeable was the sharp conflict between reason and religious authority. Philosophy emancipated itself from theology. Historical study placed the mythological gods in a delicate position. One group of thinkers relegated them to the realm of fable; others tried to identify these deities with natural forces or elements; while others claimed that they were symbols of abstract ethical precepts. Religion lost its grip on educated Greeks. Scepticism and infidelity prevailed among the higher classes, and a corresponding change in their standard of morals followed.

(2) With the loss of political independence, after the Peloponnesian War (431-404 B.C.), a great change was wrought in the general Greek outlook on life. Hitherto the individual had centered in the one comprehensive institution, the city state. The religion was a state religion, where the gods were so incorporated with the Greek city states that they were held accountable for the welfare of the commonwealth. When Athens fell (404 B.C.), and when Greece lost her political independence to Philip of Macedon (338 B.C.), Greek religion lapsed into chaos. The people lost faith in the gods because they failed to protect them against the enemy. Philosophically, the Greeks had been accustomed to thinking of the city state as the highest good to man, but this ideal was smashed when the city states were absorbed into new, vast political units. The Greek nation was obliged to follow one of two courses: either to recognize the new and broader relations to humanity, or no longer consider the state as comprehending all possible good to man, and fall back upon the resources of the individual. The typical Athenian followed the latter course. Religion and philosophy became divorced from political or state interests.

(3) Finally Greek religion and philosophy were almost entirely divorced from scientific interests, as well as from the absolute, immutable, universal laws, as set forth by men like Socrates, Plato, and Aristotle. All problems connected with philosophy and religion were approached from the individualistic point of view. People turned against the traditional laws and authority. A flood of narrow individualism was the inevitable result. Every man was a law unto himself. Individual taste was considered the sole and final judge. There were as many systems of morals as there were individuals, and this again meant that there was no system at all. The general result was a widespread moral laxity, and a general indifference toward the earlier sanctity and obligation of an oath.

Such were the general religious, philosophic, and moral conditions among the Greeks when they came into vital and intimate contact with the Romans. Many prominent Roman leaders set their faces like flint against these Greek ideas, customs, and innovations. Cato the Elder (232-147 B.C.) constantly told the Romans that Greek education and Greek literature and philosophy would bring their country to ruin.

This is briefly the general trend of development in Greek life up to the Roman period. Time and space do not permit any discussion of such representative philosophers as Pythagoras, Socrates, Plato, Aristotle, Zeno, and Epicurus. Socrates has been called "the John the Baptist of the ancient world." And Plato's lofty, spiritual philosophy has been likened unto a bridge over which many have passed from paganism toward the Kingdom of God. Aristotle has been called the greatest systematizer the world has ever known. During the first 1400 years of our Christian era no single book save the Bible exerted such influence upon the civilized world as his "Organon." His influence was particularly felt in the formulation of the Christian dogma, and in Medieval scholasticism.

b. *The Romans.* The early Romans, like the early Greeks, were dominated by the same institution, the city state, upon which their civilization was founded. From the Greeks they borrowed the idea of a confederate government, and developed it into a universal empire. They were possessed by a firm belief that they were called upon to govern the world. The genius of the Romans expressed itself along concrete, external, practical, and constructive lines. They were deficient in imaginative and esthetic power, as compared with the Greeks, but they possessed a sobriety, a dignity, and a moral sense that the Greeks lacked. The Romans were austere, practical, and utilitarian. It has been said that "the Greeks never lost their youth; the Romans were always men." The Greeks furnished certain ideals of life. The Romans furnished the institutions that made the realization of these ideals possible.

The Roman religion was abstract, practical, formal, and legalistic. The early Roman gods were mysterious, abstract, impersonal beings, without human power or feelings. They lacked the vividness of the Greek deities. The Romans had no Olympus, and though the gods were of different sexes, they were commonly childless. The gods promised no future rewards or punishments or hopes of a future life. They constituted a crowd of oppressive beings that constantly interfered with human affairs, keeping a watchful eye on all things in nature, as well as in individual, social, and political life. Hence there was a constant necessity of obtaining the favors of the gods as a practical means of getting on in the world. This worship took the form of elaborate and minutely prescribed religious ceremonies, and the Romans were exceedingly scrupulous in performing the prescribed worship with the greatest exactness.

In rendering this divine service, the Roman was entirely unconcerned with the state of his own soul. His religion had little or nothing to do with personal morality—although his loyalty to the State, and his careful observance of the religious ceremonies, produced a truthfulness, a sincerity, and a stalwart character that was almost entirely wanting among the Greeks. The Roman looked upon his religion as a sort of a contract between him and the gods. If he kept his part of the contract, the gods were bound to keep theirs. Religion was purely an external affair, and the religious Roman was the man who best knew the ritual and carefully observed it. Render unto the gods the worship due to them—nothing more, and nothing less. Excess in religious matters was hated by the Romans as much as lack of piety.

Everything centered in the State. Devotion to the State in terms of bravery was always one of the leading Roman ideals. "Rome must never conclude a peace save as a victor." But victory could not be obtained except by the favor of the gods. Religion was therefore closely interwoven with the affairs of the State, resulting in a religious patriotism that had no parallel anywhere else in the ancient world. The government officials—and not the priests—were the masters of the religious ceremonies. And the Pontifex Maximus, or head of the religious affairs, was also the head of the State. This religious patriotism resulted in an early deification of the Roman State and its official head. During the period of the Republic (up to 31 B.C.), the State was represented by the Capitolene Jupiter, and the "Dea Roma" was worshipped in his temples, not only in Italy, but also in the provinces. Smyrna had such a temple as early as 195 B.C. After the Roman Empire came into existence, the Emperor took the place of the Capitolene Jupiter, with emperor worship the result. Pergamum worshipped Rome and Augustus as early as 29 B.C.

Until about 250 B.C. the Roman character and religion remained substantially as they had been in preceding centuries. But as Rome expanded politically and gradually came into larger world relationships, the traditional ideals, as expressed in customs and religion, suffered marked modifications. The first inroads came from the Greeks. When Greece was conquered, many Romans became so infatuated with everything Greek that they came to look upon their own culture and religion as something old-fashioned and provincial. World history has perhaps no parallel to this thorough attempt of one people to assimilate the culture of another. The tragic part of it was that the Romans received only the shell of the old Greek culture and religion. The cultivated Romans caught the sceptical, hollow, unbelieving spirit of the Greeks. Yet they were very cautious, and did not openly acknowledge their lack of faith in the gods, because they found religion conducive to conservatism among the masses. They even hypocritically participated in the official, religious ceremonies after their own faith had long since died.

A number of other causes contributed to a rapid decline in morals and religion. Through the many conquests Rome came into a close communion with the degenerate life of Greece and the Orient. Wealth, luxuries, and slaves from the new provinces had a demoralizing influence upon the Romans. Religion and morality declined with alarming rapidity. Divorce became common. Wealth and influence ruled the State.

As the common people lost faith in their traditional gods, they naturally sought new cults to give them certitude or assurance. There were "gods many and lords many" to choose from, for it was a Roman maxim to tolerate all religions of the conquered nations. When the Romans besieged or conquered a city or a province, they invited the divinities concerned, with a solemn formula, to take up their abode in Rome. At the same time the provincials were required to recognize and to honor the Roman gods. The general result was a mingling of deities—a religious syncretism—that has no parallel. The rising Empire became a melting pot where not only the different nationalities were dissolved and fused into one great mass, but also local religions suffered a similar fate.

In the midst of this religious chaos, men began to seek for a reasonable religious unity. Could they find the relation between the one and the many? Was there a common denominator in all these bewildering religious systems? In the general search for an answer, the religious world of the Augustan Age witnessed a distinct trend toward a polytheistic monotheism.

The religious development in the Graeco-Roman world culminated—in its progressive degradation—in emperor-worship. The State was considered the Highest Good. The Emperor was the chief representative, the incarnation of the State. Amidst the social and religious chaos, Caesar Augustus appeared to the masses as the Capitolene Jupiter, as the visible representative of Zeus, as the World Reason or Soul. Why not worship the Emperor? The government officials recognized the advantages of a formal, universal State religion, and seized the first opportunity to deify Augustus. He did not, however, permit the people to worship him as divine, but he did permit the worship of the genius of the Emperor as being divine. This became the official ordinance. But the difference between the worship of the Emperor himself and the worship of his genius was too technical and too fine for the masses.

As Emperor worship rapidly extended to the provinces, the government officials made it the solemn duty of every person in the Empire to participate in this official worship. Not even the Christian people were exempted from such service. Refusal was considered an act of high treason, with the death penalty. Technically this universal State religion involved only a worship of the genius of the living Emperor, and of the dead apotheosized emperors. To the practical Romans, this worship served as a center of religious unity. The people could still worship their local deities, but all must participate in this central form of worship as an act of loyalty to the State. But what uplifting moral and spiritual values could the worship of such emperors as Claudius and Nero bring to the people? People began to wonder what kinds of gods they were asked to worship. And were the other gods any better? Scepticism and infidelity spread among the masses, and their religion became an empty ceremonial. "Having no hope and without God in the world"[14] was Paul's fitting description of the pagan world.

"The fullness of time" was drawing near for the Gentiles. The Graeco-Roman world had had sufficient time to display what the human mind can produce in its own strength, without a direct, divine revelation. Great things had been accomplished along various lines, but in matters of religion and morality the pagan world was

[14] Eph. 2:12.

becoming increasingly conscious of its inability to satisfy the religious cravings of the soul, and of its incompetency to effect a moral regeneration in a morally corrupt society. These concrete object lessons prepared the Gentile mind for the reception of Christianity.

It would be incorrect, however, to think that the world at the dawn of Christianity was infested with intellectual and religious dullness. A feverish tempo characterized practically all of Graeco-Roman life at the birth of Christianity. Seldom has the world witnessed such unrestrained luxury and voluptuousness among the higher classes as in the early days of the Roman Empire. Never before had there been such widespread passion among all classes for amusements, for the theatre, the circus, the chariot-races, and the gladiatorial sports. Never had there been so many public parades and public displays. There were many divine images, altars, and temples, many religious cults, many impressive religious ceremonies and processions, and much sincere religious longing. The gay, reckless outward life concealed sincere, earnest hearts and minds that despaired of ever being able to find what they looked for, a religion that would give them ASSURANCE. Mankind longed to discover the Kingdom that is from above. The mighty cultural movement of the Graeco-Roman world culminated in a universal longing for redemption. This longing prepared the non-Jewish world for "the fullness of time," for the coming of the Messiah.

c. *The Jews*. The position of the Jews in the ancient world was so unique that a special Section has been set aside for a discussion of their religious, moral, and political development.

3. REVIEW QUESTIONS

1. How did the Mosaic Law and Greek philosophy serve as tutors to bring the people unto Christ?
2. How would you characterize the early Greek religion?
3. How would you describe the character and the religion of the early Romans? Were they much different from the Greeks? From the Hebrews?
4. Why were the Romans dominated by an unparalleled religious patriotism?
5. What causes contributed to a rapid decline in Roman morals and religion?
6. Why did the Graeco-Roman world at the birth of Christianity witness such unparalleled religious syncretism?
7. Do modern nations have anything akin to Emperor worship? How do the Christians in modern Japan deal with this situation?
8. Why did the mighty cultural movement of the Graeco-Roman world culminate in a universal longing for redemption?
9. How would you compare Rome and the United States in their attitudes toward foreign born peoples?

TOPICS FOR SPECIAL STUDY

1. Study the relation between religion and reason. How did Rationalism affect the emotional and the intellectual life of the early Greeks? Why?
2. Describe the typical form of the early Roman worship.
3. Compare the mingling of religions in the ancient world and the religious "melting pot" of America.

IV. Developments in the Jewish World.—"Salvation is from the Jews."[15] Such was the general belief, not only among the Jews themselves, but also among many pagans. This salvation, as expressed in the Christian Gospel, constitutes one of the cornerstones of modern Western civilization, others being Roman law, Greek philosophy, and certain Teutonic elements.[16]

The Jews had been God's chosen people since the time of Abraham.[17] They had enjoyed unusual privileges through a direct, divine guidance and revelation. God had spoken to them through the Law and the Prophets. He had given them a special country and special institutions and ordinances so that they, as a nation, could develop according to the divine plan. How did Israel respond to these privileges?

The Old Testament shows that Israel fell away from God. General apostasy brought on a terrible punishment. The Ten Tribes were taken into Assyrian captivity in 722 B.C. The Two Tribes were taken into Babylonian captivity in 586 B.C., and of these only a small remnant, 50,000-60,000, returned in 536 B.C. under the leadership of Zerubbabel. The Temple in Jerusalem was rebuilt 520-516 B.C. During the years 456-433 B.C. Ezra and Nehemiah were permitted to come to Palestine to build up the returned Jewish remnant. Nehemiah strengthened the nation by building the walls of Jerusalem and by fortifying the city. Ezra built up the nation from within by establishing a religious and social system (theocracy) that held the nation together for centuries.

Alexander the Great (336-323 B.C.) brought Palestine under Hellenistic sway. From 323-203 B.C. Palestine was controlled by the Ptolemies of Egypt. Then the Egyptians gave way to Syrian control, under Antiochus III. His successor, Antiochus (IV) Epiphanes (175-164 B.C.), corrupted the Jewish priesthood, introduced heathen rites, and profaned the Jewish Temple (170-168 B.C.). This led to the Maccabean Revolt (167-141 B.C.). Simon Maccabeus finally established an independent Jewish government

---

[15] John 4:22.
[16] Teutonic elements such as Teutonic life and vigor, respect for woman, sense of honor, and love of liberty.
[17] Genesis Chap. 12.

which lasted from 141-63 B.C. In 63 B.C., Pompey the Great made Syria a Roman province, with Palestine an integral part.

Herod the Great was governor of Galilee and King of Judea from 37 to 4 B.C. Jesus Christ was born during the last few months of his reign.[18] After the death of Herod his kingdom was divided among his three sons. Archelaus (4 B.C.-6 A.D.) received Judea, Idumea, and Samaria. Herod Antipas (4 B.C.-37 A.D.) received Galilee and Perea. It was this Herod who beheaded John the Baptist. Philip (4 B.C.-34 A.D.) got possession of the trans-Jordan territory.[19] Archelaus was exiled by Caesar August (6 A.D.), and his territory became a procuratorial province, subject to the census. Pontius Pilate, who passed sentence upon Jesus Christ, was the fifth procurator of Judea, Idumea, and Samaria. He held office 26-36 A.D.

The Jewish people passed through a crucial development during the 500 years before Christ. Shortly after the destruction of Jerusalem in 586 B.C., the Jews were settled in three great centers of the ancient world, namely in Egypt, Babylonia, and Palestine. The Jewish colonists in Egypt settled principally in the commercial centers, in the cities. As trade was the chief occupation open to them, the former shepherds and farmers of Judea soon became traders and merchants. They kept their national integrity, however, and although their business interests were widely scattered, they soon organized into great mercantile companies with their agents and branch houses. In time, the Jewish colonists of Egypt and Babylonia gained control over a considerable part of the trade of the world.

The Jewish exiles to Babylon were settled by Nebuchadnezzar in a colony in the northern part of the plain between the Tigris and the Euphrates rivers. The active commercial life of Babylonia soon made its influence felt among them. Like their brethren in Egypt, they soon left farm and shepherd life, and turned to trade and commerce. The latent Semitic genius for trade had been aroused and brought riches to its possessors. Most of the Jewish exiles became so attached to their new homes in Babylonia that they did not care to return to Palestine although opportunities were repeatedly offered. It was during the Babylonian and the Greek periods that the Jews in the Dispersion began to lay the foundation for the "Golden Internationalism," that is, Jewish control of the world's money.

In Judea, the majority of shepherds and peasants were allowed

---

[18] Matthew Chap. 2.   [19] Luke 3:1.

to remain in the land when Jerusalem was destroyed in 586 B.C. Practically all Jewish captives to Babylonia were taken from the city of Jerusalem and from the other cities of Judea. The remaining Jews, almost entirely confined to the highlands of Judea, with the remnant that returned from Babylonia, formed the nucleus of the Jewish population in Judea at the time of Christ.

When Alexander the Great (336-323 B.C.) founded the city of Alexandria, the Jews were there, and soon occupied a position in this leading metropolis similar to that of the Jews in New York

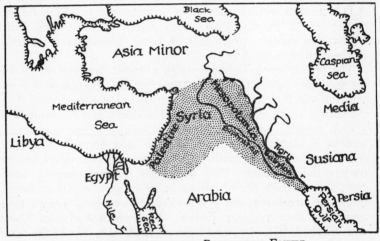

THE TERRITORY OF THE BABYLONIAN EMPIRE
(Indicated by the dotted or shaded region)

City or in London at the present time. Alexander granted the Jews and the Macedonians equal and exceptional favors. Probably one-eighth of the population of Egypt, or 7,800,000, was Jewish. The historian, Strabo, (63? B.C.-24? A.D.) states that in his time the Jews were found in every city and every place in the habitable world. There was a large Jewish Dispersion in the East and a large Jewish Dispersion in the West. Only a small minority lived within Palestine proper. Compare the account, in Acts 2:9-11, of the non-Palestinian Jews present in Jerusalem on the first Pentecost. Israel had become a world nation, with Jerusalem as its great religious center.

A natural consequence of this change from a special to a world nation resulted in a pressing demand for a Greek translation of the Old Testament. The Jews of the Western Dispersion wanted their sacred Scriptures in Greek. This translation, known as the Septuagint, may have been completed as early as the reign of Ptolemy III (247-221 B.C.). Others place it later. This Greek Old Testament was important in bringing the religion of the Old Testament to the Grecian world. Another means was the Jewish synagogue.[20]

As traders and merchants, the Jews of the Dispersion came into lively and continuous contact with all people of the then civilized world. This contact was not without its marked influence upon the Jews. Those of the Western Dispersion were attracted by certain features of Greek culture and Egyptian worship. Those of the Eastern Dispersion were influenced by Chaldean astrology, fatalism, and magic, by Persian dualism, and by Oriental mysticism. Many evidences indicate that a group of Jews began to look upon these elements as a supplementary revelation. Among such evidences may be noted: (1) the Apocrypha and Pseudepigrapha of the Old Testament, (2) the Jewish-Hellenistic literature of this period, (3) the early Kabbalistic speculations, and (4) the formation of Jewish sects.

The inevitable result of this development was a general division of the Jewish world into two large groups, analogous to the Orthodox and the Reformed Jews of today. One group, the orthodox, tried to exclude foreign influences, building "hedges" around the Mosaic Law as high as possible. Such was the attitude of the Pharisees or "Separatists." The other group, represented by the Sadducees, tried to recognize and to assimilate what was considered good in the culture and religion of other peoples. The Sadducees were the forerunners of modern Liberal Judaism.

Three stages may be distinguished in the development of the liberal group. First, certain features of the culture, science, and religion of the surrounding peoples came to be regarded as a supplementary revelation to the Old Testament. Secondly, some of these elements, especially Greek philosophy and science, were considered as valid and authoritative as the Old Testament itself. Thirdly, some finally placed these elements above the Scriptures. An interesting parallel is found in modern times. When the modern scientific movement began to assert itself, some people condemned it altogether. Others began to look upon science as a supplementary revelation. Still others placed science on par with the authority of the Bible. Finally, science was enthroned as the chief authority of

[20] The synagogue was the place where the Jews met for local worship.

Truth. Today not a few people listen to the dictates of science rather than to the words of the Bible.[21]

How much the conservatives and the liberal groups differed in their views and beliefs, may partly be understood (1) by comparing the views of the Pharisees with those of the Sadducees, (2) by comparing the writings of Philo Judeas (20 B.C.-40 A.D.) of Alexandria with those of contemporary Palestinian rabbis, and (3) by placing the Epigrapha and Pseud-Epigrapha of the Old Testament[22] side by side with the Old Testament itself. How extremely bitter the first clash was between conservative Hebrew religion and Hellenistic culture may be understood by studying the Maccabean uprising in Palestine, 167-141 B.C.

Among the best known Jewish parties or groups in Palestine at the time of Christ, mention may be made of the Pharisees, the Sadducees, and the Essenes, representing formalism, scepticism, and mysticism respectively. Mention may also be made of the Scribes, who were the religious lawyers of the day. The Scribes as such did not constitute a religious party. They were professional people. The Essenes, who numbered about 4000 in Palestine at the time of Christ, constituted a religious order that was extremely ascetic. They were forerunners of the hermits and monks. Recent investigations have proved that the Essenic doctrines were essentially gnostic.

The following diagram may prove helpful in tracing the origin and the history of these Jewish groups.

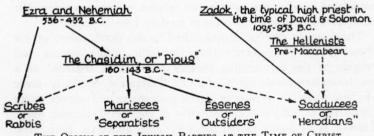

THE ORIGIN OF THE JEWISH PARTIES AT THE TIME OF CHRIST

A brief comparison of the leading views of the Pharisees and the Sadducees, the two most influential parties at the time of Christ, may also be of interest.

[21] There is, however, no contradiction between science and Christianity.
[22] cf. R. H. Charles: "Apocrypha and Pseudepigrapha of the Old Testament" Vols. I-II. Oxford, Clarendon Press, 1913.

Pharisees	Sadducees
1. They constituted the nucleus of the religious and academic aristocracy.	1. They constituted the nucleus of the priestly, political, and social aristocracy.
2. They taught that the soul is immortal. Hence there is a resurrection from the dead, and a future reward and punishment.	2. They taught that there is *no* resurrection from the dead, and *no* future reward or punishment. Hence, live for this life.
3. They believed in the existence of angels and spirits, good and bad.	3. They claimed that there were no angels and no spirits.
4. They were predestinarians almost to the verge of fatalism. Yet they asserted that man has a free will and that he is morally responsible.	4. They emphasized the absolute freedom of the human will and self-determination. The divine element had no influence upon man's choice for good or evil.
5. They coordinated the Oral Law (Tradition) and the Written Law (Old Testament) as joint rules of faith and practice.	5. They maintained that the Old Testament, as the inspired record of revelation, was the only infallible rule of faith and practice.
6. They magnified traditional Judaism and made it the basis of a vast system of minute laws which were to regulate all life in Israel. Man was reduced to a legal machinery.	6. They broke down the "hedges" around the traditional Judaism, and placed Hellenistic culture side by side, if not above Traditionalism. They were rationalists.
7. They tried to gain salvation by good works, and this externalized their entire religious and moral life.	7. They tried to live for this life only, since they denied the resurrection from the dead, and this rationalized their religious and moral life.
8. They confined their activities mostly to the synagogue. They were strong religious and political leaders.	8. They confined their activities mostly to the Temple. They were the "chief priests," and from their midst, the high priest was chosen.

Perhaps a word may be added in regard to the school system of Palestine at the time of Christ. The educational system of Palestine reached its fullest development around 75 B.C.-70 A.D. A pre-Christian rabbi, Simon ben Shetach, inaugurated a new primary school system (64 B.C.) which was based, as it seems, on compulsory attendance. Another rabbi, Joshua ben Gamala, later extended this principle, it is said, to every town and village outside of Palestine where Jews were living. In this development, one may also see a preparation for the coming of the Messiah.

The general reception of the Messiah by the Jewish world reveals that the Jewish parties at the time of Christ were all about equally far away from the central truth of the Gospel that "the righteous shall live by faith."[23] They wanted to live by their own good works. They wanted a Messiah who should establish a great temporal kingdom with special privileges for the Jews. When Jesus Christ the Messiah stated and demonstrated that his kingdom was

[23] Rom. 1:17.

not of this world,[24] the Jews as a nation rejected him. "He came unto his own, and they that were his own received him not."[25] Israel as a nation had almost become a caricature of what it should have been, according to the divine plan.

But God had, in spite of this negative aspect, used the chosen people remarkably well in preparing mankind for "the fullness of time." Israel had first of all received, preserved, and transmitted God's divine revelation, as contained in the canonical Old Testament. For about two centuries before Christ this revelation was accessible to the Greek speaking world in the so-called Septuagint translation. The many Jewish communities, dispersed throughout the world had their synagogues, their Old Testament, and their regular divine worship. They were eager, enthusiastic missionaries, trying to gain proselytes as indicated in Matt. 23:15: "ye compass sea and land to make one proselyte." God used these synagogues as so many centers for spreading the idea of one, just, holy, and loving God; for preaching the Law and the Prophets; for holding forth the idea of a future life with reward and punishment, for inculcating the Old Testament doctrine of sin and the means of the forgiveness of sins; and most of all, for holding forth the divine promises of a world Redeemer.

As "the fullness of time" approached, both Jew and Gentile had come to see—as far as they were capable of seeing—that mankind was utterly incapable of saving or redeeming itself. Salvation must come from above. The Jews held forth, though with sad limitations, the divine promise of a world Redeemer. And then, "when the fullness of time came, God sent forth his Son, born of a woman."

4. REVIEW QUESTIONS

1. Why was the "salvation" to come from the Jews?
2. How did God equip the chosen people so that they could develop according to the divine plan?
3. Why the Maccabean Revolt?
4. When and why did the Jewish shepherds and farmers transform themselves into traders and merchants?
5. Of what significance for Christianity was the scattering of the Jews over the whole inhabitable world?
6. What influence did this wide contact with the rest of the world have upon the Jews themselves? Why?
7. In what important respects did the views of the Pharisees and the Sadducees differ from those of the Christian Gospel?
8. How did God, through his chosen people, prepare mankind for the coming of Christ?

[24] John 18:36.
[25] John 1:11.

CHAPTER II

THE APOSTOLIC ERA (A.D. 1-100)

I. Jesus Christ, the Founder of Christianity.—Our knowledge of the earthly life of Jesus Christ is based primarily on the four canonical Gospels: Matthew, Mark, Luke, and John; and partly on the Book of Acts, the New Testament Epistles, and Revelation. The Old Testament may also be included, because it predicts the coming of the Messiah and his mission on earth. The earthly life of Jesus Christ was a fulfillment of that which was written about him in the Law and the Prophets.[1]

What information do the Gospels furnish concerning the Founder of the Christian Church? In the Gospel according to John the veil of the infinite past is lifted, and Christ is seen in his relation to the Godhead and to the universe. "In the beginning was the Word (Logos), and the Word was with God, and the Word was God. The same was in the beginning with God. All things were made through him; and without him was not anything made that hath been made. In him was life; and the life was the light of men."[2] This is a unique description of a unique personality. The Evangelist adds that this Logos became flesh, and dwelt among us.[3]

The genealogy in Matt. 1:1-17 connects the incarnate Word with David and with Abraham. The genealogy in Luke 3:23-38 goes beyond Abraham, and connects Christ with Adam and with God. The miraculous conception and the virgin birth—"conceived by the Holy Ghost, born of the virgin Mary"[4]—are recorded by Matthew and by Luke. The Savior was born in Bethlehem in Judea, but grew up in Nazareth in Galilee.

Some confusion has prevailed as to the exact date of the birth of Jesus Christ. It is stated in Matthew 2:1 that the Savior was born in the days of Herod the Great. This king died a few days before the Jewish Passover in the year 750 A.U.C. (anno urbis conditate), i.e., after the founding of the City of Rome; and this year corresponds to the year 4 B.C. in our present calendar.

The explanation is that our present method of numbering the years "from the Incarnation of the Lord" was introduced by Dionysius the Little about 530 A.D. and came into general use

[1] Matth. 5:17.   [2] John 1:1-4.   [3] John 1:14.   [4] cf. Apostles' Creed.

29

during the reign of Charlemagne (768-814 A.D.). Dionysius placed the Nativity or birth of the Savior on December 25, 754 A.U.C.; and the Annunciation to Mary—identified with the "Incarnation" or conception—on March 25 of the same year. Yet, he did not begin his era with the date of the Incarnation, March 25, but with the first of January preceding. Hence January 1, 754 A.U.C., is the epoch of the era of Dionysius, or our Christian era, corresponding in our calendar to January 1, 1 A.D.

From this it is evident that Dionysius made a miscalculation of several years as to the birth of Christ. Edersheim[5] has calculated that Christ was born in December 749 A.U.C. corresponding to the year 5 B.C. in our calendar. The Wise Men came from the East to worship the Lord in Bethlehem in February, 750 A.U.C.[6] As they departed, Joseph was warned in a dream to take the child and the mother and flee to Egypt.[7] Shortly after, Herod the Great killed the male infants of Bethlehem.[8] "But when Herod was dead," late in March, 750 A.U.C., or 4 B.C., the Holy Family left Egypt and settled in Nazareth in Galilee.[9] It is self-evident that this earlier date for the birth of Christ does not in the least affect the validity or reliability of the New Testament. The mistake is not with the Bible, but with Dionysius the Little, evidently handicapped by inadequate chronological data when he selected 754 A.U.C. as the year of the birth of the Lord.

Because of this earlier date of the birth of Christ, the year 30 A.D. is usually selected as the date of the first Pentecost.[10] The Lord began his public ministry when he was "about thirty years of age."[11] This was the age when Jewish Levites began their public service.[12] Hence John the Baptist, the Forerunner of Christ, also very likely began to teach and to baptize at the age of thirty. The Baptist and Christ were half a year apart in age.[13]

Luke states that John the Baptist began to preach and to baptize "in the fifteenth year of the reign of Tiberius Caesar."[14] Tiberius became co-regent—"collega imperii"—with his step-father, Caesar Augustus, in 764, or possibly early in 765 A.U.C. He became the sole ruler from August 19, 767 A.U.C., corresponding to the year 14 A.D. Luke evidently reckons, as provincials would do, from the co-regency with Augustus. The "fifteenth year" would then be 779 A.U.C. Counting back thirty years, the Baptist was born around June, 749 A.U.C., and Christ in December of the same

---

[5] Edersheim: The Life and Times of Jesus the Messiah, Volume 1, Pages 187 and 212-213.
[6] cf. Matth. 2:1-12.
[7] Matth. 2:13-15.
[8] Matth. 2:16-18.
[9] Matth. 2:19-23.
[10] Acts Chap. 2.
[11] Luke 3:23.
[12] Num. 4:3.23.
[13] Luke 1:26.
[14] Luke 3:1.

year. This checks with the figures above. The Baptist should then have begun his ministry around the middle of the year 779 A.U.C. or in A.D. 26; and Christ must have started his ministry early in A.D. 27. There is an old tradition among the Basilideans, a Gnostic sect, that the Lord was baptized on the sixth or on the tenth of January. He was probably in the public ministry for three years. Hence he was crucified just before the Passover, A.D. 30, and the birthday of the Christian Church occurred on the following Pentecost.[15]

Little is told about the childhood and youth of Jesus Christ. Luke states[16] that the child grew, and waxed strong, filled with wisdom: and the grace of God was upon him. As a man the Lord developed normally in the fullest sense of the word. He developed physically, mentally, and spiritually. He grew in wisdom. He was

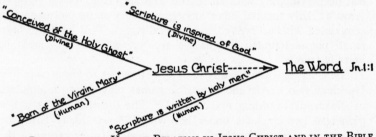

THE DIVINE AND THE HUMAN RELATION IN JESUS CHRIST AND IN THE BIBLE

in all points tempted like as we are, yet without sin.[17] He was the only perfect man that ever lived.[18] He was also true God.[19]

At the age of twelve he visited Jerusalem during the Passover feast. Try to picture in your mind's eye the young Lord—this unique personality, as he approached Jerusalem that year, and as he participated in the religious ceremonies in the Temple. Did he not, even at this early age, realize the deeper meaning of the Passover and the Paschal Lamb? He certainly astonished the learned Doctors of Divinity by his understanding, his questions, and his answers. At this time Jesus also became a "Son of the Law," according to a Jewish custom corresponding to our Confirmation. The custom consisted of tying a phylactery[20] on the forehead, and another on the arm, as a token that henceforth this youth was willing to be guided by the Word of God in thought and action.

15 Acts Chap. 1-2.   17 Heb. 4:15.   19 John 1:1; Matth. 28:18; Rom. 1:4; etc.
16 Luke 2:40-52.   18 John 8:46.
20 A phylactery was an oblong wooden box containing Scripture passages. Two leather straps were fastened to the phylactery so that it could be tied to the forehead or to the arm.

The following eighteen years are passed over in almost complete silence. He lived with his parents in Nazareth; he was subject to them; and he advanced in wisdom and stature, in favor with God and men. Justin Martyr, in his "Dialogue with Trypho" Chapter 88, evidently records a well known tradition when he states that the Lord made plows and yokes and taught people righteousness by his peaceful pursuit. In Mark 6:3 he is referred to as "the carpenter, the son of Mary."

Those silent years were no doubt rich in experience. He was an ideal son, subject unto his parents. There is a tradition that his stepfather, Joseph, died early, and that Jesus as the oldest son in the family took it upon himself to support the household. His attitude toward home life is clearly reflected in his beautiful relation to the family circle at Bethany, Martha, Mary, and Lazarus. He had deep sympathy with all sorrow and suffering. Those eighteen years of daily manual labor among all kinds of people made him acquainted with everyday life as it really was. That he "hath been in all points tempted like as we are, yet without sin" must be literally true.[21]

The Gospels contain many indirect references to his private life. He knew two of the most popular games played by the children of Nazareth: wedding and funeral.[22] The illustration "as a hen gathereth her chickens under her wings"[23] was likely based on observations in his mother's chicken yard. His reference to the leaven which a woman took and hid in three measures of meal[24] was likely based on memories from his mother's kitchen. He was well acquainted with farm life,[25] and his intimate knowledge of shepherd life indicates that he may have tended sheep during his boyhood days. He had an eye for beauty in nature, especially for the lilies of the field.[26] He was acquainted with the life of the birds, and he knew the habits of the foxes.[27] His reference to the weather forecasts[28] may refer to the many evenings he watched the beautiful sunsets, while he listened to men of Nazareth make their predictions as to the weather. As a boy he also formed the habit of frequently withdrawing himself to secluded places for prayer and meditation.

Did the Lord ever go to school? The Jews had compulsory elementary education for all children above the age of six. But before the child became of school age, it devolved upon the parents,

[21] Heb. 4:15.
[22] Matth. 11:16-17.
[25] Matth. 13:31-32; Mark 4:28; Matth. 13:3-8; etc.
[26] Matth. 6:28.
[23] Matth. 23:37.
[24] Matth. 13:33.
[27] Matth. 8:20.
[28] Matth. 16:3.

especially upon the father, to give religious instruction. Joseph and Mary would not neglect to educate their children as prescribed by law. It is reasonable to infer that the Lord finished the elementary school, possibly also the Beth 'Midrash, or advanced school. On the other hand it is quite certain that he did not attend the higher, professional schools. The Scribes and the Pharisees did not classify him among "the learned."[29]

However, Jesus had an unusual opportunity to come in direct contact with the religious life of his people. Nazareth was a center of Jewish Temple life. The priests were divided into 24 "courses." Priests living in Galilee would gather in Nazareth before they went to Jerusalem to perform their services in the Temple, and they would disband in Nazareth on their return. Both Joseph and Mary had the bluest Jewish blood in their veins. It is reasonable to infer, therefore, that these priests would frequently gather in their home. Jesus must have listened to their conversations with deep interest, for Mary had by this time told him that he was to be the Messiah.

Nazareth also came in contact with the outside world because of the highway, the Via Maris, which led through the city and down to the sea. Men of all nations, busy with another life than that of Israel, would appear on the streets of the village. Some of these travellers were Jews from distant countries. Others were typical representatives of the great Graeco-Roman culture and civilization. Two worlds—the Greek and the Jewish—met in the home town of the Lord.

Did the Lord feel the conflict between a powerful inner urge to come forward and do great things, and equally adverse outward circumstances? Did his humble circumstances ever tempt him to think that he would never have a chance to show the world that he was the Messiah? Did his recognition of his marvelous native ability ever arouse within him a desire to make a name for himself along other lines of endeavor? He "hath been in all points tempted like as we are, yet without sin."[30]

Jesus knew that John the Baptist was to be his Forerunner. From the autumn of 26 to the autumn of 27 (Tishri 779 to Tishri 780 A.U.C.) was a sabbatical year for the Jews. Hence they had unusual opportunities to gather around the Baptist. Jesus heard of John's success and evidently concluded that his own public ministry must soon begin. This concrete situation, coupled with an

[29] Matth. 13:54.   [30] Heb. 4:15.

inner conviction of the spirit, caused the Lord to enter his public ministry when he was about thirty years of age.

The baptism of Jesus Christ marks the transition from private to public life. On this occasion three remarkable things happened: first, the heaven was opened; second, the Holy Spirit descended as a dove and came upon him; third, a voice came out of heaven saying, "Thou art my beloved Son; in thee I am well pleased."[31] Straightway after his baptism, he was led by the Spirit into the wilderness, where he was tempted for forty days and forty nights.[32] A few days later he began to teach, to preach, and to perform miracles. Recognition is made of the six general periods in his public ministry: (1) an early Judean ministry; (2) the Galilean ministry; (3) the North Galilean ministry; (4) the Perean and later Judean ministry; (5) the Passion Week; and (6) the Resurrection Narratives.

What was the main motive of his Messianic mission? The answer is given in the words of John 3:16: "For God so loved the world, that he gave his only begotten Son, that whosover believeth in him should not perish, but have eternal life." He came to redeem mankind and to establish the Kingdom of Heaven upon earth. As the first Adam had brought sin, sorrow, sickness and death into the world, "so also in Christ shall all be made alive" by faith in him. "The righteous shall live by faith."

His Messianic activity had a twofold aspect: what he *said*; and what he *did*. His deeds refer to his mighty works or miracles, used by him as a key to the human heart. He healed all manner of disease and all manner of sickness among the people. He even cast out demons and raised the dead. What he said during his official ministry may be grouped under his teaching and his preaching activities. As to his teaching, the Evangelist states that the people "were astonished at his teaching; for his word was with authority."[33] His preaching was marvelous: "never man so spake."[34]

As his influence grew he felt that his work must be given a more definite and permanent form. The time had come when he must select from his few faithful friends, those whom his Father "had given" him, a number of permanent apostles. He selected twelve, corresponding to the twelve tribes of Israel.[35] These were to be

[31] Matth. 3:13-17; Mark 1:9-11; Luke 3:21-38.
[32] Matth. 4:1-11; Mark 1:12-13; Luke 4:1-13.
[33] Luke 4:32.   [34] John 7:46.
[35] This number must have a striking significance for all Jewish people because of its prominence in the Old Testament. There were really thirteen tribes in Israel, after Ephraim and Manasse had taken the place of Joseph; and there were thirteen apostles, after Paul was called.

the representatives of the new spiritual Israel.[36] Christ through this selection originated the "apostolate," the first office of the Christian Church.[37] These apostles came to have a special authority in the early Church: (1) because of their special call by the Lord; (2) because of their special training by him; and (3) because of the special revelations given to them after the resurrection of the Lord.

The ministry of Christ made a tremendous impression upon the people. Several times they tried to take him by force and make him their king. But sentiment turned against him when he repeatedly refused to establish a temporal kingdom. "My kingdom is not of this world," was his decided answer. His unsparing exposé of the hypocrisy and spiritual pride of the religious leaders of Palestine hastened and matured a deadly opposition against him. He was finally seized by his enemies, arraigned before Caiaphas and Pilate, and crucified on Good Friday, in the year 30 A.D. On Easter morn he arose from the dead. During the next forty days he appeared to a number of individuals and groups. He then ascended into heaven, after he had promised to send the Holy Spirit upon his disciples.

His earthly mission was ended. As the grain of wheat falls into the ground and dies in order that it may bear much fruit,[38] so he had been willing to suffer and to die in order that he might make atonement for the sins of mankind. "Behold the Lamb of God, that taketh away the sin of the world."[39] His resurrection from the dead sealed his victory over death, and proved him to be the Son of God with power.[40] The importance of the resurrection of Christ for the Christian Church is stressed in 1 Corinthians, Chapter 15. The Second Article of the Apostle's Creed gives an excellent summary of the life and work of the Lord.

That Christ intended to organize a Church is clearly seen from the essentials he left for a church organization. Notice that the *Augsburg Confession*[41] defines the Church as "the congregation of saints, in which the Gospel is rightly taught and the sacraments rightly administered." Christ gave to his Church the following essentials: (1) The preaching of the Word of God. Christ himself is the Word; (2) The Sacrament of Baptism, and the Sacrament of the Altar. Christ himself instituted these two sacraments, and only these two; (3) Church leaders, or Apostles, with a special

[36] Rev. 21:14.
[37] Luke 6:13; Matth. 28:16-20.
[38] John 12:24.
[39] John 1:29.
[40] Rom. 1:4.
[41] Article VII.

call and a special training; (4) The special guidance of the Holy Spirit; (5) The Power to exercise the necessary church discipline.[42]

Certain groups have been eager to claim the Apostle Paul as the real founder of the Christian Church. Such claims are not founded on facts. Jesus Christ is the founder of the Christian Church. Paul himself declares: "for other foundation can no man lay than that which is laid, which is Jesus Christ."[43] He states in another epistle: "I count all things to be loss for the excellency of the knowledge of Christ Jesus my Lord."[44] He determined to know nothing save Jesus Christ and him crucified.[45] He makes it clear, in all his writings, that the Gospel he is preaching, and the work he is doing, is based on the revelation from Jesus Christ, his Lord.

5. REVIEW QUESTIONS

1. Why is Jesus Christ a unique personality?
2. Why is 30 A.D. taken as the year of the birth of the Christian Church?
3. What can you say about the childhood and youth of the Lord?
4. Why, do you think, did God place his only begotten Son in a home in Nazareth? Do you think a more suitable place could be found? Why not?
5. Did the Lord go to school? Was he classified among "the learned"?
6. What was the main motive in his Messianic mission?
7. Why did he select and train apostles? Why did these have a special authority in the early Church?
8. Why was the Messiah rejected by his people?
9. What did Christ leave as the essentials for his Church?
10. Why is Jesus Christ, and not the apostle Paul, the real founder of the Christian Church?

TOPICS FOR SPECIAL STUDY

1. Compare the three accounts of Christ as recorded in Matthew 1:1-17, Luke 3:23-38, and John 1:1-4. How do they differ? Can you see why?
2. Outline the relation between Jesus Christ and the Word of God (cf. 2 Tim. 3:16; 2 Pet. 1:19-21; and diagram on page 31).
3. Compare the Jewish, the Greek, and the Roman systems of education at the time of Christ.

II. The Early Jerusalem Church (A.D. 30-44).—It is essential that the student should get a good perspective of the Apostolic Age. Study the outline in the Table of Contents, and the map on page 38. Notice that (1) from 30 to 44 A.D. Jerusalem was the great church center. The Apostle Peter and James, the brother of the Lord, were the great leaders of the Church at that time. (2) From 44 to 68 A.D. the Apostle Paul made Antioch in Syria the great center for foreign missions. (3) From 68 to 100 A.D. the Apostle John made Ephesus the great church center of the

[42] Matth. 18:15-20; 16:16-19.   [44] Phil. 3:8.
[43] 1 Cor. 3:11.   [45] 1 Cor. 2:2.

world. Rome did not come into prominence as a church center till after the Apostolic Age.

The Book of Acts is practically the only historical writing that gives first-hand information concerning the early Church in Jerusalem, A.D. 30-44. Only a few additional remarks may be found scattered in the New Testament Epistles.

Luke, the author of the Acts, gives an original, fresh, trustworthy, and inspiring description of contemporaneous events, based in part on his personal observation and experience. The theme of the book is found in Acts 1:8: "But ye shall receive power, when the Holy Spirit is come upon you: and ye shall be my witnesses in Jerusalem, and in all Judea and Samaria, and unto the uttermost part of the earth." Accordingly, the author devotes the first seven chapters to a description of the beginning and the development of the early Jerusalem Church. Chapters 8-12 describe the spread of the Church to Judea and Samaria; and chapters 13-28 describe the extension of the Gospel "unto the uttermost part of the earth."

The Book of Acts may be considered the earliest history of the Christian Church. The narrative centers mainly about two apostles: Peter, chapters 1-12, and Paul, chapters 13-28. The Church had its origin in Jerusalem. Then Antioch in Syria became the next great center for foreign missions. Paul spread the Gospel to the north and to the west until he reached Rome, the great capital of the world. Geographically, the narrative describes a semi-circle, starting in Jerusalem and ending in Rome. "Westward the course of Empire takes." Luke wanted to convince the learned and influential Theophilus[46] that Christianity was just the religion for this great Empire.

Acts continues the narrative where the Gospels leave off. The first chapter relates how the Lord, forty days after his resurrection, assembled his disciples on Mount Olivet, where he gave them the final charge. He was then taken up into heaven. The disciples returned to Jerusalem and assembled in a house where they remained steadfastly in prayer, waiting for the Holy Spirit which the Lord had promised to send them. The group numbered about 120. During these ten days of waiting, Matthias was chosen for the apostleship and the place in the ministry vacated by Judas Iscariot.

Why was it so essential that the disciples wait in Jerusalem for the Holy Spirit? The Lord had told his disciples that it was expedient for him to go away. Otherwise the Comforter, the Holy

[46] Acts 1:1; Luke 1:1-4.

Spirit, could not be sent.[47] When Christ had ascended into heaven, the Father would send the Holy Spirit in his (the Lord's) name. "He shall teach you all things, and bring to your remembrance all that I said unto you."[48] "And he, when he is come, will convict the world in respect of sin, and of righteousness, and of judgment."[49] The disciples would be powerless and helpless until they had received the Holy Spirit. Consequently, the Pentecost, 30 A.D., is usually taken as the real birthday of the Christian Church.

A careful study of the second chapter of Acts would now be of great help to the student. On the first Pentecost after the resur-

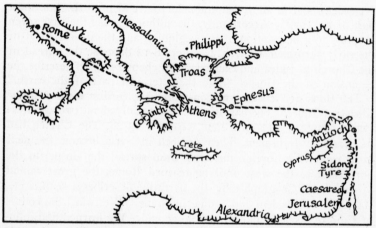

MAP INDICATING THE GREAT CHRISTIAN CENTERS IN THE APOSTOLIC AGE

rection of Christ, the 120 were all together in one place. It was the third hour of the day, i.e., at nine o'clock in the morning, designated as the "hour of prayer." "And suddenly there came from heaven a sound as of the rushing of a mighty wind, and it filled all the house where they were sitting. And there appeared unto them tongues parting asunder, like as of fire; and it sat upon each one of them. And they were all filled with the Holy Spirit, and began to speak with other tongues, as the Spirit gave them utterance."[50] The Spirit came upon disciples and apostles, men and women alike; there was no distinction among persons.

It may be of interest to note that Pentecost was a Jewish festival called the "feast of the harvest."[51] Later this festival was also

---

[47] John 16:7.   [49] John 16:8.   [51] Deut. 16:9-10; Exod. 23:16; Num. 28:26.
[48] John 14:26.   [50] Acts, Chap. 2.

regarded as the celebration of the giving of the Law from Sinai,[52] whence the incorporation of the Jewish "congregation" was to be dated. The festival lasted one day and was celebrated on the fiftieth day after the first day of the Passover.[53] Christ was crucified on Friday, the 14th of Nisan.[54] Counting the days as the Jews did, from sun-down to sun-down, the Passover started on Friday evening, the 15th of Nisan, lasting until sun-down on Saturday. Counting Sunday the 16th of Nisan as the first of the fifty days, it is evident that the ancient Church correctly placed the first Christian Pentecost on a Sunday.

The outpouring of the Holy Spirit caused a tremendous stir among the people in Jerusalem. They came together and listened to those who were speaking about the mighty works of God. In the audience were devout Jews "from every nation under heaven." Yet they heard these spirit-filled disciples "speaking in our own tongues the mighty works of God." All were amazed; some were perplexed; and others mocked.[55] Then the twelve apostles stood up, Peter acting as their spokesman. Taking his text from Joel 3:1-5, he explained what had happened in the light of the Old Testament prophecy, and connected this extraordinary event, the outpouring of the Holy Spirit, with the life and work of the crucified and risen Savior. The people were "pricked in their heart" when they heard these things, and asked Peter and the other apostles what they should do. The answer was: "Repent ye, and be baptized every one of you in the name of Jesus Christ unto the remission of your sins; and ye shall receive the gift of the Holy Spirit." About 3000 souls received the word and were baptized that day.

Were some of the visiting Jews, "devout men, from every nation under heaven," among the 3000 converts? And if so, could these Christian converts return to their respective communities and keep quiet about this most unusual and intense experience on Pentecost? The parables of the leaven and of the mustard seed[56] here find their first practical application.

Luke gives an interesting description of the early Christian community in Jerusalem. The Christian Church had, from her very birthday, all the essentials of organization, and all the distinguishing features of public Christian worship. This early church was a faithful prototype of the Christian Church of later generations. Consider the following points:

[52] Talmud: *Tractat Pesach,* 68b. [54] John 18:28. [56] Matth. 13:31-33.
[53] Lev. 23:15-16. [55] Acts 2:13.

1. The Founder of the Christian Church had given to his congregation all the essentials of organization: (a) the preaching of the Word; (b) the Sacrament of Baptism and the Sacrament of the Altar; (c) the power of discipline; and (d) trained church leaders.[57] Additional organization had been left with local congregations as a matter of expediency.

2. On the first Christian Pentecost, the Holy Spirit had been sent as the divine guide of the Church in all matters. It is significant that the early Jerusalem Church recognized the authority of the Holy Spirit in the first recorded case of discipline. The sin of Ananias was considered a "lie to the Holy Spirit," not to Peter and the other apostles.[58]

3. The Lord had arranged for the guidance of the Church through the Apostles. The early Christians recognised this apostolic authority. They continued steadfastly in the apostle's teaching.[59] The apostles differed from other charismatic persons, i.e., men who possessed special gifts of grace,[60] because of, (a) their special call by the Lord, (b) their special training by the Lord, (c) their miraculous endowments and their authority, from which there was no appeal, and (d) their special relation to the Lord—his revelations to them—after his resurrection.

4. They continued steadfastly in the "fellowship."[61] The Lord had given a new commandment to his disciples, that they love one another.[62] Martin Luther called this fellowship "the priesthood of all believers," as based on the fact of justification by faith alone. The early Christians were not bound to approach God through some ecclesiastical institution, or through some specified church official, as it later came to be in the Catholic Church. Every Christian had free, personal access to God through faith in Jesus Christ. They also believed in the Lord's promise: "Where two or three are gathered together in my name, there I am in the midst of them."[63]

5. They continued in "the breaking of bread." As the institution of the Lord's Supper had been preceded by an evening meal,[64] so the early Christians continued this custom throughout the Apostlic Age. Later the Lord's Supper came to be celebrated only at the Sunday forenoon services, because the enemies of the Christians accused them of immoral conduct in connection with the evening feasts, declaring that they killed little children and drank their blood and ate their flesh.

6. The Christians continued daily, "steadfastly with one accord in the temple."[65] They did not voluntarily separate themselves from the public, organized religious life of Jerusalem, but rather tried to put new life and new meaning into the existing order of things. They endeavored with the utmost care to win the disciples of Moses for the Lord. This relation continued under the later leadership of James "the Just," who died about 66 A.D.

7. The Christian worship had from the very birthday of the Church all the distinctive features of such worship. (1) Peter read from Scripture before he began to preach. Reciting from the Oral Gospel was equally common. "They continued steadfastly in the Apostle's teaching." (2) The Gospel was preached. Peter was the preacher on the birthday of the Church, and he preached a revival sermon in the purest sense. (3) The Sacraments were diligently used. "The Lord added to them day by day those that were saved."[66] But the people were not saved until they had repented and had been baptized.[67] And those who were saved, continued steadfastly "in the

---

[57] cf. pp. 35-36.
[58] The New Testament contains numerous references to the direct guidance of the Holy Spirit. Read also the Third Article of the Apostle's Creed.
[59] Acts 2:42.
[60] I Cor. 12:8-12 and verse 28.
[61] Acts 2:42.
[62] John 13:34.
[63] Matth. 18:20.
[64] Luke 24:30.
[65] Acts 2:46.
[66] Acts 2:47.
[67] Acts 2:38-41.

breaking of bread." (4) They made use of public prayers,[68] including some of the former Jewish prayers, as well as those formulated by the Christians. (5) They had a regular place of public worship, namely the Temple.[69] Hence these early Christian services must have been marked, not only by stirring interest and remarkable power, but also by dignity. Outside Jerusalem the synagogue was frequently used.[70] (6) They had regular times for worship. At first they met every day, but they soon set aside Sunday as the special day of worship. (7) There is no specific mention of singing on the Day of Pentecost, but the Lord had used a hymn when he instituted the Lord's supper,[71] and it would be very strange if the apostles left out this part of the original ceremony in their service. Singing became an attractive feature of early Christian worship,[72] and the Apostolic Church had the richest material for sacred poetry and music. (8) There is naturally no mention of any formal confession on the Day of Pentecost. The Apostle's Creed was formulated later, but the essentials of this Creed are stated by Peter in his sermon.

8. The Lord and his apostles had had a common community of all goods. The apostles naturally extended this relation to the whole Christian community in Jerusalem. In this manner they followed the exhortation given by their Lord.[73] They had "all things in common; and they sold their possessions and goods, and parted them to all, according as any man had need."[74] But the apostles did not make this a legal ordinance. This experiment of having all goods in common was evidently never repeated in any other congregation. Read, for instance, about the rich and the poor in the Epistle of James.

9. Those who did not belong to the youthful Church were prevented from making any premature attack upon the Christians. Fear came upon every soul.[75] Inwardly, the Church had a tremendous power. Many signs and miracles were done through the apostles.[76] The number of Christians soon grew to 5000.[77] A little later Luke states that believers were the more added to the Lord, multitudes of both men and women.[78] "And the word of God increased; and the number of the disciples multiplied in Jerusalem exceedingly; and a great company of priests were obedient to the faith."[79]

10. Outwardly, the Christians had to endure three persecutions by religious authorities in Jerusalem. The first is described in Acts, Chapter 4; the second in Acts 5:17-42; the third in Acts 7:57-8:3. But none of these persecutions could stop the victorious progress of the Christian Church.

11. The Church soon had to face the possibility of a division within its own bosom. With the increase of the congregation, the business management became extensive and difficult. And so "there arose a murmuring of the Grecian Jews against the Hebrews, because their widows were neglected in the daily ministration."[80] The congregation, under the leadership of the apostles, found it expedient to select "seven men of good report, full of the Spirit and of wisdom," whose chief duty was to take care of the poor in the congregation. It should be noted that the right to elect was vested in the congregation, while the appointment and the consecration were communicated by the apostles. This practice of electing a regular committee for the overseership of alms, and the mode of appointment, marks the beginning of the deaconate. The office of presbyter was still vested in the apostles themselves. The Seven were the assistants to the apostles, as the deacons later were the assistants to the elders.[81]

12. The Presbyterate was probably the third office to be instituted in the

[68] Acts 2:42.
[69] Acts 2:46.
[70] James 2:2.
[71] Matth. 26:30; Mark 14:26.
[72] Col. 3:16.
[73] Luke 12:33.
[74] Acts 2:44-45.
[75] Acts 2:43.
[76] Acts 2:43.
[77] Acts 4:4.
[78] Acts 5:14.
[79] Acts 6:7.
[80] Acts 6:1.
[81] The Seven are not called deacons in Acts Chapter 6. See diagram, page 66.

Church. Nothing is said of the origin of this office, but it very likely shaped itself after the synagogue. Study diagram and explanation on page 66.

13. The persecution that arose in connection with the stoning of Stephen, the proto-martyr, caused the Christians to scatter abroad throughout the regions of Judea and Samaria. Christian congregations were established in these districts. Philip baptized the Ethiopian enunch—a representative of the Hamites.[82] Peter baptized Cornelius—a representative of the Japhetic nations.[83] The universality of the Gospel began to assert itself. Some of the persecuted Christians settled in Cyrene, while others travelled to Phoenecia, Cyprus, and Antioch in Syria.[84] In Antioch a number of Greeks accepted the Gospel. Hence the establishment of the first Christian Jewish-Gentile congregation.

14. In Samaria the Church was brought in contact with Simon Magus,[85] whom the Church Fathers call the father of the Gnostic heresies. There is a tradition that this Simon had been one of thirty disciples of John the Baptist. After the imprisonment and death of the Baptist, Simon is said to have sought the leadership among John's disciples, but did not succeed. He is then said to have gone to Egypt to study magic, and to have returned to Samaria, where he was held in great esteem because of his magical art. He offered the apostles money for the power of the Holy Spirit. From this incident the word "Simony" is coined, i.e., the purchase or sale of ecclesiastical preferment.

15. The conversion of Saul took place during this early period. God used this man, more than any other human being, to extend the Kingdom of God upon earth.

16. The account of Tabitha, or Dorcas,[86] contains interesting information as to the charitable activities of the Church in some localities. Dorcas was "full of good works and almsdeeds." She helped the widows and the poor by sewing garments for them. Tabitha, or Dorcas, furnishes an example of that type of Christian charity that has since been carried on largely through ladies' aid organizations.

17. The inter-church relations are described in Chapter 11, where the Christians in Antioch sent relief to the famine stricken Christians in Judea; and in Chapter 15, where the various congregations sent delegates to the Apostolic Council in Jerusalem.

18. Acts, Chapter 12, contains the first account of the persecution of the Church by a secular authority, King Herod Agrippa I. It is evident, however, from the account that he persecuted the Christians in order to increase his popularity with the Jews, not because he had specific orders from the Roman government. This event, which took place in 44 A.D., marks a slight turning point in Apostolic history. Henceforth Peter resided only intermittently in Jerusalem. The leadership of the Jerusalem Church passed from Peter to James "the Just," a half brother of the Lord. In the literature of the second Christian century this James is referred to as the first bishop of Jerusalem.

19. The Early Jerusalem Church was a missionary church, starting "from Jerusalem" and working out toward the ends of the earth. It was also a church of power, accompanied by many signs and wonders and by special and extraordinary gifts of the Holy Spirit.

20. This early Church was truly a faithful prototype of the Christian Church of later generations. Like the grain of mustard seed it contained the sole authentic germ of the living organism, the Holy Christian Church.

[82] Gen. 9:18-27.   [84] Acts 11:19-21.   [86] Acts 9:36-43.
[83] Gen. 9:18-27.   [85] Acts 8:14-24.

6. REVIEW QUESTIONS

1. Where do you find first-hand information concerning the Early Jerusalem Church?
2. How would you describe the first Christian Pentecost? (cf. Acts).
3. How do we know that this event took place on a Sunday?
4. On what conditions were the 3000 souls saved on Pentecost?
5. Is it likely that some of the visiting Jews, "devout men, from every nation under heaven," were among the 3000 converts? If so, what would be the natural consequences as to the early spread of the Gospel?
6. How do you know that the Early Jerusalem Church had all the essentials of organization, and all the distinguishing features of Christian worship?
7. What place did the Holy Spirit have in the early Church?
8. How did the Lord provide for appropriate leadership of his Church?
9. Was the early Church schismatic? Why not?
10. What other features of interest did you notice in the life of the early church?

TOPICS FOR SPECIAL STUDY

1. Outline the characteristics of the various forms of church government, such as the Apostolic, the Primitive Episcopal, the Metropolitan and Patriarchial, the Papal, the Episcopal, the Presbyterian, and the Congregational. Which form is most Biblical?
2. Compare the charismatic persons in the Apostolic Age with the Christian lay preachers of today.
3. The administration of the Lord's Supper in the Apostolic Age and today.
4. Compare the experiment of having a community of goods with similar experiments of today? What is your conclusion?

III. Antioch in Syria as the Next Church Center (A.D. 44-68).

—The chief first-hand information concerning the Church during the years 44-68 is the Book of Acts, which carries the narrative up to the year 60, or perhaps 62. The Epistle of James and the Epistles of Paul and of Peter, give additional and supplementary information. Among the secular writers the works of Josephus are particularly valuable.

During the first fourteen years in the life of the Christian Church, 30-44, the grain of mustard seed[87] had developed into a tree of considerable proportions. Its branches reached out to communities of God's chosen people, Israel, in many parts of the world. Was this tree also to overshadow the great Gentile world? Was the Christian Church intended only for the Jews, with a few Gentile proselytes; or was it to be a universal Church, with faith in Jesus Christ as the chief requisite for membership?

Christ had frequently asserted the universality of his Kingdom on earth, but it is evident that the vision of the early Jewish Christians was much beclouded by Jewish particularism. For some time

[87] Matth. 13:31-33.

they spoke the Word "to none save only to Jews."[88] Yet, as the River Nile in due season overflows its banks and brings great fertility to the adjoining territory, so also the Lord arranged for the spread of his Gospel to the Gentile world.

Attention is again called to the gradual preparation of the Church for her great mission among the Gentiles: (1) The persecution that arose in connection with the martyrdom of Stephen,[89] scattered the Christians among their traditional enemies, the half-Gentile Samaritans. These Samaritans accepted the Gospel,[90] as some had already done in the days of the Lord. (2) The Evangelist Philip baptized the Ethiopian eunuch.[91] Henceforth the Church had a representative among the Hamites in the South. (3) Cornelius, a representative of the Graeco-Roman world—a descendant of Japhet—was baptized together with his entire household.[92] (4) Many Greeks in Antioch "turned to the Lord."[93]

To the Jewish-Gentile church in Antioch in Syria, the Church in Jerusalem had sent one of its charter members (Joseph) Barnabas,[94] a Levite from Cyprus,[95] to supervise the work of the congregation. The importance and efficiency of his service earned him the title of "apostle"[96] in the broader sense of that term. He soon secured the able assistance of his friend, Saul of Tarsus. These two worked together in Antioch "even a whole year," A.D. 43-44, before they were delegated to go with gifts to the famine-stricken Christians in Jerusalem.[97]

Henceforth the center of interest in the narrative in Acts shifts from Jerusalem to Antioch; and from the Apostle Peter to the Apostle Paul. From 44 A.D. Antioch in Syria became the center of Gentile Christianity, as Jerusalem was the center of Jewish Christianity.

How rich the mother church of Gentile Christianity was in prominent prophets and teachers, is related in Acts 13:1. Among these Manaen, a foster-brother of King Herod Antipas, is mentioned. While these prophets and teachers of Antioch "ministered unto the Lord, and fasted, the Holy Spirit said, Separate me Barnabas and Paul for the work whereunto I have called them. Then, when they had fasted and prayed and laid their hands on them, they sent them away."[98] Thus the First Missionary Journey began.

The First Missionary Journey[99] marked a new departure of exceedingly great importance for the Christian Church. The man

[88] Acts 11:19.   [91] Acts 8:26-39.   [94] Acts 11:22.   [97] Acts 11:25-30.
[89] Acts 8:1.   [92] Acts, Chap. 10.   [95] Acts 4:36.   [98] Acts 13:2-3.
[90] Acts 8:4-8; cf. John 4:4-42. [93] Acts 11:20-21. [96] Acts 14:4.14.   [99] Acts 13:4-14:28.

whom the Lord had called to be "Apostle to the Gentiles" began now in earnest to preach the Gospel among the Gentiles, not excluding the Jews. Paul and Barnabas went to the island of Cyprus, the native land of Barnabas. Hence they started "from Jerusalem," i.e., from their home community. They selected next the cities of Antioch in Pisidia, Iconium, Lystra, and Derbe. From these centers the Gospel spread to the surrounding territory. The Jews that refused the Gospel proved to be the worst enemies of the two missionaries, persecuting them wherever they could. The churches founded on this journey were carefully organized by Paul and Barnabas. Duly elected and consecrated "elders" succeeded the apostles as the spiritual leaders and general directors of the local congregations.[100]

A door of faith had been opened unto the Gentiles. Many turned to the Lord. This situation brought on a severe clash between Jewish particularism and the universality of the Christian Gospel. On what terms should these Gentile Christians be admitted to membership in the Church? Was not the transition to be made by way of Jewish Christianity, i.e., by way of circumcision and the observance of the Ceremonial Law? Or, was justification by faith in Jesus Christ alone, without circumcision and Mosaism, sufficient qualification for church membership?

The issue was settled at the Apostolic Council in Jerusalem. Acts, Chapter 15, gives a vivid account of the proceedings. James the Just, authoritative head of the Jerusalem Church, settled the problem in favor of the Gentiles—according to the witness of prophecy.[101] His verdict was sanctioned by the apostles and the elders and by the entire Church. Gentile Christianity was emancipated from circumcision and the bondage of the Jewish ceremonial law, and Paul was officially recognized as an apostle to the Gentiles. It was a great and far-reaching decision. Justification by faith alone had been recognized as a universal law in God's Kingdom on earth. It was this principle Paul re-asserted in his epistles to the Galatians and to the Romans. It was this same basic law that was re-emphasised in the Lutheran Reformation. These four: the Apostolic Council in Jerusalem, the Epistle to the Galatians, the Epistle to the Romans, and the Lutheran Reformation, constitute a four leaf clover because they all deal with the same fundamental problem: man is justified and saved by faith in Jesus Christ alone, and not by human merit.

Shortly after the Apostolic Council in Jerusalem, Paul started

<hr>

[100] Acts 14:22-23.   [101] Acts 15:13-21.

on his Second Missionary Journey. On this tour he preached the
Gospel with great success in Europe: in Philippi, Thessalonica,
Boerea, Athens, and Corinth. During his two years' stay in Corinth,
he wrote I and II Thessalonians, and probably Galatians. For an
account of this journey, read Acts 15:36-18:22.

After spending some time time at his home base, Antioch in
Syria, Paul started on his Third Missionary Journey.[102] He once
more visited the congregations of Galatia and Phrygia, and then
he came to Ephesus, where he stayed for three years.[103] From
Ephesus he wrote I Corinthians. Paul's long stay in Ephesus
shows his keen insight as a Christian leader. He evidently saw

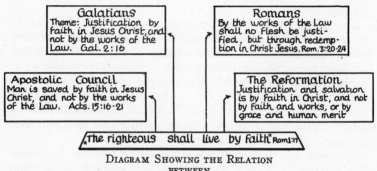

DIAGRAM SHOWING THE RELATION
BETWEEN
THE APOSTOLIC COUNCIL, GALATIANS, ROMANS, AND THE PROTESTANT
REFORMATION

that the current of history, commerce, and civilization moved
westward, and that Ephesus would become a great center for the
Church. The young but gifted Timothy was selected as leader of
this important church, after Paul's departure.

From Ephesus Paul travelled to Macedonia where he wrote
Second Corinthians. From Macedonia he travelled to Corinth,
where he stayed for three months during the winter. During this
stay he wrote his great masterpiece, the Epistle to Romans. He
felt that his main work in the East was finished, and he wanted to
turn westward for new fields to conquer. Rome had been selected
as the new base for these intended missionary activities. From
Rome he intended to go as far west as to Spain.[104] But before
he could go to Rome, the Spirit guided him first to make a trip to
Jerusalem,[105] and this trip terminated his third Missionary Journey.

---

[102] Acts 18:23-21:14.
[103] Acts 20:31.
[104] Rom. 16:24-28.
[105] Acts 20:22.

His trip to Jerusalem was followed by a two year imprisonment in Caesarea. He was then sent by ship to Rome, where he remained a prisoner for two years. During this first Roman imprisonment Paul wrote four epistles: Ephesians, Colossians, Philemon, and Philippians. Here Luke closes the narrative of the Book of Acts.

There are strong evidences that Paul was set free from the imprisonment recorded in the last chapter of Acts, among them the following: (1) The historical background and the facts implied in I and II Timothy and Titus do not fit in with the earlier life of Paul as described in Acts. These epistles must have been written after he had been set free. (2) The Book of Acts and the Imprisonment Epistles, Ephesians, Colossians, Philemon, and Philippians, indicate that Paul would probably be set free. (3) In the First Epistle of Clement of Rome, written around 95 A.D., the author states in 5:5f.: "Paul preached both in the East and West . . . taught righteousness to the whole world, and came to the extreme limit of the West." According to current usage, "the extreme limit of the West" could only mean Spain. These words were written by a Roman Christian, only 30 years after Paul's death. (4) The Muratori Canon, line 38; and the Acts of Peter, Chapter 1, mention Paul's visit to Spain. But these testimonies are late, and therefore of less value.

Assuming that Paul was set free in 62 A.D., what course did he follow? Based on statements in his last three epistles, he was released late in 62 and spent the winter in Nicopolis, where he probably wrote I Timothy and Titus. Early in the spring of 63 he probably made a hurried inspection tour to the East, including Ephesus and Crete. He then set sail for Spain. On the night of July 18-19, 64 A.D., Rome began to burn, and kept on burning for six days. The Christians were blamed for the fire and a persecution started. Peter was martyred, but Paul was evidently still in Spain, out of reach. According to the oldest tradition, Paul was martyred later than Peter.

Paul was imprisoned when he returned from Spain. When he wrote II Timothy he had been in prison for some time. From this epistle it is clear that Paul himself did not expect to be released. "I am already being offered, and the time of my departure is come."[106] He died a martyr's death in 66, or early in 67 A.D., during the reign of Nero.

No authentic information is available regarding the other apos-

[106] 2 Tim. 4:6.

tles and leaders, save in the cases of James, the brother of John, who was martyred in 44 A.D.;[107] James the Just, who was killed by fanatical Jews in 66 A.D.; and John, who died in extreme old age, after the accession of Trajan (A.D. 98-117).

Tradition assigns the following fields to the various apostles and evangelists: Andrew is said to have labored in Scythia; hence the Russians worship him as their apostle. Philip spent his last years in Hierapolis in Phrygia. Bartholomew is said to have brought the Gospel according to Matthew into India. Thomas is said to have been the apostle to Parthia, and also to India. The tradition concerning Matthew is rather confused. He is said to have preached first to his own people, and afterward in foreign lands. James Alphaeus is said to have worked in Egypt. Thaddeus is said to have been the missionary to Persia. Simon Zelotes is said to have worked in Egypt and in Britain; while another report connects him with Persia and Babylonia. The evangelist John Mark is said to have founded the Church at Alexandria.

Christianity had begun its world-wide conquest. Within less than thirty years after the death of Christ, growing Christian communities were found in all important cities along the eastern and northern Mediterranean Sea. At the time of Paul's death, in 66 A.D., it seems fairly certain that the Gospel had spread throughout all the important eastern, southern, and western parts of the Roman Empire. The regions up the Danube and the Rhine had evidently not as yet been visited by apostles or evangelists. Less than three centuries later, the Christian religion had conquered the Roman Empire, Christianity becoming the official Roman religion.

The years 66-68 A.D. terminate the second stage in the development of the Apostolic Church. All the prominent apostles and early leaders were dead save the Apostle John. When the Jewish War broke out in 66 A.D., he left Jerusalem and took up his residence in Ephesus. James the Just, who had given so much prestige to the Jerusalem Church, was killed in 66 A.D. That same year the Jewish War broke out. The Christians, who believed the prophecy of the Lord concerning the destruction of Jerusalem, left the city in great numbers. Jerusalem lost much of its former prestige as the Mother Church, and Antioch in Syria shared a similar fate. From 68 A.D. Ephesus became the leading center of Christianity, with the Apostle John as the undisputed leader.

Three different views of salvation were held in the first Christian

[107] Acts 12:2.

century. (1) The Pharisees and certain Judaizers claimed that man is saved by faith plus good works. This view was combated by Paul in Galatians and in Romans. (2) Certain sects taught that man is saved by knowledge or by education. Paul exposed and refuted this view in First Timothy and in Colossians. (3) Jesus Christ and his apostles taught that man is justified and saved by faith in Christ, and not by works or human merit, hence "sola fide."

7. REVIEW QUESTIONS

1. Where do you find reliable information concerning the life of the Church during the years 44-68 A.D.?
2. How did Jewish particularism assert itself against the universality of Christianity?
3. Why did Antioch in Syria become a new church center?
4. Why the Apostolic Council in Jerusalem?
5. Why the organic connection between the Apostolic Council, Galatians, Romans, and the Reformation?
6. Why did Paul spend two years in Corinth, and three in Ephesus?
7. What evidence do we have that Paul preached the Gospel in Spain?
8. In what fields did the other apostles probably labor?
9. Why are the years 66-68 taken as a turning-point in the Apostolic history?
10. Discuss the various views of salvation within the Church.

TOPICS FOR SPECIAL STUDY

1. Paul, the missionary and the church leader.
2. Was Peter the first bishop of Rome?
3. The Epistle of James, A.D. 49 or 50, and its relation to the Apostolic Church.
4. Church problems in Corinth.
5. James the Just as a church leader.

IV. Ephesus as a Church Center (A.D. 68-100).—The source material for this period, A.D. 68-100, is rather scattered. The Epistle of Jude, the Epistle to the Hebrews, and the writings of John date from these years. The *First Epistle of Clement of Rome*, written to the Corinthian Church around 95 A.D., is a valuable source. The *Didache*, or *Teaching of the Twelve*, may date from the first century. The *Shepherd of Hermas* was written shortly after 100 A.D. Some information may also be obtained from the secular writers, Josephus, Tacitus, Suetonius, and Cassius Dio.

Ephesus became the third center of Christianity. "Westward the course of Empire takes." The city had a population of about 225,000 and is referred to as "the first and greatest metropolis of Asia." It was also known as "the temple-keeper of the great Diana,"[108] and the Temple of Diana was known as one of the

[108] Acts 19:35.

seven wonders of the world. The city had a theatre which seated
30,000. Ephesus was at this time the great commercial, political,
and religious center of Asia.

Paul had spent three years in establishing a church here. Timothy
had succeeded him as its leader, but he had been called to Rome
during Paul's second imprisonment[109] and had evidently been imprisoned himself.[110] At this time the Jewish War had broken out
(66 A.D.), so John came to Ephesus.

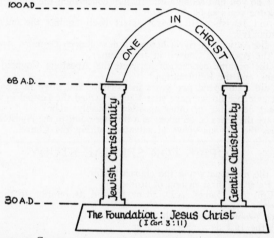

THE GROWTH OF CHRISTIANITY FROM 30 TO 68, AND FROM 68 TO 100 A.D.

John was particularly well qualified to step in as the church
leader. There had been distinct Jewish and Gentile jealousies
within the Church, but John was a man who stood above strife
and division.

The development of Christianity during the time of Peter and
of Paul may be likened to two massive pillars. During the leadership of John, these pillars were connected by a beautiful arch.
Peter and Paul had displayed remarkable ability and great aggressiveness in laying the foundation for the outward spread of
Christianity. In the meantime John's peculiar genius had developed
in mysterious silence and meditation. He had turned his attention
more toward the inner life and growth of the Church. He was
particularly well prepared to bring Jewish and Gentile Christians
into a compact unity. On the rapidly growing mustard tree, wild

[109] 2 Tim. 4:9.   [110] Heb. 13:23.

and spurious branches (sects and heresies) had appeared. John was the man to lead the Church against strong and clever spiritual foes, and to give proper encouragement in times of outward persecutions.

Shortly after John's coming to Ephesus the attention of the entire Christian Church was centered on Palestine. The Jewish War (A.D. 66-70) had placed the Holy Land in a horrible situation. Just before the Passover in the year 70 Titus started a siege against Jerusalem which lasted from April to September. On July 17 the perpetual sacrifice in the Temple ceased forever, from lack of both priests and animals.[111] On September 8 all of Jerusalem was conquered, and the Temple was burned. Fire and sword made the destruction so complete that Josephus says "there remained nothing to make those who came thither believe that the place had ever been inhabited."

The destruction of Jerusalem and the Temple influenced the development of the Christian Church in various ways, among them the following: (1) It separated Christianity and Judaism forever. Henceforth the Graeco-Roman world could not consider Christianity a mere sect of Judaism. The whole fabric of the Mosaic theocracy had been demolished and could no longer be thought of as a possible framework for Christianity. (2) This departure from a Judaism that had rejected the true Messiah did not, however, involve a departure from the spirit of the Old Testament revelation. The Christian Church merely entered into the inheritance of the spiritual Israel of the Old Testament. (3) With the Jerusalem Church established for the time being in the predominantly Gentile city of Pella in Decapolis, the overshadowing prestige of the great Mother Church was lost. Henceforth the nascent Gentile Church was not hampered in her development by intolerant and exclusive Judaistic tendencies, fostered in Jerusalem. (4) The conservative tendency of the early Church, represented by Peter, and the progressive tendency, represented by Paul, might have resulted in a wide division of the Church. This would have been a great calamity for Christianity. The destruction of Jerusalem assisted in breaking down the partition between "Jew" and "Gentile," and resulted in a new and higher spiritual and organic unity—a unity in diversity—that of a humanity which was sanctified by faith in Jesus Christ.

Information is scanty concerning the territorial progress of Christianity from 70 to 100 A.D. The main interest centers in the

[111] Josephus: *Jewish War*, VI, 2.1.

spiritual development of the Church amid outward persecutions, apostasy, and besetting heresies.

Many beginnings had been made by apostles and evangelists, in planting the Gospel in various parts of the Empire. Most of these congregations had a marvelous increase, soon becoming centers of intense missionary activities which spread to the surrounding communities. Christianity spread to western Europe.[112] There existed flourishing Christian communities in Gaul, especially in Lyons and Vienna, by the middle of the second century. Around 80 A.D. the Roman government established Roman provinces in Upper and Lower Germany, with Cologne as the center. Irenaeus (d. 202 A.D.) evidently refers to these provinces when he speaks of the preaching of the Gospel among the Germans and other barbarians who "without paper and ink, have salvation written in their hearts by the Holy Spirit." But just how extensively the Gospel was preached in these regions in the Apostolic Age cannot be definitely determined.

Everywhere Christianity proved capable of transforming the hearts and minds of men and renovating society. How remarkable this change was may partly be understood by comparing Christianity with the pagan religion. It was not the function of heathen religion to make men virtuous. "The chief objects of pagan religion were to foretell the future, to explain the universe, to avert calamity, and to obtain the assistance of the gods. They contained no instruments of moral teaching analogous to our institution of preaching, or to the moral preparation for the reception of the sacrament, or to the confession, or to the reading of the Bible, or to religious education, or to united prayer for spiritual benefits. To make men virtuous was no more the function of the priest than of the physician."[113]

The spiritual development is remarkably well reflected in the New Testament writings of this period. The readers addressed in the Epistle of Jude were in a most threatening danger because of prevalent libertine and antinomian[114] tendencies. The readers addressed in the Epistle to the Hebrews were exposed to a twofold difficulty: (1) they were under strong pressure to abandon the religion of Jesus Christ; (2) they were partly exposed to outward persecutions. In the writings of the Apostle John, incipient gnostic tendencies are clearly combated.[115]

[112] For a statement of the early traditions, see p. 48.
[113] W. E. H. Lecky: *History of European Morals*, Chapter IV.
[114] anti: *against* nomos: *law*.
[115] For a discussion of Gnosticism, see next chapter.

Ephesus and vicinity had been a field of speculative thought even in the days of Paul. This is evidenced by Colossians, and by Paul's warning to the Ephesian elders: "I know that after my departing grievous wolves shall enter in among you, not sparing the flock; and from among your own selves shall men arise, speaking perverse things, to draw away the disciples after them."[116] Paul said this, no doubt, on the basis of personal observation and experience.[117]

What Paul had predicted became a reality during John's residence in Ephesus. False teachers and unsound tendencies found their way to the city. Cerinthus, a contemporary of John, was the best known of these teachers. His teachings may be summarized as follows: There is a boundless chasm between God and the world. This chasm is bridged by intermediate beings, consisting of angels of various orders. Our world was not created by God, but by one of the inferior angels who did not know the supreme God. The Mosaic Law was given by the ministry of angels, and was consequently of a subordinate importance. The world-creating angel was the ruler of the Jewish people, the Jehovah of the Old Testament. Above him the Jewish people as a body could never rise. Only a few enlightened people had the true knowledge of the supreme God and worshipped him. Cerinthus denied the supernatural conception of Christ. He distinguished between Jesus, the lower earthly Messiah, and the heavenly Christ who came upon Jesus in baptism, and left him before the suffering on the cross. Hence Cerinthus attached no importance to the suffering on the cross as connected with Christ's work of redemption. Epiphanius states that Cerinthus also denied the resurrection of Jesus. He is also said to have entertained gross and sensual notions about an earthly millennium.[118]

In view of the fact that such doctrines were spread in Ephesus and vicinity, it is readily understood why the venerable Apostle John would endeavor to establish the Christians more firmly in what they had already experienced, namely (1) "that ye may believe that Jesus is the Christ"—not an earthly Jesus and a heavenly Christ; (2) that this Jesus Christ is "the son of God," and not merely the son of Joseph and Mary, or the son of an inferior, world-creating angel; (3) "and that believing ye may have life in his name." This was the purpose of John's Gospel,[119] which was written in conscious opposition to the doctrines of Cerinthus.

[116] Acts 20:29-30.   [117] 1 Cor. 16:9.
[118] mille: *thousand* annus: *year*, cf. Rev. 20:1-5.
[119] John 20:30-31.

The spiritual condition of the Christian communities in Asia Minor toward the close of the Apostolic Age is well pictured in the messages to the Seven Churches.[120] Persecutions from without, heresies from within, and a compromising attitude toward these heresies threatened to paralyze the spiritual life of the Church. How fortunate for the Church that the Apostle John, the bosom friend of the Lord, still lived and could interpret the person and the mission of Christ; and that he could define Christian truth in its relation to changing surroundings. The writings of John are unexcelled in their clear portrayal of Jesus Christ as the Son of God, as the Son of Man, and as the Lamb of God that taketh away the sin of the world.

John's long stay in Ephesus was roughly interrupted. He was banished to the island of Patmos during the reign of Domitian (A.D. 81-96). From Patmos he wrote Revelation,[121] the last book of the Bible. He was permitted to return to Ephesus, where he died in extremely old age after 98 A.D.

Standing on the divide of the first Christian century, looking backward, the rise and the development of the Christian Church may be considered in the terms of two symbols: (1) Up to around 70 A.D., Jewish and Gentile Christianity developed side by side, like two massive, well-proportioned pillars.[122] From 70-100 A.D. these pillars are connected by a beautiful arch. (2) A small grain of mustard seed is placed in the ground. The roots go back to the Old Testament. Then the stem and the branches and the leaves appear. The herb grows into a mighty tree. But quite early spurious and wild branches appear, and these make a decided claim to genuineness on account of their supposed connection with the root. Is the Church able to distinguish between the genuine and the spurious; will these branches be allowed to continue to grow, or will they be removed like withered branches?

8. REVIEW QUESTIONS

1. Why did Ephesus become a center of Christianity?
2. How was the Apostle John equipped to step in as the church leader at this time?
3. How did the destruction of Jerusalem influence the development of the Church?
4. What can you say about the outward growth of the Church during these years?
5. Why was not pagan religion capable of transforming the hearts and minds of men, and renovating society?

[120] Rev. 2:1-3:22.   [121] Rev. 1:9.   [122] See diagram on page 50.

6. What particular dangers threatened the spiritual life of the Church?
7. Why were the views of Cerinthus so dangerous for the Church?
8. Why was the Apostle John so particularly well qualified to interpret and to define Christian truth in its relation to the changing surroundings?
9. How would you briefly characterize the rise and the development of the Apostolic Church?

TOPICS FOR SPECIAL STUDY

1. The Apostle John as a church leader.
2. The destruction of Jerusalem and its consequences.
3. False teachings combated in the Epistle of Jude.
4. The Melchizedekian cult and the Epistle to the Hebrews.
5. The Nicolaitans (Rev. 2:12-17; etc.)
6. Does Rev. 20 clearly predict a reign of Christ on earth?

V. Persecutions in the Apostolic Era.—The Jews were the first to persecute the Christians. The people who had rejected and crucified their Messiah would naturally attack his followers. "If they persecuted me, they will also persecute you."[123] The Sadducees were the first to cause trouble in Jerusalem, because the Christians proclaimed in Jesus the resurrection from the dead.[124] Peter and John were arrested, brought to trial before Jewish religious authorities, and were charged not to speak at all nor to teach in the name of Jesus.[125]

A second attack was made upon the Christians by the Sadducees, under the direction of the high priest. This time all the apostles were arrested. They were brought before the council, and the members of the council "were minded to slay them," but Gamaliel warded off this calamity. Finally the apostles after being beaten and charged not to speak in the name of Jesus, were permitted to leave.[126]

The third attack upon the Christians was made jointly by the Sadducees and the Pharisees, as a result of the martyrdom of Stephen. Saul of Tarsus, one of the leaders of this persecution, was a strict Pharisee,[127] and no doubt had the support of his party in his vigorous attack upon the Christians. "Breathing threatening and slaughter against the disciples of the Lord,"[128] he even went to distant Damascus in order that he might bring Christian men and women bound to Jerusalem.

King Herod Agrippa I was the first secular authority to persecute the Christians. He "Put forth his hands to afflict certain of the church, and killed James the brother of John, with the sword. When he saw that it pleased the Jews, he proceeded to seize Peter

[123] John 15:20.
[124] Acts 4:2.
[125] Acts 4:5-18.
[126] Acts 5:18-40.
[127] Acts 23:6.
[128] Acts 9:1.

also."[129] This persecution occurred in 44 A.D. The cause may be sought in the policy of the king to cultivate popular Jewish favor by zealously defending the Jewish religion. There is no reason to believe that Herod acted on orders from Rome.

In Acts 18:2 there is a reference to an edict of Emperor Claudius that all Jews should depart from Rome. Suetonius[130] states that the Jews were expelled because of the constant tumults produced by one Chrestus. Some see in this name a reference to Christ and the Christians. But Chrestus was actually a current Greek and Roman name. And Suetonius[131] had definite knowledge of the sect called Christians. Hence it is inconceivable that he should have understood Christ the founder of Christianity as Chrestus the agitator. In that case he must have believed that Christ was present in Rome. That he should entertain such belief is most improbable, for not only Suetonius,[132] but also Pliny and Tacitus[133] had definite knowledge of Christ and the Christians. Furthermore, Aquila and Priscilla were still Jews—and not Christians—when Paul met them in Corinth.[134] They had been expelled from Rome as Jews, not as Christians. Hence this edict, which dated from around 50-52 A.D., was not against the Christians, but against the Jews.

Many of the slanders and insults against the Christians, and blasphemous remarks about Christianity, were caused by Jews who frequently stirred up the heathen populace against the Christians[135] by accusing the Christians of revolting against the decrees of Caesar.[136] The Apostolic Church was also troubled by false Jewish teachers, who caused much ill-feeling against the Christians.

The New Testament never presents Christ and Christianity as hostile to the State. Christ had told his disciples to render unto Caesar the things that were Caesar's, and unto God the things that were God's. Paul had repeatedly stated that the government is of God, and that the Christians should be in subjection to rulers and to authorities. Peter and the other apostles had taken the same attitude. Up to 60 A.D., when Paul came to Rome as a prisoner, the State had been in no hostile relation to the Church. The military captain in Jerusalem had saved Paul's life[137] and had given him safe journey to Caesarea. Paul had been kept a prisoner in Caesarea for two years because the governors concerned courted the favor of the Jews, not because they hated Paul or the other Christians.

[129] Acts 12:1-3.
[130] Claudius 25.
[131] Nero XVI.
[132] Nero XVI.
[133] Annals XV, 44.
[134] Acts 12:2.
[135] Acts 13:50; 14:2; 14:19; 17:5f.; 18:12; etc.
[136] Acts 17:7.
[137] Acts 21:31ff.

At his final trial the government had found that he had done nothing worthy of death or bonds.[138] He might have been set free if he had not appealed his case to Caesar. In Rome he was well treated and was even allowed to live in his own hired dwelling. As a prisoner he was allowed to preach, to write, and to receive visitors.

Gentile persecution of the Christians did not originate with the State as such, but with the *populace*. The earliest form of pagan persecution consisted mainly of slanders and insults against the Christians, in blasphemous remarks about Christianity. Such a state is reflected in the First Epistle of Peter, written around 62-64 A.D. The popular feeling toward the Christians had by this time grown quite hostile; and as every interest in the Roman Empire centered in the State, it is evident that the Roman government would sooner or later reflect the popular opinion of the populace by taking active measures against the Christians. Paul's trial at Rome in 62 A.D., and the legal hearings that preceded the Neronian persecution in 64 A.D., focused the attention of the authorities on the Christians.

A great conflict between Christianity and the Graeco-Roman world was inevitable. Christianity challenged almost everything for which the Roman world stood, and condemned or excluded many phases of the life of antiquity. There were at least sixteen points of difference.

1. In the Graeco-Roman world the State was conceived of as the Highest Good. The State included all the possible good that could come to man, even religion, which was subordinated to the State. Hence supreme loyalty to the State was the great Roman ideal. Service to the State was the purpose of life. But the Christians were citizens of a kingdom that was not of this world.[139] They recognized an authority that was higher than the State, and if the law of the Empire came in conflict with the law of God, they would obey God rather than man.[140] It was this supreme loyalty to a law outside the Roman law that irritated and worried the Roman authorities more than all other accusations against Christianity combined. Christianity struck at the very root of ancient Romanism by opposing this one-sided, all-subjecting political element. The Christians were rightly accused of inducing the Romans to renounce the existing State religion, and to believe in the only true religion, Christianity. The Romans concluded that Chris-

[138] Acts 26:31.   [139] John 18:36.   [140] Acts 5:29.

tianity was anti-national and hostile to the State and disloyal to the Emperor. Hence the Christians had no right to exist. They were accused of high treason, and punished accordingly.

2. Christianity appeared in the Graeco-Roman world as a new religion, not permitted. The guiding principle of Rome against new religions was, "Whoever introduced new religions, the tendency and character of which were unknown, whereby the minds of men might be disturbed, should, if belonging to the higher rank, be banished; if to the lower, punished with death." Another Roman law against secret meetings was turned against the Christians during the reign of Trajan. The Christian congregations were looked upon as secret associations, as unlawful corporations.

3. The Christians refused to live like other people. The Roman world advocated pleasure, happiness, and the satisfaction of the senses as personal ends. The Christians preached and practiced self-denial, and emphasized the joy of a future life. They would not decorate their houses for a pagan festival; they would not make advantageous marriages into heathen families; they would not accept government offices which included the performance of heathen religious rites. To use the words of Caecilius, "You in the meantime, in suspense and anxiety, are abstaining from respectable enjoyments. You do not visit the shows; you are not present in the solemn processions; you do not appear at public banquets; you abhor the sacred contests, and the meats and drinks a portion of which has been offered and poured out upon the altars. You do not wreathe your heads with flowers; you do not honor your bodies with odors; you reserve unguents for funeral rites, you even refuse garlands to your sepulchres—pale, trembling beings, worthy of pity, even the pity of our gods. Thus, wretched ones, you neither rise again, nor meanwhile do you live." The heathen populace, and the government, came to look upon the Christians as a race that was averse to all that is great, fair, and noble in humanity. The Christians were accused of being hostile to humanity—*haters of mankind*.

4. The Roman religion was purely external; consequently it was very impressive. The Romans could not conceive of religious services without temples and images, altars and sacrifices. The early Christians had no impressive temples or images. They had no sacrifices and no altars. They prayed to an unseen God. The Romans could not understand such worship. They reasoned that the Christians had no God and that they therefore were atheists. But atheism was a very serious offence in the Roman Empire.

Hence, *away with the atheists!* Charges of atheism and super-stition were common during the reign of Domitian, A.D. 81-96.

5. The Christians consistently refused to worship the Emperor because such worship would involve a denial of their Lord. The government considered such refusal an act of high treason and punished the offenders accordingly. They were also looked upon as anarchists.

6. Society, built on a basis of slavery, was filled with social classes. Christianity proclaimed the equality of all men before God, and thereby struck at the very root of slavery. The Apostolic Church was not in position, however, to take active measures against this evil. Consequently, this view did not invite active persecution.

7. Family life was very corrupt. Infidelity and divorce were common. Infanticide was a prevailing practice. Christianity pro-claimed the sacredness of marriage and the family life, and con-demned exposure of infants as murder.

8. There was a union of the State and religion, with religion subordinate to the State. Christianity favored a separation of Church and State.

9. The Romans worshipped many gods and tolerated the offi-cially recognized religions. The Christians excluded all other religions, and worshipped one God only.

10. Christianity honored all useful labor, and exhorted all in every class to work. "If any will not work, neither let him eat."[141] This was completely against contemporary thought.

11. The miracles of healing, and the cures of demoniacs at-tributed to the Christians brought upon them the suspicion of practicing magic; of being in possession of magical books, the Scriptures; and of being in league with the powers of darkness. The practice of magic was a serious offence.

12. Paul and Silas[142] were accused of introducing customs which the Romans could not lawfully receive or observe. Christians were later frequently accused of destroying the good old customs, on which the Empire and civilization rested. Public calamities, such as droughts, earthquakes, famine, pestilence, floods, were looked upon as revenge of the gods because the people tolerated the Christians in their midst.

13. Those who lived by pagan worship, men like the Ephesian silversmiths,[143] the people who sold cattle for pagan sacrifices,

[141] 2 Thess. 3:10. [142] Acts 16:21. [143] Acts 19:23.

the procurers, the poisoners, the fortune-tellers, etc., accused the Christians of injuring their trade.

14. Some persecution arose from family dissensions, as fore-told by the Lord.[144]

15. The secrecy of the Christian meetings in times of persecu-tions gave rise to widely circulated—and generally believed—rumors that the Christians were guilty of abominable immorality (incest and cannibalism).

16. As none but Christians would be present, they surrounded the Lord's Supper with some secrecy. Since the non-believers heard that the Christians on such occasions were eating "body" and drinking "blood," they spread stories that the Christians ate human flesh, drank human blood, and killed little children. As they credulously listened to such tales the populace stirred to blind rage, becoming a savage mob against the Christians.

The first imperial persecution, almost accidental, of the Chris-tians began in 64 A.D. From the 19th to the 24th of July, 64 A.D., the city of Rome burned. Emperor Nero wanted to divert from himself the suspicion of being the author of the fire. He knew the Christians had already become objects of popular hatred. By accusing them of incendiarism, he could furnish new entertainment for his diabolical cruelty, and make himself popular by inflicting sufferings on the hated Christians. Consequently, the Christians in Rome were accused of incendiarism, misanthropy, and unnatu-ral vice. A horrible persecution followed. Many Christians were executed in the most cruel manner. Burning alive was the ordinary punishment of incendiaries. The Christians were accordingly nailed to posts of pine, covered with combustible material, and set on fire to illuminate the public gardens at night. Some were crucified. Others were sewn up in skins of wild beasts and exposed to be torn to pieces by mad dogs. Peter is said to have suffered martyr-dom in Rome under Nero in 64 A.D. Paul was martyred by the same Emperor two years later.

This persecution seems to have been confined mainly to the city of Rome, although the example set by the Emperor may have been followed in some of the provinces. But the Christians were from then on in constant jeopardy in many parts of the Empire. Nero was followed by Vespasian (68-79), and Vespasian's son Titus (79-81). There were no official persecutions by these two emperors. Vespasian, however, demanded rigid loyalty to the State; and

[144] Matth. 10:34 ff.

Titus felt that both Christianity and Judaism had in them the same tendency of revolt against the State.

Domitian (81-96 A.D.) was a persecuting emperor, especially during the latter part of his reign. Non-Christian Jews were the immediate cause of this persecution because they refused to pay poll-tax to the Capitolene Jupiter. The resulting conflicts between government officials and Jews often involved the Christians, because the Romans did not as yet definitely distinguish between Jews and Christians. This emperor zealously suppressed all religious and secular organizations which he thought capable of political intrigue. Two grandsons of Jude, the brother of the Lord, were summoned from distant Palestine because they were relatives of the Lord, and descendants of King David. But when he saw these simple countrymen and their calloused hands, he thought them incapable of engaging in political schemes, and they were dismissed in peace.

Emperor worship was generally enforced at this time. The Christians refused to participate. Hence the general charge against them was high treason. Additional charges of atheism and superstition were quite common. It is not definitely known whether Domitian issued any edict prohibiting any one from belonging to the Church, although some think such an edict must have been prepared during the period between Nero and Trajan, and that Domitian actually prepared it. The Christians were punished, some by confiscation of property; others by banishment; others by death.

There was no general, carefully planned, widespread, and systematic persecution of the Church at large in the Apostolic Age. The persecutions under Nero and Domitian were "mere outbreaks of personal cruelty and tyrannical caprice." Trajan and his successors directed their attacks mainly against individual Christians. Decius (249-251 A.D.) was the first emperor to initiate a general widespread persecution which aimed at the complete suppression of Christianity.

9. REVIEW QUESTIONS

1. Why did the Jews, particularly the Pharisees and the Sadducees, persecute the Christians?
2. Who was the first secular authority to persecute the Christians? What was his motive?
3. How was the relation between Church and State up to around 60 A.D.?
4. How did the Gentile persecution of the Christians begin?

5. Discuss some of the causes of the Christian persecutions.
6. May the Christian leaders, in anticipation of the persecutions, have minimized the conflict by promoting a better understanding of the principles of Christianity? Give reasons for your answer.
7. What can you say about the first imperial persecution of the Christians?
8. What was the relation between Church and State during the reign of Domitian?
9. How did the persecutions in the Apostolic Era differ from the Decian persecution?
10. How did the persecutions influence the Church at large? List the possible good or evil results.
11. What does the rumor about cannibalism prove concerning the Christian conception of that time about the Lord's Supper?

TOPICS FOR SPECIAL STUDY

1. The legal status of Christianity in the Roman Empire.
2. The status of the Jews in the Roman Empire during the first century A.D.
3. Christianity versus the ancient world: a conflict of ideas and ideals.
4. The ideal relation between church and state.

VI. Organization, Life, Discipline, and Worship.—What is the Christian Church? How does this Church differ from other organizations? Externally, "the Church is the congregation of saints, in which the Gospel is rightly taught and the Sacraments rightly administered. And to the true unity of the Church, it is enough to agree concerning the doctrine of the Gospel and the administration of the Sacraments. Nor is it necessary that human traditions, rites, or ceremonies, instituted by men, should be everywhere alike."[145] Internally, "the Church is not only the fellowship of outward objects and rites, as other governments, but it is in principle a fellowship of faith and the Holy Ghost in hearts."[146]

There was an organic relation between the Old Testament "congregation" and the New Testament "church." Yet the two institutions differed considerably in matters of organization and worship. The former had a special priesthood characteristic of Old Testament times. The latter had a universal priesthood of all Christians, through the eternal mediatorship of Jesus Christ. "He made us to be a kingdom, to be priests unto his God and Father."[147] "Ye are an elect race, a royal priesthood, a holy nation, a people for God's own possession."[148]

This universal priesthood of believers was gathered into an organism under Christ, the founder and the head of the Church. God "put all things under his feet, and gave him to be the head over all things in the church, which is his body, the fullness of him that

---

[145] *Augsburg Confession*, Art. VII.
[146] *Apology of the Augsburg Confession*, IV, 5.
[147] Rev. 1:6.
[148] 1 Pet. 2:9; cf. Heb. 4:16.

filleth all in all."[149] "For as the body is one, and hath many members, and all the members of the body, being many, are one body; so also is Christ."[150] The body here refers to the Church.

The Lord gave to his Church all the essentials of organization.[151] Remember that he charged them with: (1) The preaching of the Word of God; (2) the administration of the two Sacraments; (3) the Apostolate, the first office of the Christian Church; (4) the power of discipline; (5) the promise, and the actual sending of the Holy Spirit.

Extraordinary importance was attached to the direct guidance of the Holy Spirit in all affairs of the Church. The Lord said concerning the Spirit: "he shall teach you all things, and bring to your remembrance all that I said unto you."[152] "When he, the Spirit of truth, is come, he shall guide you into all truth."[153] Luther says in his Catechism concerning the Holy Spirit that He "calls, gathers, enlightens, and sanctifies."[154]

Christ had also arranged for the guidance of the Church through the office of the *Apostolate*.[155] The apostles had been carefully selected and trained by him. They were the recognized leaders of the Church because of (1) their special call from the Lord, (2) their special training by the Lord, (3) their miraculous endowments and their God-given authority from which there was no appeal, and (4) their special revelations from the Lord after his resurrection.[156] Hence the apostles differed from other early Christians who also possessed special or extraordinary gifts of the Holy Spirit.[157] The apostolate embraced, as stated before, all the various orders or functions which the Church transmitted to later times. The functions which later were assigned to bishops, presbyters, deacons, pastors, prophets, evangelists, and charismatic persons, did all originally center in the apostles.

As the Church grew rapidly, and the work soon became too extensive for the apostles, the congregation in Jerusalem elected a committee of seven to assist them. The duties of the Seven are implied in Acts 6:1-3. From this it appears that the *Deaconate* was the second office to be instituted in the Church. The Seven in Acts 6:1-6 are not called deacons, however, and consequently some have claimed that the Presbyterate, and not the Deaconate, was the continuation of the Seven. But it should be remembered that the office and the function of the presbyters were at that time still

---

[149] Ephes. 1:22-23.
[150] 1 Cor. 12:12.
[151] cf. pp. 35-36.
[152] John 14:26.
[153] John 16:12-13.
[154] Acts 5:4.9.
[155] Luke 6:13; Matth. 28:16-20.
[156] cf. pp. 35-36.
[157] 1 Cor. 12:4-11; 12:28.

vested in the apostles themselves. The Seven were assistants to
the apostles, as the deacons later were assistants to the elders.[158]
The apostles, and later the elders or presbyters, retained the supervision and guidance of the deacons.

The Official Relation between Apostles, Deacons, and Elders:

The *Presbyterate* or the office of elders was probably the third
office to be instituted in the Church. Nothing is said of the origin
of this office, but it very likely shaped itself after the synagogue.
Christian presbyters are mentioned for the first time in Acts 11:30.
In the New Testament there are two names used interchangeably
for these officials, namely "presbyteroi" or presbyters, and "epis-
copoi" or bishops (cf. pastor, minister, elder). Some believe that
"presbyter" was a title of dignity, and that "bishop" was a corresponding title of function; but the facts presented in 1 Tim. 3:1-7
and 5:17-22 do not warrant such conclusion. The only difference
between presbyters and bishops seems to have been a difference in
name. From Acts 14:23 it is clear that Paul and Barnabas, on their
First Missionary Journey, entrusted the general leadership of the
various local churches they had founded to local elders. These succeeded the apostles as the spiritual leaders and general directors
of the local congregations.

Paul made it a practice to organize all the churches he founded,
or came in contact with, according to a definite system. His first
act was to select from each local congregation a group of elders
who should function as spiritual leaders and general directors, each
group for its own local church. This he did on his First and
Second Missionary Journeys, as also during the last years of his
life.[159] Local elders, or presbyters, succeeded the apostles as the
leaders of the churches, and the deacons assisted the elders.[160]
This was the prevailing church organization, at least in the regions
of Asia Minor and in Europe, during the time of Paul.

The monarchical episcopate, of which there was no trace in the
Pastoral Epistles, or in the time of Paul, first gained a foothold in
the provinces of Asia toward the close of the Apostolic Age. This
is evidenced in the epistles of John, and in Revelation. The
monarchical episcopate had become the highest office in the local

[158] Acts 14:23; Phil. 1:1; 1 Thess. 5:12; cf. Acts 20:17.
[159] Tit. 1:5; 1 Tim. 3:1-13; etc.   [160] Phil. 1:1; 1 Tim. 3:1-13; etc.

church, that is, the leadership of each congregation centered in one single official who was superior to the other elders and to the deacons. This is clear from the messages of the Lord to the Seven Churches.[161] At the time these messages were given (around 94-96 A.D.), the name "episcopos" or bishop had evidently not as yet become the regular title of individual bishops, as was the case in the epistles of Ignatius, written around 110 A.D. The authorized leaders of the Seven Churches are designated by two symbols: "The seven stars are the angels of the seven churches."[162] Stars, in Scriptural language, frequently designate those who govern or rule; and the name "angel" is used in the Old Testament to designate prophets and priests, whom God had sent to the people to proclaim the will and the Word of God. The officials of the Seven Churches are called "stars" because of the leadership; and "angels" because of their exalted position and their great responsibility. Notice how the Lord placed the entire responsibility for the congregation on a single official, and not on a group of elders.

Timothy and Titus were not ordinary elders or presbyters, but above them. Both acted as temporary representatives of Paul in his apostolic capacity, Timothy in Ephesus and vicinity, and Titus on the island of Crete. Paul felt himself responsible for the development of the churches in these two districts, especially with reference to doctrine and organization. In the temporary functions of Timothy and Titus one may see, perhaps, the rudiments of the Diocesan episcopacy, although this office was not formally instituted until the second century. But the position of the Apostle John in Ephesus, at the time he wrote his epistles and Revelation, had nearly all the characteristics of a later diocesan bishop. Compare also the earlier relation of James the Just to the Jewish churches in the Dispersion, as reflected in the Epistle of James.

There were also the Christians who had received special and extraordinary gifts of the Holy Spirit. These special endowments belonged to no special order or office in the Church, but they were given to believers as the Spirit willed.[163] These gifted persons, with the exception of women,[164] were allowed to teach and to preach in the congregation. Some of them were employed as special evangelists.[165] The office of the deaconesses is referred to in Rom. 16:1. From 1 Tim. 5:9 it appears that only widows above the age of 60 were admitted to this office. They took care of the poor, the sick, and the strange women in the congregation.

---

[161] Rev., Chap. 2-3.   [163] 1 Cor. 12:11.   [165] Acts 21:8; Ephes. 4:11.
[162] Rev. 1:20.   [164] 1 Cor. 14:34; 1 Tim. 2:12.

Careful instructions were given as to the qualifications of candidates for church office.[166] A brief study of the first recorded election in the Apostolic Church[167] leaves the following impressions: (1) the qualifications of those to be elected were defined by the apostles; (2) the right to elect candidates was regarded by the apostles as vested in the church; (3) the election itself was performed by the congregation, but the appointment and the consecration were completed by the apostles; (4) the final act was the imposition of hands, signifying the divine communication of power and grace. This procedure evidently became the accepted order in the early Church.

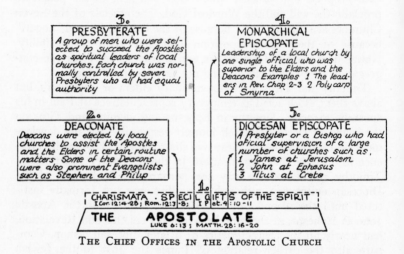

3.
PRESBYTERATE
A group of men who were selected to succeed the Apostles as spiritual leaders of local churches. Each church was normally controlled by seven Presbyters who all had equal authority

4.
MONARCHICAL EPISCOPATE
Leadership of a local church by one single official who was superior to the Elders and the Deacons Examples 1 The leaders in Rev. Chap. 2-3 2 Polycarp of Smyrna

2.
DEACONATE
Deacons were elected by local churches to assist the Apostles and the Elders in certain routine matters Some of the Deacons were also prominent Evangelists such as Stephen and Philip

5.
DIOCESAN EPISCOPATE
A Presbyter or a Bishop who had official supervision of a large number of churches such as, 1 James at Jerusalem 2 John at Ephesus 3 Titus at Crete

1.
CHARISMATA . SPECIAL GIFTS OF THE SPIRIT
I Cor. 12:4-28; Rom. 12:3-8; I Pet. 4:10-11

THE   APOSTOLATE
LUKE 6:13 ; MATTH. 28: 16-20

THE CHIEF OFFICES IN THE APOSTOLIC CHURCH

Brotherly love[168] was the guiding principle in the life of the Christians. "By this shall all men know that ye are my disciples, if ye have love one to another." This love expressed itself in tender care for the sick and needy, and in a remarkable hospitality. Their pure and unselfish living soon aroused the admiration of the non-Christians. The Christians acted as a wholesome leaven in a decaying society. Christianity checked, and gradually removed three great evils of antiquity, contempt of foreign nationalities, slavery, and degradation of womanhood.[169]

Church discipline was quite severe. Heretics, apostates, and those who had committed gross sins, were excluded from communion

166 1 Tim. 3:1-13; Acts 6:3.
167 Acts 6:1-6.
168 John 13:34-35.
169 Gal. 3:28.

with the Church. The idea was also current that certain sins committed after baptism admitted of no pardon, but involved permanent exclusion from the Church. For this reason baptism was preceded by careful instruction, not only in doctrine, but also in the things Christians were to seek and shun.

For the essential characteristics of the Christian worship, see Section 2 of the present chapter. Sunday, "the Lord's day," was set aside for worship because of hallowed associations. On this day the Lord rose from the dead. The birthday of the Church, the first Christian Pentecost, was on a Sunday. And the first day of the week God created the world and turned darkness to light.[170]

On Sundays two services were usually held. The forenoon service consisted of praise, prayer, and preaching and to this also others than Christians might be admitted. The evening service was concluded by a "love feast," or common supper, which again was followed by the Lord's Supper, or the Sacrament of the Altar. Toward the close of the Apostolic Age, or shortly after 100 A.D., these "love feasts" were abandoned, and the Eucharist was transferred to the forenoon service.

It is not likely that the various churches followed a uniform, fixed law regarding the form of worship. The form of a service would naturally depend, to some extent, on the gifts of those who took part. But even the spontaneous, unpremeditated utterances of those speaking with "tongues," and the "word of prophecy," were presented to the audience in becoming order.

Places of worship were to begin with in the Temple,[171] in the synagogues,[172] and in private houses.[173] Rented buildings were also used.[174] Special church buildings, erected in a later era, were usually in basilica style.

Artistic decorations were used by Christians in solemn resting places of the dead, toward the end of the first Christian century. Prominent church leaders admonished their followers to pay attention to things "good and lovely."[175] It is therefore reasonable to conclude that art had a place in the house of worship and in the Christian home.

VII. What the Church had at the close of the Apostolic Era.—A brief summary of the achievements and the characteristics of Apostolic Christianity may be of interest.

---

[170] Sunday was hallowed by "sunrise" service and evening "love-feast" or agape. Otherwise the Christians worked on Sunday like other people. Constantine made Sunday a day of rest for state officials, but not for everybody. Christians had begun to rest on Sunday and have forenoon services sometime previous to Constantine's official decree.
[171] Acts 2:46; 3:1-4:3.   [172] James 2:2; Acts 13:13f.; 14:1; 17:1-2; 18:4f.; 19:8.
[173] Acts 2:46; 20:7-8; Rom. 16:23.   [174] Acts 19:9, etc.   [175] Phil. 4:8.

1. The Church as a living organism had, like the grain of mustard seed, been planted, and had developed into a mighty tree, whose branches overshadowed most of the civilized world. The spiritual power of this organism had proved itself capable of transforming the hearts and minds of the believers, and of gradually renovating a decaying society.

2. The Church had taken on its own characteristic forms of organization, life, and worship. On the rapidly growing tree, spurious shoots and false branches had begun to appear in the form of sects and heresies. The inner life and vitality were partly sapped by undue compromise, apostasy, and persecutions. The Church

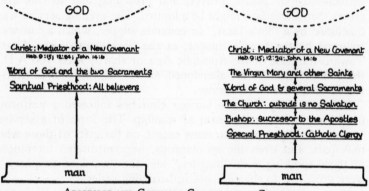

APOSTOLIC AND CATHOLIC CHRISTIANITY COMPARED

sought to adjust herself to these conditions: partly by a careful explanation of the great, fundamental Christian principles, as given in the New Testament; partly by the continued preaching of the Gospel in power and the Holy Spirit; and partly by the holy life of the Christians.

3. The life and the development of the Church became the basis of all future developments of Christianity. What the apostles taught and instituted became the model whereby all subsequent teaching or practice was to be judged. Apostolic Christianity became the authentic prototype of the Church of the future.

4. In anticipation of the development of the Church in the next centuries it may be of interest to compare Apostolic and Catholic Christianity, or apostolicity and catholicity. The following differences may be noticed: (1) the former recognized a universal,

spiritual priesthood of all believers; the latter recognized a special priesthood, which marked the division of the Christians into a "clergy" and a "laity." (2) To the question: where is the Church? the former said: "Where two or three are gathered in my name, there I am in the midst of them;" the latter said, where the bishop is, there is the Church. Outside of this Church there is no salvation. (3) The Apostolic Church held that every Christian had a direct access to God through faith in Jesus Christ; the Catholic Church held that communion with God was only possible through a communion with the bishop. (4) The former permitted any Christian man who had the special gifts of the Spirit to teach and to preach and to administer the Sacraments; the latter gave this authority to the bishop only. (5) The former maintained that a sinner received forgiveness by confessing his sins directly to God, as revealed through Jesus Christ in his Word; the latter maintained that forgiveness of sins came by mouth of a mediating priest. (6) The former conditioned personal communion with God on *faith* only; the latter conditioned such communion by strict adherence to certain outward forms. (7) The former conceived of the Church as a group of holy people who believed in Jesus Christ, a "congregation of saints;" the latter conceived of the Church as a group of believers who belonged to the episcopate, or to the Church of the bishops.

On the basis of these brief comparisons, the student will be able to anticipate some of, the subsequent developments—from apostolicity to catholicity. He will also be able to see how the accumulative effect of an extreme catholicity would inevitably lead to a Reformation, or to a demand that the Church should come back to the apostolic faith and practice.

10. REVIEW QUESTIONS

1. How does the Church differ externally and internally from other spiritual organization?
2. How did the Lord provide for the organization of his Church?
3. What place did the Holy Spirit have in the government of the Church?
4. Why the apostolate, the deaconate, and the presbyterate?
5. What was the prevailing church organization in the time of Paul?
6. What is meant by monarchical episcopate and diocesan episcopacy? Were these forms of government general in the Apostolic Church?
7. What place did the specially gifted (charismatic) members have in the general work of the congregation?
8. What general procedure was followed in the election of church officials?
9. What' was the guiding principle in the life of the Christians? Why?
10. How was church discipline practiced?
11. What can you say about the early Christian worship? What parts of the synagogue service were taken over?

12. Summarize the achievements and the characteristics of the Apostolic Church.

TOPICS FOR SPECIAL STUDY

1. Compare the Spiritual Priesthood of all Believers with the Special Priesthood (1) of the Old Testament (2) of the Catholic Church (3) of Protestantism. What is your conclusion?
2. The Christian Worship in the Apostolic Age and Today.
3. The Place of Woman in the Apostolic Church.
4. The Conception of the Church in the Apostolic Age.
5. Illustrate by a graph the theories concerning the ministry as held by the (1) Roman (2) Episcopalian (3) Lutheran Church.

A SELECTED BIBLIOGRAPHY FOR CHAPTER II

1. Ayer: *A Source Book for Ancient Church History.*
2. Rainy: *The Ancient Catholic Church, Chap. I-III.*
3. Sanday: *Outlines of the Life of Christ.*
4. Ramsay: *St. Paul the Traveler and Roman Citizen.*
5. Lightfoot: *Dissertations on the Apostolic Age.*
6. Schaff: *History of the Christian Church,* Vol. I.
7. Walker: *History of the Christian Church,* pp. 18-52.
8. Kidd: *Documents Illustrative of the History of the Church* (to A.D. 461).
9. Jackson: *Rise of Gentile Christianity.*
10. Dill: *Roman Society from Nero to Marcus Aurelius.*
11. Dobschütz: *Christian Life in the Primitive Church.*
12. Uhlhorn: *Christian Charity in the Ancient Church.*
13. Canfield: *The Early Persecutions of the Christians.*
14. Hatch: *The Organization of the Early Christian Churches.*

CHAPTER III

THE POST-APOSTOLIC ERA. A.D. 100-170

This era is called *post-apostolic* because the leadership of the Church during this era was entrusted largely to men who had enjoyed intercourse with and instruction from the apostles, among them Clement of Rome;[1] Barnabas, the fellow-missionary of Paul; Hermas;[2] Ignatius, Bishop of Antioch, and a disciple of Peter or John; Polycarp, Bishop of Smyrna, and a disciple of John; and Papias, Bishop of Hierapolis, and a disciple of John.

The sub-apostolic era may be likened to the figure of Janus, the double-faced Roman deity, with one face toward the Apostolic, and the other toward the Catholic Church. Special interest centers in the transition from apostolicity to catholicity.

The following is the source-material: Group I—Eusebius; "Ecclesiastical History," from the time of Christ (30 A.D.) to the time of Eusebius (A.D. 260-339). Group II—the writings of the Apostolic Fathers: (1) The Letter of Barnabas; (2) The Teachings of the Twelve; (3) The Letter of Clement of Rome; (4) The Shepherd of Hermas; (5) The Letters of Ignatius of Antioch; (6) The Letter of Polycarp; (7) Fragments of Papias. Group III—the writings of the Christian Apologists: (1) Quadratus (A.D. 125); (2) Aristides (A.D. 125); (3) Justin Martyr (A.D. 166); (4) Tatian the Assyrian. Group IV—the letters of Pliny and Trajan (A.D. 112).

HEAD OF JANUS

I. Christianity and the Jews.—The Apostolic Church had carefully followed the command of Christ to preach the Gospel to the Jews first. While the Christian leaders recognized the universality of the Gospel, they also realized that the Jews had priority, and that the problem of converting the Jewish nation to Christianity would have to be settled within a comparatively short time. The Jews as a nation might accept the Gospel,[3] but it seemed more likely that they would become bitter and passionate opponents

---

[1] cf. Phil. 4:3. [2] cf. Rom. 16:14. [3] Rom., Chap. 11.

of the Church. Hence the chief missionary work of the apostolic Church was to seek to win as many disciples of Moses for Christ as possible, ere it was too late. As the Church passed the first Christian century mark, the problem had largely been settled. The Jews as a nation had rejected the Gospel. Hence the chief problem of the Church during the sub-apostolic era was to settle down to the enormous task of converting the Gentile world.[4]

A terrible divine judgment[5] fell upon the Jews in 70 A.D. because they refused to accept their true Messiah and violently opposed the Church. The destruction of Jerusalem broke their national power, but not their hatred of Christianity. In the years that followed, they persecuted the Christians, as well as frequently rebelling against the Roman government.

The Emperor Hadrian, in A.D. 117, issued an imperial edict forbidding religious practices of the Jews such as circumcision, observance of the Sabbath, and public reading of the Law. A Roman colony was also to be found in Jerusalem, with pagan worship established in the city. The Jews, under the leadership of a false Messiah called Bar Cochba or "Son of the Star,"[6] started a rebellion in 132 A.D. Thousands of Jews from Palestine, Cyrene, Egypt, and Mesopotamia flocked to his standard. For three years the insurgents held the ruined fortress of Jerusalem. The Christians consistently refused to acknowledge this false Messiah, while their principles forbade them to join in the rebellion. They were therefore subjected to great cruelties by the followers of Bar Cochba. In 135 A.D. the rebellion was crushed by the Roman government after more than a half million Jews had perished. Jerusalem was rebuilt as a pagan city and called Aelia Capitolina. The Jews were forbidden to enter the city, or even to come near it.

With political independence destroyed, the Jews could not further independently persecute the Christians, but they retaliated by circulating horrible calumnies on Jesus Christ and his followers. In their learned rabbinical schools at Jabneh, Tiberias, and in Babylonia, they nourished a bitter, anti-Christian hostility. The presidents of these schools were the recognized spiritual leaders of the Jews. In these schools the Oral Jewish Tradition was consolidated and reduced to writing, a process which started in the second Christian century continuing for about five hundred years. The final result was the Talmud.

The Emperor permitted the Christians to remain in Jerusalem

cf. Rom. 11:11 ff.   [5] cf. Matth., Chap. 23-24.   [6] cf. Num. 24:17.

after 135 A.D., in acknowledgment of their neutrality during the rebellion of Bar Cochba. A Gentile-Christian congregation, headed by a Gentile-Christian bishop, was soon organized. While a small minority of Christian Jews joined this new Jerusalem church, the majority left because they were unable to brook the profanation of the Holy City, and because they were not willing to become a part of a Gentile congregation, governed by a Gentile bishop.

These events predicted the future development of the Jewish-Christian Church. A small minority gave up its specific Jewish identity being gradually absorbed in the Gentile church, but the great majority continued to live an exclusive life, with distinct tendencies away from the pure Gospel. This Jewish-Christian majority soon split up into a number of sects. From the second century these sects are easily grouped according to two general and distinct tendencies: (1) an orthodox group, including the Nazarenes, the Ebionites, and the Elkesites; (2) a group with marked syncretistic (mingled) tendencies, including the various Jewish gnostic sects. Each group furnished its own characteristic perversions of the Christian Gospel.

1. *The Orthodox Jews, or the Judaizers.* According to Acts 24:5, the name *Nazarene* was originally used by the Jews to designate all Christians. After the destruction of Jerusalem and down to the end of the fourth century, the Nazarenes were identified with a small group of Jewish Christians who held themselves bound by the Law of Moses, but did not refuse fellowship with Gentile Christians. They propagated themselves in certain churches of Coele-Syria. On an essentially Christian foundation they built a large super-structure of non-essentials, of which circumcision, observance of the Sabbath, and a carnal chiliasm were a part. Their zeal for these things, innocent in themselves, resulted in a growth in the wrong direction. The essentials of Christianity were gradually replaced by non-essentials, until the Nazarenes found themselves outside the Church. Wishing to be both Jew and Christian they were neither one nor the other.

The Ebionites had their name from a Hebrew word *ebion* which means poor, humble, oppressed. They regarded themselves as the genuine followers of Christ and his poor disciples. Ebionism had certain general characteristics. Christianity was degraded to the level of Judaism. The Law of Moses had universal and perpetual validity, and therefore it was binding on all Christians. Hence observance of the ceremonial law was necessary for salvation. The Apostle Paul was considered an apostate and a heretic whose epistles must be discarded. The Ebionites parted into two main branches: (a) the Pharisaic Ebionites, successors to the Judaizers whom Paul opposed in his Epistle to the Galatians; (b) Essenic Ebionites, corresponding to the errorists whom Paul opposed in his epistle to the Colossians.

About 220-222 A.D. a Syrian named Alcibiades of Apamea brought to Rome a book called the "Book of Elchesai," so named from two Syriac words which mean "hidden power." Elxai is said to have received this book believed to have fallen from heaven about 101 A.D. It contains a large element of pagan religion, mingled with Judaistic and Christian ideas. Some attention is given to astronomy and magic. Christ is described as an angel[7] who has been incarnated (bound up in a human body) several times. The chief characteristic of the book is perhaps the setting forth of a new theory of salvation by a new baptism. In times of persecution the Christians are allowed, according to this book, to renounce their faith. The views of the Elkesaites contributed to the origin of Mohammedanism.

2. *The Jewish Gnostics.* (a) *The name.* The name is formed from a Greek word *gnosis* which means *knowledge, enlightenment,* and sometimes *science.*[8] Compare the Christian Science movement of today. During the first three or four Christian centuries, the gnostics were identified with a group of people who proclaimed a salvation by *knowledge,* as opposed to the Christian proclamation of a salvation by *faith.*

(b) *Origin and development.* Traditionally, the gnostic movement has been considered a heathen or Gentile perversion of the Gospel, "an acute Hellenizing of Christianity." Consequently the movement could not have started until Christianity had had sufficient time to come in contact with the great Gentile world. Recent research has proved, however, that there existed a fairly well developed Jewish gnosticism even at the time of Christ, and that the prominent early gnostic leaders—Cerinthus, Basilides, Valentinus, and others—were Jews, who in turn received their main gnostic tenets from Philo Judeas, a learned Jew of Alexandria (20 B.C.-40 A.D.). Gnosticism originated on Jewish soil, and from the Jews the movement spread to the Gentiles.

Attention is again called to the Jewish adoption of foreign religious and cultural elements. In these foreign elements, taken over and cultivated on Jewish and Christian soil, the germs of gnosticism must be sought. Left to themselves and allowed to

[7] cf. Hebr. 1:4-6.   [8] cf. 1 Tim. 6:20.

develop on native soil, these foreign elements[9] would not of themselves have constituted a gnosticism. But when the Jews mixed
these elements with Jewish and Christian ideas, and moulded the
whole thing into a religio-philosophic system, a gnostic movement
resulted.

The roots of the gnostic movement can be traced far back into
pre-Christian times. The admonition in Ecclesiasticus 3:21-22 is
now—by many—considered a warning against gnostic speculations.
F. Weber,[10] thinks this book was written around 300 B.C. Rabbi
Jochanan ben Zakkai, the great contemporary of the apostle Paul,
knew of a Mishnah that warned against gnostic speculations.[11]
This Mishnah must have been formulated in pre-Christian times.
Jochanan ben Zakkai was himself well versed in gnostic speculations. There is an organic relation between the Jewish Cabala and
the gnostic speculations.

Jewish literature produced during the two centuries before
Christ, displays the following distinct tendencies: (1) stress on the
absolute majesty and sovereignty of God above the world; (2)
mediary beings—angels, and archangels, and a special divine agent
—between this far distant God and mankind; (3) development
of a remarkable Sophia or Wisdom literature; (4) a doctrine of
two primary Powers or Principles, good and evil; (5) a special
divine "dynamis" or agent, conceived of in various ways—in
Jewish-Babylonian literature as Seth, Enoch, Melchizedek, etc., in
Palestine as the Metraton, in Alexandria as the Logos, and in
Patristic literature as the Horos, Stauros, Lytrotes, etc.; (6) adoption of several extra-canonical accounts of the creation; (7) adoption, especially in Alexandria, of a doctrine of macrocosm and
microcosm, that is, that man is nothing but a small universe, and
the universe is nothing but a large man. Compare these tendencies
with the characteristics of gnosticism, as given below.

Alexandria was the great meeting place for Greek, Jew, Egyptian, Roman, and Oriental. In this great center of learning, cultural
and religious elements from the various nations could be compared,
conciliated, and fused on a larger scale than anywhere else in the
world. Alexandria became the hot-bed of early Jewish gnosticism.
A particular brand of gnosticism was developed in Syria; another,
in Samaria.

As a system of speculative thought, gnosticism centered about
two general questions: first, the origin of the universe; second,
God and his mode of governing the world.

[9] cf. pp. 22-28.   [10] Weber: Jüdische Theologie, p. xiii.   [11] cf. Chagigah 11b.

(c) *Characteristics.* Stress was laid on a transcendent, nameless, unknowable, not-being God, corresponding to "the Great Unknown" of modern times. Mediary beings—the Pleroma—were believed to furnish intercourse between this far-distant God and mankind. There was great respect for the Great Mother, called Sophia or Wisdom. In the Christian period Sophia was usually identified with the Holy Spirit. Two primary and equal Powers, Good and Evil, were recognized. The latter was co-eternal with the former; hence the marked dualism in all gnostic systems. A special divine agent was to be the Redeemer of the world. Several extra canonical accounts of the creation were advocated. God himself did not directly create the world. From him proceeded a series

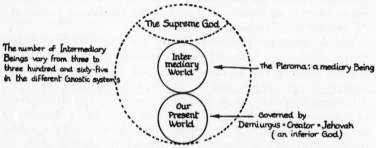

RUDIMENTS OF A GNOSTIC CONCEPTION OF THE UNIVERSE

of emanations or aeons on a descending scale. The lowest of these emanations was called the Demiurgus, or Creator. He was identified with the God of the Jews, the Jehovah of the Old Testament. Hence the Father of Jesus Christ, the God of the Christians, was vastly inferior to the Supreme God; and the apostles of Christ would accordingly be vastly inferior to the apostles of this Supreme Being. Recall the struggle in the New Testament between the apostles of Christ and those who claimed to be apostles but were found false. The gnostics would stamp the Old Testament revelation from Jehovah as far inferior to the true "gnosis" or revelation of the Supreme Being.

The doctrine of microcosm and macrocosm has, by some recent investigators, been considered the essential key to a study of gnosticism. As man consists of body, soul, and spirit, so the universe must have a corresponding division. Our visible world, limited by the sky heaven, corresponds to the human body; the region of the stars and the Holy Seven planets corresponds to the human soul; the third heaven, where God and the Sophia dwell, corresponds to the human mind. This same doctrine divided mankind into three groups; (a) the "hylics" or men of earth, who were not capable of being saved; (b) the "psychics," or men of heaven, who might or might not be saved; (c) the "pneumatics" or men of God, who alone were sure of salvation.

There were some additional beliefs. Sin was conceived of as residing in matter, or the body, and not as the Christians believed, in the heart or in the moral nature of man. The Fall was identified with the incorporation of material substance in the universe, and the fall of man simply consisted in the incarnation of spirits in material bodies, where these spirits were held as in a prison house.

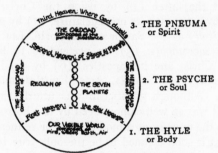

3. THE PNEUMA
or Spirit

2. THE PSYCHE
or Soul

1. THE HYLE
or Body

MICROCOSM AND MACROCOSM

Redemption consisted in the liberation of the spirit from the material body. The resurrection of the body was emphatically denied. Salvation came through knowledge (gnosis) imparted by the Redeemer. When a part of the spiritual world had fallen and had been incorporated into material substance, the Mediary beings, or inferior gods, held a council to determine how these spiritual elements could be redeemed, or brought back to the world of light. The gods decided that each should contribute the best he had, and so they created a new god, the Redeemer. His "humiliation" consisted in his leaving the world of light to come down to our world, in order that he might gather the spirits incarnated or bound up in matter.

This Redeemer could not have had a *real* body. That "the Word became flesh, and dwelt among us"[12] had to be explained away. This was done in one of several ways. (a) Christ had a phantom body. He was not truly born. Hence he did not suffer on the cross.

[12] John 1:14.

(b) Jesus was an ordinary human being upon whom the divine Christ came in baptism, and left him before the crucifixion. (c) A distinction was made between a higher, heavenly Christ and a lower, earthly Christ.

The gnostic ethics were either ascetic or libertine. If the body is evil, deny it proper care; or, if the body constitutes a prison house, abuse it in licentious living. Compare the Christian view[13] of the body as "the temple of the Holy Spirit." The gnostics had a number of sacraments, such as a baptism by water, a baptism by Spirit, and baptism by fire, anointment by oil, a supper, a sacrament of the bridal chamber, etc.

(d) *The Influence of Gnosticism on Christianity.* When gnosticism came in touch with Christianity, it rapidly adopted the outward garb of the latter (1) by using the Christian forms of thought, (2) by borrowing its nomenclature, (3) by acknowledging Christ *dualistically* as the Savior of the world, (4) by simulating the Christian sacraments, (5) by pretending to be an esoteric revelation of Christ and his apostles, (6) by producing a great number of apocryphal Gospels, Acts, Epistles, and Revelations (apocalypses). Although gnosticism was utterly the opposite of Christianity, it was so well camouflaged by this borrowed garb that it appeared to the unwary as a modification or refinement of Christianity. In fact it soon claimed to be the only true form of Christianity, set apart for the elect, unfit for the vulgar crowd.

Gnosticism, highly aggressive, became so widely diffused throughout the Christian churches that for several centuries, especially from the second to the fourth, it threatened to stifle Christianity altogether. Many of the early Church Fathers, especially Irenaeus, made great efforts to suppress and to uproot it. The gnostic leaders were excluded from membership in churches, while gnosticism was denounced as heresy by the Church as a whole.

Christianity was influenced by gnosticism in at least seven ways. (1) Amid the general confusion ushered in by the gnostics, the Church was obliged to set up certain standards to be acknowledged by any one who claimed to be Christian. These standards included the Apostles' Creed, the formation of the New Testament Canon, and the Apostolic Office, or the historic Episcopate. (2) The defence of the Christian faith led to the formation of Christian dogmas, expressed in current philosophical terminology. (3) The gnostic stress on mysteries, spiritual hymns, and impressive rites in

[13] I Cor. 6:19; cf. Rom. 12:1.

duced more elaborate liturgical services in the churches. (4) The gnostic dualism, and contempt for matter, paved the way for Christian asceticism, which in turn led to monasticism. (5) The intermediary beings of the gnostics paved the way for the Saints in the Catholic Church. Notice the relative position of Sophia and the Virgin Mary in the two systems. (6) The superficial division of mankind into elect and non-elect groups paved the way for the doctrine of predestination. (7) Although condemned by the Church, the gnostic movement has continued to live to the present day. Compare the Christian Science doctrine and the radical wing of the so-called liberal Christians.

11-12. REVIEW QUESTIONS

1. Why the name *post-apostolic*?
2. How does this period form a transition from Apostolic to Catholic Christianity?
3. Where would you look for source material for this period?
4. Why did the early Christians preach the Gospel to the Jews first?
5. Why do you think the Jews as a nation rejected the Gospel?
6. What attitude did the Christians take toward Bar Cochba and his rebellion? Why?
7. Why did the presidents of the rabbinical schools become the recognized spiritual leaders of the non-Christian Jews?
8. Why was only a comparatively small Jewish minority absorbed in the Gentile Church?
9. Along what general lines did the Jewish-Christian majority split up into sects?
10. What is your reaction toward the Nazarenes? Can you think of any modern parallel?
11. What were the chief characteristics of the Ebionites? How do you connect them with the Apostolic Council in Jerusalem?
12. Why do the Elkesaites remind you of the present day Mormons?
13. What can you say about gnosticism as to (a) name, (b) origin and development, (c) characteristics, (d) influence upon Christianity?
14. Are there any modern gnostic tendencies?
15. How would you compare the gnostic and the Christian conception of God? Could a gnostic truly say: "Our Father who art in heaven"?
16. Why can there not be two co-eternal powers: good and evil?
17. Why did the Gnostics distinguish between Jehovah and a Supreme Being?
18. How would this distinction between an inferior and a superior God influence the status of (1) the apostles of Christ? (2) the Old Testament revelation?
19. Why did the gnostics divide mankind into three large groups?
20. How did the gnostics and the Christians differ in their conception of sin, redemption, and the Redeemer?
21. Why were the gnostic ethics either ascetic or libertine? How do these views compare with those of Christianity?
22. Did the gnostics have any sacraments? How many can you name?
23. Why was gnosticism such a dangerous rival of Christianity?
24. During what centuries was gnosticism most threatening to the Church?

TOPICS FOR SPECIAL STUDY

1. Microcosm and Macrocosm in Religion.
2. Irenaeus and His Fight against Heresies.
3. Jerusalem from 70 to 135 A.D.
4. Jochanan ben Zakkai and His Influence on Contemporary Jewish Life.
5. Outline the Views of one of the following Gnostic Leaders: Basilides, Valentinus, Marcion.
6. Modern attempts to create a Jewish Christianity.
7. The fate of converts from Judaism.

II. Christianity and the Roman Empire.—1. *The Rapid Spread of Christianity.*—Christianity spread with astonishing

THE SPREAD OF CHRISTIANITY EASTWARD

rapidity during the first three centuries. It spread to all parts of the Empire, even to regions beyond Roman territory. Christian missionaries found their way eastward to Mesopotamia, Persia, Media, Bactria, Parthia, India, and Armenia; southeast, to Arabia.[14] It gained a firm foothold in Lower Egypt, especially in Alexandria; from there it spread to Middle and Upper Egypt; westward to the Roman provinces of North Africa. In Europe it spread to Gaul, up the Danube, and toward the Roman provinces in Germany. Tertullian (A.D. 160-220) holds that Christianity was brought to Britain toward the end of the second century.

[14] See map on page 9.

There were several reasons for this remarkable progress. (1) The Christians expected the speedy return of the Lord. There was but little time to organize, no time to be idle. The essential thing was to preach the Gospel "unto the uttermost part of the world" before it was too late. (2) They were imbued with a strong conviction that Christianity was the *only* true and universal religion, the only means of salvation for mankind, and they preached accordingly. (3) The life of the Christians drew the people toward the Gospel. The world at the time of Christ lacked in love. The Church practiced charity, hospitality, and brotherliness. (4) The equality of all Christians before God made a special appeal to people from the lower and the middle classes. In the Kingdom of God, the individual counted. The slave and his master were equally precious in the eyes of the Lord. The young slave girl was protected. The exposure of infants ceased wherever Christianity was firmly established. Slavery was undermined, although the Church did not at this time have the power or the means of suppressing this social evil. (5) Heathenism as a religious force was bankrupt. The best thought of the age was alienated from the pagan gods. Heathenism produced no martyrs, while the Christians were ready to die for their faith. (6) The Gospel was spread by travelling merchants who were important contacts between the various local congregations. (7) A few high government officials who belonged to the Church naturally used their influence to promote the interests of the local congregations. (8) Many prominent women helped to spread the Gospel because of the exalted place Christianity gave to womanhood. (9) Lastly, God was with his people and gave them increase.

This victorious march of Christianity attracted the attention of the world. What was the nature of this new world force, this new religion that was capable of establishing itself, not only in the remote districts, but also in the very centers of culture and civilization? Leading representatives of pagan culture and learning began to study Christianity; the Roman government was obliged to bring the Church under careful scrutiny. The first noticeable reactions were the recognition of Christianity as a religion distinct from Judaism; gradual recognition that Christianity challenged almost everything for which the Graeco-Roman world stood; and that it condemned and excluded many phases of the life of the day.[15] In consequence the Graeco-Roman world struck back at

[15] cf. pp. 57-60.

Christianity with terrific force. The attack centered in severe critical writings by the intellectual proponents of paganism, and severe persecutions by the Roman government.

2. *The Literary Opposition to Christianity.*—During the second century the Graeco-Roman world tried to suppress Christianity by enlisting its culture and learning in fierce literary and intellectual assaults upon the Christian faith. But these onslaughts proved futile, for the Church passed through its fiery trials and came out victorious.

Men like Seneca (3 B.C.-65 A.D.), the elder Pliny (A.D. 23-79), and Plutarch (A.D. 46?-120?), never alluded to Christianity. Tacitus (A.D. 55-120), and the younger Pliny (A.D. 62-112) made scanty, although contemptuous references to the Christians.

Chief among those who endeavored to discredit Christianity were: (1) Arrian, who judging Christianity according to Stoic principles, considered Christianity as "mad fanaticism and custom;" (2) Fronto in his lost oration (A.D. 166) evidently a lawyer's defence of the legal proceedings against the Christians; (3) Lucian of Samosata (b.120), "the Voltaire of Grecian literature," who not only echoed the popular prejudice, but also made Christianity an object of mockery and derision; (4) Apuleius who made some daring caricatures of the Christian mysteries; (5) Crescens the Cynic who was a formidable opponent of the Gospel in the days of Justin the Martyr; (6) Celsus, a Greek philosopher who around 170 A.D., was the outstanding literary champion of heathendom against Christianity. He was a Paine-Ingersoll of the second century. His elaborate attacks upon the Christian faith anticipate most of the objections of modern infidelity against Christianity.

Literary attacks continued far into the third century. Philostratus, a Neo-Pythagorean philosopher who died around 230 A.D., attacked Christianity by producing a positive rival to Jesus Christ in Apollonius of Tyana, a real person who died around 96 A.D. In a work called "Life of Apollonius of Tyana," Philostratus pictured the hero as an ideal man, possessing supernatural power. The most dangerous opponent during this later period was the Neo-Platonist, Porphyro (A.D. 233-305). He wrote fifteen books against Christianity, especially against the Bible.

3. *The Literary Defense of Christianity.*—Christian literature served a twofold purpose. Christian leaders resorted to writing as a medium of instruction for members of the Church. When pagan

writers from the time of Hadrian (A.D. 117-138) attacked Christianity, Christians were ready to answer. Those who wrote in defense of Christianity were called Apologists.

The Apologists may be divided into those who wrote to emperors and to other government officials appealing for toleration, and those who answered the vicious attacks of heathen and Jewish philosophers. To the first group belong: Quadratus, bishop of the Church in Athens, and "a disciple of apostles," who presented Emperor Hadrian (A.D. 125) with a written defense of the Christian faith; Aristides who wrote an "Apology" to Emperor Hadrian, possibly as early as 125 A.D.; Miltiades who wrote an "Apology" addressed to the rulers of the world; Athenagoras, an Athenian philosopher, who addressed his defense "to the Emperors Marcus Aurelius Antonius and Lucius Aurelius Commodius;" Melito, bishop of Sardis, who wrote to Marcus Aurelius; and Apollinaris, bishop of Hierapolis, who addressed the same emperor.

To the second group belongs the author of the Epistle to Diognetus, perhaps the earliest formal defense of Christianity. The epistle presents Christianity as superior to both Judaism and heathenism. Ariston of Pella wrote "The Dialogue of Papiscus and Jason" in which a Jewish Christian explains and defends his faith to an Alexandrian Jew. Justin Martyr wrote the "Dialogue with Trypho the Jew;" and Tatian, the Assyrian, a disciple of Justin Martyr, wrote a "Discourse to the Greek" (170 A.D.) in which he vindicates Christianity by comparison with paganism.

Justin Martyr belongs to both groups. He presented written appeals to the Emperors Antonius Pius (A.D. 138-161) and Marcus Aurelius (A.D. 161-180), and he also composed a "Dialogue with Trypho the Jew" as a defense of Christianity against Judaism. He is by far the ablest and most important Apologist.

Since this literary contest with heathenism and with Judaism called forth a distinctly scientific Christian authorship it paved the way for the development of a scientific tendency in Christian theology. In the third century, and even toward the close of the second, three different types of literary productions, with corresponding variations in doctrinal views, may easily be distinguished. (1) The Alexandrian School continued the tradition of the Apologists that Christianity was revealed philosophy. Pantaenus, Clement, Origen, Dionysius, and Gregory Thaumaturgus were the best known teachers. (2) The School of Asia Minor continuing the work of the Apostle John was distinguished by its conciliatory tendencies, its firm adherence to the Bible, and its fight against heretics. Its best known representatives were Melito of Sardis, Irenaeus, Hippolitus, Gaius of Rome, Hegesippus, and Julius Africanus. (3) The Latin-African School reflected the peculiarities of the Western mind. Its realism and its practical effort to apply the Gospel to the lives of men made a marked contrast to the idealism and the speculations of the Alexandrians. Tertullian, Cyprian, Minucius Felix, Commodianus, and Arnobius were its prominent leaders.

4. *Persecutions by the Roman Government.*—Emperor Trajan, 98-117, ushered in a new stage in persecutions, first by applying a Roman law against secret associations in harassing Christian congregations; and second, by his rescript to Pliny the Younger (A.D. 112) in which the Emperor, without so intending, actually shaped the policies of the Roman government toward the Christians for nearly two hundred years.

Trajan had sent Pliny, a cultivated Roman lawyer, to govern the province of Bithynia-Pontus, A.D. 111-113. Pliny, perplexed as to what to do with the many Christians in the province, decided to refer the matter to the emperor himself. Pliny wrote a letter to Trajan, from which it seems plain that he was convinced that the vulgar charges against the Christians were unfounded. But he had found "an offensive and irrational superstition." Pliny's practice, up to writing this letter, had been to ask those who were brought to trial if they were Christians. If they answered in the affirmative, he would command them to recant. If they refused as many as three times, he ordered them executed because of their "pertinacity" and "inflexible obstinacy." Trajan answered that he approved of this procedure, adding that while no general rule could be laid down, the Christians should *not* be sought out; but if brought before the government by responsible accusers, they were found guilty of being Christians, they should be executed unless they recanted. Anonymous charges should be disregarded.

This procedure was to apply to Bithynia-Pontus only, but it soon spread throughout the Empire. While the rule against the Christians was inexorable, it was to be administered cautiously. The Christians were outlaws, but the officials were not bound to notice them until some informer brought them to court. Much depended upon the temper of the provincial governors. They could do a great deal to encourage or to discourage accusers. Trajan's rescript to Pliny actually prevented a general, systematic persecution of the Christians for many years to come.

Among the many martyred during the reign of Trajan were two prominent leaders, Symeon, Bishop of Jerusalem, and Ignatius, Bishop of Antioch. Symeon, successor of James the Just and a relative of the Lord, was brought to trial, convicted of being a Christian, tormented for many days, and finally crucified (A.D. 107) at the advanced age of 120 years. Ignatius, after an audience with the Emperor, was condemned to death, transported to Rome, and thrown before wild beasts in the Colosseum, around 115 A.D.

Emperor Hadrian, 117-138, pursued the general policy of his predecessor. During his reign the mobs of the towns were wont, on occasions of heathen festivals, loudly to call for the blood of the Christians. Hadrian issued an edict against such riots, but legal persecution of the Christians continued.

Antonius Pius, 138-161, was a mild emperor, but he seems to have followed the policies of his two predecessors. During his reign a number of public calamities excited the populace against the Christians. Polycarp, aged bishop of Smyrna, died at the stake about 155 A.D.

The reign of Marcus Aurelius (A.D. 161-180) was a stormy time for the Church. This emperor with a particular dislike for religious enthusiasm, scorned the exultations of the Christian martyrs. He accused them of obstinacy and a desire for theatrical display. He had no sympathy with the Christian belief in immortality. He allowed the persecutions to revive, not only giving free reign to outbursts of popular fury, but also introducing a system of espionage and of torture to be used against the Christians. A number of public calamities occurred, such as earthquakes, inundations, famine, and a very destructive pestilence (A.D. 166) that ravaged the Empire from Ethiopia to Gaul. These events were popularly looked upon as a revenge of the gods, because the populace tolerated the Christians.

Although there was no uniform, systematic persecution throughout the Empire, many Christians were martyred, especially in Asia Minor and in Gaul. Marcus Aurelius received many written apologies in behalf of the persecuted Christians, but he turned a deaf ear to them all. The chief Apologist, Justin Martyr, was put to death in Rome in 166 A.D.

13. REVIEW QUESTIONS

1. What reasons can you give for the remarkable progress of the early Church?
2. How did the surrounding world react to this victorious march of Christianity?

3. Why the literary and intellectual assaults upon the Christians faith?
4. Could you mention some of the best known literary opponents of Christianity in this era? Any modern analogies?
5. How did the Church meet this opposition? Mention some of the Apologists.
6. Why did the Christian literature of this era serve a twofold purpose?
7. How did this literary contest with heathenism and with Judaism influence the Church?
8. How would you characterize the Alexandrian, the Asia Minor, and the Latin-African schools of Christian thought?
9. What emperors did the post-apostolic Church have to deal with?
10. How did Trajan influence the course of the persecutions?
11. How did the edict of Hadrian influence the Christians?
12. How would you characterize the reign of Marcus Aurelius with reference to the Christians?

TOPICS FOR SPECIAL STUDY

1. The Relation of Christianity to Other Religions.
2. Marcus Aurelius: Philosopher and Emperor.
3. Discuss the Views Presented in the "Dialogue with Trypho the Jew."
4. Clement of Alexandria and Origen as Representatives of the Alexandrian School.
5. Discuss One Representative of the School of Asia Minor: Melito of Sardis, or Irenaeus, or Hippolitus, or Gaius of Rome, or Hegesippus, or Julius Africanus.
6. Discuss the Life and Work of one of the following men: Tertullian, Cyprian, Minucius Felix, Commodianus, Arnobius.
7. Polycarp, Bishop of Smyrna.

III. Montanism.—The extraordinary spiritual gifts of miracle-working and prophecy did not cease with the apostles. Justin Martyr (A.D. 103-166), Irenaeus (d. 202 A.D.), and Origen (185-254) testify that miracles were performed in the name of the Lord in their time, and that the gift of prophecy had a place in the regular worship in a number of churches. But the enthusiastic prophetic element in early Christian life was gradually being replaced by a growing formalism in teaching and in worship. Moreover, with the expectation of the speedy return of the Lord growing dim in most of the churches of the second century, strictness of conduct and discipline relaxed.

Montanism arose, partly as a distorted reaction against these tendencies, partly as a product of the peculiar religio-nationalistic views of the Phrygians. It originated in Phrygia in Asia Minor about the middle of the second century, and from this region it spread westward. The founder was Montanus of Ardaba, a village in Mysia, near the Phrygian border. Jerome states that Montanus had formerly been a priest in a heathen temple dedicated to Cybele. Soon after his conversion he appeared at Pepuza in Phrygia, as a prophet and reformer of Christianity. Among his adherents were two women, Priscilla and Maximilla, who also claimed prophetic authority. The following features serve to distinguish believers in Montanism:

(1) They accepted all the books of the Bible, and held firmly to the Rule of Faith.

(2) They placed extraordinary emphasis on the miraculous gifts of the Holy Spirit, especially prophecy, making the possession of such gifts the test of the true Christian Church.

(3) They ushered in a new type of prophecy, which Eusebius says was "contrary to the traditional and constant custom of the Church," closely akin to the ecstatic visions and wild frenzies of the priests of Cybele. The prophet claimed to fall into a trance or ecstatic transport, in which his own self-consciousness ceased and his own mind was altogether passive, while God took entire possession of him and spoke through him. In this ecstatic state the Montanist prophets, according to Eusebius, "raved and began to babble and utter strange sounds," evidently much like the glossalia in the Irvingite and kindred congregations.[16]

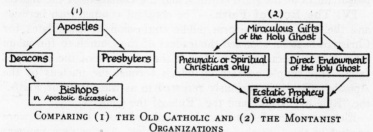

COMPARING (1) THE OLD CATHOLIC AND (2) THE MONTANIST ORGANIZATIONS

(4) The main import of the Montanist prophecy was the proclamation of the speedy coming of the Lord. He was to establish the Millennial Kingdom, the New Jerusalem, in the village of Pepuza in Phrygia, whither the believers should betake themselves.

(5) In preparation for the coming of the Lord, the Montanists imposed upon themselves a fanatical asceticism and church discipline. Women were forbidden all ornamental clothing and virgins were veiled. Worldly science, art, and all worldly enjoyments were considered a snare laid by the enemy. Fasts were numerous and severe. Married life was considered a lower plane than the single state, and second marriage was under all circumstances forbidden as adultery. Second repentance was impossible, and therefore the lapsed could not be restored to fellowship of the Church. Tertullian, the ablest convert to Montanism, considered it the main duty of the new order of prophecy to restore a severe church discipline.

(6) They maintained that the direct endowment of the Spirit of God constituted the real qualification and appointment for the office of teacher and minister in the Church, and not the outward ordination and episcopal succession. The supernatural element and the free motion of the Holy Spirit were above the fixed, ecclesiastical order. Hence they denounced the clergy as psychical or carnal in contrast to their own superior spirituality.

(7) They ushered in a new spiritual aristocracy by maintaining, like the gnostics, a distinction between psychic or *carnal* and pneumatic or *spiritual*

---

[16] For a discussion of the Irvingites, consult General Index.

Christians. To the latter belonged those who had accepted the higher teaching of the Spirit by the mouth of the Montanists, and these again constituted the real spiritual Church, which was one step in advance of the Church of the apostles. Here the Montanists assumed a schismatic character.

(8) They believed in a progressive divine revelation. This progression reached its climax not in Christ and his apostles, but in the age of the Holy Spirit which had commenced with Montanus. Hence the Montanists regarded their own dreamings and visions as more important than the written word of the Bible.

The Montanists spread so rapidly among the excitable Phrygians that the Church of that region became alarmed. Bishops and synods of Asia Minor condemned the movement as heresy, and excommunicated the Montanists. The churches of Gaul and Rome followed. Africa was for some time a stronghold of Montanism because the gifted Tertullian identified himself with it. There were many off-shoots of Montanism, but the true successors were the Novatianists of the third century, and the Donatists of the fourth.

IV. The Rule of Faith.—The constant conflict with heresies and the need of a uniform public confession by candidates for Christian baptism soon led the leaders of the Church to formulate a brief, easily grasped summary of the essentials of the Christian faith. This simple confession, which formed the nucleus of the Apostle's Creed, is variously referred to as the "Rule of Faith," the "Rule of Truth," and the "Rule of the Church."

Elements of confession and doctrinal and moral instruction were present in the Church from her beginning. At the very moment Christ stepped from private life into his public ministry, God himself declared: "This is my beloved Son in whom I am well pleased."[17] The voice from heaven was also heard on several other occasions.[18] John the Baptist made the great confession: "Behold, the Lamb of God, that taketh away the sin of the world."[19] Christ himself made many statements concerning his divine sonship and his divine mission, and he also elicited acknowledgments of faith in his Messiahship. Peter responded on one occasion by saying: "Thou art the Christ, the Son of the living God."[20] The Gospel of John was written "that ye may believe that Jesus is the Christ."[21] And in Matth. 28:19 the Lord himself gave his disciples the command to baptize "into the name of the Father and of the Son and of the Holy Spirit." Various confessions of faith were also made by those who came to Jesus to be healed.

In the Epistles the types of confessions are reproduced and extended. References to this confessional element are very numerous.

[17] Matth. 3:17.
[18] Matth. 17:5; John 12:28.
[19] John 1:29.
[20] Matth. 16:16.
[21] John 20:31.

A specific connection between faith, baptism, and a traditional confession is more or less clearly indicated in a number of New Testament passages, but nothing is definitely known as to the exact wording of this traditional confession.

The most ancient form of the Apostle's Creed is the old Roman symbol which reads as follows: "I believe in God the Father Almighty; and in Jesus Christ, His only begotten Son, our Lord, who was born of the Holy Spirit and the Virgin Mary, crucified under Pontius Pilate and buried; the third day He rose from the dead, ascended into the heavens, being seated at the right hand of the Father, whence He shall come to judge the living and the dead; and in the Holy Spirit, holy church, forgiveness of sins, resurrection of the flesh."

Irenaeus (d. 202) and Tertullian (A.D. 160-220) both claim that this identical confession was everywhere employed in the Church, since the time of the apostles. Seeberg[22] thinks that "this most ancient form still preserved and others similar to it were in common use at the beginning of the second and at the end of the first century." The current text of the Apostle's Creed has a few additions.

The Rule of Faith was useful not only as a sign of recognition among orthodox Christians, but also as a Standard of Truth against heretical opinions. Appeal to Scriptures against heresies was not in all cases conclusive because some of the heretics claimed to possess the only key to the meaning of the Bible, declaring that the interpretation made by orthodox teachers was wrong. But heretics could not easily get by this splendid summary of apostolic teaching. Even the average lay Christian could detect any serious deviation from this simple Rule of Faith.

V. Organization, Worship, and Discipline.—The Church had, from her very birthday, all the essentials of organization, all the main elements of public worship, and of discipline. Section V of the preceding chapter outlines the origin and development of the Apostolate, the Deaconate, the Presbyterate, and the activity of charismatic persons. The monarchical episcopate had gained a firm foothold in Asia Minor toward the end of the first century, and in the temporary functions of Timothy and Titus, and in the authoritative position of the Apostle John at Ephesus, the rudiments of the diocesan episcopacy were recognized. But the episcopacy was by no means universally established by the end of the Apostolic Age.

[22] Seeberg: *Text-Book of the History of Doctrines*, Vol. I, p. 84.

Clement of Rome (A.D. 95) and Ignatius of Antioch (A.D. 110-117) may have had a formative influence upon church organization in the second century. Clement, a pupil of the Apostle Paul, states in his first "Epistle to the Corinthians," Chapter 42: "The Apostles have preached the Gospels to us from the Lord Jesus Christ; Jesus Christ was sent forth from God. Christ, therefore, was from God, and the Apostles from Christ. Both these appointments, then, came about in an orderly way, by the will of God. Having, therefore, received their orders, and being fully assured by the resurrection of our Lord Jesus Christ, and established in the word of God, with full assurance in the Holy Ghost, they went forth proclaiming that the Kingdom of God was at hand. And thus preaching through countries and in cities, they appointed their first-fruits, having proved them by the Spirit, to be bishops and deacons of those who should afterward believe." Clement continues in Chapter 44: "Our Apostles knew, through our Lord Jesus Christ, that there would be strife on account of the office of the episcopate. For this cause, therefore, inasmuch as they had obtained a perfect foreknowledge of this, they appointed those already mentioned, and afterwards gave instructions that when these should fall asleep, other approved men should succeed them in their ministry." It appears that Clement traced the existence of church officers to the apostles.

Ignatius, Bishop of Antioch, and a pupil of the Apostle John, states in his Epistle to the Church of Tralles, Chapter 2: "For since ye are subject to the bishop as Jesus Christ, ye appear to me to live not after the manner of men, but according to Jesus Christ, who died for us, in order that by believing in His death ye may escape death. It is therefore necessary that just as ye indeed do, so without the bishop ye should do nothing, but should also be subject to the presbytery, as to the Apostles of Jesus Christ." Ignatius continues in Chapter 3: "In like manner, let all reverence the deacons as Jesus Christ, as also the bishop, who is the type of the Father, and the presbyters as the sanhedrin of God and the assembly of the Apostles. Apart from these there is no Church."

In his Epistle to the Church of Smyrna, Ignatius states: "See that ye follow the bishop as Jesus Christ does the Father, and the presbyters as he would the Apostles; and reverence the deacons as a commandment of God. Without the bishop let no one do any of those things connected with the Church. Let that be deemed a proper eucharist which is administered either by the bishop or by him to whom he has intrusted it. Wherever the bishop shall appear there let also the multitude be, even as wherever Jesus Christ is there is the Catholic Church. It is not lawful without the bishop either to baptize or to make an agape. But whatsoever he shall approve that is also pleasing to God, so that everything that is done may be secure and valid." Notice that Ignatius exalts the authority of the bishop, and refers to the Church as "the Catholic Church."

These views of the episcopacy as the highest spiritual office in apostolic succession seem to have been universally held by the middle of the second century. At that time, there was a distinct recognition of the three orders in the Christian ministry: bishops; elders or presbyters; and deacons. Several reasons may be given for this increasing prominence of the bishops. Ignatius, and many others, maintained that it was not lawful, without the bishop or his representative, either to baptize or to celebrate the eucharist. This practice enhanced the power and the dignity of the bishop. The bishop gradually absorbed the main functions of the former evangelists, prophets, and teachers, as a chief security for the maintenance of the unity of the teaching transmitted from the apostles. The conflict with heresy made it expedient to transfer the responsibility to a single office. False teachers claimed to possess the truth delivered to the Church by the apostles. The Church answered by investing the office of the bishop, the only direct succession from the apostles, with the power to determine and to interpret true doctrine and saving faith. As the Church came into increasingly intimate contact with the cultural and intellectual elements in the Empire, the educational standards of the church leaders had to be raised.

Local churches in a district were conscious of a certain interrelation, partly informal and partly organic. The Apostolic Church had quite early seen the need of calling together representatives from churches in various districts for the purpose of discussing matters that pertained to the whole Church. The Apostolic Council in Jerusalem is the classical evidence. In the post-apostolic age the churches in certain districts found it necessary to present a united front against Montanism, and to decide on a somewhat uniform practice of church discipline. Such synods were held in Asia Minor as early as the middle of the second century; later in the same century the churches of the East and of the West met to discuss the Easter question.[23]

Christian worship was still essentially the same with the excep-

---

[23] Eusebius: *Church History*, Book V, Chap. 16 and 24.

tion of growing formalism and a rather uniform practice of having the eucharist in connection with the Sunday forenoon service. The Sunday morning service consisting of Scripture reading, preaching, prayer, and singing, was open to everybody. Before the eucharist service began, all the unbaptized were dismissed.

Church discipline was practised according to the principles of the previous era.[24] Yet the earlier strictness of conduct and discipline relaxed considerably in many localities. A contemporary Christian writer, who identified this laxity of discipline with a deteriorating spiritual life, describes the Church as an elderly person with a wrinkled face.

14. REVIEW QUESTIONS

1. How do you account for the rise and the influence of Montanism?
2. Why did the Church condemn Montanism as heresy?
3. Is there anything in Montanism that reminds you of any contemporary religious movements?
4. Why did the Church formulate the Rule of Faith?
5. Can you see any reasons why certain religious groups of that period would try to do away with this Standard of Truth? Any modern analogies?
6. What was the general status of the Church organization at the beginning of the post-apostolic age?
7. How do you account for the transition from Apostolic to Catholic Christianity?
8. Why the interest in the formation of a New Testament Canon?
9. Why the development of regional and general synods?
10. How did the concentration of power in the office of the bishop influence the future course of the Church? Could this development have been altered?
11. What can you say about the Christian worship during this era?
12. Why the laxity in the earlier strictness of conduct and discipline?

TOPICS FOR SPECIAL STUDY

1. Ecstasy in Religion.
2. The Formation of the Apostles' Creed.
3. Early Regional Conferences in the Christian Church.

A SELECTED BIBLIOGRAPHY FOR CHAPTER III

1. Ayer: *A Source Book of Ancient Church History.*
2. Rainy: *The Ancient Catholic Church.*
3. Schaff: *History of the Christian Church,* Vol. II.
4. Mansel: *The Gnostic Heresies.*
5. Schaff: *Creeds of Christendom.*
6. Westcott: *History of the Canon of the New Testament.*
7. Ramsay: *The Church in the Roman Empire before A. D. 170.*

[24] cf. pp. 66-67.

CHAPTER IV

THE ANTE-NICENE ERA. A.D. 170-325

In a smeltery ore is reduced by fusion in a furnace. The liquid metal is poured into set forms where it cools taking on a permanent shape. The Church at this time was subjected to fiery trials, severe persecutions from without, and besetting heresies from within. As Christianity spread westward,[1] the organized life of the Church gradually was permanently moulded by the Roman genius for government, law, and order. This process resulted in Catholicism, and paved the way for the adoption of Christianity as the official state religion after 325 A.D.

I. The Rise of the Catholic Church.—What is meant by Catholicism? Viewed in the light of apostolic and post-apostolic Christianity, Catholicism involved two distinct changes, a change of church government, and a change of faith.

In the Apostolic Era the universal, spiritual priesthood of all believers was generally recognized by the Church. There was no special priesthood, hence there was no division of the Christians into "clergy" and "laity," nor was there any distinction between a higher and a lower spiritual order of believers. So far as spiritual position and privileges were concerned, ordinary church members were on the same level as church officials. Apostles, prophets, teachers, and other "gifted men," as well as ordinary church members—all alike had *immediate* access to God through *faith*.[2] A mediating priest or bishop was not necessary to salvation. A sinner received forgiveness by confessing his sins directly to God, as revealed in Jesus Christ through the Bible. Assurance of forgiveness of sins and of salvation came to the believer through the Word of God, not by the mouth of a mediating priest. There was no special priesthood which could bar or excommunicate the individual or a community from direct access to God and His grace, the Word, and the Sacraments. The Church was not identified with any specific office,[3] but rather with the assembly of believers, the "congregation of saints."[4] Christ said: "where two or three are gathered

[1] See map on page 38.
[2] See diagram on page 68.
[3] cf. pp. 89-92.
[4] cf. pp. 62-66.

in my name, there I am in the midst of them."[5] A direct, personal communion with God through *faith in Jesus Christ* was the essence and the power of the Christian life.

God gave "some to be apostles; and some, prophets; and some, evangelists; and some, pastors and teachers."[6] The local churches had elders and deacons, who supervised and directed the work of the congregation, administered its charity, took care of the sick, and saw to it that services were regularly held. But *the early church organization was not centered in office and in law, but in the special gifts of the Spirit.* The teaching, the preaching, and the administration of the Sacraments were conducted by the "gifted men" in the congregation. An elder might also teach, preach, and administer the Sacraments, but he did not do so because he was an elder, but because he was known to have the "gift." None of these "gifted men" held church office in a legal or judicial sense. The preaching and the teaching and 'the administration of the Sacraments were not *legally* confined to any specific office. The Gospel could be preached and the Sacraments could be administered in the presence of any assembly of believers, gathered in the name of the Lord.

Toward the close of the first Christian century a change took place. A general lack of confidence in the special gifts of the Spirit, a desire for more specific order, and a pressing demand for proper safeguard against heresy resulted in a gradual transfer of the preaching, the teaching, and the administration of the Sacraments from the "gifted men" to the local elders. These elders again were elected because they possessed some of the special "gifts," particularly the gift of teaching. The official functions were now performed by elders only. The ministry of the Word and the Sacraments became *official*, and which marked the beginning of the division of the Christians into "clergy" (chosen ones) and "laity" (the masses).

During the second and third centuries another important change took place. Instead of government by a group of elders, the local churches were headed by single officials for whom the name "bishop" was exclusively reserved. This change took place in certain regions of Asia Minor even toward the close of the first century, although the name bishop was not then used to designate these officials.[7] The election of the bishop became a *legal* ordinance, and the bishop alone had a right to preach, to teach, and to administer the Sacraments because he alone, it was believed, had been

---

[5] Matth. 18:20.   [6] Eph. 4:11.   [7] cf. pp. 64-65.

endowed and appointed by God to be the leader of the congregation. The presence of the bishop or his representative was now essential to every valid act of the congregation. In fact, without the bishop there could be no church. Any society, to be a church, must have a bishop, and any person desiring to be a Christian, must be subject to a bishop. Outside of this Church, the Church of the bishops, there was no salvation. The Church was no longer understood to be the holy people of God believing on Jesus Christ, but rather a group of persons belonging to the churches of the bishops.[8] The personal communion with God, and the assurance of the presence

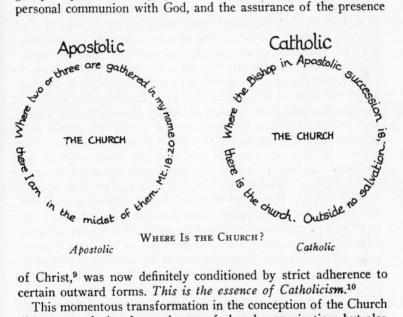

Apostolic

Where two or three are gathered in my name. Mt. 18:20. there I am in the midst of them.

THE CHURCH

Catholic

Where the Bishop in Apostolic succession is, there is the church. Outside no salvation.

THE CHURCH

WHERE IS THE CHURCH?

Apostolic   *Catholic*

of Christ,[9] was now definitely conditioned by strict adherence to certain outward forms. *This is the essence of Catholicism.*[10]

This momentous transformation in the conception of the Church did not merely involve a change of church organization, but also a change of faith. Communion with God was now possible only by a communion with the bishop. The original spiritual priesthood of all believers yielded to a special priesthood, the clergy; and the evangelical conception of the Church as "the congregation of saints" yielded to the Catholic conception of the Church as a group of believers belonging to the episcopate.

II. Organization: the Historic Episcopate.—Several facts account for the rapid rise of the historic episcopate.[11] The extraor-

[8] cf. pages 89-92.   [9] cf. Matth. 18:20.
[10] According to the new view of Sohm, the real Catholic church started at 1200 as a corporation.
[11] Make a careful study of the four reasons given on page 91.

dinary spiritual gifts of miracle working and prophecy, as exercised by the early Church, were gradually replaced by formalism in teaching and in worship. As Christianity spread westward, the Roman genius for law and order exerted a formative influence upon the organized life of the Church. The relation between God and the believer came to be looked upon as a legal contract between two parties. Compare this with the old Roman ideal, Chapter I, Section 3, and with Pharisaic Judaism. The heroic fight against the gnostics, especially as to what constituted the true Church, led to the early establishment of the episcopal office. The claim of the Montanists[12] that the direct endowment of the Spirit of God, and not outward ordination and episcopal succession, constituted the real qualification and appointment for the office of teacher and minister, strengthened the office of the bishop because the Church recognized in the episcopate a safeguard against the schis-matic character of the Montanists. The churches had come to be large bodies difficult to manage, especially as to discipline, charity, and finance. Disagreement among the presbyters would often prevent a desirable unity in the church. Hence the need for episcopal authority was strongly felt, and the vindication of such authority was sure to follow. The heroic martyrdom of a number of the bishops added to the prestige of the office. The specially "gifted" became fewer and their prophecies perhaps less reliable; the expectation of the speedy return of the Lord was no longer so general; a new generation had grown up that had not been won directly for the Church from heathenism, but had been born and educated in Christian homes. Instead of the immediate gifts of the Spirit, Christians rather relied on organizations and outward religious authority.

The gnostics claimed that they alone possessed the essential Gospel truth, and that they constituted the true Church. Hence they raised the question: *What is true Christianity?* The Old Catholic Church gave a threefold answer. (1) *True Christianity is the religion that is taught in Holy Scripture,* that is, in the canonical Old Testament, and in the Apostolic Writings. But what books were Apostolic? The efforts of the Church to obtain a unanimous agreement influenced the formation of the New Testament Canon. (2) *True Christianity is the religion that is expressed in the Rule of Faith.*[13] (3) *True Christianity is the religion that is held in the churches whose bishops are the successors to the apostles.* Where the bishop was, there was the apostolic tradition. He alone

[12] See pp. 86-88.   [13] cf. pp. 88-89.

had power and authority to speak against heresy. Gnostic errors were not overcome by clever dialectics, or by the formulation of a scientific theology, but rather *by the high, popular esteem of the office of the bishop.* The power of the bishop did not rest merely on a legal basis, but rather on the firm belief of the Christians that the bishop alone had the *charisma veritas* from God to teach, to preach, and to administer the Sacraments. The bishop, equipped and called by God, and duly elected by the Church, with outward ordination and apostolic succession, defended the faith of the Church against heresy.

Uniform adoption of the episcopal form prepared the Church for a successful encounter with certain difficulties. What the Christian faith lost in purity was gained in the strength of organization. The Church, in preparing for the conquest of the world, developed a strong hierarchy of officers, headed by a single governing official, to lead the believers and guard against the dangers of unsteady mass movements. Holding that the bishop alone was called by God to be the leader of the congregation; that only where the bishop was, there was the Church, and that only by communion with the bishop could the believer have communion with Christ, the Church developed universal government by the pope; for the local church was, after all, a miniature of the government of the Old Catholic Church as a whole, with the Bishop of Rome as a type of Christ. When the Roman Empire crumbled in 476 A.D., the Church had developed a strong organization that made it possible for her to withstand and partly to transform the flood of barbarism that swept over Europe. On the other hand, the misuse of this organization ultimately demanded drastic adjustments.

Cyprian of Carthage (A.D. 195-258) had a strong formative influence upon the development of church government. A typical high-church man of the epoch, he is said to have done more for the development of hierarchical views than any other man. His conception of the Church embraces the following:

(1) There is but one Church of Jesus Christ in the world. Seemingly there are many churches, but "just as there are many rays of the sun, but one light; and many branches of the tree, but one strength, founded on the tenacious roots; and since from one source many streams flow forth, the numerosity may seem diffused by the bounty of the surging stream, nevertheless unity in origin is preserved."

(2) To be a Christian, one must be in this Church. "Whosoever he is, and whatsoever his character, he is not a Christian who is not in the Church of Christ." "There is no salvation outside the Church." Furthermore, "it is not possible that he should have God for his Father, who would not have the Church for his Mother."

(3) "The Church is constituted of bishops, and every act of the Church is controlled by these leaders." "Whence thou shouldest know that the bishop is in the Church, and the Church in the bishop, and he who is not with the bishop, is not in the Church."

(4) The bishops are the successors of the apostles, and are chosen by the Lord himself, and are induced into their office as leaders or pastors. The bishqp is not only the successor of the historic apostolate, and hence the legitimate teacher of the apostolic tradition, but he is also the inspired prophet, endowed with the "charismata" or special gifts of the Spirit.

(5) The Church thus organized is "one and Catholic" or universal. Outside of this Church there is no salvation.

(6) The bishops constitute a college (collegium), the episcopate. Upon their unity rests the unity of the Church. This unity of the episcopate rests upon the divine election and endowment which the bishops have in common as successors of the apostles, and finds expression in their united conferences and mutual recognition.

(7) All bishops are of equal rank. Yet, apostolic authority was first bestowed upon Peter, and Peter was believed to have founded the church of Rome. Hence the Roman church is the "mother and root of the catholic church." "Does·he trust that he is in the church who strives against and resists the church? who deserts the *Cathedra Petri* on which the church has been founded?"

(8) Rebellion against the bishop is rebellion against God. The schismatic is a heretic, and heretical baptism has no validity.

(9) Cyprian also asserted the actual priesthood of the clergy, based upon the sacrifice offered by them, and their care for the poor. Notice the connection between this view and the views of legalistic Judaism and the old, legalistic Roman religion.

The Roman bishop tried to make practical use of Cyprian's theory of the *Catheara Petri*, but Cyprian firmly maintained his right of independent opinion and action. Although the Church had not yet become a hierarchy, it developed rapidly in that direction. While all the bishops theoretically stood upon the same level, the so-called "country-bishops" would not, because of the location, enjoy the direct influence and popular esteem of the bishops of the larger cities. Besides, the bishops of Rome, Constantinople, Antioch, Jerusalem, and Alexandria naturally secured special prominence because of their location, and the unusual influence of their churches. The importance of the provincial cities, and the five great cities just mentioned paved the way for the formation of the office of the Metropolitan and the Patriarch.

Synods modeled on the Apostolic Council in Jerusalem were held in certain regions of the Church from the middle of the second century.[14] Matters of heresy and discipline made them desirable. At first the churches were represented both by the bishops and by lay delegates, but toward the end of the era bishops only sat in these councils. The synods met by province, and on rare occasions before 325 A.D. there were synods attended by bishops of several

[14] cf. page 91.

provinces. After 250 A.D., these provincial synods were generally held once a year, usually in the capital city, with the bishop of that city the presiding officer.

In 313 A.D. Emperor Constantine granted full toleration to the Christians, and in 325 A.D. he issued a general exhortation to his subjects to embrace Christianity. Constantine himself continued to hold the traditional office of "pontifex maximus," or high priest for the official pagan worship, although he was baptized in 337, the year before his death. He made Christianity the Official Religion of the State, and organized the Church on the basis of the political organization of the Empire. While this new organization of the Church was not fully completed by Constantine, the parallel organization of Church and State led to the following results. (1) As the city territory (civitas) was the smallest unit in the

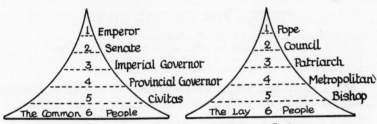

PARALLEL ORGANIZATION OF STATE AND CHURCH

political administration of the Empire, so the diocese, embracing the corresponding church territory, became the simplest unit in the ecclesiastical administration, headed by a bishop. (2) Over the city territory was the province, with its provincial governor. The corresponding church office was that of the Metropolitan (archbishop), held by the bishop of the provincial city. (3) During the fourth century several provinces were governed by an imperial governor (vicarius). The Church had a corresponding officer in the Patriarch (cardinal). (4) The Imperial Council had its counterpart, partly in the assembly of Patriarchs (College of Cardinals), and partly in the Ecumenical Councils of the Church. (5) The Emperor soon found his ecclesiastical counterpart in the Pope.

15. REVIEW QUESTIONS

1. How would you briefly characterize the development of the Church during this era?
2. What is meant by Catholicism?
3. Did the early church organization center in any certain office and in law,

or did it center in the special gifts of the Spirit? Give reasons for your answer.

4. What is meant by the statement that the ministry of the Word and the Sacraments became official?
5. Why did the church organization begin to center so much in the office of the bishop? Was this a good thing for the Church?
6. How did the historic episcopacy help the Church to conquer the gnostic error?
7. What is meant by apostolic succession?
8. In what respect did the historic episcopacy assist in the development of papacy?
9. How did Cyprian's views influence the development of church government?
10. Why did the Church come to be organized on the basis of the political organization of the Empire?
11. Was it a good thing for the Church thus to develop a State within a State (cf. ch. V, Sec. 1)? Was it a good thing for the future of civilization?
12. Why did the emphasis on form of belief supersede the emphasis on personal virtues and simple faith?

TOPICS FOR SPECIAL STUDY

1. The Roman influence on church organization.
2. What importance should be attached to Apostolic Succession?
3. Discuss the Apostolic and the Catholic conception of the Church.
4. The formation of the New Testament Canon.

III. Church and State: Persecutions.—The reign of Marcus Aurelius (A.D. 161-180) marked a turning-point in the history of Rome. Before his reign Rome was ascendent, prosperous, and powerful. During his reign the Empire was beset by many difficulties, such as pestilence, floods, famine, and heavy German inroads. After his reign the Empire was distinctly on the defensive —and on the decline. The causes had their origin in changes in national life during the two preceding centuries. Now the Empire began to feel seriously the effects of these changes. There was a general decline in mental energy, a lowered vitality, a weakened power of resistance. The birthrate was on the decline. People streamed into the cities. Slavery undermined the peasant classes. Trade and industry were fettered by heavy taxation. The leadership gradually passed out of the hands of the educated classes; the emperors themselves were no longer Romans or Italians. The army was largely recruited from distant provinces, even from districts beyond its borders. After the death of Commodius (192 A.D.) the emperors were elected by the army for nearly a century (up to 284 A.D.). Hence these rulers were known as the "Barrack Emperors." Of the twenty-five emperors who mounted the throne during this period, all but four came to death by violence. The administrative machinery of the Empire was increasingly inefficient, and to internal disorders were added the terrors of barbarian invasions.

In the meantime the Gospel had spread in every direction with astonishing rapidity; in many parts, the Church became a powerful organization with which the State had to reckon. Moreover, the general depression and distress that followed the decline of the Empire led the superstitious people to believe that it was the Christians who had called down upon the nation the anger of the gods. The Christians were hated, and many attempts were made to stamp out the new religion. Legally, Christianity was condemned from the beginning of the second century to the beginning of the fourth. Yet, the relation of the State to Church, up to the time of Decius (A.D. 249-251), depended largely on the good-will and the varying fortunes of the several emperors. With the exception of a severe persecution in Carthage and Egypt in 202 A.D., in the reign of Septimus Severus (193-211), the Christians enjoyed a fair degree of toleration up to the beginning of the reign of Decius.

The first general, systematic persecution of the Church took place during the reigns of Decius (249-251) and Valerian (253-260). In 248 the Empire celebrated the thousandth anniversary of the founding of Rome. It was a time for revival of ancient traditions and memories of the order, vigor, and splendor of former days. The celebration resulted in renewed interest in heathen religions, in a marked revival of patriotism. Meanwhile the Empire was gravely threatened by barbarian attacks and torn by internal disputes. The populace attributed these troubles to the cessation of the persecution of the Christians. Rome had grown great, they claimed, when the old gods were worshipped by all. The rejection of these gods by a portion of the populace had brought on contemporary calamities. Emperor Decius setting out to restore the unity and the vigor of the Empire, decided that the extermination of Christianity and the rehabilitation of the State religion were politically necessary. He conceived of Christianity as being radically opposed to the genius of Roman institutions, and he is said to have remarked that he would tolerate a rival emperor in Rome rather than a Christian bishop.

An imperial edict aiming at the universal suppression of Christianity was issued in 250. All Christians, men, women, and children, must give up their faith or suffer the penalty of confiscation of property, torture, and death. His policy was continued by

Valerian (253-20). Many Christians remained steadfast, but many also "lapsed," and took part in some form of heathen worship, or procured false certificates that they had done so. A few years later the re-admission of some of these into the Church gave rise to serious disputes, even to schisms. Novatian, a presbyter in Rome, refusing to re-admit the lapsed, was made bishop of a schismatic church which spread rapidly over the Empire and lasted for more than two centuries.

From 260-303 the Christians enjoyed an almost unbroken rest. The Church grew rapidly in numbers and enjoyed prosperity. Many large, well-equipped churches were built. But in 303 the State began its supreme effort to destroy the Church by starting a violent persecution that lasted until 313. Diocletian (284-305), a great statesman, determined to restore the Empire to its former greatness and splendor. He reorganized the whole machinery of the government, including the restoration of the old pagan worship. Like other statesmen of the ancient world, Diocletian could not conceive of a State without a state religion. The welfare and the unity of the Empire were bound up with careful performance of the rites of the national worship. Neglect of such service angered the gods and endangered the safety of the State, bringing drought, pestilence, and other calamities. The Christians steadily refused to worship the Roman gods and to burn incense before the statues of the Emperor. Hence they were marked as atheists and as public enemies.

In 295 all the soldiers were ordered to offer sacrifices. In 296 the sacred books of the Christians in Alexandria were sought for and burned. In 297 or 298 the Christian persecutions began in the army, but the great, general persecution broke in 303. In that year Diocletian issued three edicts in rapid succession: the first ordered the destruction of Christian buildings; the second demanded the imprisonment of all bishops and presbyters; the third subjected all Christians to torture. A fourth edict of 304 offered Christians the simple alternative of apostasy or death. During this "Great Persecution" some of the Christians "lapsed," that is, they denied their faith. Others who gave up their sacred books were called "traditors." When the persecution was over, some of these asked permission to come back into the Church. This gave occasion for several important schisms: the Meletian schism in Alexandria; the schism of Heraclius in Rome; and the Donatist schism in Carthage.

Diocletian had associated with himself Maximianus as co-emperor. He had also appointed two subordinate Caesars, Galerius and Constantine Chlorus, the father of Constantine the Great.

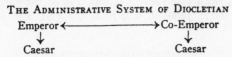

THE ADMINISTRATIVE SYSTEM OF DIOCLETIAN

Emperor ←——————————→ Co-Emperor
↓   ↓
Caesar   Caesar

Galerius, who was the real instigator of the Great Persecution, was finally satisfied that it was impossible to annihilate Christianity, and to give to the gods of Rome their old supremacy. In 311 he issued, together with his co-regents Constantine and Licinius, an edict which granted limited toleration of the Christians. Before the battle of the Mulvian Bridge in 312, Constantine made the cross his new military insignia. This act constituted, or rather signified, a turning point in the history of the Roman Empire and of the Church.

In 313 when Constantine was master of the whole eastern part of the Empire, the Great Persecution came to an end. The Edict of Milan, signed in 313 by Constantine and Licinius, recognized Christianity as a lawful religion. Licinius renewed the persecution for a short time in the East, but he was defeated by Constantine, who in 324 became sole ruler of the Empire. He openly protected and favored the Church, for he knew that the future of his Empire was bound up with Christianity, not with the old State religion. Christianity had now, after centuries of struggle, won a great victory over paganism. But this victory was not won without battle scars and many modifications in the life and organization of the Church.

A LIST OF EMPERORS

Diocletian and Maximian (A.D. 284-305).
Constantius and Galerius (A.D. 305).
Galerius and Severus (A.D. 306).

In the West:
Constantine (A.D. 306-324)
Maximian (A.D. 306-310)
Maxentius (A.D. 306-312)
Constantine, Sole Emperor in 324 A.D.

In the East:
Galerius (A.D. 306-311)
Maximian II (A.D. 307-313)
Licinius (A.D. 307-324)

How did the Christian Church gain this remarkable victory? Was it because of the heroism of the Christian martyrs? Was it because of the ideal life of the Christians in times of peace? Was it because of the powerful preaching of the Gospel? Was it because of the bankruptcy of heathenism? All these factors contributed to the complete reversal of the conditions of the Church; but the real victory came from God. He made good His promise: "In the world ye have tribulation: but be of good cheer; I have overcome the world."[15] The battle was won "not by might, nor by power, but by my Spirit, saith Jehovah."[16] It was true of the early Church as of Israel of old: "Jehovah will fight for you, and ye shall hold your peace."[17]

16. REVIEW QUESTIONS

1. Review carefully the causes of the Christian persecutions as listed on pages 57-60. Why did the Jews, and the heathen populace, and finally the Roman government persecute the Christians?
2. What important element did Emperor Trajan add to the history of the Christian persecutions? (cf. pages 84-85).
3. Why did the reign of Marcus Aurelius mark a turning point in the history of the Empire and of the Church?
4. Why did the relation of State to Church, up to the time of Decius, depend so largely on the good will of the emperors and the provincial governors?
5. Why did Decius begin a general, systematic persecution of Christianity?
6. What problems did the "lapsed" and the "traditors" give the Church? Should the resulting schisms have been avoided?
7. Why do you think the persecution from 303-313 is called the "Great Persecution"?
8. Why did this persecution terminate in a victory for Christianity?
9. What battle scars did the persecutions leave on the Church?
10. Was Christianity at the close of the Apostolic Era so well adapted to become the official State religion, as was the case after 325 A.D.?
11. Was this modification of Christian life and practice a good thing for the Church and for the future of civilization?

TOPICS FOR SPECIAL STUDY

1. "The Great Persecution."
2. The Diocletian reorganization of the Empire.
3. Constantine's position toward the Christian Church.
4. The law of Sunday rest not primarily intended for the Christians.
5. The Donatist schism in Carthage.

IV. Internal Conflicts: Controversies, Heresies, and Schisms.—The early Church passed through internal conflicts more trying than persecutions, with results far more momentous. Christianity had been given to the world as the only religion, as "the true light which lighteth every man."[18] In none other than Jesus Christ was there salvation.[19] But there existed already other systems of religion and philosophy which claimed to deal authoritatively with the destiny of man and his relation to the Deity. What contact was there between the cardinal truths of Christianity and truths already known? And how could these Christian truths be

[15] John 16:33.
[16] Zech. 4:6.
[17] Exod. 14:14.
[18] John 1:9.
[19] Acts 4:10-12.

explained, systematized, and fitted into the intellectual life of the world?

Most answers reflected the backgrounds of the various people just as the water of a river may be variously colored by the soil of the different localities through which it flows. There were different schools of Christian thought, such as the Alexandrian, the Western-Asiatic, and the African; yet most of the differences were perfectly compatible with the common Christian faith. Where churches had been formed from Jewish communities there was naturally a lingering attachment to the ancient Jewish ritual; where congregations had been formed from pagan converts, attempts were often made to reconcile the Christian faith with old pagan philosophies. Men sought to raise the Church to ideal purity in morality and discipline, but using *unnatural* methods they provoked schisms.

The principal causes of the conflicts were: (1) perversions of the Gospel and schisms occasioned by certain orthodox and syncretistic Jewish[20] groups; (2) conflicts and heresies caused by those who sought to harmonize Christianity with pagan philosophy and religion; (3) controversies concerning discipline and morality within the Church; (4) schisms that arose in regard to ecclesiastical order; and (5) disputes regarding Christian doctrine.

(1) There were various Jewish perversions. The orthodox groups, such as the Nazarenes, the Ebionites, and the Elkesaites, were troublesome enough for the Church; but the most formidable enemies were gnostic teachers and their schools, chief of whom were the Ophites, the Cainites, the Sethians, the Melchizedekians, Simon Magus and the Simonians, the Nicolaitans, Cerinthus, Basilides, Valentinus and his school, and Marcion and his school. It is beyond the scope of this book to enter into a discussion of the views of each of these men and their schools.[21]

(2) Attempts to harmonize Christianity with pagan philosophy and religion resulted in gnosticism, Neo-platonism, and Manichaeism. The first has already been considered. Neo-Platonism, founded in 241 A.D. by Ammonius Saccas of Alexandria, was set up as a rival to Christianity. Porphyry (A.D. 233-304) offered it as a substitute for Christianity. The system combined earlier Greek schools with Oriental religion and theosophy.

Manichaeism took its name from Mani or Manichaeus (A.D.

[20] cf. pp. 73-74.
[21] Special studies might well be made on such men as Cerinthus, Basilides, Valentinus, and Marcion. For a general discussion of the Gnostic movement, see pp. 74-79.

216-277), a Persian who attempted to reconcile Christianity with Zoroastrianism. It was essentially a dualistic religious philosophy, mixed with pantheistic, gnostic, and ascetic elements, and a fantastic philosophy of nature. After 280 A.D. it found many adherents also in the West, Augustine being much interested before his conversion to Christianity.

(3) Several schisms were caused by over-eager reformers keenly alive to practical defects in discipline and morality within the Church. Among these were Montanus in Asia Minor, Novatian of Rome, Novatus of Carthage, and the Donatists of the fourth century. These reformers evidently meant well, but their methods led to intolerance and fanaticism. Montanism has already been discussed.[22] The Novatian schism was caused by a controversy concerning the admission of the "lapsed" into the Church after the Decian and Valerian persecutions (A.D. 249-259). Novatian of Rome would not allow the lapsed to be restored to the communion of the Church, even on proof of penitence. During the absence of Bishop Cyprian, Novatus, a presbyter of Carthage, advocated extreme laxity regarding the lapsed. Many were re-admitted without examination or proof of repentance. When Cyprian returned to Carthage he called a council which decided to readmit the lapsed to membership only after due repentance and penance according to the offense. Novatus moved to Rome and, curiously enough, joined the Novatianists.[23]

(4) The peace of the Church was disturbed by ecclesiastical strifes, such as the Easter or Quartodeciman controversy concerning the date of Easter, and the Anabaptist controversy, involving the validity of Baptism performed by heretics.

Easter was the earliest annual festival celebrated in commemoration of the resurrection of Christ. In the East, the Christians celebrated the crucifixion of Christ at the same time as the non-Christian Jews celebrated the Old Testament Passover, on the fourteenth day of the Jewish month Nisan (Quartodecimans: 14th day observers), and the resurrection of Christ, or Easter, on the sixteenth day of Nisan, regardless of the day of the week. The West stressed the fact that Christ arose on Sunday, and insisted that Easter should be celebrated on no other day. The matter was finally settled by the Council of Nicea in 325 A.D. in favor of the Western practice.

[22] cf. pp. 86-88.
[23] The Donatist schism grew out of the Diocletian persecution, and rather belongs to that period.

A serious controversy arose over the validity of Baptism performed by heretics. Was it necessary for candidates received into communion to be baptized again if they had already been baptized by a heretic? The earlier practice had been to receive such members on imposition of hands, with prayers. But at the beginning of the third century the custom of renewing the rite sprung up in Asia Minor and in Alexandria, from which regions the Anabaptist movement was introduced to North Africa. Several synods of Carthage maintained the necessity of re-baptism; but the Bishop of Rome repudiated the Anabaptists with great force, so the practice was gradually discontinued.

(5) Differences in doctrine appeared early, especially with reference to the Holy Trinity and the divinity of Jesus Christ. Monotheism[24] was the most precious treasure of Christianity. Yet this one God was a Triune God, a holy Trinity. Some contended that this doctrine led to preaching two or three gods instead of one. Anxious to preserve the unity of God, they reduced the Trinity into a Unity, into a Monarchy of the Deity. Hence the name Monarchians, and our modern Unitarians.

The Monarchians tried to eliminate the mystery of the Trinity in one of two ways. One group denied the divinity of Christ, but ascribed to him a certain divine power or "dynamis" as a supernatural endowment. The Supreme Being simply worked upon or influenced the man Jesus Christ. This is called Dynamistic Monarchianism. This group was also later known as the "Adoptionists" because of their doctrine that Jesus Christ was not the Son of God by nature, but that he ultimately became God's Son by adoption. Another group made Christ and the Holy Spirit mere manifestations of God. They made no distinction between Father and Son, but saw in them only a difference in the *mode* in which the one divine person manifests Himself. Hence the name Modalistic Monarchians. This group was again divided into the Patripassians[25] and the Sabelians, who claimed that the Father, the Son, and the Spirit were only different names for the same person.

Origen of Alexandria (A.D. 185-254) caused another controversy. He taught that the Son, Jesus Christ, was but an emanation (outflowing) from the Father, and that the Holy Spirit was an emanation from both. On the ground of his "subordination" of the Son, Origen has been termed the father of Arianism (cf. next

---

[24] Monotheism, from *monos*, single, one, plus *theos*. God.
[25] Patripassians, from "Patris passio," i.e. "the Father's suffering."

chapter). He also taught that the future life would be a scene of probation. The punishment of the wicked was not final, the redeeming work of Christ extending even to the fallen angels. Hence Origen was the father of Universalism. His doctrine of a temporal punishment of the wicked paved the way for the Catholic doctrine of "purgatory." His views were controverted by several synods, being finally condemned formally by the Church.

There was also the so-called "Chiliastic Controversy." The word is derived from the Greek "chilias" which means "a thousand." Another name for the same movement is Millennarianism, from the Latin "mille" which means "one thousand." Many early Christians believed in the immediate coming of the Lord a second time to reign visibly on earth for one thousand years, according to Revelation 20:2-3, before the general resurrection and judgment. A distinction may be made between the Pre-Millennarians, or those who believed that Christ would appear before the Millennium, and the Post-Millennarians, or those who put the Second Coming after the Millennium. Whenever extreme chiliastic tendencies asserted themselves in the Christian life, eminent church leaders exerted a wholesome, counteracting influence. There is no account of any actual chiliastic schisms except in Nepos in Egypt, as recorded by Eusebius.

The various internal conflicts led to a number of beneficial results, in particular, the following: (1) the formation of the Rule of Faith; (2) the formation of the New Testament Canon; (3) the perfection of the church organization, including the establishment of the historic episcopate; and (4) the development of a Christian theology.

17. REVIEW QUESTIONS

1. Why do you think the Church had to pass through so many internal conflicts?
2. What claims did Christianity have to help establish itself as the only universal religion?
3. Why did not the existing systems of religion and philosophy willingly admit the claim that Christ is the true light which lighteth every man?
4. What is your reaction to the different schools of Christian thought of this era?
5. What situations promoted internal struggles during this era?
6. Do the reform movements of Montanus and Novatus remind you of any similar movements in recent times? Are such movements justified?
7. Why the Anabaptists?
8. How do you account for the origin of the Monarchians or Unitarians?
9. Why is Origen termed the father of Universalism?
10. Did anything good come out of these conflicts?

TOPICS FOR SPECIAL STUDY

1. The system of Neo-Platonism.
2. Manichaeism in contact with Christianity.
3. The Early Anabaptists.
4. The Early Unitarians.
5. Universalism in the Early Church.
6. The history of Chiliasm.

V. The Beginnings of Monasticism.—Monasticism may be defined as a system of renunciation of life in the world for the purpose of promoting the interests of the soul. This mode of life is not peculiar to Christianity, but is inherent in almost any system of religion. Monasticism has two roots: (1) the belief that the world is incurably evil; (2) the belief that the most holy men are those who do the hardest things for conscience's sake.

Early Christian monasticism grew from these roots and centered around voluntary poverty, voluntary celibacy, and voluntary seclusion from the world. There were four stages in its development: (1) ascetic tendencies within organized congregations; (2) hermit life, which involved separation from society for the purpose of living alone; (3) cloister life, which involved a rather informal association of hermits in the same locality; (4) monastic orders, where several hermit associations organized under the same rule and name. Christian monasticism reached the third stage during the Ante-Nicene Age.

The first hermit to gain world-wide fame was an Egyptian ascetic named Antonius, or St. Anthony. He was born in Memphis around 250 A.D. During most of his life, from the age of twenty to the extreme old age of 106, he lived in seclusion in the desert. St. Anthony became so popular that hermit life became a mass-movement. Hermits became so numerous in various localities that formation of hermit associations (cloisters) became necessary. The first known cloister organization was that of Pachomius on the island of Tabenna on the Nile in the year 335 A.D. And this takes us into the next period of church history.

VI. Christian Education and Theology.—The early Church was faithful to her calling to make disciples of all nations. These converts were formally taken into full church communion through the rite of baptism. But the Church at first addressed herself in her missionary preaching to adults. Hence instruction and a period of probation became necessary. This period covered two or three years, though it might be shortened in special cases. How this catechumenal instruction was carried on is shown in two sets of lectures, in the first six chapters of the "Didache" or the "Teachings of the Twelve," dating from around 100 A.D., and in the "Apostolic Constitutions" completed before the end of the fourth century.

This catechumenal training, common everywhere in the early Church, gave rise to the catechetical schools, which in turn developed into schools of Christian theology. The clergy in the Greek-speaking world felt the need of a training on a par with that of their critics, the learned Greeks. The catechetical school of Alex-

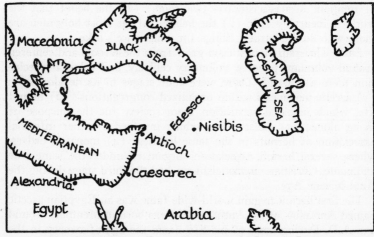

MAP SHOWING THE EARLY CATECHETICAL SCHOOL CENTERS

andria was the most famous educational institution in the early Church. Its original purpose was simply to give catechumenal training, but its scope was soon enlarged so as to give both a general secular and a religious training. Similar schools were opened at Antioch, Edessa, Nisibis, and Caesarea.

In the West the people as well as the leaders were less philosophic but more practical. They concerned themselves with the moral regeneration of society through the moral regeneration of converts. Pagan learning was gradually rejected as undesirable for Christians. Says Tertullian, "What indeed has Athens to do with Jerusalem? What concord is there between the Academy and the Church? What between heretics and Christians?" So Hellenic learning declined rapidly. A council held in Carthage in 401 forbade the clergy to read any pagan author. After the barbarian invasions, Greek learning was practically forgotten in the West for almost a thousand years.

VII. Life and Worship.—Christianity effected a great moral regeneration of society. Its influence was demonstrated most clearly in the home. Monogamy was strictly enforced. The sacredness of the marriage tie was proclaimed. Woman was elevated to a new and higher place. Exposure of infants was condemned as simple murder, and children became sacred. Christian parents made it their sacred duty to train their children and members of their household in the ways of Christianity.

True love pervaded the Christian home life, and the life of the congregations. "See how the Christians love each other" was the common remark of pagan neighbors. This love manifested itself, not only among the Christians themselves, but also in hospitality and charity toward the heathen.

The Christian idea of equality and responsibility gave the citizen a new place in the State. Christianity emphasized duty to God, unselfish service, personal morality, chastity, and honesty. Consequently, there were certain occupations that the Christians would not enter. Christians would not make images for idol worship. They would not be astrologists, magicians, or actors. On military service, opinion was divided. They did not want to be bankers because they did not think it was right to charge interest on money. Gladiatorial activities were shunned. Neither did they like to see church members become innkeepers.

Certain activities remind one of the work and mission of modern Bible societies. A learned and wealthy pastor, Pamphilus of Caesarea, circulated numerous books of the Bible, sometimes as loans, but often as permanent gifts. During the reign of Diocletian, the books of the Bible had found a wide circulation in the congregations.

Church discipline was quite severe, though cases of undue laxity were not wanting. The careful catechumenal instruction was the main safeguard against accepting unworthy members. But discipline was also exercised among the regular church members. The discipline was originally administered by the congregation as such, but during the third century this authority was gradually transferred to the bishop.

Church penance became an established practice during this period, though it was not as yet considered a sacrament. In baptism the candidate received complete forgiveness of sins up to the moment the rite was performed. But it was generally accepted that certain sins committed after baptism admitted of no pardon, while other sins would exclude the offender from church membership until due penance had been made. There were four stages or degrees in this penance, and the completion of each stage normally required one year.

The eighth book of the "Apostolic Constitutions" contains an interesting description of public worship as it prevailed in the Church at the close of the third century. The general service included prayer, praise, reading of the Bible, and a sermon. After the sermon the catechumens, the penitents, and those who were possessed were dismissed. Then followed the service for the regular church members, according to a rather elaborate ritual. The climax of this service was the partaking of the Lord's Supper.

As the Church became Romanized and partly paganized, Christians tended to emphasize the *form* of belief, rather than personal virtues and simple faith. In the endeavor to create specific forms for Christian life and worship, Old Testament models were often used. Christian clergy functioning as a priesthood was largely taken from the Old Testament, and the sacrificial theory of the Lord's Supper came from the same source. The Sacrament of the Altar came to be looked upon as the sacrifice of the New Covenant. The gifts (the elements) which the Christians brought on this occasion[26] constituted the "pure offering"[27] of the congregation *for* the Lord's Supper. The priest again, in imitation of Old Testament practice, offered these gifts *in* the Lord's Supper. The priest became the mediator between God and the congregation.

Regular church buildings became common during this period. There is a record of the existence of such buildings in Caesarea, Bithynia, Gaul, and North Africa toward the close of the third century. At the beginning of the Diocletian persecutions, there were no less than forty churches in Rome. In Nicomedia a splendid church was erected opposite the imperial palace. During the persecutions the Christians met for worship in caves, in desert places, in places of sepulture, and in the catacombs. The catacombs were underground passages, from 2-4 feet wide, frequently three or four stories deep. In the walls were openings where the bodies of deceased believers were buried.

Singing formed an essential part of the Christian worship,[28] but it was in unison and without musical accompaniment. Augustine

[26] Heb. 13:15.
[27] Mal. 1:11.
[28] Cf. Eph. 5:19; Col. 3:16; Jas. 5:13; Matth. 26:30; Acts 16:25.

(354-430) describes the congregational singing of his day as simple and non-artistic.

As private houses soon became inadequate for the ever growing congregations, and the rented buildings outgrew their usefulness, the Christians erected special buildings for worship.[29] The earliest known church buildings were erected in Edessa, Arbela, and vicinity before the year 200. They were in the form of a rectangular room with an arched roof. Later appeared the square room with cupalo or dome roof. In Rome and vicinity the churches were usually in basilica style, that is, a rectangular building divided into nave and aisles and covered with a flat roof, and often with a projecting, semi-circular addition at one end.

Christian decorative art was in this era largely confined to burial places, the catacombs.[30] Important Christian conceptions were expressed by symbols, of which the anchor as a symbol of Christ is thought to be the oldest. Another ancient symbol is the fish, because the Greek name for fish forms the initials for Jesus Christ, Son of God, Savior. The deer designates Christ as the one who tramples the serpent (death) under feet. The Tree of Life signifies the re-opened Paradise. The palm is a sign of victory. Later symbols are Christ as the Good Shepherd, and the dove.

The legal conception of the relationship between God and man paved the way for work-holiness, or the merit of good works. Let man acquire for himself *merits* before God, says Tertullian. In the Western Church there was also an ever growing tendency to subjugate the soul, for the attainment of its salvation, to the Church as a divine, mediating institution. The chasm between clergy and lay people gradually widened.

Special adoration of martyrs and saints became quite common during the Ante-Nicene Era. On the anniversaries of the death of the martyrs, the Christians gathered about their burial-places for memorial services, which usually consisted of prayers, commemoration of the good deeds and the sufferings of the martyrs, oblations, and the celebration of the Lord's Supper. Martyrdom was early lauded as baptism by blood in which sin was washed away. A very high value was attached to the intercession of the martyrs at the throne of God. The Christians did not as yet pray to the saints, nor did they worship the relics of the saints as

[29] Two names were used for a Christian place of worship, "the house of God" and the ecclesia (cf. p. 2).
[30] In Rome alone the catacombs reached a total length of 880 kilometers, and had burial space for six million people.

possessing miraculous virtues. Those practices became more common during the following period.

VIII. Retrospect.—What was the Church at the close of three centuries? It is evident that in life, doctrine, organization, and worship the congregations of 323 A.D. were somewhat different from the churches of 100 A.D. Perhaps the Christian Church at the close of the Ante-Nicene Era may be likened to a full grown person just through the most formative period of life. Childhood and youth have been molded into mature and permanent forms, but future growth and adjustments must still come.

The Church had extended to all parts of the Empire, from the Euphrates to the Atlantic, and from the Danube, the Rhine and the firths of Scotland to the African deserts. Churches were even established in regions beyond the Roman territory, especially toward the East. Christianity had gained a high social position. Many congregations and individuals were quite wealthy. Christian leaders, especially the teachers and the writers, had culture and education superior to that of the pagans. And the Christian literature of this period presupposed a well-educated Christian public.

Christianity had, like a leaven, permeated Graeco-Roman life, but paganism had in turn reacted decidedly upon the Church. The masses began to join the Church some time before Constantine, or before Christianity became the official religion of the State, some of whom remained pagan in thinking and in practice. Corrupting ideas gained undue popularity. Worldliness and externalism prevailed. There was an unfortunate distinction between a higher and a lower morality, between the clergy and the laity. The Church, through the clergy, became a necessary mediary agency between God and man. The meritoriousness of good works was advocated by prominent church leaders. Martyrs and saints gained undue recognition, and a special sanctity was attached to places and relics associated with saints. Externalism was manifested in the elaborate rituals and in the rapidly increasing number of Christian festivals.

The Graeco-Roman world was Christianized, and Christianity was partly paganized. Moral and religious corruptions in the Church began quite some time before Christianity was adopted as the state religion. It is historically incorrect to make the State Church the scapegoat for all the faults of the Christian Church of succeeding periods.

It would also be incorrect to suppose that Christianity was corrupt toward the close of the Ante-Nicene Era. There are many evidences of the existence of a healthy, vigorous Christian life, in spite of the many demoralizing tendencies.

18. REVIEW QUESTIONS

1. How do you account for the origin and the growth of Monasticism?
2. Why did the early Church place such stress on Christian education?
3. What attitude did the Church take toward pagan learning? Did the Church of the East and of the West differ on this score?
4. How did Christianity affect home life in Roman society? Why?
5. In what respect did Christianity give the citizen a new place in the State?
6. How did the Church promote Christianity by means of appropriate literature?
7. What is meant by church penance? How was it practiced?
8. Where would you seek for a first-hand description of a typical religious service for the Ante-Nicene Era?
9. Why was the Lord's Supper looked upon as a sacrifice? Does your denomination hold this identical view today?
10. What can you say about the places for Christian worship?
11. Why did the meritoriousness of good works, and the martyrs and the saints receive so much attention at this time? Compare with the practices in the Apostolic Era.

TOPICS FOR SPECIAL STUDY

1. The Monastic Ideal in the Ancient World.
2. The Early Catechetical Instruction.
3. Penance in the Ante-Nicene Church.
4. Tertullian, the Father of Western Catholicism.

A SELECTED BIBLIOGRAPHY FOR CHAPTER IV

1. Rainy: *The Ancient Catholic Church*, Chapters VI, XI.
2. Workman: *Persecution in the Early Church.*
3. Uhlhorn: *Conflict of Christianity with Heathenism.*
4. Drane: *Christian Schools and Scholars.*
5. Harnack: *The Mission and Expansion of Christianity in the First Three Centuries.*
6. Lindsay: *The Church and the Ministry in the Early Centuries.*
7. Baker: *Constantine the Great.*
8. Workman: *Christian Thought to the Reformation.*
9. Hatch: *Organization of the Early Christian Churches.*
10. Bigg: *The Church's Task in the Roman Empire.*
11. Krüger: *History of the Early Christian Literature in the First Three Centuries.*
12. Beet: *The Early Roman Episcopate to A.D. 384.*
13. Chapman: *Studies in the Early Papacy.*
14. Harnack: *Constitution and Law in the First Two Centuries.*
15. Thompson: *The Historic Episcopate.*
16. Healy: *The Valerian Persecution: A Study of the Relation between Church and State in the Third Century.*
17. Burkitt: *The Religion of the Manichees.*
18. Whittaker: *The Neoplatonists.*
19. Mackean: *Christian Monasticism in Egypt to the Close of the Fourth Century.*
20. Oesterley: *The Jewish Background of the Christian Liturgy.*

CHAPTER V

The Post-Nicene Era. A.D. 325-590

The history of the Church in this era deals primarily with three lines of development: first, the relation of the Church to the Empire; second, the development of Christian doctrine; third, the development of church organization and cultus.

(1) Christianity was established as the only authorized religion of the Empire, while heathenism and heresy were prohibited by law. The Gospel was preached among the barbaric tribes to the north and to the east. The Empire weakened, while the Church grew strong, gradually taking over the power of the State. After the destruction of the western part of the Empire, the Church was for several centuries the sole link with the past.

(2) Since Christianity was considered the chief unifying factor in the Empire, great efforts were made to unify the doctrine of the Church. These attempts led the attention to the various theological controversies; to the formulation of creeds; to the five General Councils; and to the illustrious Christian writers of the period.

(3) Efforts were made to unify the Church in organization and practice. Church government centered increasingly around the clergy; worship became ritualistic and external; secularity and corruption prevailed maturing the Church for the punishment soon to come through Mohammedanism and the great tribal movements.

I. The Church and the Empire.—The Imperial Edicts of 311 and 313 A.D. marked a great turning-point. In 311 Christians were granted a limited toleration, and in 313 the two emperors Licinius and Constantine declared: "We grant to the Christians and to all others full liberty of following that religion which each may choose." These two edicts, which some have called the Magna Charta of Christianity, are among the most important documents in the history of mankind.

It is interesting to note that as Christianity passed through the great triumphal Arch of Victory, the principle of full religious liberty was declared. Constantine saw that Christian principles could not be made a matter of law. Christianity must begin from within. But he clearly manifested, by subsequent edicts, that he favored the Christian religion, and after he became sole Emperor, he issued a general exhortation to his subjects to embrace Christianity. At the same time he avoided the alienation of the pagan majority by retaining the title, and by performing the duties of the Pontifex Maximus, High Priest for the official pagan religion.

He moved cautiously but successfully where an ordinary ruler would have rushed forward, only to stumble and to fall.

Constantine effected one of the greatest transformations in history. Before his death *the Roman Empire had largely emancipated itself from the old, pagan religions.* Christianity was established as the great unifying bond of the Empire. That does not mean that everybody by this time professed Christianity. There still existed a powerful pagan majority, and a pagan nobility; but *a fundamental change had taken place in the public consciousness* that was soon to bring visible and far reaching results.

While Christianity was not formally adopted by Constantine as the religion of the State, he virtually gave it this position. The privileges that had belonged to the religious institutions of old Rome were given to the Church, with several new ones added. He exempted the Christian clergy from military and municipal duties and their property from taxation (313). He abolished various customs and ordinances offensive to Christians (315). He gave the Catholic but not the heretical churches right to receive legacies (321). He enjoined the civil observance of Sunday (321). He contributed liberally to the building of churches, to the circulation of the Scriptures, and to the support of the clergy. The Catholic churches were given the privilege of asylum. He preferred Christians to fill the chief offices, surrounded himself with Christian councilors, and gave his sons a Christian education.

This elevation of Christianity made Constantine the first representative of a Christian theocracy,[1] a policy which involved: (1) the assumption that all subjects are Christians just as the Old Testament theocracy assumed that all subjects of that government were Israelites; (2) an intimate connection between civil and religious rights; and (3) the belief that Church and State as divine institutions were the two arms of one and the same divine government on earth. This idea was more fully developed in the Holy Roman Empire of the Middle Ages, and has re-appeared in various forms even down to the present time.

Constantine continued as the supreme pontiff of the religious affairs of the State. He called himself the bishop of bishops, and Eusebius and other church officials willingly granted him this title. When the Empire was shaken to its very foundations by internal dissensions and outward pressure by the barbarians, he relied upon Christianity as the only power capable of renovating and building

---

[1] Theocracy (*Theos*: God + *krateo*: rule).

up society and tottering political organization. He tried in every way to strengthen and to unify the Church. In 314 he called the Council of Arles to settle the Donatist controversy, and in 325 he called the first General Council of the Church, held at Nicea in Asia Minor. To this Council bishops came from all parts of the Empire, but few came from the West. They traveled by the imperial post and at government expense. Constantine himself was present at Nicea, and took part in some of the meetings.

In 330 he transferred the seat of government to Byzantium,[2] mainly because of his dislike of the heathenism still prevailing in Rome. The selection of this unrivalled locality for the building of

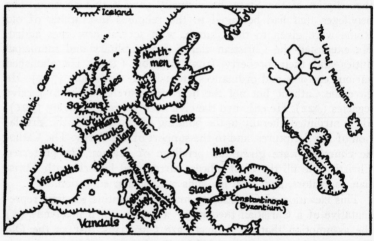

LOCATION OF TRIBES, A.D. 500

a new Christian Rome (Constantinople) profoundly affected the future course of history. One result was a divided Empire and a divided Church although Constantine tried to make the new government seat the real center of Christianity. He built magnificent churches; he had works of art brought from all parts of the world; and he elevated the Bishop of Constantinople to a position equal to that of the Bishop of Rome.[3]

All succeeding emperors, with the exception of Julian the Apostate (361-363) placed themselves on the side of Christianity. The three sons of Constantine did not follow his wise policy, but tried

[2] See map above.
[3] He also gave away 50 splendid copies of the Bible prepared under the direction of Eusebius of Caesarea.

to suppress paganism by force. Julian the Apostate tried to revive Graeco-Roman paganism, but this reaction was short-lived and futile. The immediate successors of Julian gradually restored to the churches the privileges they had enjoyed under Constantine and his sons. In 392 Theodosius the Great declared all heathen sacrifices to be high treason, and in 529 paganism lost its last support when Justinian the First closed the school of philosophy at Athens. All rivals of Christianity were vanquished. The Church enjoyed peace, popularity, and power.

Shortly after Christianity had become firmly established in the Empire, "the fullness of time" came for a large number of invading barbaric tribes. The great "Human Gateway" between the Caspian Sea and the Ural Mountains opened wide, and hordes of people moved swiftly into Europe. These invading tribes soon broke the boundaries of the Empire, and after many bitter struggles one of the barbaric chiefs, Odoacer of the Ostrogoths, dethroned the last of the western Emperors in 476. A number of barbaric kingdoms were set up: the Kingdom of the Visigoths (415-711) in Spain and Southern Gaul; the Kingdom of the Ostrogoths (493-554) in Italy; the Kingdom of the Burgundians (443-534) in Southeastern Gaul; the Kingdom of the Vandals (429-533) in North Africa; the Kingdom of the Franks under the Merovingians (486-752); the Kingdom of the Lombards (586-774) in Northern Italy. Between 443-485 the Angles, the Saxons, and the Jutes left Denmark and North Germany and settled in South Britain. Slavic tribes also moved into the Eastern Empire.

Tremendous changes took place in Europe as a result of these tribal movements. Can you see the providence of God in preparing the Church to sow the seeds of Christianity among these barbarians? What would have happened if these tribes had overrun Europe at the time of Pericles, at the time of Caesar Augustus, or even at the time of the Apostle John?

Now the Church was ready to preach the Gospel among the barbarians. All Teutonic tribes were converted to Christianity either before, or shortly after their entrance into the Empire. The beginning was made by the Visigoths (Western Goths). Christian captives taken in war brought the Gospel to them, and Ulfilas (311-383) gave them an alphabet, and translated the Bible into their tongue. From the Visigoths Christianity came to the Ostrogoths (Eastern Goths), to the Vandals, and to the Lombards. The King of the Franks, Clovis (481-511), became acquainted with Christianity through his queen, Clothilda, a Catholic Burgundian princess. After the battle with the Alemanni he decided to embrace Christianity. He was baptized, and he compelled his army to be baptized. In 587 the King of Spain, Ricarred, accepted Christianity. The Anglo-Saxons in Britain came in direct contact with Christianity through the Britons and the Celts, and the Christian Church was established in distant Abyssinia.

Did the Church of this era remain true to her divinely appointed mission by permitting herself to be adopted as the State Church? The question may not seem easy to answer. In general it may be said that while the masses were Christianized, the Church was secularized and paganized. Many other results may be registered, but the Church had no choice. Christianity had, even before Constantine, become a powerful factor in the Empire. Many worldly elements had entered the Church which now stood ready to receive the masses. Heathenism had collapsed. But people must have a religion, and Christianity was the religion that could properly take the throne.

Suppose Diocletian had succeeded and Christianity had remained the religion of a small minority. European culture would then have developed under the influence of the Mithra religion (Sun-worship), the most powerful rival of Christianity at that time. Would this have given the Church a better opportunity to fulfill her mission? The Church of Europe might have been obliged to exist under much the same conditions as the Christian Church in the Mohammedan lands during the last twelve centuries.

19. REVIEW QUESTIONS

1. What general lines of development did the Church follow?
2. Why was Christianity for two centuries an unlawful, persecuted, and despised religion?
3. Why are the edicts of 311 and 313 called the Magna Charta of Christianity?
4. Why did Constantine succeed in bringing about such a marvelous transformation in society?
5. What is meant by the statement that Constantine became the first representative of a Christian theocracy?
6. Do you discover any difference between the theory of religious liberty to Constantine and that of the modern Protestantism? How do the two theories differ?
7. Why did Constantine transfer the seat of government to Constantinople? Did this transfer have any effect upon the future course of the Church?
8. Why, do you think, did the "fullness of time" come for the Teutonic tribes at this particular time, and not earlier?
9. What did the Church do for these barbarians?
10. Was it a good thing that Christianity became a State religion?

TOPICS FOR SPECIAL STUDY

1. To what extent may Christian principles be legislated?
2. Constantine as the first representative of a Christian Theocracy.
3. The founding of Constantinople.
4. Map the movements of the principal tribes from A.D. 100 to A.D. 500.

II. The Formation of Christian Doctrine.—The chief causes which contributed to make the Post-Nicene Era (325-590) pre-eminently one of theological controversies and doctrinal formulations were:

(1) Christianity had to appear in systematized or scientific form to prove its claim as a universal religion. But constant persecutions had not given the Christians much opportunity to examine critically the grounds of Christian belief, and to formulate Christian doctrines.

(2) When persecutions ceased and the Church enjoyed peace and popular favor, there arose a demand for reason to penetrate the truths of Christian revelation, and to formulate these truths in definite language. But men apprehended variously the great cardinal truths of Christianity, which gave rise to serious controversies, which threatened to break up the unity of the Church.

(3) Constantine and succeeding emperors looked upon the Church as the great unifying force. Hence great efforts were made to keep unity and to suppress heresy. But where was the true Church? The criterion was formulated and defined by the five General or Ecumenical Councils of this period. The doctrinal definitions of these Councils, especially those of the Nicene and the Athanasian Creeds,[4] have always since been accepted by the main body of the Church.

THE GENERAL OR ECUMENICAL COUNCILS

1. Nicea (I), 325
2. Constantinople (I), 381
3. Ephesus, 431
4. Chalcedon, 451

5. Constantinople (II), 553
6. Constantinople (III), 680
7. Nicea (II), 787

There were four principal doctrinal controversies. Two of these, the Arian and the Nestorian, of a *speculative* nature, had their origin in the Eastern or Greek-speaking Church. They centered in the question "What think ye of Christ? Whose son is he?"[5] The deity of the Holy Spirit was also involved. The other two disputes, the Donatist and the Pelagian, had their origin in the Western or Latin-speaking Church, and dealt more with *practical* subjects, such as, how is man saved? what is the Church? who are the true ministers? what are the Sacraments?

Arianism takes its name from Arius, a presbyter of Alexandria who, coming before the public in 318 or 320 claimed that Christ was neither true God nor true man, but a sort of demi-god, half way between men and the Father. Christ was "different from and

---

[4] See diagram on p. 125.   [5] Matth. 22:42.

unlike the substance and peculiar nature of the Father in all respects." He was also unlike man because he had no human soul. It will be seen that Arius gave the worst possible answer to his own question.

Propagating his theory with great activity, political sagacity and tact, he involved the Eastern Church in bitter controversy for nearly a century. Athanasius, the Father of Orthodoxy, was the great opponent of Arius. The first Ecumenical or General Council at Nicea in 325 condemned Arianism and accepted as the general creed of the Church that "Jesus Christ is very God of very God, of one substance with the Father and begotten of the Father from eternity." The second General Council at Constantinople in 381 endorsed this doctrine.

Semi-Arianism took a mediary position between Arius and Athanasius. Another group called Macedonians from Macedonius, their leader (also called Pneumatomachians), held that the Holy Spirit was of an essence inferior to that of the Father and of the Son. The second General Council at Constantinople in 381 formulated and subscribed to the doctrine that the Holy Ghost "proceeds from the Father and is to be worshipped and glorified together with the Father and the Son."

(b) *Nestorianism* centered about the two natures of Jesus Christ. Nestorius, a presbyter at Antioch, and later Patriarch of Constantinople (428-435) made a distinction between the divine and the human natures in Christ which amounted almost to a separation into two persons. Christ himself was not born, but only the man Jesus. Hence Mary was not to be called the mother of God. Only to the human Jesus could birth, suffering, and death be ascribed. Hence certain acts of the Lord were ascribed to his divine, certain others to his human nature. But this distinction might easily lead to a denial of the absolute value of the suffering, death, and resurrection of Jesus Christ. Hence the Church condemned Nestorianism as heresy at the third General Council, held at Ephesus in 431. A lengthy creed was officially adopted, the first part of which reads as follows:

"We, therefore, acknowledge our Lord Jesus Christ, the Son of God, the Only-begotten, complete God and complete man, of a rational soul and body; begotten of the Father before the ages according to (his) divinity, but in the last days . . . of Mary the Virgin according to (his) humanity; that he is of the same nature with the Father according to (his) divinity, and of the same nature with us according to (his) humanity. For a union of the two natures has taken place; wherefore we confess one Christ, one Son, one Lord." Cyril, Bishop of Alexandria, was the great opponent of Nestorius.

Monophysitism[6] claimed that though Christ was both human and divine, he had but one nature, that of God. This view was prominently advocated by Eutyches, an abbot of Constantinople, who added that Christ was so completely divine he had no real human body, but only the outward appearance of a man. The fourth General Council at Chalcedon in 451 rejected this doctrine and declared that in the person of Christ there are two natures, the divine and the human, united without confusion or change. But the doctrines of the Monophysites continued to be taught in one form or another. One group advocated that the two natures in Jesus Christ had mixed into a third and new theanthropic (God-man) nature. The fifth General Council at Constantinople in 553 forcibly suppressed Monophysitism.

Monotheletism[7] followed, declaring that though Christ had a human nature, he had not a human but only a divine will. The sixth General Council at Constantinople in 680 condemned this doctrine.

(c) *Donatism* originated in Carthage, North Africa, shortly after the Diocletian persecution. The Donatists, who were the High Churchmen of the fifth century, took issue with the Catholic Church in matters of church discipline and martyrdom. The party held that the traditors, or those who had surrendered copies of Scripture in the recent persecution, had committed a mortal sin.

In 311 Caecilian was hastily elected and consecrated Bishop of Carthage. The consecration service was performed by Felix of Aptunga, whom the Donatists declared to be a *traditor*. This offense, they declared, rendered all the official acts of Felix invalid, including the ordination of Caecilian. A group of 70 bishops assembled at Carthage and elected Majorinus as a rival bishop in 312. He died the following year and was succeeded by Donatus the Great, from whom the schismatic party took its name. For many years the North African Church was rent by two warring and sharply opposing parties, the Donatists and the Catholics.

After Augustine had been elected Bishop of Hippo in 395 he addressed all his energy to reconciling the opposing factions. He entered the controversy on the Catholic side and declared that the character of a minister does not affect his official acts. All the acts

---

[6] Monophysitism (*monos*: single + *physis*: essence or nature).
[7] Monotheletism (*monos*: single + *thelema*: will).

of the Church are valid acts, though the officials may be unworthy men.[8] The true Church is recognized by her possession of the Creed, the Sacraments, and the apostolic succession of bishops. He also defined the Sacraments. Augustine's answers and definitions gave Donatism its deathblow. The schism was outlawed in 411, and when the Vandals invaded Africa, the Donatists disappeared in the ensuing chaos.

(d) *Pelagianism* centered in the question: how is man saved? Three general answers were given. Pelagius ascribed the chief merit of conversion to man. Augustine gave God all the glory and made freedom the result of divine grace. The Semi-Pelagians co-ordinated the human will and the divine grace as factors in the work of salvation.

Pelagius (370?-440?), a British monk, appeared in Rome and in Africa and set forth the following views: (1) Man has no original sin inherited from Adam. Sin is not a fault of nature but is purely a matter of will. (2) Each person is created like Adam, with perfect freedom to do good or evil. Hence an entirely sinless life is possible, and man can save himself by his own good works. (3) Infant baptism is useless because man has no hereditary or original sin. New-born children are sinless. (4) While salvation is possible without the Law and the Gospel, or by divine grace, these greatly facilitate the attainment of salvation. Christ helps us by his good example, as Adam hurt us by his bad example.

Augustine appeared as the great opponent of Pelagius. He asserted: (1) Man was created in the image of God, with freedom of will. All of this Adam lost in the fall, and the character of the fallen Adam passed over to his posterity, not by way of imitation but by generation. Hence all have original sin, even new-born children. (2) Through the fall of Adam man lost his freedom of choice in matters pertaining to salvation, which must be attributed solely to divine grace. (3) Infant baptism is necessary because new-born children have original sin which involves divine penalty. Infants dying without baptism are damned. Original sin is taken away in baptism; yet the sinful nature remains after baptism. (4) The salvation of man is attributed to grace and faith. Even faith is a work of grace. It depends solely upon the omnipotent will of God whether any one shall will, or not will; that is, God has mercy upon some and effectually calls them while He leaves others to their merited fate.

The views of Augustine were generally accepted by the Catholic

[8] For Luther's view in this matter, see Chap. X, Sect. V.

Church, while Pelagianism was condemned by the third General
Council at Ephesus in 431. A few years later an attempt was made
by a group called Semi-Pelagians to find a middle ground between
Augustine and Palagius, but this movement soon spent its force.[9]

It is significant that the General Councils became the open battlefields upon which the victory of orthodoxy was decided. The growing importance attached to these General Councils and to the decisions of the Church Fathers gave additional confirmation to the
old Catholic principle of tradition. The Catholic Tradition was
soon co-ordinated with Scripture, and at times even placed above
it as a norm for faith and conduct.

To this era belong a number of illustrious Christian writers.
Athanasius (300-373), the Father of Orthodoxy, was a bishop at

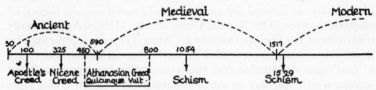

THE THREE GENERAL ANCIENT SYMBOLS

Alexandria. The Athanasian Creed has its name from him. *St.
Ambrose* (340-397) was a bishop of Milan, the greatest pulpit
orator of the Western Church and a great champion of Catholicism
against Arianism. *Chrysostom* (347-407), or "the Golden Mouth,"
was so called because of his unrivalled eloquence. He was a presbyter at Antioch, and later a patriarch at Constantinople, and one
of the foremost champions of truth in the early Church. *Augustine*
(354-430) has been called "the Teacher of the Christian Occident." He was a great writer of apologetical and dogmatical works.
He seems to be regarded equally great by Catholics and Protestants.
Jerome (343-420) translated the Old Testament directly into Latin
from Hebrew and prepared a conservative Latin revision of the
New Testament by the aid of the "Itala" and other existing translations. His completed Bible work is known as the *Versio vulgata*,
or the Vulgate.

III. Augustine's "City of God."—Augustine's unfinished
masterpiece was his "City of God" (De Civitate Dei) consisting

---

[9] Semi-Pelagianism, however, became the prevalent conception during the latter part of
the Middle Ages.

of twenty-two books; it was written between 412 and 426 A.D., in the dark days after the capture of Rome by Alaric. In the first ten books he presents a remarkable defense of Christianity against paganism and the encroaching Roman patriotism. In the last twelve books he contrasts the *Civitas Terrena*, or secular State, founded on conquest and maintained by fraud and violence, with the *Civitas Dei*, or Kingdom of God. The Civitas Terrena, or Earthly City, has as its highest representatives heathen Babylon and Rome. The Civitas Dei, or City of God, is represented by the Christian Society, that is, by the visible, hierarchically organized Church. Augustine's vision of the gradual extension of the City of God over the world is magnificent. The Earthly City must pass away as the City of God grows. The Earthly City has no right to exist unless it is definitely subordinated to the City of God.

The "City of God" exerted a profound influence upon Western Christianity. It formed the religious background for the theory of medieval papacy. The Roman Curia of the Middle Ages actually transformed the Civitas Dei into a Civitas Terrena, represented by the visible church empire ruled by the Bishop of Rome. The "City of God" also accentuated that sharp distinction between sacred and secular which still has so much influence in Western civilization.

20. REVIEW QUESTIONS

1. Why was the Post-Nicene Era pre-eminently an era of theological controversies and doctrinal formulations?
2. Why were the controversies of Eastern origin so different in nature from those of the West?
3. How did the Arians and the Semi-Arians differ from Athanasius?
4. Why was the issue finally settled by a General Council?
5. Why did Nestorianism and kindred views cause so much disturbance in the Church? Can you see why such views would be harmful? Explain.
6. Discuss the Donatist schism. Do you agree with the decision of Augustine?
7. Compare the views of Pelagius and Augustine. Has Pelagianism anything in common with present-day Humanism?
8. Why was Catholic Tradition coordinated with Scripture and even placed above it in some cases?
9. Are you in position to say what attitude Protestantism takes toward Tradition?
10. Mention some of the illustrious Christian writers of this period. Have you taken time to study one or more biographies of some of these men?
11. What can you say about the Latin Vulgate?
12. Discuss Augustine's "City of God."

TOPICS FOR SPECIAL STUDY

1. May serious doctrinal errors coexist with true personal faith?
2. The Nicene Creed.
3. The Athanasian Creed.

4. Outline the main events of the first five General Councils.
5. Augustine, the father of Western Catholicism of the Medieval Period.

IV. The Development of Church Organization.

—There was a great transformation in church government, especially with reference to the position and the privileges of the clergy. Before the time of Constantine the clergy, especially the bishops, enjoyed an ever-increasing power and influence. Yet the clergy had been co-ordinated with the laity in a true Christian brotherhood. In the course of the fourth and fifth centuries an ever-widening chasm developed between clergy and laity, until the view prevailed that only the clergy constituted the Church proper. Several causes contributed to this strange development.

(1) The clergy became an economically independent order. Many new privileges were gradually added. The privilege of receiving legacies and donations made the Church wealthy. This property was generally divided so that the bishop received one fourth; the priests in his territory received one fourth; one fourth was used for the maintenance of the congregations; and one fourth was given to charity. These donations, added to the income of the clergy, promoted their interests in secular affairs. The income of the country churches was also under the supervision of the bishop and his clergy.

(2) The Church became a legal tribunal with a very extensive jurisdiction. Constantine gave the episcopal tribunals right to settle all legal disputes within the Church, and also civil matters which did not involve criminal cases. The clergy could henceforth avoid altogether the secular courts. Through the peculiar privilege of intercession, which formerly also had belonged to the heathen priests, the clergy could often obstruct the course of justice in the civil courts.

(3) The clergy became a special order, with special customs and a distinct career. The clergy was separated from the laity not only by their official capacity, but also, as it was believed, by higher religious and moral gifts and an *indelible character* imparted through ordination. Once a priest, always a priest. Enforced celibacy does not belong to this period; yet certain restrictive measures in family life were expected of the clergy. Official penance was abolished in favor of private penance before the clergy, later also before the monks. In dress, in shaving the crown of the head, and in other external ways the clergy manifested their distinction.

(4) Codification of church (canon) laws and traditions began. Some of the doctrines and practices of the Church did not have any support in Scripture, so the officials sought support, like the Pharisees of old, in Tradition.

The clergy was organized quite differently from the earlier eras. The country bishops disappeared as their official duties were taken over by the city bishops. In the cities the presbyters continued in office, but they were entirely dependent upon the will of the bishop. A new office, that of arch-presbyter, was created. The deacons also continued to function as a part of the inferior clergy. Their activities were supervised by an arch-deacon. The sub-deacons and the lectors constituted the lowest orders of the clergy.

The clergy of a city, territory, or diocese was ruled by a bishop[10] who had complete control of church affairs. He decided all legal matters, supervised the finances, arranged for the transfer of the priests to new places, and sanctioned their journeys. Increased worldly goods often caused the bishops to take an active part in politics. They surrounded themselves with a court, a body-guard, and a host of servants. Quite different from the shepherd bishops of earlier periods!

The Council at Nicea in 325 had recognized and sanctioned the office of the Metropolitan. The essential duties of the metropolitan bishop was to sanction or to reject the ordination of bishops in his province and to preside at the provincial synods. The autocratic

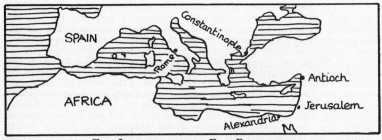

THE LOCATION OF THE FIVE PATRIARCHS

tendencies of the metropolitans became more marked as the Church increased in wealth and in secular power.

But there was still room for additional offices above that of the metropolitan. The Council of Nicea in 325 had designated the bishops of Rome, Alexandria, and Antioch as *superior* metropolitans or patriarchs, although the Roman bishop refused this title. The General Council of Constantinople in 381 designated the bishop of that city a patriarch, and the General Council of Chalcedon in 451 gave the same title to the bishop of Jerusalem. After the middle of the fifth century the Church had four patriarchs, located in Alexandria, Jerusalem, Ephesus, and Constantinople, and one *monarchical* bishop in Rome. How long would these five officials be content to remain on the same level? Would not some of these patriarchs demand first place?

V. The Theory of Papal Power.—The Bishop of Rome and the patriarch of Constantinople became leading rivals for church supremacy. After the Western Empire was destroyed in 476, the

[10] cf. pp. 95-99.

emperor of Constantinople became the sole emperor of the world, and this new dignity naturally added some prestige to the patriarch of that city. But as the ruler of the world the emperor assumed, in imitation of Constantine, the title of Bishop of Bishops. A secular ruler had become the nominal head of the Church. Was there any power in all Christendom that could wrest this title from the emperor and assert the inherent right of the Church to govern her own affairs?

Only the Bishop of Rome dared to come forward with an open challenge, and through the great and long conflict that followed, the Roman bishop laid the basis for the world leadership of the Roman See. Among the causes contributing to make the Bishop of Rome the outstanding leader of the whole Christian Church were :[11]

(1) Rome as the geographical and political center of the world gave the Roman bishop a unique prestige. In the minds of the people Rome was still the capital of the world—yea, even the world's mistress—long after Constantinople had become the seat of the imperial government, and Milan had become the seat of government of Western Europe. There was universal reverence for all things Roman.

(2) Ever since 100 A.D. the congregation in Rome was probably the largest in Christendom. It was wealthy, hospitable to strangers, and generous to the poor.

(3) Successful resistance to Gnosticism and to Montanism gave added strength and prestige to the Roman church.

(4) But the main prop to the prestige of the Roman church was the claim to apostolic tradition and to the *cathedra Petri*.[12] The Apostle Paul had written to this church that her faith was "proclaimed throughout the whole world."[13] He had spent some time in Rome, and had died a martyr's death there. Shortly after 100 A.D. it was generally believed that the Apostle Peter had also lived in Rome and that he had been martyred by Nero in 64. Before 170 the tradition spread that Peter had been the first bishop of Rome. Several prominent Church Fathers, including Cyprian and Irenaeus, had strongly asserted the primacy of the Roman bishop.

(5) Pope Leo the Great (440-461) gave the theory of papal power its final form. This theory rested on three Scripture passages : Matth. 16:18-19; John 21:15-17; and Luke 22:31-32. The Apostle Peter was set forth as the vicar or earthly representative of Jesus Christ. The bishop of Rome was the direct successor of Peter and consequently enjoyed all the privileges of that great apostle. As Peter was thought of as the Supreme Teacher who corrected the other apostles, and from whom the other apostles got their authority, so the Roman bishop claimed a corresponding recognition. The church of Rome had apostolic tradition, a claim which could not be made by the church of Constantinople.

(6) The many missionaries of the Roman church naturally transplanted to the new churches a feeling of affection for, and loyalty to the Mother church.

(7) During the barbarian invasions, when the emperors failed to defend Rome, the popes saved the city through their intercession. Attila (452) and Geisric (455) were both routed by Pope Leo the Great.

[11] cf. pp. 97-98.   [12] cf. page 98.   [13] Rom. 1:8.

(8) When Constantine moved to Constantinople, the Roman bishop became the foremost personage in Rome; and after the Western Empire fell to pieces (476), the Roman popes became the most important persons of Western Europe, gradually taking over the power of the State and establishing a secular as well as a religious supremacy over Europe.

(9) The bishop of Rome remained faithful to the Nicene Creed, and reinstated Athanasius as bishop. Arianism was finally condemned and the Nicene Creed became the creed of the whole Church, a great victory for Rome.

(10) During the Mohammedan conquests (which did not take place until the next period) the cities of Antioch, Jerusalem, and Alexandria fell into the hands of the Moslems, and this again eliminated three possible candidates and cities from the struggle for church supremacy.

At the General Council of Chalcedon in 451 the patriarch of Constantinople had been voted the chief bishop of the entire Church. All protests by the Roman bishop and his delegates proved futile. The two rivals faced each other. The struggle between them was to have profound influence. The basis was laid for the differences that later were to divide the Church into the Roman and the Greek Catholic divisions.

The Christian Church was still an organic *unity* with a world wide horizon. The grain of mustard seed had truly developed into a mighty tree whose branches reached out to all parts of the inhabited world. But a threatening cloud was seen on the horizon, and a streak of lightning was about to split the mighty tree into two halves, Greek and Roman Catholic. Was this merely a result of inordinate ambitions of two bishops? Was it because the civilized world was divided into one Greek and one Latin speaking group, each with its world capital? These causes played a part, no doubt, but the division of the Church came as an *inherent* necessity which made it possible for the Western Church to liberate herself from the stagnating Church of the Orient.

21. REVIEW QUESTIONS

1. Why an ever-widening chasm between the clergy and the laity?
2. Why did the clergy become an economically independent order?
3. How did the right to have episcopal tribunals affect the Church?
4. Why do you think the clergy tried, by external means, to indicate their distinction as a special order?
5. Why the beginning of the codification of church (canon) laws?
6. The three orders of the clergy: bishops, presbyters, and deacons, continued during this era. What changes do you notice in their relative importance? Account for this change.
7. How would you compare the bishops of this era with the shepherd bishops?
8. Why the metropolitans and the patriarchs? How did they try to find a Biblical basis for their claims?
9. Account for the rivalry between the bishop of Rome and the patriarch of Constantinople.

10. Why did it mean so much for the church of Rome to have apostolic tradition?
11. What part did Pope Leo the Great play in the development of the theory of papal power?
12. How was the Church prepared for a division into Greek and Roman Catholic groups? Was this division good or bad for Christianity?

TOPICS FOR SPECIAL STUDY

1. The place of Tradition in Judaism and in Western Catholicism.
2. The rise of the prince bishops.
3. Clergy and Laity at the close of the Ancient Period.
4. The change from official to private penance.
5. The rise of the episcopal tribunals.
6. Leo the Great's theory of papal power.

VI. Worship, Life, Discipline, and Manners.—The general transformation was naturally reflected in the public worship and in the general discipline and manners. Christian worship was left free to develop according to inherent tendencies. But the large number of unconverted, worldly persons who made a profession of Christianity necessarily exercised a most detrimental influence. Many nominal Christians sought compensation for their heathen beliefs and their heathen deities in veneration of angels, martyrs, saints, images, and relics.

Pagan polytheism[14] and the worship of the emperor, naturally led to a worship of angels among nominal Christians. The archangel Michael was particularly popular. Pagan hero worship soon found its counterpart in the worship of Christian martyrs and saints. These had enjoyed a special veneration even before the time of Constantine.[15] The Church developed an elaborate doctrine of the saints as heavenly beings who shared in the omnipotence and omniscience of God. The number of canonized saints increased every year. Every province and every town had its tutelary saint. Altars and churches were erected over their graves, and the practice of praying *for* the saints[16] was now converted into entreaty for their *intercession*.

As martyrs became canonized saints, their relics were conceived as possessing miraculous power. Their application, it was believed, restored the sick, exorcized demons, detected crimes, averted plagues, and even raised the dead. The worship of relics was the counter-part to pagan fetishism. No altar and no church was built that did not possess its own relics. The principal relic was the cross of Christ which *Helena*, Constantine's mother, is said to have discovered in 326. Pious pilgrims were allowed to carry with

---

[14] Polytheism (*polys*: many + *theos*: god).   [16] cf. page 113.
[15] cf. page 113.

them from Jerusalem splinters of the cross into all lands, and soon there were splinters enough for several crosses. A special festival was instituted in honor of the discovery of the cross of Christ. Other relics included bones of the martyrs, their garments, their utensils, and the instruments with which the martyrs had been tortured. Traffic in relics became so wide-spread that Theodosius I in 386 had to prohibit the sale of relics as merchandise. Transfer of the bones of martyrs to new places was commemorated by special festivals.

The adoration of Mary, the mother of the Lord, originated later than the veneration of angels and saints and relics. From the first Mary was regarded as the highest ideal of maidenhood. This veneration grew steadily, and the notion that Mary remained a virgin after the birth of Christ became an article of faith as early as the fourth century. During the great doctrinal controversies[17] the absolute divinity of Christ was strongly emphasized, which belief enhanced respect for Mary to a point beyond the veneration paid to the saints. She was the "mother of God." Augustine did not number her among sinners. Ambrose designated her the second Eve who co-operated with Christ in his atonement. A legend spread that Mary, immediately on her decease, was raised by angels and carried to heaven, where she was elevated as the heavenly queen. As such she became the object, not only of veneration, but also of *invocation*. People looked on her as the real helper in heaven, and they prayed to her for intercession, rather than to God through Jesus Christ. They prayed in Mary's, and not in the Lord's name.

The worship of Mary was the counter-part to the worship of a female divinity, the Great Mother, by all pagans in the lands around the Mediterranean. It was a fatal inheritance. A little later the mother of Mary, Anna, also became the object of special adoration. Several festivals, such as the Feast of the Annunciation, the Feast of Purification, the Feast of the Ascension of Mary, and the Feast of her Birth were instituted in honor of the mother of the Lord.

In view of the religious development, as indicated above, it was only natural that the pagan worship of images should be transformed to Christian image worship. The early Christians had manifested a very strong dislike for images because they were considered prohibited in the first commandment. And adoration of images was strongly opposed by certain Church Fathers as late as the fourth century. But Greek love of art, strengthened by popular

[17] cf. pp. 121-125.

traditions, allowed pictures and images of Christ, Mary, and the saints, not only in the churches and palaces, but in practically every home. These images were thought to possess even more miraculous power than the relics. The common people worshipped, not the divine and abstract representation, but the image itself. The customary forms of worship were the lighting of candles before the images, kissing them reverently, bowing before them, prostration, and the burning of incense.

Pilgrimages to sacred places such as Palestine, Mount Sinai, the tombs of Peter and Paul, became general because of the excessive merit or work-righteousness attached to such acts of devotion. The visit of Constantine's mother, Helena, to Palestine in 326 stirred up much interest for such journeys. Several Church Fathers vainly tried to oppose this sickly zeal for pilgrimages because it endangered genuine religion and morality.

Paganism came to have a most fatal influence upon the development of the doctrine of the seven sacraments. Originally only two sacraments had been recognized, namely, Baptism and the Lord's Supper. By 1215 the number was definitely fixed at seven, namely, Baptism, Confirmation, Lord's Supper, Penance, Extreme Unction, Ordination, and Marriage, but this official decision came as a climax of a long development.

The simple rites of Baptism and the Lord's Supper were greatly elaborated, and new sacraments were added. Confirmation became a sacrament toward the close of the fourth century. The idea of the Christian priesthood as a divine institution led to the establishment of Ordination as a sacrament. Augustine regarded Marriage as a sacrament. The sacrament of Extreme Unction began to be recognized during the pontificate of Innocent I (401-417). But the Catholic sacramental system was not definitely formulated until the Middle Ages.

Many ceremonies were added to the rite of baptism. Exorcism was pronounced for the candidate. Then the officiating priest breathed on him[18] and touched his ears, saying *Ephphata*![19] He then made the sign of the cross on forehead and breast. In some regions salt[20] was given to the candidate. A piece of money was often given as a symbol of the talent of baptismal grace.[21] The new name given in baptism indicated entrance into a new life.

The Lord's Supper came to be regarded, not only as a sacrament (divine assurance to man), but also as a sacrifice (act of worship

---

[18] John 20;22.
[19] Mark 7:34.
[20] Mark 9:50.
[21] Luke 19:12.

toward God), and this led to the Graeco-Roman doctrine of the sacrifice of the mass. The Lord's Supper came finally to be regarded as "an unbloody repetition of the atoning sacrifice of Christ by the priesthood for the salvation of the living and the dead." The consecrated elements of bread and wine were literally changed, it was believed, into the body and blood of Christ, and this body of Christ was literally offered every day and every hour upon the many altars of Christendom. Several altars were erected in the same church at which specially designated priests would say mass, or offer intercessory prayers for the living and for the dead. To order a mass came to be regarded as a meritorious deed. Finally, the idea of the *sacrifice* in the Lord's Supper completely overshadowed that of the *sacrament*.

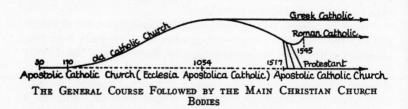

THE GENERAL COURSE FOLLOWED BY THE MAIN CHRISTIAN CHURCH BODIES

Worship developed an extraordinary wealth of forms and an indescribable ceremonial beauty. The whole service centered around the celebration of the Eucharist (Lord's Supper).[22] Church music and congregational singing became more general.[23] Preaching was rather rhetorical and formal. Christmas, Easter, and Pentecost became the principal festivals of the Church, while many lesser festivals were instituted in honor of Mary, angels, martyrs, and saints. The Confessional was gradually recognized as a part of the church system. Many magnificent church buildings were erected, mostly in the style of the basilica.[24]

While church life had many gloomy aspects, brighter sides were not wanting. The Gospel remnants acted as a powerful leaven in the communities and exerted a many-sided influence upon the moral, the social, and the civic relations. Church discipline was naturally much more lax than in previous periods. Excommunica-

[22] cf. page 112.
[23] The singing in the churches was homophonic during the first ten centuries.
[24] In the Orient the arch and cupola roofed churches were about equally popular until the seventh century when the latter became predominant. Pictures decorated Occidental and Oriental churches alike, except in Central Asia where they were prohibited. Greek speaking churches also prohibited the use of sculpture. Representative art found its way to many Christian homes.

tion was only exercised against those guilty of gross sins which had occasioned scandal.

VII. The Monastic Life.—The monastic movement received a new impulse, for various reasons. Many pious Christians looked upon the invading barbarians as a threatening cloud from which they must flee. The adoption of Christianity as a State religion seemed to many to threaten the purity of the Church which caused them to seek seclusion with like-minded men in desert places. Events immediately before and after the fall of the Western Empire in 476 gave many serious-minded men the impression that the world was falling to pieces, morally and politically. To flee from this evil world, they sought retreat in cloisters and monasteries.

Some extreme forms of monasticism developed. The Stylites (Pillar-monks) lived on pillars. Symeon the Stylite (390-460) is said to have lived for thirty years on a pillar sixty feet high. The Bosci (Grazers) withdrew from civilization and lived in uncultivated fields.

Monasticism at first was opposed by educated people. Christianity was intended to develop and to complete the human personality, not to mar and cripple it. Taste for harmony, beauty, art, and science revolted against the self-inflicted tortures, the neglect, and the lack of culture of the adherents of monasticism. But their opposition was more secular than religious. They lacked the clear, evangelical conception and conviction of the un-Christian features of monasticism. Hence they lost ground in this struggle, and monasticism prevailed.

From Egypt the movement spread to Asia Minor, thence to the Western Church where it took on a more practical character. The cloisters and monasteries founded in Italy, Gaul, Britain, Ireland, and Scotland became important centers of learning. The Rule of St. Benedict of Nursia was so successful at the monastery of Monte Cassino (founded in 529) that it became the pattern for practically all the monasteries of the Western Church. In a series of seventy-three rules covering all phases of monastic life, the forty-eight prescribed at least seven hours of daily labor and two hours of reading "for all able to bear the load." Benedictine monks became the most expert farmers and craftsmen of the Middle Ages. The requirement of daily reading formed the beginning of the monastic schools, which preserved learning in the West during the long intellectual night of the medieval period.

VIII. On the Threshold to the Medieval World.—Many deteriorating influences were operating within the Church. The cessation of the persecutions caused a distinct decline in Christian enthusiasm. When Christianity became a mass-movement, many accepted the new faith without any real spiritual change. Riches and prosperity attracted worldly-minded men to church offices, and avarice became one of the besetting sins of the clergy. The many doctrinal disputes estranged certain groups from the Church. The adoption of a double standard of morals, one for the clergy and one for the laity, and extreme asceticism, were signs of a deteriorating spiritual life. The Church and other existing institutions were getting ready for that long and gloomy period, "the Dark Ages." The barbaric invasions and the conquests of the Mohammedans caused the spiritual and intellectual life of Europe to be obscured for several centuries.

22. REVIEW QUESTIONS

1. In what respect did nominal Christians find compensation for their heathen beliefs in Christian worship?
2. Can you see why nominal Christians would feel the need of worshipping angels and saints?
3. Did pagan religions have anything that corresponded to the worship of relics? Explain.
4. How do you account for the worship of the Virgin Mary?
5. Why did early Christians oppose images, and why did image worship become so common?
6. What is meant by pilgrimages? Why did these become so popular?
7. Why did the Catholic Church develop a system of seven sacraments?
8. How did the Lord's Supper come to be connected with the sacrifice of the mass?
9. How would you compare the divine worship of this era with that of the Apostolic Era?
10. Why did monasticism become so popular? Is this movement still with us?

TOPICS FOR SPECIAL STUDY

1. Work-righteousness and its relation to Church life.
2. Pagan parallels to the Catholic worship of the Virgin Mary.
3. The observance of church festivals about 500 A.D.
4. The origin of the Catholic Mass.
5. Pagan parallels to Catholic monasticism.

A SELECTED BIBLIOGRAPHY FOR CHAPTER V

1. Walker: *History of the Christian Church*, Pages 112-194.
2. Rainy: *The Ancient Catholic Church*.
3. James Orr: *Progress of the Dogma*.
4. Workman: *Evolution of the Monastic Ideal*.
5. Warfield: *Augustine and the Pelagian Controversy*.
6. DuBois: *The Ecumenical Councils*.
7. Fisher: *A History of Europe*, Vol. I.
8. Hefele: *A History of the Councils of the Church* (5 vols.).
9. Kruger: *The Papacy: The Idea and Its Exponents*.
10. Leigh-Bonnet: *Handbook of the Early Christian Fathers*.

PART II

THE MEDIEVAL WORLD

From Gregory the Great to the Reformation A.D. (590-1517)

INTRODUCTION

1. **Limits and Epochs of the Medieval Period.**—The Medieval Period is so-called because of its chronological position between ancient and modern times. It forms the transition from Graeco-Roman civilization to the Romano-Germanic civilization destined to control the future of the western world.

Invading Teutonic tribes caused the downfall of the western Roman Empire in 476 A.D.; which event marks the great divide—politically—between the ancient and the medieval periods. But in the history of the Church, the medieval period dates from the accession of Pope Gregory the G. at (A.D. 590) who stood on the confines between the old and the new order of things. He was the last Church Father as well as the first medieval theologian. He was the last Roman bishop and the first medieval pope.

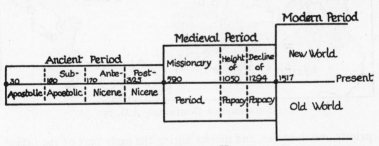

PERIODS IN CHURCH HISTORY

Three stages may be distinguished in the development of the Church during the medieval period: (1) the rise of papacy, from Gregory I to Gregory VII (590-1050); (2) the Era of Absolute Papacy, from Gregory VII to Boniface VIII (1050-1294), (3) the Decline of Papacy and Signs of Reformation, from Boniface VIII to Luther's Theses (1294-1517).

137

2. **General Character of the Medieval Period.**—The theater of medieval Christianity was limited almost entirely to the Occident. World history moved toward the west, to Italy, Spain, Gaul, Great Britain, and Germany, where the Teutonic-Latin peoples developed the western civilization.

Destructive invasions ushered in the medieval period. The two centuries which brought the Teutonic tribes into Europe appeared like the doom of Judgment Day—as a catastrophe to civilized society. Unspeakable disorder and frightful destruction existed everywhere in the western Empire. The Church was the sole surviving force capable of exerting any constructive influence upon the invaders. The importance of the services rendered by bishops,

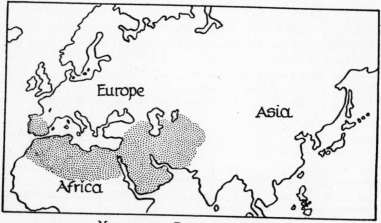

MOHAMMEDAN DOMINIONS, A.D. 750

priests, missionaries, and monks during the early part of the period can hardly be over-estimated.

In the Orient destruction was even more complete, because the power of the Church was broken, and the Cross was supplanted by the Crescent, the standard of Mohammedanism. In the seventh century a great wave of Semitic people, the Mohammedans, starting in Arabia, swept rapidly over Syria, Palestine, Egypt, and Persia (633-651), destroying everything in its wake. Twice the Mohammedans laid siege to Constantinople (669-676 and 717-718), but without success. In 707 they conquered North Africa, and Spain in 711. In the great Battle of Tours in 732 Charles Martell finally defeated the Mohammedans and saved western civilization.

The Mohammedans robbed the Greeks of their marvelous vitality and stifled their genius. Greek culture was suppressed and trampled under foot, while Saracenic[1] civilization was imposed upon the subdued peoples. This new civilization possessed considerable vitality, being remarkable for its development of mathematics, natural science, and philosophy. Saracenic civilization was also a powerful factor in the formation of medieval Scholasticism. But it was, after all, a culture far inferior to the Hellenic, and medieval Europe had to free itself from its grip before it could experience the Renaissance, the Reformation, and the development of the modern mind.

Islam paralyzed and partly annihilated the life of the Church in the Eastern Empire. Mohammedan toleration permitted the patriarchal seats at Alexandria, Antioch, and Jerusalem to remain for some time, but the Church's progress and expansion were completely arrested. The Greek Church became petrified and has remained in cadaveric rigidity to the present day. When shall the Spirit from on high again restore this Church to its former glorious life? Enough vitality remained to enable the Church to give the arriving Slavic tribes the alphabet, the elements of education, and the doctrine of the Church. But the Slavic nations did not in turn have the ability to revive the Greek world. The only event that stirred the eastern Church was the iconoclastic controversy in the eighth and the ninth centuries. After that the life of the Greek Church seemed to stagnate. The candlestick had toppled over.

Europe on the other hand was destined not to have Saracenic, but Teutonic-Latin civilization. For three or four centuries the lamp of learning burned very low, and Europe presented a dreary spectacle of ignorance, lawlessness, and violence. It was an era of transition and reconstruction. The Church transmitted to the Teutonic tribes the inheritance of the Graeco-Roman civilization plus the Christian religion, and these elements, together with the Teutonic life and vigor, their respect for woman, their sense of honor, and their love of liberty became the leading principles of the new Teutonic-Latin civilization.

Slowly this new civilization developed. The Papacy and monasticism were the important stepping stones from the old to the new. The Latin spirit attained its majority during the Renaissance, and the Teutonic spirit emancipated itself during the Reformation.

[1] Saracen: "children of the desert."

CHAPTER VI

The Rise of Papacy

FROM GREGORY I TO GREGORY VII (590-1050)

The discussion of this era will center around the following topics: (1) Missionary endeavors among Celtic, Teutonic, and Slavic peoples; (2) Islam and the Greek Church; (3) the Holy Roman Empire; (4) the growth of Papacy; and (5) Monasticism.

I. Missionary Endeavors among Celtic, Teutonic, and Slavic Peoples.—Before the tribal movements, Europe was chiefly settled by Celtic tribes which had been conquered by the Romans and amalgamated with them. The Celts still held on to the western edge of the European continent, but existed as a distinct race only in Ireland and in Scotland. The Teutonic tribes conquered continental Europe, mingled with the Romans, and set up a number of independent kingdoms.[1] In the rear of the Teutons were the Huns, the Slavs, and the Magyars. The Mongols and the Turks appeared late in the eleventh century mostly as proselytes of Mohammedanism.

How a number of the Germanic tribes came in contact with Christianity has already been told. All save the Franks and Burgundians had accepted Christianity in its Arian form.[2] But the native population of western Europe was orthodox Catholic. Hence for some time there were two rival Christian churches in regions where these tribes ultimately settled. The Catholics were usually in the majority, but the Arians were the rulers, and the religion of the ruler was usually the religion of his tribesmen. In the competition between these two forms of Christianity, orthodox Catholicism won out mainly because the Germanic conquerors were conscious of their cultural inferiority. They greatly reverenced Roman culture and desired to become Romanized. Accepting the orthodox Catholic faith was one step in that direction. The Romanizing process was greatly facilitated by intermarriage with the native stock. However most important was the fact that the Franks, the most

---

[1] Ostrogoth, Visigoth, Vandal, Frankish, Lombard and Burgundian; cf. p. 119.
[2] See page 120. In Burgundy the princes were Arians, but the Roman property owners and the rest of the natives were Catholics or pagans.

influential Germanic tribe, came forward as a Catholic power. Their example was soon followed by the other tribes.

The church organization of the Franks was also copied by other tribes. The king was head of the national church, and all clergy gave oath of allegiance to him. He controlled property, appointed bishops, called national synods, and placed before these synods important matters to be discussed. Bishoprics were subdivided into parochial churches, each under a priest. In consequence papal supremacy was largely suppressed during the early centuries of the Middle Ages.

By the middle of the eighth century, the church had reached a very low ebb. The old civilization had been swept away, and the new had not taken its place. The clergy was intolerant and spent most of its energy in acquisition of riches and secular power. The bishops became great landowners and peers. The Kingdom of the Franks continued to expand territorially, but it failed to carry on a corresponding mission work. With few exceptions, the great missionaries of the early Middle Ages came, not from southern Europe, but from Britain and Ireland.

Between 443 and 485 the Angles, Saxons, and Jutes took possession of Britain, driving the native Christianized Celts into the mountains of Wales and Cornwall. It is not definitely known when these Celts had first accepted Christianity. St. Patrick labored in Ireland from 431 to 461, organizing the Irish Church, but Christians were there before him. The Celtic race accepted Christianity with ardent enthusiasm. A number of famous monasteries were established, and these became the centers of Iro-Celtic Christian life. The Monastery of Armagh in Ireland and the Monastery of Iona on an island southwest of Scotland, were great centers of Christian learning for more than two centuries. The Monastery of Iona has been called "the Nursery of Saints and the Oracle of the West."

Characteristic of the early British Christians was their zeal and success in missionary work. Among the best known early missionaries were St. Patrick (Patricius, 378-460), the "Apostle of Ireland," and Columba (521-597), the "Apostle to Scotland." He organized the Caledonian[3] or Scottish Church. Columbanus (543-615) spent many years as missionary to Burgundy, Switzerland, and Northern Italy. He founded several monastic mission stations of which the Luxovium (Luxeuil) Monastery was the best known. He exerted great influence, not only through teaching and preach-

---

[3] Scotland was at that time called Caledonia and was inhabited by Picts.

ing, but especially through the use of the private confessional for lay people as well as for monks. Columbanus was likely among the first to prepare handbooks for use in the private confessional. Through his influence, Celtic Christianity spread rapidly south and east; and it appeared that Armagh and Iona—not Rome—were to become the great spiritual centers of the new Europe.[4]

But Gregory the Great soon turned the tide in favor of Rome. He selected Benedictine monks to start well organized and successful missionary propaganda. The Benedictines were well equipped for this task. Their military and monarchical organization appealed to the Teutonic warriors, giving them ready access to the royal courts. The sending of Augustine and forty other Benedictine monks in 596 to the court of King Ethelbert of Kent in Britain was an event of world historic significance.

Augustine baptized King Ethelbert of Kent in 597 and this virtually meant the winning of all his people. Augustine was consecrated "Archbishop of the English people" that same year. He started to build the Canterbury Cathedral which, after thirteen centuries, still remains the Mother Church of England.

The Catholic mission made great progress in England during the next forty years. King Oswy, in 655, introduced Iro-Celtic Christianity into all parts of England, save Kent and surrounding territory. The cause of the Roman Church seemed hopelessly lost until Wilfrid, a British Benedictine monk, finally succeeded in turning the interest of Oswy in favor of Rome. At the Synod of Whitby in 664, the differences were settled in favor of Roman practice. The necessary adjustments were quickly made, and Roman practice rapidly replaced the Iro-Celtic even in Ireland. The Abbot of Armagh placed his famous monastery under *unitas catholica*. Iona was the only remaining center of Iro-Celtic Christianity, and this monastery received its death knell at the beginning of the ninth century.

Theodorus, a Greek monk from Tarsus, became the new Archbishop of Canterbury. His Greek training and culture and his 22 years as Archbishop of England was to have a permanent influence on English church life. At the Synod of Hertford, 672-73, the basic plans were adopted for organized church life in England, including

[4] Iro-Celtic Christianity differed from that of the Roman Church of the time of Gregory the Great in certain respects: (a) Iro-Celtic Christians did not recognize the authority of the Bishop of Rome; (b) they recognized the supreme authority of the Scriptures and did much to promote Bibl⸱ study; (c) they had no Mariolotry and saint worship; (d) they had a different form of tonsure, cutting the hair on the forehead and temples to form a crescent, while the Romans cut a circle on top of the head; (e) they celebrated Easter according to the Eastern method, keeping it on the Sunday following the full moon in March.

the primacy of the Archbishop of Canterbury, 16 bishoprics, cathedral chapters, synods, Benedictine monasteries, and the beginning of organized parishes. Theodorus made the private confessional apply, not only to the monks, but to lay people as well. He promoted institutions of learning where three cultural streams, the Graeco-Roman, the Celtic, and the Anglo-Saxon, mingled, and produced a remarkable and for its time unsurpassed culture which culminated in the Renaissance.[5]

To these victories the Roman Catholic form soon added another one. Anglo-Saxon missionaries planted the Church of Rome in the heathen parts of Germany and Scandinavia. The churches in Europe were henceforth to be in loyal submission to the pope of Rome, a significant factor in the rise of the papacy.

Wilfrid left England because of opposition to Theodorus. On his way to Rome he made a forced landing in 678 on the coast of Friesland where he started mission work. Willibrord (657-739) "Apostle to the Frisians" and first missionary to Denmark, continued the work of Wilfrid. In 690 he worked in the region at the mouth of the Rhine. Supported by the pope and the Frankish Kingdom, he established the Archbishopric of Utrecht with Willibrord as its occupant.

Winfrid (672?-755), better known as Boniface, "Apostle to the Germans," continued the work of Willibrord in Friesland, but the principal scenes of his activity were East Franconia, Bavaria, Thuringia and Hesse. He was imbued with a tremendous conviction that a central authority was essential to the best interests of the Church, and that this authority must be the pope at Rome. He really conquered northwestern Europe and *laid the foundation for medieval papacy.* He Christianized Central Germany, Hesse and Thuringia during the decade 722-32 and as a reward he was consecrated Archbishop of Mainz in 732. In the following decade he organized churches, schools and monasteries in Central Germany and Bavaria according to Roman pattern, always tying these institutions to the Church of Rome.

Pope Gregory III now asked him to subjugate all erroneous forms of Christianity in the Frankish Kingdom and to unify and organize the Frankish Church in absolute obedience to the pope. Boniface succeeded in having a synod assembled in 742, and this synod recognized the Archbishop of Mainz as the Primate of Austria. The synod also sanctioned the Benedictine order and con-

---

[5] Mention may be made of men like Caedmon (c. 670), Bede Venerabilis (673-735), Aldhelm (640?-709), Alcuin (735-804), Cuthbert (d. 687) the ascetic, and the many prominent missionaries to the Continent.

demned the Iro-Celtic form of Christianity. A later synod, held in 747, recognized papal supremacy over the Frankish Church. But synodical decisions were not legally valid unless they were sanctioned by the king, and Pepin the Little, who that year became sole king, refused such sanction. The king continued the reformatory work of Boniface, as evidenced by the reform synods of 755-57, but Boniface himself was shoved aside. He had, however, by this time already instilled permanent obedience to the pope in the hearts of the majority of bishops and clergy.

Ansgar (801-65), a French Benedictine monk, became the "Apostle to the North." He preached the Gospel in Denmark and Sweden, later continuing to superintend missionary work as Archbishop of Bremen. Christianity gained final victory in Denmark during the reign of Canute the Great (1014-25). Norway was Christianized from England through the efforts of two Norwegian kings, Olaf Tryggvason (995-1000) and Olaf Haraldson "the Saint" (1015-30). In Sweden the first Christian king, Olaf Lapking, was baptized in 1007. From the Scandinavian countries Christianity spread to Iceland, Finland, and Greenland.

The Slavic peoples were Christianized mostly by Greek missionaries. Two brothers, Cyrillus and Methodius, preached the Gospel in Moravia about 860. A Christian princess brought Christianity to Bohemia, and from there it spread to Poland and Hungary. But all these countries, save Bulgaria, turned from the Greek to the Roman Catholic Church, and acknowledged the pope of Rome as the supreme head of their churches. Russia was Christianized during the reign of Vladimir the Great (d. 1015) "the Clovis of Russia." He received Christian baptism and compelled his subjects to do the same. Russia became a loyal subject of the Greek Catholic Church.

23. REVIEW QUESTIONS

1. Why is medieval church history mostly concerned with the Occident?
2. Do you think Rome would have been better able to withstand the barbarian invasions if Christianity had not arisen?
3. How did Saracenic civilization influence the Greek Catholic Church?
4. Why was the victory of Tours in 732 so important for Europe?
5. Mention the main elements in the Teutonic-Latin civilization. When did this civilization attain its majority?
6. Why did orthodox Catholicism conquer the Arians?
7. Why did the Roman Catholic form of Christianity prevail over the Iro-Celtic?
8. How did St. Boniface help to lay the foundation for medieval papacy?
9. What can you say about the Apostle to the Frisians? the Apostle to the Germans? the Apostle to the North? the "Clovis of Russia"?
10. How was Christianity brought to the Slavic nations?

TOPICS FOR SPECIAL STUDY

1. Saracenic Civilization.
2. Early Celtic Centers of Christian Learning.
3. Use of the Private Confessional in the Early Middle Ages.
4. English Culture at the Time of Theodorus.
5. Early German Bishoprics.

II. Islam and the Greek Church.—While Christianity was gaining mastery over the barbarian tribes of western Europe, a new Theocracy[6] arising in Arabia expanded to tremendous proportions. It was modeled on that of Moses. Mohammed (570-632) was its founder, its prophet, and its military leader. Sprung from the distinguished tribe of the Koreish, the custodians of the sacred shrine of the Kaaba (cube), he was born in the holy city of Mecca. Within this temple was preserved the sacred black stone which the Mohammedans say was originally white as milk, but turned black because of the sin of man. Mohammed, epileptic in childhood, was brought up by his relatives without any education. First a shepherd, he later became a merchant and a camel driver. The religion of his people was heathenism, but Mohammed and his tribe came in frequent contact with Judaism and degenerate forms of Christianity (Ebionism, Arianism, and Sabellianism). A commercial journey through Syria with an uncle brought Christianity and Judaism to his special attention.

In 610, at the age of forty, Mohammed appeared as a prophet, proclaiming a new religion sometimes called *Islam*, meaning "submission to Allah," sometimes Mohammedanism after its founder. The religious system of Islam may be summed up as follows: God, or Allah, is one. He is omnipotent and omniscient. Submission to Him is the central principle in the system. Hence the name Islam. All events are foreordained, and men must submit to this unchangeable order of things without a murmur. There are two classes of angels: good and bad. Allah has given His revelation in the Scriptures, that is, in the *Quran* and in the *Sunna*, a great body of traditions of Mohammed's sayings. God has sent prophets such as Adam, Abraham, Moses, and Jesus. But the greatest of them all is Mohammed, the Paraclete[7] promised by Jesus. The soul is immortal. In the final judgment God will reward the faithful and punish the unbelievers. No atonement is necessary. Man can gain Paradise by his own good deeds. Paradise is a place of the richest sensuous

---

[6] Theocracy. (*Theos*: God + *krateo*: rule).
[7] Paraclete or Comforter, John 14:16.

pleasures. The good works consist of prayers, fastings, the giving of alms, and at least one pilgrimage to Mecca. But the best of all is war—even to death—against the unbelievers. A drop of blood shed in sacred war is of more avail than two months of fasting and prayer. Polygamy and concubinage are encouraged because they were practiced by Mohammed himself. Islam is a strange admixture of heathenism, Juadism, and Ebionite Christianity.

His teachings arousing the hatred of some of his kinsmen, Mohammed fled with difficulty to Medina. This flight or "Hegira," July 15, 622, is adopted by Mohammedans as the beginning of a new era. At Medina he organized a remarkable theocracy in which he was the prophet, lawgiver, judge, and king. The inhabitants of Medina received his system with great enthusiasm, and from that moment began the "holy war" of the spread of Islam.[8]

Although the original Mohammedans were not well educated, they possessed great absorptive power for learning. In their conquests they came in contact with survivals of Greek civilization and with Christian learning. They came in contact with educated people in Babylonia, Assyria, and Egypt. Damascus, the Mohammedan capital, became renowned for its learning. When Bagdad superseded Damascus as the capital in 760, the Mohammedans absorbed much of Hindu mathematical knowledge. Bagdad became an intellectual center of first importance. Eastern Mohammedan learning was gradually carried to Spain by traveling scholars. Around 1050 Mohammedan reactionaries succeeded in driving the Hellenic Mohammedans out of Bagdad, and they fled to Africa and to Spain. In Spain they developed a skillful agriculture. They cultured the silk worm, and manufactured silk and cotton garments. They also manufactured paper from cotton, and prepared morocco leather. Moslem learning in Spain assisted in the intellectual awakening of Europe.

III. The Holy Roman Empire.—For centuries, the Roman Empire in the West was the great political ideal of the conquering Teutons. During the "Dark Ages" this ideal appeared like a brilliant sun, seeming to cast a magic spell, not only upon great leaders, but also upon the masses of the peoples. Amidst the chaos of civil wars, lawlessness, and violence the people longed for concentration of all secular power in one head. They longed for a strong, protective arm. These longings resulted in the establishment of the Frankish, and somewhat later, of the German Empire.

---

[8] The rapid spread of Islam marked the beginning of a new era, the middle ages, for the Orient.

The Ancient World bequeathed to posterity not only the idea of a world monarchy but also the idea of a world religion. The Roman Empire had developed a co-ordinate religious organization in the Roman Church,[9] and this religious counterpart, continuing after the secular empire crumbled, became a most important factor in the formation of the new Teutonic-Latin civilization. The Roman pope, the chief representative of the old imperial power in Italy, played a prominent role in the public affairs of western Europe.

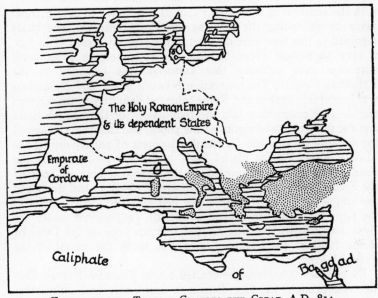

EUROPE IN THE TIME OF CHARLES THE GREAT, A.D. 814.
(The dotted region indicates the Roman Empire in the East)

It was only natural that as a new western Empire arose on a Teutonic-Latin foundation it should seek a firm alliance with the pope of Rome. The Church was a divine institution, but it was also believed that the Empire was eternal and that it would exist, by divine decree, until the end of time. The empire and papacy were regarded as the two arms of God in governing the world. God had set the emperor over the temporal affairs of the world and the pope over its spiritual interests. A harmonious co-operation of the two great world-rulers was necessary so that each in his own sphere could promote the kingdom of God on earth.

[9] See pages 99 and 116-20.

When the kingdom of the Ostrogoths (493-554) fell, the Emperor of the East became the ruler of Italy and the *ex officio* Lord Protector of the Church. But he was too weak to defend the western Church against her enemies, while he often meddled unduly with her internal affairs. Hence the popes of Rome began to look toward the Franks for better defense and for greater liberty. When Charles Martell (714-741), savior of Christian civilization of western Europe died, his son, Pepin II "the Short" (741-768), set aside the Merovingian dynasty and assumed the name of king with the *sanction* of the pope. Pepin II was quick to return papal favor by defending the pope against the Lombards. The lands regained in this war were donated to the pope by Pepin II in 756 a very significant event because the pope became a temporal sovereign over territory that formerly had belonged to the Byzantian Empire. The connection between Rome and Byzantium was henceforth broken and Rome belonged definitely to the western world. This endowment laid the foundation for the Church State and the temporal sovereignty of the popes, and this in turn formed the *material* background for the development of papacy during the Middle Ages. Papacy placed itself under the protection of the Frankish State and acknowledged the Frankish king as head of the Frankish Church. After Charlemagne (768-814) had destroyed the kingdom of the Lombards and had enlarged Pepin's gifts to the pope to include the entire Exarchate (a province under the Byzantian Empire), it was decided that the pope as the Duke of Rome (and of the Church State) was to be the vassal of the Frankish king.

By conquest Charlemagne created a new Frankish-Roman Empire and brought his vast domain in uniformity and articulation with the Roman Church. Few rulers have done more than he for the diffusion of Christian learning.

Desiring officially to sever papacy from the Eastern Empire and to secure a legal basis for his own power in Italy and western Christendom he made plans for his papal coronation, and on Christmas day in the year 800 Pope Leo III placed a crown of gold upon his head and proclaimed him Emperor and Augustus.[10] This was the official beginning of the Roman Empire of the Middle Ages. Henceforth Teutonic-Latin civilizations recognized two divine and co-ordinated institutions, the Holy Roman Empire and the Holy Roman Church, each supreme within its own sphere. The

[10] Hampe and other historians think that the coronation came as a distinct surprise to Charlemagne; that he did not intend to receive the royal crown from the pope as this might indicate papal supremacy; but that he finally yielded for political reasons.

history of these two powers, their struggle with each other for supremacy, and their relations to the rulers and the people of Europe, make up a large part of medieval history.

Charlemagne assumed active leadership in Christian mission work, ecclesiastical legislation, church government, election of bishops, establishment of schools and monasteries, and the formulation of educational standards. His best known missionaries were *Arno*, Bishop of Salzburg, and *Willehad*, Bishop of Bremen. *Alcuin* and *Paul Warnefrid* were his constant advisers in matters of education and monastic life.

In his famous *Libri Carolini*[11] he boldly opposed the Eastern Church and the pope in the question of image worship. He held the Germanic view that images are useful for ornamentation of the churches and for the perpetuation of holy deeds; yet they are by no means necessary, and they must not be worshiped. In consequence, image worship was not practiced in churches north of the Alps until the beginning of the eleventh century. Libri Carolini also introduced the *filioque*[12] into the Frankish Church, and it was officially sanctioned by the Synod of Aix-la-Chapelle (Aachen) in 809, in opposition to the pope.

The ancient metropolitan church organization[13] was adopted by Charlemagne with the modification that the metropolitan was called archbishop. He divided his empire into twenty-one archbishoprics and increased the number of bishoprics. The regular diocesan bishops were assisted by so-called chorbishops who had no diocese. The large country dioceses were divided into parishes headed by parish priests. Several parishes were supervised by a dean who served as a mediary between the parish priest and the bishop. Each parish was granted landed property to support the parish clergy. Monasteries also received large land grants, and many monasteries and princes had their private churches. Church property was tax exempt and legal church matters were settled in ecclesiastical and not in secular courts. Chapters[14] were organized at all cathedrals.

[11] Charlemagne dictated the main contents of the Caroline Books, but they were formally prepared by his theologians.

[12] In the original Athanasian Creed the Holy Ghost is said to proceed "from the Father." Influenced by Augustinean theology the Synod of Toledo of 589 added "filioque" (i.e. "and the Son"). The pope protested, not for dogmatic reasons, but because he considered it technically incorrect to add this word to an official document of an ecumenical council. Leo III, the contemporary of Charlemagne, also opposed the filioque. By the middle of the eleventh century the Roman Church included the filioque in the symbol or creed.

[13] See pages 99 and 127-28.

[14] A chapter is an ecclesiastical corporation consisting of the clergy of a cathedral. Its principal function is to provide for public worship in the cathedral to which it is attached.

Provisions were made for regular visits by the bishop to his parishes. On such occasions all people of the parish were called together and the bishop would catechise, hear confessions of sin, and exercise church discipline. By decree of 802, all laymen were to learn thoroughly the Creed and the Lord's Prayer. The first medieval catechism dates from Charlemagne's reign.

Divine services were planned so as to make the greatest and most favorable appeal to the public mind. The sermon was the central and the Roman mass the subordinate part of the service. Two volumes of carefully collected and edited sermons "suitable for the whole year and for each separate festival, and free from error" were sent to the churches for use at their services.[15] Much attention was given to the esthetic side of the worship, including architecture, sacred ornamentation, music, and liturgy. Church bells became quite common, and the first church organ was sent for to Byzantium.

Charlemagne manifested great interest in public education and in Christian literature. With the help of Alcuin he reorganized the palace school so effectively that it became a forerunner for the modern university. He had no interest in asceticism, but tolerated monasteries because of the monastic schools. In 801 he made the Benedictine order and the canon collection of Dionysius the Little authoritative standards within their respective spheres. He organized and improved monastic and cathedral schools. Foundation for the modern library was laid by the collecting and copying of manuscripts in the monasteries. The learned literary works of Alcuin and Paul Warnefrid made medieval literature a world literature and learning became international. Charlemagne's enthusiasm for schools went so far that he directed that "every one should send his son to school to study letters, and that the child should remain at school with all diligence until he should become well instructed in learning." In saying this, however, he addressed the freemen of the court and the official classes. Hence it may be doubted that he thought of compulsory education for children of the laboring classes.

The actual results of Charlemagne's work were rather meager. He was a man far ahead of his time. General ignorance and superstition prevailed. Traffic in relics increased. Angelology, demonology, white and black magic flourished among the newly Christianized people. Teutonic *wanderlust* gave impetus to pilgrimages,

---

[15] This pericope system, adopted by the Roman Church, was perpetuated also by some of the Protestant churches.

and the Teutonic ideal of womanhood found a reasonable expression in Mariolotry.

The empire of Charlemagne was divided between three grandsons. One was given the part east of the Rhine; another the part west of the Rhone and the Meuse; the third was given the narrow, central strip between these along with the *imperial title*. The rich lands of the lower Rhine, the valley of the Rhone, and Italy belonged to the emperor. For a century and a half this

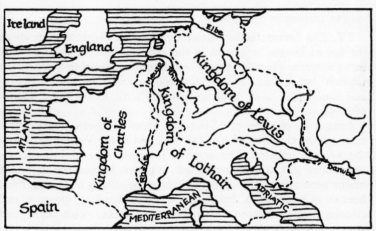

THE WESTERN EMPIRE AS DIVIDED AT VERDUN, A.D. 843

imperial title was the emptiest of honors. In 962, Otto the Great revived it as he was crowned Emperor of the Romans. Henceforth the prince whom the German Electors chose as their king also had a right to the crown of Italy and to the imperial title. After this the Empire was known as "the Holy Roman Empire of the German Nation."

24. REVIEW QUESTIONS

1. What can you say about the life of Mohammed?
2. Discuss the main characteristics of his religious system.
3. What part did Mohammedan religion and civilization play in the life of the early Middle Ages?
4. Why did the idea of a world monarchy make such strong appeal to the invading Teutonic tribes?
5. Why did the empire and papacy come to be regarded as the two arms of God in governing the world?
6. What part did these two institutions play in the history of the medieval period?

7. Discuss the rise of the Holy Roman Empire.
8. Why was the donation of Pepin II to the pope in 756 so significant for the future of Europe? Was this donation good or bad for the Church?
9. Why did Charlemagne receive papal coronation?
10. Why the Caroline Books?
11. How did Charlemagne organize the Frankish Church?

TOPICS FOR SPECIAL STUDY

1. The Significance of Charles the Great.
2. Libri Carolini as a Settlement with the Orient.
3. Origin and Development of the Chapter.
4. Why Charlemagne's Empire Collapsed.
5. The Carolingian Renaissance.

IV. The Iconoclastic[16] Controversy.—A violent dispute about the use of images broke out in the eighth cenutry and lasted well into the ninth. The controversy was largely confined to the Eastern Church but it had far reaching consequences for the Western, and contributed more than any single factor to the great schism of 1054.

Images or pictures of Christ, the apostles, saints, and martyrs crowded the churches both in the East and in the West long before the seventh century. The original intention was to instruct the uneducated in Christian truth, but they soon became the object of undue veneration. Bowing down before the images or kissing them became quite common. Images were asked to act as sponsors, and coloring-matter scraped from them was mixed with bread and wine in the sacrament. Often images were actually worshiped.

Jews and Mohammedans criticized the Christians severely for their worship of images. Several bishops declared themselves against the practice, and a number of Christians in the Moslem world believed God had given the Church into the hands of infidels because the Christians had departed from the true worship and had fallen into idolatry. They also felt that image worship was a chief obstacle to the conversion of the Jews and the Mohammedans to Christianity.

In 723 the Caliph Jezid commanded the removal of all pictures from Christian churches within his realm. In 730 Emperor Leo the Isaurian[17] issued a similar edict, which gave rise to a bitter controversy. Germanus, Patriarch of Constantinople, immediately opposed the imperial edict, and he was promptly deposed by the emperor. John of Damascus was the next great champion of image worship and he was enthusiastically supported by the monks. He

---

[16] Iconoclasts (*eikon*: image + *klao*: break).
[17] His defense of Constantinople, 717-18, against the Mohammedans was practically as important for Europe as the victory of Charles Martell at the Battle of Tours in 732.

lived within Mohammedan territory and was therefore beyond the jurisdiction of the emperor. God, he declared, is present in the image as He is in the Lord's Supper. The image as a symbol is the actual representation of things invisible. Christ is not a real Christ unless He is pictured or portrayed.

The emperor, however, soon cleared the churches of the East of images, and he issued a decree that the same should be done in the churches in the West. Pope Gregory II sent him a denunciatory letter, and in 731 Pope Gregory III not only excommunicated the emperor, but all iconoclasts in Eastern and Western churches.[18] The emperor retaliated by annexing the churches of Illyria to the patriarchate of Constantinpole.

Constantine VI became emperor at the age of nine, but his mother, Irene, put herself in possession of the throne, and through her influence a Council of Nicea in 787 declared image worship to be in accordance with apostolic tradition. But a wave of reaction soon swept over the Church, and Emperor Leo the Armenian issued a new edict in 814 against image worship. Images—paintings and mosaics only—were finally restored permanently to the Eastern Church by the "Resident Synod" of Constantinpole in 843, during the regency of Theodora; and the *Feast of Orthodoxy* was established in commemoration of the triumph of image worship.[19]

V. The Growth of Papacy.[20]—Papal dominion over Europe was advanced during this era, 590-1050, by prominent popes, by missionary endeavor, by the iconoclastic controversy, by the donations to papacy by Pepin II and Charlemagne, by the *Donations of Constantine* and the *Pseudo-Isidorian Decretals*, and by the decline of imperial power. After the division of the Frankish Empire, papacy remained for a century and a half the only real international power in Europe, until the coronation of Otto the Great in 962.

Gregory the Great (590-604) was Rome's greatest pope. Coming from a wealthy patrician family, he was eminently gifted as an administrator, as a skillful diplomat, and as a practical man of affairs. He served as imperial prefect of Rome, and as ambassador to the imperial court at Constantinople, and as an abbot of a cloister he had founded before he was chosen pope. His pontificate

[18] This decision was made at the synod called by Gregory III and attended by ninety-three bishops.
[19] This feast practically marked the close of the development of the Greek orthodox dogma. The celebrated victory indicated (a) Greek monasteries as the bearers of Byzantian cultural and religious life and doctrine, (b) termination of the monastic struggle for complete independence of the Church, and a consistent submission to Byzantian Caesar-papism, (c) a compromise with the iconoclasts: sculpture was prohibited, and all images and mosaics had to conform rigorously to traditional and conventional models.
[20] Review pp. 95-99 on the historic episcopate, and pp. 128-30 on the theory of papal power.

was full of trouble. Famine and epidemics devastated Rome. The Lombards and the Eastern Romans threatened from without. The Franks had established a national Church which, at the best, recognized the pope merely as a moral authority. The Christianized Visigoths in Spain took a similar attitude. The prestige of the Bishop of Rome had almost reached a vanishing point in Italy itself. The Church was torn by internal dissensions, while a deepseated moral corruption prevailed. As a pope Gregory distinguished himself in a number of ways. He, and not the military officers, raised an army, paid the expenses of war, and made peace with the Lombard king. He re-established church discipline, organized church finances, and improved the ritual of the services and the church music. He won his conflict with the patriarch at Constantinople who had assumed the tittle of "universal bishop." Gregory caused this title to be revoked, and adopted for himself the title of "servant of servants of God." He was untiring in sending out missionaries. The Archbishopric of Canterbury was established during his pontificate. He extended the influence of the Roman See to France, England, Spain, and Africa. He was a strong supporter of monastic orders and showed special favors to the Benedictines. He was the founder of the theology of the Middle Ages and produced a large number of writings. Special mention may be made of his doctrine of Purgatory, good works, and the mass and the eucharist. In his successful efforts to extend papal authority be built on the foundation laid by Pope Leo the Great.[21] It was Gregory the Great who laid the foundation for the military power of the popes by maintaining an army.

Mention has been made in previous sections of missionary endeavor, the material donations of Pepin II and of Charlemagne, and the iconoclastic controversy as contributing factors in the rise of papacy. As the Church became more involved in secular affairs there was a strongly felt need for adequate documentary support of the claims of papacy. Such support was found in a spurious document called the *Donations of Constantine*, appearing some time between 751 and 774. This document claimed that the Emperor Constantine the Great had received absolution from Pope Sylvester, and that the emperor in turn had given to the pope absolute supremacy over all the churches in Christendom, a great deal of worldly goods, and secular supremacy over Rome, all of Italy and western Europe. These claims were not at first taken

[21] See p. 129.

very seriously by anyone except by the popes themselves. The idea of *papal world supremacy* appears in this document.

Three ecclesiastical tendencies struggled for supremacy in western Europe from the time of the reign of Lewis the Pious (814-40) and onwards, namely (1) adherence to Charlemagne's policy of imperial supremacy over the Church, (2) development of a Frankish national Church to be independent of State control, (3) papal supremacy. The first of these lost prestige during the fierce contention among Lewis' sons and the division of the Frankish Empire in 843. The second was for some time successfully promoted by the archbishops (metropolitans) who desired to be independent of secular princes and the pope alike. The secular princes retaliated by cultivating friendship with the bishops, and these in turn would rather have supervision by a distantly residing pope than by a nearby resident archbishop. Hence increased episcopal prestige meant increased power for papacy.

In the early part of the ninth century three successively published collections of spurious and genuine canons and decretals appeared.[22] By 850 they were gathered into one collection known as the *Pseudo-Isidorian Decretals*.[23] This document, which has been characterized as "the boldest and most magnificent forgeries of history," had a threefold purpose: (1) to emphasize papal[24] supremacy, (2) to suppress the power of archbishops and to add prestige to bishops and the lower clergy as an aid to greater papal power,[25] and (3) to improve the moral and spiritual life of the Church.

Contemporary archbishops opposed the Pseudo-Isidorian Decretals. Archbishop Hinkmar rejected them as spurious and called them "a mouse-trap for metropolitans." But Pope Nicholas I made official use of them as early as 864, and toward the end of the century nobody questioned their genuineness. Hints at forgery were made by Cardinal Nicholas of Cusa in the 15th century, and in the 17th century the Reformed theologian Blondel proved them to be spurious. But by this time they had rendered their service to the Roman Church. In a time of felt need, they had lent the author-

[22] They were most likely prepared by clerics from the Archbishopric of Reims, where the dominant Archbishop Ebo and his more powerful successor, Hinkmar, threatened the liberty of the lower clergy.
[23] The name is from the supposed author who designated himself as Isidor Mercator.
[24] The spiritual power as exercised by the pope is infinitely superior, it is claimed, to the secular power of emperor and princes.
[25] The Pseudo-Isidorian Decretals maintained (a) that bishops stand in the same relation to the pope as the other apostles stood in relation to Peter, (b) that provincial synods cannot be held without being summoned by the pope, and that their decrees are only valid after they have been sanctioned by the pope, (c) that the clergy constitutes the "divine family" while the lay people constitute the "carnales," and (d) that none of the clergy may be summoned before a secular court. A layman may not even accuse a priest, and it requires at least seventy-two trustworthy witnesses to substantiate a charge against a bishop.

ity of apostolic and early Catholic antiquity to certain doctrines and practices until these had become too firmly imbedded in Catholicism to be shaken or destroyed.

Pope Nicholas I (858-67) was one of the strongest representatives and promoters of medieval papacy. He fully appropriated the teachings and implications of the Pseudo-Isidorian Decretals and pushed the claims of his office in every direction. He definitely formulated the medieval idea of papacy and carried out in part the papal claim to world supremacy. He deposed and excommunicated Photius, Patriarch of Constantinople. He humbled Archbishop John of Ravenna to complete submission to papacy. He won a similar victory over Archbishop Hinkmar of Reims who had to reinstate a deposed bishop by order of the pope. He also ordered King Lothair II to take back his divorced queen, Teutberga. As a missionary organizer he compared favorably with Gregory the Great. He established the Hamburg-Bremen Archbishopric and gained dominance over the Moravian Church through the support of Cyrillus and Methodius. He appreciated the influence of literature and contemplated the establishment of clerical censorship of books. His contemporaries hailed him as a "second Elijah," and his death was generally mourned. Nicholas I was the last great link in the development of papacy from Gregory I (the Great) to Gregory VII.

The popes made little use of their temporal power during the tenth[26] and the first half of the eleventh centuries because papacy had sunk to a low level of moral degradation. Rival feudal factions in Rome for some time set up and pulled down popes at will, frequently elevating unworthy men to the papal chair. The intervention of the imperial power finally rescued papacy from this unfortunate situation.

VI. Monasticism.[27]—About 600, Christian Europe had reached a very low intellectual and spiritual level. During the seventh and eighth centuries conditions grew worse. Inter-communication largely ceased and trade and commerce died out. The spirit of Christian Europe of this period is characteristically reflected in monasticism with its ascetic, external, legalistic view of religion, its stress on obedience and authority, and its love for seclusion, order, system, and regularity.

The most influential monastic order was the Order of St. Benedict of Nursia. Pope Gregory the Great had been a Benedictine abbot before he occupied the papal chair. He did much to promote this order throughout Italy, Spain, France, Germany, and England.

---

[26] The tenth century was the *saeculum obscrum* for Rome, the *"dark century"* for Italy.
[27] See pages 113 and 135-36.

Each Benedictine monastery was a self-supporting community. To the traditional duties of meditation and prayer, Benedict added manual labor such as agriculture, gardening, and manual training, and two hours every day for reading and study. The daily work was so planned that all the monks of a monastery should cooperate to the largest possible extent. The monks became permanent inmates of the monastery in which they took their vows. The Rule of Benedict of Nursia was revised and adopted for conditions of western Europe by Benedict of Aiane (750-821) and by Berno in Burgundy (927) and finally by Odo of Cluny (942), culminating in the ascendancy of the famous monastery of Cluny in Burgundy.

Monasteries established on the pagan frontier or in heathen territory became centers of missionary activities. The Church owed her signal victory over the barbarians mainly to the zeal and devotion of the monks. Many of the monasteries remained as farming, charitable, and ascetic institutions and became the centers of agricultural development, of works in arts and crafts, and of Christian hospitality. A small number of monasteries gradually accumulated libraries and became celebrated for their literary and intellectual activities. These monasteries have been called "the publishing houses of the Middle Ages" because the monks copied and transmitted manuscripts and preserved books. Some of the monasteries became centers of learning, and the monastic schools became teaching institutions of first importance. The monks became the chroniclers of the events of their own times, and posterity is indebted to them for a great part of its knowledge of the early medieval centuries. The development of the convents for women was another achievement of monasticism. The monasteries helped to establish Latin—the medium of expression of Graeco-Roman civilization—as the language of the Church. Unity of language made for greater unity in culture and religion.

VII. Religious Art and Worship.—At the beginning of the medieval era the majority of churches in Latin Christendom were built in basilica[28] style. From the 5th to the 12th centuries this basic type of architecture was developed into the so-called *Romanesque basilica* which was characterized by the round arch, general massiveness, and grouping of the interior and the exterior so as to produce the effect of rhythm rather than uniformity. Religious art was given the freest scope. Sculpture was encouraged as well as painting, and each artist was allowed to depict Christ and the saints according to his own ideals.

The Renunciation, the Apostles' Creed, and the Lord's Prayer

[28] See pp. 112-13 and 134.

were definite parts of the public worship. Public singing in the church service was restricted to the choir of priests, the congregation joining in the responses only. Ambrosian music was supplanted by the Gregorian. The Roman mass[29] gradually replaced the sermon as the main part of the service. A comparatively rich Greek and Latin hymnology grew up, echoing the monastic life in subdued tones of contemplation and devotion. Among the Latin hymnists of this period may be mentioned Gregory the Great, Venantius Fortunatus (d. 609), the Venerable Bede (d. 735), Notker of St. Gall (d. 912), and Peter Damian (d. 1072).

25. REVIEW QUESTIONS

1. Name the reasons for the steadily growing power of the popes of Rome.
2. What is meant by the Iconoclastic Controversy and how did this feud affect the Roman Catholic Church?
3. When and how was the temporal power of the popes founded? What is meant by the Church State?
4. How do you account for the appearance of the Donations of Constantine?
5. What claims did the Pseudo-Isidorian Decretals set forth?
6. How did these counterfeit documents affect the papacy?
7. What was the condition of the papacy during the tenth and the first half of the eleventh centuries?
8. How do you account for the four stages in the development of monasticism?
9. Discuss the prominent characteristics of the Benedictines.
10. Enumerate the achievements of medieval monasticism.

TOPICS FOR SPECIAL STUDY

1. Gregory the Great and his influence on the Church.
2. The establishment of the Archbishopric at Canterbury.
3. The basis for the temporal sovereignty of the popes.
4. The Order of St. Benedict of Nursia, and its difference from Eastern monasticism.
5. Influence of invading Northmen.

A SELECTED BIBLIOGRAPHY FOR CHAPTER VI

1. *Cambridge Medieval History*, Vols. I-II.
2. Adams: *European Civilization During the Middle Ages.*
3. Robinson: *Conversion of Europe.*
4. Dudden: *Gregory the Great.*
5. Bury: *Life of St. Patrick.*
6. Howorth: *St. Augustine of Canterbury.*
7. Kurth: *St. Boniface.*
8. Bryce: *The Holy Roman Empire.*
9. Krüger: *The Papacy: the Idea and Its Exponents.*

---

[29] At the beginning of the Middle Ages, Milan and vicinity and the Ambrosian liturgy; the Franks used several variants of a Gallic mass; Spain had its own mass, and so did the Celts in Ireland and Britain. All were written in Latin; only the Slavs used the mass in the vernacular. As papacy increased in power, the Roman mass gradually replaced all other forms for mass in Latin-Teutonic Christendom.

CHAPTER VII

The Era of Absolute Papacy

FROM GREGORY VII TO BONIFACE VIII (1050-1294)

I. The Three Theories Concerning the Relations of Pope and Emperor.—The most interesting and instructive chapters of the history of the Middle Ages concern the development and the mutual relations of the Holy Roman Empire and the Holy Roman Church. From the middle of the eleventh to the middle of the fifteenth centuries the empire and papacy, each theoretically the counterpart of the other, were for the most part in mortal combat.

Three general theories were gradually developed regarding the relations of pope and emperor. (1) Pope and emperor were each independently commissioned by God to rule supreme, each within his own world-wide dominion. These two dominions, the Holy Roman Church and the Holy Roman Empire, were co-ordinate, divine institutions. Neither was set above the other. Both were to co-operate in mutual advancement of each other's interest. Church and State constituted a double sovereignty emblemized in the dual nature of Christ. (2) The emperor was superior to the pope in secular affairs. Appeals were made both to Scripture and to history in support of this theory. Jesus Christ had paid tribute money, and he had also said: "Render unto Caesar the things that are Caesar's." Advocates of this theory also claimed that the gifts of Pepin II and Charlemagne to the Church had made the popes vassals to the emperors. (3) The temporal power was subordinate to the spiritual even in secular affairs. The soul rules over the body and the sun is superior to the moon; hence the spiritual must be over the temporal power. Appeals were also made to such Scripture passages as First Corinthians 2:15 and Jeremiah 1:10.

Their relative strength was further tested during the great struggle which ended in a permanent division between the Eastern and the Western Church.

II. The Schism Between East and West in 1054.—As the center of gravity of the new European civilization moved towards the west, certain differences between Oriental and Occidental

Christianity became increasingly apparent. These differences were due partly to various inherent characteristics and partly to different environment.

The Second Trullian Synod, held in 692, laid the first tangible foundation for the division of East and West. The 102 canons[1] issued excited the antagonism of the Western Church which was greatly intensified during the iconoclastic controversy.

Political and religious alienations were caused by the rise of the Frankish empire and the promotion of papal supremacy. Constantinople looked upon the connection with papacy and empire as a manifestation of revolt, while Rome on the other hand pressed her claim to papal world supremacy. Undue emphasis on minor variations in worship and practice tended to widen the breach between the two branches of the Church, and final separation seemed imminent during the controversy of Photius and Pope Nicholas I, but two additional centuries passed by before the schism was permanently affected.

Photius, twice patriarch of Constantinople, 858 (857?)-867, and 878 (877?)-886, has been called "the Luther of the Greek World" because he, more than any other, helped the Greek Church to understand and appreciate her distinction from the Latin. Using the strength the Eastern Church had gained after the iconoclastic controversy, he pressed his propaganda against the Western Church in two ways, (1) by Greek missionary expansion among the Slavs towards the north and the west, and (2) by bold and powerful attacks on the pope's claim to primacy.

Photius tried to win these Slavs for the Greek Church, but he met with powerful rivalry from Frankish and papal missions. When the line of demarcation was finally drawn, Byzantian Christendom retained permanently the countries of Montenegro, Serbia, Bulgaria, and Russia.

In the struggle, Photius and Pope Nicholas I excommunicated each other. Photius accompanied his excommunication by an encyclical which is rightly called the *magna charta* of Byzantine Christianity. Photius changed the differences in worship and practice between the Eastern and the Western Church into a difference between *orthodox* and *heretical* Christianity. To minor differences in observance of fasts, celibacy, anointing with oil, and the like,

---

[1] Canon 13 sanctioned marriage of the lower clergy; canon 36 made the patriarch of Constantinople equal in rank with the pope in power and privileges; canon 55 repeated the Oriental prohibition of fasting on Saturdays during Lent; canon 67 prohibited the eating of blood and suffocated animals; and canon 82 forbade the pictorial representation of Christ as the Lamb of God. These and other canons practically ignored Western synods and papal decrees.

Photius added the doctrinal difference implied in the *filioque*. The Nicene Creed stated that the Holy Ghost "proceedeth from the Father," while the Latin Church, without sanction of an ecumenical council and without consultation with the Greek Church added *filioque* ("and the Son"). Photius made filioque and papacy the great wall of division between the Greek and the Latin Church.

The breach was healed temporarily by the Synod of Constantinople of 869, and for the next hundred years the Byzantine empire enjoyed a remarkable renaissance while western Europe suffered a distinct decline, except in England. During this Byzantine renaissance the Eastern Church took on her final characteristics. A collection of church laws, the *Nomocanon* completed in 883, has since the Synod of Constantinople in 920 been declared binding for the entire Greek Orthodox Church. In the *West* the main task of the bishops was to promote good church government, while theological learning was left largely to monks and the lower clergy. In the *East* the church leaders were primarily concerned with the promotion of the cult, that is, the adherence to prescribed religious observances. Theology was promoted by the prelates, although monks also made some contributions. Four episcopal orders were recognized, namely the patriarch, the metropolitan, the archbishop, and the bishop. Influenced by Oriental mysticism, the Greek Church came to differ considerably from the Latin in the conception of the Sacraments by aiming at a physical-mystical union with the Deity. The ritual, especially the Greek mass, was considerably enriched. Sermons preached in the language of the people were still common, and the congregation took part in the singing during worship. Much attention was given to the mystic side of religion.

During the political decline, 1025-81, Emperor Constantine IX Monomachus needed Rome's help to defend his possessions in Italy against the Normans. In return he prepared to recognize Pope Leo IX's claim to primacy. But Michael Cerularius, Patriarch of Constantinople, 1043-58, had other plans. He wanted to make himself pope of the Eastern Church and to make the Church independent of the State. In order to realize these ideals, he planned a definite break or schism between the East and the West. When Pope Leo IX had been defeated by the Normans in Italy in 1053, Cerularius began his schismatic work. The Latin churches and monasteries in Constantinople were closed. He also influenced the Bulgarian patriarch, Leo of Achrida, to write a circular letter to the bishops of Southern Italy in which he recited all the alleged errors of the

Latin Church. The letter had the *intended* effect of stirring up
Pope Leo IX to anger, and to a bitter controversy between Rome
and Constantinople. The emperor, *Constantine Monomachus,* in an
effort to restore peace, induced the Roman pope to send Cardinal
Humbert and two other legates to Constantinople in order to settle
the controversy.

At first the delegates discussed certain differences of ritual
between the Greeks and the Romans, including such items as the

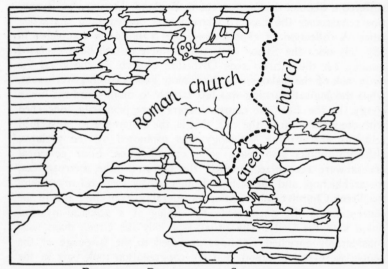

PERMANENT RESULT OF THE SCHISM OF 1054

Roman use of unleavened bread in the Lord's Supper, omitting
the "Hallelujah" from the liturgy during Lent, confessing that
the Holy Ghost "proceeded from the Father and the Son" while
the Greeks said "from the Father," and the Roman injunction of
clerical celibacy and the permission of the Greek clergy to marry.
Other differences arose concerning the Roman's refusal to acknowledge the validity of the chrisma if administered by presbyters, their use of milk, butter, and cheese during the week of
Quadragesima, and their introduction of the expression "filioque"
which implied the existence of two supreme principles. Of these
differences the one most offensive to the Greek Catholics was the
use of unleavened bread in the Lord's Supper.

Cerularius irritated the hot-tempered Cardinal Humbert, who

had prepared a written dialogue between a representative of Constantinople and a representative of Rome. This controversial tractate was burned in the presence of the Roman legates. Finally, on July 16, 1054, the Roman legates, on behalf of the Roman pope, placed on the high altar of the Church of Sophia a decree of excommunication. As the legates left the church they shook the dust off their feet against it. Michael Cerularius and the other eastern patriarchs replied by excommunicating Rome. The schism between East and West was complete, and has remained so to the present day.

III. The Holy Roman Empire and Papacy.—The empire of Charlemagne soon disintegrated. After the death of his son, Lewis the Pious (814-840), the empire was divided. One part formed the nucleus of modern Germany, another part formed the nucleus of modern France, while the third part constituted a narrow, central zone which became a mingling place and a battle ground for the two races. A genuine central government could not be maintained. The three kingdoms broke up into a number of little states, largely independent of one another. This situation gave rise to the *feudal system.*

Feudalism became the characteristic institution of the eleventh, twelfth, and thirteenth centuries. In this system all political and military power was connected with the holding of land. Any man was the independent sovereign of as much territory as he could hold or obtain. Attention is called to the following features of feudalism: (1) the holding of land from a lord or landowner; (2) the existence of a close personal bond between the grantor of an estate and the receiver of it, whereby the landlord was bound to give protection, and the tenant had to take an oath of "homage" or personal allegiance; (3) the full or partial rights of sovereignty which the landlord had over those living upon his estate. The estate, which might be large or small, was called a feud, whence the term *feudalism.* Theoretically all the kings on earth were considered the vassals or tenants of the emperor, and he in turn was God's vassal. According to some the pope, not the emperor, was God's vassal on earth. The kings might in turn parcel out their domains to subordinate vassals who had the titles of count, duke, marquis, and so on. The feudal system, it will be seen, greatly promoted the growth of the medieval papacy.

While France, Burgundy, and Italy were still broken up into many feudal states, a new empire was being formed in Germany. Henry the Fowler was elected king of the Germans in 919, which marks the beginning of modern Germany. He consolidated the German duchies and principalities into some semblance of unity and order. His son, Otto the Great (936-973), restored the Holy Roman Empire. Otto the Great sought to counteract the disintegrating tendencies of feudalism by trying to bring the German duchies and principalities under the control of members of his own family, and by establishing the new Holy Roman Empire upon *the power of the Church.*

His efforts to secure unity were only partially successful because the emperor's brother, the Duke of Bavaria, and the emperor's son, the Duke of Swabia, proved to be stubborn and self-willed rulers. The second method involved a dubious element. Otto tried to counteract the influence of the German feudal lords by donating large estates to the Church and by elevating certain bishops to feudal lordship. He felt that he could rely more upon princely bishops than upon the secular German princes. Furthermore, the secular duchies and principalities were *hereditary*, while those of the church were not. The bishops were not married, and when they died, the emperor had the privilege of appointing their successors. Even the church estates belonged, in a certain sense, to the Empire, and taxes were paid to the emperor in the form of "gifts." Thus the emperor raised the Church to secular power. But what would happen when the Church through the Pope felt strong enough to assert her independence, or when the third theory of papal power should be put into practice? For the time being the empire found a material foundation in the power and favor of the Church, and the Church was in turn attached to the emperor through imperial *investiture*.

The term "investiture" designated the ceremony of inducting an abbot or bishop into office. From the time Otto the Great the ceremony usually consisted of giving the new bishop or abbot his predecessor's pastoral staff and the delivery of the episcopal ring. These tokens conveyed not only spiritual but temporal jurisdiction. The investiture was granted by the emperor, who claimed to be God's supreme representative on earth.

While the Carolingian Empire disintegrated papacy also suffered a distinct decline. The national churches of France, England, and Germany largely governed themselves, and the time seemed at hand when the Roman Catholic Church should be broken up into distinct national churches tolerating little or no interference from the pope. But the newly created German Empire saved the Church from such disintegration, for the emperor was generally considered the nominal head of all Christendom. This again involved the following relations and obligations: (1) the imperial synods of the tenth and eleventh centuries represented the entire Church of the West, regardless of nationalities; (2) the emperor was obliged to promote the interests of papacy.

It was the imperial power that raised papacy from the low moral degradation which had been caused by rival feudal factions in Rome. In 1046 Henry III deposed the three rival popes and promoted the election of a German bishop as pope. The German emperor appointed not only Pope Clement II, but the three succeeding popes. The Empire had reached its zenith. The German Church was the obedient servant of the imperial power, and the entire Church acknowledged the emperor as the supreme head. For the time being the Church needed the help of the imperial power, but the inherent tendencies of papacy would naturally demand that the Church be *independent* of the Empire, yes, even superior to it in both spiritual and secular affairs. The Empire had raised the Church materially from her decadence. A great reform movement was soon to raise her spiritually. Papacy was on its way to absolute supremacy.

IV. Reform Movements Within the Church.—Culture of the tenth and eleventh centuries was largely a result of the Carolingian Renaissance and the Carolingian revival of Latin culture. The cultural trend was indicated by the predominant use of the Romanesque architecture, characterized by the rounded arch and dome. Virgil (70-19 B.C.) was the most celebrated author. Latin was used, not only as the language of the Church, but also as the language of polite intercourse. The chief representatives of this Virgilian culture were found at the royal courts and in the monasteries, especially in the monastery of St. Gall. The monastic professors were interested not merely in religion, but also in art and science, and in the national and political life. They did not believe in self-abnegation or destruction of human individuality but in its harmonious development. The world was to be subdued, not to be shunned. The good things in life were to be enjoyed, and an active part should be taken in the social and national life.

These ideas and practices were diametrically opposite to the original ideals of monasticism.[2] The severe ascetic practices gradually ceased. The strict monastic discipline was not enforced. A life

[2] See page 109.

of leisure and luxury prevailed in most of the European monasteries. The monastic salt had lost its savor, and as such it was ready to be thrown out and trodden under foot of men.[3]

Meanwhile an important movement for reform was started by *Odo*, the abbot of the monastery of Cluny. His reform program consisted of (1) the absolute liberation of the Church from secular control both with reference to the church estates and the appointment of candidates for church offices, (2) the abolition of "Simony"[4] or the custom of paying large sums of money for the appointment to office, (3) the abolition of clerical marriages, and (4) the elevation of papacy as the real governing power of the Church. From this it will be seen that the Cluniac Reformation aimed at nothing less than a reformation of the entire Church on the basis of Canon Law. And here the Donations of Constantine and the Pseudo-Isidorian Decretals served their purpose.

The Cluniac Reformation, spreading to the entire Western Church, gained an unusual popularity with the common people because of the strict asceticism and the acts of charity of the Cluniac monks. The order was well organized with a common constitution for all the monasteries concerned and a general "archabbot," the abbot of Cluny. The German emperor did much to promote this reform movement in his empire. The reformers soon asserted their influence in politics by prohibiting Hugo Capet and his Synod of Rheims in 991 from separating the French Church from Rome. They also tried to abolish war, but when this was impossible they proposed in 990 the "Truce of God" which commanded all men to cease from warfare from Thursday evening to Monday morning. This proposal was formulated into an edict by the Council of Clermont in 1095.

In Rome the Cluniac Reform found the least favor. But Emperor Henry III forced the reform upon the Roman Church when he deposed the three rival popes and appointed Clement II to the chair of St. Peter in 1046. Two years later the following pope, Benedict XI, was deposed, and Henry III placed Leo IX (1049-1054), one of the most prominent Cluniac Reformers, in the papal chair. Pope Leo IX selected Hildebrand, the later Pope Gregory VII, as a cardinal, and Humbert as his diplomatic representative. And now a thorough and speedy reform of papacy was effected in harmony with the Pseudo-Isidorian Decretals.[5]

[3] Matth. 5:13.
[4] Acts 8:9-24.
[5] See p. 155.

26. REVIEW QUESTIONS

1. Why is Photius called "the Luther of the Greek World"?
2. In what ways did the Byzantine renaissance influence Eastern church life?
3. Why the schism between East and West in 1054? How do you think this division affected Christianity?
4. Who were the principal characters involved in this final schism? Did their individualities influence the proceedings?
5. What do you think of the listed differences between the two divisions? Did these differences justify the schism?
6. Why did the empire of Charlemagne disintegrate so rapidly?
7. What happened to papacy during the collapse of the Empire?
8. Discuss the feudal system. How did this system affect papacy? Why?
9. How did Otto the Great counteract the distintegrating influences of feudalism?
10. In what ways did the German Empire strengthen papacy?
11. What was the general condition of the European monasteries before the Cluniac Reform?
12. Discuss the program of Odo of Cluny. Why was this reform program so influential?

TOPICS FOR SPECIAL STUDY

1. The Byzantine Renaissance.
2. Greek, Frakish, and papal missions among the Slavs.
3. Essential differences between Greek and Latin church life.
4. Feudalism and its influence on the Church of the Middle Ages.
5. The influence of the Carolingian Renaissance on the monastic life.
6. Odo of Cluny.

V. The Age of Gregory VII.*—Pope Gregory VII (1073-1085), better known by his earlier name of Hildebrand, is the most noteworthy character after Charlemagne that the Middle Ages produced. In 1049 Pope Leo IX brought him from the monastery of Cluny to Rome where he was made a cardinal. From 1049 to 1073 he was the maker and the adviser of popes, and from 1073 to 1085 he himself held the papal chair.

As adviser he labored diligently with his colleague from Cluny, Pope Leo IX, to reform papacy according to the ideals of the Pseudo-Isidorian Decretals and the spirit of the Cluniac reform. They made special efforts to suppress simony and to enforce the celibacy of the clergy. The Cardinal College, which had consisted of the presbyters and the deacons of the papal churches in Rome together with the seven bishops who lived closest to Rome, was now expanded to an international institution with representatives from the various countries. This new institution, created by a decree of

---

* Use the name "Hildebrand" before his election as pope, and "Gregory VII" as pope only.

the Lateran Synod of 1059, became most important for extending and maintaining papal world supremacy.

In 1056, Cardinal Humbert published his great book against simony. It is significant that Humbert expanded simony to include the Investiture. He opposed secular interference in appointments to church offices, even when money was not paid. The imperial practice of appointing German bishops was stamped as a gross sin. The common people should be stirred up against the princes so that they could be deposed if the practice could not otherwise be stopped.

Pope Nicholas II (1058-1061) and Hildebrand put Humbert's program into effect. The Lateran Synod of 1059 decreed that the pope should be elected by the Cardinal College. Nicholas II appointed papal legates to the various countries. These legates soon became important assets of the international Roman Church. Hildebrand formed an alliance with the Normans of southern Italy. This gave papacy the backing of a strong army; from it originated the Norman Conquest of England in 1066; from it the spirit of medieval chivalry and the crusades originated. Hildebrand also gave valuable aid to the revolutionary activities of the papal party (designated *Pataria*) in northern Italy.

When Nicholas II died in 1061, the Empire tried to appoint a pope antagonistic to the policies of Hildebrand. But he induced the College of Cardinals to appoint a candidate in sympathy with his program. In Germany the feudal lords took advantage of the minority of the Emperor, Henry IV, to oppose the government and its candidate. Hildebrand's candidate, Pope Alexander II (1061-1073) was elected, and through him papacy became the great central power in world affairs.

Alexander II and his adviser, Hildebrand, formed a firm alliance with the king of France as the most effective means of subduing the troublesome feudal lords. In Spain the papal legates allied the church with Rome. In England, William the Conqueror claimed the throne on the advice of Hildebrand, and William brought the schismatic church of England back to Roman control. The archbishop Adalbert of Hamburg-Bremen was deposed in 1066 because he tried to establish an independent Nordic Patriarchy. The next step was to bring the German Church under complete papal control, which led to the Investiture Controversy.

Gregory VII, who had been the moving spirit in the development of papacy for more than twenty years, was elected pope in 1073. His conception of the papal office may be stated in his own words: "The Roman Church was founded by God alone; the Roman pope alone can with right be called universal; he alone may use the imperial insignia; his feet only shall be kissed by all princes; he may depose the emperors; he himself may be judged by no one; the Roman Church has never erred, nor will it err in all eternity." He believed that all the Christian states should form a world empire with the pope at its head as God's representative on earth. He made the claim to absolute world supremacy the central idea in papacy.

The newly elected pope strengthened his position with the reform party by causing the Lateran Synod of 1074 to decree that celibacy of all the clergy should be strictly enforced. This decree, which was not enforced during his lifetime, eliminated the hereditary principle in the holding of church offices, and strengthened the authority of the pope over the clergy.

Through the Lateran Synod of 1075 Gregory VII issued a decree forbidding any of the clergy to receive a bishopric or abbey or church from the hands of a secular prince or lord, even from the king or emperor. Gregory VII insisted that henceforth investiture should be received from the pope as God's supreme representative in the world, and this claim involved a complete revolution within the medieval legal and political world.

The "Investiture Controversy" was first waged between Henry IV and Gregory VII. Henry IV hastily declared Pope Gregory VII deposed. The pope answered by excommunicating the emperor in 1076; then he started to Germany for the purpose of bringing the German Church under complete papal control. At Canossa he was met by the emperor who came to have the sentence of excommunication removed. The pope refused to admit the emperor to his presence, and for three successive days Henry IV stood in penitent garb in the courtyard of the castle, waiting for permission to kneel at the feet of the pope and receive forgiveness. On the fourth day he was admitted, and the sentence of excommunication was removed.

Henry IV avenged his humiliation by reducing Rome almost to ruins, driving Gregory VII into exile where he died in 1085. But the investiture controversy was not settled before 1122 when it ended as a drawn battle. In the Concordate of Worms pope and emperor agreed (1) that all elections of bishops and abbots should be conducted according to the laws of the Church, but under imperial supervision; (2) that the right of spiritual investiture by ring and staff belonged to the pope, and (3) that the emperor should exercise the right of investiture by the touch of a scepter as an emblem of secular rights and authority.

Gregory VII's idea of the pope's spiritual and temporal world supremacy had not been realized. It was well for Europe that the two opposing parties were so evenly balanced. A victory for the empire would have secularized the Church, and a victory for the pope would so far have rendered every throne in Europe insecure.

VI. The Crusades, 1096-1270.—Historically, a crusade[6] designates (1) one of the warlike expeditions undertaken 1096-1270 by Christians of western Europe to reclaim the Holy Land, particu-

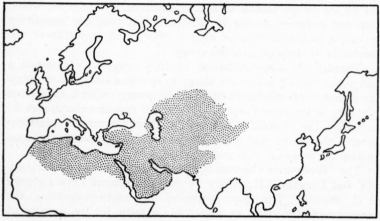

EUROPE AND THE ORIENT ON THE EVE OF THE CRUSADES, A.D. 1098
(The dotted regions indicate Mohammedan territory)

larly the Holy Sepulchre, from the infidel Turks; (2) a vigorous concerted movement of the Church against heathens or heretics.

Pilgrimages to the Holy Land had been made since the fourth century. Christians longed to see the land where Jesus Christ had lived, died, and risen from the grave. Such pilgrimages soon acquired a peculiar meaning as meritorious works. Pilgrims were treated considerately even after the Mohammedan Arabs took possession of Palestine in the seventh century, but the Seljuk Turks who captured the Holy Land in 1073 were of a different stamp and greatly increased the hardships of the Christian pilgrims. Appeals were made to Gregory VII who in turn planned a war for the double purpose of driving the Turks out of Palestine and of re-

---

[6] The name *crusade* is from the word *crux* = cross. A red cross sewed on the outer garments was the insignia of a crusader.

uniting the Greek Church with the Latin; but the Investiture Controversy prevented him from carrying out his plan.

Alexius I, Byzantine emperor, made an urgent appeal to western Christendom for help against the Turks. Pope Urban II received his ambassadors and in a stirring address of Nov. 26, 1095, at the Council of Clermont in France, the pope made a strong and successful appeal to the lords, knights, and foot soldiers of western Europe to cease their private warfare and to turn their strength of arms against the Turks and rescue the Holy Land. The crusade was to take the place of penance for sin, and the pope accorded many other privileges to those who went, and those who died on the journey, and those who died in battle against the infidels.[7]

Deus lo vult or "God wills it" was the enthusiastic answer of the multitude, and this enthusiasm soon spread to all of France and to England. One great central ideal had suddenly seized the imagination of the people of western Europe. They felt united in one great common purpose which seemed to lift the individual above the generally prevailing misery and hopelessness of the impoverished classes. Insolvent debtors were promised liberation from their obligations. European prisons were emptied of all who cared to join the crusade. Many nobles, filled with a desire for adventure and inspired by the *viking instinct* and the example of Norman knights who about 1090 had rescued Sicily, Sardinia, and Corsica from the grasp of Mohammedanism, enlisted in the crusade. Bishops and priests, inspired by the *monastic ideal* of sacrifice, addressed the multitudes in the fields and in the squares, urging them to enlist. The joining of a crusade came to be looked upon by many as the surest way to acquire merit and to atone for the most grievous sins.[8]

The first crusade set out in 1096. A second started in 1144, and a third in 1187. These were the great crusades, though six others were undertaken during the thirteenth century, including a children's crusade which started in 1212. A Latin Kingdom of Jerusalem was established in 1099 and lasted until 1187, and co-extensive with it was a Latin patriarchate. The history of this kingdom and of each crusade need not be traced here. The important matter

[7] Pope Urban II said in part: "Strong in our trust in the divine mercy, and by virtue of the authority of Sts. Peter and Paul, of whose fullness we are the depository, we hereby grant full remission of any canonical penalties whatever to all the faithful of Christ who from motives of devotion alone and not for the procurement of honor or gain shall have gone forth to the aid of God's church at Jerusalem. But whosoever shall have died there in true repentance shall undoubtedly have the remission (indulgentiam) of sins and the fruit of eternal reward."

[8] The almost universal expectation among Christians that the year 1000 would bring the end of the age had stimulated, not only a yearning for the heavenly Jerusalem, but also a general desire to see the earthly capital.

for the present purpose is to estimate the consequences of the crusade movement.

(1) The old isolation was broken and intercommunication and some common ideas and feelings were promoted. Christendom became a great international community with a common ideal and a common fight against the infidel Turks.

(2) The fall of Constantinople was postponed for more than three centuries, giving the young Christian civilization of central, Europe time to consolidate its strength against the returning tide of Mohammedanism.

(3) Feudal artistocracy was undermined and the growth of monarchy was promoted because the estates of French and English nobles who did not return and who had no heirs, were given to the crown. German knights and nobles refused as a class to participate in the crusades. Hence they were not killed off or improverished, but continued to rule in feudal fashion. This is one reason why nationalism developed so much slower in Germany than in England and in France.

(4) Revival of trade, commerce, manufacturing, and industry promoted the rise of cities and the evolution of a new class of merchants, bankers, and craftsmen.

(5) The stimulated intellectual life in Europe found expression in the organization of universities for study, in more extensive travel, in geographical exploration, and in the production of literature.

(6) The pope became the supreme ruler of Western Europe. He was the head of armed Christendom, and the princes became accustomed to follow his leadership and to obey his orders. Financial contributions to the crusades became the basis for a regular tax which, after the Lateran Council of 1215, was claimed by the pope.

(7) The crusades promoted a spirit of religious intolerance and paved the way for the Inquisition. Popes proclaimed crusades, not only against Mohammedans, but also against heretics within the Roman fold.

(8) Campaigning for the crusades stimulated a spirit of devotion and a fervent, imaginative popular preaching which later found expression in the mendicant monks.

(9) The crusades stimulated interest in relics and sacred places. When Palestine again was lost to Christendom, the people concerned developed sacred places and relics of their own. Influenced, possibly, by the Mohammedan worship known as *tasbih*, the use of the Rosary became more general during the thirteenth century.

(10) The crusades influenced the system of absolution. Immunity from the penalties of transgression was originally granted only to those who personally participated in a crusade. Celestine III (1191-98) granted at least a partial absolution to those who contributed money towards a crusade, and Innocent III (1198-1216) granted complete absolution to those who sent a substitute to the field.

(11) Certain moral features of the crusades were discouraging. Many crusaders came from prisons and from morally corrupt homes. They preferred the less restrained life of a crusade to a more strict disciplinary life at home.

(12) The stimulation of a new intellectual life in Europe, the growth of freedom of thought, commercial and manufacturing enterprises, strong national governments, and increasing suspicion as to the motives of the Church in promoting wars against the Mohammedans, tended to weaken and undermine papal absolutism. The crusades were therefore neither an unmixed evil nor a pure benefit to the Church and to the world.

27. REVIEW QUESTIONS

1. What influence did Hildebrand exert upon the Church and the world before he became pope?
2. How was the Cardinal College modified?
3. What significance did Humbert's book against "simony" have?
4. How was the papacy strengthened during the pontificate of Nicholas II?
5. Why was Alexander II elected pope, and not his rival German candidate?
6. Discuss the world policies of Alexander II.
7. What convictions did Gregory VII have as to the dignity of papal office?
8. How did he try to realize his great ideals? Did he succeed?
9. What is meant by the investiture controversy?
10. Why the crusades? How did these strengthen papacy?

TOPICS FOR SPECIAL STUDY

1. The Age of Pope Gregory VII.
2. The Cardinal College as an International Institution.
3. Papacy and the Norman Conquest of England in 1066.
4. The rise of nationalism and its influence on papacy.
5. Conversion of the Normans to the Catholic faith.
6. The crusades as an outward manifestation of the great change in thinking and ideals in western Europe.

VII. The Monastic Orders.—*Asceticism* was the highest ideal of medieval piety. To renounce the world and all its pleasures, to retire into monasteries in a sincere search after holiness was praised as the highest form of earthly existence. The monk was considered the Christian ideal in the medieval world. Hence monasticism reached its highest stage during this era and earned, more than ever before or since, the title of "Knighthood of Asceticism."

From the eleventh to the thirteenth centuries a large number of monastic orders were founded. The monastery of Cluny, which dominated the Western world for nearly two centuries, furnished a pattern for these orders, especially in placing themselves directly under the protection of the pope, free from all outside interference from secular nobles or local bishops. Hence the popes formed the closest alliance with the monastic orders and promoted their interests. The monks became the loyal standing army of papacy.

The popes granted the following privileges to the favored monastic orders: (1) exemption from the payment of tithes; (2) exemption from the jurisdiction of papal legates; (3) exemption from excommunication by any one lower than the pope; (4) exemption from the interdict over the regions where they were situated; (5) permission to the abbots to wear the episcopal ring and gloves; and (6) freedom from obligation to attend councils if not summoned by the pope.

Among new orders, the most important was the Cistercian which dominated the Western world during the twelfth century. The order took its name from the monastery of Citeaux (Cistercium), founded in 1098 by Robert of Molesme. In 1113 Bernard of Clairvaux, one of the most imposing men of the Middle Ages, joined the order and made it famous. The Cistercians placed themselves under episcopal control and became a part of the regular church machinery; each monastery governed its own affairs through its own local abbot, and these abbots came together once a year for general conferences. The order insisted on a very severe asceticism, simplicity in divine worship, mystic piety, and a marked worship of the Virgin Mary, to whom all their monasteries were dedicated. They built their monasteries in remote and uncultivated districts and used much of their time to cultivate fields, gardens, and orchards. Inmates were divided into monks and lay-brothers, the latter doing most of the manual labor while the former devoted themselves to more strictly spiritual tasks.

Attempts were also made to give monastic regulations to the parish clergy. Each cathedral and each prominent church needed the services of several priests. Why should not these live under a common rule of discipline? The rule most commonly used was "The Rule of St. Augustine," and those who adopted it were called Augustinian Canons. These had a community of goods; they ate together and slept in one dormitory; and they wore a common

dress. Thus the regulations ordinarily applied to the monks were
expanded to the priests. Finally a regular order for such clergy
was founded in 1119 at Premontre. This order was named the
Premonstrants.

The most peculiar outcome of the monastic movement was perhaps the combination of the ascetic ideal with that of chivalry in
the formation of the Knightly or Military Orders. These orders
originated in Palestine. The Hospitalers or the Order of the
Knights of St. John took its name from a building in Jerusalem
which was dedicated to John the Baptist. The original purpose
was to take care of the sick and destitute pilgrims and to defend
them against the infidels.

The Knights Templars (1119) organized for the purpose of
protecting the pilgrims along the dangerous road from the sea-

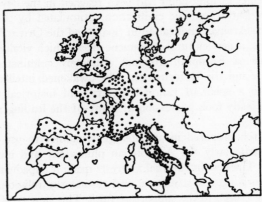

EUROPEAN MONASTERIES ABOUT 1300 A.D.

coast up to Jerusalem. These military orders became very influential in Europe. They devoted their energies to the promotion
of social welfare, and in the twelfth century the Knights Templars
exerted a strong control over the world's money exchange. The
order of German or Teutonic Knights (1190) was made up almost
exclusively of German elements.

Monastic orders multiplied so rapidly that the pope through the
Fourth Lateran Council, 1215, prohibited additional orders. A little
later the pope felt obliged, however, to make an exception in the
case of the Mendicant Orders: the Dominicans and the Franciscans. The leading characteristics of these orders were: (1) They
gave all their goods to the poor and preached the Gospel, with

special emphasis on repentance and love; (2) they traveled from place to place and lived from alms; (3) they placed themselves directly under the authority of the pope; (4) they interested themselves in art, science, and learning in general and soon occupied the foremost places in the schools and universities; (5) they restored preaching to the divine worship of the medieval period, and through their preaching they exerted an influence over the people partly paralleled by that of the modern press; (6) their interests were identical with those of papacy; and these orders became the pope's best agencies for the suppression of heresies. As teachers, preachers, confessors, and administrators of charities, the Mendicants exerted a tremendous influence upon the life of western Europe.

VIII. Scholasticism and the Rise of Universities.—About 1100 a distinct turning-point had been reached in the development of the new Latin-Teutonic civilization. Stimulated by the contact with Graeco-Arabian civilization in Spain and the Orient,[9] through the crusades, a new cultural movement arose which vitally affected every phase of European life and ultimately culminated in the Renaissance and the Reformation. The awakened intellectual life gave rise to a spirit of rational inquiry and historical curiosity which manifestly took possession of many of the leading minds of Europe.

The Church prepared in an intelligent manner to use the new learning, particularly the Aristotelian philosophy and method, in her service. The new intellectual interests made it expedient for the Church to organize, systematize, and restate the religious beliefs and to bring *reason* to the support of *faith*. This new type of intellectual activity gave rise to the great era of scholasticism, which reached its height during the latter part of the twelfth and in the thirteenth century. Scholasticism, which literally means the method of thinking worked out by the teachers in the cathedral schools, did not produce new doctrines but rather concerned itself with the *systematization* and *organization* of the faith and doctrine of the Church. When this work was done, scholasticism declined rapidly, and the spirit which gave rise to its labors was inherited by the new universities.

Most of the great Schoolmen were Mendicant monks, that is,

[9] These stimuli came through three principal sources, (a) the writings of Solomon ben Gabriol and Moses Maimonides who represented a Semitic form of Aristotelianism, (b) Eastern Arabian Aristotelianism as represented in the writings of Avicenna of Bokhara (980-1037), and (c) Western Arabian Aristotelianism as represented in the writings of Avarrhoes of Cordova (1126-98).

they belonged to either the Dominican or the Franciscan Order. Their theological-philosophic work was guided by the following basic principles: *first,* the Bible as the only absolutely reliable divine revelation; *secondly,* the Bible must be interpreted in the light of Tradition, that is, in harmony with decisions of popes and councils and the views of the Church Fathers, even those of the late Hugo of St. Victor and of Peter the Lombard; *thirdly,* recognition of Aristotle as a greater authority than some of the Church Fathers.

With the new emphasis on reason as an aid to faith came a new interest in man, or in the anthropological problems of religion. The

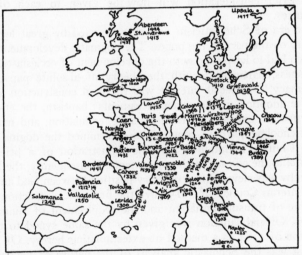

LOCATION OF THE CHIEF EUROPEAN UNIVERSITIES FOUNDED BEFORE 1500

Schoolmen did not pay so much attention to the Trinitarian and Christological problems of old, but rather addressed themselves to the analysis of *grace* as expressed in the Sacraments, and of *merit* as expressed in law and good works. In consequence the Christian dogma, as formulated by the Schoolmen, took on a rather legalistic character; and their conclusions were formulated so well —especially those of Thomas Aquinas—that they have ever since been accepted as an authoritative statement of the Roman Catholic Church.

From the fourteenth century certain differences arose among the Schoolmen as to the nature of knowledge. One group, the *nomial-*

ists, held that ideas or concepts are only names for real things, and that reality consists in the individual concrete objects. Hence truth can be reached only through investigation and the use of reason. The other group, the *realists,* held that ideas, concepts, universals, constitute our real existence; that the human senses are deceptive; and that revealed truth alone is reliable. The Church decided in favor of the realists, and this decision had an important bearing on the development of church doctrine, especially the eucharist.[10]

Scholasticism exerted a considerable influence on the formulation of Christian doctrine, on the development of canon law, on religious life and practice in the late Middle Ages, and on education. Brief consideration will now be given to each of these influences.

The era of Scholasticism was characterized by great legislative activity on the part of the popes. The dogmatic development of the Church had to keep pace with the development of ecclesiastical consciousness, particularly with the theory of absolute papal world supremacy. Of special interest was the final construction and the definite adoption of the seven sacraments: baptism, the eucharist, confirmation, extreme unction, penance, ordination, and marriage. The Schoolmen, whose conclusions determined the dogma of the Latin Church, maintained that the ministration of a priest was *essential* to the efficacy of the sacraments. Consequently, the Roman hierarchy was elevated to a mediary position between God and man. The Lateran Council of 1215 gave the first official sanction to the doctrine of transubstantiation and the requirement of annual confession. Official sanction was given by the same synod to the Inquisition of 1184 as a method of exterminating heresy. Of special interest was the Scholastic analysis of the nature of penance and the consequent laws concerning indulgence.

Canon law was also organized, systematized, and restated so as to be in full accord with the absolute primatial power of the pope. The *Decretalium Gregorii IX compilatio,* published in 1234, became the standard laws for the Church until they were superseded by the *Corpus juris canonici* of the sixteenth century. Through these laws, the Church assumed the position of a legal institution or corporation. Furthermore, these laws were placed on par, if not above, the Roman *Corpus juris civilis.*

[10] If ideas or substances are realities, they are independent of the attributes or qualities which identify them in the concrete. Hence it is possible, according to the realist, to distinguish between the idea or substance of the eucharist and the elements which identify this idea in the concrete. It is also possible, according to this view, to conceive of a change in the substance without a corresponding change in the attribute. In this way the Church justified the doctrine of transubstantiation.

Medieval piety reached its highest development in a mystic type[11] of Scholasticism as represented by Bernard of Clairvaux, Hugo of St. Victor, Francis of Assisi, Anslem of Canterbury, and Abelard. Bernard of Clairvaux is rightly called "the Father of western mysticism." His *imitatio-Christi* ideal found expression in an Evangelical emphasis on faith and salvation by grace alone. The Christian life proceeded from the forgiveness of sins through Christ. Hence an all-consuming love for the crucified Savior burned in his heart. But he found the highest expression of the religious life, not in a personal relation with Christ through faith, but in asceticism, Mariolatry, and a mystical relation with Christ in which all personal activity finally ceased. He made mysticism the central moment in religion and laid the foundation for a scientific mystic theology. Hugo of St. Victor made himself the representative of a Neo-Platonic mysticism which, in his followers in the thirteenth century, often branched out into pantheism. Francis of Assisi exerted the greatest influence through his suffering-love-of Christ ideal which found expression in his stress on poverty, brotherly love, and popular preaching. Asceticism was still the great religious ideal, but instead of fleeing from the world and into desert places, the monks were now admonished to go out into the world to preach and to do good works. The good life was thought of as strict adherence to the laws of the Church: obedience to the clergy, use of the Sacraments and Sacramentals,[12] Mariolatry, and saint worship, use of the Rosary, acts of mercy, pilgrimages, adoration of relics, and the like.

The Schoolmen were also great promoters of education. They occupied practically all the leading teaching positions in the prominent schools of their time, and in several respects they paved the way for greater intellectual freedom and secular educational interests. Thomas Aquinas for instance, following Aristotle's doctrine of the State, had to admit the right of the State to independent existence, although he naturally subordinated it to the Church. John Duns Scotus admitted that some of the Church doctrines were beyond the grasp of human intelligence. He asserted, however, that their absurdity did not lessen, but rather added to their value. They were above reason and had to be grasped by faith.

[11] There were three dominant types of medieval churchly mysticism, (a) the bridegroom-bride mysticism of Bernard of Clairvaux, (b) the Neo-Platonic mysticism of Hugo of St. Victor, and (c) the suffering-love-of-Christ mysticism of Francis of Assisi.

[12] Sacramentals refer to certain benedictions and consecrations, including exorcism, sprinkling with holy water, making the sign of the cross, and the like, as used in Greek and Roman Catholic churches.

Hence reason could no longer be used in undivided support of faith. The *credo ut intelligam* ("I believe in order that I may understand") was now changed to *credo quia absurdum* ("I believe because it is absurd"). Faith and knowledge were separated, and this paved the way for empirical, secular sciences.

The great Schoolmen were Anselm of Canterbury (1033-1109), Peter Abelard (1079-1142), Bernard of Clairvaux (1091-1153), St. Victor Hugo (1097-1141), Peter Lombard (1100-1164), Alexander of Hales (1185-1245), Albertus Magnus (1193-1280), Thomas Aquinas (1227-1274), Bonaventura (1221-1274), Duns Scotus (1265-1308), Roger Bacon (1214-1294), Raymond Lull (1234-1315), William of Occam (d. 1349), and Gabriel Biel (d. 1495).

Intimately connected with the new cultural movement was the rise of universities. Some of these developed out of the cathedral schools while others took their rise from student and teacher guilds. The term *university*, analogous to our modern *corporation*, was at first applied to any chartered association, but later it came to be restricted to its present meaning. Practically all universities of western Europe took as their model either Bologna or Paris. Bologna University was the model for practically all Italian universities; for some of the Spanish universities; for Montepellier and Grenoble in France; and for Glasgow and Upsala. The University of Paris became the university mother of most of the northern French and Spanish universities; for Prague, Vienna, Heidelberg, and Cologne, and through her Copenhagen; for Oxford, and through her Cambridge, and through her the University of Harvard.

28. REVIEW QUESTIONS

1. Why did the monastic orders make such progress?
2. Discuss the order of the Cistercians, the Rule of St. Augustine, and the Premonstrants.
3. Why the Knightly or Military Orders?
4. What characterized the Mendicant Orders?
5. What causes promoted the rise of Scholasticism?
6. What general principles did the Schoolmen follow?
7. Why did the Schoolmen pay so much attention to the Sacraments and to Sacramentals and human merit?
8. How do you explain the difference between *nominalists* and *realists*?
9. What practical influence did the realist philosophy have on the formulation of the doctrine of transubstantiation?
10. What part did the Schoolmen have in the development of Christian doctrine?

TOPICS FOR SPECIAL STUDY

1. Asceticism as a religious ideal.
2. Transforming church schools into universities, in Europe, and in America.
3. The Seven Sacraments.
4. Scholasticism and Education.

IX. Papacy at Its Height.—Papal power which for centuries had been in process of growth was brought to its pinnacle during the pontificate of Innocent III (1198-1216). Slowly and gradually papacy had risen to its dizzy height of absolute world supremacy. Innocent III added the finishing touches, after which the finished structure stood there throughout the rest of the century.

Pope Innocent III was the great pope of the thirteenth century. He was capable of gathering under favorable conditions all the favorable trends of medieval development into one great, unifying organism which gave papacy its universal power. He insisted that the pope was not merely God's deputy or representative on earth; he was *vicarius Christi*; and while the pope was inferior to God, he was superior to all men. As the vicar of Christ he could wield two swords, the spiritual and the temporal. Kings and princes received their power from the pope as the moon receives its light from the sun; hence the pope could make or depose kings at will. Peace and justice should reign on earth, a slogan which appealed to the people. Pope Innocent also developed the interdict so that it became a dreaded moral, economic, and political weapon. He centralized the institution of papal legates so that it was under complete papal control. He brought the German Church under complete papal control, and thereby robbed the German Empire of its best support. He promoted powerful reforms within the Church, especially with reference to simony, the high living of the clergy, monastic decadence, superstition, etc. Heretics were effectively suppressed, especially the Albigenses and the Waldenses. His world supremacy was acknowledged and his great reforms were sanctioned by the Fourth Lateran Synod in 1215 which was the greatest church convention in the Middle Ages.

It was the fortune of this great pope to live in a time when his convictions could be practically applied. He built for the present, but he failed to adjust the great papal machinery to the needs of the immediate future, or to the changes that were going on in Europe. His less gifted successors had to struggle to maintain the power he had gained, and finally the crash came during the pontificate of Boniface VIII (1294-1303).

X. The Albigenses and the Waldenses.—The Church had drifted far from the life and practice of the Apostolic Church. Jesus Christ had been rejected because he would not found a kingdom of this world. And now his supposed representative, the pope, reigned supreme in secular as in spiritual affairs. Many spurious elements had been introduced in church government, doctrine, discipline, and worship. Spurious asceticism, work-righteousness, lax and demoralizing discipline, secularism in the Church, and other abuses had made heavy inroads in the Church. Reactionary and reformatory tendencies were sooner or later bound to appear. Among the many such sects of the period, the best known are the Albigenses and the Waldenses.

The Albigenses were so-called because they were numerous around the city of Albi. They constituted a widely distributed sect with very marked anti-churchly tendencies. Their religion was more Manichean than Christian. Innocent III induced the king of France to start a crusade (1208-1213) against them. In this persecution many men, women, and children lost their lives, but the sect was only suppressed in France and in Italy.

Peter Waldo, a prosperous merchant of Lyons, was the founder of the Waldenses. He died before 1218. The Waldenses had the following program: (1) the Church must return to the pure teaching of Scripture; (2) there is no purgatory; (3) the Church is not infallible; (4) Christian laymen are entitled to preach; (5) selling one's goods and giving the proceeds to the poor is an act of Christian consecration; the Waldenses were not schismatic but intended to carry out their program within the Church.

In 1179 two Waldenses appeared at the Third Lateran Council and asked papal sanction to their mode of life and that they be allowed to continue to preach. Upon careful examination, Pope Alexander III excommunicated them and they were also severely persecuted. The Waldenses were the forerunners of the Hussites and the Bohemian Brethren. The sect is still found in Italy, and since 1870 its members have enjoyed the rights of Italian citizenship.

XI. Ecclesiastical Art, Life, and Worship.—The life of the Church was characteristically reflected in contemporary church architecture and religious art. The lofty theories of papacy and the impressive intellectual system of Scholasticism found fitting expression in Gothic architecture which, after the twelfth century, rapidly replaced the Romanesque. Gothic architecture was characterized by rectangular floor space, pointed arches, cross-vaulting, and construction of the superstructure in such a way as to render the roof independent of the walls. Being no longer essential to the support of the roof, the walls gave place for large windows between the supporting pillars. Gothic churches were lofty, impressive, attractively decorated, and light.

Religious art, especially sculpture, painting, and mosaic enjoyed a remarkable renaissance. Scholastic analysis and formulation of the central doctrines of the Church furnished the main motives and inspiration. Transubstantiation, the miracle of the incarnation in mass, and Mariolatry were the central motives selected. All decorative art aimed to depict life and motion in varied and brilliant colors, and the leading tendency was to impart instruction. Special attention was given to the decorations of the halls for mass. The two leading painters of the period were Cimabue of Florence and his disciple, Giotto. They presented in painting the story of Mary, the mother of Jesus, beginning with the legends concerning her birth, and ending with her coronation as Queen of Heaven. Toward the close of the thirteenth century the passion story of Christ was also depicted in sculpture and in painting.

The mystic element was prominent in literature and worship. Some of the choicest Roman Catholic poems and hymns date from this era. Pageants representing scenes from the life of Christ, or of saints, or of Old Testament characters were given simply and impressively in a number of churches, especially during Christmas and Easter seasons. These miracle or mystery plays became very popular. The casts became larger and the presentations more elaborate and the plays increased in liveliness. Fun and hilarity began to predominate even in the most sacred presentations, especially where the stage was set in the public city square. Many priests finally forbade plays on church grounds, and by 1300 the control of these plays had largely passed into secular hands.

Worship was surrounded by ceremonial beauty, mysticism, and superstition. Special adoration of the host came into use in the thirteenth century, and also the custom of not giving the cup to lay communicants but the consecrated bread only, dipped in consecrated wine. Use of indulgence was widespread. Forgiveness of sins was more easily obtained through absolution because of the accepted Scholastic distinction between *contrition* and *attrition*.[13] The religious life of the multitude was perhaps most character-

---

[13] *Contrition* indicated sorrow for sin proceeding from *love* to God, in connection with repentance. *Attrition* indicated sorrow for sin proceeding from *fear* of punishment, and hence an imperfect repentance. The Schoolmen, especially Duns Scotus, maintained that attrition was sufficient.

istically reflected in the extensive use of Sacramentals, in pilgrimages, and in traffic in relics. Adoration of the Virgin Mary became more general. Mary, as the "holy relic" in which the incarnated Christ had dwelt, must have possessed divinity, they thought. Franciscan monks formulated the doctrine of the immaculate conception. Well informed church members should not address God directly, but through the worthy mediation of Mary, the Queen of Heaven. Her images were supposed to have miraculous and healing powers. The Virgin Mary was so highly exalted that the common people sought a more human mediator in her mother, the Holy St. Anna.

XII. Rise of the Third Estate.—The burgher and the peasant classes of medieval Europe had practically no influence on world affairs prior to 1300. Leadership in Church and State was entrusted entirely to the clergy and the nobility. The Church and the secular nobles were the great landowners in western Europe, and land was the basis of wealth and influence. But the revival of trade, commerce, manufacturing, and industry in the rising cities promoted the development of a middle class which, to begin with, consisted of merchants, bankers, and craftsmen. In the fourteenth century this new class made its modest appearance on the scene of world history, and gradually it came to play a very important role. It was this Third Estate which centuries later instigated the Scottish-English and the French revolutions and wrested the control from the nobility and the clergy. The Third Estate has been the ruling class since the middle of the eighteenth century.

29. REVIEW QUESTIONS

1. When did papacy reach its greatest height?
2. Compare the views and practices of Pope Innocent III with those of Jesus Christ.
3. Why did strong, anti-churchly sects appear?
4. Who were the Albigenses? the Waldenses?
5. Why do you think the cathedral schools developed into universities? Do you know of any modern parallels?
6. Why did Gothic architecture replace the Romanesque?
7. Why the miracle and the mystery plays?
8. How do you explain the special adoration of the host? The use of indulgence?
9. Why the special adoration of the Virgin Mary? of St. Anna?
10. How do you explain the rise and the importance of the Third Estate?

TOPICS FOR SPECIAL STUDY

1. Pope Innocent III.
2. The Albigenses.
3. The Waldenses.
4. Gothic Architecture.

5. Byzantine influence on religious art.
6. Religious poetry and music in the 12th and 13th centuries.

A SELECTED BIBLIOGRAPHY FOR CHAPTER VII

1. Lagarde: *The Latin Church in the Middle Ages.*
2. *Cambridge Medieval History*, Volume II.
3. Workman: *The Church of the West in the Middle Ages*, Volume I.
4. Robinson: *Readings in European History*, Volume I.
5. Thatcher and McNeal: *Source Book for Medieval History.*
6. Bryce: *Holy Roman Empire.*
7. Mann: *Lives of the Popes of the Early Middle Ages.*
8. Ludlow: *The Age of the Crusades.*

CHAPTER VIII

The Era of the Decline of Papacy and Signs of Reformation

From Boniface VIII to Luther's Theses (1294-1517)

I. Abuses of the Papal Power.—The successors of Innocent III were not capable of interpreting the signs of the time; consequently they failed to adjust themselves and their administration to changing conditions in Europe.[1] They continued the policies of Innocent III and even tried to effect a still greater centralization of temporal and spiritual power in the office of papacy. All opposition was ruthlessly suppressed. Some of the most horrible chapters in the history of persecutions belong to this era.

After the close of the war against the Albigenses in 1229, Gregory IX made heresy a capital offense, and insisted that the State must assist the Church in supressing heresy. All the kings of Europe agreed to make heresy punishable by death, except in England where it was made a capital offense in 1401. Torture was used (after 1252) as a means of bringing the accused to confess, and impenitent heretics were burned at the stake. *Inquisition* became an authorized department of church administration. The laws were changed so that it would be easy to accuse people of heresy by classing all kinds of opposition or criticism as "heresy," and difficult for the accused to clear themselves. As the pope found the episcopal inquisition too lenient, he instituted special inquisitional tribunals in charge of monks under direct papal supervision. These special tribunals had unlimited power in matters of heresy.

Roman law was, during the greater part of the Middle Ages, the basic law. By the thirteenth century Church law was placed on a par with it. In a new collection called *Drecetalium Gregorii IX compilatio*[2] Church law was placed above the old imperial law of Rome. In 1234, a number of administrative offices were created at the papal court, including the *Rota romana* or highest Church court,

[1] The most prominent successors were Gregory IX (1227-41) and Innocent IV (1243-54).
[2] These laws were compiled under the direct supervision of the capable Spanish canonist, Raimond de Penaforte. They form the main portion of the *Corpus juris canonici* of the sixteenth century.

and the *Camera apostolica* or Department of Finance. The maintenance of papal world supremacy and the administrative machinery cost tremendous sums of money. The resulting policies of raising money caused the Church a great deal of harm, especially simony and the sale of indulgences. Soon the people began to react unfavorably toward the Church because of the strong financial oppression.[3]

From the twelfth century the pope claimed the exclusive right to appoint candidates for church offices. Such appointments necessitated knowledge of local conditions and of the fitness of the candidates. The local bishops, not the distant pope, would have such information. Office-seekers came to Rome, and the pope frequently appointed candidates who perhaps had never seen the land nor the community they were to serve. Some held office, but a representative did all their official work. Some of the pope's favorites held a number of offices in various countries, and consequently the proper personal attention could not be given to each office. At times a certain office would be given to two candidates, to the first one immediately, to the second in the case the first one died. Sometimes, several candidates were on the waiting list for the same office; and when the vacancy occurred, law suits resulted.

The pope himself demoralized the office of the bishop and of the parish priest. The bishop had no appointive power, and the mendicant monks had unlimited access to any pulpit or any parish. The mendicant monk could exercise pastoral care toward any church member; he could preach; he could act as a father confessor; he had papal privileges of absolution; and he had papal power to exercise a stricter church discipline than either bishop or parish priest.

Whatever was left of episcopal authority was abolished when the pope established the court of appeal. From the time of Gregory VII, appeals to the pope had usually brought favorable results. Appeals from every country were brought to Rome. But how could cases of local administration be given proper attention at a single court? Consider the long journeys of those appealing to the court, their disadvantage of being in a strange land, the long time of waiting, with some of the arbitrary decisions made.

Simony flourished openly at the papal court. Church offices and decisions were sold for money. The entire personnel around the

---

[3] Pope Gregory IX also waged an uncompromising warfare against the German emperor, Frederick II. In a papal bull of 1239 the pope designated the emperor as the "Beast" of the Book of Revelation. Pope Innocent IV declared Frederick II deposed and instigated a crusade against him. When Frederick II died in 1250, papacy enjoyed a greater momentary power than during the pontificate of Innocent III. But the means used in the acquisition of this power tended to lower the popular estimation of papacy.

pope, from the porter to the cardinal, demanded fees. Popes and cardinals enriched their relations, especially their illegitimate children. Nepotism was practiced to such an extent that it scandalized the Church. Celibacy was enforced upon the clergy and upon the monks, but lack of proper ethical principles led to an appalling immorality.

II. **The Babylonian Captivity of the Church (1305-1376).** —When Boniface VIII (1294-1303) ascended the papal chair, the see of St. Peter still possessed the power and influence with which Gregory VII and Innocent III had invested it. Boniface continued the arrogant assertions of papal supremacy without taking due notice of the new spirit of nationalism which began to resent the dominion of the universal Church. The new conception of monarchy was presented by Dante's "De Monarchia" in which he insisted that the empire derived its existence directly from God and not from the Church. The revival of city-life created demands for self-government and freedom from monastic control; the revival of trade, commerce, industry, and banking, also developed a spirit of independence averse to papal dominion.

Boniface began his reign by expelling the influential Colonna family. He tried to restore Sicily to the king of Naples, but failed. During the war between Philip the Fair of France and Edward I of England the pope claimed to be arbiter between them (1295), but neither would listen to him. He retaliated by issuing a papal bull, the *Clericis Laicos* which prohibited England and France, on pain of excommunication, from taxing the Church and the clergy for military purposes. Edward forced the payment of these taxes through his parliament, and he disregarded the papal claim to Scotland as a feud. In France the pope fared still worse. Philip the Fair answered the papal bull by prohibiting the export of money from his kingdom, a severe financial blow to the pope.

Besides simony and the sale of indulgences the pope had the following financial resources: (1) The *Annates* or first fruits, the first year's income in office, exacted of bishops and abbots; (2) the *Reservations*, the richest benefices in each country, were reserved for the use of the pope and the cardinals; (3) the *Expectancies*, in which the pope sold to the highest bidder the nomination as successor to rich benefices before the death of the incumbent; (4) the *Commendations*, consisting of indefinite, provisional appointments on condition of payment of an annual tax; (5) the *Jus spoliorum*, or the claim that the pope was the rightful heir to all property acquired by officials of the Church during their tenure of office; (6) *tithing* of church property for urgent wants. And now the French king prohibited these large sums of money from being sent out of the country.

The pope issued a bull of excommunication and interdict.[4] The excommunication was directed against the French king. He was cut off from all relations with his fellow-men, and his subjects were released from their oath of allegiance. The interdict was directed against the kingdom of France. The churches were to be closed; no bell could be rung, no marriage celebrated, no burial ceremony performed; only the sacraments of baptism and extreme unction could be administered. But these terrible weapons had lost their force. The king had the pope seized and confined in prison where he died in 1303.

Benedict XI (1303-1304) annulled the decrees against Philip and the French nation. Nine months after his assumption of office he died, and was succeeded by Pope Clement V (1304-1314), a Frenchman who previously had promised to support the French policy. He transferred the papal Curia to the French city of Avignon[5] where papacy had its headquarters for about seventy years. Hence the term "Babylonian Captivity" in commemoration of the exile of the Jews in Babylonia. During this period papacy was manifestly subservient to French interests, seven successive popes being Frenchmen.

The Babylonian Captivity weakened papacy, because papacy was made subservient to State interests. The prevailing immorality at the papal court undermined papal prestige, and led to demands for reform. The heavy financial burdens imposed by papacy and the questionable methods of raising money alienated the nations from the pope and the Church. Pope Clement V dissolved the Order of Knights Templars in 1312 and confiscated the estates of the members, an unpopular action which aroused serious opposition to papacy.[6] Several popes promised under oath before their election

[4] The *Unam sanctam* bull of November, 1302, is the classic expression of the papal claim to the world supremacy. If the king resists the pope, he resists God Himself. The following sentence of Thomas Aquinas was incorporated in the bull: "We declare, define, and affirm that every man must obey the pope or forfeit his salvation." A synod held at Rome declared this bull to give a correct expression of the view of the Roman Catholic Church.

[5] The transfer was made in 1309. Avignon belonged to the king of Naples, but the Roman Curia bought it in 1348 and added it to the Church State.

[6] After the final loss of Palestine, the Knights Templars turned their energies from military activity to exchange of commodities and world finance. Their Temple in Paris soon became the center for the international money market. Philip IV of France, who greatly feared their power, was the main instigator against them. The Grand Master, Jacques de Molay, as he stood ready to be burned at the stake, denied under oath that the Order was guilty of ungodliness and immorality.

that they would restore the papal court to Rome, but after the election this oath was violated.[7]

III. The Papal Schism (1378-1417).—Pope Urban V (1362-1370) made a brief break in the Babylonian Captivity by returning to Rome, but he soon went back to Avignon. Gregory XI (1370-1378) put a definite end to the exile. He returned to Rome in 1377 and died there the following year. His successor, Urban VI (1378-1389) was elected on the distinct understanding that he would return to Avignon. When he later declined, the French fled and declared the election illegal. They elected a Frenchman, Clement VII (1378-1394), who took up his residence at Avignon. For the next forty years the Roman Catholic Church had two popes and two colleges of cardinals, each pope anathematizing the other.

This state of affairs was intolerable so an Ecumenical Council was called at Pisa in 1409. This Council laid down the principle that a General or Ecumenical Council was superior to the pope. The two popes were deposed, and a new one, Alexander V (1409-1410), was elected. Now there were three, instead of two, popes anathematizing each other!

The Council of Constance (1414-1418) ended the schism. All three popes were deposed, and Martin V (1417-1431) was elected pope by this Council. Efforts made to heal the disgraceful papal schism had finally proved successful.

30. REVIEW QUESTIONS

1. How did torture, burning at the stake, and Inquisition harmonize with the spirit of Christianity? Why do you think the pope made use of these means?
2. Why did Church or Canon Law supersede the Roman Law? List good and bad effects of this change.
3. In what ways did the prevailing method of appointing church officials prove harmful to the Church? Compare this method with that of electing the Seven (Acts: Chapter 6) deacons in the early Jerusalem church.
4. How did the mendicant monks demoralize the general order of the Church?
5. Did the papal court of appeal prove useful to the Church? Give reasons for your answer.
6. How did Simony, Nepotism, and Celibacy affect morality within the Church?

[7] Pope John XXII (1316-34) needed more money to support his papal court. He reserved for himself the right to appoint all higher church officials; patriarchs (cardinals), archbishops, and bishops. Each appointee had to pay a set fee, usually one-third of one year's income from that office. Sale of indulgence became more general. With the termination of the Crusades, the plenary indulgence offered during the Crusades was transferred to the Jubilee Years, of which the first was held in 1300. John XXII's system of church taxation made the Church the international money power in Europe. The *Curia* became the central administration system in the Church.

7. What changes were taking place in Europe during the pontificate of Boniface VIII?
8. Why the "Babylonian Captivity" of the Church?
9. Why the papal schism of 1378-1417?
10. How was the breach finally healed?

TOPICS FOR SPECIAL STUDY

1. The Rota romana and the Camera apostolica.
2. The establishment of the Court of Appeal.
3. Enforced Celibacy.
4. Dante's "De Monarchia."
5. The "Babylonian Captivity" of 1305-1376.
6. The Papal Schism of 1378-1417.

IV. Reformatory Movements.—The Medieval Church had through her most characteristic institutions, papacy and monasticism, reached the peak in her development. Papacy had reached absolute power, only to use that very power for selfish interests, allowing abuses which finally undermined it. Monasticism had pressed the ascetic ideal so far that moral bankruptcy ensued. The Church and the world longed for a moral and spiritual regeneration. A reformation was needed in "head and members" of the Church, and a general desire for such reformation existed during the entire period. This desire for reform found expression in movements which will now be briefly considered.

In 1324 a book called "Defensor pacis" was written by two men, Marsilius of Padova and John of Jandun. It was the most important contribution on the relation between Church and State in the later Middle Ages. A new ideal for the Church was set forth: the Church should become more democratic and limit herself to her proper sphere—the spiritual welfare of mankind. Much disturbance had come to European society because the Church had unduly meddled with the affairs of the State.

A new conception of the State was also set forth: the State should rest on the sovereignty of the common people. The people should control the legislature through popularly elected representatives. The executive power should be left in the hands of an elected king who should rule according to an accepted Constitution.

The book promulgated the sovereignty of the common people as applied to the Church. The Church should first of all address herself to her proper duties, the spiritual welfare of mankind. The church people should themselves elect their priests and officials. These popularly elected church officials should constitute the General Council which should be the highest spiritual power on earth. The priests should not have property or secular power; their salaries should be paid by the State. The entire Canon or Church Law should be abolished, and the Church should be placed under the control of the State. The essential duty of the priest was to preach the Gospel and to administer the Sacraments. The priest and the Church were not an essential medium through which man must approach God. Every individual had direct access to God through faith. In summary it may be said that the book asserted: (a) the need of a reformation; (b) the State-Church principle; (c) religious individualism; (d) political liberalism; (e) modern democracy; and (f) Holy Scriptures as the only source of faith.

William of Occam (1280-1349), the most influential theologian of his time, made some of these ideas better known through his writings. Occam asserted that (a) the pope is not infallible; (b) that the General Council and not the pope is the highest authority in the Church; (c) that Holy Scripture is the only infallible source in matters of faith and conduct; (d) that in all secular matters the Church and the pope are subordinate to the State. Occam's philosophy exerted a strong influence upon Martin Luther.

In France the reform movement was fostered chiefly in the University of Paris. The most prominent was perhaps John Charlier of Gerson (1363-1429), the moving spirit in the Council of Pisa, 1409. He believed that (a) a visible head of the Church at Rome was necessary, but that a General Council was superior to the pope, (b) a genuine reformation was necessary in "head and members" of the Church, and (c) the Bible was the only source and rule of Christian knowledge.

Several Germans, Henry of Langenstein, Theodore of Niem, Nicholas of Cusa, and Gregory of Heimburg, insisted on church reform. But of more importance was the German mysticism, as represented by Meister Eckhart (1260-1327) and John Tauler (1290-1361). The mystics were dominated by two specific sentiments: (a) genuine sorrow for the decay of the Church; and (b) a strong longing for a reformation.

The so-called Reform Councils should also be mentioned. The men responsible for calling the Council of Pisa, 1409, had in mind not only to heal the papal schism but also to reform the Church. But the newly elected pope, Alexander V, adjourned the Council before any reformatory work could be done. At the next Council, in Constance (1414-1418) a number of reforms were proposed, but Pope Martin V skilfully avoided any reform measures. He made separate agreements—known as concordats—with individual nations. It was evidently easier to bargain with each nation than to meet them all in joint assembly. At the Council of Basel (1431-1449) the Council at first took an independent position by declaring that the real authority resides in the General Council and not in the pope. But the pope retaliated by declaring this decision void, and the Council was dismissed. Papacy in the end was triumphant against the reforming councils.

John Wyclif (1320-1384) became the leader of a strong reform movement that spread over England and certain parts of the Continent. This movement contended that the reform must aim, not merely at correction of outward corruptions of the Church, but also at the removal of the hidden causes. The movement addressed itself to the people rather than to the learned, the reformers, Wyclif and Hus, proclaiming the Biblical doctrine of justification by faith in the crucified Savior. The Bible was acknowledged as the only source of truth. Emphasis was placed on the invisible Church at the expense of the visible Christian community. The pope was not believed infallible, and his bulls and decrees had no authority except as they were based on Scripture. The clergy were not to rule but to serve and help their people. Wyclif declared the pope to be Antichrist. He declared that the bread and wine in the Lord's Supper were not changed into the body and blood of Christ. He gave England the first complete version of the Bible in the English language. It was due to his initiative that England got the first complete version of the Bible in the English language, in 1380. The first part of this version, from Genesis to Baruch 3:20, was translated by Nicholas de Hereford. The translation of the balance of the Old Testament, the Apocrypha, and the New Testament, is credited to Wyclif. He also sent out lay evangelists to instruct the people. Wyclif was condemned by Pope Gregory XI in 1377, but the English Parliament protected him. He retired to his parish at Lutterworth where he died. His followers, called the Lollards, numbered many nobles. But in 1401 heresy was made a capital offence in England, and the mere possession of Wyclif's writings was punishable by death. Wyclifism was suppressed by force.

John Hus (1369-1415), a professor at the university of Prague, was a follower of Wyclif who placed himself at the head of a reform movement in Bohemia. He was also a powerful preacher and occupied the most influential pulpit in Prague. After 1409 he became the head of the national Bohemian party in the university. The whole nation rallied around him in the cause of church reform. Hus was excommunicated, first by the Archbishop of Prague, and next by the pope. He was summoned before the

Council of Constance where he was condemned as a heretic and burned at the stake. The Emperor Sigismund had promised him safe conduct to and from the Council, but failed to keep his promise. Likewise his colleague, Jerome of Prague, was burned at the stake, and this event precipitated the Husite War. Unfortunately, the Husites were divided into two parties, the Calixtines and the Taborites. The Calixtines were enticed to reunite with the Catholic Church, and the Taborites were defeated in the battle of Prague in 1434.

Girolamo Savonarola (1452-98) headed a remarkable movement in the city of Florence. He was educated in medical study, but religious inclinations caused him to enter a monastery in Bologna in 1475, and he remained there quitely for seven years. His religious life in the monastery developed along the line of visionary mysticism and he soon felt called to become an itinerant preacher. His superiors sent him out, but he had little success to begin with. By 1486 he seems to have found the right form and content for his preaching, namely (a) the Church shall be punished; (b) then the Church shall be renewed; and (c) this shall soon come to be. His preaching had great influence on his audiences. Lorenzo Medici called him to Florence in 1490. He died two years later as Savonarola's disciple. Michelangelo who later became famous as sculptor, painter, and poet, was a frequent listener to Savonarola. The coming of Charles VIII of France with an army to Italy in 1494 brought Savonarola into politics. Piero Medici was driven from Florence, and Savonarola became dictator of the city in 1495. This furnished him an opportunity to reform the city much according to his own liking.[8] But his denunciation of the authority of the pope and the corruption of the Church caused Alexander VI to place him under papal ban in 1497 and he also threatened Florence with the interdict. Savonarola was condemned as a heretic[9] and put to death in 1498.

The Brethren of the Common Life, originally a society of pius clergymen founded in the Netherlands by Gerhard Groot, had no intention of breaking with the Roman Catholic Church, but devoted themselves primarily to teaching and to preaching in order to

[8] He urged that Florence be made a theocracy and that Christ be proclaimed king. He enlisted the help of about 4000 young people, 12-20 years of age, as crusaders against luxury and immorality. People read the Bible and went to church instead of enjoying the customary games and theater productions. Business people returned what they had gained illegally. Savonarola was not an Evangelical Christian in the modern sense of the term.
[9] Neither his reform plans nor his theology contained anything heretical. His views on doctrine were so thoroughly in accord with the Catholic Church that his *Trionfo della croce* of 1497 was used by the Catholic *Propaganda* more than a century later as a textbook.

reform the Church from within. They formed voluntary associations on the basis of devout living, and labored for their support. The original association became the nucleus of similar institutions throughout northern Europe. These associations admitted not only clergymen but also lay people. Several well-known schools were founded, and through these institutions as well as through their earnest and evangelical sermons, they exerted a wide and beneficial influence among the people. Thomas à Kempis who wrote the "Imitation of Christ," and John of Wessel, Luther's forerunner in theology, belonged to the Brethren of the Common Life. Similar institutions for Sisters of the Common Life were also founded.[10]

These many movements indicate how widespread and general was the demand for a church reform in Europe. But "the fullness of time" had not yet come for the great Reformation of Luther, Zwingli, and Calvin.

31. REVIEW QUESTIONS

1. Account for the general desire for a church reform.
2. What ideas were set forth in "Defensor pacis"? Why did not these ideas find a wider and more immediate application?
3. Discuss the views and the influence of William of Occam.
4. Who was John Charlier of Gerson? What did he do with reference to church reform?
5. What ideals dominated the Mystics?
6. Discuss the reform councils. Why did the popes set their faces like flint against these councils?
7. What characterized the reform movement of Wyclif and Hus?
8. Why did not Wyclif exert a more immediate influence in England?
9. How did John Hus influence Bohemia and the general course of the history of the Church?
10. Who was Savonarola?
11. In what ways did the Brethren of the Common Life influence the people of northern Europe?

TOPICS FOR SPECIAL STUDY

1. The influence of William of Occam.
2. John Wyclif and John Hus.
3. Savonarola as a Reformer.
4. Meister Eckhart and John Tauler.
5. The early history of the Brethren of the Common Life.

V. The Renaissance and Papacy.—The Renaissance revealed some characteristic differences between Latin and Teutonic elements. In Italy the Renaissance was *classical* and *scientific*, and

---

[10] By 1500 the Low Countries (Netherlands) alone had twenty-two large houses for Brethren and at least eighty-seven houses for Sisters.

awakened little or no tendency toward a religious reformation. In northwestern Europe the Renaissance was *religious* and *moral*.

The Renaissance for a whole century (1333-1443) was almost entirely an Italian movement, but gradually it spread to all of Catholic Europe and survived until the Counter-Reformation. The Crusades and the Italian contact with Saracenic culture had promoted a general transformation in the economic, social and cultural life of Italy and the rest of Europe. A revival of patriotism, of national self-consciousness, and of Italian language and literature; a scientific connection with Graeco-Roman culture, Aristotle,

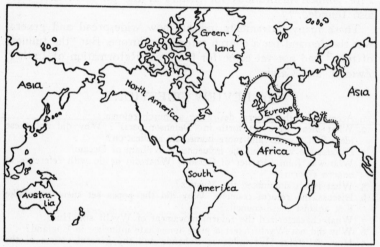

THE KNOWN WORLD IN 800 AND THE KNOWN WORLD OF TODAY
(The Known World in 800 is limited by a heavy line accompanied by dots)

Corpus juris, and Neo-Platonism; a revival of art and of the old Greek esteem of the individual; the moulding of the Italian national spirit with the ancient, pagan view of life into a new culture essentially different from the culture and the ascetic ideal of the central Middle Ages;—in short, all these are a part of the great movement known as the Renaissance. The human spirit was awakened to the greatness of the world in which man lives.

The Crusades had furnished the people of Europe an incentive for geographical exploration, and contact with Saracenic civilization had stimulated the intellectual life of the West. The Crusades had revived Western trade and commerce, and these again led to travel, exploration, and discovery. Marco Polo and Sir John

Mandeville travelled extensively in the Orient, and their travel descriptions (around 1295) astonished all Europe. By the beginning of the fourteenth century the compass had been perfected in Naples, an event which ushered in a great era of exploration. The Canary Islands were discovered in 1402; the Madeira Islands in 1419; the Cape Verde Islands in 1460; Vasco da Gama sailed around the southern point of Africa in 1487. The chief motive of these sea voyages was to discover a trade-route by sea to India. Europe soon realized that the route discovered by Vasco da Gama was too long and dangerous, and this stimulated the search for a shorter route. With this in mind Christopher Columbus sailed westward and discovered America in 1492. Magellan sailed around the earth in 1519-1522 and proved conclusively that the world was round. Man's notions of the physical world had changed completely.

A transformation in economic, social, and cultural life was inevitable. The lively trade and commerce brought great wealth to certain cities, causing a rapid increase in city population. Industry was revolutionized. The strict isolation of the early Middle Ages had limited arts and industries to the particular needs of the townsman. The new contact with the outside world permitted a surplus production which could be sold at fairs in exchange for other products. The old barter system of exchange of commodities was superseded by the exchange of money, which in turn gave rise to the banking system, the beginning of modern *capitalism*. The great bankers of Europe soon had more power than leaders of armies.

The rapid increase in the population of the cities gave rise to a new class, the citizens. The wealthy cities, purchasing their freedom from the feudal lords, organized their own city government. The people constituted a new social order consisting of merchants, bankers, tradesmen, artisans, and craftsmen. This new class, the *citizens*, demanded certain rights and obtained certain privileges regarding the education of their children, which gave rise to guild or apprenticeship education and the burgh or city schools of Europe. The training in these schools was naturally somewhat different from that of the church schools, for this new type of education naturally promoted the ideals and the culture of the Renaissance.

Closely connected with the Renaissance were such great inventions as the improvement of the compass which has already been referred to, the use of paper and the invention of the printing press, and the invention of gunpowder. The manufacture of paper is very likely a Chinese invention. The Greeks obtained the process from the Mohammedans about 1250 and the first paper mill was set up in Italy in 1276. By 1450 paper was in common use in Europe. The invention of the printing press by John Gutenberg of Mayence in 1450 marked a turning point in the development of civilization. The first book that came from his press was a Latin Bible printed about 1453. The invention of gunpowder revolutionized warfare. The costly armor and the fortified castle were rendered almost useless, and the feudal levy was replaced by a regular, standing army, a change which aided the royal power.

The Renaissance stimulated patriotism and the production of a national literature. This new spirit found expression in the evolution of the modern European States. With the rise of strong, national governments the dominion of the universal Church was greatly curbed. The pope and the clergy were more and more confined to their original functions of spiritual and religious service.

Italy considered herself heir to the political and intellectual Rome of the great past. To understand this inheritance the Italians began to reconstruct their own literature, history, mythology, and their political and social life on the basis of the life of ancient Greece and Rome; and these ideals were pagan, rather than Christian.

Classical interest exerted a marked influence upon learned or educated people and caused them to break away from medieval Scholasticism. Their interests centered in historical and philological studies and gave rise to Humanism. The Renaissance reacted strongly against the ascetic ideal, and yet the movement did not alienate itself from the Church because it did not have any corresponding religious or social elements on which to build.

Classical ideals soon found their expression in art, in sculpture, in architecture, and particularly in painting. But classicism was particularly influential in promoting the *new individualism*. The medieval ideal of the individual was self-abnegation; the new ideal promoted self-expression. Not repression but expression of the inherent tendencies in man. Not ascetic seclusion but the use and the enjoyment of all the world can offer. Man should be self-confident, conscious of his powers, enjoy life, feel his connection with the historic past, and realize the potentialities of accomplishment.

The rational inquiry, with historical and philological studies, made men subject documents of the Church to critical examination. In 1440, Laurentius Valla proved that the spurious "Donations of

Constantine" were a forgery. He also made a critical comparison between the Vulgate and the original Greek text. The apostolic origin of the Apostle's Creed was contested. Representatives of the Renaissance began to undermine the Catholicism of the Middle Ages.

From 1450 to 1520 papacy entered into the spirit of the Renaissance. The popes endeavored to make Rome the center of the new culture, and in keeping with this ambition they surrounded themselves with a brilliant court of artists and scholars, poets and sculptors. The inevitable result was *the secularization of papacy*, which in turn increased a demand for a reformation of the Church in head and members.

One very beneficial result of the Renaissance was the revived interest in the study of Hebrew and Greek. This promoted a better understanding of the Bible on which the great reformatory work of Luther, Zwingli, and Calvin was based. Without this preparation their work would not have been possible.

VI. The Church and the People.—The Renaissance had awakened a new religious and moral consciousness among the people of northern Europe. German humanism had paved the way for a general religious crisis and reform (1) by exposing the abuses of the Church and the work-righteousness, (2) by claiming the Bible as the only form for faith and by placing the Bible in the hands of the people, (3) by undermining and refuting the method and the theology of Scholasticism, (4) by placing a greater emphasis on real, practical Christianity, and (5) by strengthening the national, anti-papal party. The printing press made possible a wide circulation of the Bible and devotional literature. Many attempts were made to translate the Bible into the language of the people; by 1520 there were 18 German, 2 Dutch, 11 Italian, and 4 Bohemian translations. Evangelical preaching and the teaching of reform parties, especially the Brethren of the Common Life, exerted a wide influence.

Superstition and fear dominated the religion of the common man. Fear of the Devil and his world, God's awful Judgment Day, hell and purgatory, exerted a tremendous influence upon him. How could he protect himself against Satan? And how could he obtain salvation, thereby escaping the torments of hell? He looked to the Church, and the Church gave the following answer:

(1) Protection against the forces of evil and salvation reside in the Church, and in the Church only. It had been asserted for many centuries that "there is no salvation outside the Church."

Communion with God and the forgiveness of sins were possible only through a communion with the Church, represented by the clergy.

(2) The Church had a great number of means whereby man could protect himself against Satan and the evil spirits. Charms and amulets were sold to the people for such purposes. Prayers to the Saints and to the Virgin were particularly effective.

(3) The Sacraments were necessary to salvation. They were in the pope's power, and could be withheld if the organization of the Church did not approve. The pope had the power of excommunication and of placing cities, provinces, or kingdoms under interdict.

(a) Excommunication was directed against individuals. The lesser excommunication deprived a person of the sacraments; the greater cut him off from all rights. If a king, his subjects were released from their oath of allegiance. Mass could not be celebrated in the presence of the excommunicate. He could not hold a benefice, exercise jurisdiction, or take part in an election pertaining to the Church. Anyone who provided him with food or shelter incurred the penalties of the Church. Christian burial was denied him.

(b) The interdict was directed against a city, province, or kingdom. The total interdict forbade public worship, the administration of the sacraments, and Christian burial. The churches were closed; no bell could be rung; no marriage celebrated; no burial ceremony performed. The sacraments of baptism and extreme unction alone could be administered.

(c) The ban of the Empire was a secular punishment, a declaration of outlawry, upon any excommunicated person or community.

(4) Penance consists of contrition of the heart, confession, and satisfaction. Auricular confession was necessary before absolution could be received. All known sins must be enumerated before the confessor. Satisfaction and release from punishment could usually be secured by means of good works, such as prayers, alms, pilgrimages, and the like.

(5) All arrears of temporal punishment were inflicted in Purgatory, a place of punishment before the resurrection. Souls in Purgatory might be delivered by masses, intercessions, alms, and good works. No one needed to be in fear of hell if he had rightly used the sacrament of penance.

(6) Punishment for the sins of the living and for those in Purgatory could be lightened or remitted altogether by securing indulgence from the Church. These indulgences were sold for money. The practice of indulgence rested on the theory that Christ and the Saints had performed more good works than were needed.

These surplus merits were at the disposal of the Church and could be given or sold to less fortunate people.

(7) The merits of good works were greatly extolled. This work-righteousness had its roots in Pharisaic legalism and in the legalistic religious conceptions inherited from the old Romans.

VII. Retrospect.—For many centuries the Church had insisted on being a kingdom of this world in distinct opposition to Jesus Christ, the founder, who emphatically had stated: "my kingdom is not of this world." The accumulative effects of this sinful state of affairs were bound to be keenly felt. Many pagan and worldly elements had come to exert an undue influence. While the simple Gospel was obscured, the pope and church officials set their faces like flint against any reforms. In the meantime the new Teutonic-Latin civilization was emerging from the chaos of the Middle Ages. The dawn of a new day had come; the modern mind of a new world began to assert itself. The "fullness of time" had come for a successful Reformation.

32. REVIEW QUESTIONS

1. What causes promoted the rise of the Renaissance?
2. How did the Italian Renaissance differ from that of northern Europe?
3. Why was this an age of geographical discoveries? How did these discoveries influence the life of Europe?
4. Why the great transformation in industry and art? Why the rise of the banking system and of modern capitalism?
5. Who was the citizen? What caused the rise of this new class?
6. How did the improvement of the compass, the introduction of paper, the invention of the printing press, and the invention of gunpowder influence European life?
7. Why did the Renaissance promote patriotism, national literature, and the development of the modern European States?
8. Compare the ideals of the Renaissance with the ideals of Christianity.
9. Why the new individualism?
10. How did the Renaissance prepare for the Reformation?

TOPICS FOR SPECIAL STUDY

1. The influence of the Renaissance on the Church.
2. The geographical discoveries between the years 1295 and 1500.
3. The rise of the Third Estate, the Citizens.
4. How the Church reacted toward a changing world.
5. Compare the Christian Church of 100 with the Roman Catholic Church of 1500.

A SELECTED BIBLIOGRAPHY FOR CHAPTER VIII

1. Workman: *The Church of the West in the Middle Ages*, Volume II.
2. Workman: *The Dawn of the Reformation.*
3. Ullman: *Reformers before the Reformation.*
4. Gasquet: *The Eve of the Reformation.*

5. Hyma: *The Christian Renaissance.*
6. *The Cambridge Modern History,* Volume I, *The Renaissance.*
7. Flick: *The Decline of the Medieval Church.*
8. Trevelyan: *England in the Age of Wyclif.*
9. Locke: *The Great Western Schism.*
10. Pastor: *History of the Popes from the Close of the Middle Ages.*
11. Gierke: *Political Theories of the Middle Ages.*
12. Jarrett: *Social Theories of the Middle Ages.*
13. Huizinga: *The Waning of the Middle Ages.*
14. Arrowsmith: *The Prelude to the Reformation.*
15. Loserth: *Wycliffe and Huss.*

PART III

THE MODERN PERIOD

From the Reformation to the Present

SECTION 1

THE CHURCH IN THE "OLD WORLD"

CHAPTER IX

EUROPE ON THE EVE OF THE REFORMATION

I. General Observations.—The Protestant Reformation in the sixteenth century constitutes one of the most powerful spiritual movements in history. October 31, 1517, the day when Dr. Martin Luther nailed his 95 theses to a church door in Wittenberg, is correctly designated the birthday of the Reformation; yet this single event must not be isolated from the general historical setting of European life.

The Teutonic-Latin civilization had finally reached its majority. First came the Revival of Learning, or the Renaissance, which marked the first definite break with medievalism. Opening up aspects of life hitherto practically unknown, three almost entirely new worlds were revealed to the people of western Europe, namely, (1) the great Graeco-Roman world of the past, expressed in literature and art, science and religion; (2) the world within each individual, with its innate, latent possibilities, the subjective world, the world of emotions; (3) the great physical world as revealed through the amazing geographical discoveries.

A proper perspective of this tremendous expansion is necessary. In the ancient world, civilization had been confined to river valleys such as the Nile, the Tigris, and the Euphrates. In the medieval world, civilization centered around the Mediterranean. From the beginning of the modern era the Atlantic and the Pacific became the natural highways of the world's intercourse and commerce.

The Renaissance affected Italy and Northern Europe differently, because the Italian got his main inspiration from ancient Rome and Greece, while the North-European centered his interests on Palestine, the birth-place of Christianity. The Italian was interested in self-culture and self-development which leads toward an extreme individualism, while the North-European was interested in education as a means to social and religious reform. In Italy the movement was essentially pagan; in the North it was essentially Christian, so much so that in Germany the Renaissance and the Reformation can hardly be distinguished. In the South the movement was aristocratic; in the North, democratic.

The German Renaissance is most frequently referred to as a Reformation, but it is also called the Protestant Revolution. These two terms describe two phases of the same movement. It was a Reformation in that it brought its adherents back to the three great and original principles of Christianity: (1) Holy Scriptures as the sole normal authority for faith and life; (2) justification by faith alone without any merits of good work; (3) the priesthood of all believers. It was a Revolution in that when the Catholic Church refused to be reformed according to the principles just indicated, half of Europe broke away from papacy and formed the Protestant Church.

Only a small portion of the world belonged to Christendom at the time of the Reformation. Palestine, Syria, Asia Minor, Egypt, and North Africa had been lost to the Mohammedans. And ever since the great schism of 1054 the Christian Church had been separated into East and West. This situation had been made permanent by the Mohammedan conquests which had come like a wedge between the two divisions of Christendom. Constantinople had fallen into Mohammedan hands in 1453, and in 1529 only the most heroic efforts in the battle at Vienna had stayed their advance into Europe. Isolation was so complete that the Greek Catholic Church remained almost entirely outside the influence of the Reformation.

The transition from the medieval to the modern world was not an abrupt one; change came about gradually in the religious, intellectual, moral, social, economic, and political life of western Europe. How these various factors prepared for the Reformation will be considered in the following sections. Someone has said that John Wyclif was the morning star of the Reformation; John Hus and Hieronymus of Prague were its first martyrs; Savonarola was its great prophet; and, it may be added, Luther, Zwingli, and Calvin were the great reformers. There is an organic connection between the Apostolic Council in Jerusalem, the Epistle to the Galatians, the Epistle to the Romans, and the Protestant Reformation.[1] They constitute a four-leaf clover.

Modern church history presents four separate stages: (1) the Reformation and the Counter-Reformation, in the sixteenth century; (2) the Age of Orthodoxy, in the seventeenth and part of the eighteenth centuries; (3) the Age of Deism, Rationalism, and Naturalism, in the nineteenth century; and (4) the Age of Pantheism, Materialism, and Communism, beginning with the present century.

II. The Political Conditions in Europe.—In western Europe the chief political development was the formation of nations with strong, centralized governments. Feudalism broke down; the royal power tended to become absolute. New national languages and literatures were also coming into being. At the beginning of the sixteenth century the four great Christian powers in Europe were England, France, and Spain, with strong national governments, and Germany where the tendency toward national unity was evident. Italy was without a national government. But Europe had to reckon with a great non-Christian power, the Mohammedans, a threatening cloud on the political horizon.

England was the first country to become a compact nationality. The Wars of the Roses (1455-1495) had ruined the feudal lords of England, so the following kings, Henry VII (1485-1509) and Henry VIII (1509-1547), were free to rule as they pleased, although under parliamentary forms. This strong monarchical power naturally tended to curb the dominion of the universal Church and the pope. The English king had been the supreme head of the English Church ever since the time of William the Conqueror (1066); but the greatest respect was shown to the pope who was recognized as the head of the Church of England "insofar as the laws of the land permitted." A new estate, the commons, had had a voice in the English government ever since 1265 when the House of Commons was formed. The middle class constituted the main prop of the English throne during the Reformation period.

In France the Hundred Years' War (1338-1453) had practically ruined the French nobility, during which the royal power had been consolidated. The few feudal lords still retaining their power were crushed by Louis XI (1461-1483). His son, Charles VIII (1483-1498), planned to make France instead of Germany the head of the Holy Roman Empire. Succeeding kings, especially

[1] See diagram on page 46.

Francis I (1515-1547), had a similar ambition. The strong royal government was supported by the commons who had had representatives in the National Assembly ever since 1302. In 1516, Francis I and Pope Leo X made an agreement known as the Concordat of Bologna, which made the king the virtual head of the church organization in France.

Spain had for several centuries been under Mohammedan domination, but from the northwestern corner of the peninsula a few Christian chiefs had gradually pushed the invaders back until the Moors were finally driven out of the country in 1492. The marriage

EUROPE ON THE ACCESSION OF THE EMPEROR, CHARLES V, 1519 A. D.

of Ferdinand of Aragon and Isabella of Castile brought two rival principalities into a union which laid the basis for the Spanish monarchy. Portugal remained an independent kingdom until 1580. Spain was rising to its era of glory through expansion and consolidation at home and by means of a rapid colonization which started with geographical discoveries. King Ferdinand died in 1515 and was succeeded by his grandson, Charles I of Spain. Charles inherited not only all the Spanish possessions of Ferdinand, but also the crowns of Austria and Burgundy. In 1519 he was elected emperor of the Holy Roman Empire. Henceforth he was known as Emperor Charles V, the man who played such a prominent role in affairs during the Protestant Reformation. In 1478 the Inquisition was established in Spain for the purpose of suppressing heretics, especially Moors and Jews. The severities of the Inquisition plus the despotic rule of King Ferdinand brought on a series of revolts which lasted from 1504 to 1522, when Charles V inaugurated a reign of personal despotism. These Spanish troubles prevented the Emperor from giving the desired attention to the Lutheran Reformation in Germany. The consolidation of the kingly power had naturally prompted the formation of a national Spanish Church. Ferdinand and Isabella desired not only to reform the church, but also to bring the church under the submission of the State, or the crown. They practically forced such an agreement, or Concordat, with the pope in 1482.

Germany had a political organization similar to the American union under the Articles of Confederation. Ever since the German Carolingian line had become extinct, the great nobles of the kingdom had assumed the right to elect their king; and from the coronation of Otto the Great in 962 the chosen king also had a right to the crown of Italy and to the imperial title.[2] By the close of the Hohenstaufen period (1138-1254), Germany was divided into about three hundred virtually independent states, but seven of the leading princes had usurped the right to elect the king. These seven Electors, four of whom were secular and three of whom were prince-bishops, exercised a strong influence over Germany until the Holy Roman Empire was dissolved by Napoleon in 1806. From 1438 the imperial crown had become hereditary in the Austrian House of Hapsburg, although the Electors continued a formal function. Maximilian I (1493-1519) was the greatest medieval emperor of this line. He made great efforts to consolidate Germany, but the Electors refused to invest the emperor with greater authority. Maximilian I, in turn, divided his attention between the interests of the Empire and the interests of the House of Hapsburg. He married Mary of Burgundy, the sole heiress to the possessions of Charles the Bold. He arranged for the marriage of his son and daughter with the daughter and son of Ferdinand and Isabella. The son, Philip, died in 1506, leaving two sons, Charles and Ferdinand. Maximilian I arranged before he died to have Charles elected emperor, and he also negotiated a marriage for Ferdinand with Anne of Bohemia, the heiress to the crowns of Bohemia and Hungary. When Maximilian I died in 1519, he left for his two grandsons, Charles and Ferdinand, a vast dominion which included Austria, Tyrol, Styria, Carinthia, a part of Swabia, Holland, Brabant, Flanders, and the other Burgundian lands, Spain, and a hereditary claim upon the crown of Naples and Sicily. Although the pope was nominally the head of all the churches, consolidation in Germany promoted the formation of a national church under state control.

Italy by the middle of the fifteenth century was divided into five so-called Great States, the duchy of Milan, the two republics of Venice and Florence, the Church State, and the old kingdom of Naples. But inter-state jealousy and discord, plus the traditional struggle between papacy and the Empire, prevented the unification of Italy for three more centuries.

The great migrations in the ninth and tenth centuries had drained Scandinavia of some of the best elements of their population. Consequently, these northern countries did not play a prominent part in the history of medieval Europe. The Treaty of Calmar in 1397 had united the kingdoms of Norway, Sweden, and Denmark under one sovereign, the king of Denmark, but each country retained its own constitution and made its own laws. This union involved Finland, a Swedish dependency, and Iceland and Greenland, which belonged to Norway. The treaty was soon violated and jealousies, feuds, and wars soon disrupted the treaty. King Christian II made serious efforts to subdue rebellious Sweden, but he disgraced his victory by a massacre of Swedish notables in Stockholm in November, 1520. Gustaf (Erickson) Vasa raised the standard of revolt against Denmark and was acclaimed king of Sweden in 1523.

Russia had emerged as a really great power. Ivan the Great (1462-1505) had freed the country from the hateful Tartar domination. However, Russia belonged to the Greek Catholic Church, so it did not play any active part in the Reformation.

Turkey was the great Mohammedan power in Europe. Most of what is known as Turkey in Europe was conquered by Amurath I (1360-1389). The conquest of Europe was continued by Bajazet I (1347-1403) who vowed that his horse "should eat oats on the high altar of St. Peter's in Rome." His rapid advance spread the greatest alarm in central and western Europe. The kingdom of Hungary was destroyed between 1526 and 1529. For years the church bells of Germany called the people to pray against the coming Turks. In 1529 they laid siege to Vienna but were finally checked by the united efforts of the European princes. The Turkish menace occupied so much of the attention of Emperor Charles V and the Catholic princes that they were unable to concentrate their attacks on the Reformation movement.

From this brief survey it appears that consolidation and nationalism were everywhere in the ascendency. The increased power of the kings curbed the dominion of the pope by slowly depriving the universal Church of her governmental functions. On the eve of the Reformation the rising national States were demanding control of the church government.

This transition to government control of the Church did not, however, promote any reformation. The kings of England and France were not concerned with any church reform; but the formation of national churches curbed the power of the pope, and made his efforts to crush the Reformation less effective.

33. REVIEW QUESTIONS

1. Why is the birthday of the Reformation usually identified with the beginning of the Modern Period?
2. Why did the Teutonic-Latin civilization need so much time to reach majority?
3. What indications did European life give of a general transition to modern times?
4. Account for the differences produced by the Renaissance in Italy and in Northern Europe.
5. Why is the German Renaissance sometimes called a Reformation and sometimes a Revolution?
6. What relation do you see between the Reformation, the Epistle to the Romans, the Epistle to the Galatians, and the Apostolic Council in Jerusalem?
7. Compare or contrast the political development in England, France, and Spain.
8. Why had not Germany and Italy formed strong national governments at this time?
9. What was the political situation in Scandinavia, in Russia, in Turkey? Why did Russia not take any part in the Reformation?
10. How did the Mohammedan menace affect the Reformation?

TOPICS FOR SPECIAL STUDY

1. Origin and Characteristics of Western Civilization.
2. The supremacy of the Bible, the supremacy of faith, and the supremacy of the Christian people.
3. The rise of nationalism and its influence on the Reformation.

III. The Intellectual Ferment.—The Renaissance brought radical changes in the intellectual life of Christian Europe. The revival of the liberal culture of the classical era, new aspirations for free moral personality, the awakening of a critical and self-reliant spirit, new influences stimulated by the geographical discoveries, inventions, revived industry, trade, commerce, and banking,—all tended to shake off European medievalism.

In northern Europe the new humanism was rapidly diffused, primarily in the universities, but also in many of the secondary schools. The university of Paris became a center for Greek scholarship for two centuries. The universities of Vienna, Heidelberg, Erfurt, Tübingen, and Leipzig were among the first to introduce the new learning, while four new universities, Wittenberg (1502), Marburg (1527), Königsburg (1544), and Jena (1558) were established. In England the new learning was introduced at Oxford by Grocyn, Linacre, and Colet, and at Cambridge by Erasmus, who taught there for four years (1510-1514). John Colet reconstructed the cathedral school of St. Paul's in London in 1510; other secondary schools of England followed suit. The enthusiasm for the new learning led to a similar reconstruction of secondary schools in Germany, in the Low Countries, and in France, and to the establishment of new types of secondary schools wholly expressive of the new spirit.

Among the best known humanists were John Reuchlin (1455-1522), Desiderius Erasmus (1467-1536), John Colet (1467-1519), Sir Thomas More, author of "Utopia," and Philip Melanchthon (1497-1560). Emperor Maximilian I and King Henry VIII of England were also greatly interested in the new learning.

The introduction of the Renaissance in the North also awakened a new zeal for religious reform. The northern leaders turned back to the writings of the Church Fathers and to the original Greek and Hebrew Testaments for authority in religious matters, but the Church did not adopt an intelligent attitude toward these progressive tendencies. The pope and the cardinals were influenced by the Italian Renaissance which rather resulted in a paganization of religion. Hence the papacy and the Church of southern Europe suffered a distinct decline in morality at the time when the great religious revival took place in the northern lands. The official Church entrenched herself in the dogmatic, restrictive, and pedantic scheme of scholasticism, which position caused the great conflict with the modern scientific spirit of inquiry and reason. The humanistic campaign against ignorance, traditionalism, and exploitation, the demand for religious reform, and the insistence upon saner methods of historical research and Bible study, prepared Europe intellectually for the Reformation.

IV. The Economic Unrest.—*Land* was the economic basis of wealth, and the land was owned by the Church and by the nobility. One-third, perhaps nearly one-half, of all the land of

Germany was owned by the Church. The tillers of the soil, the serfs and the peasants, were subject to those who owned the land. Their annual income was hardly large enough to keep them and their families alive, and they had no freedom on the land they worked. Cutting down a tree without permission involved capital punishment, while hunting on the land they worked, or fishing in the brook that might·run through the farm, was strictly prohibited because the land did not belong to them.

Up to the thirteenth century there was no middle class in Europe. The clergy and the nobility constituted the upper class, and the serfs and the peasants formed the other. But the revival of industry, and commerce created a new Estate—the citizens, the freemen, the bourgeoisie, the burghers—forming the nucleus of the great general public of modern times. The members of this new class controlled the increasing trade through their well-organized arts-and-crafts guilds; but the chief offices of these guilds tended to become hereditary in a few families who later exerted a dominant control over the workmen. Increasing commerce caused cities to form trading confederations, such as the Hanseatic League of northern Germany. These great merchant companies, with their world trade and their enormous capital, soon superseded the local guilds. A capitalist order, consisting primarily of merchants and bankers, created a proletariat class within the cities, causing a great cleavage between rich and poor. The growing hatred between the rich merchant and the poor was intensified by ostentatious display of burgher wealth, by luxurious living, and by corrupt morals.

The tillers of the soil and the laborers in the cities made moderate demands for rights and just treatment, but their petitions usually went unheeded. The result was a strong undercurrent of restlessness and discontent among the lower classes of society. Taxes had become an almost unbearable burden; and besides the money paid for the support of the local government a stream of gold was drawn into the papal treasury for the use of unworthy pontiffs. The priests exacted tithes of all the income of the peasants; and demanded money for all their services such as baptism, marriage, confession, extreme unction, and burial. Even the forgiveness of sins could be bought for money, in direct·contradiction to the words of Scripture that man is redeemed, not with silver and gold, but with the precious blood of Jesus Christ.

Increasing dissatisfaction with the existing order caused peasants in various lands to start insurrectionary movements, and there were many such in the northern countries from the time of the English uprising in 1389 to the Peasant War in Germany in 1525. However, all peasant revolts, generally local and badly organized and poorly financed, were suppressed by the princes amid terrible carnage. During these uprisings the general watchwords were, "down with the priests!" and "down with the lords!"

Sale of indulgences had been revived by Pope Leo X (1513-1521) to finance the building of the church of St. Peter in Rome. Vast sums of money were collected for the papal treasury in all lands. This coincided with a feeling of nationalism and a demand for religious reform in the northern countries. Many civil rulers watched this shameless exploitation with growing impatience, for they themselves needed larger revenues for the maintenance of their standing armies and for other public purposes. The economic situation prepared for the secession from Rome. Consider the successful appeal of Luther "To the Nobility of the German Nation" in 1520 and the subsequent political development in northern Germany.

V. Social and Religious Conditions.—The age was *religious*, not *materialistic*. There had awakened a new religious zeal which was evidenced (1) by an almost feverish anxiety to gain a work-righteousness through all sorts of mechanical performances such as the recital of Ave Maria and Pater Noster, alms-giving, confession to the priest, and pilgrimages; (2) by an increase in mystical religion, or rather by a growing interest in the inner life of the spirit; (3) by an increasing alienation of the lower classes from an oppressive Church; (4) by a growing scepticism of the Humanists toward certain doctrines and practices of the Church; (5) by various attempts to bring about a religious reformation.

1. Much of the piety of the age was turned outward. The people were eager to build and to decorate churches. Practically every village had its chapel, and every town of fair size had several churches. The city of Cologne with its 50,000 inhabitants had 11 great churches, 19 parishes, 22 monasteries, 12 hospitals, and 76 convents. Nürnberg with its 30,000 citizens had 15 churches and 12 monasteries. These religious institutions received numerous gifts from the rich and the poor alike.

Such institutions were the centers for religious activities. An astonishingly large number of masses were said in the various churches. In the city of Cologne more than a thousand masses were said every day at the church altars. There was a revival of preaching such as the medieval Church had never witnessed, but the preaching contained very little of the Gospel message. Religious externalism expressed itself in all sorts of scenic display, including an extraordinary wealth of form and an indescribable fullness of church ceremonial, elaborate church festivals, magnificent processions, and Passion and Miracle plays. Bookkeepers kept careful record of the number of Ave Marias and Pater Nosters said in a day and in a year. In Germany every seventeenth person belonged to some religious order.

Belief in the miraculous power of relics was universal. Ever since the seventh General Council, held in 787, the bishops were forbidden under penalty of excommunication to consecrate new churches which possessed no relics. Buying and collecting relics had become a popular mania. Frederick the Wise, who later became a friend and a protector of Luther, possessed more than 5,000 relics, including among others the hair and bones of departed saints, Aaron's rod, bits of the burning bush which Moses viewed, and two jugs of wine from the wedding in Cana.

Remorse and fear drove thousands of people on pilgrimages. People travelled to Rome and to other celebrated places as a means of soothing troubled consciences. In the year 1300 more than 200,000 pilgrims visited Rome because the pope had promised all penitents who visited the churches of the apostles that year absolution from all their sins. Such jubilees were later declared every twenty-fifth year. In 1450 about 1,000,000 pilgrims visited Rome in one week. By way of contrast, it is interesting to note that in the year 1900 the "Eternal City" had only about 500,000 visitors in a whole year.

These recurring jubilees, one of the most striking features of the religious life of the later Middle Ages, were intimately connected with the Catholic doctrine of penance and the practice of indulgences. Penance, which had been an established *institution* in the Church since the Ante-Nicene Age, had consisted of four practices: (1) contrition of the heart; (2) auricular confession to the priest wherein all sins known must be confessed; (3) satisfaction or penance, which consisted of outward works as prescribed by the Church, including alms, fasts, pilgrimages, and fines; (4) absolution or the forgiveness of sins pronounced by the priest in the name of God. The satisfactions were the external signs of sorrow for sin demanded of the penitent by the congregation or by the priest as a condition of absolution and re-admission to the Church. During the seventh century it became a general practice to commute satisfactions of penances by substituting pecuniary

Lutheran	Reformed	Anglican	Catholic
1483, November 10 Birth of Martin Luther	1484, January 1 Birth of Ulrich Zwingli	1485-1509 Reign of Henry VII	
			1492 Columbus discovered America 1493-1519 Emperor Maximilian I
	1509, July 10 Birth of John Calvin	1509-1547 Reign of Henry VIII	
1512 Luther becomes Doctor 1517 Luther's 95 Theses			
	1519 Zwingli's protest against indulgence preached by Sampson		1519-1556 Emperor Charles V
1521 Diet of Worms	1522 Zwingli's breach with Rome		
1525 Peasants' War	1525 Mass abolished by Zwingli		
1530 Diet of Augsburg	1531 Death of Zwingli 1536-1538 Calvin's first stay at Geneva 1541 Calvin's return to Geneva		1545-1563 Council of Trent
1546 Death of Luther Schmalkald War 1555 Peace of Augsburg		1547-1553 Reign of Edward VI 1553-1558 Reign of Queen Mary 1558-1603 Reign of Queen Elizabeth	1556-1564 Emperor Ferdinand I
	1564 Death of Calvin		1564-1576 Emperor Maximilian II 1576-1612 Emperor Rudolph II
1580 Book of Concord			

compensation for punishment of religious offences, which was the origin of the indulgences.

At the beginning of the thirteenth century when the institution of penance was changed into a *sacrament*, the order was changed so that the absolution followed immediately upon the confession, with the satisfaction last. The penance or satisfaction was no longer an outward manifestation of sorrow and the necessary precedent of the forgiveness of sins, but it came to have a new meaning, which throws light on the practice of indulgences at the time of the Reformation. In the absolution that followed the auricular confession to the priest, God, it was thought, forgave the *guilt* of the sins confessed and the *eternal* punishment. But the sinner had to bear the *temporal* punishment either in this life or in purgatory, as heaven could not be entered until this punishment had been endured. The people, therefore, naturally wanted to know how they could get remission of temporal punishment for sins, due either in this life or in purgatory, and it was here that the idea of indulgences came in. An indulgence was the remission of that temporal punishment which remained due on account of sin after its guilt had been forgiven. It was granted on condition of penitence and the performance of prescribed good works such as alms, prayers, fasts, pilgrimages, but more often by payment of money to the Church.

This practice of indulgences, which pervaded the whole penitential system of the later medieval Church, was based in part on the theory of a treasury of merits. Christ and the saints, it was thought, had earned an unlimited treasury of merits which was at the disposal of the Church. Out of this treasury the Church could bestow merits to anyone who met certain prescribed requirements much in the same fashion as money can be drawn and credited or given by check.

The practical value of indulgences consisted in the remission of penalties that were due after a person had received the absolution. But at the time of Martin Luther the popular idea prevailed that indulgences procured the *forgiveness of sins* as well as the remission of penalties. Sale of indulgences tended, therefore, to lead the people away from true repentance.

2. There was a widespread evangelical faith among the simple, pious, medieval Christians. Consider the influence of the Lollards, the Hussites, the Brethren of the Common Life, the wide circulation of the Bible and devotional literature, and the evangelical preaching and teaching of the reform parties.

The attitude toward the spiritual world which characterized these groups is usually called *mysticism*. The Mystics emphasized contemplation, emotions, direct vision, and religious intuition as immediate avenues of approach to God. The priest and the rites of the Church were utilized as aids to the spiritual life, but they were not regarded as necessary intermediaries. Mystic religion was less a matter of intellect than of heart and feeling; it was not so much a knowledge of God as a life communion with him through self-denial. The Mystic desired to be lost *in* God rather than to be saved *through* Jesus Christ.

Mysticism helped to pave the way for the Reformation in several ways. The intensely religious devotion acted as a wholesome check on the prevailing religious formalism and officialism. The genuine sorrow of the Mystics for the decay of the Church spread to the masses, and this sentiment led to a longing for a reformation.

3. Because of oppressive taxes and religious abuses the lower classes were gradually alienated from the Church. The many peasant uprisings were directed against the Church as well as against the nobility. When Luther started the Reformation the peasants hailed him as their friend and liberator.

4. The knowledge of the earliest sources of Christian truth and history led the Humanists to see the great contrast between the early and the contemporary Church in doctrine and practice. They openly criticized the prevailing religious corruption, and tried to bring about reform. Erasmus thought a reform could best be effected by acquainting the public with the earliest forms of Christianity. Hence his publication of the Greek New Testament and the Latin editions of the Church Fathers. This going back to the first principles of Christianity prepared the people to accept Scripture as the supreme authority in matters of faith and life.

5. Many attempts had been made before the time of Martin Luther to bring about a religious reformation, but the Church had absolutely refused to be reformed. Meanwhile some of the best minds of northern Europe had come to see that the Church had become the embodiment of a religious world-view which was *false*. The great reformers primarily did not break with the Catholic Church because it was corrupt in life and practice, but rather because the Church steadily refused to base its doctrines and its religious life entirely on the principles of Holy Scripture. The Catholic Church refused to accept the three great Reformation principles: (a) Holy Scriptures as the sole normal authority for faith and life, (b) justification by faith alone without any merits of good works, and (c) the priesthood of all believers. The

Reformation had to come, therefore, in opposition to Rome, and this finally led to the great secession, to Protestants and Catholics.

34. REVIEW QUESTIONS

1. What general changes did the Renaissance effect in the intellectual life of northern Europe?
2. Through what agencies was the new humanism diffused among the people of the North?
3. Why did the new humanistic studies develop religious fervor in England and in Germany instead of the patriotic fervor of the scholars of Italy?
4. How do you account for the serious economic unrest just before the Reformation?
5. In what ways did the economic situation prepare for the secession from Rome?
6. Why do you think the age was religious rather than materialistic?
7. How do you connect the stress on work-righteousness with the general religious world-view?
8. Explain carefully the practice of indulgences. Did this practice prevail toward the close of the Apostolic Era? Why not?
9. What is meant by mystic religion? How did Mysticism pave the way for the Reformation?
10. What general attitude did the lower classes of people take toward the existing Church and toward Martin Luther? Why?
11. Why was the Protestant Reformation essentially a revolution against a certain religious world-view?
12. How do you explain the fact that the Church refused to be reformed?

TOPICS FOR SPECIAL STUDY

1. The influence of Desiderius Erasmus.
2. The influence of John Reuchlin, the Humanist.
3. John Colet and Sir Thomas More as promoters of the new learning in England.
4. The interest of Maximilian I, Henry VIII, and Francis I, in the new learning.
5. Peasant revolts in Europe between 1389 and 1525.
6. The condition of the world in 1500 compared with the time of Christ.

A SELECTED BIBLIOGRAPHY FOR CHAPTER IX

1. Rowe: *History of the Christian People*, Pages 241-250.
2. *Cambridge Modern History*, Volume I, Chapters XVII-XIX.
3. Lindsay: *A History of the Reformation*, Volume I, Pages 1-188.
4. Gasquet: *The Eve of the Reformation*.
5. Smith: *The Age of the Reformation*, Chapters I-II.
6. Hulme: *The Renaissance and the Reformation*.
7. Hyma: *The Christian Renaissance*.
8. Schaff: *History of the Christian Church*, Volume VI, Pages 1-15.
9. Thompson: *The Middle Ages, 800-1500*, Vol. II.
10. Deansley: *A History of the Medieval Church, 590-1500*.
11. Lagarde: *The Latin Church in the Middle Ages*.
12. Pullan: *From Justinian to Luther*.
13. Coulton: *Life of the Middle Ages*.
14. Workman: *Christian Thought to the Reformation*.
15. Emerton: *The Beginnings of Modern Europe*.
16. Mackinnon: *History of Modern Liberty*.

CHAPTER X

Luther and the Reformation down to 1530

I. Luther's Youth and Training.—When Martin Luther appeared as a reformer, there had been for two centuries an increasing criticism of the Church. The demand for reform was general and of long standing. The Protestant Reformation was peculiarly favored by a timely convergence of forces as to time, place, persons, circumstances, and religious and political relations. Yet this favorable environment did not produce the Reformation. Luther worked out his own position (by himself), regardless of previous rebellions and repeated refusals of reform. The origin and the genius of the Reformation must be sought not in a favorable environment, but in the *personal experiences* of Martin Luther of the truth of the Gospel and in the growth of his religious convictions based upon the Word of God.

Martin Luther was born November 10, 1483, at Eisleben in what is now Prussian Saxony (a bronze tablet on his grave has 1482, while Melanchthon would have it 1484). According to prevailing custom he was baptized on the next day and named Martin after that day's saint.

His parents were Hans Luder (Ludher, Lüder, Leuder, Lothar) and wife Margaret, born Ziegler. They had recently moved from their ancestral home at Möhra in Thüringia, and six months after Luther's birth they settled at Mansfeld, a rich mining town several miles distant from Eisleben. Hans Luther was a farmer's son, and Margaret came from a burgher family in Eisenach. They are described by contemporaries as of small stature with rugged features and of a "brownish hue." Martin Luther was proud of his ancestors. He said on one occasion: "I am a farmer's son; my father, grandfather, and ancestors were all real farmers."

The father of the great reformer was self-reliant, enterprising, and energetic. He possessed a boldness which was characteristic of the Luther family, and a vigorous humor. In Mansfeld he soon acquired a respectable official position. The mother of Martin Luther was a hard-working, faithful, but strict woman who did not have time to be happy. She was pious but superstitious and taught her children not only to pray to God and to "the dear

Saints," but also to fear and shun all the diabolical spirits which the people of that age believed in almost more than they believed in God.

From his parents Martin Luther received hereditary traits that were of great value to him in his work. The vigorous peasant nature, the powerful physical and mental energies, helped him to survive the abuses of the monastic life and the titanic work connected with the Reformation. He also inherited that fearless, fight-

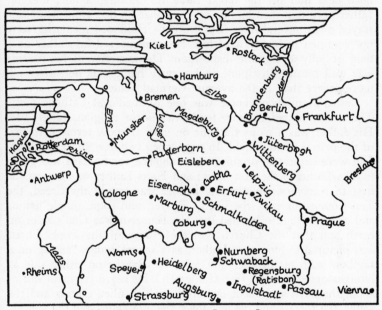

MAP ILLUSTRATING THE LIFE OF LUTHER

ing spirit, that vigorous humor, and that rustic rudeness which marked his ancestors. He possessed a love for hard work, a determination of will, and a peculiar common-sense conservatism. His intimate knowledge of the language of the common people, his close contact with nature and with the people of the lower classes, his knowledge of the popular religious life, and his thorough education made him a man of the people in the best sense. The German people recognized him as one of their own; they listened to him and loved him as few German leaders have ever been loved.

Luther's childhood home was austere and exacting. His parents encountered many difficulties in Mansfeld before they finally attained to economic independence. To begin with there was grinding poverty in the household. Luther himself once said, "my father was a poor hewer (i.e. miner), the mother carried all her wood upon her back, so that she might warm and rear us; their life was one of severe toil and extreme privation; at the present day, people would not hold out long in the midst of such suffering." The children shared in these privations. They were also frequently subjected to the immoderate severity of the parents. Luther's mother once beat him till the blood came for stealing a nut; and his father once punished him so severely that he fled from home and stayed away several days. But Luther's childhood memories were not confined to bodily hardship. He remembered his father as a man of jolly and gentle disposition. The austerity of his parents was well meant. Discipline in his early home was not, after all, more severe than in the average German home.

Luther's childhood home was one of medieval Catholic piety. There were no reformatory tendencies in the religious family life. His father was a pious Catholic on very friendly terms with two of the priests of Mansfeld. In 1497 when two new altars in Mansfeld were dedicated, promise of indulgence for 60 days was given to all who heard the first mass; and Hans Luther was among the first to receive an indulgence. Luther was taught the Creed, the Ten Commandments, the Lord's Prayer, and some simple hymns and chants. He also learned that the Emperor was God's ruler on earth and that the Church was the House of the Pope. Christ was pictured to him, says Luther, as a severe Judge, "sitting on a rainbow with his Mother and John the Baptist on either side as intercessors against his frightful wrath." He heard frightful stories about the devil and about evil spirits which filled the air and the water, the forests and the meadows, the mountains and the valleys, and did a lot of harm to the people and to their cattle. Even more dangerous were the witches whose secret power over the people could accomplish terrible things. He knew of some miners and old women who practiced sorcery. He saw the many groups of pilgrims who came through Mansfeld. All these things made strong impressions upon the sensitive mind of young Luther.

He received his elementary education in the village school of Mansfeld which he attended from the age of six or seven to fourteen. At school he was taught reading, writing, religion, and the elements of Latin. The school discipline was very severe. Luther was whipped fifteen times in one forenoon without sufficient cause. The magistracy of the village demanded that the school children should go to church and that the choirmaster should teach them to sing. All the school boys had to attend the church festivals where the impressive ceremonies and especially the singing made lasting impressions upon the young minds. The people of Mansfeld were good Catholics who honored the pope, attended the church services, believed in the Saints and in relics, and bought indulgences. Luther grew up in this pious environment.

The severe discipline at home and in school and the strict legalism of the Catholic religion as taught implanted in Luther a feeling of religious *uncertainty* and *fear*. God was not presented to him as a loving Father but as a terrifying, unapproachable Being; Christ was not a merciful Savior but a threatening and severe Judge. Salvation was to be gained through the mediation of saints and of the Church and by good works. These impressions and views were common. But Luther did not stop here. His deeply religious and somewhat introspective nature, his passion for the absolute, and his invincible urge to examine the very essence of his own religious life separated him from his contemporaries and gradually led him to work out his own position. He was painfully conscious of his personal responsibility toward God and wanted to know presently if he would be saved or condemned.

By 1497 the economic condition of Hans Luther had improved to such an extent that he could send his son to a school in Magdeburg for one year. The teachers of that school belonged to the society called Brethren of the Common Life. Their stress upon practical Christianity coupled with mystical piety might have exerted a wholesome and formative influence upon the young student. Magdeburg was the seat of the archbishop of that region. The city had a beautiful cathedral and many churches and monasteries. Luther was greatly impressed with the ceremonies in the cathedral and with the great religious processions in the city. He also remembered seeing on the streets a young nobleman (prince of Anhalt) with a bag on his shoulders who had become a novice in the local Franciscan monastery. This man, who was thin because of excessive fasting and mortification of his body, walked about in penitent garb, begging. Luther wondered if this did not constitute the perfect Christian life.

The next three years (1498-1501) were spent at the St. George's School in Eisenach. Luther had some maternal relatives there, but they were evidently unable to help him financially. He contributed to his support by singing in the church choir and that gave him the privilege of singing on the streets, a form of scholarship in that age. For some time he was a ward in the home of Frau Ursula Cotta (born Schalbe), who took interest in him because of his singing and his fervent praying. In this pious home he came under the influence of the Renaissance in culture and refinement of manners. His connection with the Cotta home also gained him many friends among the Franciscan monks of the Schalbian Monastery, located at the foot of Wartburg near Eisenach. This intimate contact with people who devoted their whole lives to religious interests no doubt strengthened Luther's impression from Magdeburg that the monastic life was perhaps the ideal Christian life. At Eisenach he acquired a full knowledge of Latin, the principal qualification for entrance into the university.

From Eisenach he, at the age of 18 years, went to the University of Erfurt, the most celebrated institution of learning in Germany at that time. The enrollment was a little above 2,000. Luther distinguished himself as a university student. Melanchthon states that "the extraordinary talents of the young man were at that time the admiration of the whole University." His fellow students referred to him as "the learned philosopher" and as "the musician." He took his Bachelor of Arts degree already in 1502 and his Master of Arts degree in 1505. The degree of Master was usually bestowed with great solemnity. "What a glorious and exciting time we used to have of it," says Luther, "when they conferred the degree of Master and honored the recipients with a torchlight procession; I hold that no temporal worldly happiness was equal to that."

As a university student Luther was a good, pious Catholic. He continued to observe his daily religious devotions by beginning every day with prayer and by going to early mass. *To pray well is half the study,* was his motto. The wealthy city of Erfurt had an abundance of churches, chapels, monasteries, and relics. Possession of a supposed *drop of blood* from Christ added special glory to Erfurt and drew thousands of people to the city. The Festival of the Holy Blood was celebrated with great pomp in the Church of St. Mary, and at this time indulgences were granted. During this celebration none but the church bells of St. Mary's would chime. Not only were all the other bells silenced, but all religious services in the other city churches ceased. Since Luther took part in the many religious festivals of that period, he must also have helped to celebrate a special festival held in Erfurt in 1502. A papal representative had come to the city to proclaim a Papal Jubilee, which included sale of indulgences. This man was taken into the city and through the streets of Erfurt by a magnificent procession in which the city officials, the university rector, the professors, and the entire student body took a leading part. The students were fond of hearing Sebastian Weinman, a powerful preacher who sharply rebuked the prevailing vices. Luther listened to him and to the other preachers in Erfurt but said later that he had never heard one truly evangelical sermon from any pulpit of that city. It seems reasonably certain, therefore, that the general religious environment in Erfurt did not bring Luther in contact with any reformatory tendencies.

Any specific reformatory tendencies were also conspicuously lacking in the University of Erfurt. This institution of learning had been among the foremost in Germany to introduce the new learning, and the Humanistic influence had created a general desire for a more liberal intellectual culture and an aspiration for improvement in the affairs of the Church; but there existed a close and strict alliance between Church and University, and each professor had to swear to teach nothing contrary to the doctrines of the Roman Church. No one dared to depart from tradition and no one ventured to strike out into any independent course. There was, as in all humanistic circles, much severe criticism of prevailing vices and corruptions, but this criticism did not lead any one to the Gospel way to God and to salvation.

Luther took a complete course of philosophy at Erfurt, but he also found time to study the classics and some natural science. His university friends knew him as "a gay, merry, young fellow." He applied himself with characteristic energy to his studies, but his deeply pious nature would frequently turn his thoughts from the abstract, speculative realm to the practical and religious. He was conscious, not only of the austere requirements of God, but also of his own small offences in thought, word, and deed. One of his fellow students relates that Luther would frequently say as he washed his hands, "the more we wash ourselves, the more unclean we become." Luther was not guilty of any peculiar sins, but as he took inventory of his own religious life, his conscience told him that many seemingly unimportant things were transgressions against God's holy law. How could he get a clean heart?

During the summer semester in 1505 he began to study for the profession of law at the University of Erfurt, but the religious problem evidently became more and more acute for him. His friend Melanchthon relates that Luther's agony of fear at times left him almost physically and mentally exhausted. All his efforts to find peace with God were seemingly of no avail. Several external events seem to have increased his religious tension. (1) His casual acquaintance with the Bible in the university library may have helped him to see some of the differences between the Word of the New Testament and the practices of the contemporary Church. (2) During his early student days at Erfurt he accidentally cut one of his arteries and was in grave danger of bleeding to death twice in 24 hours. This event awakened in him thoughts of dying. (3) Similar thoughts came to him during a serious attack of sickness somewhat later. (4) A friend of Luther named Lang became a monk. (5) The sudden death of another friend, Hieronymous Buntz, made a profound impression upon him. (6) A pestilence which at that time raged in and around Erfurt turned his thoughts toward the future life and the destiny of man. (7) The study of law did not appeal to him, and he is quoted as saying: "show me a lawyer who loves the truth." (8) His Damascus hour came on July 2, 1505, as he returned alone from Mansfeld to Erfurt. Near the village of Stotterheim, Luther was caught in a terrible thunderstorm, and he became so frightened by a sudden crash of lightning that he fell to earth and tremblingly exclaimed, "Help me, holy Saint Anna, I will become a monk!" Saint Anna, the supposed mother of the Virgin Mary, was the patron Saint of the miners.[1]

There is no record that Luther had for some time previous to this event thought seriously of becoming a monk. A timely convergence of forces had prepared him for this great decision, but he later declared that his monastic vow was made involuntarily and unexpectedly and partly because of the terror of death. His many friends had the impression that he had been subject to a sudden catastrophe. A university friend named Crotus Rubeanus said in 1519 about Luther's experience that "a heavenly light had thrown him to the ground like a second Paul." Another friend, Justus Jonas, expressed himself in similar terms. When the remark was made to Hans Luther at the banquet after Luther's first mass, that he had become a monk admonished by a heavenly vision, he replied: "Just so it was not a trick of the devil." It seems evident, therefore, that "a revelation from heaven" (Erscheinung vom Himmel), "a heavenly call," was the deciding factor for Luther. Many years later he stated that he had become a monk "by compulsion." His friends advised him against going to the monastery, since his vow had not been made after due and sober consideration,

---

[1] The story that a fellow student "Alexis" was killed by that lightning must be consigned to the class of "legends" as Luther calls such later inventions.

and for a very brief period Luther himself "regretted" his vow. But on July 16, 1505, he said good-bye to his friends, and on the following day they accompanied him to the gates of the Augustinian monastery at Erfurt. Luther became a monk and "was entirely dead to the world, as long as it seemed good to God."

The future Reformer had had his Damascus hour. Like Paul of old he had seen a heavenly light and had heard a heavenly call; and as the Apostle had been "three days without sight, and did neither eat nor drink" (Acts 9:9), but prayed fervently (Acts 9:11), so Luther had to spend three years, 1505-1508, in the monastery at Erfurt before he saw the first rays of spiritual light and experienced the dawn of a new day.

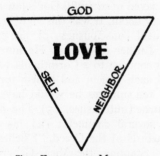

THE ESSENCE OF MORALITY
(As Luther understood it)

In the gigantic spiritual struggles of Luther, 1505-1508, five factors are easily distinguished. (1) He had entered the monastery in order that he might live a life that was pleasing to God. Hence Luther's main concern was to gain divine approval. (2) This led to the problem of sin, which became the central concern in the spiritual struggles of Luther. He came to the conclusion that his essential sin was a lack of love toward God and toward his fellow men, and he also discovered that even his "good works" were tainted with this sin. Like Paul of Old he exclaimed, "Wretched man[2] that I am! who shall deliver me out of the body of this death?" (3) But according to the theology of Occam[3] and of Gabriel Biel, and even of Bernhard of Clairveaux (cf. also the Pharisaic views of Paul before his conversion), man was

[2] Rom. 7:24.
[3] Man must, according to this view, first do his part (meritum congrui), then God will reward him by "grace" (divine power) and later by "infused love."

capable of giving to God what man *willed* to give. Luther had been trained in the doctrines of Occam and of Biel, and consequently he thought that his particular trouble was that he did not *want* to give up sin. He painfully realized that he was utterly incapable of proper repentance, and that he could not of himself produce the unselfish love which God required of every righteous person. (4) Seeing that he utterly failed to attain to a valid righteousness, he turned to another phase of Occam's theology, the doctrine of predestination. Why did not God do His part and give him the due reward, namely love? He came to believe that the motive for the divine redemption of mankind must be sought in God's *will* and not in God's *love*. He believed, during these years of struggle, that God had selected some to be lost and some to be saved, and that those who were saved *must* fulfill God's law and the ordinances of the Church in every detail. It was this view of God and religion, coupled with a painful consciousness of his own shortcomings, which almost drove Luther to despair. He himself has described these experiences, in contrast to 2 Corinthians 12:2, by saying that at times he suffered such violent and hellish tortures that if they had lasted even for ten minutes he would have perished and his limbs would have turned into ashes. (5) The dawn of day came to Luther through several channels: (a) his novice-master reminded him of the words of the Creed, "I believe the forgiveness of sins;" (b) John Staupitz, the Vicar-General of the Augustinians in Germany, intensely encouraged Luther to read the Bible, and he gradually turned Luther's attention away from the works of the law to a gracious[4] Savior; (c) in 1508 he began to study the writings of St. Augustine,[5] and paid special attention to Augustine's views on *sin* and *grace*. Faint rays of the Gospel light began to penetrate his troubled soul. For three years, 1505-1508, he had groped about in spiritual darkness, while at the same time he had lived the monastic life with more thoroughness than any other known person of his time. His experimental knowledge of divine truth told him that man *can not* be justified by good works, but he did not as yet see the full meaning of the statement in Romans 1:17, "the righteous shall live by faith."

After Luther had finished the customary probation period in the Augustinian Monastery at Erfurt, he became consecrated monk, evidently in September, 1506. He had been assigned a cell in the

---

[4] His advice was: "first find yourself in the wounds of Christ, and God's predestination will give you the greatest comfort."
[5] See pages 125-26.

monastery which could not be heated. It was a small room, six by nine feet, with a bed, a chair, a window facing the cemetery, and a door which could not be locked from the inside because the cell should always be open for inspection. The following year he was consecrated priest, and on May 2, 1507, he read his first mass in "fear and trembling" because a single mistake either in word or in movement constituted a mortal sin. In 1508 he was called to teach at the University of Wittenberg where Staupitz was the Dean. Luther was at this time recognized as one of the most talented monks among the Augustinians in Germany. He was transferred to the Augustinian Monastery in Wittenberg where he was assigned a cell in the tower of the Black Monastery.[6] He lectured at the university and preached in a small chapel and also studied for the "Baccalaureus Biblicus" degree which he received in March, 1509. In the fall of 1509 he was recalled to teach at the University of Erfurt, and he remained there for three semesters. At Erfurt he took the second examination in theology, that of "Sententarius." He returned to Wittenberg where he passed his third examination which led to the "Baccalaureus Formatus" degree.

In the winter of 1510-1511, (October 1510-February 1511), he was sent to Rome on an important mission for the Augustinian order.[7] He stayed in Rome for about four weeks and during this time studied the religious life of the Holy City with the true devotion of a pilgrim. This visit was highly instructive. "No one," said he, "can believe the scandalous acts which are openly done, unless you have seen or heard them." Luther returned to Germany without having found the much desired satisfaction for his mind and soul. In a letter written some time after his return from Rome, he exclaims, "O my sin, sin, sin!" indicating that the religious struggle was still going on within.

Upon the return to Wittenberg he was sent by Staupitz to Erfurt to complete his training for the doctorate in theology.[8] On October 4, 1512, he passed the "Licentiate" examination, and two weeks later, on the 18th and the 19th, he passed the examination for the Doctor biblicus degree. Three weeks later he succeeded Staupitz as Professor in Theology in the University of Wittenberg, a position he held until his death in 1546.

[6] The monastery really was red, but the monks in the same wore a black cloak.

[7] Luther was sent by his Erfurt brethren as a representative of the seven monasteries that opposed the plan of Staupitz to merge the two factions of the non-observant and observant Augustinians.

[8] Staupitz planned to resign and wanted Luther as his successor as professor of exegesis.

35. REVIEW QUESTIONS

1. Why must the origin and the genius of the Reformation be sought in the personal experiences of Luther, rather than in the favorable circumstances?
2. How did heredity help Luther in his great work as a Reformer?
3. Describe the childhood of Luther as to home life and training. How did he differ religiously from his contemporaries?
4. In what ways did Luther's training at Magdeburg and at Eisenach prepare him for his life work?
5. What impressions did you get of Luther as a university student at Erfurt?
6. Why did not Luther during his academic training come in more direct contact with reformatory or revolutionary tendencies?
7. Why did Luther suddenly become a monk?
8. Compare the religious experiences of Luther and the Apostle Paul. Can you explain why Luther had to go through such terrible struggles?
9. Who was the Ananias (cf. Acts Chap. 9) who brought Luther help?
10. Why was Luther permanently removed to Wittenberg?
11. Why, when, and for what purpose did Luther visit Rome?
12. How did Luther's visit to Rome influence his future work?
13. At what time did Luther become a Doctor and a Professor of Theology at the University of Wittenberg? How long did he keep this position?

TOPICS FOR SPECIAL STUDY

1. What makes a great man: (1) is it primarily native ability, or (2) is it primarily favorable environment, or (3) is it a specific combination of native ability and environment?
2. Superstition in Luther's childhood community.
3. The early religious training of Luther.
4. The Schalbean Monastery at Wartburg, near Eisenach.
5. Luther as a university student at Erfurt.
6. Luther's spiritual struggles, 1505-1512.
7. Legends concerning Luther.
8. Origin of Wittenberg University and its history before 1508.
9. Chronology of Luther's Life, 1483-1512.

II. **Luther's Development from 1512-1517.**—It was the duty of Luther as a Doctor of *biblicus* to lecture at the university on books of the Bible. He lectured on the Psalms in 1513-15, on Romans in 1515-16, on Galatians in 1516-17, and on Hebrews in 1517-18. In 1512 he was appointed Sub-Prior of the Augustinian monastery at Wittenberg; he was already the appointed preacher for that monastery. In 1515 he was made District Vicar over the eleven Augustinian monasteries in Meissen and Thüringia, a position which involved considerable correspondence and travel. That same year he was also requested by the city council to assist the sickly priest, Simon Heinz (brother of chancellor Brueck) at the city church, in preaching and hearing confessions, and by 1516 he had become so popular as a preacher that the people demanded to hear him once every day. He became equally popular as a professor. Students from all parts of Germany came to hear him, and even grave burghers of Wittenberg matriculated as students in order to hear his lectures.

Why did Luther become so popular? Consider the following reasons: (1) "He was the first German professor who, in the academic lecture room made use of his mother-tongue" (Ficker) to explain technical terms. He was truly a man of. the people. (2) He had become famous as a great scholar who based his lectures on the Greek and Hebrew text of the Bible, and not on the traditional scholastic theology. (3) Luther was more than a great teacher; he was a prophet; and his constant appeal to the Bible made his lectures and his sermons remarkably original and refreshing. (4) He simplified the religious language (from the scholastic to the mystic terminology) and laid it much closer to the common people. (5) But the main reason for Luther's power and influence must be sought in his heroic faith; he gave them the bread of life instead of the straw of philosophy and legend.

When did Luther first clearly understand the Biblical doctrine of Justification by Faith as set forth in Romans and Galatians? Luther himself declares that he did not know the light at the time he became a Doctor of Theology in 1512. But it is evident, from his lectures on the Psalms, that he had experienced this new revelation by the time he started these lectures. In his preparation for his lectures on the Psalms he constantly turned to Romans for help and, illumined by the Holy Spirit, he saw the prophetic word in Romans 1:17 in the same light as Paul himself had seen it,[9] and like Paul he made justification by faith the fundamental principle of the Christian life.[10] Luther had for many years tried to take the Kingdom of Heaven "by force,"[11] like Jacob of Old he had "striven with God;"[12] and now a word from Scripture brought him the solution. The Bible had done for him what Staupitz, Bernhard of Clairveaux, St. Augustine, and others could not do. No wonder, therefore, that Luther came to consider the Bible as the only source and standard for faith and life. In this momentous revelation which Luther experienced in the tower of the Black Monastery at Wittenberg during the winter of 1512-13, the birth of the Lutheran Reformation took place. And in the light of this experience of Luther the following Reformation principles may be understood: (1) Man is justified by faith alone

[9] Rom. 3:25.
[10] Luther realized that "justification" did not mean (a) the righteousness which God has; (b) nor the righteousness of life by God's aid (i.e. sanctification); but (c) the righteousness which God gives us in Christ and which we grasp by faith.
[11] Matt. 11:13.　　　　　[12] Gen. 32:28.

and not by works. (2) Consequently, there is a general priesthood of all believers; that is, God is accessible to every Christian without the mediation of a priest or of the Church. (3) The Bible is the only source and standard for faith and life. (4) The Bible must be interpreted by the aid of the Holy Spirit.

Luther's discovery of the Biblical doctrine of salvation did not immediately cause him to break with Rome. He was still a good, pious Catholic who did not feel himself in opposition to the system of doctrine of the Church, and he attacked as yet only the evils and the abuses which were not sanctioned by the Catholic Church herself. Four additional years, 1513-17, were required before Luther had matured as a reformer, and during these years he adjusted himself to the evangelical system of salvation by ridding himself of certain strong traditional influences, including (1) the papal authority in so far as this was contrary to Scripture, (2) the theology of Occam, especially the doctrine of predestination unto damnation, and (3) the idea that monastic piety and good life gained special favor with God.

Four main factors influenced Luther's theological development during the years 1513-17, namely (1) Occam's School of Theology, (2) the writings of St. Augustine, (3) the epistles of the Apostle Paul, and (4) German mysticism. Occam's theology helped him to build his faith upon positive facts of revelation and to mistrust reason; but this same theology caused him much trouble by its strong accentuation of the will of God and the resulting doctrine of absolute predestination. In Luther's written lectures on Romans in 1515-16, it may be observed how the thoughts connected with this doctrine at times overwhelmed him and seemed to crush him to the ground; but these same lectures also reveal how he in the midst of such struggles invariably threw himself over on God's saving grace in Christ Jesus and rested there. His legalistic religion was replaced by a religion of grace, and he re-established that direct, personal relationship with God which had characterized the original Christian faith and life.[13]

His diligent study of the writings of Augustine and of Paul helped him to comprehend fully the Scriptural doctrines of human sin and of the righteousness of the law, and of the true righteousness of God. Luther was painfully conscious of the fact that the Humanists did not fully comprehend Paul's doctrine of salvation. By working out his own position and on the basis of his personal experiences he was able to discover how Paul had felt and thought

[13] See pages 66-69.

—something the Church of the Middle Ages had not been able to do. He based everything on the promises of God in the Gospel (Word and Sacraments).

The last important factor in Luther's long development as a reformer was his ability to acquire *full certainty of God's grace and his salvation.* The Roman Church of the Middle Ages had never been able to give to its adherents that certainty.[14] The believers could only *hope* to be saved. Luther himself had up to this time thought that certainty of his own salvation would lead to abominable pride or to false assurance, but through the study of Paul and through the influence of the German mystics, he came to realize that it was the privilege of every Christian to have the blessed assurance of salvation in the Gospel message. What a happy discovery! Without this assurance Paul could never have become the great Apostle to the Gentiles, and Luther could never have become the great Reformer and the giant of faith.

A brief summary of Luther's religious convictions in 1517 may be of interest. Consider the following: (1) Man is justified or saved by faith in Christ without any merits of good works. Justification is a single act of God, following conversion and preceding sanctification, while justification according to the Catholic Church is a gradual process conditioned by faith and good works. (2) Every Christian has a direct access to God through faith in Jesus Christ. Personal communion with God and the forgiveness of sins are not conditioned by the *mediation of a priest,* but by faith in Christ only. Hence there is a general priesthood of all believers. (3) The Bible is the sole normal authority for faith and life. Tradition has value only in so far as it is based on Scripture. (4) God asserts His actual and full presence in the Holy Ghost. The Bible can not be understood from human speculation but must be interpreted, by the illumination and aid of the Holy Spirit, from the context according to the laws of language. (5) The essence of God is love. Religion is not based on a legal contract between God and man, but on God's gift of grace, or God's love to the sinner. This grace is free for all and may be accepted and enjoyed by all of faith. Consequently, there is no absolute predestination. (6) It is the blessed privilege of every Christian to have full certainty of his or her personal salvation in Christ Jesus.

Luther had been led, step by step, to an experimental knowledge of the basic Christian principles. The Renaissance appeal to

[14] Council of Trent, Canon 13.

the sources had led him to re-discover the Apostolic Christianity in all its purity and effervescence. No wonder that he held the attention of most of Germany even in 1517. But Luther had as yet no thought of separating himself from the Church of Rome. He called the Bohemians who had renounced the church "wretched heretics." He still believed in the divine origin and the divine right of papacy, the episcopacy, the priesthood, and the infallibility of the Church. He was "loaded" with reformation ideas, but he attacked as yet only the abuses which the Church herself did not sanction.

After this survey of Luther's life and activity it becomes evident that by 1517 he had been fully prepared for his great reformation work. The law of the Spirit of Life[15] had truly made him a free man. Like the great apostle he could say, "I know him whom I have believed."[16] His preaching and his teaching were with authority, coupled with great personal conviction that he was now a true witness of Christ. In April, 1517, he published 151 theses on justification. In September, 1517, he published 97 theses, "Contra scholasticam theologicam," for the purpose of improving the curriculum and the methods of study[17] at the University of Wittenberg. But the Lutheran Reformation dates from October 31, 1517, when Luther nailed his 95 theses against the sale of indulgences to a door of the Castle Church in Wittenberg.

III. Luther's 95 Theses to the Diet of Worms, 1517-21.— Pope Julius II (1503-13) started the building of the magnificent church of St. Peter in Rome in 1506, but the work was interrupted and threatened with failure for lack of funds. Pope Leo X (1513-21) tried to raise the necessary means for the completion of the church building by proclaiming a general sale of indulgences.[18] England, France, and Spain refused to be taxed in this manner, but Germany under Maximilian I yielded to the papal demands. The pope divided Germany into three districts and appointed Albert of Brandenburg, the archbishop of Mainz and of Magdeburg, as chief manager of one district which included Albert's own provinces. His chief salesman was John Tetzel, a Dominican Monk, who travelled from place to place and offered the papal indulgences for sale.

Indulgence salesmen were usually received with dignified solemnity. An eye-witness has described Tetzel's entry into a

---

[15] Rom. 8:2.   [16] 2 Tim. 1:12.
[17] Luther named it "the Wittenberg Theology."
[18] The contract made through the pope's banker, Fugger in Augsburg, was that first of all the immense debt of Albert for the pallium fees should be paid by crediting him with 50% of the net receipts, and 50% was to be credited to the pope.

certain city in the following words: "When the Commissary or
Indulgence-seller approached the town, the Bull (proclaiming the
Indulgence) was carried before him on a cloth of velvet and gold,
and all the priests and monks, the town council, the schoolmasters
and their scholars, and all the men and women went out to meet
him with banners and candles and songs, forming a great procession; then all the bells ringing and all the organs playing, they
accompanied him to the principal church; a red cross was set up
in the midst of the church, and the Pope's banner was displayed;
in short, one might think they were receiving God Himself"
(Lindsay). In front of the cross was placed a large iron chest to
receive the money, and then the people were induced in various
ways, by sermons, hymns, processions, bulletins, to buy indulgences.
Tetzel would frequently say,

> "Sobald der Pfennig im Kasten klingt,
> Die Seel' aus dem Fegfeuer springt."[19]

Freely translated this means, "as soon as the money (gold) tinkles
in the chest, the soul springs out of purgatory," or in couplet,

> "Soon as the groschen in the casket rings,
> The troubled soul from purgatory springs."

The theory and practice of Indulgences at the time of Luther have
been briefly explained in Chapter IX, Section 5.

Frederick the Wise, Elector of Saxony, did not permit Tetzel
to enter his territory for fear that too much money might be ex-
ported without real return, and since it was collected by the rival
house of Brandenburg. Hence Tetzel set up his trade at Jüterbock
on the border of Saxony and only a few miles from Wittenberg.
When many of Luther's own parishioners bought indulgences, in
spite of his repeated warnings, he could not help protesting against
this ungodly and soul-destroying method of gathering money.
As Christ had expelled the profane traffickers from the court of
the Temple, so Luther now wanted to rid the Church of this
profane and degrading practice of selling indulgences. On October 31, 1517, he nailed, in strict conformity with academic
etiquette, 95 theses to a door of the Castle Church in Wittenberg
as a basis for an academic debate which he, when his turn came,
would have to conduct. On the same day he sent a copy of the
95 theses and a letter to Archbishop Albert, and in a sermon to the
townspeople Luther called attention to his theses. This was the

---

[19] Also quoted as follows: "Sobald das Geld im Kasten klingt,
Die Seel aus dem Fegfeuer in den Himmel springt."

beginning of the Protestant Reformation. The resulting struggles which ended with a complete rupture with Rome may be discussed in connection with the following topics: (1) Luther summoned before the General Chapter of the Augustinian Order, at Heidelberg, April-May, 1518. (2) Luther before Cajetan at the Diet of Augsburg, October, 1518. (3) The Leipzig Disputation, June-July, 1519. (4) The second heresy-trial and the Bull of Excommunication, January-June, 1519. (5) Luther's answer: the three famous Reformation treatises, August-November, 1519, and the burning of the papal bull in December, 1519. (6) Luther at the Diet of Worms, 1521.

1. Luther's 95 Theses received an immediate and widespread publicity. The opponents stamped his views as Bohemian poison, as Hussite heresy. Luther answered by explaining his Theses in popular language in a "Sermon on Indulgences and Grace," and the demand for this writing was so great it went through 12 editions before the end of that year. The opponents tried to have Luther's monastic order silence him. He was summoned before the General Chapter of the Order at Heidelberg in April, 1518. In the debate which was arranged between Luther and the Dominican monks of Heidelberg, Luther defended his position with such eloquence and learning that his own Order placed itself on his side, and he won many influential friends, such as Bucer, Brenz, and Schnepf; but Luther resigned all offices he held in the order. On May 15 he returned to Wittenberg and prepared the remarkable "Resolutions" in which he attacked the authority of the pope and demanded a church reform.

2. A regular action of inquisition was now started against Luther. The pope ordered Luther to appear in Rome within sixty days, and Cardinal Cajetan was ordered to get Luther into his power. But the eagerness to crush this dangerous monk caused the pope to declare Luther—scarcely sixteen days later—to be a heretic who was placed under papal ban unless he recanted. Additional papal orders demanded that Luther's adherents be captured, and that the places which cherished him be put under interdict. But the political situation immediately forced the pope to be more lenient. At the Diet of Augsburg in the summer of 1518, Charles I of Spain had been proposed as a candidate for emperor by Maximilian I, and this was entirely against the political interests of the pope. Elector Frederick the Wise did not favor the candidacy of Charles I, and the pope tried to win this Elector over to his side. Hence he yielded to the demand that Luther be tried in

Germany and ordered him to appear before Cardinal Cajetan at the Diet of Augsburg. Cajetan pointblank demanded that Luther should recant his heresies without any argument and that he should place himself in absolute submission to the pope. Luther refused by declaring that he could do nothing against his conscience. On the night of October 20, he escaped from the city on horseback. He then appealed his case to a General Church Council, after he had in due form appealed his case to the pope for a fair hearing.

3. The pope decided to delay the proceedings against Luther because of the delicate political situation in Germany.[20] Meanwhile he sent his nuncio and chamberlain, Charles von Miltitz, to Frederick the Wise for the purpose of winning him for the papal political policies. Miltitz had a cordial meeting with Luther in January, 1519, and Luther promised to refrain from controversy provided that his opponents remained silent. But then John Eck, a professor at the University of Leipzig, challenged Professor Carlstadt, and indirectly Luther, to a debate. The disputation was held at Leipzig June-July, 1519. Carlstadt could not hold his ground against the skillful Eck, and Luther soon took his place. The superiority of Luther over Eck was apparent, but Eck finally forced Luther to admit that General Councils could err and that not all of the Hussite doctrines were heretic. Eck replied: "If you believe that a general council, legitimately convoked, can err, you are to me a heathen and a publican." He then hastened to Rome to secure a bull[21] of excommunication against Luther. A rupture with Rome seemed unavoidable. Luther had gained a tremendous popularity. He kept three printing shops busy printing his manuscripts. The German Humanists, headed by Erasmus, allied themselves for the time being with Luther's cause, and the popular German literature also took his side.

4. It was now high time for Rome to crush Luther. A second heresy-process was started against him in January, 1520. But Luther's opponents found it difficult to formulate his heresies. Statements from theologians of the universities of Cologne and Louvain, an elaborate treatise by Eck, a personal visit of Eck to Rome, three different Commissions of the foremost theologians of the Curia, and four consistories of the Cardinals were necessary before acceptable formulations could be made. The Bull of Ex-

[20] Emperor Maximilian had died, the election of a new emperor was imminent, and Frederick the Wise was administrator of the empire, so he must not be offended. The pope sent von Miltitz with the order of a golden rose to Frederick.
[21] The old leaden seals of the official papal documents resembled bubbles. Hence the name *bull* from the Latin word for *bubble* or *knob*.

communication was signed by the pope on June 15, 1520. Luther was declared a heretic, his writings were ordered burned, and he himself was threatened with the ban unless he recanted within sixty days. On the third day of January, 1521, Luther was excommunicated and the places where he labored were placed under interdict. But before this could happen, Luther had already severed his relations with Rome by burning the papal bull on December 10, 1520.

5. When Luther was informed as to how the trial was carried on against him in Rome, he wrote a treatise which was published in August under the title, "To the Christian Nobility of the German Nation." It was a summons to Germany to unite against Rome, and a platform for a reformation of the life in church and state. In October, 1520, he published a second treatise, "On the Babylonian Captivity of the Church," in which he attacked certain doctrines of the Roman Church. In response to a request by the Augustinian Order that Luther make a final attempt to effect a peaceful settlement with Rome, he published *The Liberty of a Christian Man*[22] in November, 1520. This treatise emphasized the priesthood of all believers. A copy was sent to the pope. Meanwhile a copy of the Bull of Excommunication had reached Wittenberg. Luther did the wisest thing he could do. He burned the bull and the papal books of law, as mentioned above.

6. On January 28, 1521, Charles V, the new emperor, opened his first Diet at Worms. Frederick the Wise demanded that Luther be given a fair hearing at this Diet, and he finally persuaded the emperor to have Luther appear in person before the assembly. On his way to Worms Luther was reminded of the fate of Huss, but Luther replied: "Huss has been burned, but not the truth with him. I will go on, though as many devils were aiming at me as there are tiles on the roof." He arrived in Worms on April 16, 1521, and on the following day he was called before the Diet. Frederick the Wise had advised Luther to mark time and to seek to delay the final answer. Consequently, he asked permission to postpone answering the questions put to him, and he was granted 24 hours. The next day, April 18, 1521, was the greatest day in Luther's life. Standing before the most powerful and influential assembly in the world at that time, he gave a well prepared speech which made an indelible impression upon the audience. When finally asked if he would recant he answered: "Unless I am

[22] For a possible influence of this writing on the American Declaration of Independence, see Chap. XXII, Section II.

refuted and convicted by testimonies of the Scriptures or by clear arguments . . . I cannot and will not recant anything, since it is unsafe and dangerous to do anything against the conscience." With Scripture in hand Luther had defied the entire Roman Catholic Church and the Holy Roman Empire of the German Nation. The pope had already excommunicated Luther. The emperor and the Diet of Worms put Luther under the ban[28] of the Empire, May 26, 1521, commanding his surrender to the government at the expiration of his safe-conduct, and forbidding all to shelter him or to read his writings.

36. REVIEW QUESTIONS

1. Why had Luther to assume so many official duties?
2. How do you account for his popularity as a preacher and as a teacher?
3. When did Luther fully understand the Biblical doctrine of justification by faith?
4. Why did not Luther contemplate any break with Rome? Why did the rupture come?
5. What factors influenced Luther's religious development, 1512-17?
6. Give a brief summary of Luther's religious convictions in 1517. How do these compare with the views of the Christian Leaders in the Apostolic Era?
7. What event marks the beginning of the Lutheran Reformation? Why?
8. Explain the theory and practice of the sale of indulgences.
9. How did Luther's discussion at Heidelberg help the Reformation cause?
10. In what ways did the political situation in Germany favor the Lutheran Reformation?
11. How do you think the disputation at Leipzig in 1519 influenced Luther personally?
12. How did Luther anticipate and respond to the papal bull?
13. Why did Frederick the Wise want Luther to appear in person before the Diet of Worms, 1521?
14. How do you account for the fact that Luther, in his endeavors to bring the Church back to the simpler ideals and practices of Christianity, was excommunicated by the pope and placed under the ban of the Empire by the emperor?
15. Did Luther receive a fair trial? Explain.
16. Was the ban against Luther technically correct and valid?
17. Why was Luther's appeal to a general church council disregarded?

TOPICS FOR SPECIAL STUDY

1. Luther, the teacher and the preacher.
2. "Justification" as defined by Luther and by the Roman Catholic Church.
3. Luther's idea of predestination in his former and latter years.
4. Luther's experience as to certainty of salvation.
5. The origin of indulgences and their abuses in Luther's time.
6. The trial of Luther.
7. A synopsis of the three pamphlets of 1520.
8. St. Peter's Cathedral: its predecessor, architect, execution, and completion.

[28] See page 200.

9. Luther's 95 theses.
10. Luther excommunicated and put under the ban of the empire.

IV. From the Diet of Worms to the Peasant's War, 1521-25.—Luther had endeavored, in the most critical moment of his life, to promote the growing Evangelical movement in three ways: (1) by appealing to the Word of God as the final religious authority; (2) by requesting a trial before a General Council; and (3) by appealing to the dictates of a conscience bound by the Holy Scriptures. Papacy and the Holy Roman Empire—the two supposed arms of God in governing the world—had answered by making Luther a legal outlaw whose life was to be taken and whose books were to be burned.

He left Worms on April 26, 1521, and a few days later he was secreted by friends in the Wartburg Castle near Eisenach where he was kept in seclusion for ten months. During this time he dressed in the garb of a knight and took the name of Squire George. At Wartburg he produced some of his most important literary works. He explained the new Evangelical movement and gave it a more definite form. Luther had no thought of founding a new church. He wanted to reform the existing church by bringing it back to the fundamental ideals and practices of the church of the New Testament times. His most important works at Wartburg included the treatise "On Monastic Vows," in which he urged all priests, monks, and nuns to leave the monastic life and to marry; his "Epistle and Gospel Postil," completed at Wittenberg, and written as a help for pastors; and his translation of the New Testament which appeared in print in September, 1522. A translation of the Old Testament followed in four parts, the last being published in 1532.

Luther's Bible translation was epoch-making. The previous German Bible translations were based on the partially corrupted Latin text. Luther based his New Testament translation on the original Greek text, published by Erasmus in 1516, and his Old Testament translation was based on the original Hebrew text. His intimate knowledge of the spoken, written, and printed language of his people enabled Luther to make the Oriental thoughts and illustrations of the Bible understood by the German mind. He gave Germany a unified language, the modern High German. His numerous German writings, especially his German Bible, his Small Catechism, and his hymns, exerted a singular and unique influence on the development of the German tongue.

At Wittenberg a number of friends carried on the work of the Reformation during Luther's absence. Melanchthon[24] formulated the fundamental conceptions and doctrines of the Bible in a work called "Loci communes rerum theologicarum," wherein he laid the foundation for the Dogmatics of the Evangelical Church. But the Reformation was also endangered by the destructive zeal of men who tried to turn the reformation into a revolution. Luther's old colleague, Carlstadt, took the leadership from Melanchthon and began to institute a social reform in Wittenberg that bordered on communism. He advocated that all the ceremonies and usages of the medieval religious life be abolished in order that the new evangelical liberty might be fully exercised. He bitterly attacked the monastic vows, celibacy, the use of a distinctive dress for the clergy, the use of pictures and images in churches, the withholding of the cup from the laity in the Lord's Supper, the Confessional, and the Mass. Carlstadt was ably seconded by Gabriel Zwilling, an Augustinian monk who preached in the cloister church in Wittenberg. He maintained that the communicants should partake of the Lord's Supper in groups of twelve, in imitation of the twelve apostles. Carlstadt and Zwilling expressed contempt for theology and human learning and effected the discontinuance of the city boys' school.

A more fanatical spirit began to manifest itself in the village of Zwikau, sixty-four miles south of Wittenberg. Three of the so-called Zwikau prophets, Nicholas Storch, Thomas Marx, and Marcus Stübner, were forced to leave the village. On December 27, 1521, they arrived at Wittenberg where they immediately began to proclaim their visions and revelations in a manner similar to that of the Montanists.[25] Infant baptism was denounced as an institution of Satan. They stirred up excitement which bred fanaticism. Disorders and riots increased daily and spread to other towns. Melanchthon and other sober-minded Lutherans were unable to check the tumults, so they eagerly pressed the return of Luther. Without official permission Luther returned to Wittenberg in March, 1522. After a careful study of the situation he preached in the city church for eight successive days and thereby made himself master of the situation. He made no personal references; he

[24] Luther described Melanchthon in these words: "I am rough, boisterous, stormy, and altogether war-like. I must remove the stumps, cut away the thistles and thorns, and clear the wild forests; but Master Philip comes along, softly and gently, sowing and watering with joy." But his desire to avoid strife made him too ready to compromise with Reformed and Catholic views. He was largely responsible for the doctrinal controversies within the Lutheran church in the sixteenth century.

[25] See pages 86-88.

blamed no individuals for the disorders; but he made it clear that the evangelical faith must be promoted and accepted without force or compulsion or revolution. "The Word created heaven and earth and all things; the same Word will also create now," said Luther. When order had been restored, he took up his former home in the monastery and resumed his monastic life, in order to live down the reproach of his enemies that he broke down all churchly order.

The Zwikau prophets came to Luther and proudly demanded that he recognize their higher spiritual authority. He describes a part of the interview in these words: "I have caught them even in open falsehoods, when they sought to escape by miserable, smooth words. I finally requested them to establish their doctrines by miracles, of which they boasted contrary to Scripture. They, however, declined, but boasted that I must some time believe them; whereupon I warned their God, not to work a miracle against the will of *my* God. Thus we separated."[26] They left Wittenberg for good after denouncing Luther as a new pope and as an enemy of true religion. Carlstadt submitted silently for the time being, but his feelings of revenge against Luther soon involved him in a religious controversy which resulted in his expulsion from Saxony.

Shortly after his return to Wittenberg, Luther gave a sharp answer to charges made against him by King Henry VIII of England. The latter had not only ordered Luther's books to be burned in England, but in 1521 he had also written a defence of the seven sacraments against Luther's "Babylonian Captivity of the Church." This controversy formed the prelude to Luther's break with Erasmus. Luther had for some time been impatient with Erasmus, likening him to a Moses who had led his people out of Egypt to die in the plains of Moab, never to enter the promised land. Erasmus, under obligation to Henry VIII for many favors, resented Luther's fierce reply to the English King. In 1524 he published an attack on Luther in the "Freedom of the Will." Luther answered in his book "On the Will in Bondage." The breach between the two, Luther and Erasmus, was complete after Erasmus had published his second attack called "Hyperaspistes." This rupture also alienated Luther from the majority of the humanists.

Luther's new theory of individual judgment and individual responsibility called for a general education of all citizens. In his great reformation program he had substituted the religious authority of the Bible for the religious authority of the Church; he had substituted individual judgment in the interpretation of Scrip-

[26] Köstlin: *The Life of Martin Luther*, page 250.

tures and in formulating decisions for the collective judgment of the Church; and instead of collective or institutional responsibility for salvation he had substituted individual responsibility for salvation through personal faith in Jesus Christ. According to the older theory only a few needed to be educated, but according to Luther's theory education was necessary for all. Each person should be able to read and to study the Bible, participate intelligently in the church services, and take an intelligent part in the affairs of the state. In two pamphlets, "Letter to the Mayors and Aldermen of all the Cities of Germany in behalf of Christian Schools" (1524), and his "Sermon on the Duty of Sending Children to School" (1530), he set forth the ideas of freedom of judgment and personal responsibility and individual participation in religious and governmental matters and the consequent need for the education of all. Luther's educational ideas were put into practice by two of his colleagues, Philip Melanchthon, the formulating genius of the Reformation, and Johannes Bugenhagen, the organizer, who has been called the father of the German "Volksschule." Luther urged a German State School system to include vernacular primary schools for both sexes, Latin secondary schools, and universities.[27]

The rapid spread of Luther's teaching, and the consequent alienation of many communities, even entire regions from the Church of Rome, made it necessary for the Reformer to arrange an evangelical order of Divine Service, and to organize evangelical churches. He made no plans for the formal establishment of a new church, but simply urged "that the Word should have free course among Christians." The congregations were to be put in possession of the pure Word of God, and this simple Word would in turn transform the hearts and minds of men and would renovate society. Luther cherished the hope that the evangelical principles would gradually be adopted, not only by certain German provinces, but possibly also by the existing German episcopate.

In arranging the form of worship, Luther preserved historic continuity by retaining those ceremonies in the Catholic worship which he did not consider contrary to Scripture; but certain elements, such as the sacrifice of the mass and the thought of meritoriousness of church attendance, were definitely removed. Emphasis was shifted from the things that may be seen to the things that may be heard, from elaborate pompous ceremonies which appealed to the eye and to the emotions to evangelical preaching which appealed to the intellect and to personal faith. German

---

[27] Cubberley: *History of Education*, pages 313-14.

was substituted for Latin, and the sermon was substituted for the mass. The preaching of the Word of God became the central factor in the worship, while congregational singing of German church-hymns was made the second main factor because singing led the congregation to a more active participation in the service. Luther himself composed at least thirty-eight hymns, twenty-four of which were written in 1523-24. In 1524 a German hymnary containing thirty-two hymns was published by Luther. He also revised the Order of Baptism and the Solemnization of Marriage. The private Confessional was retained as an important means for doing pastoral work. The cup was given to the laity in the Lord's Supper. Catechetical instruction of the young was made a necessary part of the evangelical service. As Luther expressed it, "One of the principal

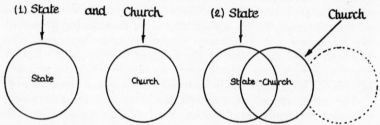

LUTHER'S CHURCH GOVERNMENT IN THEORY AND PRACTICE

parts of a right German order of worship is a plain and good instruction of the youth."

Luther had no intention of founding a new Church. His attitude is expressed in the Augsburg Confession, Article XXVIII, 77: "It is not our design to wrest the government from the bishops, but this one thing is asked, namely, that they allow the Gospel to be purely taught, and that they relax some few observances which cannot be kept without sin." But when the Church refused to make any concession, and the bishops, devoted to the pope, defended "godless doctrine and godless services" and "wrested the jurisdiction from pastors" and refused to ordain evangelical pastors, he saw valid reasons why the evangelical churches should not recognize bishops. The churches in the evangelically disposed communities had to be reorganized on a Scriptural basis. Luther drew a sharp distinction between secular and spiritual power. The Church must recognize the supremacy of the State in temporal affairs; the State must acknowledge the sovereignty of the Church in spiritual matters. But Luther's idea of the separation of Church and State was entirely too advanced for the time. The people were not capable of governing their own church affairs, and Luther's faith in the "common man" was somewhat shaken after the Peasant War. So Luther saw no other way but to place the Church under the general supervision of the State. As the central government in Germany was very weak, the control of the Church was actually placed in the hands of the evangelical princes and the evangelically disposed city-councils. State-control over the Lutheran Church in Germany was continued until the revolution in 1918. In Scandinavia state-control is still maintained.[28]

Division of Germany into Lutheran and Catholic camps could be distinctly noticed in 1524, although actual parting occurred later. By the Edict of Worms, 1521, the Reformation had been thrown into German politics. The Supporters of the old Church becoming alarmed at the rapid spread of Lutheranism, at the diets of Nürenberg in 1522-23 and 1524, representatives of pope and emperor urged the territorial princes to enforce the imperial edict. As a partial answer they received a list of one hundred grievances which Germany held against the Roman Curia. It was evident that even the regency of the empire had become decidedly favorable to the Reformation. The Catholic princes of South Germany decided, therefore, to form an alliance for the purpose of suppressing and excluding Lutheranism for their dominions. They also promised mutual help in their common danger. This Catholic alliance called forth a Lutheran party smaller, but more compact than the Catholic. The possibility of a civil war was eliminated at this time because (1) the Turks were threatening the eastern frontier of Europe; (2) because the emperor and the king of France were at war with one another between 1521 and 1528, and the emperor needed money and soldiers of the Lutherans; and (3) because the relations between pope and emperor were so strained that an imperial army even marched against Rome, in 1527, captured the pope, held him a prisoner for several months, and sacked Rome as it had rarely been sacked before.

Meanwhile, a social-economic revolution, the Peasant's War of 1524-25, broke out with unexpected force and violence. The peasants had long been suffering under heavy burdens laid upon

[28] The various systems of church government may be classified, as to form, as Papal, Patriarchal, Episcopal, Consistorial, Presbyterial, Congregational, Synodical, etc. There are three main systems with regard to the relation between Church and State, namely, the Church-State, the State-Church, and the Free-Church. In the Church-State system the Church is superior to the State; in the State-Church system the State dominates the Church; in the Free-Church system State and Church are reciprocally independent and mutually helpful.

them by their heartless masters, the secular nobles and the princely bishops who owned or controlled the land of Germany.[29] Drawing their own inferences from Luther's doctrine of Christian liberty, the peasants raised the banner of revolt against the territorial princes. They were spurred on by fanatic revolutionary preachers, especially by Thomas Münzer, but the underlying causes of the revolt were economic, not religious. The peasants stated their grievances in twelve articles, and also appealed to Luther. When these articles reached Luther at Wittenberg, he protested most emphatically against any kind of revolution. "Let every soul be in subjection to the higher powers: for there is no power but of God; and the powers that be are ordained of God."[30] The peasants must show respect for the constituted lawful authority, which in this case resided with the princes. The sword had been given by God to the civil government only, and for the purpose of punishing the evil-doers. There was no excuse for insurrection even when the government was wicked, and those who set themselves against the government would bring judgment upon themselves.[31] He made a distinction between religion and politics, between spiritual and temporal or civil affairs, and he told the peasants that their social-economic grievances had little or nothing to do with the Gospel. The demands stated in the twelve articles were moderate and reasonable, but if the peasants would try to get their requests granted by insurrection or by force of arms, he would tell the princes to put them down. On the other hand, Luther rebuked the princes and the bishops in frightful terms for their oppression of the common man and urged that they yield to demands for a re-adjustment, lest God should suffer the devil to stir up an insurrection against them. He finally advocated that the opposing parties should seek a peaceful settlement of the disputed matters by submitting to a committee of arbitration. But when he heard that the peasants had risen in open revolt, and had committed shocking outrages, he urged the princes to put them down without mercy because they defied the laws of God and the lawfully constituted authority. Between a hundred and a hundred and fifty thousand people lost their lives in the Peasant's War. Castles, convents, villages, and agricultural implements were destroyed, and several agricultural districts were turned into a wilderness.

The Peasant's War had a marked influence upon the Lutheran Reformation. Large numbers of peasants who had looked to Luther as a prophet of liberty now became indifferent or hostile to him.

[29] See pages 210-12, and 127-28.   [30] Rom. 13:1.   [31] Rom. 13:3.

Nevertheless, the Reformation gained its strongest support among the peasants *after* they had been defeated. Luther lost some of his faith in the "common man," in the ability of the masses to govern their own affairs, which prevented him from giving the evangelical churches a democratic organization. He relied upon the upper classes to take the lead in making reforms, and placed the Church under their supervision.

Luther continued to live in the Augustinean monastery at Wittenberg, although nearly all the monks had left by 1525. In 1524 he exchanged the monastic gown for a clerical robe given to him by his Elector. On June 13, 1525, he married Catherina von Bora, a poor ex-nun of noble birth. The old monastery was given to the couple as a home. Luther's marriage was an important public event because by this act he founded the evangelical parsonage.[32] His happy and beautiful family life became a model. His home became a center of intellectual and religious life and a generous Christian hospitality. Luther loved music and singing, poetry and fine arts, legends, fables, and proverbs. An attractive feature of his home life was his celebration of Christmas, when he would sit with his family to sing Christmas hymns, including his own.

> "Von Himmel hoch da komm ich her"
> (translated)
> "From heaven above to earth I come."

V. From the Peasant's War to the Diet of Augsburg, 1525-30.

—During the next five years, 1525-30, Western Christendom permanently divided into Protestant and Catholic groups. The Catholic alliance at Ratisbon in 1524 marked the definite beginning of the separation, and the Diet of Augsburg, 1530, marked the conclusion. The League of Ratisbon, which united the Catholics of the South German principalities, was soon followed by a similar alliance of the Catholics of North Germany known as the League of Dessau, 1525. But the most threatening alliance against the Reformation movement was the Treaty of Madrid, January, 1526, in which the emperor and King Francis I agreed to exterminate Lutheranism. The emperor sent an order to the German princes that they should make preparations for the enforcement of the Edict of Worms. In consequence of these threatening movements a number of princes who favored the Reformation entered into a

---

[33] Luther gave the New Testament in the vernacular to the congregations in 1522; he gave them an Evangical Order of Worship in 1523; in 1524 he gave them a hymn book; in 1525 he restored the Evangical parsonage; and in 1526 he began to send out visitors to the congregations.

defensive confederation known as the League of Torgau. The Reformation also benefited by "The Holy League" which Pope Clement VII formed with King Francis I, the Venetians, and the Duke of Milan against the Emperor, Charles V. The resulting war gave a temporary respite to the Lutherans. This change in the imperial policy concerning the Lutherans strengthened the Reformation cause to such an extent that the Lutheran minority at the imperial Diet of Spires in the Summer of 1526, almost succeeded in having the Edict of Worms abrogated. This Diet did, however, resolved unanimously that, until the meeting of a general Christian council, every State affected by the Edict of Worms should be allowed to control its own church and civil affairs as it might answer to God and his imperial majesty. An imperial decree of August 27, 1526, sanctioned this resolution.

The decision of the Diet of Spires in 1526 was a triumph for the territorial system as well as for the Reformation, and the Lutheran states and cities interpreting the resolution in their favor lost no time in organizing territorial churches, in reorganizing the public worship, and in establishing evangelical schools. The Elector John, who succeeded his brother Frederick the Wise in 1525, engaged Luther and Melanchthon to draw up a body of laws relating to the form of church government, the method of public worship, the revenues of the clergy, the education of the young, and similar matters. The resulting ordinances were established by law in the dominions of the Elector John in 1527, with other princes and states and cities of Germany following his example.

Jacob Sturm, a member of the city council of Strassburg, conceived the idea of uniting all the Evangelical groups in Germany and in Switzerland into a political alliance based on a common anti-Roman confession of faith. He was ably seconded by Martin Bucer, the Evangelical pastor of Strassburg. They succeeded in winning Landgrave Philip of Hesse, the ablest political leader of the German Reformation. Philip soon discovered that the Elector of Saxony would not join the proposed league without the consent of Luther, and Luther's consent could not be obtained except on the basis of doctrinal agreement. The Landgrave arranged, therefore, for a religious conference known as the Marburg Colloquy. At this conference, from October 30 to November 5, 1529, fifteen doctrinal points were presented. Luther, Zwingli, and the others agreed to the first fourteen points, but frankly stated their disagreement concerning the Real Presence of Christ in the Lord's

Supper. Zwingli taught that the words, "This *is* my body," must mean "This *signifies* my body," and that the same is essentially a token by which Christians may be known; while Luther held to the literal interpretation and maintained that the Sacrament is essentially an assurance of God to man that life and salvation has been prepared for him. Zwingli maintained that the Lord's Supper was a memorial feast only, and that the bread and the wine in the Supper were purely emblematic and symbolical. Luther insisted that God does not mock believers with empty signs. The communicants truly ate the body of Christ and drank his blood in the Lord's Supper.[33] He found Zwingli's theory unspiritual, unchurchly, and unscriptural. The conference between the two reformers failed. Luther parted with Zwingli saying, "You have a different spirit from us."[34]

Philip next tried to unite the Lutheran cities of South Germany with the Lutheran princes of the North. Luther drew up a confession consisting of seventeen articles, which were laid before an assembly of Lutherans in Swabach, October 1529. But the cities of Ulm and Strassburg refused to sign this confession because they rather favored Zwingli's doctrine. The attempts to unite Protestant Germany failed a second time. At the time when the Roman Catholics had gained their greatest strength, the Protestants split up into groups, with the Zwinglian and the Lutheran division kept up at the Diet of Augsburg in 1530. The cause of Luther was not to be based upon or fought by the sword of steel, but by the Word of God.

But emperor and pope came to an agreement in 1529, whereupon the Catholic party immediately revived its policy of repression. At the Diet of Spires in 1529 an imperial edict was read virtually forbidding all progress of the Reformation. The edict revoked the right of the princes to manage their church affairs. They were forbidden to introduce or tolerate any changes whatever in doctrine, discipline, and worship until a general Christian council could be held. The Edict of Worms was to be enforced; Catholics in Lutheran states were to have full religious liberty; and the Zwinglians

[33] Luther wrote in his book, *Of the Supper of ʿChrist*, published in 1528: "Similarly I also speak and confess of the Sacrament of the Altar, that therein the body and blood in the bread and wine are truly eaten and drunk orally, even if the priests who administer it or those who receive it, do not believe or otherwise misuse it; for it does not stand upon the belief or unbelief of men, but upon the Word and Ordinance of God." Compare the controversy between Augustine and Donatus (p. 123).

[34] This was true to a higher degree than Luther realized at that time. But he declared himself willing to continue the negotiations in the hope of reaching a full agreement in the future. He also offered an armistice. Zwingli on his part repudiated the agreement after his return to Switzerland and thereby made the division permanent.

and the Anabaptists were to be suppressed by force. The Evangelical members of the Diet presented a formal protest that the unanimous decision of the Diet of Spires in 1526 could not be rescinded by a majority vote in a second diet. From this protest, issued April 19, 1529, the Evangelical party received the name "Protestants."

But 1529 was not merely a year of Protestant separation. Luther published his two catechisms which, next to his Bible translation, constitute his most enduring and influential works. They have become symbolical standards of doctrine in the Lutheran Church. The *Large Catechism* begun first, was prepared for parents and teachers. The *Small Catechism*, intended chiefly for the instruction of children, has ever since been used as the foundation for instruction, especially before confirmation in all Lutheran churches. Both catechisms are gems of simple and lucid explanation. It has been said that the explanation of the Second Article of the Creed in the Small Catechism is the most comprehensive sentence in all literature.

The imperial Diet of Augsburg in 1530 had for its object to restore the unity of the Church and to prepare for war against the Turks. The emperor, needing the assistance of the Evangelical groups against the Turks, promised a fair hearing to all, inviting the Protestants to present in writing their views. Accordingly, the Protestants prepared three confessions. The Lutherans prepared the Augsburg Confession (Confessio Augustana), written by Melanchthon and approved by Luther. The Lutherans of Southern Germany under the leadership of Bucer, presented the Confessio Tetropolitana which was influenced by Zwinglian views. Zwingli presented a separate confession, thus separating himself permanently from the Lutherans. The emperor, however, refused to give the Zwinglians a hearing, and he likewise refused to accept the Confessio Tetrapolitana, although both confessions were later "refuted" by Catholic Theologians. The Augsburg Confession was read before the Diet on June 25 in the hall of the Episcopal Palace. This document consisted of twenty-eight articles, of which twenty-one clearly defined the tenets of the Lutherans, while seven pointed out the errors and abuses which had been abolished by the Lutherans. It was written in a conciliatory spirit and presented in the hope that it might be accepted as satisfactory by the emperor and the other Romanists, but this hope was not fulfilled. The Catholics presented a refutation known as the Confutation to the Diet. An attempt was then made to arrange a compromise through a committee of theologians, but the negotiations were unsuccessful. Melanchthon prepared an answer to the Confutation known as the Apology of the Augsburg Confession, a document about seven times longer than the Confession. The emperor refused to receive the Apology. The Diet voted that the Augsburg Confession had been refuted by the Confutation and that the Protestants were bound to recant. The old ecclesiastical institutions were to be restored, and if the Lutherans had not come into submission to the Catholic Church by April 15, 1531, they would be suppressed by force. This effected the Protestant-Romish schism.

Luther had brought a portion of the Christian Church back to the three great original principles of Christianity.[35] The Augsburg

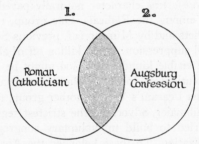

RELATION OF LUTHERANISM AND ROMAN CATHOLICISM

Confession is based on these principles which are in full harmony with the Old Christian Church.[36] "This is the sum of doctrine among us, in which can be seen nothing which is discrepant with Scripture, nor with the Catholic or even with the Roman Church, so far as that Church is known from the writings of the Fathers." Luther had simply demanded that the Roman Catholic Church should eliminate certain unscriptural doctrines and practices in order that he and his adherents might remain in the Romish Church and worship God according to the dictates of a conscience bound by the Word of God. But the Romish Church not only refused to be reformed, but even threatened to suppress Lutheranism by force. Consequently, the Catholics forced the schism as much as the Lutherans. The Lutherans did not form a new Church after the schism with Rome. They merely formed a continuation

[35] cf. page 204.   [36] cf. pages 67-69.

of the early Christian Church[37] as we know it from the New Testament and from the early Church Fathers. The Augsburg Confession[38] still remains the fundamental position of Lutherans in all lands.

Thus the years 1525-30 were years of separation, not only of Protestants and Catholics, but also of Lutherans and Catholic Humanists (Erasmus), of Lutherans and Zwinglians, and of Lutherans and Radicals.

The Radicals embraced a wide variety of religious opinions, but they had at least two common characteristics: (1) they rejected every form of Christianity connected with the State, and insisted on the strictest separation of church and state; and (2) they tried to promote a spiritual religion by proclaiming immediate, divine revelations which they frequently placed above the authority of the Bible. This *subjective* character naturally paved the way for several divisions among the Radicals. One group, represented by the Zwikau prophets and by Münzer (cf. previous Section), advocated the forceful suppression, or the killing off of all the ungodly, in order that the visible kingdom of God might be established on earth. This revolutionary form of Radicalism was temporarily crushed during the Peasant's War. Another group, represented by Carlstadt and Hübmaier, advocated the strictest segregation from the world and tried to build up voluntary congregations into a permanent organization. To these belonged the Anabaptists (also called Catabaptists, or Baptists) who rejected infant baptism. A third group, represented by Denck, Franck, and others, claimed that it was impossible to gather Christians into an outward, visible organization. Members of this group spiritualized the authority of the Bible and the value of the Sacraments. The freedom of the Spirit was the essential thing. But how could they recognize the voice of the Spirit? Here the adherents followed two[39] opposite directions: some listened to the voice of the Spirit through their *reason*, paving the way for religious rationalism; others identified the voice of the Spirit with extreme *mysticism*, which again paved the way for the later religious mysticism. Luther took a decided stand against these immoderate forms of spiritualism.

---

[37] See diagram on page 134.

[38] The Augsburg Confession has existed in two forms, the Unaltered *Invariata* of 1530 and the Altered *Variata* of 1540, both of them written by Melanchthon. The Invariata rejects synergism and teaches the Real Presence. In the Variata of 1540 Melanchthon, on his own accord, made several essential changes in order to compromise with Catholic and Reformed views. These alterations gave rise to many doctrinal controversies during the sixteenth century and since. Luther himself rebuked Melanchthon for tinkering with the confession. The Variata is not used as a Lutheran confessional basis.

[39] See diagram on page 328.

37. REVIEW QUESTIONS

1. In what ways did Luther's stay at Wartburg promote the interests of the Reformation?
2. What importance should be attached to Luther's German translation of the Bible?
3. Discuss the program of the Radicals at Wittenberg. Why was Luther so successful in restoring order?
4. How do you account for Luther's alienation from the Humanists?
5. Why did the Lutheran Reformation furnish such powerful incentive for the establishment of schools and the education of all citizens?
6. What changes did Luther make in the form of Christian worship? Why?
7. What principles did he follow in his organization of evangelical churches?
8. Discuss the causes and the progress of the Peasant's War. How did this war influence the progress of the Reformation?
9. Why did Luther plead for obedience to the constituted lawful authority? What about the Soviet government? What about the Roman government during the Christian persecutions?
10. How did the Diet of Spires in 1526 promote the progress of the Reformation?
11. Why did not the Evangelical groups form a defensive league?
12. Why are Luther's two catechisms listed among his most enduring works?
13. Why the Protestant-Romish schism in 1530?
14. Why did Luther take such a decided stand against the Radicals?

TOPICS FOR SPECIAL STUDY

1. Luther at Wartburg.
2. Carlstadt and the Zwikau prophets.
3. Melanchthon's incapacity as a leader.
4. Luther versus Henry VIII.
5. Luther's interest in public education.
6. Luther's attitude toward civil government.
7. Luther's view of the Lord's Supper.
8. The Augsburg Confession and its sources.
9. The relation of the Augsburg Confession to later Confessions.

A SELECTED BIBLIOGRAPHY FOR CHAPTER X

1. Sheel: *Martin Luther.*
2. Lindsay: *A History of the Reformation,* Vol. I, pages 189-368.
3. Smith: *The Age of the Reformation.*
4. Schaff: *History of the Christian Church,* Vol. VI, pages 97-555.
5. Ranke: *History of the Reformation in Germany.*
6. Smith: *Life of Erasmus.*
7. Köstlin: *Life of Luther.*
8. Richard: *Philip Melanchthon.*
9. McGiffert: *Protestant Thought before Kant.*
10. Reu: *Thirty-five Years of Luther Research.*
11. Boehmer: *Luther in the Light of Recent Research.*
12. Fife: *The Young Luther.*
13. Dau: *The Great Renunciation.*
14. Creighton: *History of Papacy during the Period of Reformation.*
15. Fisher: *History of the Reformation.*
16. Grisar: *Luther.* (3 Vols.—Catholic viewpoint.)
17. Holl: *Luther.* (5th ed.)
18. Mackinnon: *Luther and the Reformation.*
19. Kidd: *Documents Illustrative of the Continental Reformation.*
20. Dorner: *History of Protestant Theology, Particularly in Germany.*

CHAPTER XI

THE COMPLETION OF THE REFORMATION IN GERMANY AND IN SWITZERLAND, 1530-80

I. The Reformation of Zwingli at Zurich, 1519-31.—
While the Lutheran Reformation gained momentum in Germany, a similar movement started in Switzerland. The first leader of this movement was Ulrich Zwingli, who centered his activities in and around the city of Zurich. After his death in 1531 the Swiss Reformation was continued, completed, and made of world-wide significance through the activities of John Calvin at Geneva.

Ulrich Zwingli was born January 1, 1484, at Wildhaus, an obscure town in the district of Toggenburg, Switzerland. His father was the principal magistrate of Wildhaus, and his uncle was the local parish-priest. Zwingli was a bright-minded boy who eagerly embraced every opportunity to study and to cultivate his extraordinary talent for music. He was early distinguished for his clear and logical mind, his love of liberty and truth, and his esteem of the great pagans of antiquity. He was first educated in the schools at Basel and Bern, and later at the universities of Vienna and Basel, where he became a full-fledged Humanist. Receiving the degree of Master of Arts at the University of Basel, he was appointed parish-priest at Glarus in 1506.

For ten years, 1506-16, he served this large and wealthy parish, laboring incessantly for the moral uplift of his congregation. He also cultivated his love for letters by a diligent study of the Latin classics. In 1513, he began to study Greek in order that he might make a scientific study of the New Testament in the original. He also studied the writings of the early Church Fathers, although theology did not interest him as much as the humanities. During this period he became an outspoken *patriotic politician*, of great consequence in his future career. His experiences as field chaplain of the Swiss mercenaries at the battles of Pavia, Novaro, and Marignano made him keenly aware of the political and moral dangers lurking in the mercenary service and in the system of pensions whereby foreign princes secured the military support of the Swiss cantons. Zwingli's outspoken opposition to this service brought him so much trouble at Glarus that he accepted a subordinate vicarship at Einsiedeln.

Zwingli had by this time developed remarkable power as a preacher, and he had also become one of the foremost classical scholars in Switzerland. At Einsiedeln he matured as a Bible Humanist of the Erasmian type. He explained the teachings of the Apostle Paul in the light of Platonic or Stoic philosophy. While Luther centered his interest in Paul's doctrine of salvation, Zwingli concerned himself with the Pauline ethics. Religion was

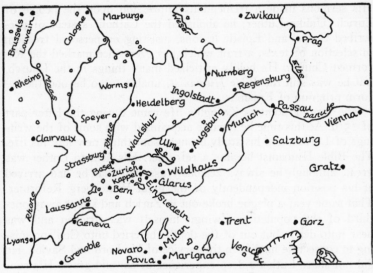

MAP ILLUSTRATING THE LIFE OF ZWINGLI

for Zwingli, as for Erasmus, a system of morals, a "philosophy of Christ." He combined a strong sense of moral responsibility with a peculiar laxity in private life. His moral conduct at Glarus and at Einsiedeln was not above reproach. Zwingli himself even spoke lightly of it. At Einsiedeln there was great opportunity for the "people's priest" to preach to large audiences. More than one hundred thousand pilgrims came annually to visit the shrine of the black image of the Virgin Mary. Miraculous virtues were attributed to this image, and over the entry to the shrine blazed the inscription, "Here the full forgiveness. of all sins may be obtained." Zwingli preached against these superstitious absurdities, and he also openly attacked Bernard Samson, who at this time offered indulgences for sale throughout Switzerland. But Zwingli was as yet a good Catholic with no thought of breaking away from the Church. He still hoped that the Church would abolish these abuses.

In December, 1518, he was elected to the position of chief pastor in the Great Minster Church at Zurich. Zwingli had by this time come to recognize the Bible as the absolute authority in matters of faith and life. He was also fully convinced that the Church needed a thorough moral reformation, and that the way to effect it was to place the Word of God in its entirety upon the candlestick. His sermons made a tremendous impression upon the people of Zurich. Unlike Luther, he abolished the Catholic system of pre-scribed Gospel and Epistle lessons, insisting on personal freedom in selection of texts, a trait which has ever since marked the Re-formed Church. He boldly criticized many things in the Church, but he was still the *Bible Humanist*, unable to go beyond the re-form program of Erasmus.

The turning-point in Zwingli's life came during the latter part of 1519. At this time he became acquainted with some of the writ-ings of Luther, and his study brought something new into his life. The Bible Humanist became a reformer. His debt to Luther was great, although he always zealously asserted that he had arrived at his position independently of the great Wittenberg Reformer. That same year a plague broke out in Zurich and swept away one-third of the population. Zwingli himself was stricken and was near unto death, but out of the depths he cried unto God[1] promis-ing to consecrate his life in the service of his Lord and Savior. He did not share Luther's deep experience of sin and grace. His con-version consisted of a clear and logical resignation to the will of God.

What qualifications did Zwingli have as a reformer? In spirit he was a thorough evangelical Protestant who subscribed to the three fundamental principles of the Reformation. But his temperament, training, and environment differed considerably from Luther's, which differences affected the life and work of the two reformers to the extent that the German and Swiss Protestants never fused into one great organization.

Both were born, baptized, confirmed, and educated as Roman Catholics, and both were consecrated to the Catholic priesthood They were as closely connected with the Catholic Church as the

[1] cf. Ps. 130:1.

apostles were with Judaism; both left the Catholic communion as the apostles left Judaism.

Both were of humble origin. Both possessed unusual physical and mental energies and a fearless, upright spirit. They were cheerful, and loved the society of their fellow-citizens. But Luther grew up in the rough and harsh surroundings of the peasants, while Zwingli was subjected to the influence of Humanism from his childhood. He was superior to Luther in refinement and manners and in tolerance, but inferior to him in originality and force, and in ability to inspire others.

Both loved poetry and music, and both were excellent scholars, great preachers, and heroic characters. Luther studied scholastic theology and passed through the severe discipline of monasticism. He experienced terrible spiritual conflicts because of a deep conviction of sin and the failure to attain to a satisfactory work-righteousness, before he accepted the Gospel as the power of God unto salvation. He finally had to wrestle with German mysticism before he fully matured as a reformer. Zwingli had little or no contact with these elements. He passed directly from the heathen classics to a scientific study of the Scriptures, combining the spirit of the Renaissance with the ideals of the Reformation. The Bible was to him the revelation of God's *will* for mankind and for the individual. He matured as a reformer because of a gradual intellectual process involving increased *insight* into the Gospel truth and a corresponding *volition* to use this knowledge for the betterment of the religious, social, and political conditions of his people.

The two reformers accepted the Word of God as the infallible rule of faith and practice, in opposition to the Catholic co-ordination of Scripture and church tradition. Both translated the Scriptures (Zwingli with the aid of Leo Judae) into their mother-tongues, to make the Bible the book of the people. But in their reform activities, the two men used the Bible quite differently. Luther, with a deep reverence for the past and deeply rooted in the Catholic faith, used the Bible as a corrective, retaining those rites and ceremonies of the Medieval Church which were not positively anti-scriptural. Hence he retained images, altars, ornaments of the churches, organs, church bells, and the like. Zwingli used the Bible as a *code of laws*, rejecting everything not expressly enjoined in Scripture. His rationalizing tendency caused him to reject everything which he thought smattered of mysticism and superstition.

Zwingli's rationalistic leanings caused him to give a purely spiritual interpretation to the rites and ceremonies retained in his church order. Luther held that the Divine Spirit operates only through the Word of God and the Sacraments, but Zwingli severed the influence of the Spirit from these Means of Grace and maintained an immediate operation of the Spirit upon the human heart.[2] He consequently claimed that the lofty ideas of heathen poets and philosophers were divinely inspired, and believed that the pious heathen were saved. Socrates, Seneca, Cato, and Hercules were included in his catalogue of saints. He regarded the Sacraments as commemorative signs only, until after 1529.*

Luther proceeded from the *subjective* or material principle, that is, from the doctrine of justification and salvation by faith, without human merit. Zwingli proceeded from the *objective* or formal principle, that is, that the Bible alone is the absolute authority in matters of life and faith, and must not be co-ordinated with or subordinated to church tradition. Luther consequently centered his whole interest on the religious aspect of the Reformation and would not permit its association with political issues. Zwingli felt that his mission had as much to do with politics as with religion so he aimed at a political as well as a spiritual regeneration. Zwingli approached the Gospel from the point of view of social reform, while Luther concerned himself with the soul's salvation. Luther maintained that the Church and the State were independent of each other and that religion should not be mixed with politics, while Zwingli effected the closest union of politics and religion and subordinated state to Church. Luther believed the sword was given to the State only and that it was wrong[3] to promote the interests of the Gospel by means of revolution or war, but Zwingli resorted to various political combinations and schemes in the interest of his reform work and even appealed to war as a means of promoting the cause of the Reformation. In reference to these matters it may be said that Luther lived in the spirit of the Sermon on the Mount, while Zwingli breathed the spirit of the Old Testament.

Zwingli's theology centered around God as the absolute *Will*, while Luther's theology centered around God as the absolute *Love*. Starting with the doctrine of God as Absolute Will, Zwingli concluded that God's decrees were absolute and that man's salvation was utterly dependent upon these decrees. Human merit and moral freedom had no standing whatever. God had from eternity *elected* certain individuals to eternal life and others to eternal death or

[2] See diagram on page 328.
* Cf. his Expositio Fidei (De Eucharistia) IV:51, 63, 64; Niemeyer Edition.
[3] cf. John 18:36.

damnation. Certainty of salvation was therefore to be sought in God's will and election, as revealed in love and mercy through Jesus Christ, and appropriated through the efficacious influence of the Holy Spirit. Luther emphasized the love and grace of God in Christ and the *objective efficiency* of the Means of Grace (the Word and the two Sacraments) in such a way that the doctrine of an absolute predestination would gradually be undermined.

Finally, the two Reformers differed in their explanations of original sin and guilt. Zwingli did not deny the terrible curse of the fall and the fact of original or hereditary sin, but he regarded this sin as a moral disease only, which of itself did not involve personal guilt. Luther taught that original sin did involve personal guilt, even in new-born children, and that infant baptism was necessary. Zwingli paid less attention than did Luther to personal evil, and he seemed to have but little thought of a personal devil.

Zwingli's work as a reformer began late in 1519 when he successfully opposed Bernard Samson and his scandalous sale of indulgences at Zurich. In 1520 he preached against the doctrine of purgatory, the intercession of saints, the system of tithes, fasting, and monasticism. He revised the Breviary (a prayer book) and made plans for a liturgy in the vernacular. That same year he persuaded the city council to issue an order that all the preachers should teach only what they could defend by Scripture.

The breach between Zwingli and the Roman Church came in 1522 in connection[4] with a controversy about fasts. In March, 1522, he preached a sermon in which he undertook to show that the prohibition of meat in Lent had no foundation in Scripture. Several of his followers made practical use of this liberty by eating meat and sausage during the Lenten season. The bishop of Constance prohibited such innovation, but Zwingli defended the new practice in a tract, published in April, 1522, which also included a discussion of the theory of good works and the authority of the Church. The Council of Zurich finally made a compromise decision in the matter by declaring that the New Testament imposed no fasts, but fasting in Lent was a very old custom which must not be abolished for the sake of good order. This resolution, which set aside episcopal authority, really constituted a revolt against the Roman Church. Zwingli's open break with Rome came with his publication of "Architeles" ("Beginning and End") in August, 1522, in which he rejected the Catholic co-ordination of Scripture and Tradition, and maintained that the Bible was the only infallible

[4] See chronology on page 212

authority which a Christian could accept. He also defied the authority of the Church by his secret marriage to Anna Reinhart in July, 1522. He made public this marriage in 1524.

These daring changes led Zwingli and the city of Zurich into conflict with the church authorities. The friends of the reform movement met·the issue by arranging for several public debates, the favorite method of that day. Zwingli prepared sixty-seven articles as the basis for the first disputation, held in the Town Hall of Zurich on January 29, 1523. These Theses, which contained the summary of his doctrinal teaching, were directed against the system of the Roman Church. The authority of the Gospel was substituted for the authority of the Church. He attacked the primacy of the pope, the worship of saints, the meritoriousness of good works, fasts, festivals, pilgrimages, monastic orders, celibacy of the clergy, auricular confession, absolution, indulgences, penances, and purgatory as human inventions, with no foundation in Scripture. The civil government of Zurich endorsed his teaching. As a result of this disputation the monasteries in and around Zurich were forsaken, and priests and nuns married.

A second public debate was held October 26-28, 1523, to discuss the use of images in the churches, and the Romish doctrine of the Mass. Zwingli maintained that statues and pictures in churches should be removed because they led to idolatry,[5] or to sin against the First Commandment. The Mass was not a *sacrifice* but a *memorial* of the death of Christ; consequently, the elaborate rite of the Mass should be abolished. The city government favored Zwingli, but the presence of Anabaptists at the debate and their radical public statements cautioned the Council to move slowly. Two of Zwingli's associates were asked to enlighten the people by preaching and writing. Zwingli himself published a "Short Christian Introduction" November 17, 1523, in which he explained the principles of the Reformation.

This paved the way for a third public debate, held January 20, 1524. Zwingli's views were publicly endorsed by the Council, and advocates of the old order were given the choice of conformity or banishment. Between Pentecost and June 20, 1524, all pictures were removed from the churches, frescoes were cut out, the relics, crucifixes, altars, candles, clerical robes, tapestry, and other ornaments were removed, and the walls were whitewashed. Latin chants and songs, the playing of organs, and the ringing of church bells were abolished. A new liturgy in the mother-tongue was intro-

[5] See pages 152-53.

duced, in which the sermon was made the chief part of the service. In recent time the Reformed churches have reacted against this Swiss iconoclasm by favoring the use of Christian art in their houses of worship.

Zwingli had abolished every church practice not expressly commanded in the New Testament. The Mass alone was left, and this was so intimately connected with the life of the people that he would not abolish it until the people were prepared to accept a substitute. Mass continued to be said until Wednesday of Holy Week, 1525. On Maundy Thursday, April 13, 1525, it was replaced by the first Evangelical communion service in the Great Minster Church. On that eventful occasion men and women were seated on opposite sides of a table which extended down the middle aisle. After the consecration of the unleavened bread and the wine by the pastor, the deacons distributed the bread upon wooden platters and served the wine out of wooden beakers.

With this last radical step and with the abolition of episcopal jurisdiction, the Zwinglian Reformation was essentially completed. Zurich had definitely severed relations with the Roman Church. Zwingli now turned his attention to the more constructive side. In 1525 he published his principal work called "Commentary on True and False Religion." He tried to foster Christian learning and encouraged the formation of elementary schools. He wrote a treatise on "The manner of instructing and bringing up boys in a Christian way" in 1524. Most important for the Reformation was the translation of the Bible into the vernacular by Zwingli and his colleagues.

Between 1524 and 1529 the Swiss Reformer became involved in a conflict with the radical Anabaptists.[6] Zwingli opposed them with great vigor. They were cruelly persecuted and suppressed or driven out of the land. The Anabaptist movement has revived in modified form among the Mennonites and the Baptists.[7]

The Zwinglian Reformation spread rapidly from Zurich to other parts of Switzerland, but the Catholic cantons formed a league against the Reformation and finally moved with armed force against Zurich. The peace of Kappel in 1529 was favorable to Zurich and the Zwinglians. In 1531 hostilities were renewed; the Protestants were defeated; and Zwingli was slain on the battlefield. At the peace concluded soon after, Zurich was compelled to abandon its alliances, while each canton was given full right to decide its own religious questions. This peace drew the lines be-

[6] cf. the Zwikau prophets.   [7] cf. the "Holiness people" of to-day.

tween Protestants and Catholics in Switzerland as they have substantially remained to the present day. With the death of Œcolampadius in 1531, the second great leader, the Zwinglian movement fell back into a slower pace, and was finally absorbed by Calvinism.

38. REVIEW QUESTIONS

1. How did environment and training of Zwingli distinguish him from Luther?
2. Discuss the life of Zwingli up to the time he became a reformer. How did he become a reformer?
3. Compare Luther and Zwingli, and their respective movements. Why did not the Lutherans and the Zwinglians unite into one visible brotherhood?
4. Why did Zwingli bring the religious questions before the tribunal of the people through public debates? Can you see any reason why the Catholic Church would try to prohibit such disputations?
5. Why did Zwingli favor an extreme iconoclasm? Do the Reformed churches of to-day continue this policy?
6. In what ways did Zwingli's administration of the Lord's Supper differ from Luther's? Why?
7. Discuss the more constructive phase of the Zwinglian Reformation. How did he educate the general public? Why was he so anxious to have the Bible translated into the vernacular? Why did the Catholics discourage the reading and study of the Bible?
8. Why did Zwingli try to control the life of Zurich according to the ideals of the Old Testament theocracy? Why did not Luther try this mode of government?
9. Discuss the program of the Anabaptists. Why did Zwingli oppose them?
10. On what basis could Catholics and Zwinglians engage in mutual warfare in order to enforce their own particular beliefs?

TOPICS FOR SPECIAL STUDY

1. Zwingli's view of the relation of church and state.
2. Zwingli's view of religion and morality.
3. Zwingli's attitude toward the Word and the Sacraments.
4. Zwingli's conflict with the Anabaptists.
5. The lasting influence of Zwingli.

II. Calvin's First Stay at Geneva, 1536-1538.—The Swiss Reformation had by this time been firmly established in other parts of the country, including the strong city Bern in the southwest. As Protestantism moved westward, the movement soon spread from German to French Switzerland. Geneva, the "gate of Western Switzerland," became a new focal point for the Evangelical movement, with John Calvin as leader. He continued, improved, and completed the Swiss Reformation and gave it a world-wide significance. Zwinglianism was practically absorbed by Calvinism. Zurich was eclipsed by Geneva, which became the metropolis of the Reformed faith.

John Calvin was born on July 10, 1509, in the city of Noyon in Picardy, about sixty miles northeast of Paris. He was the second son in a family of four sons and two daughters. His father, a man of hard and severe character, was a highly esteemed lawyer who occupied a prominent position as secretary of the bishopric, attorney of the cathedral chapter, fiscal agent of the county, and registrar of the government of Noyon. His mother, a very beautiful woman, was noted for her piety and her motherly affection. She died early, and the husband, who did not care for children, sent John to a noble family to be educated. With the children of

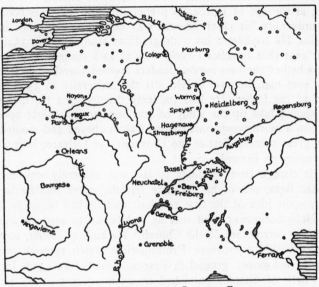

MAP ILLUSTRATING THE LIFE OF CALVIN

this family John Calvin was sent to a college in Paris at the age of fourteen. In his association with people of prominent families he acquired a refinement of manners, a knowledge of polite society, and an aristocratic bearing which distinguished him from Luther and Zwingli.

Calvin, trained as a pious Catholic, was early distinguished for his extraordinary intellect and his strength of character. He was a man of moderate stature, with pallid face, black hair, and sparkling eyes. His fellow students called him "the accusative case" because he censored their faults. Like other Picards, he combined German depth of feeling, thought, and soberness with French fire, practical good sense, and fondness for plain logic. He was physically timid, irritable, stern, and grave, but capable, nevertheless, of lifelong and affectionate friendship. He had a genius for organization, the spirit of an Old Testament lawgiver, and the mind of an invincible ruler.

His father destined him for the priesthood and procured for him, from his twelfth to his twentieth year, the income from several church-positions. In 1523, at the age of fourteen, he entered the College de la Marche in Paris. His remarkable ability as a student enabled him to enter the University of Paris a few months later, at the age of fifteen, in preparation for the priesthood. At the university his chief interest was not in theology but in the classics. He completed his undergraduate study early in 1528, the same year that Ignatius Loyola entered as a student. It is uncertain whether the two famous leaders studied together or whether they ever met, because Calvin left the university in 1528 at the wish of his father. He had suddenly decided that his illustrious son should take up the study of law because this might open up for him a more prosperous career. Calvin obeyed and studied law with great success, first at the University of Orleans, later at the University of Bourges.

The change from theology to law was evidently welcome for Calvin. Beza, one of his intimate friends, states that he had already some idea of the true religion; that he had begun to study the Holy Scriptures; and that he had begun to separate himself from the ceremonies of the Church.[8] He had, no doubt, come in contact with the incipient Protestantism which through various inroads had gained ground in France, even before 1530. Jacques Le Fèvre of Etaples published in 1512 a commentary on the Epistles of Paul, in which he anticipated some of Luther's teachings. He denied the saving merit of good works, declared salvation to be the free gift of God, and believed in the sole authority of Scripture. In 1523 he published a translation of the New Testament. He gathered about him a group of notable disciples who were interested in a reformation of the Church from within. Another group was in sympathy with the Humanistic reform program of Erasmus, including a purification of the Church from moral abuses and a return to the Bible. After 1520 the writings of Luther were circulated in France. The University of Paris condemned the Lutheran tenets in 1521 and prohibited the printing and distribution of his writings and the teaching of his doctrines.

[8] Lindsay: *A History of the Reformation*, Vol. II, page 95.

But the Lutheran ideas spread in France in spite of prohibition and persecution. At the University of Orleans Calvin came under the influence of two Protestants, his cousin, Pierre Robert Olivétan, who translated the Bible into French in 1532-35, and the German Melchior Volmar, who seems to have explained to Calvin the Lutheran conception of salvation. Volmar also supplied Calvin with Luther's "The Liberty of a Christian Man," his two Catechisms, the Marburg Articles, and the Augsburg Confession of 1530.[9]

On May 26, 1531, Calvin's father died, and he was left master of his own fortune. He now turned his attention to the classics, and decided to become a man of letters. He returned to the University of Paris to become a pupil of the Humanist professors whom the French king had invited to that institution.[10] Besides devoting himself to the study of the Humanities he was hard at work on his first literary production, a "Commentary on Seneca's Treatise on Clemency." This book, published in April, 1532, at the age of twenty-three, shows that Calvin was at that time a cultivated Humanist within the Roman Church.

Shortly after the publication of this book he experienced his "sudden conversion," or change from Romanism to Protestantism. Little is known as to place and circumstances, but it evidently occurred in 1533. Calvin himself states that "After my heart had long been prepared for the most earnest self-examination, on a sudden the full knowledge of the truth, like a bright light, disclosed to me the abyss of errors in which I was weltering, the sin and shame with which I was defiled. A horror seized my soul, when I became conscious of my wretchedness and of the more terrible misery that was before me. And what was left, O Lord, for me, miserable and abject, but, with tears and cries of supplication to abjure the old life which Thou condemned, and to flee into Thy path?" The essential feature of this experience was Calvin's consciousness of the all-powerful will of God which practically forced him into absolute obedience to the divine Will. "God himself produced the change. He instantly subdued my heart to obedience," says Calvin. His conversion resembles that of Luther and of Paul of Tarsus. After this experience he "conferred not with flesh and blood"[11] but burned the bridges behind him, and gave his life entirely to the cause of the Gospel.

He joined a little group of Protestants in Paris, where he

---

[9] Holmquist: *Kirkehistorie*, Vol. II, page 130.   [10] See page 208.   [11] Gal. 1:16.

quickly became a leader. At the secret meetings, he was frequently called upon to preach and to teach. He craved seclusion and quiet, but the people constantly invaded his retreats to get instruction and comfort. In 1533 the prospects were rather bright for the Protestants in Paris. Nicolas Cop, the bosom friend of Calvin, was elected Rector of the University. Cop thought the time was ripe for Protestant propaganda and used his inaugural address for that purpose. This address, largely prepared by Calvin, was a plea for a reformation on the basis of the New Testament. There were many secret sympathizers in the audience, but the opponents stirred up a great commotion. Calvin and Cop escaped arrest by a hasty flight from the city.

Calvin went to the city of Angouleme where he spent almost a whole year under the protection of Queen Marguerite of Navarre, sister of the French King. In May, 1534, he made a brief visit to Noyon where he resigned his benefices, thereby severing his relation with the Roman communion. That same year he issued at Orleans his second publication, the "Psychopannychia" or the "Sleep of the Soul," to refute the theory that the soul sleeps between death and the last Judgment. When the bloody persecution broke out in October, 1534, he left France going first to Strassburg and thence to Basel.

In the city of Basel he remained in scholarly seclusion from January, 1534, till March, 1536. The call had come to him to promote the cause of the Gospel by his pen. The French king, Francis I, cruelly persecuted the Protestants in his own kingdom, while he courted the friendship of the German Lutheran princes for political purposes, posing as a protector of the German Protestants. The king tried to justify the persecutions in France by accusing the French Protestants of being fanatical Anabaptists who sought to overthrow all civil order. Aroused by this double-dealing, Calvin published his "Institutes of the Christian Religion," March 1536, a dignified, forceful presentation of the beliefs of the Protestants, and a defense of the persecuted Evangelicals in France against the royal slanders that they were fanatical and rebellious Anabaptists. Keenly aware of the tremendous significance of this masterpiece, the Roman Catholics condemned it and burned it publicly in France and other places in 1542.

The "Institutes of the Christian Religion" was a brief manual of Christian doctrine, but it grew through the subsequent edition of 1539, the French translation of 1541, and the final edition of 1559, into the most famous and influential text-book of systematic theology the Reformation produced. Calvin's religious views underwent little or no change from the time of his conversion until his death. Consequently, the final revision of the Institutes of 1559, though five times larger than the original of 1536, fully preserved the identity of doctrine of the first edition. In this book the doctrinal and ethical views of the coming Calvinistic Church were expressed. The book also had great apologetic value since in it Calvin proved with irresistible logic that the Protestants, when tested by the standard of the Apostle's Creed and by Scripture were truer Catholics than the Romanists.

After the publication of this book he made a brief visit to Italy in the interest of the Evangelical movement. He spent some time at the court of the Duchess Reneta of Ferara, a daughter of Louis XII of France, and a sister-in-law of the French king. She was known as a friend of the Protestants, and Calvin came to solicit her interference on behalf of the persecuted Evangelicals in France. Calvin impressed her so deeply that she selected him as her spiritual adviser and corresponded with him freely until the time of his death, but she failed to interfere with the persecutions. After a brief visit to Paris, he returned to Strassburg where he intended to settle and devote himself to a life of quiet study. As the direct route to Strassburg was blocked by wars, he chose to travel by way of Geneva, where he arrived on August 5, 1536. He intended to spend but one night in this city, but a certain incident changed his plan and his whole future. William Farel, a former acquaintance from Paris, came to him that evening and begged him to stop in the city and help to organize the Genevan church. To use the words of Calvin, Farel threatened "that God would curse my retirement and the tranquillity of the studies which I sought, if I should withdraw and refuse assistance when the necessity was so urgent." Calvin finally decided to stay.

The international character of Geneva favored the work of Calvin. At the beginning of the sixteenth century the city had passed through a political crisis which paved the way for the Reformation. Geneva had formed an alliance with two Swiss cantons, Bern and Freiburg, to protect its liberties against foreign oppression, especially against the encroachments of the Dukes of Savoy. These Genevan patriots were called *Eidguenots* (Eidgenossen, or Confederates). Later this word degenerated by mispronunciation into *Eignots* and *Huguenots*,[12] the French nickname for the Protestants. The regained political independence of Geneva resulted in the expulsion of the Catholic bishop and the introduction of the Reformation. Bern sent William Farel, a powerful Protestant preacher, to Geneva in the Fall of 1532.

William Farel has been called " the pioneer of Protestantism in Western Switzerland," and "the Elijah of the French Reformation." He had been driven out of his native land by persecution. Endowed with remarkable gifts as an orator, he proclaimed his Protestant beliefs with tremendous conviction and force. But he lacked the calmness, the moderation, and the discretion necessary for the administration of affairs, and Farel himself admitted it. Provoking opposition in Geneva by his violent agitation and reckless zeal he was forced to leave. But he returned and held a public discussion in January, 1534, which ended in a partial victory for Farel. He continued his work at Geneva, and by August, 1535, the city decided to become Evangelical. In May, 1536, the citizens took a solemn oath to cast off the Roman doctrine and to live according to the Gospel. Saint worship and the reading of mass were abolished and forbidden, and images and relics were removed from the churches. But an influential group of citizens, the so-called Libertines, were strongly opposed to the new restraints. They frequently shouted out openly against the preachers and demanded a return to the old customs and the former liberties. Geneva was soon torn by internal strife and confusion, and Farel was unable to restore order. This was the state of affairs when Calvin arrived in August, 1536.

Calvin's first task was to prepare a plan for the educational and religious reorganization of the City-Republic. He recognized three essential needs. The people were ignorant and needed a general, religious instruction. Calvin supplied this need by arranging for lectures and sermons, and by publishing a catechism (1537) which expounded successively the Ten Commandments, the Apostle's Creed, the Lord's Prayer, and the Sacraments. This catechism, which was an extract of Calvin's *Institutes*, was larger than Luther's, but less adaptable for children. It was later superseded by the Anglican, the Heidelberg, and the Westminster catechisms. Geneva needed a brief and easily comprehended Confession of Faith which could be sworn to and maintained by all. A condensed summary of Calvin's *Institutes* was prepared for that purpose and

[12] It is more likely, however, that the name originally designated the followers of Hugues, the man who from 1507 onward fought for the liberty of Geneva.

adopted by the city in 1537. All who refused to take the oath were banished. This creed prepared the way for the later Gallican, Belgic, and Second Helvetic Confessions. He had to prepare a draft of the specific reforms he wished to have introduced, and to have this plan ratified by the city. The resulting church-law embodied all the characteristics of the system which was afterwards to be known as Calvinism.

The attempt to enforce the severe church-laws led to serious troubles. The people were not sufficiently prepared for such reforms. The problem of excommunication was the real bone of contention. Calvin insisted that unworthy persons should not be permitted to partake of the Lord's Supper, while the Councils of Geneva decided that the Holy Communion should be refused to no one who desired it. On Easter Day, 1538, Calvin and the other city pastors refused to administer the Lord's Supper because of the prevailing profligacy and immorality and also because it was a "popish holiday." The General Council ordered the pastors to leave within three days.

This apparent failure at Geneva wounded the pride of Calvin, and yet those subsequent years of banishment worked for his greatest good. He intended to settle down to quiet literary work at Basel, but Bucer induced him to accept a position as pastor for the French exiles in Strassburg. This city offered marvellous opportunities. He came in contact with people of different religious views, Scholastics, Humanists, Lutherans, Zwinglians, and Radicals. From each group he absorbed some useful element. In 1536 Johann Sturm had founded the gymnasium (college) of Strassburg, the most famous classical school in Germany. Calvin lectured at this school and learned to know Sturm, the most successful pedagogue of his day. At Strassburg Calvin also became acquainted with Jacob Sturm,[13] "the keenest and most unselfish statesman[14] of the Reformation." But of greatest consequence for Calvin's future work was his intimate acquaintance with Bucer, the great churchman and theologian of the Lutheran Reformation. As a churchman Bucer took a mediary position between Luther and Zwingli. He arranged for pastoral conventions, introduced a sound church discipline, organized works of charity, effected a close cooperation between secular and religious government, introduced a simple liturgy, and arranged for congregational singing. Calvin studied these ideas and tried out some of them in his own little congregation at Strassburg. Bucer's peculiar church organization and system of Christian doctrine strongly influenced Calvinism and paved the way for Anglicanism, Puritanism, and Pietism. During his stay at Strassburg Calvin also attended the religious union conferences at Hagenau, at Worms, and at Regensburg. On these occasions he met leading German Lutheran theologians, and put himself right with them by signing, without solicitation, the Augsburg Confession. He formed a life-long friendship with Melanchthon, and enjoyed the esteem of Luther. Calvin always regarded Luther as the great founder of Protestantism.

39. REVIEW QUESTIONS

1. Why was Zwinglianism absorbed by Calvinism? Why was Zurich eclipsed by Geneva as a center of Reformed faith?
2. Through what influences did Calvin become a Protestant?
3. Why was Calvin so quickly recognized as a leader of the Evangelicals?
4. What caused Calvin to write his first edition of "Institutes of the Christian Religion"? Why did the Catholics condemn it?
5. Why did this book have such great doctrinal and apologetic value?
6. Explain Calvin's visit to Italy. Did he succeed in his mission?
7. In what ways was Geneva suited for Calvin and his great mission?
8. Why did Farel insist on securing the help of Calvin?
9. Discuss Calvin's first plan for the educational and religious reorganization of Geneva. Why did the plan end in apparent failure?
10. Did Calvin benefit by his stay at Strassburg? Why?

TOPICS FOR SPECIAL STUDY

1. Compare Wittenberg, Zurich, and Geneva as centers of Protestant faith.
2. What Calvin owed Luther.
3. William Farel.
4. The origin of Calvin's Theology.

III. Calvin's Second Stay at Geneva, 1541-1564.—Calvin's stay at Strassburg was a fruitful period in his life. He prepared a second edition of his *Institutes* in 1539. He wrote a Commentary on the Epistle to the Romans, a popular Treatise on the Lord's Supper, and a brilliant *Reply to Sadoleto*, a cardinal who tried to induce Geneva to return to Catholicism. In 1540 he married a widow, Idelette de Bure. Meanwhile things were not going so well at Geneva. The party that ousted Calvin discredited itself and was overthrown. The new city government, torn by factions, was unable to exercise effective control. In this condition of imminent anarchy the people of Geneva turned to Calvin and humbly begged him to return. He finally consented, and on September 13, 1541, he arrived at Geneva where he was received with great joy. During the next twenty-three years he dominated the religious City-Republic of Geneva and made it the Rome of Protestantism.

Calvin immediately addressed himself to the task of organizing and superintending the religious City-Republic of Geneva. He created in Geneva a new ecclesiastical and civil order and a system of religion which came to have world-wide significance.

Calvin, like Luther and Zwingli, accepted the Bible as the sole rule of faith and life. He placed an infallible and verbally inspired Bible in opposition to the Catholic belief in an infallible Church headed by an infallible pope. On the basis of an inerrant Bible, Calvin took as the starting point of his system God's sovereign *will* or *power*, revealed through Jesus Christ as *love* and *grace*. The controlling motive in this divine will was the revelation of God's own glory. Hence the furtherance of the glory of God was always to be the prime concern of man. Calvin spoke of the glory and the majesty of God in a spirit akin to that of the Old Testament prophets. He laid equal stress on the *omnipotence* of God and the *impotence* of man.

As a logical consequence, Calvin asserted that God had from eternity foreordained all things that should come to pass. Absolute predestination was the divine program of human history, involving a decree of the *election* of certain people unto salvation, and a decree of *reprobation* for others unto eternal damnation. This was the way Calvin understood the teaching of the Bible. He admitted that it was a "horrible" decree but "the will of God is the highest rule of justice; so that what he wills must be considered just, for this very reason, because he wills it." The elect were made willing to be saved by God's grace which was irresistible. They were regenerated by the Holy Spirit, and *once saved, always saved*. The saved ones could not finally fall away from a state of grace.

The doctrine of predestination influenced Calvin's doctrine of the sacraments. Accepting the two sacraments which the Lord had directly instituted, he taught that these produced their intended effect only in the elect. To the non-elect the sacraments were empty and meaningless. All the elect received the forgiveness of sins in baptism, but since salvation depended on sovereign election alone, the sovereign will of God might work regeneration without baptism. Hence water baptism was not strictly necessary, and elect children who died without baptism were sure of salvation. In the Lord's Supper the elect were brought in communion with Christ. On the question of the Real Presence of Christ's body and blood, he rejected the Catholic doctrine of transubstantiation, and took a mediary position between Luther's realism and Zwingli's spiritualism. The elect communicants participated in the body and the blood of Christ, but the non-elect communicants participated in bread and wine only. Luther extended the participation in the body and the blood of Christ to all communicants, but with opposite effects upon the worthy and the unworthy.

Calvin's program demanded the education of all. This education did not merely include religious instruction, but also a general learning which Calvin held was "a public necessity to secure good political administration, sustain the Church unharmed, and maintain humanity among men." He maintained that "the liberal arts and good training are aids to a full knowledge of the Word." His Geneva plan included the publication of a simplified catechism in 1541, the so-called Geneva Catechism, a system of elementary education in the vernacular for all, including reading, writing, arithmetic, grammar, and religion, and the establishment of secondary schools for the purpose of training citizens for civil and ecclesiastical leadership. Such schools were organized in Geneva and in neighboring places. The famous Geneva Academy was founded by Calvin in 1555 after the pattern of Sturm's College at Strassburg. Theodore Beza, a man after Calvin's own heart, was elected president of the school. This Academy of Geneva became the great "Mission-House" of Calvinism. More than a thousand students from all parts of Europe attended daily the lectures of Beza and of Calvin. Many left the institution as learned men, eager to introduce the Calvinistic religious and educational ideas into their respective countries. Among these was John Knox, the leader of the Scottish Reformation.

Calvin introduced, with little modification, the simple church service of Strassburg. He discarded everything that savored of Catholicism, including pictures, images, vestments, bells, candles, and the like; but unlike Zwingli, he introduced congregational singing. Preaching took the most important place in the service. The Lord's Supper was administered four times a year. All church festivals, including Christmas and Easter, were abolished.

The Church was to Calvin the total number of the elect, both living and departed. Around this inner circle of the elect, the visible organization was formed for the purpose of working out the divine plan for all the relationships of men. Since many were called, but few chosen[15] the outward church or congregation would naturally include a number of nominal Christians or non-elect. The essential purpose of the Church was to glorify God, and the

15 Matt. 22:14.

glory of God centered in holiness. Hence, *holiness* was the goal the elect should strive for, and holiness was to be promoted by a rigid puritanical regulation of life. This is why the Calvinists have been among the most stalwart and ethically insistent Christians in the history of the Church.

Certainty of salvation was the privilege and the comfort of every believer. The proof of election and the certainty of salvation were to be found in the fact that the human will co-operated with the divine will in reflecting the glory of God on earth by bringing the *holiness* of the individual to a relative perfection. "Work out your own salvation with fear and trembling."[16] Consequently, predestinarianism and the struggle for a relative perfection became the strongest motives for human activity and for active

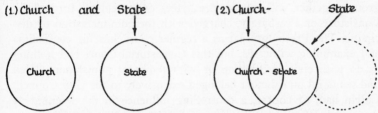

CALVIN'S CHURCH GOVERNMENT IN THEORY AND PRACTICE

participation in the work for the Kingdom of God on earth. To the individual freedom and the divine call to service, as stressed by Luther, Calvin added activity or aggressiveness, which, because of its desire for expansion, its fighting spirit, its demand for submission and obedience, and its incipient fanaticism, became the strongest bulwark against Ignatius Loyola and his troop of Jesuits.

Calvin made a clear distinction between the spiritual and the secular powers, between the church and the state. Theoretically, each was independent and sovereign in its own sphere, but, since all power was ordained of God,[17] both state and church were governed by the will of God, and all their activities reflect the glory of God. Consequently, the two theoretically independent powers had to work in such intimate co-operation that Calvin thought of the Christian community as a *unit* where the church and the state were *one*. In this co-operation of church and state, the pastors were best qualified to know the will of God as revealed in Scripture. Calvin urged, therefore, that the secular government seek the advice of the pastors and actually submit to their decisions. Christ was to govern the entire city or state by his law, but this law was to be interpreted by the pastors. Hence, the Calvinistic mode of government was truly a *theocracy*, based on the ideal of the Old Testament Israel. The entire city of Geneva was turned into a single congregation.

The congregation had the right of self-government under the sole headship of Christ. Calvin tried to institute synods, but did not succeed. The congregation was to recognize four ordinary officers instituted by Christ, namely, pastors, teachers, presbyters or lay-elders, and deacons. These were responsible to the congregation. The central church authority was vested in the city pastors who collectively were referred to as the Venerable Company. This group, together with twelve presbyters or lay-elders, formed the Consistory or Presbytery, charged with the administration of discipline. The Presbytery sat as a regular court, hearing complaints and examining witnesses, but this Consistorial Court had nothing to do with civil jurisdiction or with temporal punishment. Civil and temporal punishment belonged exclusively to the City Council. Calvin had, of course, a controlling influence in the framing of the civil laws.

Severe discipline was exercised upon high and low. The Calvinistic rules and regulations, based largely on the Mosaic legislation, aimed at the creation of "a Church without spot or wrinkle or blemish."[18] Every Christian should be consistent with his profession and show his faith by his good works.[19] The Calvinistic ordinances were not only prohibitive and protective, but also coercive. Crimes and sins were severely punished. In five years, 1542-46, Geneva, with 16,000 inhabitants, had fifty-seven executions and seventy-six banishments. All these sentences were sanctioned by Calvin. Innocent merriment was sternly checked. Attendance on public worship was enforced. Watchmen reported all breaches of discipline. There was no thought of religious toleration. Servetus, a famous Spanish physician, was condemned and burned on October 27, 1553, because of his anti-Trinitarian doctrine. This is the darkest blot in the history of Protestantism.

Calvin exerted a marked influence on the economic life of Geneva. Like Luther, he would not tolerate lending money for

---

[18] Compare diagrams on pages 242 and 271.   [19] Eph. 5:27.

gain. He even identified banking with usury. Interest on borrowed money should be taken only from those who could afford to pay it. He opposed capitalism, and yet Calvinism became a nursery for capitalism and modern industry.[20] Geneva was a commercial city whose commerce had suffered severely because of the economic policy of France. Calvin saw that its very existence would be threatened unless commerce and industry could be revived. He consequently addressed himself to the task of building up economic life by reviving trade and commerce and by starting several new industries. But his most successful appeal was to the individual citizens for work, order, honesty, thrift, contentment, and co-operation. It was the duty of every citizen to work, and the fruits of one's labor, money, and capital, were not evil but blessed result of dutiful work. The capital thus gained should be used, not for luxury and easy living, but as an investment in additional industrial and commercial undertakings for the purpose of more gain. As Calvinism spread to the different countries, it was invariably connected with the ever growing industry and commerce of those countries.

Calvinism spread not only to Switzerland, France, Holland, Belgium, Scotland, England, and America, but also to other lands. Calvinism was spread by means of the many refugees who stayed for some time in Geneva and then followed the inner urge to extend the influence of this new theocracy to other lands, by the many students who spent some time at the Academy of Geneva, and by the numerous writings of Calvin.

Calvin set forth his system in a whole literature which, as to volume, was surpassed only by Luther. His "Institutes of the Christian Religion" was printed in seventy-four full editions. fourteen partial editions, and in nine different languages before 1630. His Geneva Catechism went through seventy-seven editions, and might be had in nearly all the languages of Europe before 1630. It was adopted by the Scotch, the French-Swiss, the Huguenots, and the Dutch churches; it was used extensively in Holland, England, and America. Calvin was the author of a great number of exegetical works. Several formal confessions of faith took shape under his dominant influence. The "Consensus Tigurinus" was a formula of doctrine which united the Zwinglians and the Calvinists of Switzerland in 1549 upon a common doctrinal basis, giving Calvinism a foothold also in Germany. Lutheranism and

[20] The Fugger Banking House (Catholic) was the first great capitalistic manipulator, dealing in futures, etc.

Calvinism became competitors in all the lands into which Lutheranism had spread, especially in Germany and in Sweden. Calvin's immense and constant correspondence enabled him to mould the thought and shape the ideals of the Protestant leaders of Europe.

The success of Calvinism must be explained on the basis of its own intrinsic merits. Calvinism was an extreme form of anti-Romanism which made no compromise with the Roman church. Luther, because of his deep historic sense, retained those customs and institutions of the Roman church not forbidden in Scripture. Calvin declared the whole Roman order corrupt and purged the Reformed church of everything not expressly allowed in Scripture. Hence Calvinism, rather than Lutheranism, appealed to the aggressive anti-Romanists, especially during the period of the Counter-Reformation. Calvinism also took a firm and sober stand against the fanatic Radicalism by declaring that the Bible was the infallible source of truth. By excluding the fanatic and extravagant elements of Radicalism, Calvinism commended itself to the people as a religion of order, system, and sobriety. Finally, Calvinism produced strong, well trained, and aggressive men who took an active part in secular and religious affairs and defended Protestantism against aggressive Romanism.

Calvin was permitted to labor uninterruptedly for twenty-three years, from September, 1541, until May, 1564. In this period of unique activity, three successive stages may be distinguished: first, five years of peaceful preparations, 1541-46; second, nine years of threatening conflicts, 1546-55; third, nine years in which he enjoyed the fruits of his labors, 1555-64. On the evening of May 27, 1564, he was called to his rest. When he felt the end approaching, he took a touching leave of the Council, the city pastors, and the seventy-nine year old Farel, who had come all the way from Neuchatel. Calvin requested that his funeral should be simple, and that no monument should be erected on his grave.

40. REVIEW QUESTIONS

1. Why was Calvin recalled to Geneva?
2. What conditions favored Calvin in his unique work at Geneva?
3. Discuss Calvin's religious ideas. Calvin made the eternal election of God, Luther made the temporal justification by faith, the article of the standing or falling church. Can you see why?
4. How did the doctrine of predestination influence Calvin's doctrine of the Sacraments?

5. Discuss Calvin's educational program. Why did the Geneva Academy become the "Mission-House" of Calvinism?
6. Compare Calvin and Luther as to the order of church service. Why did they differ so much?
7. Why did Calvin place so much emphasis on holiness and a rigid puritanical regulation of life?
8. In what ways did the Calvinistic doctrine of certainty of salvation promote individual activity and aggressiveness?
9. Why did Calvin place the State under Church control?
10. Discuss the functions of pastors, teachers, presbyters or lay-elders, deacons, the Venerable Company, the Presbytery, the City Council, and the congregation. Why did Calvin recognize but four ordinary officers in the congregation?
11. How do you explain the extremely severe discipline, the many executions, the banishments, and the other forms of punishment? Would Luther go to such extremes? Explain.
12. Why did Calvin have such marked influence on the economic life?

TOPICS FOR SPECIAL STUDY

1. Compare the Lutheran, Zwinglian, Calvinistic, and Catholic view of the Lord's Supper.
2. Calvin's view on education.
3. Calvin's and Luther's view of the nature of the Church.
4. Calvin's City-State of Geneva and Augustine's *City of God*.
5. Calvinism as a world force.
6. Calvin's and Luther's ideas of justification.

IV. The Lutheran Reformation from 1530 to 1555.—After the Diet of Augsburg in 1530,[21] the Catholics threatened the Lutherans with open warfare. This menace led the Evangelical princes and cities to form a defensive league at Schmalkald in February, 1531. Luther finally gave his consent on the ground that the princes and the free cities constituted the government to which the Christians concerned owed their allegiance. The emperor was elected by the princes, not by God; and the princes had a right to oppose the emperor if he violated their rights. The relation between the princes and the emperor was a political question which the jurists, not the theologians, should decide. The Christians were in duty bound to take up arms in defense of their princes, when these were unlawfully assaulted.

The Schmalkald League, which originally included ten princes and eleven cities, soon developed into one of the most formidable powers of Europe. The league united almost all of North Germany and the more important imperial cities of South Germany. Overtures were made to France and to the Catholic Dukes of Bavaria, who were jealous of the Hapsburgs. Denmark wished to join, and Thomas Cromwell endeavored to have England join the League.

[21] See pages 248-49.

Sweden turned officially[22] Protestant in 1527. The emperor soon realized that the league was too formidable to be attacked. Furthermore, the Turks threatened a new invasion, the pope was hostile, and France and certain German Catholic princes were strongly anti-Hapsburg. These circumstances forced the emperor for the time being to give up his repressive policy. At the Diet of Nürenberg in 1532, a religious peace was concluded which granted freedom to the Protestant states until a General Church Council should decide the religious controversies. This religious peace actually lasted until 1546.

During the next ten years, 1532-42, the emperor left the Protestants undisturbed, because of his wars with the Turks and with France. This gave the Lutherans an opportunity to make new gains. The death of Zwingli and of Œcolampadius in 1531,[23] alienated South Germany from Zwinglianism in favor of Lutheranism. Before the end of the decade all of South Germany, with the exception of Bavaria, was Lutheran. By 1540 all of North Germany was Lutheran, with the exception of the territories which belonged to the prince bishops. The Catholic princes of Western Germany drove the Anabaptist communists out of the country, 1533-35, freeing the Lutheran cause from Anabaptist rivalry. Western Germany was still Catholic, but around 1540 the archbishopric of Cologne, under the leadership of the venerable Hermann von Wied, made plans to leave the Catholic church. This evidently meant a Protestant majority in the Electoral College, with the possibility that the next emperor would be Protestant. For a few years, 1540-43, the center of the Western world history focussed on the Cologne-Ruhr district. The emperor acting quickly suppressed the reform movement in Cologne and its vicinity by strong, military force in 1543. The next year the Palatinate turned Protestant. A religious discussion in 1546 revealed that in that year, at least nine-tenths of Germany was Lutheran. From Germany the Lutheran movement spread to other countries. In 1545 more than two-thirds of Austria was Lutheran. Large portions of Bohemia, Moravia, and Poland, turned Protestant, and from them the Evangelical movement spread to surrounding nations.

Meanwhile, Lutheranism passed through certain modifications with reference to church *tradition* and *organization*. Up to the time

---

[22] The severance of the Church of Sweden from Rome really occurred in November, 1523, when the Swedish king refused to confirm the bishops-elect of the Roman Curia and also refused the payment of annates. But the climax came in 1527 at the Diet of Vesteras. The first Protestant archbishop of Sweden was elected in 1531.

[23] See page 260.

of the Diet of Augsburg in 1530, Luther had no plans for a new church organization.[24] But after 1530 the situation was different. The great territorial expansion of the Lutheran faith, the bitter Catholic opposition, the severe struggle with Radicalism, and the inherent forces of Lutheranism, called for a definite organization. This work was started in Lutheran universities and colleges, under the dominant influence of Melanchthon. The Augsburg Confession, the Apology, and Luther's two catechisms were accepted as standards of the Lutheran doctrine. The Schmalkald Articles of 1537 enjoyed a similar recognition in Germany, and after 1535 the members of the Schmalkald League were required to subscribe to the Augsburg Confession. But Melanchthon's influence reached much further. "The Preceptor of Germany," as he was called, brought about an intimate relation between Evangelical religion and culture. He formulated the Lutheran views into clear, concise, and easily understood statements. At heart he was essentially a Humanist, although he always tried to agree with Luther. But Melanchthon's Humanistic interests, coupled with his ever increasing influence among the Lutherans, resulted in a rather unfortunate modification of Lutheranism. Melanchthon's interest in the classic philosophy and literature caused him to make inroads on the Lutheran world for Aristotle whom Luther called "a condemned heathen," and for a new Lutheran scholasticism; his love for the classics led him to entertain an increasingly high regard for church *tradition*, and in 1543 he practically gave tradition an independent position, in coordination with Scripture; he influenced the Lutherans to accept the three oldest symbols, the Apostle's Creed, the Nicene Creed, and the Athanasian Creed, as binding; his fear of the religious ideas of the Radicals caused him to place additional emphasis on tradition and the office of the church; he influenced the Lutheran church to follow a course of development which reminds the student of the early stages in change from Apostolicity to Catholicity.[25]

In 1535 Luther introduced the Rite or Order of Evangelical Ordination at Wittenberg. Candidates for the Evangelical ministry were to be examined and ordained by the "learned men of Holy Scriptures." The Theological Faculty at Wittenberg elected Bugenhagen as Ordinator, but the ordination was often performed by Luther himself, especially during the two years Bugenhagen was in Denmark, 1537-39. Luther had requested the princes to protect

[24] *Augsburg Confession*, Art. 28.
[25] See pages 93-99.

the church against the Catholic aggression. This *aid* was gradually turned into *dominion*. The prince became the recognized head of the church in his territory.[26] He controlled all activities of the church, even doctrine and form of worship, although decisions on doctrinal matters were usually left in the hands of the clergy. In 1539 a special ecclesiastic court was established at Wittenberg for the purpose of deciding such matters as church discipline, divorce, and the like. The members of this court, or "Consistorium" as it was called, consisted of theologians and jurists selected by the Elector. After the death of Luther this Consistorium was changed from a court to a governing body which functioned much like the former Catholic episcopacy. The majority of the Lutheran churches in Germany copied this form of church government.

Charles V continued to negotiate with the Lutherans. He practically compelled the pope, Paul III, to call a General Church Council at Mantua, in 1537. The pope insisted, however, that the Protestants should pledge unconditional submission to the decrees adopted by the majority at this Council. When the Lutherans refused to pledge themselves, the pope decided to postpone the meeting.

Meanwhile Luther had been asked to prepare a new confession of faith for the Protestants to place before the proposed General Church Council at Mantua. Luther was sick when he wrote this document, and he prepared each sentence and paragraph and article as parts of a confession of faith for which he was willing to live or to die. The resulting document, which is the most important of Luther's later writings, was ready in December, 1536. At a general meeting of the members of the Schmalkald League, in February, 1537, the Confession was signed by a majority of the theologians present, and named the Schmalkald Articles. These articles constitute the third symbolical book of the Lutheran Church. At this February meeting in Schmalkald, the Protestants also renewed their defensive league against the emperor and the Catholic princes, and subscribed anew to the Augsburg Confession and the Apology.

Alarmed at the growing strength of Lutheranism, the Catholic princes formed the Holy League of Nürenberg, July 10, 1538, for the purpose of defending the interests of Catholicism. Civil war seemed inevitable. But the threatening advances of the Turks saved the situation. The emperor was forced to negotiate with the Protestants, in order to get their indispensable military support against

[26] He had previously held a somewhat similar position in the Roman Catholic Church.

the Turks. During the next three years, 1538-41, attempts at a reunion of Protestants and Catholics were made. A number of religious conferences were held, but they ended with a conviction that the gulf between the parties was impassable. Pope and emperor finally made the firm resolve to use force, though they had to wait until the emperor could conclude successful peace with the Turks and with France.

The emperor concluded a peace with France in November, 1544. In the treaty the emperor and the French king agreed that they would wipe out heresy (Protestantism) in their dominions, and they would compel the pope to call a General Church Council. In October, 1545, the Turks made a truce with the emperor. In December, 1545, the pope was obliged to summon a Council at Trent, an Italian city although nominally within Germany. The emperor intended to use this Council as a means of re-uniting Christendom, by forcing both the pope and the Protestants to a reasonable compromise. The situation seemed to favor his carefully worked-out plan. But the pope soon made it plain that no doctrinal concessions would be made to the Protestants; and the Protestants not only refused to be bound by the decisions of the permanent majority in the Council, but they also decided not to send delegates to Trent. This gave emperor and pope an excuse to proceed against them with military force. But before the actual war broke out, Luther was permitted to go to his rest.

Early in 1546 the counts of Mansfeld, two brothers, called Luther to Eisleben to settle a dispute. The journey was made in bitterly cold weather, and he contracted a cold which made him a victim of apoplexy. He spent three weeks in Eisleben, the place of his birth, and finished the arbitration, to the mutual satisfaction of the parties concerned, on February 17. The following night he became alarmingly ill. A friend asked him: "Reverend Father, wilt thou stand by Christ and the doctrine thou hast preached?" To this Luther answered "Yes." It was his last word. He died early in the morning of February 18, 1546. His body was laid to rest in a grave made to the right of the pulpit of the church in Wittenberg, upon whose door he had nailed the 95 theses.

Charles V took the field against the Schmalkald League shortly after the death of Luther, in 1546. The Council of Trent induced the pope to declare the war a crusade. Indulgences were offered to all who would take part in it. The pope also sent an army into the field, and gave the emperor 200,000 ducats in support of the efforts to exterminate Protestantism. The Schmalkald League placed three armies in the field; but Duke Maurice of Saxony, won by the‹ emperor's offer of the electorate and other inducements, went over to the emperor's side. The Schmalkald League was defeated in 1547, and two of the princes, the Elector John Frederick, and the Landgrave Philip of Hesse, were taken prisoners. The cause of the Reformation in Germany seemed lost.

The emperor now demanded that the Protestants should leave the decision on the religious matters to the Council assembled at Trent. But a new quarrel between pope and emperor saved the situation for the Protestants. The pope feared that an absolute triumph of the emperor might endanger the temporal power of papacy. He consequently embarrassed the emperor by withdrawing his troops, by forming a new alliance with the French king, and by adjourning the Council from Trent to Bologna in order to bring it under complete Italian control. The Council was thereby in effect dissolved, and the pope refused to reassemble it. The emperor then decided to introduce a reformation of his own into his empire. He prepared a provisional scheme, the Augsburg Interim, which, if carried into effect, would have given Germany a reformed Catholic church. But neither Protestants nor Catholics were satisfied with his program. Melanchthon prepared a compromise, the Leipzig or Small Interim, but the strict Lutherans denounced the Leipzig more than the Augsburg Interim. Melanchthon lost his position as the recognized leader of Lutheranism.

In 1551-52 the Council of Trent was reassembled by the new pope, Julius III. The emperor wanted a reformed Catholic church, and he had a definite reform program, but he soon realized that he could look to neither pope nor to Council for any co-operation because of the dominant influence of the Jesuits. His efforts were thwarted by Catholics and Protestants alike. Additional opposition developed among the German Catholic princes when they discovered that the emperor and his brother, Ferdinand of Austria, had made plans to secure the imperial crown as the permanent possession of the Hapsburgs. The emperor was again occupied in wars with the Turks and with France. Duke Maurice of Saxony turned suddenly against him and became the leader of a conspiracy of German princes. A military campaign headed by the brilliant Maurice forced the emperor to conclude the Peace of Passau, in 1552. This peace treaty stipulated that the religious situation should be restored to its status in 1545. The Catholic gains through the Schmalkaldic War were taken away. That same year, 1552, the

Council of Trent was dissolved and did not reassemble for ten years.

Three years later, at the Diet of Augsburg in 1555, the Lutheran Reformation finally received legal recognition. The principles agreed on may be stated as follows: (1) two religions were permitted to exist within the empire, namely Catholicism and the religion of the Augsburg Confession, while Zwinglianism, Calvinism, and Radicalism were excluded from toleration. (2) Each prince had a right to decide which of the two religions he and his state should have, in accordance with the principle, "one local government, one religion." (3) A Catholic government was not required to tolerate Lutherans, nor was a Lutheran government required to tolerate Catholics, but the dissenting minority should have a right to emigrate. (4) The religious Peace of Augsburg was not to involve the Netherlands and the Catholic church territories in Germany. If a prince of the church became a Protestant, he should resign his position, and his territory should remain under the Catholic church. In return for this concession, the Protestants should be tolerated in the dominions of the church territories.

41. REVIEW QUESTIONS

1. Explain why the Reformation in Germany after 1530 was military and political, rather than religious.
2. Why was Luther willing to leave the rightfulness of armed resistance to the decision of the lawyers?
3. Discuss the origin, growth, and influence of the Schmalkald League. Why did not this league become the nucleus of an Evangelical German Empire?
4. Study the territorial expansion of Lutheranism during the decade 1532-42. Did this expansion cause any modification of Lutheranism?
5. What influence did Melanchthon exert upon Lutheranism? Do you expect to find that the differences between Luther and Melanchthon re-appear in the subsequent history of the Lutheran church? Why?
6. Why did Luther introduce the Act of Evangelical Ordination, and the religious court or Consistorium?
7. Discuss the origin and the influence of the Schmalkald Articles.
8. How was civil war between Catholics and Protestants avoided in 1538?
9. Why did the emperor force the pope to call the Council of Trent in 1545?
10. Why could the emperor make so little use of his victory over the Protestants in 1547?
11. Why was the emperor's church reform opposed by Catholics and Protestants alike?
12. What importance should be attached to the Religious Peace of Augsburg in 1555? Do you see any seeds of future conflict in this peace treaty?

TOPICS FOR SPECIAL STUDY

1. Luther's view on the rightfulness of armed resistance.
2. The Lutheran attitude toward Tradition.

3. Melanchthon as the "Preceptor of Germany."
4. Lutheranism and Apostolic succession.
5. The Peace of Augsburg.
6. The Augsburg and the Leipzig Interim compared.
7. The threefold policy of Charles against Lutheranism.

V. Controversies within the German Lutheran Churches, 1555-80.

—The Peace of Augsburg definitely fixed the political and national frontier between Roman Catholicism and Protestantism and established outward peace between the contending parties. But the Lutheran unity was weakened by bitter doctrinal controversies destined to absorb the energies of German Protestants for the next twenty years. The great creative and prophetic age of Lutheranism was followed by a didactic age much as the period of the Old Testament prophets was followed by the age of the great Synagogue. Doctrine threatened to swallow up life, while the followers of Luther fought for his spiritual heritage. Most of the controversies centered around points of doctrine on which Luther and Melanchthon had partly disagreed. Hence one party was called Gnesio-Lutherans or Genuine Lutherans, and the other party was called Philippists or Melanchthonians. But Flacius, the leader of the Genuine Lutherans, went to such extremes that many left him and formed a third or Middle Party which finally settled the controversies with the help of the princes.

The Antinomistic (*anti:* against + *nomos:* law) Controversy concerned the place of the Decalogue in the plan of salvation. Luther had maintained that both the Law and the Gospel should be preached because "through the law cometh the knowledge of sin."[27] But "how is it possible to preach about the forgiveness of sins where sin is not present?" John Agricola and others held that the Decalogue belonged to the hall of justice, and not in the pulpit. The Gospel only should be preached because this alone was capable of producing a real change of heart and life.

The Adiaphoristic (*adiaphoron:* matters of indifference) Controversy was caused by Melanchthon's attitude toward Roman ceremonies in the Leipzig or Small Interim. Melanchthon had introduced almost all of the Roman ceremonies for the sake of compromise under the pretext that these rites were neither commanded nor forbidden in God's Word, and hence were non-essentials, *adiaphora*, or matters of indifference. He also compromised with Rome on the doctrine of justification and the seven Sacraments. The Peace of Augsburg in 1555 removed the cause for this controversy, but no agreement on the principle had been reached.

The Majoristic Controversy started with the contention of George Major, a disciple of Melanchthon, that good works were necessary to salvation. Forgiveness of sins was obtained by faith alone, but no one would be saved without good works. The Gnesio-Lutherans raised a vigorous opposition on the ground that this was a return to the Roman doctrine of salvation by faith and good works. Old Amsdorf, for one, even went so far as to say that good works (reliance on good works) were injurious to salvation.

[27] Rom. 3:20; Smalc. Art. Part III, Art. 2.

The Eucharistic or Crypto-Calvinistic Controversy concerned the doctrines of the Lord's Supper. The Philippists held views similar to those of Calvin. The Gnesio-Lutherans stirred up such violent opposition that many of the Philippists were driven over to the ranks of the Calvinists.

The Synergistic (*syn:* together + *ergon:* work) Controversy centered around whether or not the human will or effort co-operated with divine grace in conversion and salvation. Some contended that the sinner was completely dead to good impulses, and even "contrary, resisting, or hostile toward the work of God." Man could contribute nothing whatever toward his conversion. Others maintained that the human will was a co-agent with the Word and the Spirit of God in man's conversion and salvation. Sinful nature had the freedom either to resist or to accept the grace of God. Consequently, man was responsible either for his own salvation or damnation.

The Osiandrian Controversy centered around a theory of justification proposed by Andrew Osiander of Nürenberg. According to the accepted Protestant view, justification is a single, forensic act of God, definitely distinguished from sanctification which follows as a gradual process. In the Catholic system justification is *merged* with sanctification as a gradual process, conditioned by faith and good works. Osiander identified the two. He taught that Christ, "the Personified righteousness of God" received by faith into the heart overcomes all unrighteousness and impels man to all kinds of good works, and thus man is justified by the indwelling, living Christ. Osiander's views differed from the Catholic mainly in this respect that he did not take any account of human merit or good works,[28] but only the merit and power of Christ.[29]

The Christological Controversy arose in connection with the Lord's Supper. The real question was whether or not Christ could give his body and blood in the sacrament. Some said with the Reformed that he could not, since his body was a real body and was confined to a space in heaven; others taught that he could, because his body by the personal union with the divine nature, was a glorified body and on account of the *communicatio idiomatum* could be made present.

Such disputes filled the years 1548 to 1577. So pernicious was the spirit of conflict that the Gnesio-Lutherans denied the Philippists, after 1557, the right to claim adherence to the Augsburg Confession, thereby excluding them from the benefits of the Religious Peace of Augsburg, secured in 1555. As this made for political as well as for religious disunity, the Lutheran princes felt themselves compelled to use every legitimate means of restraining these theological conflicts and, if possible, bring about a German Lutheran concord. The Jesuits claimed that the Lutherans would soon collapse, for there were, they claimed, as many kinds of Lutherans as there were ministers.

The resulting concord movement went through three successive stages. The Lutheran princes tried in vain at various peace-synods to ignore the theological differences, and to bring about a concord by merely subscribing to the Augsburg Confession. As these efforts ended in utter failure, they succeeded together with prominent

[28] Rom. 4:6.   [29] Rom. 10:4; 1 Cor. 1:30.

theologians, in securing a fixed doctrine for the separate territorial churches. The body of doctrines usually subscribed to consisted of the three ancient symbols, the Augsburg Confession and Apology, Luther's two catechisms, the Schmalkald Articles, and various smaller local confessions and writings. Having secured a fixed doctrine for the separate territorial churches, the Lutheran princes and theologians made plans whereby all of these churches could be united by a common confession. They addressed themselves to a two-fold task. Their *first* problem was to prepare a formula of concord which would settle the disputed religious questions of the preceding decade. Leading theologians, including Nicholas Selnecke of Wittenberg, Jacob Andreae of Tübingen, Martin Chemnitz of Brunswick, and Chytraeus of Rostock, prepared the document which in its final form in 1577 became known as the Formula of Concord.[30] This document received the support of the overwhelming majority of Lutheran states in Germany, and immediately assumed a position among the regulative symbols of Lutheranism. Their *second* task was to construct a Body of Doctrine which would not only be accepted by all Lutherans in all lands, but which would also define Lutheranism as against Catholicism and Calvinism. With this in mind they prepared the Book of Concord, which included the Apostle's Creed, the Nicene Creed, the Athanasian Creed, the Augsburg Confession in 1530, the Apology, the Schmalkald Articles, Luther's two catechisms, and the Formula of Concord. The Book of Concord was published in 1580 on the fiftieth anniversary day of the presentation of the Augsburg Confession to the Diet of Augsburg, in 1530. This collection of confessions was signed by fifty-one princes, thirty-five cities, and about nine thousand theologians. The publication and the signing of the Book of Concord marked the doctrinal completion of German Lutheranism.

Up to 1580 the Catholics had used the term "Lutheran" as a nickname for the *heresy* of Luther and his followers.[31] Shortly after 1580 the Lutherans adopted "Lutheran" as a name of honor. Formerly they had designated themselves as members of the

[30] The various forms of revision of the Formula of Concord may be remembered by code as follows:
A—Andreae's first draft.
C—Revised by Chemnitz.
R—Considerably enlarged by Rostock theologians (Chytraeus).
T—Edited at Torgau by a Commission of Five.
B—Bergen, the final form.
[31] The name was first used on July 4, 1519 by Luther's opponent, Dr. John Eck, at the Leipzig Disputation. Luther himself preferred to have his followers called simply Christians, or Evangelicals.

"ecclesia apostolica catholica," or the Apostolic Catholic or Evangelical Church.[32]

VI. Consequences of the Reformation.—The Protestant Reformation had started as a purely religious movement, stimulated by the all important question: "What shall I do to inherit eternal life?"[33] Yet the movement resulted in much more than a religious reformation. It produced wide, immediate, and permanent changes in practically every department of human life.

The first cardinal principle was the recognition of the absolute supremacy of the Bible as the norm for life and doctrine. Luther, Zwingli, and Calvin rejected the Roman Catholic coordination of the Bible and Tradition as joint rules of faith and conduct. The reformers accepted the Bible as the Word of God, inspired by the Holy Spirit. Through the truth revealed in the Bible did the Holy Spirit come to men, and not through the church organization. All the church could do for men was to bring them the Word, through preaching and the Sacraments. The teaching of the church had no authority except insofar as it was grounded in the Bible. Since the Bible was of such vital importance to the people, it had to be available in the language the people could read. Hence the Bible was translated into the vernacular tongues of Europe, becoming a book of the people.

The second cardinal principle was the proclamation of justification by a living faith in Jesus Christ. The reformers rejected the Roman Catholic doctrine of salvation by faith and good works, or salvation by divine grace and human merit. Justification by faith was made the very soul of the Protestant religion. It was not a new doctrine, but merely a rediscovery of the message of the Apostle Paul.[34] Faith was not merely a form of knowledge, or cold intellectual assent to religious truth, but a personal experience in which man threw himself over upon the mercy of God and surrendered life and will. Luther asserted that such faith was not merited by good works, but that it was a "pure gift of God." Good works were, however, the necessary evidence of justification. Through this doctrine the Reformers set men free, not only from their anxious dependence upon their own works and merit, but from the dependence upon the Catholic church which claimed to dispense salvation through the Sacraments and a storehouse of merits. Man could come directly to God through the mediation of Scripture.

[32] See diagram on page 134.   [33] Luke 10:25.
[34] Rom. 1:17.

The third cardinal principle was the priesthood of all believers. God, as revealed in Jesus Christ, was accessible to every believer without the mediation of a priest. The believer was a member of "an elect race, a royal priesthood, a holy nation, a people of God's own possession."[35] But this was directly against the Roman Catholic doctrine that a mediating priest was essential to salvation.[36] In the Medieval Church a gulf separated the clergy and the laity. The Roman clergy held the keys to heaven and hell. The clergy could refuse to communicate the grace of God to the laity, yes, even bar lay people from all access to God. By a stroke of the pen, the pope could excommunicate the individual, and he could place a city, or province, or kingdom under interdict. In the Medieval Church laymen had no voice in spiritual matters, and they could not even read the Bible without the permission of the priest. Luther struck directly against a special, mediating priesthood by proclaiming the spiritual priesthood of all believers. This made for a spiritual democracy, and for religious and civil liberty. Lay people were again given a voice in spiritual matters, and in the government and administration of the church.

Protestantism dealt a death blow to the double standard of medieval piety by reconstructing the domestic life, including the home life of the evangelical clergy. This was a new chapter in the history of civilization. In the Catholic communion there existed an unscriptural distinction between a lower morality for the common people, and a higher morality for priests and monks who formed a spiritual nobility. Marriage was considered inconsistent with this special priesthood because married life was of an inferior order. The reformers pointed out that perpetual celibacy was unscriptural and unnatural. It was unscriptural because the Jewish priesthood, including the high priests, married; and the apostles and other church leaders of the Apostolic period married, even Peter whom the Catholics claimed as the first pope. Perpetual celibacy was also unnatural because God had created man for marriage, and He had sanctified and blessed the family life. Hence Luther, Zwingli, and Calvin married, and they urged the Protestant clergy to do likewise. Protestantism changed the moral ideal, and elevated domestic and social life.

Universal education became necessary because of the new theory of individual judgment and individual responsibility. The reformers protested against the human authority of church and pope and

---

[35] 1 Pet. 2:9; Exod. 10:6.   [36] See diagram on page 68.

substituted the supreme authority of the Bible. They protested against the collective judgment of the church and substituted the right of individual conscience and judgment. They protested against *institutional* responsibility for salvation and substituted *personal* religion and individual responsibility for salvation. Medieval piety had caused men to flee from the world. Evangelical Christianity urged men to transform the world. This called for an active participation in all departments of life, including government and religion. But individual participation in and responsibility for the conduct of government and church involved adequate education. The ideal of supplying an education for all could not be generally realized, however, until the nineteenth and twentieth centuries.

The rise of democratic governments, a powerful impetus to progress of all sorts, an active participation in industrial and commercial undertakings, a growing emancipation of thought, the rise of a spirit of criticism and free inquiry, were natural and ultimate consequences. In the realm of literature the names of Luther and Calvin stand pre-eminent. In the realm of hymnody Luther's name will live as long as song and music endure, especially in connection with the great battle hymn of the Reformation, "A Mighty Fortress Is Our God."

Protestantism divided into three general confessions, the Lutheran, the Reformed, and the Anglican, and these three communions again produced a number of smaller divisions. The collectivism of the Middle Ages was followed by a Protestant tendency toward individualism. Unfortunately, narrowness, bigotry, and exclusiveness often prevented the Protestant groups from cooperating. Yet these groups have proved to be a source of rich blessings. Medieval collectivism is static, while Protestant individualism is dynamic. Progress thrives best in an age of individualism. Each Protestant group has developed certain individual characteristics, according to the God-given, inherent tendencies. The Lutherans have made their contribution along the line of deep, spiritual insight and investigation into the divine mysteries, such as the person of Jesus Christ and his atoning work. The Calvinists have been able to spread the Gospel far and wide in the Roman and Anglo-American world by means of marvelous organizing power, fused with great religious enthusiasm. The Anglicans have moulded Lutheran, Zwinglian, Calvinistic, and Roman elements into a distinctly new religious organism, the Anglo-Catholic church, whose special contribution has been theological and religious moderation and comprehension, coupled with great institutional strength. In the Anglican church the office and the cult hold the central places, and the religious life concentrates on practical activities.

42. REVIEW QUESTIONS

1. Explain why so many doctrinal controversies arose among the Lutherans between 1548 and 1577.
2. What part did the Gnesio-Lutherans, the Philippists, and the Middle Party or the moderate Lutherans play?
3. Give a brief account of the leading doctrinal disputes. Why did these doctrinal divisions also involve a political disunity?
4. Were the Crypto-Calvinistic plans or intrigues justifiable?
5. Discuss the three stages in the Lutheran concord movement. Distinguish between the Formula of Concord and the Book of Concord.
6. How did the name "Lutheran" orginate? When was it generally adopted by the Lutherans as a name of honor?
7. Mention the three cardinal principles of the Protestant Reformation. Why did the reformers assert the supremacy of the Bible? And why were they so anxious to make the Bible a book of the people?
8. In what ways did the Protestant doctrine of the supremacy of faith, or justification by faith, set men free from a yoke of bondage?
9. How does the principle of the priesthood of all believers differ from the principle of special priesthood, in theory and in practice?
10. In what ways did the Reformation change the moral ideal and elevate domestic and social life?
11. Why did Protestantism pave the way for universal education?
12. How do you account for the Protestant diversity? In what ways do you think these various groups may be a blessing, or a hindrance to the progress of the Kingdom of God on earth? Explain.

TOPICS FOR SPECIAL STUDY

1. The creative and prophetic age of Lutheranism, followed by a didactic age.
2. Catholic control of the lay people by the teaching priesthood versus Protestant Bible societies.
3. Protestantism and universal education.
4. The difference in the conception of "grace" in Protestantism and Catholicism.
5. The Roman Catholic idea of Tradition.
6. The Protestant Reformation as a source of political freedom.
7. The difference between the unity attained by the Formula of Concord and other unions.

A SELECTED BIBLIOGRAPHY FOR CHAPTER XI

1. *Cambridge Modern History,* Vol. II, Chap. VII, VIII.
2. Lindsay: *A History of the Reformation,* Vol. I, pages 369-416; 426-488; Vol. II, pages 21-135.
3. Smith: *The Age of the Reformation,* Chap. XVII.
4. Jackson: *Huldreich Zwingli.*
5. Walker: *John Calvin.*
6. Reyburn: *John Calvin, His Life, Letters and Work.*

7. Beza: *Life of Calvin.*
8. Doumergue: *Jean Calvin* (5 vols.)
9. Schmauck, Bentze, and Kolde: *The Confessional Principle and the Confessions of the Evangelical Lutheran Church.*
10. Fritschel: *The Form of Concord.*
11. Krauth: *The Conservative Reformation and its Theology.*

CHAPTER XII

The Lutheran Reformation Outside of Germany

Luther's influence went far beyond Germany. Within the first twenty years the Lutheran Reformation had penetrated Scandinavia and the countries around the Baltic, including Livonia, Esthonia, and Courland.[1] The movement took root in England, Scotland, Holland, France, Poland, Bohemia, Moravia, Hungary and Transylvania. Even Italy and Spain had a few Evangelical believers, although these were soon suppressed by the Inquisition or by other means of force. Many of these countries did not, however, accept Lutheranism as the official religion. England followed an independent course of reformation. Scotland, Holland, and France finally accepted Calvinism. The countries of Middle and Southern Europe were practically forced back to Catholicism. But in the Scandinavian countries and their dependencies the Lutheran Reformation was permanently established.[2]

After a long period of separate government, the three Scandinavian kingdoms, Denmark, Norway and Sweden, were united by the Union of Calmar in 1397. This treaty provided that the three lands should forever be united under one sovereign, although each country should retain its constitution and make its own laws and share in the election of the king. Denmark was the dominant member of the union. Sweden broke away in 1523. Norway continued in union with Denmark until 1814. Within the Scandinavian countries there was a continuous triangular conflict between the crown, the secular nobles, and the prince bishops. For this reason the Reformation in Scandinavia was intimately bound up with political and social movements. The Reformation offered the king a means of crushing the power of the great prince bishops by confiscating the church-property and by bringing the church directly under the control of the crown. The replenished royal treasury offered the king additional means of subduing the secular nobility.

[1] See map on page 206.
[2] The Evangelical Lutherans in all parts of the world comprise to-day the largest confessional group in the non-Roman Evangelic Christendom, with a population of between 80,000,000 and 100,000,000, and with about 70,000 congregations and 49,000 pastors.

I. Denmark.—Christian II (1513-23) was the king of Denmark when the Lutheran movement began. As the nephew of Frederick the Wise, and the brother-in-law of Emperor Charles V, he was connected with the political leaders on both sides of the Reformation controversy in Germany. He had marked Renaissance sympathies and enjoyed the reputation of being the most learned king in Christendom. He came to the throne as a papal champion, however, and soon formed a league with the Catholic hierarchy for the suppression of the Swedish national party. In 1520 he was crowned king of Sweden. On the day of his coronation he massacred over eighty of the first men of Sweden, whom the archbishop had pointed out as enemies of the Danes, under the

PRESENT POLITICAL MAP OF EUROPE
(1. Netherlands; 2. Belgium; 3. Czecko-Slovakia)

pretext that they were hostile to the pope. This horrible act, called the "Stockholm Bath of Blood," provoked the revolution of 1521, which led to the permanent independence of Sweden.

In Denmark the king took sides with the friends of the Reformation against the powerful Catholic clergy and the prince bishops. There is also good reason to believe that Christian II favored the cause of church-reform for its own sake. He wrote to his uncle, Frederick the Wise of Saxony, to send him preachers trained by Luther. Martin Reinhard came in 1520, and Carlstadt made a brief visit in May-June, 1521. After the Edict of Worms was published, the king even had in mind to give Luther a place of refuge in Denmark, but this plan did not materialize. In 1521 he published, partially as a result of the advice of Carlstadt, two sets of laws dealing with the church and the secular nobles. In the one he tried on his own authority to establish the Church of Denmark as a state-church under the control of the crown. He also included other Lutheran reforms, such as the marriage of the clergy, the enlightenment of the lower classes, and the state inspection of all the convents. The other set of laws subjected the secular nobility to the king. Immediate and powerful opposition prevented the actual enforcement of these laws. Christian II was compelled to flee from Denmark in 1523. The next few years he lived in exile. At the Diet of Augsburg in 1530 he is said to have renounced his Lutheran faith in order to get help from the emperor. In 1531 he conquered Norway, where he also pledged to support the Catholic church. In 1532 he was captured and imprisoned by Frederick I, the Danish king. He died in 1536.

Frederick I (1523-33), an uncle of Christian II, was elected king of Denmark in 1523, and of Norway in 1524. According to the terms of his election he was to protect the privileges of the nobles and to prevent any heretical preaching of "Luther's disciples and others." Frederick was favorably disposed toward the Reformation, but he did not repeat the mistake of the previous king. He soon found means of evading his election pledge by saying that he had never promised to protect the errors of the Catholic church, by pitting the secular nobility against the prince bishops, and by neglecting to enforce the Danish laws against heresy. In 1524 he imposed mutual toleration on Catholics and Protestants in the duchies of Schleswig and Holstein. From these regions Lutheranism spread rapidly to the Danish cities through the capable leadership of Hans Tausen, "the Danish Luther," and Claus Mortensen. In 1526 the king came out openly in favor of the Reformation, perhaps as much from policy as from conviction. He was ably supported, not only by the secular nobility, but also by the common people. The Danish nobles favored the king's policy because they were jealous of the powerful prince bishops and desired to possess themselves of some of the church property. The common people had become disgusted, not only with the life and practice of the clergy, but particularly with the shameless sale of indulgences which had been going on since 1516 under the supervision of Arciboldi.

The cities of Viborg, Malmö, and Copenhagen were the early

Reformation centers in Denmark. Claus Mortensen and others worked in Malmö. Hans Tausen was active in Viborg until 1529, when he was called by the king to be preacher in the St. Nicholas church in Copenhagen. Tausen, the Danish Reformer, had been educated in the universities of Rostock, Louvain, and Cologne. He had also spent two years at the University of Wittenberg where he often heard Luther. In 1524 he returned to Denmark where he began to preach the Lutheran faith. He was greatly aided in his work by a Danish translation of the New Testament, published in 1523. Preaching and Bible study in the vernacular were the means of promoting Protestantism in Denmark and in Norway. The king issued letters of protection to the Lutheran preachers in order to shield them against the threatened armed assaults by Catholic bishops.

At the Diet of Odense in 1527 the king practically tore the Danish church loose from Rome by the decree that the bishops should in the future seek confirmation of their appointment from the king, and not from the pope. The Diet of Odense in 1527 decreed that Lutherans should be recognized on equal terms with the Catholics and that the clergy should have permission to marry. At the Diet of Copenhagen in 1530 the Lutherans, under the leadership of Hans Tausen, presented a confession of faith in forty-three articles, the Confessio Haffnica, which they offered to defend in a public Danish disputation. But the Catholic clergy refused to debate in Danish, and this was not taken up in the best meaning by the Danes. From 1530 Lutheranism spread rapidly among all classes of people, in spite of Catholic opposition. In 1532 Frederick was admitted to the Schmalkald League. Denmark was fast becoming a stronghold of Lutheranism.

After the death of Frederick I in 1533, there was a serious dispute as to the successor to the throne. The Lutherans wanted the deceased king's oldest son, Christian, Duke of Schleswig-Holstein; and the Catholics wanted the younger son, John. After a distracting period of civil conflict, Christian emerged the victor. He ascended the Danish throne in 1536 as Christian III, king of Denmark and of Norway. The new king was a strong Lutheran. He had been present at the Diet of Worms in 1521, and Luther had made an indelible impression upon him. One of his first official acts was to make Lutheranism the religion of Denmark and of Norway. At the Diet of Copenhagen in 1536 the Reformation was formally legalized, and the Catholic religion was abolished by law. The bishops were forced to renounce their dignities, and all church property was confiscated for the crown and for the temporal nobles. The entire church organization was brought under the direct control of the crown. John Bugenhagen was called in from Wittenberg in 1537 to organize the Danish church along Lutheran lines. He appointed and consecrated seven superintendents who afterwards took the title of bishops. The "apostolic succession" of bishops was broken in Denmark through the ordination of these superintendents or bishops by a Lutheran preacher from Germany. The new Church of Denmark subscribed to the Augsburg Confession and to Luther's Catechism. The Reformation was carried on in a conservative way. Revised services were introduced and the entire nation was gradually instructed in the Lutheran faith.

II. Norway and Iceland.—Norway was a separate kingdom with Iceland as a dependency. Since the Calmar Union of 1397 the kingdoms of Norway, Denmark, and Sweden had been united under the Danish crown. Sweden managed to break away in 1523 while Norway remained united with Denmark until 1814. The Reformation in Norway was, therefore, largely a sequel to the Reformation in Denmark.

The city of Bergen was the early center of the Reformation in Norway. A German monk named Antonius preached the Lutheran doctrine with some success to the German speaking population of the city. He soon secured the assistance of two other evangelical preachers, Herman Frese and Jens Viborg. The bishop of Bergen, Olav Thorkelsson, tried in vain to stem the rising tide of Lutheranism. His efforts were almost completely arrested by the powerful Vincents Lunge, captain of the Bergenhus fortress, who not only supported the king against the Catholic clergy, but also tried to have the rights of Norway fully respected by the dominant Danish government. After 1528 some of the church property in and around the city was confiscated by the crown. In several of the city churches, including Hallvard's church, Morten's church, and Maria's church, Lutheran services were introduced. After a long and hopeless struggle the bishop finally left the city in 1535, and after this date the Reformation met with no serious opposition in Bergen.

From Bergen the Reformation movement soon spread to other cities. In 1529 the bishop of Stavanger complained of the inroads that Lutheranism was making into his bishopric. The movement gradually took root in the southern and the eastern parts of the country. Merchants and fishermen spread the Lutheran views even to the distant north. In 1530 "a few Lutherans" were found in western Finmark.

The archbishop of Nidaros, Olav Engelbrektsson (1523-37), and the Catholic bishops tried to suppress the Reformation, but they were largely checked by the nobility, especially by the influential Vincents Lunge. The archbishop himself was not a strong leader. On his way to Rome for the pallium in 1523 he had sworn allegiance to the deposed Christian II, but on his return from Rome he transferred his allegiance to Frederick I. His unsteady policy was again revealed in 1531 when he helped Christian II with church silver and with soldiers in order that the exiled king might regain his throne. In the civil conflicts of 1533-36 the Norwegian bishops supported John, and not Christian. Hence the new king naturally looked upon Norway as being hostile to him and to his policies.

Before Christian III was crowned king, he promised the Diet to subdue Norway by the force of arms. An army was sent in 1537. The archbishop fled to the Netherlands, taking with him the church archives and much of the movable church property. The bishops were forced to renounce their dignities. New Lutheran bishops were appointed and consecrated, but the "apostolic succession" of bishops was broken also in Norway. The new Danish Church-law was imposed upon the land for the time being, although hints were made in the legal ordinance that Norway would get its own church-law. By 1540 the formal process of establishing the Reformation in Norway had been completed.

Norway was granted its own church-law in 1607, during the reign of Christian IV. The land continued as a separate kingdom united with Denmark under the same crown, but the rights of Norway were often sadly violated or disregarded by the Danish government. From 1814 to 1905 Norway and Sweden were united under the Swedish crown. In 1905 Norway declared its independence and elected its own king.

In 1933 Norway had about 2,800,000 Lutherans, which is about 98.5% of the entire population. Of these about 20,000 belong to the Lutheran Free congregations, and the rest belong to the State Church.

In 1540 the Reformation was introduced into far-distant Iceland by Gissur Einarsson, a stepson of one of the two bishops of the island. Gissur Einarsson had studied in Germany and had, without the knowledge of his stepfather, come under the influence of Luther at the University of Wittenberg. He returned to Iceland in

1533, but when the Icelanders noticed that he had become contaminated with the Lutheran heresy, they would have nothing to do with him. But he soon regained the favor of his old, blind stepfather and even succeeded in being appointed his successor as bishop of Skalholt. He was consecrated bishop in 1540 and immediately began to introduce the Reformation into his bishopric. He was greatly helped by an Icelandic translation of the New Testament published that same year by Odd Gottskalksson, the son of an Iclandic bishop. In 1548 the other bishop of the island, Jon Arason, started a strong Catholic reaction. He was accused of high treason against the king of Denmark and put to death in 1550. Four years later the Catholic rebellion was forcibly suppressed and Lutheranism was established as the religion of Iceland. Gudbrandur Thorlaksson, the bishop who succeeded Jon Arason, translated the Bible into Icelandic in 1584.

Iceland had a Lutheran population of about 105,000 (in 1933).

III. **Sweden and Finland.**—Lutheranism was introduced into Sweden by the great Swedish reformer, Olavus Petri (1493-1552) in 1519 or 1520. Like his brother Laurentius Petri (1499-1573), the first Protestant archbishop of Sweden, he likely received his early education in the school of the local Carmelite monastery, and possibly at the University of Upsala. His father later sent Olavus to the University of Leipzig, but the growing fame of the University of Wittenberg soon attracted him, and he spent between two and three years at this institution, from 1516-19. During his stay at Wittenberg he received the baccalaureate and the master's degree. Recent investigations have disclosed that Laurentius Petri also studied at Wittenberg.[3] These two highly gifted brothers evidently became zealous disciples of Luther during their stay in Germany. Olavus states in his autobiographical remarks that he returned from Germany to Sweden in 1519. The bishop of his native diocese, Mattias Gregorii, commonly called Bishop Matts, consecrated or ordained Olavus a deacon in September, 1520, and placed him at the head of the Cathedral School of that region. About the same time he also became the secretary or chancellor of the bishop. The activity of Olavus as scholasticus of the Cathedral School, and his permission to preach, marked the beginning of the Reformation in Sweden. Among his many Lutheran converts, Olavus numbered his archdeacon, Laurentius Andreae, who became the second prominent Swedish reformer.

The Reformation in Sweden was quickly bound up with the political and economic interests of the country. In the Stockholm

[3] H. Lundström, *Undersökningar och aktstycken*, pp. 1-6.

Bath of Blood (cf. Section I), Bishop Matts had lost his life, and the government of his diocese was largely left in the hands of the archdeacon, Laurentius Andreae. That same year, 1520, the young Gustavus Vasa raised the standard of revolt against Denmark. In 1521 he was declared regent, and in 1523 he was elected king of Sweden.[4] But the early years of his reign were extremely difficult for him and for his government. His immediate problems were to pay back the money he had borrowed for his work of liberating Sweden, and to finance the new kingdom. Sweden was at that time impoverished by wars. Two thirds of the land belonged to the church and practically all the rest of the land was owned by the secular nobility. The church and the nobility claimed tax exemption. The trade of the country was largely in the hands of the Danes and the Germans. What could the king do to raise money?

He had heard and approved of the preaching of the Petri brothers before he was called to deliver his country. He had protected them against the attacks of the Catholic clergy, and there is good reason to believe that he favored the Reformation from genuine conviction. At the elective diet of Strängnäs in 1523 the king formed the acquaintance of Laurentius Andreae. On that occasion Andreae not only explained the aims and purposes of the Reformation more fully to the king, but he also suggested that Gustavus Vasa crush the power of the prince bishops by placing the church and its wealth under the immediate control of the crown. This could be done by introducing the Reformation. The king rewarded Andreae and his two colleagues by promoting them to positions of honor. Andreae was made chancellor of Sweden. Laurentius Petri was appointed professor[5] at Upsala University, and Olaus Petri was appointed preacher[6] in the large St. Nicholas church of Stockholm, and secretary in the City Council of the capital.

The king proceeded very cautiously with his reform program because the peasants who had helped him gain the throne were as yet strongly attached to the Catholic church. The bishops demanded that the Lutheran preachers be silenced, but Olaus Petri answered by issuing a challenge to a public disputation. In August, 1526, a Swedish Protestant translation of the New Testament was published.[7] With the New Testament in hand, the reading public was

---

[4] King Gustavus I was crowned on January 12, 1528.

[5] Laurentius Petri was appointed *ludimagister* at Upsala.

[6] Olavus Petri was appointed deacon-preacher of St. Nicholas in 1524. In that same year this church received a new pastor, Nicolaus Stecker, who also was German Secretary to Gustavus I. Stecker was a native of Eisleben, Germany, and a Lutheran.

[7] It is not definitely known who the translators were, but it appears that Olavus Petri was the chief translator, and that Laurentius Andreae was the chief editor of the Translation.

able to tell whether the teaching of the bishops or the preaching of the Lutherans was in harmony with Scripture.

At the Diet of Vesterås in 1527 matters were brought to a crisis. The king submitted the alternative of his abdication or the legal introduction of the Reformation. After three days of heated debate the Diet yielded to his wishes. Resolutions were adopted that the Word of God should be preached in its purity throughout the land, and that the king, and not the pope, was to be the highest authority in the Church of Sweden.[8] The Reformation was introduced into the whole land without resistance or force. As nearly all the bishops fled the country, new bishops were appointed in their places. These new bishops were consecrated in 1528 by Peter Magni, bishop of Vesterås.[9] He was the only remaining bishop who had been canonically ordained in Rome. He was ordained by a cardinal bishop in May, 1524. Bishop Peter Magni also consecrated Laurentius Petri as the first Protestant Archbishop of Upsala in 1531. Hence the "apostolic succession" of bishops was retained in Sweden. This fact was recognized by the Lambeth Conference of 1920. Duly ordained ministers of the Church of Sweden are admitted to preach in the churches of England. A Swedish Church-Book or Manual was published in 1529. A Hymn Book was adopted in 1530, and the "Swedish Mass" was issued in 1531. The Swedish Bible was printed in 1541.

During the long reign of Gustavus Vasa (1523-60), Sweden became thoroughly Lutheran,[10] with a marked conservatism in doctrine and in practice. The next king, Eric XIV (1560-68), allowed Calvinism to gain strong influence in the kingdom, mostly through the influx of the Huguenots. John III (1568-92) gave Catholicism a full opportunity to regain the land. But neither Calvinism nor Catholicism could alter the Lutheran character of the Church of Sweden. At the Church Council of Upsala in 1593, it was unanimously decreed that "the Bible is the sole rule of faith, and that its doctrines are correctly set forth in the three symbols and the unaltered Augsburg Confession." This completed the formal side of the Swedish Reformation. Sweden is to-day one of the most intensely Protestant countries in the world, with a Lutheran

[8] The Parliament at Vesterås in 1527 marked the beginning of the modern era in Sweden; but the severance of the Church of Sweden from Rome really occurred in November, 1523, when the King refused to confirm the bishops-elect of the Roman Curia and also refused the payment of annates.

[9] Gustavus I wanted duly ordained bishops present at his coronation on January 12, 1528.

[10] The Roman Church had ceased to exist in Sweden by 1552.

population of 6,096,551 (in 1933). All of these belong to the State Church except 113,721 who belong to the Swedish Mission Alliance.

From Sweden the Reformation spread quickly to Finland, where the movement took practically the same course as in Sweden itself. After 1528 the Bishop of Finland was obliged to swear allegiance to the Swedish king. The leading Finnish reformer was Michael Agricola, who later became Bishop of Abo. He published a number of religious writings, including a Finnish translation of the New Testament. By the cession of Finland to Russia in 1809 an independent Finnish Church was created, with the Archbishop of Abo as the recognized head.

Finland had in 1929 a Lutheran population of 3,514,036, which is about 97% of the entire Finnish population. About 90% of these Lutherans speak Finnish, the rest speak Swedish.

43. REVIEW QUESTIONS

1. In what countries was Luther's influence particularly felt?
2. Account for the fact that so few of these countries established permanent Lutheran churches.
3. Discuss the general condition of the Scandinavian countries at the time of the Reformation.
4. Explain why Christian II formed a league with the Catholic clergy of Sweden, at the same time favoring the friends of the Reformation in Denmark. Why did he fail in his attempt to introduce the Reformation?
5. Who was "the Danish Luther"? Discuss his reform program.
6. In what ways did Frederick I evade his election pledges?
7. At what time, and under what circumstances, was the Reformation legally established in Denmark?
8. How was the Reformation introduced into Norway? What part did Antonius, Olav Thorkelsson, Vincents Lunge, and Olav Engelbrektsson play?
9. Discuss the Reformation in Iceland. Who was Gissur Einarsson, Odd Gottskalksson, Jon Arason, and Gudbrandur Thorlaksson?
10. In what way was Lutheranism first brought into Sweden?
11. Why was the Reformation in Sweden so quickly bound up with the political and economic interests of the land?
12. How was the Reformation legally introduced into Sweden?
13. Why did Calvinism and Catholicism later fail to change the Lutheran character of the Swedish Church?
14. Why did Finland establish a national Lutheran Church?

TOPICS FOR SPECIAL STUDY

1. Hans Tausen, the "Danish Luther".
2. Bergen, the early Reformation center in Norway.
3. Gissur Einarsson and the Reformation in Iceland.
4. Gustavus Vasa and the Reformation in Sweden.
5. Michael Agricola, the Finnish Reformer.

IV. Poland.—The kingdom of Poland embraced the vast plain extending[11] from the Carpathian mountains to the river Düna, and from the Baltic almost to the Black Sea and the Sea of Azov. The country was inhabited by a variety of races, Ruthenians in the south, Lithunians in the northeast, and Poles in the northwest. In the cities there was a strong German population. Poland was theoretically an absolute monarchy, but the power of the king had been so limited that the monarch could pass no laws without the sanction of the powerful nobility. Sigismund I (1506-48) succeeded, however, in augmenting his power. During the reign of the next king, Sigismund II (1548-72), Poland was the most powerful kingdom in Eastern Europe, with a tendency toward the formation of a national church.

Poland was quite open to the inroads of new ideas. John Hus[12] and the Humanists[13] had exerted a powerful influence upon the population during the fifteenth century. The people had been awakened to the need of religious reform. The wealthy and indolent church and the immoral character of the clergy increased the general desire for reform. Fugitive Bohemian Brethren (Husites) helped to prepare the way for the Reformation in Poland. Returning students from the Lutheran universities, travelling merchants, and the German merchant-corporations in the Polish cities, invited Lutheran preachers from Germany, who brought Lutheranism into the land.

The Reformation spread with amazing rapidity. Danzig had a Lutheran preacher in 1518, and by 1525 the Catholic council was driven out of the city. This example was followed by the cities of Elbing and Thorn. Lutheranism was established in Prussian Poland (West and East Prussia) by 1525. A Protestant college was founded in the city of Posen for the purpose of educating the sons of the nobility in the Evangelical faith. Two Lutheran preachers were sent to Königsberg in 1523. Around 1540 a printing press was established in that city, and from this printing house the zealous Jan Seklucyan published a confession of faith, several catechisms, a hymn book, and a number of Evangelical writings in the mother tongue. A Protestant university was founded in Königsberg in 1544. In Wilna, the capital of Lithuania, a Protestant college was founded in 1541. Many young men went to the University of Wittenberg returning as enthusiastic disciples of Luther. By 1545 the Lutheran movement had taken root in all parts of Poland, except in the region of Masovia and its chief city, Warsaw; but a

[11] See map on page 206.   [12] See page 194.   [13] See pages 205-210.

Protestant church was not officially organized until John Laski, the great Polish reformer, returned in 1556.

After 1540 the Calvinist movement gained momentum in Poland. In 1555 the Lutherans and the Calvinists were about equally strong in the land. The Anabaptists also arrived and carried on as they had done in Germany and in Switzerland. After 1548 there was a large influx of Bohemian Brethren who had been expelled from their native country. These exiles strengthened the Protestant interest. A little later a large group of Unitarians found a home in Poland. The official religion of the land was Roman Catholicism, but few countries in Europe had at this time so great a variety of anti-Roman organizations.

King Sigismund I and the Catholic party tried in vain to stem the rising tide of Protestantism. A large number of the nobles and the gentry flocked to the Reformation standard because in it they saw a weapon against the dominant prince bishops and the church, as well as a key to a higher spiritual life. When Sigismund II (1548-72) became king, the future of Protestantism in Poland seemed much brighter. The king was officially a Catholic, but both he and his queen were friendly to the evangelical doctrine. Sigismund read Calvin's "Institutes of the Christian Religion" and carried on a correspondence with Calvin and with Melanchthon. Calvin dedicated his Commentary on the Epistle to the Hebrews to this king. At the Diet of 1555 the Protestants were strong enough to pass a law abolishing the jurisdiction of the ecclesiastical courts, which meant freedom for the friends of the Reformation. The Diet influenced the king to request that the pope call a Polish National Council, that the clergy be permitted to marry, that the cup be given to the laity in the Lord's Supper, that Mass be said in the vernacular, and that the Annates to Rome be abolished. A strong wish was also expressed for a national, Protestant church, but the king did not dare to take this step.

The pope answered the king by sending a papal legate to Poland to suppress the "heresy." This legate was ably assisted by Hosius, bishop of Ermeland. These antagonists took good advantage of the Protestant dissensions. The Protestant nobles of Poland turned to their famous countryman, John Laski, for help. He returned in 1556 and began at once to promote a union of the Lutherans, the Calvinists, and the Bohemian Brethren. With the assistance of friends he translated the Bible. His efforts to promote a Protestant union were crowned with success, although he

did not live long enough to see the fruits of his labors. At the
General Synod of Sendomir in 1560 the three dissenting parties
finally united, after Luther's doctrine of the Lord's Supper had
been recognized.

Meanwhile King Sigismund yielded to Catholic propaganda.
Members of the Order of the Jesuits were called in to establish
schools and to do other professional work. Sons of the Catholic
nobility were induced to attend famous Jesuit schools of other
countries. After the death of Sigismund in 1572 the crown became
elective. During the interregnum the Protestants formed a confederacy which guaranteed equal rights to all churches in the kingdom. Protestants and Catholics were pledged perpetually to maintain peace and to respect their mutual civil rights. The new king,
Henry of Anjou, tried in vain to avoid this pledge. He left Poland
secretly the next year to ascend the vacant French throne as Henry
III. The next Polish king, Stephen Barthori (1576-87), kept his
promise to the Protestants, but the next king, Sigismund III, violated his election pledge. During his reign Poland was completely
reconverted to Catholicism.

V. Bohemia-Moravia.—The great bulk of the population belonged to the Slavonic race, but numerous German merchants had
located in the various cities. Bohemia and Moravia were united
historically and dynastically with the Empire.

Bohemia was the homeland of John Hus and Hieronymus of
Prague, the two prominent precursors of the Reformation. During
the Husite War the followers of Hus had divided into two
parties, the Utraquists or Calixtines (calix: cup in the Lord's
Supper), and Taborites named after a fortified city.[14] Bohemian
Calixtiness had been present at the Leipzig Disputation in 1518,
and they had been greatly cheered when Luther demanded that the
cup should be given to the laity in the Lord's Supper. Bohemian
and Moravian Brethren received the Lutheran doctrine with favor,
although a large portion of the Calixtines for some time maintained
a conservative position. After the death of the great conservative
leader, Lukas of Prague, in 1528, the Bohemian Brethren came under the recognized leadership of Jan Augusta, "the Bohemian Luther," consecrated bishop in 1532. This highly gifted leader, who
frequently corresponded with Luther, gradually transformed his
party from a narrow, secluded sect to a large and influential section
of the Evangelical church. In 1535 he presented King Ferdinand
with a Confession of Faith which in several points corresponded

with the Augsburg Confession. Luther caused this confession to be printed in 1538 and wrote an introduction to it. After 1538 Bohemian and Moravian adherents of this confession came to be regarded as a special church within the Lutheran Reformation.[15] At an interview in 1542, Luther offered their delegates his hand as a pledge of perpetual friendship. The organization included numerous Bohemian nobles and the majority of the nobility in Moravia.

Ferdinand of Austria, brother of Emperor Charles V, was king of Bohemia from 1526 to 1564. He was a zealous Catholic, violently opposed to all religions other than Catholicism. He was unable, however, to suppress the Reformation. The Bohemian Protestants refused to fight against the German Lutherans in the Schmalkald War of 1546. When Ferdinand tried to inflict a heavy chastisement upon them, many fled to Poland and to Prussia. During his closing years, Ferdinand was compelled to be more considerate toward his Protestant subjects. The following king, Maximilian II (1564-76), did not disturb them. During the reign of Rudolph II (1576-1612), the Jesuits won back the country officially for Catholicism, but in the Letters of Majesty of 1609, the Protestants were granted unconditional religious liberty.

VI. Hungary and Transylvania.—The Magyars constituted the main bulk of the population, but there was also a liberal sprinkling of Slavs; German merchant-corporations had been organized in practically all of the cities.. A strong German' colony had existed in Transylvania since the latter part of the Middle Ages.

Lutheranism was brought into the country by travelling merchants and by returning students. The movement gained rapidly among the German speaking population, but the Magyars were, to begin with, rather anti-Lutheran. The Diet of 1523 decreed that the adherents of the new "heresy" were to be punished by death. But the invasion of the Turks in 1526 altered the situation completely. The greater portion of Hungary came under Turkish control, and the Turks favored the Hungarian Protestants for political reasons. A large portion of the Hungarian nobility also became interested in the Lutheran faith because they saw in this movement a means of getting a share of the secularized church property, as well as a key to a higher spiritual life, and to a national revival. Lutheranism was again permitted to spread throughout the land. Large numbers of Hungarian students flocked to the University of Wittenberg. Melanchthon was given the honorable

[15] Holmquist: *Kirkehistorie*, Vol. II, page 105.

title of "Preceptor of Hungary." The prominent Reformation leaders were Leonhard Stöckel, Matthias Biro Devay, called "the Hungarian Luther," and John Honter. At two large church conferences of 1545-46 the Hungarian Protestants subscribed to the Augsburg Confession, and organized the Evangelical Church of Hungary. In this newly organized church there was no division between the Magyars and the Germans, or between the nobility and the cities. They were all one in the Gospel. Hungary was fast becoming a purely Lutheran country.

But Calvinism and Zwinglianism soon gained considerable popularity, especially among the Magyars. Anabaptists and other Radical sects also gained ground. Active, and sometimes hostile, competition between these groups proved detrimental to Protestantism. The Unitarians came in somewhat later and found their greatest stronghold in Transylvania. Unitarianism almost wrecked the cause of the Reformation in this region. The Diet of Clausenburg in 1557, which proclaimed Transylvania an independent principality, also proclaimed universal religious liberty.

Toward the close of the century a strong Catholic reaction set in. Under the Jesuits the greater part of the country was won back to Catholicism.

VII. Croatia and Slavonia.—Croatia and Slavonia at that time were crown lands under Austria. Also to these countries did the Lutheran Reformation reach. The great reformer was Primus Truber. In 1530 he began to preach the Lutheran faith in the city of Laibach with great success. The movement spread, first to Croatia, later to Slavonia. Ferdinand of Austria instigated a strong Catholic reaction during which Truber had to flee to Germany. He continued his reform work by translating parts of the Bible and numerous Reformation treatises into the languages of these two countries. Since Slavonia had no fixed alphabet, Truber used the Latin alphabet and published at least twenty-five different books in the language of Slavonia, the most important of which were the New Testament and Luther's Catechism. He published at least thirty similar books in the language of Croatia.

Truber later returned to Croatia and Slavonia to organize a Lutheran church. This church held its own against the pressure of the Catholic Counter-Reformation for the next fifty years.

VIII. Italy.—Lutheranism spread to Italy by various agencies. Practically all the writings of Luther were translated into Italian shortly after their publication. These translations, which were anonymous, were widely circulated. The Bible was translated into Italian in 1530 by Antonio Brucioli, but the pope placed this translation on the Index of Prohibited Books. Many Italian cities had a lively commercial intercourse with Germany, and travelling merchants frequently propagated the Lutheran views.

The famous Spaniard, Juan de Valdes, had about 1530 been chosen secretary to the Viceroy of Naples. Valdes had gained world fame as a literary genius. His study of Luther's writings gradually won him over to the view of the Saxon Reformer, although he remained in the Catholic church. He published "The Alphabet of Christianity" in which he emphasized salvation by faith in Christ alone, without the merit of good works, as the essential element in religion. He also published a number of other writings, including commentaries on practically all of the Epistles of Paul. In all these, he expressed clear, Evangelical views. He escaped persecution because he did not attack papacy. His Lutheran views exerted a strong influence upon a number of prominent Italians. When he died in 1541, he had a following of at least thirty-three hundred Evangelicals in Naples alone.[16] Even Contarini and several other cardinals were influenced by his Lutheran views.

The Augustinian monk, Peter Martyr Vermigli, accepted the pure Lutheran doctrine largely through the influence of Valdes. Vermigli ranked as one of the most learned priests of Italy. Compelled to flee, he became a professor, first at Strassburg, then at Oxford, England. When Mary Tudor ascended the English throne, he returned to Strassburg. He exerted a powerful influence upon the religious life of Europe.

Bernardino Ochino, famed for his holy life and his marvellous oratory, was the general of a monastic order called the Capuchins. When he preached, no church was large enough to hold his audience. Ochino studied the writings of Luther and Zwingli for the purpose of refuting them, but they refuted him instead. He embraced the Protestant faith in 1542 after which he preached the Gospel with such power and simplicity that even the street cleaners discussed the Pauline Epistles.

Peter Paul Vergerius, Bishop of Capo d'Istria, and papal legate to Germany, was called upon by the pope to negotiate with Luther. The bishop made a careful study of Luther's writings for the purpose of refuting them and their author, but he was gradually led to embrace the Evangelical faith. He fled from Italy, later accepting a professorship at the University of Tübingen.

Flaminio, an Italian noble, published "Del benefizio di Christo," a summary of the views of Juan de Valdes. This book became as

[16] Holmquist: *Kirkehistorie*, Vol. II, page 109.

popular as some of the "best sellers" of Luther's books. In a short time 40,000 copies had been printed in Italy alone. Several of the Reform-Cardinals read it daily for meditation.

In 1542 a special Inquisition was set up for the purpose of suppressing Protestantism. The Evangelical groups were persecuted with fanatical fury, but the movement was not completely crushed until toward the close of the century.

In Spain the Reformation had a considerable following, but the Spanish Inquisition suppressed it within twenty or thirty years.

44. REVIEW QUESTIONS

1. Why was the Greek Catholic church so little affected by the Protestant Reformation?
2. Discuss the causes which promoted or hindered the establishment of the Reformation in Poland.
3. Who were the following: (1) Jan Seklucyan? (2) John Laski? (3) Sigismund II? (4) Hosius? (5) Stephen Bathori? (6) Sigismund III?
4. How was the Reformation established in Bohemia-Moravia?
5. What can you say about the following: (1) Lukas of Prague? (2) "The Bohemian Luther"? (3) Ferdinand of Austria? (4) Maximilian II? (5) Rudolph II?
6. Did the invasion of the Turks in 1526 suppress or promote the Reformation in Hungary and Transylvania? Explain carefully.
7. Why did the majority of the Magyar nobility favor the Reformation?
8. How did the inrush of Calvinists, Zwinglians, Anabaptists, and Unitarians affect the Protestant cause in Hungary and Transylvania?
9. Discuss the Reformation in Croatia and Slavonia.
10. By what general agencies did Lutheranism spread to Italy?
11. What connection did the following men have with the Reformation in Italy? (1) Juan de Valdes? (2) Peter Martyr Vermigli? (3) Bernardino Ochino? (4) Peter Paul Vergerius? (5) Flamino?
12. Why did the Reformation make so little progress in Italy?

TOPICS FOR SPECIAL STUDY

1. Jan Seklucyan.
2. John Laski.
3. Jan Augusta.
4. Matthias Biro Devay.
5. Primus Truber.
6. Prominent Evangelical Italians of this era.

A SELECTED BIBLIOGRAPHY FOR CHAPTER XII

1. *Cambridge Modern History*, Volume II, Chapter XVII.
2. Lindsay: *A History of the Reformation*, Volume I, pages 417-425.
3. Lövgren: *Church History*, pages 218-230.
4. Walker: *A History of the Christian Church*, pages 382-386.
5. Kurtz: *Church History*, Volume II, pages 114-128.
6. Bergendoff: *Olavus Petri and the Ecclesiastical Transformation in Sweden.*
7. Fox: *The Reformation in Poland.*
8. Loserth: *Die Reformation und Gegenreformation in den inneröstreichischen Ländern in 16. Jahrhundert.*

CHAPTER XIII

The Spread of the Swiss Reformation

The Protestant Reformation produced three[1] main types of evangelical communions or confessions, the Lutheran, the Reformed, and the Anglican. The Lutheran communion includes the churches which bear Luther's name and subscribe to the Augsburg Confession. The Reformed group traces its origin to Zwingli and Calvin. The Anglican group, occupying a position between Protestantism and Catholicism, includes the Established Church of England and its branches in Scotland, Ireland, India, and the colonies, and also the Protestant Episcopal Church in the United States of America.

From Switzerland, particularly from Geneva, the Swiss Reformation spread to practically all countries of Europe. Reformed churches were established in Poland, Bohemia, Hungary, Moravia, and Transylvania.[2] For some time the Swiss gave the Lutherans in Germany and in Sweden considerable competition. But the Reformed church gained its greatest strength in northwestern Europe where its adherents were known by various names: in northern France as the Huguenots; in the Netherlands as the Dutch Reformed; in Scotland as Scotch Presbyterians; and in portions of central England as Puritans.

I. France.—The Bible Humanists were the forerunners of the Reformation in France. These men believed that a return to the Christian sources was the chief need of the time. Consequently, the Bible should be given to the French people in the vernacular. The chief representative was Jaques Le Fèvre, of Etaples (1455-1536), a professor in the University of Paris. Between 1509 and 1522 he published several Bible commentaries in which he anticipated many of the teachings of Luther, especially the rule of the Scriptures and justification by faith. In 1523 he published a French translation of the New Testament in order that the people might be able to read it. A French translation of the Psalms followed in 1524, and by 1530 he had translated the whole Bible.

Le Fèvre had many devoted pupils, of whom the most promi-

---

[1] See pp. 287-88. [2] See map on page 290.

nent were William Briconnet, bishop of Meaux; William Budé, a prominent Greek scholar and one of the founders of the Collége de France; Louis de Berquin who later died as a Protestant martyr; and William Farel who became an associate of Calvin at Geneva. By 1523 a considerable group of priests and laymen, known as "the Meaux Group," had gathered around Le Fèvre and Briconnet for the purpose of promoting a reform from within the Church. The members of this group, especially William Farel, were strongly influenced by Luther. Meaux, as it seemed, was about to become a second Wittenberg. But the Parliament of Paris started a severe persecution against all who departed from the accepted doctrines and traditions of the Catholic Church. Briconnet, bowing before the storm, forsook his Evangelical friends. Le Fèvre fled to Strassburg, although he was recalled later by the king. The reform efforts of the Meaux Group as such were completely arrested.

Luther's works in French translation began to circulate as early as in 1519. They were eagerly read, especially in Paris. In 1523 a Dutch evangelical preacher at Leyden published "Summa der godliker Scrifturen," one of the most influential and widely circulated books of the Reformation period. A French translation, published in 1524, exerted a great influence upon the educated people. The French Catholics were determined, however, to crush Lutheranism by force. In 1521 the University of Paris formally pronounced Luther a heretic and a blasphemer. At the same time the Parliament of Paris made it unlawful to print and distribute Luther's writings or to teach his doctrines. This law resulted in bitter persecutions and in a number of executions. Yet sentiment in favor of the Reformation continued to grow so that by 1530 a number of isolated groups of evangelicals were found in many parts. The severe Catholic persecutions gradually caused these evangelical groups to accept the most extreme form of anti-Romanism, the great majority becoming Calvinists.

At a synod in 1532 the Waldenses[3] accepted the principles of the Protestant Reformation. The addition of this group gave a new impetus to the movement. The synod also decided, at the instigation of William Farel, to prepare a new French Bible translation based on the original text. By 1535 Pierre Robert Olivétan, a cousin of Calvin, had translated the entire Bible into excellent French. Meanwhile William Farel tried, from Switzerland, to supply evangelical pastors.

[3] See page 182.

The inconsiderate zeal of certain radical reformers brought on a severe persecution in 1534-35. Anthony de Marcourt had prepared some placards denouncing the Catholic mass. On the night of October 17-18, 1534, these placards were posted in Paris, Orleans, Rouen, Tours, Blois, and on the door of the royal bed-chamber at Amboise. The king was greatly aroused. Francis I was not opposed to a reformation of the Erasmian type, but he feared the revolutionary effects of a Protestant reformation. He believed in the old maxim, "One king, one law, one faith," so he started a persecution immediately. Two hundred persons were arrested within the first month, of which twenty were martyred; the rest were banished and their property confiscated. It was this persecution which drove Calvin out of France.[4]

Meanwhile the increasing menace of the Hapsburgs under Charles V forced Francis I to make an alliance with the infidel Turks. He also courted the friendship of the Schmalkald League, but the German princes would make an alliance with him on no terms save those of tolerance to French Protestants. Consequently, the king published an edict in July, 1535, ordering the persecution to cease. Yet, to the end of his reign in 1547 he followed the policy of tacit opposition to Protestantism. In 1545 he did not lift a finger to prevent the horrible massacre of the Waldenses, when twenty-two villages were burned and about four thousand persons ruthlessly killed. His son, Henry II (1547-1559), was determined to extirpate heresy by burning the heretics as well as their books, but persecution failed, for the number of Protestants increased steadily. "For one martyr who disappeared in the flames, there presented themselves a hundred more; men, women, and children marched to their punishment singing the psalms of Marot or the canticle of Simeon."[5]

Clemens Marot (1497-1544) was a French poet who had made a poetic translation of the Old Testament Psalms. His hymns were tremendously popular. The first Calvinistic hymnal of 1539 contained but eighteen psalms, twelve of which were composed by Marot. The completed French Protestant hymnal of 1562 included forty-nine of Marot's hymns. Between 1562 and 1565 this hymnal went through sixty-two editions, being ultimately translated into twenty-two languages. Marot's "Que Dieu se montre seulement," often called "The Marseillais of the Huguenots." gained a prominence similar to that of "Ein feste Burg" among the Germans. Marot himself renounced Protestantism in 1536.

[4] See page 264. [5] Luke 2:29-32.

The Protestant movement was without a recognized head and without organization until Calvin published his "Institutes of the Christian Religion" in 1536. Up to around 1560 the French Protestants were usually nicknamed "Lutherans" or "heretics of Meaux," although after 1536 the real leadership was supplied by Calvin. Up to 1536 they had sought to reform the Church from within, after that date they tried to promote a reformation outside the Church. They were greatly helped by Olivétan's French Bible, by Marot's evangelical hymns, and by Calvin's French theology.

In 1559 the French Protestants had about forty-nine regular congregations with more than two thousand "conventicles" or preaching places. At the first Protestant Synod, held in Paris in 1559, the "Reformed" Church of France was formally organized. Calvin had prepared forty articles which were adopted as a Confession of Faith, the "Confessio Gallicana." The synod agreed on a uniform church constitution and a formal discipline. The Church, being forced out of connection with the State, became democratic and self-governing. A synodical form of church government was adopted. Each local congregation was governed by a consistory composed of pastors and laymen. The congregations of a circuit were governed by a corresponding circuit consistory. The circuits were governed by provincial synods, and these were controlled by the national synod.

During the next two years the number of congregations grew from 49 to 2150. About one-fourth of the population had become "contaminated" with Protestantism. A large number of the great nobles, including the Coligny family, joined the Reformed Church. Even a powerful branch of the royal family, the Bourbons, embraced Protestantism. This gave to the French Reformation a peculiar mingling of religious and political aims which in 1562 plunged the French nation into a religious warfare which lasted for thirty-six years.

II. The Netherlands.—At the time of the Reformation the Netherlands comprised seventeen provinces, nearly co-extensive with the territory included in the present kingdoms of Holland and Belgium. Charles V considered these Low Countries a most valuable portion of his great realm. Agriculture, manufacture, and commerce flourished. The territory included three hundred and fifty cities. Of these Antwerp was the greatest trading center in Europe. The population, half Teutonic and half Latin, was noted for its industry and skill, and for its proficiency in science and letters.

The Netherlands had been a center of reform tendencies even before the time of Luther. The Brethren of the Common Life,[6] and the Bible Humanists had their original home in the Low Countries. Erasmus of Rotterdam, Prince of the Humanists, hailed from that same region. The famous Spanish educator, Juan Vives, had been very active in the Netherlands since 1512. He demanded a thorough reformation of the Catholic clergy, and a general church council. Luther's writings began to circulate among the Dutch in 1518, and before 1521 the Antwerp printers had issued at least a dozen of his tracts and books. Antwerp, next to Paris the largest printing center in Europe, became a stronghold of Protestant propaganda. In 1523 the first Dutch translation of the New Testament was published in Amsterdam. The "Summa der godliker Scrifturen" was published in Leyden that same year. Augustinian monks in the Netherlands accepted Luther's doctrines and carried on a rousing propaganda in favor of reform. German commercial colonies in various Dutch cities became distributing centers of the Reformation ideas.

By 1520 evangelical groups were established in all Dutch provinces. Modern Dutch historians do not, however, characterize these groups as specifically Lutheran. The early Dutch Reformation was partly Lutheran and partly a survival of older reform movements. After 1525 the more moderate Lutheranism began to give way to radical Anabaptism; after 1540 the Reformation became increasingly Calvinistic in character. When the Catholic Counter-Reformation commenced (after 1550), more than half of the Protestants were Calvinists. The Anabaptists constituted the next largest group, while the Lutherans formed a small minority.

A vigorous Catholic counter-propaganda was started in 1520, and in 1521 a special inquisition was organized to deal with heresy. The first attack concentrated on the Augustinian monastery at Antwerp. From this Lutheran center two young Lutheran monks, Henry Voes and John Esch, were taken and burned at the stake on July 2, 1523. They became the first Lutheran martyrs. The inquisition failed, however, for Protestantism spread in spite of it. The Reformation had become a popular mass movement. The commercial interests and the relative independence of the provincial government largely checked Catholic opposition. But the horrible persecutions which followed later made the Netherlands a world theater in miniature.

Increasing Catholic pressure caused the Dutch to embrace Calvinism. The Lutherans stood for passive resistance, and the Anabaptists advocated a revolutionary communism, but Calvinism gave its adherents the will to resist tyranny by force About 1550 the Protestants separated into a Lutheran minority outwardly living under existing Catholic forms, and a Calvinistic majority which organized conventicles. Calvin advised his adherents that "the Church under the Cross" must take the organized form of "house-churches." In 1559 there were enough of these Calvinistic congregations to hold a synod and to adopt a creed. This creed was adopted in 1562 as the Confessio Belgica, the Dutch Reformed Church thereby being formally organized. A synodical church government, similar to that of France, was adopted. William the Silent, Prince of Orange, tried to unite the Reformed and the Lutherans, but failed because Theodore Beza, Calvin's successor at Geneva, definitely opposed the plan.

Philip II of Spain (1555-98) succeeded his father, Charles V, as the ruler of the Netherlands. The main article of his creed was political and religious absolutism. His policy was to make the Netherlands a mere dependency of the Spanish crown, and to wipe out Protestantism. In the first year of his reign he gave the Jesuits control of the Inquisition in the Low Countries.

III. Scotland.—Scotland was a poor and backward country at the beginning of the Reformation era. Social and political conditions were medieval. The powerful nobles were extremely rough, and the clergy were ignorant and profligate. Humanistic influences had been slightly felt in the three universities, St. Andrews, Glasgow, and Aberdeen, but educational standards were weak compared with continental seats of learning. Prominent Scotch humanists accepted teaching positions in continental universities rather than stay to advance the native culture. Scotland had no centralized government. The prince bishops owned about one half of the land, and the secular nobility owned or controlled the other half. The king had very little power. He had no standing army of his own and no personal body-guard, but had to depend on the feudal militia for protection and support.

The Reformation movement reached Scotland partly by way of England, partly through the activities of returning Protestant students, and partly through the circulation of Lutheran and Reformed writings. Tyndal's and Coverdale's Bible translations were popular. Luther's writings were so eagerly read that the Parliament found it necessary, in 1525, formally to prohibit the printing and distribution of Lutheran literature. Patrick Hamilton returned from the Continent in 1528 and began at once to preach the Gospel. He had studied at Marburg, and later at Wittenberg where he had formed a close friendship with Luther. Archbishop David Beaton of Scotland had Hamilton arrested and burned at the stake in 1528. There were other early Protestant martyrs in Scotland. Prominent among these was the noble and learned George Wishart. He preached the Gospel in various places of Scotland for

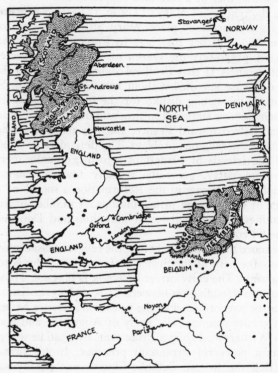

CALVINISM AS ESTABLISHED IN THE NETHERLANDS AND SCOTLAND BY 1580

about two years before he was burned at the stake in 1546. After this date the progress of the Reformation was intimately bound up with the political fortunes of the land.

Henry VII of England had formed a marriage alliance with his neighboring kingdom to the north when his elder daughter, Margaret, was married to James IV, King of Scotland. The patriotic Scotch nobility feared that this was but the beginning of a policy to make Scotland a dependency of England. Hence the nobles formed alliances with France against England. King James V (1513-42) married Mary of Lorraine, a sister of the Duke of Guise. This powerful French house was violently opposed to Protestantism. When James V died in 1542 he left the crown to his infant daughter, Mary Stuart, but the Dowager Queen, Mary of Guise, was Queen-regent of Scotland until her death in 1560. Her policy was that of Protestant suppression.

During the regency of Mary of Guise, 1542-60, a political change of great significance took place. Mary Stuart was sent to France to be educated, and her marriage to Francis II made her for a brief period (1559-60) the Queen of France. Her secret agreement with Francis II that Scotland should be given to the crown of France in case she died without heirs was sensed in Scotland. Furthermore, the strong dislike for the licentious French officers and French soldiers stationed in Scotland developed an intense and widespread hatred toward France, and this political change naturally affected the religious problem. The defenders of Scotch freedom and the friends of Protestant reform gradually merged into one powerful party, generally friendly toward England. The secular nobility also saw in the Reformation a means of crushing the power of the detested prince bishops. A number of prominent noble families, including those of Hamilton and Douglas, openly proclaimed Protestantism.

A little more than a decade before the religious issue was brought to a climax the hero of the Scotch Reformation, John Knox, made his appearance. The early career of Knox is obscure. He was born in a suburb of Haddington between 1505 and 1514. Knox himself states that he was ordained to the priesthood. Hence he very likely had a university training. His study of Augustine and his association with Wishart made him a Protestant. By 1546 he was generally known as a powerful Protestant preacher. In his preaching he asserted that the Roman Catholic Church was the Synagogue of Satan and that the pope was the anti-Christ. French soldiers captured him in 1547 and made him a galley slave for nineteen months. After his release he spent five years in England where he exerted a considerable influence. He declined the bishopric of Rochester in 1522 because he foresaw trouble under Mary. After Mary "the Bloody" ascended the English throne, he fled to the Continent and spent some time, first at Frankfort, later at Geneva, where he became an ardent disciple of Calvin.

In 1556 the future Reformer of Scotland returned to England

to marry. He subsequently went to Scotland where he preached the Gospel for several months. Knox was by this time an extreme Calvinist. He preached passionately against the mass, and presented a written petition to the Queen-regent, Mary of Guise, begging her to favor the Gospel. The petition did not meet with favor. It was evident that Scotland was not yet ready for a rupture with Rome. Knox, obliged to leave the country, returned to Geneva. But the brief stay in his native land had been of great significance for the progress of the Reformation. In 1556-57 a number of Protestant congregations, with a Presbyterian form of church government, were definitely organized in Scotland. On December 3, 1557, a number of Scotch nobles decided to sever their relations with "Satan's Synagogue." Together with a number of laymen they entered into a Covenant to stand by one another with life and fortune to "establish the most blessed Word of God and His Congregation." This is usually referred to as the First Scottish Covenant.

The next year, 1558, Elizabeth became the Queen of England. Mary Stuart, "Queen of the Scots" and potential Queen of France, denounced Elizabeth as an illegitimate usurper, proclaiming herself the rightful occupant of the English throne. This claim threatened· not only to make Scotland a part of France but to draw England into the same relation. Knox and his friends realized that a political and religious crisis was near, and that they might expect some assistance from Queen Elizabeth. On May 2, 1559, Knox was back in Scotland where he immediately began to preach. He combined, in a masterly way, the glowing passion of a great agitator with an intuitive knowledge of actual possibilities. He received excellent political and military assistance from John Erskine, the leader of the First Scottish Covenant. Wherever Knox went, his preaching was like a match set to kindling wood. The people openly revolted against the Roman Catholic Church. Images were destroyed, monasteries were stormed and looted, and the priests were commanded, under pain of death, to desist from saying mass. The Queen-regent, who regarded this procedure as rank rebellion, ordered French troops to quell the revolt. Knox induced the Protestants to meet force with force, and the armed combat ended in a draw. When France sent reinforcements, the Queen of England was finally induced to interfere. She sent an army which compelled the French to withdraw and to leave the government of Scotland in the hands of the Council of Lords. The treaty was signed on July 6, 1560. Shortly before this the Queen-regent died.

Protestantism had won an almost complete victory. The Scottish

Parliament of 1560 officially proclaimed the Reformed faith the religion of Scotland. Knox became the recognized church leader. At the request of the Parliament he prepared a Confession of Faith, the Confessio Scoticana, which was adopted on August 17, 1560, with only eight dissenting votes. A week later the Parliament passed the Laws of the Estates involving a complete rupture with Rome. In January, 1561, the Parliament adopted the "First Book of Discipline," prepared by Knox. The system worked out by Calvin was applied to the entire nation. In each parish the pastor and the presbyters constituted an administrative and disciplinary board. The presbyters were elected by the congregation. In the larger centers meetings for discussion were held which later developed into "presbyteries." Pastors and congregations within specified regions were governed by synods, and over all was the "General Assembly."

Mary Stuart tried to restore Roman Catholicism upon her return, but her unfortunate policy and her complicity in the murder of her second husband, Lord Darnely, caused her expulsion from Scotland in 1567. She was forced to abdicate in favor of her infant son, James, and her Protestant half-brother, Murray, was appointed regent. When Elizabeth died in 1603, England and Scotland were united under one crown, with James as the joint king. When Knox died in 1572, his work was ably continued by Andrew Melville (1545-1622).

45. REVIEW QUESTIONS

1. What is meant by the Reformed Church? This Church is the mother of how many evangelical denominations?
2. Why was Lutheranism gradually supplanted by Calvinism in France, in the Netherlands, and in Scotland?
3. Who were the prominent French Bible Humanists? How did these men prepare the way for the French Reformation?
4. Discuss the progress of Protestantism in France up to 1536. Who supplied the leadership?
5. What was the status of the French Protestants between 1559 and 1562?
6. What conditions in the Low Countries favored the introduction of new movements?
7. Through what agencies was the Reformation established in the Netherlands?
8. Why the Dutch "house-churches"?
9. What part did Patrick Hamilton, David Beaton, George Wishart, and Mary of Guise play in the early history of the Reformation in Scotland?
10. Why was the Reformation in Scotland so intimately connected with national and European politics?
11. Discuss the life of John Knox and his relation to the Scotch Reformation.
12. What type of church government did Knox establish in Scotland?

TOPICS FOR SPECIAL STUDY

1. "The Meaux Group" and its Evangelical influence.
2. The French Bible translation of Pierre Robert Olivétán.
3. Clemens Marot, the French hymn-writer.
4. Henry Voes and John Esch, the first Lutheran martyrs in the world.
5. The Dutch "house-churches."
6. Patrick Hamilton and George Wishart.
7. John Knox, the Reformer of Scotland.

A SELECTED BIBLIOGRAPHY FOR CHAPTER XIII

1. *Cambridge Modern History,* Vol. II, Chap. IX; Vol. III, Chap. I, VI, VII.
2. Lindsay: *A History of the Reformation,* Vol. II, pages 61-314.
3. Smith: *The Age of the Reformation,* Chap. IV, V.
4. Browning: *History of the Huguenots.*
5. Baird: *The Rise of the Huguenots.*
6. Blok: *History of the People of the Netherlands,* Vol. I-II.
7. Knox: *History of the Reformation in Scotland.*
8. Fleming: *The Reformation in Scotland.*
9. Brown: *John Knox.*
10. Brown: *History of Scotland,* Vol. I-III.
11. Robinson: *Readings in European History.*
12. Tawney: *Religion and the Rise of Capitalism.*

CHAPTER XIV

The Reformation in England

The English Reformation[1] took on certain peculiar characteristics, because the political and personal interests of Henry VIII caused him to sever the English church from Rome before Protestant doctrines had been generally accepted by his people. When the Anglican church assumed final form during the reign of Queen Elizabeth[2] it proved to be a communion half way between evangelical Protestantism and Roman Catholicism. It developed into a national church, for the English people only, while the Lutheran and the Reformed churches were international in character. The rich Renaissance culture permeating English life during the Elizabethan period, impressed itself strongly upon the Anglican church, giving to its divine worship a wealth of forms and a fullness of ceremonial beauty far surpassing those ordinarily found in Lutheran or Reformed churches.[3]

I. Early Reform Influences.—William of Occam (1280-1349), the most influential theologian of his time, was one of the early forerunners of the English Reformation. He asserted that the pope was not infallible, that the General Council and not the pope was the highest authority in the Church, that Holy Scripture was the only infallible source in matters of faith and life, and that in secular matters the Church and the pope were subordinated to the State. Occam exerted a strong influence upon John Wiclif and Martin Luther.[4]

John Wiclif (1324-84), English professor, preacher, and patriot, was the "morning star of the Reformation." He translated the Bible into English in 1382, and organized groups of travelling lay preachers who explained the Bible to the people. When his followers, called the Lollards, petitioned the Parliament for a reform of the Church, a severe persecution broke out against them. They lost their influence as a party, but they continued to meet in secret to read the Gospel together in English. The essential influence of Wiclif and the Lollards was to make the people better acquainted with the contents of the Bible.

---

[1] See map on page 313.
[2] See chronology on page 214.
[3] See pp. 287-88.
[4] See page 192.

The Renaissance was brought to England in the closing years of the fifteenth century by William Linacre (1460-1524), William Grocyn (1446-1514), and John Colet (1467-1519), who introduced humanistic learning at the University of Oxford. From Oxford the new learning was transmitted to the University of Cambridge, and over a century later, to Harvard University. Humanism made little impression, but it gained considerable prestige when the distinguished Erasmus came to the University of Cambridge to lecture for four years (1510-14). John Colet found the time ripe for reconstructing the cathedral school of St. Paul's in London along humanistic lines in 1510, and other secondary schools of England followed suit. Erasmus wrote several textbooks to introduce the new learning, and in 1516 he published his first Greek edition of the New Testament because he wanted to lead the people back to the Biblical sources. He foresaw the Reformation, stating in a letter dated September, 1517, "I am afraid that a great revolution is impending."

Luther's writings began to circulate quite early. His "Babylonian Captivity of the Church of Christ" was studied by Lollard groups at Oxford and Cambridge. Henry VIII attacked this book in his "Defence of the Seven Sacraments," published in 1521, receiving from the pope the title "Defender of the Faith." A committee of the University of Cambridge examined Luther's writings and quickly condemned and burned them. The government did the same a little later. In May, 1521, a crowd of thirty thousand watched the burning of Luther's books at St. Paul's in London, and listened to the church officials who pronounced Luther a heretic. Some of the leading humanists, including Sir Thomas More and Cardinal Wolsey, joined in the fight against the "damnable heresy." But Lutheranism spread rapidly despite the severe opposition. Evangelical groups were secretly formed. The Cambridge group numbered men like William Tyndale and Thomas Cranmer.

Tyndale's English New Testament, published in 1526, became the chief source of early English Protestantism. William Tyndale (1484-1536) had become a proficient Greek scholar while attending Oxford and Cambridge. The Greek New Testament of Erasmus and Luther's books had awakened a desire to give the common people the Bible in their own language. He went to Hamburg where he studied Hebrew with some prominent Jews. Then he went to Wittenberg to confer with Luther. His English New Testament was printed in Worms in 1525-26. English merchants smuggled his New Testament into England. After 1526 a number of prominent English nobles began to favor Protestantism. Anne Boleyn, later the wife of Henry VIII, was early pointed out as a Lutheran. Tyndale also exerted a strong influence through his book, "The Obedience of a Christian Man," published in 1528. In this book he explained and defended the Reformation. His translation of parts of the Old Testament followed later. Tyndale himself was condemned as a heretic and burned at the stake in 1536.

II. The Reign of Henry VIII, 1509-47.—The Reformation made slow progress up to 1527. Severe opposition from the king, the clergy, and some of the humanists forced it down as a deep undercurrent in the English national life. Then the castastrophe occurred which gave it such a peculiar turn, and made Henry VIII the very center of the Reformation movement there.

Henry VIII has been described as a "tyrant under legal forms." He was a man of learning and a devoted son of the Church of Rome. The people held him in high esteem because he tried to promote the interests and the welfare of England. But he was obstinate, egotistic, and self-seeking. He did not try to suppress the parliament, the convocations, the tribunals, or the national freedom, but he made them all his willing tools. In the early part of his reign he had Cardinal Thomas Wolsey (1475-1530), a prominent politician and a man who knew his people. Wolsey had two great ambitions: to make England an international power; and to become pope. He succeeded well in his first purpose, but he was not elected pope. As a consequence, Wolsey turned his hatred toward Charles V and toward the emperor's aunt, Queen Catherine of England. This hatred had important bearings on the divorce suit of Henry VIII and Catherine a few years later.

Catherine of Aragon, daughter of Ferdinand and Isabella of Spain, had been married to Henry VIII's older brother, Arthur, who did not live to inherit the crown. Pope Julius II had in 1503 granted Henry a special permission to marry his deceased brother's wife. Six children were born to this union, but only Princess Mary survived infancy. By 1527, the king desired to divorce Catherine because he was convinced that she would not bear him a son. The absence of a male heir would probably cause civil war, as no woman had ever sat upon the throne of England. Henry declared in his petition to the pope that the marriage of his brother's widow had been a sin. He had fallen in love with one of the ladies of the court, Anne Boleyn, but this he failed to mention to the pope. The fact that the lady was a Protestant put Wolsey in a delicate position, because he was an ardent Catholic. His fall seemed certain whether Catherine or Anne Boleyn was Queen of England.

Wolsey was assigned the difficult task of negotiating with the pope to have the marriage of Henry and Catherine annulled. Pope Clement VII might have granted the divorce, had it not been for recent political victories of Charles V, king of Spain and emperor of Germany. This powerful ruler was determined that his aunt Catherine should not be set aside, and the pope did not dare to offend him. Wolsey failed. Henry, greatly angered, accused him of high treason. The great cardinal died, November 30, 1530, on his way to trial.

The king was determined to have things his own way, in spite of pope and emperor, so he formed friendly relations with the Reformed and the anti-clerical parties to gain the necessary popular support. Protestant books were allowed to circulate at court, Easter, 1529. These books advocated the confiscation of church property and the return to a simpler religious life. Thomas Cromwell, an ardent Protestant, replacing Sir Thomas More, was prime minister from 1532 until 1540. Thomas Cranmer, the first Protestant archbishop of Canterbury, was appointed in 1532 and consecrated in 1533. With these appointments, the king relying on the national feeling of hostility to foreign rule, proceeded to make the parliament the willing tool of his church policies.

Cromwell suggested that the king renounce papal jurisdiction and proclaim himself supreme head of the Church of England, and then get a decree of divorce from his own courts. Henry acted swiftly. The parliament in 1532 gave the king authority to abolish the payment of annates to Rome. Later in 1532 the Act of Submission of the Clergy was passed, decreeing that the clergy in convocation could pass no laws without the king's permission. This act completely reversed the previous relation between church and state in England. In 1533 the Act in Restraint of Appeals was passed, making it a crime for an Englishman to carry any appeal to a court of Rome. All appeals had to be made before English tribunals. This marked a turning point in English constitutional history. Henry VIII had secretly married Anne Boleyn in January, 1533. Cranmer had performed the ceremony. In May, Cranmer held a court which formally adjudged Henry's marriage to Catherine null and void. Anne Boleyn was recognized as Queen of England. The pope excommunicated Henry in 1534, relieving his subjects from their allegiance. The king answered by the Act of Supremacy, passed by parliament in November, 1534, by which

Henry and his successors were declared "the only supreme head on earth of the Church of England." The breach with Rome was complete. Finally, the Act of High Treason was passed which decreed that anyone who denied the title given to the king by the statute, or anyone who ventured to call him a schismatic, was guilty of high treason. This act was as a banner hoisted over the new royal supremacy in England.

As the supreme head of the Church of England the king abolished the smaller monasteries in 1535. Five years later monasticism was abolished altogether, the property being confiscated by the crown. About six hundred and forty-five monasteries were broken up. The chantries were suppressed and confiscated in 1547. A portion of the monastic wealth was used for public purposes, such as the founding of schools and colleges, and the establishment of new bishoprics. But the greater portion of the landed property was sold or given to the favorites of the king. The new aristocracy, thus created, opposed any return to Rome, and became the very backbone of the coming Parliamentarism and Puritanism.

Much attention was given to the inner life of the Church. The Ten Articles, published in 1536, set forth the religion of the English Reformation. Cranmer, deeply saturated with Lutheran teaching, based the Ten Articles mainly on the Augsburg Confession, but statements concerning mass, celibacy, and the Catholic ceremonies, were carefully left out. Cranmer and other theologians also prepared the first English Protestant catechism, the "Institution of a Christian Man." Several Bible translations were published. Coverdale's appeared in 1535. The Great Bible, also called "Cranmer's Bible" because Cranmer wrote the preface, was published in 1539. Henry ordered all congregations to buy Bibles and all the priests to exhort the people to read the Scriptures. Within two years the Great Bible passed through seven editions.

But Henry had, strangely enough, no intention of introducing Protestant doctrine or practice in England. What he wanted was a reformed Roman Catholic church, national in character, strictly under royal control. For several years after the passing of the Act of Supremacy, he found it wise, however, not to stress his Catholic faith. The pope might induce France and Spain to move against him, and then he would need the support of the Lutheran princes of Germany. But his negotiations were not successful. These princes refused to make any alliance except upon the basis of agreement in Lutheran doctrine. This Lutheran atmosphere finally became intolerable to the king. By 1539 he forced parliament to pass or sanction the Six Articles, which forbade anyone to teach Protestant doctrines in England.

The cruel nature of this Catholic reaction, during the closing years of Henry VIII's reign, earned him the dubious title of "the Nero of England." Many sealed their faith with the martyr's death. Cranmer was strangely enough permitted to retain his office. In the midst of the severe persecutions he succeeded by masterly diplomacy in checking the Catholic reaction at its half way mark.

III. The Reign of Edward VI, 1547-53.—Edward VI was less than ten years old when he succeeded his father on January 28, 1547. He was a remarkably mature and mentally precocious lad who, at the wish of Henry VIII, had been trained in the faith of the Reformers. Henry had insured that the Council of Regency would be made up of a Protestant majority. Edward Seymour, maternal uncle of Edward VI, was chosen as Protector, and created Duke of Somerset. He was a man of Protestant sympathies. Cranmer was still archbishop of Canterbury, and his convictions were still Lutheran, although he had recently developed a leaning toward Calvinism. In the six year reign of Edward VI, the incomparable Cranmer took the initiative in creating the great literary monuments of the English Reformation.

One of the early acts of the new parliament in 1547 was to repeal Henry VIII's treason and heresy laws, including the Act of the Six Articles. This was one of the remarkable decisions in English church history. For the first time a limited freedom of thought and liberty of the press was officially permitted. The press fairly teemed with books and pamphlets. There were three new translations of Luther's books, two of Zwingli's, and four of Calvin's. The writings of Melanchthon, Oecolampadius, Bullinger, and other Continental Protestants were translated and read by the English public. Prominent foreign theologians, including Martin Bucer and Paul Fagius of Germany, Peter Martyr and Bernardino Ochino of Italy,[5] and John Laski of Poland[6] were called to England as professors and preachers. Nicholas Ridley and Hugh Latimer, two outspoken English Protestants, were appointed to bishoprics.

The liturgy and the doctrines of the Church were carefully revised. The First Prayer Book prepared by Cranmer, the "devotional genius," was authorized in March, 1549. This Prayer Book aimed at greater simplicity of the rituals, a divine worship in English, a worship that was based on the Bible and Bible reading, and

---

[5] See page 305.   [6] See page 30:.

an active and intelligent participation of the congregation in the worship. The threefold division of the clergy into bishops, presbyters, and deacons was retained. Cranmer combined in this First Prayer Book elements from Roman Catholicism, and from Lutheran, Zwinglian, and Calvinistic liturgies into something distinctly new and original. The revision in 1552 in a Calvinistic direction resulted in the Second Prayer Book. The two prayerbooks became the basis for the present English Book of Common Prayer. Between 1550 and 1553 England gave up most of its medieval Catholicism. The clergy were even allowed to marry. Cranmer prepared a Confession of Faith, the Forty-two Articles, in harmony with the Second Prayer Book. These Articles, formally adopted in 1553, were later reduced to thirty-nine, and became after several subsequent revisions the official creed of the Church of England. But the English people were not as yet ready for such drastic changes. A strong Catholic reaction was soon to set in under Queen Mary.

IV. The Reign of Queen Mary, 1553-58.—Mary, oldest daughter of Henry VIII, was proclaimed Queen of England after the death of Edward VI in 1553. She was a devout Catholic with strong Spanish affinities. Emperor Charles V and his son, Philip II of Spain, were among her chief counsellors. At their advice, she at once began to restore the old system, and to undo the reform work of the two preceding reigns. But she chose an unfortunate course which soon made her very unpopular. Her marriage to Philip II of Spain in 1554 created tremendous opposition because the English felt they were being annexed to Spain. Furthermore, giving up the royal supremacy which had made Henry VIII so popular, and to come once more under the dominance of the pope, was unwelcome. But Mary had her good reasons for this marriage. Besides personal grounds, she thought this union would restore Catholicism in England and make it a permanent Catholic country. Politically, she felt she needed Spanish protection against the pretensions of Mary Stuart and the French.

The first parliament under Mary repealed the Reforming Acts of Edward VI and Henry VIII, and restored the *status quo* of 1529 on the eve of the Reformation Parliament. But the parliament of 1553-54 refused to yield on two points. The Lords and the Commons were unwilling to restore the confiscated church lands, and they refused to give up the royal supremacy of England. Mary quickly proceeded to re-establish Catholic worship in her realm.

Thirteen evangelical bishops and other clergy who refused to return to the Catholic order, were deprived of office, and some were put to death. Cardinal Reginald Pole was sent to England in 1554 to succeed Cranmer as archbishop. Cranmer was imprisoned and finally martyred. Ridley and Latimer met the same fate. In the severe persecution under "Bloody Mary" there were 290 known martyrs. Many Protestants left England and took refuge on the Continent.

V. The Reign of Queen Elizabeth, 1558-1603.—Elizabeth, daughter of Henry VIII and Anne Boleyn, succeeded Mary in 1558. She had been brought up in the Anglican Catholicism of her father, and was a good Greek and Italian scholar. When she notified the pope of her election, he haughtily declared her illegitimate, and indicated that he would consider the claims of Mary Stuart to the English throne. Elizabeth found it necessary, therefore, to favor Protestantism from policy rather than from conviction, because it was from the Protestants alone that she could look for support. She was determined, like Henry VIII, to possess supreme authority in religious as well as in civil matters.

The parliament of 1559 sanctioned the legal succession of Elizabeth to the throne. New Acts of Supremacy and Uniformity were passed, and the religious laws passed under Mary's reign were repealed. Romanism was outlawed, and the Anglican Church was definitely established. The Elizabethan Settlement involved the following measures: (1) The Act of Supremacy of 1559 placed the Church of England directly under the control of the crown, and designated Elizabeth "supreme Governor." (2) The Act of Uniformity of 1559 accepted the Common Prayer Book of Edward VI, with a few minor revisions, as the standard Anglican liturgy, and forbade any clergyman to use any other liturgical form. (3) The Anglican Church retained the episcopal form of church government, with its Chapters, threefold division of the clergy, and Convocations. Apostolic succession was secured when the first Anglican bishop was consecrated in 1559. (4) The Forty-two Articles were revised, and reduced to Thirty-nine. These Thirty-nine Articles of Religion received the assent of the Convocation in 1563, and were sanctioned by parliament in 1571, after the pope had published a bull of excommunication the year previous.

VI. The Puritans and the Independents.—The persecutions under Queen Mary had driven many of the English Protestants into exile, either to Scotland or to the Continent. A number of these exiles, who returned during the early reign of Queen Elizabeth, had become thorough-going Calvinists in doctrine and in worship. They were not satisfied with the Elizabethan Settlement, because they thought her reforms did not go far enough. They desired the following changes: (1) a *purer* form of worship than the Anglican, and hence the name "Puritans;" (2) the displacement of Episcopacy by Presbyterianism which, they claimed, was the only form of church government known to the New Testament; (3) a revision of the standards of doctrine to bring about a larger incorporation of Calvinism.

Puritanism had its academic center at the University of Cambridge. Pastors educated at this university were frequently trained in the Calvinistic doctrines. The Puritans took a leading part in the economic, industrial, and commercial life of the nation,[7] and eventually amassed great wealth. They became great land-owners, and this admitted them to participation in the affairs of parliament. The gradual fusion of the Lollard movement with Puritanism resulted in a marked interest in Bible reading, and in the production of a rich and extensive devotional literature.

Thomas Cartwright (1535-1603), and Walter Travers, joint-authors of the "Book of Discipline," declared the Puritan platform. They did not withdraw from the Established Church of England, but worked from within for the accomplishment of their purposes.

A party of non-conformists called Independents or Congregationalists began to make its appearance around 1580. The Independents were Calvinists in doctrine, but severed all connections with the Established Church of England and refused to have anything to do with it. Robert Browne organized the first congregation of English Independents at Norwich in 1580. John Greenwood, Henry Barrowe, and John Robinson further unfolded the Independent plan. They rejected presbyterianism and episcopacy maintaining that the local church or congregation was the true unit of church government. Each congregation had a right to set up its own standards in harmony with New Testament models. This was the beginning of Congregationalism. Persecuted with great severity by the government, many of the Independents fled to the Continent, especially to Holland. From these exiles, gathered in Holland, came most of the passengers of the "Mayflower" and the "Speedwell" to the New World.

[7] See pp. 272-73.

46. REVIEW QUESTIONS

1. How did the course of the Reformation in England differ from other lands? How are these differences reflected in the Anglican church?
2. Discuss the early reform influences in England. Compare the early leaders of the Reformation in England with those of Germany, Switzerland, and Sweden?
3. What circumstances made Henry VIII the center of the English Reformation?
4. Discuss the important resolutions passed by the parliament of 1529-36. What other reform measures did Henry VIII take up to 1539?
5. Account for the Catholic reaction during the closing years of Henry VIII's reign.
6. In what ways did the reign of Edward VI promote the Reformation in England?
7. Might not Queen Mary have brought the English Church back to Rome, if she had chosen a more diplomatic course? Give reasons for your answer.
8. What determined the general religious policies of Queen Elizabeth?
9. When was the Anglican Church permanently established?
10. Discuss the origin and the program of the Puritans. In what ways did the contact with the Lollards make Puritanism different from Calvinism in the rest of the world?
11. Distinguish between Independents, Puritans, and Calvinists.
12. What part did the Puritans and the Independents play in the early history of the United States? Have other Protestant denominations in America adopted the congregational form of church government? Which?

TOPICS FOR SPECIAL STUDY

1. The influence of Tyndale's Bible on the English Reformation.
2. Cardinal Wolsey and the English Reformation.
3. Thomas Cranmer as the first Protestant Archbishop of Canterbury.
4. Thomas Cromwell and the Reformation in England.
5. The great literary monuments of the English Reformation.
6. The origin of Puritans and Independents.

A SELECTED BIBLIOGRAPHY FOR CHAPTER XIV

1. *Cambridge Modern History,* Vol. II, Chap. XIII and XIV; Vol. III, Chap. VIII-X.
2. Lindsay: *A History of the Reformation,* Vol. II, pages 315-420.
3. Smith: *The Age of the Reformation,* Chap. VI, VII.
4. Stephens and Hunt: *History of the English Church.*
5. Perry: *History of the Reformation in England.*
6. Pollard: *Henry VIII.*
7. Creighton: *The Age of Elizabeth.*
8. Pearson: *Thomas Cartwright and Elizabethan Puritanism.*
9. Gardner: *History of the English Church in the Sixteenth Century.*
10. Frere: *History of the English Church in the Reigns of Elizabeth and James I.*
11. Wakeman: *History of the Church of England.*
12. Brewer: *The Reign of Henry VIII from His Accession to the Death of Wolsey.*
13. Marti: *Economic Causes of the Reformation in England.*
14. Arrowsmith: *The Prelude to the Reformation.*
15. Salzman: *England in Tudor Times.*

CHAPTER XV

RADICAL REFORM MOVEMENTS

The Protestant Reformation produced three large communions, the Lutheran, the Reformed, and the Anglican. But the Reformation was accompanied by a number of radical religious revolts which demand a brief consideration. Several extremist groups claimed that Luther, Zwingli, and Calvin had not gone far enough in their religious reforms. These groups tried, therefore, to complete the evangelical Reformation by exalting either a deformatory mysticism or a deformatory rationalism, or by giving free play to revolutionary and liberalist tendencies. The doctrines and

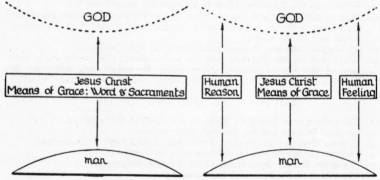

COMMUNION BETWEEN GOD AND MAN AS UNDERSTOOD BY (1) THE
REFORMERS (2) THE RADICALS

practices of these religious radicals were abhorred by the great reformers quite as cordially as by the Roman Catholic Church.

I. The Anabaptists.—Anabaptism was the collective name of a wide variety of religious opinions held by various groups. The promoters were representatives of the mystical piety of the closing Middle Ages, with which they frequently combined socialistic principles and sometimes apocalyptic visions. The Anabaptists had their largest following among the artisans and the working men of the towns.

While the groups differed widely from one another in many respects, they had at least three things in common: (1) They all rejected infant baptism and rebaptized members who had been baptized as children: hence the name "Anabaptists" which means Rebaptizers. (2) They would have nothing to do with state churches or national churches because these, they claimed, numbered many nominal Christians, while the true Church should be an association of true believers only. (3) They subordinated the outward Word of God and the Sacraments to the subjective experience of the "inner light" of the Spirit. The Spirit did everything, and had no need of infant baptism or the "bodily" Word.

The Anabaptists had no general organization. Traveling evangelists spread all over the Continent and even reached across to England. They formed smaller, or larger, praying communities which frequently organized into regular congregations with deacons, elders, and pastors; but each group was independent of the rest. These groups reproduced what seemed to them to be the beliefs, usages, and social practices of the early Christians. In some communities they used a common catechism for the instruction of their young. This catechism was published in German, French, Bohemian, possibly also in Italian.

Two general types of Anabaptists were distinguished, the quietists and the revolutionaries. The quietists sincerely devout were peaceful in spirit. They believed in passive resistance and maintained that no real Christian could be either a civil official or a soldier. The revolutionaries were fanatics who advocated the abolition of all existing authorities in Church and State, and the substitution of a visible kingdom of God on earth, controlled by the saints or true believers.

1. *The Quietists.*—Balthasar Hubmaier was a highly gifted man who, as a devout Catholic, had studied philosophy and theology under the guidance of John Eck, the famous opponent of Luther. At the age of thirty Hubmaier was called to the University of Ingolstadt as professor of theology. His fame soon secured him a new position as preacher in the cathedral of Regensburg. An unfortunate conflict with the Jews of Regensburg caused his expulsion from that city. He accepted a call to Waldshut, a town of Lower Austria. In 1522 or 1523 he made an open profession of the Reformed faith and was, for some time, a staunch supporter of Zwingli. But his Anabaptist views soon caused a parting of ways. Hubmaier's prestige in Waldshut was so great that nearly all the inhabitants accepted his views. On Easter, 1525, he and three hundred men were baptized in a milk-dish filled with water. From Waldshut the movement spread rapidly to surrounding terri-

tories. The adherents often claimed to be the recipients of immediate, divine revelations, visions, and dreams. Catholics and Zwinglians started a violent persecution against them. Hubmaier fled to Moravia, where he founded a large congregation which absorbed practically all the Zwinglians of that region. Hubmaier was finally imprisoned, tortured, and executed in Vienna in 1528.

Caspar Schwenkfeld was a pious nobleman who ardently embraced the Lutheran Reformation. But his extreme emphasis upon an inward mystical religion caused him to sever relations with the Lutherans. In 1525 he claimed to have received, through a special revelation, a new understanding of the Means of Grace, that is, the Word and the Sacraments. He exalted the inner word of the Spirit above the written Word of the Bible. The Word of God which was read and heard and preached at the church services was not a means whereby God and the Holy Spirit taught men and worked in them a saving knowledge of Christ, conversion, repentance, faith, and a new obedience. These things were accomplished by the inner word of the Spirit alone. The water and the Word in baptism were not the means whereby God sealed His covenant and worked regeneration. This was done by the Spirit. The bread and wine in the Holy Supper were not means whereby Christ distributed his body and blood.[1] Schwenkfeld was opposed to all outward church forms, and disapproved of infant baptism. He was in discord with every doctrine of the Augsburg Confession. After 1539 his followers called themselves "Schwenkfeldians" and grouped themselves in individual congregations. A Schwenkfeldian colony of about two hundred members settled in Pennsylvania in 1734.

2. *The Revolutionaries.*—The Zwikau prophets were among the early revolutionary Anabaptists.[2]

Their chief exponent was Thomas Münzer. He boasted like the others of prophetic visions, dreams, and direct communications with God. Münzer claimed that he held secret dialogues with God in a chamber of a church tower. His ultimate aim was to establish a kingdom of saints where all goods should be held in common. To do this it was necessary to overthrow the existing order of society. He preached insurrectionary sermons in which he advocated a literal application of the commandment in the third chapter of Deuteronomy that the images and the altars of the Canaanites should be destroyed and the ungodly should be killed without mercy. He also sent secret emissaries to various communities to gather his "elect" into a general secret

---

[1] cf. The Formula of Concord.   [2] See pp. 239-341.

league. His inflammatory speeches were reduced to writing and sent to the people. Münzer, more than any other individual, was responsible for the fanaticism leading to the Peasant's War. Note his exhortation on the eve of the Peasant's War: "Now on, on, on! Show no quarter, no matter what terms Esau may propose! Pay no regard to the distress of the ungodly, tho' they plead friendship, and beg and weep and implore like children. Have no mercy, as God has commanded in Deuteronomy 5:7, and has likewise instructed us. On, on, while the fire burns! Keep your swords warm in blood: On, while it is yet day! God leads you on. Follow him." No wonder that Luther urged the princes to make common cause to put down the insurgents. The revolutionary form of Anabaptism was temporarily crushed during the Peasant's War, Münzer himself being beheaded.

Melchior Hoffmann, "the evil genius of the Anabaptists," was a traveling lay preacher who spread his views in Germany, Livonia, Esthonia, Sweden, Denmark, and Holland. He founded a large Anabaptist congregation in the city of Emden, but made Strassburg the center of his activity. Besides holding the usual Anabaptist views, Hoffmann claimed to be one of the "two witnesses" mentioned in Revelation 11:3. He also predicted that Christ would return to reign over his saints in 1533, and that Strassburg was to be the New Jerusalem, the seat of Christ's universal dominion. He soon gained a large number of followers called "Melchiorites." The authorities at Strassburg had Hoffmann arrested in 1533, and he died in prison ten years later.

Jan Matthys, a baker from Haarlem, appeared in Strassburg in 1533 claiming to be the other "witness" mentioned in Revelation 11.3. But he transferred the New Jerusalem to the city of Münster, and advocated the forcible setting up of the new kingdom of saints and the slaughter or expulsion of the ungodly. He sent out apostles in various directions, but especially to Holland and to Westphalia. Four of these apostles were sent directly to Münster to prepare for his coming. Münster had since 1529 been under Anabaptist influence through the activities of the gifted preacher Bernhard Rothmann. Toward the close of February, 1533, the Anabaptist element was strong enough to elect a new City Council. Meanwhile the troops of the Catholic bishop had laid siege to the city. When Matthys arrived, he soon made the City Council his obedient tool. He commanded all adults to be baptized or leave town. He also introduced a community of goods. All books were burned except the Bible which became the law book for the "New Jerusalem."

Opposition was suppressed by the sword. In obedience to a supposed revelation, Matthys and twenty others went out through a city gate, and made a fierce attack on the bishop's soldiers. They were overpowered and killed, scarcely three months after his arrival at Münster.

John of Leyden, one of the four apostles sent to Münster in advance of Matthys, became the·new leader of the "New Jerusalem." He dismissed the old City Council and selected twelve elders to rule the people. He himself was proclaimed king. He established his court and selected Divara, the beautiful widow of Matthys, as his queen. Polygamy was proclaimed. The "king" had sixteen wives and his court preacher had nine. But the reign of John of Leyden was of brief duration. In June, 1535, the city was captured by the bishop's soldiers, and the dream of the "New Jerusalem" was at an end. Münster was restored to the Catholic fold.

3. *The Mennonites.*—After the catastrophe at Münster, the Anabaptist forces were so scattered that their disappearance seemed certain. But in 1536 appeared the man who was to bring order out of confusion and actually save the movement. This man was Menno Simons (1492-1559). He was before his conversion to Anabaptism a Catholic priest in Wittmarsum, Friesland. A diligent study of the Scriptures caused him to doubt many Catholic doctrines, and the martyr-like courage of the Anabaptists turned his attention toward them. He resigned his priesthood, accepted the Anabaptist views, and was baptized anew in 1536.

Menno Simons, a wise, peace-loving, anti-fanatical organizer and leader, soon purged Anabaptism of its apocalyptic and revolutionary elements. For nearly twenty-five years he traveled from place to place in Holland, Frisia, and Northwestern Germany, preaching to the dispirited Anabaptist communities. He organized them into a simple brotherly association known as the Mennonite church. These early Mennonites agreed to the following views and practices: (1) the need of personal conversion and of adult baptism as its sign and seal; (2) denial of the guilt of original or transmitted sin, and hence the rejection of infant baptism; (3) refusal to bear arms, to hold civil office, to take oath, to take revenge, and to participate in worldly amusements; (4) obedience to civil magistrates in all things not contrary to conscience and the Word of God; (5) rejection of state control over the church; (6) the exercise of strict supervision over the lives of the members; (7) introduction of feet-washing in accordance with the thirteenth chapter of John; (8) a low estimate of the Sacraments and a nearly unitarian view of the incarnation of Christ.

The Mennonites spread into England after 1625, and formed a close connection with the English Independents.

4. *The Baptists.*[3]—The Baptist church originated in England near the beginning of the seventeenth century. The Baptists differed from the Anabaptists of the Continent by retaining the Congregationalist constitution, and from the English Independents by rejecting infant baptism. In other respects they generally adhered to the Calvinistic doctrines. But the Arminian views[4] caused a general Baptist division in 1791. The larger number, which held to the Calvinistic doctrine of predestination, were called "Regular" or "Particular" Baptists. Those who held to the Arminian views were called "General" or "Free-will" Baptists. Toward the close of the seventeenth century Francis Bampfield organized a new group known as "Seventh-day Baptists" because they observed the seventh day as the day of rest.

From England the Baptists spread to America and to various countries of Europe. In England and America they are found in practically every town and city. They are divided into many different groups, some of which do not adhere to any general confession of faith. The "Confession of the American Free-will Baptists," last revised in 1868, is the most authoritative statement of the Arminian Baptist views. The historic manifesto of the Particular Baptists is the "Confession" of 1677, as reissued in 1689.

II. The Libertines.—During his early labors at Geneva, John Calvin had much opposition from a party known as the Libertines. This particular party was made up of two elements, one political and one religious, but in other regions the Libertines or Spirituals were usually thought of as a religious sect.

The Libertines made their first appearance in the Netherlands where they called themselves the Spirituals. From the Netherlands they spread to France, about 1529, and to Switzerland, Germany, and England. Their main tenets may be stated as follows: (1) There was but one spirit in the universe, the Spirit of God, who lived in all creatures; hence there could be no devil and no angels, good or bad. (2) Since there was but one Spirit, nothing could be essentially bad, and sin was merely an illusion. (3) Regeneration consisted in the knowledge that the distinction between good and bad was baseless, and those who had this knowledge had attained

---

[3] Their lineage is Anabaptist, but they have departed from the early apocalyptic and revolutionary elements of Anabaptism.

[4] See page 351.

to the innocence which Adam had before the fall. (4) Salvation consisted in the deliverance from the phantom of sin. (5) There was no truth in Gospel history, and the crucifixion and resurrection of Christ had, at the best, only a symbolical meaning. (6) The Word of the Bible was a dead letter which must either be entirely rejected, or else be interpreted according to Libertine views. (7) Spiritual marriage was superior to legal marriage which was merely carnal and not binding; hence there was to be a community of women as well as a community of goods. It was this lax view of the marriage relation which stigmatized them as Libertines.

This pernicious sect, which made some progress among the higher classes in France, and in Holland, was practically driven out of Geneva by Calvin and his associates. Calvin said it was the most pernicious sect that had appeared since the ancient Gnostics and the Manicheans. He likened them to the errorists described in the Second Epistle of Peter and in the Epistle of Jude. In England the sect was known as the Familists.

III. The Unitarians (Socinians).—The modern Unitarian (Socinian) movement originated during the Reformation period, although the roots may be traced back to the Monarchian movement of the second and third centuries of the Christian era. A number of Humanists of Central and Southern Europe began to register their intellectual objections to various doctrines of the Church, and especially to the belief in the divinity of Christ. Prominent among these were Lelio Socini (1525-1562) and his nephew, Faustus Socini (1539-1604).

Lelio Socini was a prominent Italian lawyer who left his country in 1547 because he was suspected of heresy. He traveled widely and made the acquaintance of leading Protestant theologians, including Melanchthon and Calvin. He was in Geneva during the trial of Servetus[5] and listened to the debate which preceded the death sentence of the famous Spanish physician. Socini recorded his impressions and thoughts but did not dare to have them published. This manuscript was bequeathed to his nephew, Faustus Socini, who practiced law at Siena, Italy.

Faustus Socini was a man of high moral character. He had studied not only law but also theology. The manuscript of his uncle made a great impression upon him. He left Italy and visited some of the groups which shared the anti-Trinitarian views of his uncle. In 1579 he went to Poland where he organized a Unitarian community known as the Polish Brethren. His activities soon ex-

[5] See page 272.

tended to Hungary, Transylvania, and neighboring countries. Transylvania became the great stronghold of the Unitarians.[6] He purged the Unitarian groups of their Anabaptist leaven, and ironed out a number of minor differences. At the Unitarian Synod, held at Krakau in 1603, it was decreed that rebaptism was not necessary for entrance into a Unitarian church. In 1600 he founded a Unitarian college at Racow. Thousands of students came to this school every year. Yearly Unitarian synods were also held at Racow. Many Unitarian books were printed, including the famous Racovian Catechism of 1605. The name "Unitarian" seems to have been coined in Transylvania about the year 1600.

These early Unitarians held to following doctrines: (1) God's plan of salvation is revealed in the New Testament, but not in the Old. (2) This divine revelation supplements human reason, but does not contradict it; hence all religious teaching must be tested by human reason. (3) The doctrine of the Trinity and the eternal divinity of Christ conflicts with reason and must be denied; Christ was only a man, although divine honors are due him. (4) Man has no original sin and guilt; hence the reality and the necessity of an atonement must be denied. (5) The natural worth and dignity of man make it possible for him to obtain salvation, provided he gets the proper instruction in the truth. (6) This truth has been imparted through the man Jesus Christ. (7) There is no predestination and no eternity of hell.

The Unitarian doctrines were repudiated by Catholics and by Protestants alike. Modern or present-day Unitarians have entirely eliminated the supernaturalistic element in religion. They have no formal creed but form a free fellowship under the authority of reason and conscience.

47. REVIEW QUESTIONS

1. Why did so many groups try to bring about a more radical reform than the Lutheran, the Reformed, and the Anglican Communions?
2. What general traits had all Anabaptists in common?
3. In what ways did the Quietists and the Revolutionaries generally differ?
4. Discuss the views of Hubmaier and Schwenkfeld. How did they differ from the accepted Lutheran and Reformed doctrines?
5. The Jews tried several times to make Jesus Christ their earthly king. Compare these attempts with the endeavors of the Revolutionary Anabaptists to establish a kingdom of saints on earth.
6. How did the revolutionary Anabaptists defend their insurrectionary activities? Did they seek support in Scriptures? How?
7. Why did the "New Jerusalem" at Münster fail?
8. Discuss the views of the Mennonites.

[6] See page 304.

9. What made the Libertines so pernicious?
10. Compare the Unitarians and the Monarchians. Did they hold exactly the same views? Explain.
11. Why were the early Unitarians called Socinians?
12. Discuss the Unitarian doctrines. Why were they repudiated by Catholics and Protestants alike?

TOPICS FOR SPECIAL STUDY

1. Socialistic and communistic tendencies among the radical reform groups.
2. Balthasar Hubmaier.
3. Caspar Schwenkfeld and his followers.
4. Thomas Münzer.
5. Melchior Hoffmann and his associates.
6. The early history of the Mennonites.
7. The rise of the Unitarian movement.
8. The early history of the Baptist movement.

A SELECTED BIBLIOGRAPHY FOR CHAPTER XV

1. Lindsay: *A History of the Reformation*, Vol. II, pages 430-483.
2. Vedder: *Balthasar Hübmaier.*
3. Walker: *A History of the Christian Church*, pages 366-370.
4. Kurtz: *Church History*, Vol. II, pages 218-225.
5. Newman: *A History of Anti-Paedobaptism.*
6. Vedder: *A Short History of the Baptists.*
7. Horsch: *Menno Simons, His Life, Labours and Teaching.*
8. Various Encyclopedias.
9. Schubert: *Der Kommunismus der Wiedertäufer in Münster und seine Quellen.*
10. Bergmann: *Die Täuferbewegung im Kanton Zürich bis 1660.*
11. Burrage: *History of the Anabaptists in Switzerland.*
12. Dosker: *The Dutch Anabaptists.*
13. Coutts: *Hans Denck.*
14. Sachsse: *Doctrov Balthasar Hubmaier als Theologe.*
15. Vedder: *Balthasar Hubmaier.*
16. Smith: *The Mennonites.*
17. Fock: *Der Socinianismus.*
18. Wallace: *Antitrinitarian Biography.* (3 vols.)

CHAPTER XVI

The Catholic Counter Reformation

The Protestant Reformation had swept like a tidal wave over the greater part of Europe,[1] reaching its high-water mark around 1572. But by 1575 this tidal wave began slowly to subside. Roman Catholicism was at last able to check the progress of Protestantism and to win back parts of Europe which it had lost. This Catholic reaction, called the Counter Reformation, aimed at three specific things: first, to bring about certain reforms in life and discipline; secondly, to arrange the teachings of the Catholic church into a compact, authoritative system as over against Protestantism; thirdly, to reorganize the whole political and institutional machinery of the Church to meet the new situation. These aims were partly realized between 1545 and 1648.

I. Early Reform Efforts.—The need of reform within the Church was admitted by thoughtful men within the Roman Catholic fold at the beginning of the sixteenth century. The religious needs of modern man demanded a readjustment of the Church to the new conditions of the modern world. But Catholics did not at first have the same conception of reform. A small group of mystics declared that the one reformation needed was the rediscovery of true religion, which they claimed had been lost. The Bible Humanists advocated a reformation of life and doctrine by a return to the New Testament and to the Christian Fathers. They also favored the formation of national Catholic churches, as well as an educated clergy, Church Councils, and more spiritual freedom within the institutions of the Church. The orthodox leaders went to the opposite extreme in demanding only such reforms as would strengthen the absolute papacy with obedience and subjection to the Church. This lack of a united Catholic front prevented an earlier check on the Protestant development.

John Colet of London, Jacques Lefevre of Etaples, France, and Desiderius Erasmus of Rotterdam, Holland, were among the prominent Bible Humanists who advocated a return to the Bible and to the early Church Fathers. They wanted a reformed Catholic church, but no schism. Their program was largely adopted by

Emperor Charles V,[2] by Henry VIII of England,[3] and partly by Francis I of France. Other princes found it advantageous to take a similar position until they could determine the actual course of events. This mediary position naturally tended to check the repressive policies of the papal circle.

Meanwhile several organizations were formed within the Catholic church for the purpose of stimulating a healthier spiritual life. The "Oratory of Divine Love" was founded in Rome about 1517 by fifty or sixty persons who came together for worship and mutual edification. Among the leaders was Giovanni Pietro Caraffa of Theate, who later became Pope Paul IV (1555-59). Another member was Jacob Sadoleto, who later became a cardinal. Several new orders for Inner Mission work were created. Among these were the Theatines, an Italian association of pious clergymen, which received papal sanction in 1524. The Theatines were the precursors of the Jesuits in their activities in suppressing heresy, but their main aim was to reform the clergy. Their regulations required that the members should devote themselves to preaching, to the temporal and spiritual aid of the sick, and to the salvation of criminals. The sack of Rome in 1527 scattered the Theatines to various parts of Italy.

But these reform groups had accomplished very little up to the time Paul III ascended the papal chair (1534-49). Pope Hadrian VI (1522-23) had exhibited much reform zeal, but his efforts proved ineffective. His successor, Pope Clement VII (1523-34), was elected partly because he opposed such reforms. Yet he had to listen to clamorous demands for a Catholic reformation. Emperor Charles V persistently demanded a General Council where the whole situation could be discussed.

Pope Paul III (1534-49) was fully aware of the gravity of the situation. He fostered the reform movement by placing in the College of Cardinals men who were seriously interested in reform. Among these were Gaspar Contarini, John Peter Caraffa, Jacob Sadoleto, and Reginald Pole.[4] The pope appointed these and others as a Commission of Nine to investigate the state of the Church and to recommend reforms. This Commission met and drafted a report which was presented to the pope in the fall of 1537. The report, revealing many scandals connected with the papacy, emphasized the urgent need of a radical reform.

All members of the Commission advocated administrative and moral reforms, but they did not all agree as to the method of procedure. Contarini advocated a policy which might conciliate the Protestants, while Caraffa urged a stern repression of all doctrinal divergences. For some time the pope yielded to a policy of conciliation. He called a General Council at Mantua in 1537,[5] although this meeting was postponed. He also permitted several religious conferences with the Protestants,[6] but the gulf between Catholics and Protestants was apparently impassable. He appointed a commission to introduce certain reforms, but the commission never acted. The Catholic reformers did not at this stage have sufficient strength to carry out a conciliatory reform. The pope finally adopted the repressive methods of Caraffa, a policy followed by the later popes of that period.

The efforts to bring about a Catholic reformation in the spirit of Erasmus, Charles V, and Contarini had failed. The Roman church was not willing to move in that direction. But the work of the Commission of Nine had brought its members into power at Rome. The next three popes were chosen from among these "reformers." This was very significant because men were given a chance to bring about readjustments of the Catholic church without becoming heretics.

II. The Society of Jesus.—The year 1540 is a turning-point in the history of the Christian Church. In that year the Lutheran Reformation received its greatest setback because of the double marriage of Philip of Hesse. In 1540 the English Reformation began to lose much of its Lutheran character. In 1540 John Calvin was called back to Geneva to start his world-famous work. In that same year the Society of Jesus received its papal sanction.

Ignatius Loyola (1491-1556), the founder of the Society of Jesus, was a Spanish nobleman who had prepared himself for a military career. A severe wound received at the battle of Pampeluna in 1521 made further military service impossible. During his slow recovery at the Loyola castle he read books dealing with the life of Christ, St. Dominic, and Francis of Assisi. Loyola was moved to make the greatest decision of his life: he dedicated himself as a spiritual knight to the service of the Holy Virgin.

In 1522, before he had even fully recovered, he journeyed to the Dominican monastery at Montserrat where he hung his military outfit before an image of the Virgin. From there he went to the Dominican monastery at Manresa where he passed through a great religious crisis. His sinful heart and the problem of the forgiveness of sins brought him to the very brink of despair. He finally found peace in complete subjection to the authority of the Church and its Tradition. Luther had found peace by a complete subjection to the Word of God. Loyola found religious truth primarily in Church Tradition. Luther found religious truth in the Word of God, and he accepted the Tradition only in so far as this agreed with Scripture. Loyola's religion demanded the crucifixion of the individual conscience in complete obedience to the authority of the Church. The evangelical Christianity of Luther advocated a conscience bound by the Word of God.

Loyola subjected himself to the most severe self-discipline. He also claimed to have had remarkable divine visions. These exercises and visions he recorded in "Spiritual Exercises," one of the most

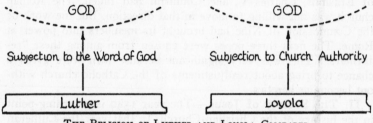

THE RELIGION OF LUTHER AND LOYOLA COMPARED

influential books in the world. But Loyola still had much to learn before he could become the leader of the Counter Reformation. He made a journey to Jerusalem in 1524, but returned the next year with the conviction that his life-work could not be accomplished without an education.

At the age of thirty-three he began to prepare for the priesthood. For two years he sat among the school boys of Barcelona to study Latin. He then attended two universities in Spain, and in 1528 he entered the University of Paris where he remained for seven years. At Paris he gathered around him a little group of younger students who became absorbed in his "Spiritual Exercises." On August 15, 1534, this little group of seven promised by an oath to live in chastity and poverty, to do mission work among the Mohammedans, and to subject themselves in absolute obedience to the pope. These four vows, together with the "Spiritual Exercises," constituted the basis of the order.

Four years later the missionary program was exchanged for another. The war with the Turks temporarily barred the way to the Mohammedans, so Loyola decided to change his missionary order into an order of parish-priests to promote the interests of the Catholic church both at home and abroad. In this revised form the Society took on a fourfold program. The members of the Society became active as teachers, preachers, confessors, and directors of works of mercy. They also took up the foreign mission program as soon as this was feasible. In this Society of Jesus, commonly called the "Jesuit Order," the papal church acquired a most efficient instrument for the suppression of Protestantism.

The constitution called for carefully selected men. Each applicant had to prove his worth by a long period of preparation, and each member promised absolute obedience to the superiors. At the head of the organization was the "General" to whom all members owed absolute obedience. The General, who lived at Rome, appointed his associates in the administration. Loyola firmly believed that his constitution was founded on direct revelations from God. In considering the almost unlimited power of the General over his members it should be remembered, that Loyola himself as well as all other Jesuits were under the complete control of the pope. Loyola himself was under the constant surveillance of five sworn spies who carefully watched his activities.

The Jesuits' motto was "All for the greater glory of God." This meant to them the extension of God's Kingdom upon earth. This Kingdom was condensed in the Roman Church and represented by the pope. All doctrines which deviated from the papal church were heresies. Consequently, Luther, Zwingli, and Calvin were emissaries of Satan whose influence had to be destroyed by any means. This frequently involved the Jesuits in unethical procedure. The doctrine of "intentionalism" frequently meant that the end justified the means. The doctrine of "mental reservation" meant that a man was not bound to state the whole truth on oath. The doctrine of "probabilism" meant the probability of a thing made it good. Finally, personal responsibility was undermined by blind, unconditional obedience to authority.

The Society of Jesus became powerful almost at once. Remarkable results were obtained in all lines of endeavor, but especially in its educational propaganda. Jesuit colleges and universities and training seminaries were established in France, Belgium, Holland, Germany, Austria, Hungary, and Poland. These schools, usually large and well-supported institutions, did much to roll back the tide of Protestantism. The Jesuits also gained much favor because of their acts of mercy. Loyola established "Martha-Houses" for fallen women. Ransom was paid for Christian captives among the

Mohammedans. Help was given to the poor. Francis Xavier became a world-famous missionary to the Far East. Jesuit missionaries also went with Spanish colonists to Mexico and South America. Jesuit preachers used the pulpit and the confessional very effectively for the spread of their convictions.

In 1773 the Order was for a time abolished by the pope because of its unscrupulous methods and its interference in European politics. At that time the Society of Jesus had 22,589 members, about half of whom were teachers. The Order was re-established by the pope in 1814.

III. The Inquisition.—The "Holy Office," usually called the Inquisition, was a church tribunal whose objective it was to discover and to eradicate heresy. Those suspected of heresy or spiritual offences against the Roman church were brought before this court. Confession frequently was wrung from the victims under torture as cruel as imagination could devise. Penalties usually consisted of confiscation of property, imprisonment, banishment, or death. The sentences were executed by the secular government.

This terrible institution, which had prevented Protestantism from getting any foothold in Spain, was set up in Italy in 1542 on recommendation of Caraffa, and under the supervision of Pope Paul IV. Six cardinals were appointed Inquisitors-General with full power to act in cases of heresy on both sides of the Alps. The inquisitorial courts were so successful in the suppression of Protestantism in Italy that the pope decided to use them also in Corsica and Sardinia and in the Low Countries. In time, the Inquisition became a world-wide institution.

How could such cruel coercion and infliction of pain enter into the Catholic propaganda? The Catholics justified the use of this terrible machinery on the ground that the Catholic church, as they said, was the only true Church, outside of which there was no salvation. When the people were led astray by Protestant "heresy," it was the duty of the Church to bring those people back again. Heresy was to the church body as cancer was to the human body. The physical tortures of the Inquisition were like painful operations, absolutely necessary in order that the body might be kept in a sound condition.

IV. The Council of Trent, 1545-63.—The second great agency of the Counter Reformation was the Council of Trent which, during its three separate sessions, decided to close the door of the Roman church firmly against all forms of Protestantism. The Council had three specific purposes: first, to define and codify the

Catholic doctrine; second, to reform the life of the Catholic church; third, to suppress heresy.

The Council of Trent co-ordinated Scripture and Tradition as joint rules of faith. Tradition was inspired as truly as the Scriptures, and should therefore enjoy equal authority. The Church alone had the right of interpretation. The apocryphal books of the Old Testament were acknowledged. The doctrine of justification left room for work-merit. Sanction was given to the seven medieval sacraments. The Council emphatically rejected any compromise or modification of the medieval Catholic doctrine. But the Catholic theology was adorned with the embellishments of modern humanistic learnings, stated in such a way as to repudiate the views of the Protestant reformers. The doctrine of papal supremacy was implied in the twofold provisio that "the Pope was to be the sole exponent of the decrees henceforth, and that no one, on pain of anathema, was to impeach the accepted usages and order of the Church."

The reform-decrees of the Council provided for a stricter church discipline, a better education of the clergy, more preaching, more pastoral care of the laity, and more constant and helpful oversight over the clergy by the bishop. Clerical celibacy was made binding. An official statement of the faith approved at Trent in the form of the Roman Catechism was published in 1566. The liturgy and the breviary were revised, and arrangements were made for a new edition of the Latin Bible. The resulting text, known as the Sixtine edition, was published in 1590.

The suppression of heresy included not only the destruction of the heretics but their writings as well. Pope Paul IV drafted the first papal Index or list of prohibited books in 1559. A Commission selected by the Council of Trent drew up more definite rules for the construction of the papal Index, and a new list, the Tridentine Index, was published by Pope Pius IV in 1564. Pope Sixtus V (1585-90) amended this Index to include objectionable passages in books. This final revision was known as the Index Expurgatorius.

Roman Catholicism had by 1565 mobilized its forces against Protestantism. Catholic doctrines and practices had been formulated into a compact authoritative system. The Inquisition and the Index had been perfected for the use of the Catholic authorities. With Paul IV (1555-59), the former Caraffa, the Counter Reformation reached the papal throne. Some allowance had been made for an inner reformation of the Church. There had been a remarkable revival of the mystical piety of the Middle Ages, resulting in the formation of new religious societies and new orders of monks and nuns. Much Catholic zeal went forth in the work of foreign missions. A new theological literature had come into existence. But most important of all, the faith and the self-denying work and enthusiasm of the Jesuits served as an inner spark that set the whole anti-Protestant machinery in motion. The Jesuits revived, not only intense opposition to Protestantism, but also a spirit that was willing to suffer and to fight for its faith.

Five years after the closing of the Council of Trent, the Jesuits began to build the *Il Gesù* church in Rome in *Barocco* style, characterized by an impressive portal, a massive cupola, numerous side chapels, an almost bewildering richness of marble decorations and statues, subdued but uniform light, elaborate gold inlays, and the blending of exceptionally striking colors on walls and ceiling. To these artistic surroundings the Jesuits added marvellous music and impressive sacramental mysticism which all tended to make favorable and lasting impressions on the worshipper.

V. Wars of Religion.—The main characteristic of the revived Catholicism was its effort to regain by force the territory lost to the Protestants. The history of this armed struggle, which lasted for nearly a hundred and fifty years, falls into three main periods: the attack on the Calvinistic regions of Western Europe, 1562-98; the attack on the Lutheran regions of Central Europe, 1618-48; the struggle which finally led to the establishment of the English world supremacy.

1. *France.*—After the death of Henry II in 1559,[7] the throne was occupied successively by his three sons, Francis II (1559-60), Charles IX (1560-74), and Henry III (1574-89). None of these was a strong ruler. The ambitious and crafty queen-mother, Catherine de Medici, and the great French nobles usurped the real power. The French nobles were divided into two parties, one Catholic and one Protestant. The Catholic party rallied around the house of Guise, while the Protestant party rallied around the house of Bourbon, of which the King of Navarre was the chief representative. The queen-mother tried to increase her power by skillfully playing off one party against the other. In three savage wars, 1562-63, 1567-68, and 1568-70, neither side gained much advantage.

In 1572 the massacre of Saint Bartholomew night occurred in Paris. All notables of France had been gathered to celebrate the

[7] See pages 308-309.

marriage of Henry of Navarre to the sister of the king. A careful plot had been laid against the Huguenots. On a given signal the Catholics killed all the Protestants they could find in the city, including Admiral Coligny. Couriers were sent to various parts of France, instigating similar massacres in other cities. Two thousand Protestants were killed in Paris and twenty thousand in the rest of the land. But the massacre did not destroy Protestantism in France.

Henry of Navarre, who had escaped death by embracing Catholicism, placed himself at the head of the Protestant party, and a new series of wars began in 1576. After the death of Henry III in 1589, Henry of Navarre was King by right of inheritance. But his succession was bitterly contested by the Catholics. He was firmly established on the royal throne, as Henry IV, after he had once more renounced Protestantism. But he remembered his former co-religionists. In 1598 he issued the Edict of Nantes, which granted the Huguenots not only toleration but certain political rights and several fortified cities. This Edict was revoked by Louis XIV in 1685, at which time about fifty thousand Huguenot families were driven out of France.

2. *The Netherlands.*—Philip II of Spain, who succeeded as ruler of the Netherlands in 1555,[8] was distrusted and feared by the Dutch. His political schemes and his cruel suppression of Protestantism finally provoked a series of local uprisings culminating in open revolt in 1572. The war lasted until 1609. William of Orange was the leader of the Protestant party. After his assassination in 1584, his place of leadership was taken by Jan van Oldenbarneveldt. In 1581 the northern provinces broke away from Spanish rule, and proclaimed their independence as the United Netherlands (Dutch Republic). Calvinism was proclaimed the official state-religion. Their independence was officially recognized by Spain in the Peace of Westphalia in 1648.

48. REVIEW QUESTIONS

1. Why was Roman Catholicism so slow in checking the progress of Protestanism?
2. What would have happened to the Protestant and the Catholic groups if the reform program of the Bible Humanists had been adopted? Why?
3. Why did the Roman church refuse the reform measures of Erasmus, Charles V, and Contarini?
4. Compare Loyola with Luther and Calvin as to character, training, conversion, and life purpose.
5. What were the peculiar strength and the peculiar weakness of the Society of Jesus?

[8] See page 312.

6. In what way did the Catholics justify the extensive use of the Inquisition?
7. Why should the Council of Trent be mentioned as a great agency of the Counter Reformation?
8. Why do Catholics co-ordinate Scripture and Tradition?
9. How does the Catholic doctrine of justification differ from the Protestant?
10. Compare the reform-decrees of the Council of Trent with those of Luther, Zwingli, and Calvin.
11. Discuss the movement leading to the establishment of the Index Expurgatorius. What do you think of it?
12. The Reformation involved Europe in several wars of religion. How long did this armed struggle last? Mention the three successive stages.
13. Discuss the situation in France during these religious wars. How did the expulsion of the Huguenots affect France?
14. How is the rise of the Dutch Republic related to the Counter Reformation in the Netherlands?

TOPICS FOR SPECIAL STUDY

1. The origin of the Theatines.
2. Gaspar Contarini and John Peter Caraffa.
3. Why the reform program of the Bible Humanists failed.
4. The Society of Jesus and its organizer.
5. The use of the Inquisition.
6. The Council of Trent as a landmark in the history of Catholicism.
7. The Massacre of St. Bartholomew night in 1572.

A SELECTED BIBLIOGRAPHY FOR CHAPTER XVI

1. Lindsay: *A History of the Reformation*, Volume II, pages 484-610.
2. Smith: *The Age of the Reformation*, Chapter VIII.
3. *Cambridge Modern History*, Volume II, Chapter XVIII.
4. Walker: *A History of the Christian Church*, pages 422-429.
5. Sedgwick: *Ignatius Loyola.*
6. Campbell: *The Jesuits.*
7. Ward: *The Counter Reformation.*
8. Thompson: *The Wars of Religion in France.*
9. Harrison: *William the Silent.*
10. Froude: *The Council of Trent.*
11. Schmidt: *Studien zur Geschichte des Konzils von Trient.*
12. Boehmer: *Studien zur Geschichte der Gesellschaft Jesu.* Vol. I.
13. Dyke: *Ignatius Loyola, Founder of the Jesuits.*
14. Gothein: *Ignatius von Loyola und die Gegenreformation.*
15. Hoensbroech: *Der Jesuiterorden. Eine Encyclopädie aus den Quellen zusammengestellts.* (2 vols.)
16. Jourdan: *The Movement towards Catholic Reform in the Early Sixteenth Century.*
17. Ranke: *History of the Popes, Their Church and Their State, in the Sixteenth and Seventeenth Centuries.*
18. Pastor: *History of the Popes from the Close of the Middle Ages.*
19. Whitehead: *Gaspard de Coligny, Admiral of France.*
20. Rocquain: *La France et Rome pendant les guerres de religion.*
21. Vienot: *Histoire de la Réforme française des origines à l'édit de Nantes.*
22. Blok: *History of the People of the Netherlands.* (Vols. III-V.)
23. Motley: *History of the United Netherlands, 1548-1609.* (4 vols.)

CHAPTER XVII

THE AGE OF THE THIRTY YEARS' WAR AND THE ENGLISH REVOLUTION

I. Causes Leading up to the Thirty Years' War.—The terms of the Peace of Augsburg, 1555,[1] were soon violated by the Lutherans as well as by the Catholics in a series of quiet tug-of-war contests. The real bone of contention was the "ecclesiastical reservation" which provided that if a prince of the Catholic church in Germany became a Protestant, he should resign his position, and his territory should remain the property of the Catholic church. The Catholics resented loss of this church property to Lutheran control, and tried to win it back. War might have broken out sooner had it not been for the conciliatory policy of the reigning emperors. Ferdinand (1556-64) and Maximilian II (1564-76) granted many liberties to the Protestants in their territory. Protestantism spread mightily in many Catholic states, especially among the nobility, in spite of the agreement, "one local government, one religion."

While the Catholics mobilized all their forces in preparation for their carefully planned counter-attack, the Protestants were sadly weakened by intestine conflicts. Lutherans and Calvinists struggled for mastery of the Continent. They carried on a bitter contest in Poland, Hungary, and Bohemia. In Germany the Calvinists converted the Palatinate into a Reformed state, with Heidelberg as the religious center. From this center came the famous hand-book of Reformed doctrine, the "Heidelberg Catechism" in 1563. The acceptance by Frederick V, the Elector of the Palatinate, of the crown of Bohemia, was the immediate cause of the Thirty Years' War.

Increasing friction between Catholics and Protestants prepared both parties for open warfare. After 1570 the dukes of Bavaria began to persecute the Protestant minorities in their territories. The Hapsburg princes in Austria, Bohemia, and Hungary adopted the same policy after 1580. In Bohemia and Hungary the Protestants formed the majority of the population, including the nobility and the land-owners. When the Hapsburg princes, who were

[1] See page 281.

all Catholics, began to enforce the law of "one local government, one religion," these Protestant nobles and land-owners refused to give up their old rights, and they were strong enough to put up a most determined opposition. War seemed inevitable.

Open hostilities of a local character broke out in 1606-07 in the city of Donauwörth. This free city, with an overwhelming Protestant population, was put under the ban of Emperor Rudolph II because the Protestants had stoned a Catholic procession. Maximilian, Catholic duke of Bavaria, seized the city on imperial command and annexed it to his territory. At the Imperial Diet of 1608 the Catholics demanded the restoration of all church property confiscated since 1555. A number of Protestant princes, anticipating further troubles, formed a Protestant Union in 1608, headed by Elector Frederick IV of the Palatinate. The Catholic princes formed a Catholic League in 1609, headed by Maximillan of Bavaria. War was delayed, however, by the assassination of Henry IV of France in 1610 and by the uncertainty of the imperial succession in Germany.

II. The Thirty Years' War, 1618-48.—The Thirty Years' War began with a local revolt in Bohemia in 1618. The large Protestant population of Bohemia had in 1609 secured from the Emperor Rudolph II (1576-1612), a Letter of Majesty granting a high degree of Protestant toleration, including the permission to build Protestant churches. Matthias (1612-19), who succeeded Rudolph both as king and emperor, was bound by oath not to molest the Protestants of Bohemia. But when he, in violation of this oath, prohibited the building of certain churches, the Protestant Union was ready to interfere. Matters were gravely complicated in 1617 when the feeble and childless Matthias recognized his cousin, Ferdinand, as his legal successor to the Bohemian throne. Ferdinand was a staunch supporter of the Counter Reformation. But the real trouble started in May, 1618, when a group of dissatisfied Protestants flung two Catholic regents from a high window in the city of Prague. The Catholics looked upon this as an act of rebellion. Violence was met with violence. Soon the revolt spread to Austria and Hungary. When Ferdinand II (1619-37) was elected Emperor of Germany and King of Bohemia in 1619, the Protestant Bohemians refused to recognize him. They elected a Calvinistic prince, Frederick V of the Palatinate, to be their king, an act bound to lead to open warfaie.

The first stage of the war, 1618-23, concerned the status of Protestantism in Bohemia, Moravia, Austria, and the Palatinate.

Frederick V, Elector of the Palatinate, failed to get the necessary Protestant support. Lutheran Saxony even took the field against him. In the battle near the White Mountain in 1620 the Bohemian and Hungarian nobles were crushed. The Catholics took advantage of this victory by closing all Lutheran and Reformed churches and schools in Bohemia, Moravia, and Austria. The Protestant pastors were driven into exile. A little later all non-Catholics living in these lands were given six months in which to change their religion or leave the country. Meanwhile the Catholics had centered their attack on the Palatinate. This Reformed State was conquered in 1621-23, and Catholicism was enforced. In 1623 the electoral title, together with a large portion of the state, was transferred to the Duke of Bavaria. This gave the Catholics a majority in the Electoral College.

In its second stage, 1623-29, the war took on an all-European character. The Catholic League selected Tilly as general of its army, and the emperor entrusted his army to the brilliant Wallenstein. The Lutheran princes of North Germany, with the exception of Saxony and Brandenburg, mobilized their forces in defence of Protestantism. Christian IV of Denmark put an army in the field against the Catholics. England and Holland sent some help. Richelieu, the prime minister of France, planned a defensive league composed of France, Protestant Germany, the United Netherlands, and Denmark, in opposition to the growing Hapsburg power; but the league did not materialize. The Catholics decisively defeated the Protestants in a succession of battles. In 1629 the emperor could practically dictate his own terms of peace. The Edict of Restitution, issued in March, 1629, recognized the Peace of Augsburg in 1555, which excluded Calvinists and Zwinglians from toleration.[2] All Protestants were to be excluded from Catholic lands, and all church property which had come into Protestant possession since the Peace of Passau in 1552 was to be restored. This involved two archbishoprics, nine bishoprics, and a great many monasteries. The Protestants rightly looked upon the Edict of Restitution as the first step in a process which would finally recatholize all of Protestant Europe.

At the beginning of the third stage of the war, 1630-32, the Catholic forces were weakened by mutual quarrels and jealousies. They disagreed concerning the spoils, and certain members of the Catholic League demanded that the emperor should dismiss Wallenstein who had so greatly increased the imperial power. He was

[2] See page 281.

dismissed in 1630. In that same year Gustavus Adolphus, the "Lion of the North," landed a Swedish army in Germany. He came to save Protestantism as well as Sweden. At first the lukewarm Protestant princes were jealous of his leadership, and did not join forces with him until the city of Magdeburg had been captured by the Catholics in 1631, and the inhabitants had been cruelly maltreated. Then the Margrave of Brandenburg and the Duke of Saxony finally threw off their neutrality and helped the Swedish King with troops, while anti-Austrian France helped him with money. At the battle of Breitenfeld in 1631, Gustavus Adolphus routed the Catholic League, and then he marched victoriously to the Rhine where he spent the winter. Meanwhile the Saxons had taken the city of Prague. In the spring of 1632 the Swedish King marched against Bavaria. The Bavarian capitol was taken, and Tilly was mortally wounded. Wallenstein, who had been recalled by the emperor, met Gustavus Adolphus with a large army at Lützen, near Leipzig. In a fierce battle, November 16, 1632, the Protestants won a decisive victory, but Gustavus Adolphus was slain. Protestantism was saved. The Catholic empire was broken into fragments, and the Edict of Restitution became a dead letter.

In its fourth and final stage, 1632-48, the war degenerated into a struggle for political advantage. Catholic France became an active ally of Protestant Sweden, while certain Protestant states of Germany fought on the imperial side. The war continued as savagely as ever. Mercenary troops devastated Germany. Sheer exhaustion and war-weariness finally forced the contending parties to conclude peace. The Peace of Westphalia, October 27, 1648, provided that Lutherans, Calvinists, and Catholics should have equal religious and civil rights. The religion of each state was to be Protestant or Catholic according to its position in 1624, the "normal year." But the princes, and not the people, were to decide the kind of religion.

The Peace of Westphalia fixed the future alignment of Europe. France, Spain, Portugal, Italy and South-Eastern Europe remained Catholic. Germany and Switzerland remained partly Catholic and partly Protestant. In England, Scotland, Holland, and the Scandinavian countries the Protestant religion remained as established. In a general way, those countries which had formed an integral part of the ancient Roman Empire, remained within the Catholic fold. No privileges were accorded to the Protestants in Austria and Bohemia. The pope, who emphatically denounced the Peace of Westphalia, continued the re-catholizing process under Jesuit leadership, especially in Poland, Hungary, and Transylvania.

III. The Arminian Controversy.—With the declaration of independence in 1609,[3] the United Netherlands (Dutch Republic) proclaimed Calvinism as the official state-religion. But some of the ministers did not take kindly to the predestinarian views of Calvin. They claimed that the Calvinistic doctrine of predestination made God responsible for human sin, and denied man his freedom of will. The resulting discussion brought Jacob Arminius (1560-1609) and his system to the front. He summarized his views in five articles in opposition to the five points of Calvinism.

The views of Jacob Arminius and his followers may be stated as follows: (1) Election was *conditional* upon, and inseparable from Divine *foreknowledge* of those who would believe and persist to the end. Calvinism taught *unconditional* election, based on the sovereign *will* of God. (2) Christ died for all the people, and not only for the elect, but not all men accepted this atonement. Hence believers only received the actual benefit. Calvin limited the atonement to the elect only. (3) Man was not totally depraved and could therefore co-operate with God in the spiritual regeneration. Calvin held to the doctrine of the total depravity of man. (4) God's grace was not irresistible for the elect, and withheld from the reprobate. Calvin held the opposite view. (5) Against the Calvinistic doctrine of "Once in grace, always in grace," Arminius emphasized the possibility of a lapse from grace.

At the Synod of Dort, November, 1618, to May, 1619, the Arminian views were condemned. The Arminians were deposed and excluded from communion, and some were even banished from the country. The Synod endorsed the Belgic Confession of 1562[4] and the Heidelberg Catechism. Arminianism was the historic forerunner of Methodism.

IV. The Scottish-English Revolution.—James VI of Scotland[5] came to the English throne as James I in 1603. He reigned as king over England and Scotland until his death in 1625 and was succeeded by his son, Charles I, who was executed in 1649. These two sovereigns, like the other Stuarts, were firm believers in the *divine right of kings*, while the Commons of the Parliament and a large portion of the English people asserted the *divine right of the common people*, especially in matters of taxation and religion. In these differences of view lay the germs of the Scottish Revolution and the Civil War.

[3] See page 345.   [4] See page 312.   [5] See page 316.

Four religious parties existed in England during that period, Romanists, Anglicans, Puritans, and Independents. Queen Elizabeth had outlawed Roman Catholicism, but the law had not been uniformly enforced. A group of Catholics remained in England, and in 1605 some of these entered into a plot to blow up the Parliament building on the opening day of the sessions of the Houses, when king, lords, and commons would be present. The plot was discovered, the offenders were punished, and severe laws were enacted against the Catholics. After this event the Romanists were an almost negligible factor. The Anglicans supported the king and the episcopal form of church government. The Puritans,[6] the staunch supporters of the Parliament, aimed to displace episcopacy by Presbyterianism. The Independents or Separatists rejected the episcopal and the presbyterian forms of church government and maintained that each local congregation was the true unit of church government.

In 1603, while James I was on his way to London to assume his position in the government, a large number of puritan ministers presented him with a petition in which they modestly complained of the "burden of human rites and ceremonies," and asked for a purer doctrine and a better ministry. James answered, "I will have one doctrine, one discipline, one religion in substance and ceremony." This meant that he would have the Separatists and the Scottish Church in all respects conform to the model of the Church of England. The Puritans were admonished "to conform or they should hear of it." James I proceeded very cautiously, however, to substitute a royally controlled episcopacy for the Scottish Presbyterianism. Several bishops and two archbishops were consecrated and given full diocesan jurisdiction in Scotland; but the king waited many years before he attempted any changes in the Scottish worship. In 1621 he finally secured, by the Five Articles of Perth, the introduction of certain English customs of worship. This act occasioned widespread discontent among the Scots.

Charles I (1625-49) was more despotic and tyrannical than his father. During the first four years of his reign he dissolved three Parliaments, and during the next eleven years he governed without that body. His most active supporters were Thomas Wentworth, later Earl of Strafford, and William Laud, Bishop of London until 1633, and later Archbishop of Canterbury. Laud was the chief religious and political adviser of Charles I after 1628.

William Laud was a prominent representative of the Anglican

party and an ardent supporter of the crown. He believed in the divine right of kings, and also in the divine right of bishops. There could be no true church without bishops. He attached great importance to externals in religion and to uniformity in ritual, vestments, and the like. In theology he was an Arminian. As Archbishop of Canterbury he made it his aim to crush all nonconformism in England and in Scotland, and the royal support enabled him to enforce conformity with a heavy hand.

When Charles I and Archbishop Laud began to force the Anglican liturgy upon the Church of Scotland, 1634-37, the entire Scottish nation flared in opposition. At Edinburgh the attempt of a bishop to read the service led to a riot in 1637. In February, 1638, the National Covenant of the Scots was formed for the defence of Presbyterianism. In December, 1638, a General Assembly decided to restore the Presbyterian system of 1581. This was rebellion, and Charles I decided to crush it by force.

The king was forced to call a Parliament in April, 1640, in order to obtain a vote of supplies. Three weeks later he dissolved it, and a brief war followed with the Scots. In November, 1640, he was compelled to summon a Parliament again. This was known as the "Long Parliament" because it remained in existence for twelve years. One of the first acts of Parliament was to impeach Strafford and Laud. Both were later executed. Another early act was the passing of a law which declared that no taxation could be imposed without the consent of Parliament. The king interpreted these acts as sedition. In January, 1642, he tried to seize five of the leaders of the Commons by force of arms, and this act precipitated the Civil War of 1642-49.

Parliament appealed to the Scotch for help, but Scotland refused to combine forces against the king unless England would make Presbyterianism the religion of the realm. Parliament agreed to this in the Solemn League and Covenant of 1643, so a Scottish army crossed the border the following year. Episcopacy was abolished by Parliament in 1643, and provisions were made to give the Church of England a Presbyterian creed and government. The Westminster Assembly, 1643-1647, framed the Westminster Confession, the Longer and the Shorter Westminster Catechism, a Directory of Worship, and a Presbyterian form of church government. All were adopted by the General Assembly of Scotland and by Parliament. It was a great victory for the Calvinistic system as well as for Presbyterian Puritanism.

But Presbyterianism was never fully established in England.

Oliver Cromwell was unwilling to force this system upon the nation. To him forms and ordinances were secondary to personal piety. He maintained a national Church in accordance with the Westminster Assembly, but he also granted toleration for Baptists and Independents. This brought him into conflict with the Scots.

Cromwell subdued the Scots, and in 1648 the army took control over the Parliament. An officer named Pride was stationed at the door to arrest all who opposed the army's policies. "Pride's Purge" kept one hundred and forty-three members from their seats. The purged Parliament sentenced Charles I to be executed, which sentence was carried out on January 30, 1649. A few weeks later the Commons abolished the office of king, and the House of Lords. A free state was established under the name of "The Commonwealth." It lasted from 1649 until 1660. In 1653 Cromwell was given the title of "Lord Protector of the Commonwealth of England, Scotland, and Ireland." After his death in 1658, the Protectorate was filled for two years by his son, Richard Cromwell. In 1660 the monarchy was restored, and Charles II (1660-85) was placed upon the throne.

Charles II was a Catholic, but the party that brought him upon the throne prevented him from restoring Catholicism in England. The Anglican order was reconstructed as far as possible. Charles II was succeeded by his brother, James II (1685-88). He was an outspoken Romanist who at once began to restore the Catholic worship. His policy finally precipitated another revolution in 1688. James II was driven out, and his Protestant daughter Mary, and her husband William, Prince of Orange, were placed upon the English throne. The Bill of Rights, adopted in 1689, rehearsed the old rights and liberties of Englishmen. The Toleration Act, adopted the same year, granted freedom of public worship to all Protestant Dissenters, but not to Catholics and Unitarians. The Established Church of England subscribed to the Thirty-nine Articles, and practical control of it was vested in Parliament. As a result of this religious settlement, the people of England organized themselves under the names of Presbyterians, Independents or Congregationalists, Baptists, Quakers, and Anglicans.

The final settlement in Scotland in 1690 ratified the Westminster Confession and recognized Presbyterianism as the Church of Scotland. But Episcopalians and Independents were also tolerated. The Scotch population was finally divided into three general groups which were known as the Established Church, the

United Presbyterian Church, and the Free Church of Scotland. All these groups held to the Westminister standards.

V. Retrospect.—By 1689 the three successive stages of the Counter Reformation[7] had come to an end. The armed conflict between Catholics and Protestants had practically ceased, though religious antagonism continued to exist. The religious map of Europe had assumed practically the same character as it has to-day.

49. REVIEW QUESTIONS

1. Discuss the causes of the Thirty Years' War.
2. What was the status of Protestantism at the end of the first stage of the war?
3. Why did the cause of Protestantism seem so hopeless in 1629?
4. How did the hostility of one type of Protestantism toward another affect the course of the Thirty Years' War?
5. Why did Gustavus Adolphus of Sweden and Richelieu of France take such interest in this war?
6. Why was the Peace of Westphalia a prominent landmark in European history?
7. Discuss the Arminian controversy. In what ways did Arminianism influence Holland, England, Scotland, and America?
8. What do you think of the divine right of kings, the divine right of the common people, the divine right of episcopacy, the divine right of Presbyterianism, and the divine right of congregationalism?
9. What part did these doctrines play in the Scottish Revolution and the Civil War?
10. Why did "The Commonwealth" end in failure?
11. Account for the fact that the English nation again followed the "middle way" by adopting Anglicanism?
12. At what time had the Counter Reformation spent its force? Summarize its final political and religious results.

TOPICS FOR SPECIAL STUDY

1. Gustavus Adolphus, "the Lion of the North."
2. Consequences of the Peace of Westphalia in 1648.
3. Arminianism and its general influence.
4. Why England preferred Episcopalianism to Presbyterianism.

A SELECTED BIBLIOGRAPHY FOR CHAPTER XVII

1. *Cambridge Modern History*, Volumes IV-V.
2. Rowe: *History of the Christian People*, Pages 321-336.
3. Gardiner: *The Thirty Years' War.*
4. Harrison: *Beginnings of Arminianism.*
5. Tulloch: *English Puritanism and Its Leaders.*
6. Gregory: *Puritanism.*
7. Gardiner: *Oliver Cromwell.*
8. Gardiner: *History of the Commonwealth and Protectorate.*
9. Hutton: *History of the English Church from Charles I to Anne.*

[7] See pages 343-45.

CHAPTER XVIII

PROTESTANT LIFE AND THOUGHT IN THE XVII AND XVIII CENTURIES

The great formative period of the Protestant Reformation was followed by three specific movements known as Orthodoxy, Pietism, and Enlightenment. The first emphasized pure doctrine at the expense of a healthy spiritual life; the second emphasized spiritual life at the expense of pure doctrine; and the third made human reason the highest authority in religious matters. The Age of Orthodoxy revived the spirit of Scholasticism; the movement called Pietism revived in part the spirit of Monasticism; and the Period of Enlightenment revived the old pagen ideal of the worth

Reason	Faith	Reason	Faith	Reason	Faith	Reason
Renaissance	Reformation	Orthodoxy	Pietism	Rationalism	Confessionalism	Scientism
Classicism	Melanchthonian (1530)	Syncretism	Latitudinarianism	Unitarianism	Unionism	Liberalism
Mysticism	Humanism	Quietism	Formalism	Supernaturalism	Criticism	Fundamentalism
Faith	Reason	Faith	Reason	Faith	Reason	Faith

THE CONFLICT OF RATIONALISM AND FAITH IN THE MODERN PERIOD[1]

of man. All three movements exerted a vital influence upon the life and the thought of Europe and America during the seventeenth and the eighteenth centuries.

I. The Age of Orthodoxy.—The truth which the great reformers of the sixteenth century had re-discovered in the Scriptures had been stated by them in the several Protestant confessions of faith. Hence the sixteenth century was a period of creeds. But the need was soon felt to have the Protestant doctrines formulated in a more systematized or scientific form, to match the systems of Roman and Greek Catholicism, and to define and differentiate

[1] This diagram, suggested by Dr. O. M. Norlie, should not convey the impression that the historical movements are mechanical. The intention is merely to show that faith and reason are frequently at odds, and that each new appearance of faith and reason has a new complexion. Within these epochs are, of course, many other conflicting currents. cf. diagram, page 470.

them from all divergent Protestant views. This was largely accomplished during the seventeenth century. By this activity the Roman and the Greek Catholic communions were also stimulated to modify or re-define their doctrines. Jesuitism fought its great battle with Jansenism and Quietism in the Roman church, and in the Greek church the doctrines were formulated anew by Petrus Mogilas.[2] The seventeenth century was, therefore, the Age of Orthodoxy.

Protestant schoolmen, mostly professors in the universities, set themselves to organizing and systematizing the Evangelical faith and doctrine into good teaching form. Hence theological science, especially dogmatics, flourished in the various Protestant communions during the seventeenth century. The most prominent of the new schoolmen were John Gerhard (1583-1637) among the Lutherans, and Gysbert Voetius (1589-1676) among the Reformed. This new Protestant scholasticism contained much that was good and commendable, but the whole movement was conspicuously one-sided. The Bible became an arsenal from which doctrines were to be proved. The Gospel was treated as doctrine rather than as a power of God unto salvation,[3] and Christianity was presented as a religion of right thinking without a corresponding emphasis on the right condition of the heart. This one-sided emphasis on right thinking made the age of orthodoxy an age of great theological controversies.

But orthodoxy did not merely produce quarrelsome theologians and a parched Protestantism. It also produced strong religious personalities, men who knew whom they believed and what they believed. It was a most wholesome counter influence. Orthodoxy laid great stress on the Christian education of the young and on the building up of strong Christian homes. Perhaps the most beautiful trait was the devout family spirit and the widespread practice of family worship. In conformity with the spiritual priesthood of the believer, each family head would daily gather his family to a common worship consisting of the reading of Scripture, prayer, and song. The Evangelical parsonage set the example and proved to be the center of true christian culture.

Simultaneously with the orthodox movement came several counter-acting tendencies known as Mysticism, Theosophy, and Syncretism. These were followed by Pietism which represented the opposite extreme of Orthodoxy.

1. *Mysticism.*—The Lord and his Apostles had laid great stress

on a personal living faith in God. This primacy of a personal communion with God, and the resulting assurance of the forgiveness of sins, had also been emphasized by the reformers, especially by Luther. In the seventeenth century there were many advocates of this type of Christian mysticism, such as John Arndt (1555-1621), Henry Muller, Christian Scriver, and the hymnwriter Paul Gerhard, among the Lutherans, and John Bunyan (1628-88) and Richard Baxter (1615-91), among the Reformed. The Christian mystic was essentially concerned with God and his own soul. He would generally conform to the external conditions of the Church, unless these seriously threatened his spiritual life. Such churchly or conformist mysticism has always formed a vital part of a normal Christian life.

But by the side of this normal Christian mysticism, a one-sided and deformatory mysticism frequently developed, sometimes in a mild form, sometimes as a caricature of truth. This separatist or unchurchly form[4] is generally referred to historically as *Mysticism*. The Mystics subordinated the Word of God and the Sacraments to the subjective experiences of the "inner light" of the Spirit. Their immediate divine revelations, visions, and dreams were generally placed above the authority of the Bible.[5] Church organization was repudiated as inimical to the Spirit. Freedom of the Spirit was the essential thing. But how could they recognize the Divine voice? Some recognized the Voice through human reason, and this paved the way for a religious rationalism. Others listened to the Voice through their inner, emotional experiences, and this frequently paved the way for a dwarfed religious life.

a. The Society of Friends (The Quakers). The most notable product of the seventeenth century Mysticism was, perhaps, the society of Friends, started at Nottingham, England, by George Fox. After 1650 the opponents in ridicule called them Quakers because of a certain incident. A judge at Derby, threatened by a Friend with the prophecy, "Thou shalt quake at the Last Judgment," is said to have retorted, "No, thou shalt be the quaker." This term of derision later became a name of honor.

George Fox (1624-91) was the son of a Presbyterian weaver of Drayton. He was an honest and sincere man, but strongly inclined to go to extremes. As a youth he had been carefully trained in the Puritanic religion, though many of his early associates were Anabaptists. He was employed as a shoemaker when an incident caused him to seek spiritual help from a clergyman. The advice he

---

[4] See diagram on page 328.   [5] See pages 250 and 330.

received did not satisfy him, so he turned against the organized church and its ministry. Years of spiritual struggle followed until in 1646 he had a transforming experience, a revelation which opened his mind to the importance of the "inner light" of the spirit in man. It seemed like a baptism of the Spirit, accompanied by special gifts of grace.

Following the immediate prompting of the Spirit, he started his work as a wandering preacher in 1647, and for the next forty years he spread his Quaker views by writing and by itinerant preaching. He travelled extensively in England and in Scotland, and he also visited Holland and America. In 1649 he interrupted an English pastor in the midst of his sermon and proclaimed the need of the "inner light" of the Spirit for the right understanding of the Bible. For this public disturbance he was imprisoned, under the Blasphemy Act, and this was but the beginning of a series of imprisonments for similar disturbances. He travelled about in clothes made of leather. He refused to take oath or to do military service. His outspoken and defiant opposition to all forms of organized Christianity made him appear a dangerous foe of the established church law and order. Hence Fox and his followers met with fiery opposition.

The followers of Fox increased rapidly. In 1648 a dissolved Anabaptist congregation at Nottingham, England, rallied around him. In 1652 a Quaker community was gathered in Preston Patrick, England. During the first four years Fox was the only minister of the various Quaker groups. In the fifth year he had twenty-five assistants, and in 1656 he had not less than fifty-six assistant travelling preachers. In 1661, there were more than forty-two hundred Quakers in the English prisons. Quaker missionaries found their way to Continental Europe, to parts of Asia and Africa, to the West India Islands, and to America. William Penn founded a Quaker colony in Pennsylvania in 1682.

Fox finally saw the need of organizing the movement. A constitution was prepared in London in 1660 which included rules regarding the formation of local congregations, Sunday services, church discipline, and Elders as leaders of the flock. The next year, 1661, Quaker synods with advisory authority assembled. Much against the original intentions of George Fox, congregations were formally organized, and a Quaker Free Church sprang into existence. Robert Barclay, the theologian of the movement, reduced the doctrinal views of the Quakers into a system. His *Catechism* of 1673, and his *Fifteen Theses* as stated in the *Apology* of 1675, are the nearest approaches to an authoritative Quaker confession of faith.

The distinguishing features of the Quakers and their system may be summarized as follows: (1) The Bible is the Word of God, but its religious authority is subordinate to the divine inward revelations of the Holy Spirit through the "inner light" in man. These revelations or promptings of the Spirit contradict neither the Scriptures nor Reason. (2) The Sacraments are purely spiritual and symbolic. The outward elements are not only unnecessary but misleading. Hence Baptism and the Lord's Supper are not observed among them. (3) Every member is a priest unto God. Hence there is no need of a special ministry or of theological training. (4) Since the Spirit is regardless of sex, women may preach and teach as well as men. (5) Any specified liturgy or formal worship is abominable idolatry in the sight of God. There is no music or singing. The members come together and sit in complete silence until someone is prompted by the Spirit to speak, pray, or exhort. If none is thus prompted, they remain in silent meditation and contemplation for some time, and then quietly separate. (6) Individual eccentricities such as visions, dreams, ecstasies, hysteria and the like have at times found expression in the Quaker meetings, but these extravagances have been checked by the corporate experience of the group concerned. (7) The earlier Quakers refused to take oath and to do military and civil service. This is still true of the Evangelical Friends, but not of all of the members of the Hicksite Quakers. (8) The Quakers magnify the worth of human personality. They are industrious and sincere and live in utmost simplicity. Quakers are generally to be found in the front ranks of social reformers and philanthropists. They strongly oppose intemperance and war.

All other Protestant communions acknowledge the Bible as the supreme religious authority. The Quakers, on the contrary, find their supreme religious authority in the inner religious experiences of man, or in religious empiricism. The immediate illumination of the Holy Spirit through the "inner light" in man gives the necessary strength and guidance.

b. The Swedenborgian Church. Another product of Mysticism was the Swedenborgian or New Jerusalem Church which arose in the revelations of Emmanuel Swedenborg (1688-1772), a distinguished Swedish scientist. At the age of fifty-five he claimed to have a revelation which opened his sight to a view of the spiritual world, and granted him the privilege of speaking with spirits and angels. Of the rest of his life he could write, "I have been for thirty years in open communication, by the Lord's mercy, with the spiritual world." This first revelation was followed by others in which he claimed the secrets of the universe were unveiled to him. He experienced a direct call to give up all wordly learning and to write down his revelations.

Swedenborg did not present his system as a substitute for the revelation of God as given in the Bible. But he claimed to have the true key to the understanding of the Bible, which he interpreted allegorically. He revived the Gnostic doctrine of correspondences between the natural and the spiritual world. Man was a small universe, and the universe was a large man.[6] There was no original sin. Hence no justification by faith was possible. Christ was the Savior of the world in the sense that he defeated the hosts of evil and won freedom for man. There was no bodily resurrection from the dead. After the physical death, men continued to live in the spiritual world in which they really existed now. Swedenborg also claimed that the Second Coming of Christ, as foretold in the Bible, really occurred in the year in which the spiritual world was revealed to him. And the New Jerusalem, foretold in Revelation, came to earth in 1771 when the first Swedenborgian church was started. Hence the name "New Jerusalem Church."

His views exerted a considerable influence in Sweden, Germany, England, and North America. A "Church of the New Jerusalem" was founded in London in 1788. In the United States of America Swedenborgian churches are found in about thirty states.

2. *Theosophy.*—Theosophy, which means "divine wisdom," is concerned with mystical speculations concerning God and the universe. It seeks to find the essential truth which underlies all systems of religion, philosophy, and science; it rests upon an inner revelation which is superior to sensible experience and reason; and it is in constant search for secret doctrines which will furnish the best key to truth.

Mystical speculations of this type found expression through such men as Valentine Weigel, Jacob Bohme, and Johann Valentine Andreae. Valentine Weigel (1533-88) was a German Lutheran pastor in good standing. Some manuscripts published after his death disclosed that he was really a theosophist who adhered to the doctrine of the "inner word" or the "inner light." He claimed that everything external, including heaven and hell and even history, inhered latently in man, in his personality and subjectivity.

Jacob Bohme (1576-1624), "the German Gnostic," was one of the greatest, most profound, and most ingenius theosophists that ever lived. Outwardly he adhered to the Lutheran Church, but his speculations were anything but churchly. He claimed to have frequent visions and revelations, and that he for days would be encompassed by a divine light. He dated his fuller theosophical illumination from a time when he beheld the mysteries of the Deity and of the universe in the reflection of the sun from a brightly polished pewter plate. His speculative system, too extensive to explain in a few words, has ever since exerted a strong influence upon certain religious groups.

Johann Valentine Andreae (1586-1654), a Lutheran court preacher, founded the secret brotherhood known as the "Rosicrucians."[7] The name signifies the union of science and Christianity, as symbolized by the rose and the cross (*rosa:* rose + *crux:* cross). Besides nourishing certain mystical speculations, the Rosicrucians aimed to combat alchemy and Roman Catholicism. The movement has since undergone a recrudescence in connection with freemasonry. Rosicrucian organizations are found today in various parts of Europe and in America.

3. *Syncretism or Latitudinarianism.*—The exaggerated zeal and the contentious spirit of orthodoxy provoked a number of protests. The advocates of a broader religious toleration in England were called "Latitudinarians." William Chillingworth (1602-44) was the ablest English representative of this conciliatory tendency. Efforts were also made on the Continent to reconcile Lutheran and Reformed theology. George Calixtus (1586-1656), a Lutheran professor at Helmstadt, tried to promote mutual denominational forbearance by recognizing the three ancient symbols, the Apostolic, the Nicene, and the Athanasian creeds, as containing the essentials of Christianity. But he found a very small hearing. His opponents accused him of underestimating the importance of the truths which the Lutheran Reformation had brought to light. Dutch Arminianism[8] was also a protest against the extreme Calvinistic orthodoxy.

4. *Immortal Church-hymns.*—Attention should be called to the many beautiful church-hymns of this period. The intense suffering and the varied experiences of Protestant Christians during and shortly after the Thirty Years' War found expression in a number of immortal hymns. Paul Gerhardt (1607-76), the foremost Lutheran hymn-writer in Germany, composed one hundred and twenty hymns. A large number of other Lutheran hymn-writers of

[7] Holmquist: *Kirkehistorie*, Vol. II, page 348.   [8] See page 351.

this period could be mentioned. The Reformed church furnished but few religious poets during this period. Mention may be made of Louisa Henrietta, Joachim Neander, Richard Baxter, and John Milton.

50. REVIEW QUESTIONS

1. Can you see any reasons why the formative period of the Reformation should be followed by such movements as Orthodoxy, Pietism, and Enlightenment? Does this development compare with the prophetic era of the Old Testament which was followed by the era of the great Synagogue? Explain.
2. Why was the sixteenth century an epoch of creeds, and why was the seventeenth century the epoch of orthodoxy?
3. In what sense did orthodoxy revive the spirit of Scholasticism? Why was the movement so one-sided? What good results did it produce?
4. Describe the movement called Mysticism. How is this related to the normal Christian mysticism?
5. Discuss the Quaker movement. Account for the rapid growth of the movement. Why the fiery opposition to the Quakers?
6. Mention the distinguishing features of the Quakers. How do they differ from other Protestant communions?
7. Do you know of any distinguished members of the Quaker church of today?
8. Discuss Swedenborg and his system. How did he deviate from the accepted Protestant views?
9. Do you see any difference between Mysticism and Theosophy? Why?
10. Why may such men as Weigel, Bohme, and Andreae be numbered among the theosophists?
11. Who are the Rosicrucians?
12. Why did orthodoxy of the seventeenth century leave so little room for religious toleration?

TOPICS FOR SPECIAL STUDY

1. John Gerhard and Gysbert Voetius, the Protestant Schoolmen of the seventeenth century.
2. Deformatory Mysticism.
3. The place of human reason in religion.
4. Religious poets and hymn-writers of the seventeenth century.

II. Pietism.—Pietism is the name given to a great religious awakening within the Protestant churches of the seventeenth and the eighteenth centuries in behalf of practical religion. From religious gatherings called *collegia pietatis* the movement was nicknamed "Pietism." This movement, combining the mystical and the practical tendencies within the Lutheran and the Reformed churches, came as a reaction against the inordinate stress of orthodoxy on pure doctrine and formalism. The movement started almost simultaneously in Holland, Germany, and Switzerland, but the earliest traces appeared in Holland about 1660. Certain members of the Dutch Reformed Church who revolted against the extreme Calvinistic-Puritanic Orthodoxy, formed small groups of "regenerates" who cared but little for pure doctrine or formal confessions. They stressed a living faith made manifest in practical and upright living. Religion was an affair of the heart rather than of the head.

Philip Jacob Spener (1635-1705), a Lutheran clergyman, was the founder of German Pietism. He saw many evils in the church-life of his time and made proposals for improvement. The Word of God should be more widely diffused through religious gatherings (*collegia pietatis*) of lay-people where the Bible was read and discussed under the guidance of the pastor. The Christian lay-people should be encouraged to take a more active part in practical church work, such as religious instruction, mutual edification, and care for the salvation of others. Due attention should be given to the fact that Christianity is far more a life than an intellectual attitude. More gentleness and love between denominations should be manifested, and all theological controversies should be purged of personal, selfish polemics. The theological training should be thoroughly revised, and an experimental knowledge of religion should be required of all theological students. A complete change in the current method of preaching should be effected. Sermons should be prepared for the purpose of building up the Christian life of the hearers. Undue rhetorical art and the controversial and argumentative elements should be eliminated from the sermon.

Spener promoted interest in the Sunday School, in catechetical instruction, and in Protestant confirmation. He quickened interest in prayer-meetings and Bible study, and fought for the privilege of private devotional meetings. He opposed dances, cards, and the theatre, and inculcated moderation in food, drink, and dress. He stirred up much interest in missions among Jews and heathen. But he underestimated the authority of the Protestant creeds by basing his religious views and practices exclusively on the Bible. He also maintained that serious doctrinal errors might coexist with true personal faith of the heart. He emphasized a personal spiritual life rather than a mere intellectual acceptance of the doctrines of the Church.

August Herman Francke (1663-1727) brought the Pietistic movement to its great climax in Germany. His life-work was done in connection with the University of Halle. John Wesley, the founder of Methodism, was much influenced by him. Francke promoted the general religious program of Spener, but added the work of Inner Missions as a central factor of Lutheranism. A special feature of his Inner Mission work was the establishment of his famous "Institutions" at Halle. The first of these was a school for poor children. He soon added a pay school for the well-to-do, another school for the children of the nobility, and a little later an orphan school. At the time of his death these "Institutions" had more than twenty-two hundred pupils, and over three hundred teachers and workers and attendants. He also established a printing press, a book store, and a boarding house where needy students could get free board. A wealthy friend paid for the establishment of a Bible Institute. The University of Halle became the great Pietistic center which supplied Europe with teachers, pastors, foreign missionaries, and influential laymen.

From Germany the movement spread to the Scandinavian countries. King Christian VI favored the introduction of Pietism into Denmark and Norway. Prominent among the Danish Pietists were Hans Adolph Brorson (d. 1764), one of Denmark's great hymn-writers, and Erik Pontoppidan (d. 1755) who wrote an explanation to Luther's Catechism which is still used in abbreviated form. In Norway the movement produced such men as Hans Egede (d. 1758), the great missionary to Greenland, Thomas von Westen, who was active in educational and Inner Mission work and Hans Nielsen Hauge (1771-1824), Norway's great lay-preacher and revivalist. In Sweden the Pietistic movement was suppressed by a royal decree in 1706.

Lack of organization and certain inherent defects shortened the history of Pietism. Pietism was not an organized movement. Spener and Francke did not want their adherents to form a new church. They should form *ecclesiolae in ecclesia*, or groups within the constituted church and serve as a spiritual leaven for the larger group by promoting a "living Christianity." The Pietists claimed that the regeneration of man took place, not in Baptism, but in a specific conversion. Francke had in 1687 experienced a very sudden conversion, preceded by a great spiritual struggle and a conviction of sin. His conversion was so real and so vivid that he could state accurately its time and place. The Pietists of Halle soon insisted that Francke's experience furnished the standard whereby all real conversions should be tested. This insistence on a methodical form of conversion frequently led to a narrow, severe, and unjust judgment of the "unconverted." As a "congregation within the congregation" the Pietists frequently caused much friction by magnifying the contrast between "converted" and "unconverted." If the pastor did not adhere to their views, they would at times nourish a conscious opposition of the spiritual priesthood of the lay-people to the special priesthood of the clergy. The Pietists formulated a code of conduct which bordered on Pharisaism. Their Christianity was gloomy, austere, and legalistic. The Pietists paid inordinate attention to the study of the Second Coming of Christ and the Millennium.[9] Their reliance on visions and dreams led, at times, to an unbridled subjectivism.

But these glaring defects should not lead the student to underestimate the central values of the Pietistic movement. Pietism came as a one-sided reaction against the one-sidedness of Orthodoxy. The gradual fusion of these two movements produced a healthy, vigorous type of Christianity.

1. *The Moravians.*—A notable result of Pietism was the establishment of the Moravian or "renewed fraternity" (Unity of the Brethren) in 1727. The charter members of this communion were Moravian and Bohemian Protestants who had been driven from their homes by the Counter Reformation. Count Nicholas Ludwig von Zinzendorf (1700-1760) invited them to settle on his estate of Berthelsdorf in Saxony. The first group settled there in 1722. Two years later a larger group arrived, and this was followed by a third group of settlers. The village of Herrnhut was the center of their colony. Religious differences between the Bohemian and the Moravian settlers threatened a disruption of the colony, but Zinzendorf succeeded in uniting them by magnifying the interests they had in common. On May 12, 1727, the little community was organized as a "renewed fraternity."

The peculiar nature of the religious organization reflected some of the peculiarities of the founder, Count Zinzendorf. He had been brought up under Pietistic influences, and had spent six years in study at one of the "Institutions" of Francke at Halle. At this place he had acquired the interests which furnished him with the two great purposes of his later life, the evangelization of foreign lands, and the formation of an international association of true Christians with membership in all Christian churches, including the Roman and the Greek Catholic communions, and with Herrnhut as the general headquarters. This second motive explains why he did not want to organize an independent church at Herrnhut. He wanted the Moravian colony to form a special group within the Lutheran church of Saxony. The colony at Herrnhut should formally belong to the Lutheran congregation of Berthelsdorf. They should attend the regular Lutheran services, and the Lutheran

⁕ See page 108.

pastor should perform all their ministerial acts. But the colony should also have an additional organization of its own, headed by twelve "Elders." This special "congregation" should meet for daily worship by itself. In these special gatherings they introduced the love-feast, and feet-washing, and the fraternal kiss. They also used daily watch-words from the Old Testament and doctrinal texts from the New Testament to control and direct their feelings and meditations.

This Moravian community attracted immediate and widespread attention. Its membership increased rapidly, not only by the arrival of additional Moravian exiles, but also by the flocking thither of religious refugees of all Protestant nations. Zinzendorf, the general director of the colony, managed to keep these diverse elements together. The "renewed fraternity" manifested an astonishing ability to propagate itself. Members of the society were sent to various Protestant countries to form *ecclesiolae in ecclesia* or groups within the established churches. Such organizations were soon formed in various parts of Germany, in Holland, Denmark, England, and North America. The Herrnhut colony sent out missionaries to the West Indies in 1732 and to Greenland in 1733.

Zinzendorf secured ordination for his missionaries by introducing the episcopacy into his organization. Jablonsky, a court-preacher at Berlin and a former bishop of the Moravian church, ordained David Nitschmann as bishop of the Moravian community at Herrnhut. Zinzendorf himself was ordained as a Lutheran Minister in 1724. In 1737 he received ordination as Bishop of the Moravians from the hand of Jablonsky. Zinzendorf's intimate connection with England, and the increasing importance attached to episcopal succession caused him to take this ordination. By this act he established a formal connection with the Husite church.

But Zinzendorf's indifference toward doctrinal formulas and confessions of faith brought him into discredit with the Lutheran church and the government of Saxony. He was exiled from Saxony for more than ten years, 1736-47. During this period he travelled extensively. Among many other places he visited the West India Islands, 1738-39, and America, 1741-43. Meanwhile the Moravian community organized, much against the will of Zinzendorf, into an independent church in 1742. The new church, known as the "Unity of the Brethren," was formally recognized by the Saxon government in 1742. By 1745 the group was a fully organized church with bishops, elders, deacons, and a special liturgy. In 1749 the English Parliament recognized the Unity of the

Brethren as "an ancient Protestant Episcopal Church." It was in England that the adherents of this communion were first and generally called "Moravians."

August Gottlieb Spangenberg (1704-92), the "second founder" of the Unity of the Brethren, perfected its organization and assisted in the formulation of the generally accepted doctrines of that communion. The Moravians have subscribed to the Augsburg Confession since 1749, but the cardinal points of their doctrine are stated in their Catechism, the "Easter Litany," and the "Compendium of Doctrine." It was partly through Spangenberg's influence that Moravianism became the connecting link between German Pietism and English Methodism.

III. English Methodism.—English Methodism came as the last great wave of the religious revivals which swept over the Protestant world. The movement came largely as a reaction against English rationalism and the general spiritual and moral decline of the English nation. John Wesley (1703-91) was the man who called the revival into existence, but he was ably assisted by his brother, Charles Wesley (1708-88), and by George Whitefield (1714-70). John Williams Fletcher (1729-85) was also prominently connected with the founding of Methodism. John Wesley was the great organizer, Whitefield was the great pulpit orator, Charles Wesley was the great hymn-writer, and Fletcher was the prominent theologian of the early Methodist movement.

A just appreciation of the place and the value of the Methodist revival can only be obtained by a careful study of the historic background of the movement. England had undergone a remarkable change during the eighteenth century. The great colonial expansion had made England a world empire, with control over millions of colonists and natives. The great Industrial Revolution had transformed England from an agricultural to an industrial nation. The old social and economic structure of England had to give way to a new social and economic order. Large cities sprang into existence. Much wealth was accumulated in a few hands, while large masses suffered from extreme poverty. These rapid changes were at first disastrous to life, morals, and religion because the necessary readjustments were made neither by the church nor by the state. The Anglican church had largely failed to take up its special and world-wide mission when the Methodist revival started. Methodism satisfied to a large extent the religious needs which the Anglican church had failed to meet, and this accounts in part for the world wide scope and the international character of the Methodist church.

Four outstanding experiences of John Wesley impressed themselves indelibly upon the early Methodist movement. As the son of an Anglican clergyman, rector of the county parish of Epworth, John adopted his father's high-churchly views, including a marked interest in an elaborate ritual. William Law's ideals of a consecrated life influenced him to the extent that he accepted the doctrine of entire sanctification or sinless Christian perfection in the present life. His connection with the academic club which provoked the nickname "Methodists," and his later contact with William Law, induced him to study the devotional literature of the Mystics. His attention was turned inward, to the development of his inner spiritual life. His contact with the Moravians provoked a strong desire to obtain a full assurance of his salvation. This assurance came on the evening of May 24, 1738, at a quarter of nine o'clock, as he listened to the reading of Luther's preface to the Epistle to the Romans. Whitefield and Charles Wesley had already had similar experiences. In these specific conversions the evangelical Methodism was born. A dignified ritual, the attainableness of Christian perfection, a marked interest in Mysticism, and present assurance of salvation were four cardinal features of early English Methodism.

John and Charles Wesley and George Whitefield had all studied at the University of Oxford, and all three had taken ordination as ministers in the Established Church of England. The Wesley brothers left England in 1735 to serve as missionaries in the newly established colony of Georgia, but their work was so unsuccessful that they soon returned, Charles in 1736 and John in 1738. After their "conversion" in 1738 they began to preach evangelical revival and "Biblical holiness." They presented the order of salvation as follows: A sudden conversion preceded by great spiritual struggles leads to true Christianity. Faith opens the door to true religion, but sanctification and relative perfection is religion itself.

The Church of England did not look kindly upon this revival movement. The Wesley brothers received few invitations to preach, and the invitations were seldom repeated. A number of Anglican clergymen definitely closed their doors against the movement. But these closed doors proved a blessing in disguise. Whitefield, who had just returned from America, pointed the way by starting meetings in open places. His outdoor meetings near Bristol gathered audiences that at times numbered twenty thousand. John

Wesley hesitated at first, but he soon followed Whitefield's example. Immense audiences gathered to hear him. This was the beginning of the world-wide Methodist crusade to free human souls from the bondage of Satan, the world, and one's own sinful flesh.

Organization was soon deemed necessary. John Wesley had no desire to break with the Church of England. Hence he did not form independent congregations, but organized "societies" on the Moravian model. Each Methodist society was again divided into "bands" or groups for mutual cultivation of a Christian life. A little later he divided these bands into "classes" of about twelve members, each class with a "class leader." Wesley also issued "society tickets" to worthy members. Others who wished to join were received on trial. These tickets were renewed quarterly, and unworthy members were carefully sifted out. In this manner the Methodists enforced a discipline which was characteristic of the movement.

After 1742 some of these "societies" owned property, which necessitated further organization. "Stewards" were elected to care for the property. As the scope widened, a number of preachers had to be taken into the Methodist service. The number of the societies increased so rapidly that Wesley had to delegate much of the supervision to others. In 1744 he called the first Annual Conference in London. In 1746 he divided England into circuits. Each circuit was carefully supervised by a superintendent. From 1744 to 1784 the Methodist societies formed a complete church organization except in two important respects; they ordained no ministers, and they administered no sacraments.

Important changes took place in 1784. Conditions in America caused John Wesley to assume the right to ordain ministers. He also gave the societies the right to administer the Sacraments. He reorganized the English Annual Conference to a "legal one hundred" preachers only and vested in this Conference some of the authority he had personally exercised. He insisted, however, that Holy Communion be received in the Established churches only. Toward the end of 1784 the Methodist Episcopal Church in America was formally organized in Baltimore.

John Wesley never formally renounced allegiance to the Thirty-nine Articles of the Established Church of England, but he objected to the Calvinistic element in these Articles. Wesley was an outspoken Arminian.[10] Whitefield, on the other hand, was an outspoken Calvinist who strictly adhered to the doctrine of predestina-

[10] See page 351.

tion. This caused an estrangement resulting in the formation of two kinds of Methodism, Wesleyan Methodists who constituted the larger group, and Calvinistic Methodists who followed the lead of Whitefield. After the death of Whitefield the Calvinistic Methodists divided into three groups, Lady Huntingdon's Connection, the Tabernacle Connection, and the Welsh Calvinistic Methodists.

Methodism exerted a world-wide influence. It quickened the spirit of English evangelism. It awakened a new spirit of humanitarianism, especially by its prison reforms and by its fight against slavery. It promoted the modern Sunday School, and founded tract and Bible societies. It greatly stimulated Protestant interest in foreign missions. Wesley originated the idea of popular and inexpensive libraries. He established free labor bureaus, poor relief, medical dispensaries, orphanages, and widow's homes. The Salvation Army issued from Methodism.

IV. The Age of Rationalism.—The eighteenth century marked a turning-point in human thinking and progress, culminating in a new world-view and in a new outlook on life. This new attitude found expression in an undue emphasis on human reason, in the formation of modern constitutional governments including the United States of America, and in the French Revolution. These changes prepared the way for the remarkable religious, intellectual, political, and social activities of the nineteenth century.

Three specific lines of thought combined to form a new philosophy of life which, to begin with, was rather critical of the traditional religion. The humanistic idea of the dignity of man, the freedom of the human will, and the ability of man to do the will of God, came as a revival of the ancient Greek philosophy of man. Human reason was made the final test of all things. Bacon's inductive method and Descartes' "hypothetical doubt" gave rise to a general demand that all things received as true must be capable of proof. The revolutionary discoveries in science, especially by Copernicus, Galileo, and Sir Isaac Newton, cautioned men to discover new truth by observation of known facts.

The thrill of the new discoveries gave rise to a spirit which was less conscious of God and more conscious of man and his inherent powers and possibilities. Man became the measure of all things, and human reason, *ratio,* was enthroned as the only religious authority. This gave rise to Rationalism. A system of "natural religion" replaced the traditional religion. In England this system ran out into Naturalism or Deism. In France it led to the actual worship of the Goddess of Reason. In Germany it produced the

"Illumination" (Aufklärung). The whole period was called "The Age of Rationalism."

English Deism[11] must not be confused with Atheism or Pantheism. Deism recognized human reason as the only source of knowledge. Reflection upon the world of nature and of man led the Deist to the conclusion that there is a God, that the human soul is immortal, and that man must pursue virtue to attain to a state of bliss after death. The Deist also believed that in the Godhead there was but one person, the Father. God created the universe, and then he withdrew, leaving it to the control of the "laws of nature." True religion consisted of a knowledge of God and the pursuit of virtue. The practice of virtue was again largely identified with humanitarianism. Deism was also called a "natural religion" because the Deists claimed they did not need a divine revelation to support it.

Rationalism exerted a paralyzing influence upon Protestant and Roman Catholic church life during the latter half of the eighteenth century. The movement ran its course in all countries. Its climax as well as its termination was marked by Kant's philosophy. Kant took his followers, as it were, to the very summit of pure reason to point out its marvellous possibilities as well as its distinct limitations. He actually pointed reason back to its own territory by showing that pure reason could neither demonstrate nor overthrow the objects of belief. He even rose to the support of Christianity by emphasizing the validity of Christian experience.

Rationalism produced some practical results. Its emphasis on intellectual freedom and individual liberty paved the way for political democracy. People trained to think independently demanded to govern themselves, demonstrated by the French Revolution and by the establishment of independence in the United States. It also promoted religious toleration, and affected the temporary abolishment of the Society of Jesus.

51. REVIEW QUESTIONS

1. What is meant by Pietism? Compare it with Methodism.
2. Discuss the general reform program of Spener. Do you agree with him?
3. Mention the specific religious influences of Francke and his connection with the University of Halle.
4. Why was the duration of Pietism so brief? Why did it not take the form of a world crusade, like English Methodism?
5. Discuss the origin and the development of the Moravian church. In what ways did Zinzendorf's peculiar views affect it?

[11] See page 449.

6. Describe the background of Methodism. What possibilities did Methodism have, from its very beginning, of becoming a world-wide organization?
7. Mention the outstanding characteristics of the early English Methodism.
8. Explain the gradual organization of the Methodist movement.
9. Discuss the general and the specific influences of Methodism.
10. What is meant by the Age of Rationalism?
11. Account for the rise of Rationalism. Discuss its essence.
12. What practical results did Rationalism produce?

TOPICS FOR SPECIAL STUDY

1. The religious views of Spener and Francke.
2. Count Zinzendorf and the Moravians.
3. John Wesley, the Founder of English Methodism.
4. "Natural religion" versus traditional Christianity.

A SELECTED BIBLIOGRAPHY FOR CHAPTER XVIII

1. Walker: *A History of the Christian Church*, pages 481-529.
2. Kurtz: *Church History*, Volume II, pages 196-206, 238-275.
3. McGiffert: *Rise of Modern Religious Ideas.*
4. McGiffert: *Protestant Thought before Kant.*
5. Nagler: *The Church in History*, pages 171-194.
6. Wilkinson: *Emanuel Swedenborg.*
7. Thompson: *Moravian Missions.*
8. Simon: *Revival of Religion in England in the Eighteenth Century.*
9. Winchester: *Life of Wesley.*
10. Townsend, Workman and Eyeres: *New History of Methodism.*
11. Hurst: *History of Rationalism.*
12. Dorner: *History of Protestant Theology, Particularly in Germany.*
13. Guericke: *Life of A. H. Francke.*
14. Spangenberg: *The Life of Nicholas, Count Zinzendorf.*
15. Holmes: *History of the Protestant Church of the United Brethren.*
16. Lecky: *History of England during the Eighteenth Century*, Vol. I-VIII.
17. Bornkamm: *Mystik, Spiritualismus und die Anfänge des Pietismus.*
18. Heppe: *Geschichte des Pietismus und der Mystik in der reformierten Kirche, nämentlich der Niederlände.*
19. Ritschl: *Geschichte des Pietismus.* (3 vols.)
20. Grünberg: *Philipp Jacob Spener.* (3 vols.)
21. Herpel: *Zinzendorf.*
22. Kramer: *August Hermann Francke.* (2 vols.)
23. Seeberg: *Gottfried Arnold.*
24. Hoffmann: *Die Aufklärung.*
25. Hagenbach: *German Rationalism in Its Rise, Progress, and Decline.*
26. Merkle: *Die kirchliche Aufklärung im katolischen Deutschland.*
27. Parton: *Life of Voltaire.* (2 vols.)
28. Torrey: *Voltaire and the English Deists.*
29. Leland: *A View of the Principal Deistic Writers.* (5th ed., 2 vols.)
30. Sorley: *A History of English Philosophy.*
31. Eayrs: *John Wesley, Christian Philosopher and Church Founder.*
32. Lunn: *John Wesley.*
33. Colligan: *Eighteenth Century Noncomformity.*
34. Dimond: *The Psychology of the Methodist Revival.*

CHAPTER XIX

CATHOLIC LIFE AND THOUGHT IN THE LAST THREE CENTURIES

I. Roman Catholicism in the XVII and XVIII Centuries.
—The Catholic Counter Reformation, having done much to regain the prestige and the power of the Roman Church, had spent its force by the end of the seventeenth century. Austria and Spain, its chief supporters, had been shorn of much of their power by the Peace of Westphalia. The Jesuits, the very soul of the movement, had lost much of their earlier zeal. The popes, although uniformly capable and forceful, were not great leaders of men. The Roman church seemed unable to adapt herself to the new life of Europe. The eighteenth century was, therefore, a period of decline for Roman Catholicism.

1. *Church and State.*—The leading powers of Europe had established national Catholic churches largely controlled by the kings.[1] Royal church control naturally gained support by the theory of the Divine Right of Kings. The divinely appointed king claimed a right to govern the church in his own land. The result was a series of sharp conflicts between monarchs and popes, in which the authority of papacy was steadily weakened.

In France this emphasis on national independence was called Gallicanism. Certain "Gallican liberties" had been granted to the Church of Gaul in the fourth century. Additional rights had been granted from time to time, always in close connection with the French monarchy. Louis XIV had these Gallican liberties restated by an assembly of the French clergy in 1682. The Four Gallican Articles asserted that the pope had no right to interfere in French national affairs, that the spiritual authority of the pope was subject to the regulations of canon law, that the pope could not change the laws of the French church, and that general councils were of higher authority than the pope. The quarrel finally ended in a compromise. The clergy practically withdrew the Four Gallican Articles, but the king kept the disputed income from certain church positions.

The close connection between the Church of France and the

[1] See pages 205-207.

tyrannical French court proved disastrous. When the French Revolution burst upon the Government, the Church went down with it. All French church property was confiscated in 1789, and in 1793 the National Convention adopted a law abolishing Christianity in France. Two years later religious freedom was proclaimed, but the State recognized no religion. Napoleon transformed the states of the Church into a Roman Republic in 1798, and imprisoned the pope. Papacy came to the end of the eighteenth century shorn of its secular power.

2. *Jansenism.*—Jansenism was a movement within the Church of France similar to the Puritan movement within the Church of England. Cornelius Jansen, Bishop of Ypres, revived the Augustinian doctrine of sin and grace. This opened the eyes of many to the falsity of the prevalent Semi-Pelagian opinion[2] of the meritorious nature of good works, and gave rise to an attempt to reform the Roman Church. A number of scholarly men, including Jean du Vergier, Antoine Arnauld, and Blaise Pascal, joined.

The Jesuits, strict Semi-Pelagians, made a violent attack upon the Jansenists, and secured their condemnation by a papal bull of 1653. Blaise Pascal responded by exposing the base moral principles of the Jesuits in his "Provincial Letters." Louis XIV, finding the Jansenists useful in his own disputes with papacy, protected them. The controversy entered its second stage in 1693 when Pasquier Quesnel, a Frenchman living in the Netherlands, published his "New Testament with Moral Reflections." This book contained the text of the New Testament, accompanied by excellent edifying remarks, many of which were taken verbatim from Augustine. Powerful opposition by the Jesuits resulted in the condemnation of this book and of Jansenism by a papal bull of 1713. One hundred and one sentences, some of which were direct quotations from Augustine, were condemned as heretical by the pope. The doctrines of Augustine appeared to be officially rejected by the Roman church.

Twenty French bishops and three theological faculties, protested against this papal bull, but their protest proved unavailing. The Jansenists who failed to conform to the decree of papacy were driven from France. The majority withdrew to Holland, where they formed a Jansenist Catholic church which still exists.

3. *Quietism.*—The Catholic Quietists were to the Roman church what the Anabaptist Quietists[3] and the Quakers[4] were to the Protestant churches. The early Quietist movement had its strong-

hold in Spain, where its essence was explained by Miguel de Molinos (d. 1697) in "The Spiritual Guide." He claimed to find peace and assurance by a quiet, mystical surrender of self into the hands of God. This mystical union, which recalls the "inner light" and the "inner word" of the Protestant Mystics, appeared to render superfluous the rites, ceremonies, and institutions of the Roman church. The Jesuits quickly recognized this feature of the Quietist movement, and secured the condemnation of Molinos by a papal bull of 1687.

Quietism found a new stronghold in France. Madam Guyon (d. 1717) popularized it by her writings. Fénelon, Archbishop of Cambrai, adopted the Quietist views. A new Catholic revival began to sweep over France, but the severe opposition of the Jesuits soon reduced it to a mere ripple. Madame Guyon was imprisoned for ten years. Fénelon was permitted to retain his position as archbishop, but a number of his Quietist statements were officially condemned by a papal bull of 1699.

4. *Suppression of the Jesuits.*—The Jesuits were very active. Their power increased steadily in Europe and in foreign mission fields. But toward the end of the eighteenth century a number of causes combined to bring about their temporary downfall. They were intolerant. They left no room for a legitimate variety of religious interpretation. Catholic Christianity was forced into a Romanism of the narrow Jesuit type. This was done while the rapidly rising tide of the new rationalism demanded religious tolerance and intellectual freedom. The policy of accommodating Christianity to the heathen notions by permitting the "Malabar customs" brought strong protests, not only from other Catholic missionaries, but even from the popes themselves. Constant interference in political affairs made the order notorious. Lively participation in colonial trade, in spite of its prohibition by the constitution of the order, brought about a sharp moral decline. Jesuitism had further come into popular disfavor in its conflict with Jansenism.

Suppression of the Jesuits started in the best strongholds of the order. Portugal expelled them in 1759; France in 1764; and Spain and Sicily in 1767. Pope Clement XIV was finally forced to abolish the order in 1773. Refusing to dissolve, the order continued in non-Catholic lands, especially in Protestant Prussia and in certain parts of Russia.

II. **Roman Catholicism in the XIX and XX Centuries.**— The Roman Catholic Church was in a torn and distracted condition at the opening of the nineteenth century. The Society of Jesus, which had constituted the very backbone of the Church, had been abolished; much of the church property had been confiscated by the French Revolutionaries; monasteries were abolished; the priests were despised and persecuted; church services were frequently disturbed; and Pope Pius VI had been left to die in a French prison in 1799. But a century later this whole situation had changed. At the opening of the twentieth century the Roman church had been restored to a strength and splendor such as it had not enjoyed since the central period of the Middle Ages. The pope was proclaimed the *infallible* head and the *universal* bishop of Christendom. All schismatics were declared heretics.

1. *The New Awakening, 1800-30.*—Pope Pius VII (1800-23) was of a humble, introspective, and stubborn nature. He pursued a policy in thorough accord with the spirit of the Council of Trent and the Jesuit order. He selected as his secretary a jurist named Consalvi who, next to Napoleon himself, was considered the most capable diplomat of that period. His reactionary policy was indicated by the formal restoration of the Jesuit order in 1814, and by the condemnation in 1816 of Bible societies and of translations of the Bible for the use of the people.

Napoleon did not care for religion personally, but he realized its value for society. As a measure of statecraft, he reorganized the French Church to suit his own policies. In 1801 he concluded a *Concordat* with Pope Pius VII, and in 1802 he formulated a new church constitution known as the *Organic Articles*. These two documents decreed the Roman church to be the religion of the majority of the French people; but Calvinists, Lutherans, and Jews were to be tolerated. The bishops in France were appointed and maintained by the State, but were to be confirmed by the pope. All bishops had to swear to support the constitution of the nation, and the Church was excluded from all political activity. The Concordat and the Organic Articles was the church-law in France until 1905.

The Roman church received a heavy blow in 1803 when all church territory in Germany was given to the secular states. The Catholic church in Germany lost more than three million members, as well as its basis for political power. The Holy Roman Empire[5] ceased to exist in 1806.

A new era began after the fall of Napoleon in 1814. The pope was again at liberty to select his own policy. The Congress of

[5] See pages 146-51.

Vienna, 1814-15, restored to the pope the States of the Church. Consalvi's clever diplomacy acquired a new legal status in many European lands. The urgent wish of all nations to restore and maintain religion, peace, and order, caused the majority to look to the pope for help, for he was the traditional head of Christendom. Papacy was also greatly aided by the new Romanticism and Ultra-Montanism.

Romanticism especially affected literature, art, and religion. The Romanticist laid a new emphasis on the emotions, pleading for a return from the complexities of a modern civilization to the simpler life of earlier days. This involved a new appreciation of the ancient and the medieval, and the rejection of that spirit which dominated the French Revolution. The new appreciation naturally involved the Catholic church with its history running back in an unbroken line for about seventeen hundred years. The Roman church was idealized. A number of Protestants decided to return to Catholicism. The most conspicuous example was the Oxford Movement. John Henry Newman (1801-90), the leader of this movement, brought more than one hundred and fifty clergymen from the Church of England to the Church of Rome.

Ultramontanism arose in 1820. Its main purpose was to assert the papal supremacy. All religious and moral authority and power should center in the office of the pope at Rome ("ultra montes" or "beyond the mountains," from French and German viewpoints). It asserted that the pope's decisions regarding faith and morals were infallible. The typical Ultramontanist reasoning was that without an infallible pope there can be no Church; without a Church there can be no Christianity; without Christianity there can be no religion; and without religion there can be no civilized society. The Jesuits were powerful advocates.

2. *Liberalism and Ultramontanism, 1830-70.*—Liberalism[6] may be characterized as the reappearance of Rationalism in a modified form. The principles of Rationalism were applied more specifically by the Liberals to the sphere of politics. Its principles were freedom of the press, freedom of conscience, freedom of organization, and strict separation of Church and State. Several prominent Ultramontanists, including Lamennais, Lacordaire (d. 1861), and Montalembert (d. 1870) thought that these ideals might be used to promote papal supremacy. They tried, therefore, to promote a Catholic or Ultramontanist Liberalism. But could papal supremacy

6 Liberalism was condemned by the pope in 1864.

and infallibility be reconciled with religious tolerance, political freedom, and modern science?

The Jesuits raised the question, and Lamennais turned to Pope Gregory XVI (1831-46) for an answer. In a papal bull of 1832, the *Mirari vos*, the pope definitely condemned these liberal views, and advocated the rigid use of the Index[7] and a strict book censure. This forced a choice between Liberalism and Ultramontanism. Lamennais chose the former. He broke with papacy, and devoted the rest of his life to promoting Christian socialism.

But papacy benefited greatly through Liberalism. The "Catholic Emancipation Act" of 1829 gave Catholics and Protestant dissenters in England equal privileges. The Catholic church of Ireland was formally liberated from English government control in 1869. Frederick William IV made the Catholic church independent of Prussian state control in 1850. Austria followed in 1855. The French school law of 1850 was a victory for papacy. The Pope was rapidly gaining direct and universal control of the Catholic Church in all lands.

Ultramontanism won its culminating victories during the pontificate of Pius IX (1846-78). It made it possible for the pope to proclaim that "the doctrine which holds that the blessed Virgin Mary was, from the moment of her conception, by the singular grace of God . . . preserved free from every taint of original sin, has been revealed by God, and is therefore to be firmly and constantly believed by all faithful." Henceforth every good Catholic was to believe in the Virgin Mary as a mediator and intercessor with God. This was also clearly asserted in the encyclical of Pope Pius XI, the *Lux veritatis*, issued on Christmas day, 1931.

Another victory was won in 1864 when the Pope published his "Syllabus of Errors." This encyclical refuted eighty serious errors, including freedom of conscience, freedom of the press, Protestantism, Communism, Bible societies, civil marriage, free scientific investigation, separation of church and state, non-sectarian schools, and religious toleration. The Syllabus of Errors closed by condemning the claim that "the Roman Pontiff can and ought to reconcile himself to, and agree with, progress, liberalism, and civilization as lately introduced."

The crowning act came in 1870 when the Vatican Council declared that the pope is *infallible* when speaking *ex cathedra* on questions of faith and morals. This dogma, which sealed the triumph of Ultramontanism, was accepted by practically all Catholics.

[7] See page 343.

A small group, headed by Ignaz Döllinger, protested against the dogma insisting that the Church Councils should retain their traditional significance. This group separated from the Papal Church and organized under the name of "Old Catholics."

3. *Roman Catholicism from 1870 to 1938.* — The pope suffered a political loss when King Victor Emmanuel II captured Rome on September 30, 1870, and incorporated it with the Kingdom of Italy. The pope became a voluntary prisoner of his Vatican palace, continuing until 1929 when the Lateran treaty was signed.

A strange cult gained much popularity during the closing years of the pontificate of Pius IX. A morbid nun claimed she saw in Christ's body his bleeding heart, and that she received a commission from him to institute a "devotion to the Sacred Heart." The pope authorized this cult, because he found it conducive to church loyalty. It was so popular in France that the National Assembly built a Sacred Heart Church at Montmarte in Paris. The pope initiated all faithful Catholics into this worship in 1875.

Pope Leo XIII (1878-1903) governed with outstanding ability. He addressed himself to two chief problems, to promote cordial relations between papacy and the secular governments, and to define the proper attitude of Roman Catholicism toward modern culture.

He made papacy a dominant influence in the affairs of Protestant Germany. The Protestants of Austria and Hungary were systematically suppressed in spite of the religious toleration granted in 1866. Belgium became a stronghold of Ultramontanism, with the University of Louvain as its center, and with Cardinal Mercier (1851-1926) as its head. Spain gave the Jesuits free play. The French Republic was formally recognized by the pope in 1890, and the French people were urged to support the government, an act which won the good will of France. Five Catholic universities were founded, of which the *Institut catholique* in Paris was the most prominent. England was brought into closer relations by the appointment of John Henry Newman as Cardinal in 1879, and by sympathetic interest in English social problems. But he also revealed his papal absolutism by pronouncing the Anglican orders invalid in 1896. He established the Roman Catholic episcopate in Scotland in 1878. Russia established an embassy at the Vatican. Relations with the United States were particularly successful. The Catholic University in Washington was established in 1899. Prominent Cardinals, such as John Ireland, were appointed, and the organization of the Roman church was greatly improved. Leo XIII created approximately one-fourth of all the present Catholic bishoprics and archbishoprics. He also sought the reunion of the Roman and the Oriental Churches.

His attitude toward modern science and social problems was that of an Ultramontanist with scholarly tastes and wide sympathies. Scientific investigations, freedom of speech, and freedom of press were to be controlled by the Church. Biblical study was to be limited and checked by the verbal inspiration theory. The Index was enlarged. Religious tolerance was to be practiced in Protestant countries, but not where Catholicism had the upper hand. Much interest was shown in the Catholic Youth Movement. He revived the Catholic belief in miracles, saint worship, Virgin Mary worship, indulgences, and the Holy Rosary. He laid special stress on acts of mercy and a holy life. Great interest was shown in monastic life and in foreign missions.

Pope Pius X (1903-14) continued Leo's policies, but with less ability. There were four outstanding events in his pontificate. Aristide Briand advocated the abolition of the Concordat of Napoleon and the complete separation of State and Church in France. This was formally decreed by the French Government in December, 1905. The pope had set his face against Modernism. By a "Syllabus" and an "Encyclia" of 1907 he condemned Modernism and took stringent measures for its suppression. By the decree of December 20, 1905, a great change was wrought in the administration of the Holy Eucharist. All Catholics, even little children, are invited to come often, daily if possible, to the chief channel of grace. The Eucharist, it is said, is not merely a reward for the good, but also a medicine for the spiritually ill. Children have a right to it as an antidote against temptation and sin. The Biblical Institute was founded in Rome in 1909, as a school for biblical studies, leading to the doctorate in Sacred Scriptures.

Pope Benedict XV (1914-22) had the difficult position of governing the Catholic church during the world war. He maintained a strictly neutral attitude, because papacy had about equal interests on both sides. He gave much attention to the relief of suffering, especially among prisoners of war. He continued the papal fight on Modernism and on Protestantism, and issued a new edition of Canon Law known as *Codex juris canonicis*, in 1917. This code of laws became effective in May, 1918.

The creation of Czecho-Slovakia, October 18, 1918, presented a serious problem. The Catholic clergy started a powerful reform movement and demanded that the Catholic worship be conducted in the vernacular, and that the clergy be permitted to marry. Benedict XV refused these requests. The friends of reform responded by forming a National Catholic Church of Czecho-Slovakia in 1920. Dr. K. Farsky was chosen Patriarch. Apostolic succession was obtained from the Orthodox Church of Jugoslavia.

During the reign of Benedict XV, England and Holland sent representatives to the Vatican for the first time since the Reformation. The Prince of Wales, the Prime Minister of England, and the President of the United States visited the Pope. Turkey established an embassy, and France and Portugal resumed diplomatic relations with the Vatican. The German Imperial Government abrogated the Anti-Jesuit Law in 1917. A German embassy replaced the former Prussian embassy in Rome, and an Apostolic Nunciature was established in Berlin.

The establishment of the independent Republic of Poland in 1918 furnished an opportunity for Roman Catholic expansion. Achille Ratti, later known as Pope Pius XI, labored successfully for several years as Apostolic Visitor and Nuncio to the newly constituted Polish State, and prepared the way for the Concordat of 1925 which regulates the relations of Church and State. The Roman Catholic church in Poland is organized into five Metropolitan Sees, with fifteen suffragans; and provisions are made for maintaining a Papal Nuncio at Warsaw, and a Polish Ambassador at the Vatican.

Pope Pius XI (1922-1938) has promoted the interests of papacy[8] with great ability, especially in foreign missions. In his first encyclical he emphasized the need of promoting peace and good will among the people, the need of carrying on a systematic and determined fight on Protestantism, and the need of a united Catholic action (*actio catholica*) of clergy and lay people.

The Lateran Pact of 1929 marked a new era, according to the pope himself. "We now begin to put into force the things we have established, and there is still much work to be done." Harmony was restored between Italy and the pope. His local sovereignty was slightly enlarged. This diplomatic victory has added a great deal to papal prestige, and it has opened the way for important relations between the pope and the governments of the world. The Vatican State is restricted to about 160 acres.

In an encyclical of January 18, 1930, the pope proclaimed papal supremacy in matters of education. He condemned exclusive state control of education as the cause of great evils. He denounced

---

[8] During the jubilee year 1925 over a million pilgrims visited Rome.

Naturalism, early sex information, athletics for girls, licentious books, and films. In an encyclical of December 26, 1931, called the *Lux Veritatis*, the pope urged a union of Protestants and Catholics in invoking the protection of the Virgin Mary as a mediator and intercessor with God. Pope Pius XI was a strong Ultramontanist.

The municipal elections held in Spain on April 12, 1931, resulted in the proclamation of the Spanish Republic. King Alphonso XII left the country. A new Republican Constitution was adopted on December 9, 1931, and immediately became the law of the land. This Constitution provides for complete separation of church and state; abolition of the Concordat with the Pope; state monopoly of education; and suppression of all state subsidies to Catholic worship. The Jesuit Order in Spain was dissolved by official decree of the Spanish Republic on January 23, 1932, and all its property was confiscated. All other Religious Orders in Spain have been subjected to an arbitrary regime.

III. The Greek Catholic Church.—After the great schism in 1054,[9] the Eastern division took the official name of "the Holy Orthodox Catholic Apostolic Eastern Church." The word "Eastern" (Oriental) designates its origin and geographical territory. It is usually referred to as the Eastern Church, or the Greek Orthodox Church. Its present membership is about one hundred and ten millions, or seven percent of the world's population.

It consists of a large number of independent churches in eastern Europe, in western Asia, and in northeastern Africa, of which the more important are, the Russian Orthodox Church, the churches under the patriarchate of Constantinople, the churches under the patriarchate of Alexandria, the churches under the patriarchate of Antioch, the churches under the patriarchate of Jerusalem, the churches under the archbishopric of Cyprus, and the churches under the abbotship of Sinai. These churches are held together because they subscribe to the same "Canon Law," based on the first seven General Church Councils.[10] They have remained static, because their people have remained static.

There are important differences between Eastern Catholicism and Romanism. Oriental Catholics do not recognize the supremacy of the pope, but are governed by a patriarch. The Lower clergy of the Eastern Catholic churches are permitted to marry, but not the higher clergy. To the words in the Nicene Creed, "And in the Holy Ghost," the Greek and Roman churches later added the words, "who proceedeth from the Father," and there the Greek church stopped; while the Roman church added, without the authority of the General Council, the words "and the Son" (filioque). The Greek church has protested ever since against the "filioque." The Oriental church gives the cup to the laity in the Lord's Supper.

In 1800, practically all the territory of the Eastern Church, with the exception of Russia, was under Mohammedan control. As people who possessed holy Scriptures and as people who worshipped one God, the Christians were permitted to exist in the Turkish dominions, but they had no voice in the affairs of the government. The patriarchs were valuable to the sultan, because they induced the Christians to pay the heavy taxes, and because they were a protection against Roman propaganda.

1. *The Balkan States.*—The Balkan Peninsula had its immigration problem of Slavs, like the states of western Europe; and it was not until the nineteenth century that the national Balkan churches were able to gain their independence. The Greek Church declared its independence at a national synod at Naupalia in 1833. The Greek king, together with a permanent synod, governed the church instead of the patriarch at Constantinople. The independent national church of Bulgaria was recognized by the sultan in 1870. The metropolitan in Bucharest was elevated to patriarch of Rumania in 1925, and the metropolitan of Belgrade was elevated to patriarch of Jugoslavia in 1924. There are altogether fifteen such independent orthodox church bodies. Their inter-relation, and their relation to the patriarch of Constantinople, have been formulated as "complete liberty for each group to arrange its internal affairs, and complete solidarity of all groups in negotiations with other communions." Consequently the Turkish Government recognizes the patriarch of Constantinople as the head of the Christians.

2. *Separate Oriental Churches.*—The Orient has also a number of separate churches that have been in existence since the Ancient Period.

The Armenian Church numbered about three million members in 1800. After 1820 nearly one-half of its territory came under Russian control, and the members were gradually absorbed by the Russian Orthodox Church. The church property was confiscated by the Russian government in 1903. The other half was under Turkish control. In 1896 the Turks massacred about 50,000 Armenians. Similar massacres followed. During the world war, particularly from 1915 to 1918, the Turks deported or massacred more than one-half of the Armenian nation. To-day the Armenian Church is practically a heap of ruins.

The Syrian-Nestorian church, with a membership of about 150,000, has its main territory in the borderland between Turkey and Persia. The patriarch, who has his residence in Mosul in Mesopotamia, has also political control of his people. This group has suffered a great deal because of Mohammedan persecutions, Greek Orthodox opposition, and Roman propaganda. Many adherents have found refuge in America.

The Jacobites, with a membership of nearly 150,000, live in the same territory as the members of the Syrian-Nestorian church, but their patriarch lives at Antioch. This group has an elaborate church organization, and stresses the importance of "successio apostolica." There is much rivalry between the Jacobites and the Nestorians. On September 20, 1930, two Jacobite bishops of Southwest India and nearly all members of their congregations were received into the Roman Catholic church by Bishop Benziger of Quilon. The two bishops were Mar (Bishop) Ivanos, Metropolitan of the Bethany Congregation of Jacobite monks, and his suffragan, Mar Theophilos, Jacobite Bishop of Tiruvella.

The Coptic church in Egypt numbers about half a million members. The patriarch lives in Cairo. This group is strongly pressed by the Mohammedans.

The Abyssinian church numbers about three million members. This group has yielded considerably to Evangelical influences and is favorably inclined toward western civilization.

3. *The Russian Orthodox Church.*—The Church in Russia was dependent on the patriarch of Constantinople until 1589, when a patriarch was established in Moscow. In 1721 Peter the Great substituted the Holy Synod for the patriarchate, which arrangement knit the Church and the State more closely together. At times the Orthodox Church had to meet a powerful rivalry from Roman Catholicism.

In 1811 the historian Karamzin published the slogan, "one God, one czar, one people," in line with the general policy to gather all the orthodox in the Balkans and in the Turkish dominions under Russian control. This led to a movement similar to Ultramontanism. The Russian Orthodox Church pursued a policy of ruthless suppression and persecution. The Doukhobors were driven from the country. Other sects, especially the Stundists and the Baptists were persecuted. The Lutherans in Esthonia and Lithuania were systematically suppressed, while millions of white Russians and Ukranians who came under Russian control when Poland was divided were forcefully absorbed.

About 1880 a strong reaction set in. Students returning from German universities introduced the socialistic ideas of Karl Marx, formulating a social religion that made a strong appeal to the industrial workers in Russia. A very different tendency—a Gnostic-Spiritualistic Christianity—found its popular expression in the books of Leo Tolstoï (1828-1910). He severed relations with the Orthodox Church, and promulgated his own Christianity which abolished state, church, and nationality.

The world war brought many trials to the Orthodox Church. An all-Russian church meeting in August 1917 re-instated the patriarch at Moscow. Tichon, who had been orthodox bishop in America, was elected patriarch. But the revolution in November, 1917, brought the Bolshevik party into control under Lenin. In January, 1918, state and church were completely separated. The various churches were permitted to exist as cultural groups, but all church property was nationalized. The priests, classified as "non workers," were to be starved. All theological schools were closed, and religious instruction in the public schools was transformed to instruction in Leninism. When Tichon protested, the government waged one of the most cruel and extensive persecutions in history. Thousands were martyred.

In 1922 "The Living Church" was organized by the lower clergy of northern Russia. This organization was favored by Lenin because of its friendly attitude toward the Bolsheviki regime. Bishop Antonin became the recognized leader. The Living Church re-established the "Holy Synod" which was recognized by the Bolsheviki as the highest church authority in Russia. Tichon was imprisoned.

When Lenin withdrew in 1922, all religious toleration ceased. In the twenty-two theses formulated by the Third International. the government declared open war on religion. An illustrated magazine, "Besbosjnik" (the Godless) was used as Bolshevik propaganda.[11] In 1923 religious processions, funerals, meetings, and images were prohibited, and Sunday was abolished. In the edict of July, 1924, all under eighteen years of age were prohibited from attending religious services. In the homes, religious instruction was forbidden in groups of more than three. All teachers in the public schools had to swear that they were anti-Christian.

Unfavorable reaction caused the Soviet government to assume a more liberal attitude toward religion after 1924. Atheism was stamped as a part of the inheritance of the corrupt culture of the bourgeoisie. The government pursued this general policy: let the old generation with its traditional religious views die in peace, but train the coming generation in the positive views of Leninism, and Leninism shall finally bring salvation to all mankind.

Forceful means have since been used[12] to suppress religion. The Living Church was dissolved in 1925, and several "red" churches were organized. In 1929 nearly fifteen hundred churches were

---

[11] From 1923 to 1930, twenty million copies were distributed broadcast throughout Russia.

[12] See Oscar Schabert: *Baltisches Martyrerbuch*.

closed to divine worship and converted into club houses for the "Club of the Godless," or into power houses, fire stations, granaries, moving picture halls, gymnasiums, and the like. Yet, the Russian Orthodox Church is still in existence and may, in the end, come out of the fiery trials victorious.

52. REVIEW QUESTIONS

1. How did the theory of Divine Right of Kings affect the relation between Church and State?
2. What is Gallicanism? How did Louis XIV make use of Gallican liberties?
3. Why did the French Revolution turn against the Church?
4. Discuss the Jansenist movement. How did the suppression of Jansenism affect the Roman church?
5. Why were the Jesuits so eager in suppressing Quietism?
6. Account for the temporary downfall of the Jesuits.
7. Account for the rapid restoration of the Roman church in the nineteenth century.
8. What particular benefit did the Roman church receive from Romanticism?
9. What is Ultramontanism?
10. Discuss the conflict between Liberalism and Ultramontanism. Why did the Ultramontanists so zealously promote the doctrine of papal infallibility?
11. What has characterized the development of Roman Catholicism from 1870 to 1933?
12. Discuss the history of the Oriental Catholic churches.

TOPICS FOR SPECIAL STUDY

1. Cornelius Jansen, the Bishop of Ypres.
2. The Roman Catholic Quietists.
3. The pope as the infallible head and universal bishop of Christendom.
4. John Henry Newman and the Oxford Movement.
5. United Catholic Action (actio catholica).
6. Eugenios Bulgaris the "Melanchthon of Balkan."
7. Fedor Dostoievski (1821-81) and the Church of Russia.
8. The Stundists of Russia.
9. Leo Tolstoi and his religion.
10. Anti-religious propaganda in Russia.

A SELECTED BIBLIOGRAPHY FOR CHAPTER XIX

1. Kurtz: *Church History*, Volume II, pages 226-237.
2. Rowe: *History of the Christian People*, pages 459-475.
3. Sloan: *The French Revolution and the Religious Reform.*
4. Nielson: *History of the Papacy in the Nineteenth Century.*
5. Williams: *Newman, Pascal, Loisy, and the Catholic Church.*
6. Manning: *The True Story of the Vatican Council.*
7. Loeppert: *Modernism and the Vatican.*
8. Cadoux: *Catholicism and Christianity.*
9. Adeney: *The Greek and Eastern Churches.*
10. Spinka: *The Church and the Russian Revolution.*
11. Fedotoff: *The Russian Church since the Revolution.*
12. Miller: *The Power and Secret of the Jesuits.*

CHAPTER XX

Protestantism in the XIX and XX Centuries

The drift of history in the nineteenth and twentieth centuries has been toward world unity, toward a world organized for common effort and common accomplishment. This tendency has been fostered by many influences. The railway, the steamship, telegraph and telephone, wireless telegraphy, radio, electricity, airships, airplanes, and the like, have drawn once isolated nations closer together. Development in the *political* realm has been from the federal state toward international federation. Examples of national federalism are the United States of America, the Dominion of Canada, the Commonwealth of Australia, the Swiss Confederation, the Soviet Union of Russia, and the German Republic. The tendency toward international federalism has found expression in the World Court at Hague, in the League of Nations, and in the proposed plan of a United States of Europe. In the *moral* realm the consciousness of mankind as a large community has developed into a sentiment which recognizes the universality of moral law, and the need of international amity and good-will. *Education* has made thought and scholarship international. Ease in *transfer of commodities* has made the world a single mart of trade, where nations are brought in intimate and constant contact. These influences have profoundly affected the realm of *religion*. The various religious systems of the world have been subjected to careful historical study and comparison. Whole continents have been opened for Christian missions. Numerous religious federations have been formed, from the Holy Alliance in 1815 to the Federal Council of Churches of Christ in America in 1908. Successful attempts have been made to bring about organic union of certain church bodies. Organic church unity, or at least church federation, seems to be the slogan of the day.

There has been a distinct tendency toward complete separation of Church and State. From the middle of the eighteenth century to the present, the tendency has been to make Church and State mutually independent. A free Church unhampered by State control, and a free State unhampered by Church control, appears to be the desired goal.

A similar relation has developed with reference to religion and philosophy. The new intellectualism which Rationalism ushered in during the eighteenth century emancipated philosophy from traditional theology. Traditional authority was shaken off, and human reason and experience became the measure of all things. This independent philosophy has since, on the basis of natural science, formulated a mechanical or materialistic world-view directly antagonistic to Christian thought. The traditional Christian worldview recognizes a personal God as the Creator and Governor of the universe. But according to the mechanical or materialistic world view, the universe is the product of a strictly mechanical development or evolution of the inherent forces of nature. God and mind are identified with matter. Human thinking is to the brain what gall is to the liver. There is no spirit. It remains to be seen how these two conflicting world views, the Christian and the materialistic, will affect the future of civilization.

There has been the steady ascendency of the *proletariat* in its great conflict with the *bourgeoisie*. The proletariat constitutes about ninety percent and the bourgeoisie is about ten percent of the entire population. It was the middle class, the *ten percent*, that instigated the Scottish-English and the French revolutions, and wrested the control from the nobility and the clergy. It has been the ruling class since the middle of the eighteenth century. But what about the proletariat, the *ninety percent*? This large class has discovered itself and makes demands for "Liberty, Equality, and Fraternity." These demands are, rightly understood, in full accord with the Gospel; but the means advocated by the proletariat are not always in harmony with Christianity. The Third International, representing a considerable portion of the proletariat, advocates a world revolution to destroy the established governments and eliminate the Christian Church and the Christian home. The struggle between the middle class and the proletariat is pregnant with great and fatal possibilities.

Religious thought presents a welter of cross-currents. Religion has been strongly influenced by the advancement of knowledge, for man's knowledge has seemingly grown beyond his own power to organize it properly. The newly discovered forces and facts are in most cases too near, as yet, to be seen in their true perspective. But out of the apparent confusion three leading types of Evangelical Christianity have developed, the *revivalistic*, the *churchly*, and the *liberal*. The revivalist type developed during the first third of the nineteenth century, while the other two developed after 1830.

I. The General Awakening, 1800-1830.—The political situation in Europe exerted a powerful influence upon religious development. The French Revolution and the Restoration of 1815 were the first great forces.

1. *The French Revolution, the Napoleonic Age, and the Restoration of 1815.*—The French Revolution came like a tremendous storm which threatened to sweep away the Church, the throne, the nobility, and the whole established order of things. Europe was shaken to the very foundations. But the French Revolution also bequeathed three principles which modern society has generally recognized, namely, the principle that all men are equal in the civil realm as they are in the religious realm, the principle that governments derive their just powers from the consent of the governed, and the principle of nationality that the state coincides with the nation.

These ideas were temporarily shelved because the destructive elements of the French Revolution caused the whole movement to end in terror. People saw what would become of the modern world without God and Christianity; and the suffering brought on by the Napoleonic Wars caused the people to long for peace, stability, and a return to religion. A strong reaction set in, so the Congress of Vienna restored everything as nearly as possible to its condition before the Revolution. Some of the disillusioned turned to nature after the precepts of Rousseau, but the great majority lifted eyes and hearts to God in prayer for help. Christianity was restored to its honored position. The Holy Alliance of 1815 was formed with the object "to make Christianity the highest law of national life, in spite of all confessional dissensions," and all the princes of Europe joined it except the pope, the sultan, and the king of England. A spirit of evangelism awoke once more in the Protestant countries of Europe.

2. *Romanticism.*—Romanticism[1] came as a powerful reaction against Rationalism. Romanticism was a wholesome counter influence because it recognized the emotional as well as the intellectual side of personality, and gave due attention to the poetic, the imaginative, and the esthetic elements in life. Romanticism made religion a matter of feeling of absolute dependence upon God. This brought the comfort and strength of religion, and the renewed confidence in God which people yearned for. Protestantism as well as Catholicism awoke to a new life.

3. *Schleiermacher.*—Several great theologians served as medi-

[1] See pages 377-78.

ators between philosophy and theology and made Christianity acceptable to the "cultured despisers of religion." One great mediator was Friedrich Daniel Ernst Schleiermacher (1768-1834), German pastor and university professor. He has been called the Origen of the nineteenth century because his reinterpretation of Christianity had such far-reaching and lasting influence on religious life and thought. Kant had made religion a matter of the *will*. Schleiermacher defined religion as *feeling*, as the immediate consciousness of absolute dependence on God. This Christian *consciousness* was alone the true interpreter of religion and the standard for testing the truth.

Schleiermacher wrested the scepter of theological learning from Rationalism, but failed to restore Protestantism to Biblical Christianity. He became, in fact, the founder of a new Rationalism which has largely dominated the religious thought of the nineteenth and twentieth centuries. The human intellect, as compared with an ordinary light, has two distinct qualities; it gives *light*, and it gives *warmth*. Eighteenth century Rationalism stressed the first of these qualities, while nineteenth century Rationalism stressed the second; which accounts for the peculiar emphasis on feeling as the seat of all religion. Feeling in this sense is not merely sense and taste for the Divine, but the immediate *consciousness* of absolute dependence on God.

The God revealed in the "feeling" of Schleiermacher was not a personal Being, but rather according to the pantheistic view, an impersonal force which was immanent in the world. God was to him "the absolute unity," and permanency, the universal, the absolute, the eternal principle indwelling in the world. The life of this universe was mirrored in each individual. Man was a microcosm, a reflection of the universe. In his relation to God as the eternal principle, man felt himself finite, limited, temporary, and dependent. This feeling of dependence was the true basis of religion. Christianity was not the final form of religion, but it was the best religion known to men because it produced the best God-consciousness and brought man into harmony with God.

Jesus of Nazareth was not conceived of as "God revealed in the flesh," but only as an ideal, sinless man, unique in his God-consciousness. Christ redeemed man, not so much from sin as from ignorance of God. Atonement in the ordinary sense was not admitted. Christ realized in himself the ideal of humanity, and in his consciousness he realized the perfection of fellowship with God. The Christian consciousness of God was created and sustained by

Christ through the Church. Schleiermacher's theology was strongly Christo-centered, though not in the Orthodox sense. He gave a new recognition of the importance of the person of Christ and the Church, and stirred up much discussion regarding the Christ of history as compared with the Christ of experience.

Three schools of theology resulted in Germany, namely, the extremely conservative Confessional School with renewed emphasis on the historic creeds of Lutheranism, and consequently opposed to the union of Lutheran and Reformed churches; the Mediating School which tried to smooth out the differences between the conservatives and the older radicals without surrendering to either group; and the Ritschlian School which stressed religious pragmatism and the use of historical or "higher" criticism. The influence of these schools soon extended to other lands, especially Scandinavia, England, and America. Schleiermacher was interpreted to the English-speaking world by Samuel Taylor Coleridge (1772-1834), and he in turn influenced Horace Bushnell, the Congregational leader in America.

4. *Foreign Missions and Works of Mercy.*—There was a renewed interest in works of charity and mercy and a remarkable expansion of foreign mission activity. Protestant churches founded and maintained foreign mission societies, inner mission societies, Bible societies, tract societies, Christian alliances, Sunday schools, institutions of mercy, training schools for nurses, and the like. Foremost of these practical enterprises was the foreign mission work. The nineteenth century was the great missionary century.

The missionary motive was inherent in Protestantism from the time of the Reformation, but lack of geographical contact and the need of building up the churches from within delayed the preaching of the Gospel in heathen lands. Protestant missions in the sixteenth and seventeenth centuries were confined to narrow fields. The city of Lübeck sent a missionary to Abyssinia in 1634. The Dutch sent missionaries to Ceylon as early as 1636. Sweden did mission work among the Lapps after 1559. Eliot and Campanius worked as missionaries among the American Indians. But these missionary efforts were rather sporadic and individual. Protestantism had not as yet been aroused to a world-wide interest in non-Christian peoples.

A more extensive Protestant missionary activity commenced at the beginning of the eighteenth century. The German Pietists not only recognized the missionary obligation, but founded the Halle-Danish mission in 1705. Halle University furnished at least sixty foreign missionaries during the eighteenth century. Moravian missions[2] started in 1732, and Quaker missionaries[3] found their way to Europe, Asia, Africa, and America. But Protestant missions still lacked the propaganda spirit, the careful organization, and the world-wide outlook which have characterized the foreign missionary work of the nineteenth century. The Protestants in the home lands had not as yet organized into local and private mission societies.

William Carey (1761-1834) initiated this new state in Protestant world missions. The voyages of discovery by Captain James Cook, from 1768 to 1779, aroused his interest in the heathen world. He persuaded a group of twelve Baptist ministers in England to organize the Particular Society for Propaganda of the Gospel among the Heathen (later called the Baptist Missionary Society) in 1792, and the next year he was in India as its first missionary. This organization was followed by the formation of the London Missionary Society in 1795, interdenominational at first, but later Congregational. Its first missionaries went to Tahiti in 1796. Robert Morrison was sent to China in 1807. He was the first Protestant missionary to that country. John Williams was sent to the South Sea Island in 1816. Robert Moffat was sent to South Africa in 1818, and William Ellis was sent to Madagascar. David Livingstone, the famous son-in-law of Moffat, also entered its service. The growing sense of missionary obligation caused a group of Anglicans to form the Church Missionary Society of the Evangelicals in the Church of England in 1799. This is today the largest Protestant mission society. The Society for the Propagation of the Gospel in Foreign Parts, a high-churchly English mission society, was founded in 1701.

General interest in foreign missions was aroused in other Protestant countries. The Scottish Missionary Society was organized in Edinburgh in 1796, and in that same year the Glasgow Missionary Society was founded. The Church of Scotland Mission Boards came into being in 1825, and Alexander Duff was its first missionary to India. Duff's arrival on the mission field in 1829 marked a turning point in the history of Protestant world missions. The age of revival, 1792-1830, was about to be followed by an age of confessionalism, 1830-70. Other Protestant mission societies founded before 1830 were the Basel Evangelical Missionary Society, 1821; the Danish Missionary Society, 1821; the Berlin

Missionary Society, 1824; the Paris Missionary Society, 1824; the American Board of Commissioners for Foreign Missions, 1810; and the Baptist Missionary Union, 1814. Today there are more than sixty American and over seventy European foreign mission societies, but the majority of these have been founded after 1830.

The foreign mission movement created a demand for a wider circulation of the Bible. A pioneer in this field was the Canstein Bible Institute at Halle, founded in 1704. The British and Foreign Bible Society was formed one hundred years later, in 1804, and the American Bible Society was organized in 1815. After the "Apocrypha controversy" of 1827-28, the British and Foreign Bible Society decided to print its Bibles without the Apocrypha of the Old Testament. This decision proved unsatisfactory to the German branches of the society, which seceded to form the Berlin Bible Society. The Bible societies became important connecting links between foreign and inner missions.

It is difficult to estimate the results of this remarkable missionary activity. Many savage tribes were Christianized and adopted modern civilization. The Christian missionaries became pioneers in education, medical science, and sometimes in industrial organizations. The missionaries made vast contributions to the advancement of human knowledge, especially in geography, ethnology, sociology, and philology. Foreign missions stirred up much interest in practical Christian enterprises in the home lands.

Some attention has now been given to the general situation existing in practically all Protestant countries of Europe during the first third of the nineteenth century. Brief attention will now be given to the development of church-life in specific countries from 1800-30, including England and Scotland, Germany, and Scandinavia.

5. *England and Scotland.*—The Established Church of England experienced three religious awakenings, the Evangelical revival which produced the Low Church party, the Anglo-Catholic revival which strengthened the High Church party, and the Social revival which promoted the formation of the Broad Church party. The first made its appeal to the individual; the second, to the higher classes of society; and the third gripped society in general. The Evangelical awakening ran its course from 1800 to 1830, while the other two movements took their rise around 1830. In addition, England had various groups of dissenters, Methodists, Baptists, Quakers, Congregationalists, and Presbyterians, whose total num-

ber rapidly approached that of the Established Church. The action and reaction of these groups, and the general influence of the great cultural and political movements, furnish the interesting but complicated material for English church history.

John Newton (1725-1807) and William Wilberforce (1759-1833) were the outstanding leaders of the Evangelical revival in England. They were ably seconded by Joseph Milner (1744-1797) and his brother, Isaac Milner (1750-1820). All of these men had been strongly influenced by English Methodism. Wilberforce was the recognized lay leader of the Evangelical branch of the Church of England for nearly fifty years. In 1787 he began his agitation against slavery. His efforts resulted in the abolition of the slave trade in 1807, and three days before his death he had the pleasure of knowing that slavery itself had been abolished throughout the British dominions.

Two new branches of Christian activity grew out of the Evangelical revival, the modern Sunday School, and the work connected with modern Young People's Societies. Robert Raikes founded the modern Sunday School as a "new experiment" in 1780 at Gloucester, England. William Wilberforce, John and Charles Wesley and others came and studied the experiment, "caught the fire," and extended the movement. Its growth was phenomenal, not only in Great Britain, but also in other European countries and in America.

The Evangelical revival strengthened the Protestant element in the Anglican Church by placing Luther and Calvin above the Church Fathers and above the Anglican Scholasticism, by giving the sermon the main place in the religious worship, and by the strong emphasis on the use of the Bible. The Low Church party formed an important contact between the Church of England and the large number of dissenters. A new spirit of humanitarianism was awakened, especially regarding slavery, prison reforms, sanitary conditions in insane asylums, better protection for factory workers, and regulated hours of work in factories for women and children. More attention was paid, however, to the *effects* of the social and economic evils than to the underlying *causes*. The Evangelical revival also promoted great interest in home and foreign missions. But the movement gradually lost its first impetus, and by 1830 the Low Church party had ceased to grow.

In Scotland the Evangelical movement was led by two brothers, Robert and James Haldane. After their conversion in 1794, they applied their energy and wealth to evangelize Scotland. Being opposed by the Presbyterian General Assembly, the Haldane brothers built tabernacles throughout Scotland, and James Haldane established seminaries for the training of preachers, all at his own expense.

6. *Germany and Scandinavia.*—The Congress of Vienna, 1815, decreed that all Christian denominations in the German states should enjoy equal toleration. This caused considerable confusion, especially in states which had been partly Lutheran and partly Reformed. Some state governments tried to end the confusion by uniting the two churches, the Lutheran and the Reformed. Frederick William III, in 1817, decreed a Union for the churches in Prussia. Several smaller German states followed suit. The Union was later reduced to an administrative organization under which Lutherans and Reformed lived and co-operated within the same congregations.

But the Union soon met with vigorous opposition from the Lutherans. The leader of the opposition party, often referred to as the Confessional School, was Claus Harms (1788-1855). The Romantic movement had led him to a new appreciation of the historic creeds of Lutheranism and the seventeenth century Orthodoxy. On the three hundredth anniversary of the Reformation, October 31, 1817, he published Luther's ninety-five theses, and also ninety-five theses of his own in which he pleaded for a return to the fundamental principles of the Reformation. The Catholics, he said, had only the Sacraments; the Reformed had only the Word; but the Lutherans, he said, had both the Word and the Sacraments. His theses aroused a violent controversy, but the movement for confessional Lutheranism grew rapidly because it was coupled with a deep spiritual awakening in the congregations. The Confessional School stressed, not only pure doctrine, but also practical Christian work. Fliedner's Deaconess Institute at Kaiserwerth served as a model of that type of Christian activity for other Protestant countries.[4]

A number of dissatisfied Lutherans seceded from the Prussian state-church in 1841 and organized the Evangelical Lutheran Church of Prussia. This church was divorced from state control, and it was self-supporting and self-governing. Henceforth Germany had three Protestant churches instead of two.

Denmark passed through a period of distress early in the nineteenth century. In 1807 the English seized the Danish fleet and

⁴ See pages 401-402.

naval stores because of Napoleon's Continental Blockade. In 1813 the Danish State went bankrupt, and in 1814 Denmark lost possession of Norway. Yet this period of tribulation brought a remarkable regeneration to the inner life of the nation. Danish literature enjoyed its Golden Age, and the Danish church experienced one of its strongest religious revivals. The four outstanding churchmen of the period were Jacob Peter Mynster (1775-1854), Nicolai Frederik Severin Grundtvig (1783-1872), Hans Lassen Martensen (1808-1884), and Sören Kierkegaard (1813-1855).

Grundtvig, Danish clergyman, poet, and hymn-writer, was one of the greatest men in Scandinavian church history. He believed himself called to be a religious reformer. From 1810 to 1830 he fought against the prevailing rationalism, and advocated a return to the old Lutheran Christianity. But he did not find the rule of faith and conduct in the Bible but in the Apostles' Creed which was the rock foundation and the "living word" of the church. Almost coordinate with the Apostles' Creed as a rule of faith were the Lord's Prayer and the words of institution to the Sacrament of Baptism and the Sacrament of the Altar. The rest of the Bible he referred to as "the written word" and even as "the dead word." He magnified the importance of the Baptismal Covenant and minimized the need of conversion.

Sweden was less affected by rationalism than Denmark and Germany. Rationalistic tendencies crept into the Altar Book of 1811, but they were almost entirely lacking in the great Hymn Book of 1819. Prominent among the Swedish churchmen of this period were Johan Olof Wallin (1779-1839), Esaias Tegnér (1782-1846), Henrik Schartau (1757-1825), Lars Linderot (1761-1811), Lars Levi Laestadius (1800-1861), and Carl Olof Rosenius (1816-1868).

Schartau was a strong Evangelical preacher of the Old Lutheran type. He exerted a lasting influence on the entire Swedish Church. He strongly opposed all forms of lay preaching, all forms of free Christian associations, and all free Christian activity. The Church was the only association for Christians, and every member should get his spiritual advice from his own pastor. Members of each congregation were to be instructed in the fundamentals of Christianity through catechization in the church, through pastoral examination in the home, and through the sermon.[5] Linderot and

---

[5] Schartauism is best known for its strong tendency toward orthodox piety, for the emphasis it gives to lawfulness in private religious development ("the order of grace"), and to priestly authority (private confession). cf. Westman in *The Lutheran World Almanac*, 1923, p. 27.

Laestadius[6] were powerful revivalistic preachers of the old Pietistic type.

The increasing religious enlightenment of the lay people of Sweden resulted, as in Denmark and Norway, in strong revivals among the laity. Adherents of these revivalistic groups were nicknamed "Läsare," i.e. "Readers," because they spent much time in reading the Bible and religious literature. After 1842 these "Readers" got a prominent leader in Rosenius, the father of the New Evangelism in Sweden.

Norway experienced a widespread Evangelical revival through the efforts of Hans Nielsen Hauge (1771-1824), lay preacher and revivalist. Converted in 1796, he was resolved to preach for the conversion of others. He preached in his home community the first year, but from 1798 to 1804 he traveled through Norway preaching twice and some times four times a day. He gained many followers, and these formed a chain of small brotherhoods, closely interlinked, and strongly attached to the State Church.

Hauge's religious activity encountered strong opposition from the clergy and the state officials. He was imprisoned from 1804 to 1811 on the charge of violating the conventicle act which forbade lay preaching. But this opposition was, no doubt, a concealed blessing for Hauge and his religious movement because it checked his rather inordinate interest in the promotion of trade and industry. His imprisonment forestalled a possible financial disaster to his friends and a general discredit to the whole movement. As it was, Hauge became a national hero.

The Hauge revival movement was of the old Pietistic type. It had very little in common with the Methodist movement in England. Hauge was neither an organizer nor a separatist. He advised his followers to affiliate with the church pastors and the existing church order. But he initiated that voluntary lay activity which ever since has characterized the religious life of Norway.

53. REVIEW QUESTIONS

1. Describe the drift of history in the nineteenth century.
2. Is the tendency toward complete separation of church and state in harmony with the teaching of the New Testament? Give reasons.
3. Compare the Christian and the materialistic world view.
4. What problem does the proletariat constitute to modern society?
5. Discuss the three leading principles of the French Revolution.

[6] The followers of Laestadius believe that forgiveness of sins can be obtained only in the Christian congregation, and not directly from Heaven, as the "Spiritualists" believe. Forgiveness is received only through the Means of Grace, particularly through "the word of reconciliation" as heard in public sermon or private absolution. Laestadianism is perpetuated in America in the Finnish Apostolic Lutheran Church of America.

6. How did Romanticism influence religious life during the first half of the nineteenth century?
7. How did Schleiermacher influence church history?
8. Why did the nineteenth century become the great missionary century?
9. Estimate the results of this remarkable missionary activity.
10. What characterized the church life of England and Scotland during the first third of the nineteenth century?
11. Discuss the church life of Germany and Scandinavia during this same time.
12. What new branches grew out of the Evangelical revival?

TOPICS FOR SPECIAL STUDY

1. The parting of the ways of religion and philosophy in the nineteenth century.
2. The proletariat and the bourgeoisie in modern history.
3. The life and work of some of the great missionaries of the nineteenth century.
4. Claus Harms and his influence on the Lutheran church.
5. The study of comparative religion and its results.

II. Orthodoxy, Liberalism, and Revival, 1830-70.—Protestant church life of this period was characterized by a powerful struggle between orthodoxy, liberalism, and revivalism. Confessional orthodoxy gained the upper hand about the time the romantic movement was displaced by realism. The work of inner and foreign missions experienced a remarkable expansion during these years.

1. *The Lutheran World: Theology and Inner Missions.*—Lutheran Germany had three schools of religious thought about 1830, the rationalistic, the confessional, and the "mediating." The most notable representatives of the first group were Heinrich Eberhard Gottlob Paulus (1761-1851) and J. F. Röhr. The best known leaders of the confessional group were Claus Harms (1778-1855), Ernst Wilhelm Hengstenberg (1802-69), Louis Harms (1808-65), Adolf von Harless (1806-79), Theodor Kliefoth (1810-95), F. C. Vilmar (1800-68), Franz Delitzsch (1813-90), and C. E. Luthhardt (1823-1902). Among the leaders of the mediating school were August Neander (1789-1850), August Tholuck (1799-1877), Isaac August Dorner (1809-84), Richard Rothe (1799-1867), Wilhelm Meyer (1800-73), G. C. F. Luecke (1791-1855), and Julius Mueller (1801-78).

The rationalistic school had by 1830 lost much of its former prestige because of the overpowering opposition from romanticism, Hegelian philosophy, Schleiermacher, and confessional orthodoxy. Lutheran orthodoxy had, on the other hand, gained in influence among the people and at the universities. After the death of Schleiermacher, his influence at the Berlin University was transferred to Hengstenberg, and his pulpit was offered to Claus Harms. German rationalism finally received its death blow from the criticism (1834-37) of Karl von Hase.

Lutheran confessionalism vigorously opposed the Prussian Church Union[7] of 1817. Prior to 1870 this Union was condemned in all Lutheran circles. The king tried to quiet this opposition by declaring, in 1852, that the union of Lutherans and Reformed was not a union in doctrine, but only an administrative organization. Several other German states followed the example of Prussia; other states made the union include also doctrine; while others retained the traditional Lutheran or Reformed state churches. Consequently, Protestant church life in Germany took on an unparalleled complexity which the political union of Germany in 1871 failed to eliminate.

The opposition of the united Protestant churches of Germany to confessional intolerance was greatly strengthened by the rise of Liberalism.[8] It was a powerful political and religious reaction against the suppressive policies inaugurated by the Congress of Vienna in 1815. The "July Revolution" of 1830 and the "February Revolution" of 1848 were results of political liberalism; and liberal theology was a result of religious liberalism. Liberal theology failed entirely to sense the need of the confessional element in religion; its interest centered in a critical study of the Bible.

David Friedrich Strauss (1808-74) was the first important representative of this new "critical" or liberal school. In his "Life of Jesus" published in 1835, he denied the historical validity of many of the Gospel narratives. His book, which caused great controversy, set others to work upon the books of the New Testament, in an effort to establish their historical value.

Ferdinand Christian Baur (1792-1860), the founder of the new "Tübingen school" of theology, became the leader of this new line of investigation. Following Hegel's theory of development, he believed that all historical progress must be through the three stages of thesis, antithesis, and synthesis. Applying this criterion to the New Testament, he concluded that the historical Jesus had presented the thesis of Christianity. The struggle between Pauline and Petrine views constituted the antithesis, which lasted far into the second century. The writings of John, with the exception of Revelation, presented the synthesis. Baur concluded, therefore, that

[7] See page 396.
[8] See pages 378-79. The name liberalism appeared in Spain as early as 1812.

the greater part of the New Testament books were written in the second century.[9]

Baur's method, the historical or "higher criticism," soon became fashionable. Many scholars of the Church began to study the books of the Bible as historical documents. Much attention was also given to the study of the text of the Scriptures and to the history of Christianity and of the Church. But the radical consequences of this liberal theology soon limited its direct influence and shifted the center of the scientific theological study to the orthodox group. This gave rise to the so-called New Lutheranism which based its allegiance to the Lutheran confession on a deep, strong conviction. The new orthodox Lutheran school, which laid great stress on the importance of the sacraments and the office of the Church, controlled the Protestant theology of Germany for more than two decades, 1848-70.

General interest in foreign missions resulted in a considerable expansion of the existing mission societies[10] and in the organization of new groups. The most prominent societies organized during this time were, (1) the Leipzig Society, 1836, with missions in India and Africa; (2) the Gossner Society, 1836, with missions in India; (3) the Swedish Missionary Society, 1835, with orphan homes and schools in Lapland; (4) the Norwegian Missionary Society, 1842, with missions in South Africa and Madagascar; (5) the Hermannsburg Missionary Society, 1849, founded by Louis Harms, with missions in India, Africa, New Zealand, and Persia; (6) the Evangelical Fatherland Association (Swedish), 1856, with missions in East Africa and Central India; (7) the Finnish Missionary Society, 1859, with missions in Africa and China; (8) the India Home Missions to the Santals, 1867, founded by Skrefsrud and Börresen; (9) the Swedish Church Missionary Society, 1868, with missions in South Africa and India.

The most important contribution was, however, the remarkable development of inner mission[11] work, which came as a result of the pietistic and the orthodox revivals. Johann Hinrich Wichern (1808-81) was the great organizer of the inner mission work in Germany. He established a rescue home for desolate and wretchedly poor boys of Hamburg in 1833. A similar home for small girls was soon founded, and other institutions of mercy were added later. He also organized city missions and training schools for

---

[9] Only about five of Paul's Epistles were considered genuine.
[10] See pages 392-94.
[11] The term "inner missions" was first used in 1818 to designate mission work among heathen people living in Christian lands.

inner mission workers. He provided lodging houses for some of the homeless and spiritual care for prisoners. Religious tracts and papers were distributed among the people. Trained mission workers preached on the streets and visited the homes, carrying the Bible in their hands. The interests of the inner missions were effectively furthered by Wichern's pen and by his stirring lectures. He even accepted a position as a minister in the Prussian government in order that he might further the inner mission cause. His system was quickly copied, not only by the rest of Protestant Germany, but by foreign countries as well.

Of epoch-making importance was the founding of the modern Protestant order of deaconesses by the Lutheran pastor, Theodor Fliedner (1800-64) in 1836, and the building of the Kaiserwerth Deaconess Institute that same year. Amalie Sieveking (1794-1859), who first suggested an organization of this kind, became the first superintendent. A corresponding organization for deacons (men) was later founded by Fliedner. At his death the Protestant deaconess order had 30 institutions and 1600 deaconesses. An important branch of the German inner mission movement was the organization of the Gustavus Adolphus Society in 1842 to help suffering Lutheran congregations in Catholic lands.

But anti-Christian forces also exerted a powerful influence upon western Europe. Karl Marx (1818-83), the founder of modern socialism, developed a social philosophy which rested on the following principles: (1) The life and the history of mankind are the products of a strictly mechanical development of the *material* forces of nature, and not[12] of the spiritual. (2) Possession of material prosperity and immediate happiness is the highest good. (3) Since this prosperity should be enjoyed by all, and not merely by the "privileged" classes, it is necessary for labor to fight capital to the point of a social revolution, after which the state takes over all production. (4) "Religion is the opiate of the workers" because it suppresses the revolutionary tendencies of the workers and promotes obedience to constituted authority. Marxian socialism was frankly hostile to the established churches, and usually agnostic and atheistic.

2. *The Reformed World: Formation of Free Churches.*— Within the Reformed world the same general cultural and religious influences prevailed. The Reformed had corresponding schools of religious thought, corresponding revival movements, and

[12] See pages 388-89.

the same drift toward a rigid orthodoxy. This strict Calvinistic orthodoxy caused a number of Reformed groups to leave the established state-supported churches to form free church organizations.

In Switzerland each canton had its Protestant state church since the political restoration of 1815. This situation caused much religious complexity, because each state church developed more or less in isolation and without the wholesome influence of a confederate Swiss church union. The government of these Swiss state churches fell, after 1835, largely into the hands of radical liberals. Trouble started in 1817 when "The Venerable Compagnie of the Genevan Clergy" refused to ordain candidates for the Christian ministry if they believed in the divinity of Christ, original sin, and predestination. Several orthodox groups protested by organizing free, independent congregations. The free church movement soon spread to other parts of Switzerland. The Free Church of Pays du Vaud was organized in 1847; the Free Church of Geneva was organized in 1848; and the Free Church of Neuchatel was organized in 1873. Alexandre Vinet (1797-1847) and Frederic Godet (1812-1900) were the prominent leaders of the Swiss free church movement.

The Evangelical revival in Switzerland produced a new branch of Christian charity work of world-wide significance. Henri Duant, a citizen of Geneva, organized the International Red Cross society in 1863. The red cross emblem signified the Swiss flag and the love of Christ.

After the July Revolution of 1830, Protestants obtained the same rights as Roman Catholics. France had scattered Lutheran congregations, but the bulk of French Protestantism belonged to the Reformed church. After 1830 the liberal religious movement gained a controlling influence in the French Reformed Church. This provoked opposition from Reformed orthodoxy and finally led to the organization of the French Reformed Free Church in 1849, under the direction of Frederic Monrod and Count Gasparin.

The Reformed national church in the Netherlands experienced a strong Evangelical revival about 1830. It was started by the poet William Bilderdijk and continued by Henry de Cock, a fiery young clergyman, and by two converted Jews. Henry de Cock, who conducted Calvinistic revival meetings in his own congregation, was deposed in 1834 because he violated the ecclesiastical order by ministering in congregations belonging to other clergymen. The majority of de Cock's congregation and four other congregations and their pastors, left the state church and organized a free church.

This organization, which kept on growing, was persecuted by the government until the "February Revolution" in 1848. It was finally sanctioned by the government in 1869 as the "Christian Reformed Church."

In the Established Church of Scotland an old system of lay patronage and the relation of church and state were the chief topics of agitation and irritation. The right of the land proprietors to elect pastors was particularly troublesome to the leaders of the Evangelical revival because this right was often exercised to force undesirable pastors upon the congregations. Thomas Chalmers (1780-1847), the most notable leader, finally persuaded the Assembly of 1834 to pass the Veto Act, conceding local congregations the right to reject pastors placed over them by lay patrons. The civil courts, however, protected the patrons in their hereditary rights. At the meeting of the Assembly in 1843 the majority of the opponents of the lay patronage withdrew from the Established Church of Scotland and organized the Free Church of Scotland, under the leadership of Thomas Chalmers. This new organization, to which about two fifths of the pastors of Scotland belonged, was friendly to the state church idea and strove to maintain cordial relations with the Mother Kirk. Another group, consisting of about one fourth of the population of Scotland, organized the United Presbyterian Church in 1847. This organization, which insisted upon the strict separation of state and church, was largely supported by the wealthy middle class.

3. *The Anglican World: Anglo-Catholicism and Broad Churchism.*—England has, since 1830, had three parties[13] within the Established Church. (1) The High-Church party, with influential representatives among the aristocracy, seeks to maintain the most intimate connection between church and state, and zealously preserves all churchly forms and institutions in government, worship, and doctrine. (2) The Low-Church or Evangelical party, more or less Methodistic, advocates Evangelical freedom and the independence of the church. (3) The Broad-Church party, not an organized group in the sense of the High and the Low church groups, seeks to make the Established Church as comprehensive as possible and to make it really the Church of the nation.[14] In addition to these parties, the English nation has a large number of dissenters.

---

[13] High and Low Church parties flourished long before 1830.

[14] The Broad Church party regards all people as being the children of God. Phillips Brooks, the great representative of the American Broad-church movement said that man is a child of God that the devil has laid his hands on, and not a child of the devil that God tries to steal.

The Oxford movement and its perpetuation in Anglo-Catholicism was, perhaps, the most conspicuous development in the Anglican church during the nineteenth century. A number of causes contributed. The efforts of the Broad Church party to include in one national Church all Christians except Unitarians and Catholics sanctioned, according to the High-Churchmen, an undesirable religious toleration. The increasingly close connection between the Low Church party and the dissenters appeared as a reaction against orthodoxy and hierarchy. The newly awakened sympathy with the life of the Middle Ages caused some to look to the Roman church as the only secure lifeboat. As political liberalism admitted an increasing number of dissenters, Catholics, and anti-clerically minded representatives in Parliament, the High Church party felt that the best interests of the Church were jeopardized.

John Henry Newman (1801-90), John Keble (1792-1866), Edward B. Pusey (1800-82), Richard Hurrell Froude (1803-36), Henry E. Manning (1808-92), and Frederick W. Faber (1814-63) were the prominent leaders. They believed that the best way to create new interest in the Church was to issue tracts on religious subjects, or *Tracts for the Times*. In these they attacked the growing laxity of the Church in matters of doctrine and polity, and insisted on the apostolic origin of the episcopate, the necessity of apostolic succession, and baptismal regeneration. The majority in the High Church party kept the *via media* between Catholicism and Protestantism, but Newman, Faber, Manning, and others joined the Roman Catholic church.

The Broad Church party took special interest in the social reforms of the nation. Thomas Arnold (1795-1842) and Richard Whateley (1787-1863) were early leaders. Later leaders were Frederick Denison Maurice (1805-72), Charles Kingsley (1819-75), Henry H. Milman (1791-1868), Arthur P. Stanley (1815-81), F. W. Robertson (1816-53), and Julius C. Hare (1795-1855). Interest in the social problems caused Maurice to establish *The Working Men's College*. His younger friend, Kingsley, organized the Christian Socialist movement. He claimed that Jesus Christ had proclaimed the principles of "Liberty, Equality, and Fraternity." The Bible was the source of liberty; baptism produced equality; and the Lord's Supper furnished the fraternity. Liberal religious tendencies of the German brand caused the leaders of the Broad Church party to depart from the common beliefs of the Church in theology. When one of the group, Bishop Colenso of

Natal, Africa, questioned the Mosaic authorship of the Pentateuch in 1862, the Archbishop of Cape Town deposed him. The Archbishop of Canterbury, however, sustained Bishop Colenso and maintained that the African Church was independent of the English mother church.

Congregationalists and Baptists had much the same ideal as to church polity. An official manifesto of 1833, the Declaration of the Congregational Union of England and Wales, created a greater harmony among the Congregational churches, while the Baptists were more divided. Prominent among the Congregational leaders of this period were Ebenezer Henderson, R. W. Dale, and A. M. Fairbairn. The great pulpit orator of the Baptists was Charles Spurgeon (1834-92), who preached in a great tabernacle in London. After 1870 this great preacher used much of his energy to fight the liberal tendencies within the Baptist fold.

English Methodism had lost much of its national influence because of internal divisions. But after it succeeded in closing up its disordered ranks by drawing closer in doctrine and in Christian effort, it grew until it now constitutes the largest Protestant church, next to the Lutheran and the Anglican.

The most conspicuous offshoot of Methodism is the Salvation Army, started by William Booth (1829-1912) in 1865 and definitely organized in 1878. It started as an evangelizing agency but broadened to include social service. After 1889 the Army established rescue homes, farm colonies, and labor bureaus. Booth, who formerly had been a Wesleyan Methodist pastor, retained for his organization the Methodist demand for a sudden conversion and a relative perfection. He adopted Charles Finney's method of bringing the converts up to the altar ring. From Zinzendorf he adopted the idea of an international organization which was above denominationalism and nationality. Anglican high-churchism taught him the value of organization and of dignified officialdom, and Ignatius Loyola seems to have led his thoughts in the direction of a religious militarism. He introduced the military features into his organization in 1878. Women took a prominent part in the official work of the Salvation Army.

The Apocalyptic-Pentecostal movement gained considerable influence after 1820. The catastrophe connected with the French Revolution and the Napoleonic wars caused many to believe that the Last Judgment was fast approaching, and from the Apocalypse (Revelation) many tried to figure out the day and the hour of the coming of the Lord. This movement was frequently accompanied by ecstasy and an inordinate desire to speak in tongues as the Christians did on the first Pentecost.

Out of this movement two new organizations were formed, the Catholic Apostolic Church of 1835 and the Darbyites or Plymouth Brethren of 1831. The first group was organized by Edward Irving (1792-1834) who looked upon the entire development of the Church since the days of the Apostles as a great apostasy. He proclaimed that the Last Judgment was near and that all true Christians were to be blessed with the supernatural gifts and endowments of the Apostolic church before the coming of the Lord. In 1836 the Irvingites organized all of Chirstendom into twelve tribes with an apostle for each tribe. After 1867 all true Christians were "sealed," on the basis of Rev. 7:3 f., by the laying of hands. The second coming of Christ was to occur as soon as 12,000 had been sealed in each tribe.

John Darby (1800-82) differed from Irving mainly in that he did not wish to form a definite organization. But the followers disregarded their leader and organized a special church, the Plymouth Brethren.

The Inner Mission movement produced a great variety of forms of Christian activity. Elizabeth Fry (1780-1845) continued her great work among prisoners and ex-prisoners. Charles Dickens aroused the public, through his novels, to see its social responsibilities. Florence Nightingale (1820-1910) started her epoch-making work in connection with the training of professional nurses and the care for the wounded on the battlefields. Miss Nightingale had herself taken a course of training at the Deaconess Institution at Kaiserwerth. George Williams founded the Young Men's Christian Association in London in 1844.

The scope of the foreign mission work widened considerably. Alexander Duff initiated a new method of carrying on mission work by the founding of the school mission among the higher castes of India. School mission work was soon begun in all foreign mission fields. David Livingstone and Stanley laid the foundation for mission work in Central Africa. Hudson Taylor founded the China Inland Mission in 1866. Japan was opened for European culture in 1859 and a rudimentary evangelical mission was started there. Henry Grattan Guinness founded the East London Training Institute for inner and foreign mission workers.

While these movements were in progress, the center of the world's thought was shifting. Science and mechanical inventions transformed the conditions under which men lived, and created new problems and raised many questions for the Church to answer. In natural science men were finding a great new field for investigation and study. Men began to think of the universe as a playground of vast mechanical forces. In 1859 Charles Darwin published his *Origin of Species* which was soon followed by the *Descent of Man*. These two books formed the starting-point for his famous "theory of evolution." The ramifications of this evolutionary principle were felt widely. Thomas Huxley and others applied the principle to Christian theology and to history of religion. Some enthusiasts even made evolution take the place of God. Darwin's theory brought to many people a complete change in their view of the universe, and this new world-view was generally hostile to the traditional Christian religion.

III. Materialism, Communism, and Churchly Revival, 1870-1914.—The year 1870 was a great landmark in European history. The Franco-Prussian War resulted in the formation of the New German Empire. Italy was unified into one kingdom. The Vatican Council proclaimed the dogma of papal infallibility. A materialistic world view and a new culture based on the modern economic and political structure, capitalism, imperialism, democracy, and socialism—exerted an ever increasing influence upon society. Under the influence of Realism, the scholarly world turned away from Romanticism and the speculative elements, and limited the scientific studies to actual experience and detailed exact investigations. This was especially true of the natural sciences. The historical sciences and their many branches gave rise to new social, political, and religious ideas and to a new psychological orientation. Out of the study of comparative religions arose a school of teachers who deny the absolute truth of Christianity. They merely look upon Christianity as the highest and best development of the general religious consciousness of the human race.

The new Biblical criticism threatened to bring about a considerable change in Protestant theology. Two great English scholars, Joseph Barber Lightfoot (1828-89) and Brooke Foss Westcott (1825-1901) led the Biblical scholarship of the Anglican church along the traditional *via media* route. In Lutheran and Reformed countries, certain groups made a distinct departure from traditional Christian views. Julius Wellhausen (1844-1918) advanced the theory that the Pentateuch is post-exilic, with a denial of the Mosaic authorship. A correspondingly radical investigation of the New Testament was made by K. A. Weizsäcker, Bernhard

Weiss, Heinrich Holtzmann, and A. Jülicher; and Adolf von Harnack applied the same critical method to church history and to history of dogma. The most influential theologian of this period was Albrecht Ritschl (1822-89). His new scheme influenced the theological thinking of both Europe and America for at least forty years.

The new social, political, and religious ideas resulted in many openly anti-Christian attitudes. The first organized movement to leave the Church started in 1905. About 31,000 people had left the evangelical church of Germany in 1909, and by 1914 the number had reached 44,000. In the Netherlands about half a million people left the organized churches. To-day there is hardly a Christian country that can claim its entire population, even nominally, for the Christian church.

But this general apostasy aroused the men of the Church to do greater and better things. A strong evangelical revival gripped especially the youth of the Church and found expression in organizations like the Young Men's Christian Association, the Young Women's Christian Association, and the World's Student Christian Federation. In Germany the revival movement produced a great Christian laymen's movement, the so-called "Gemeinschaftsbewegung," whose adherents worked in harmony with but independently of the organized churches. A corresponding movement in England organized the "Church Army" to bring the Gospel to the outcasts of the great cities. Much interest was also aroused in regard to foreign missions. John R. Mott formulated the slogan, "The evangelization of the world in this generation." Efforts were also made to unify the many evangelical free churches.

Groen van Prinsterer (1801-76) and Abraham Kuyper (1837-1920) promoted a strong churchly revival in Holland. The latter founded the free University of Amsterdam as a center of orthodox Calvinism. His followers were organized in the 'eighties into a large free church which united, in 1892, with the Christian Reformed Church of 1869 to form the "gereformeerde Kerken in Nederland."

IV. Protestant Developments after 1914.—The world events of the last two decades are still so near that they do not admit of proper historical perspective. Yet a certain orientation is possible. The independent national churches have flourished during the last two decades. World-wide efforts have been made to bring about a greater Protestant solidarity. On the foreign mission fields, native Protestant free churches have been organized. World-wide anti-Christian propaganda has been carefully planned and executed by the Third International.

After the World War a series of independent national states were created along the border line between the orthodox and the western world. Within these states new national independent churches were organized. In Germany the church was separated from the state in 1919, while in other Protestant countries the national churches generally enjoyed more freedom from state control. This has developed within the Protestant churches a better organization of the church, the centering of this organization in the office of the pastor or the bishop, the encouragement of an active lay participation in the work of the church, the rallying around the evangelical confessions of faith, and the development in the divine worship of forms and fullness of ceremonial beauty in harmony with the demands of modern man.

Aggressive Catholic propaganda, anti-churchly activities of the Third International, and the general chaos created by the World War, have made the Protestant world more conscious of the need of greater solidarity. In 1921 the German Evangelical Church Alliance ("Deutscher evangelischer Kirchenbund") was organized. It includes all the German evangelical churches and also the Moravian church. About 40 million German Protestants belong to this alliance. Similar national federations were organized in France, Belgium, and Czecho-Slovakia. The first Lutheran World Convention was held in Eisenach, Germany, in 1923, and a similar convention was held in Copenhagen in 1929. The Lambeth Conference of 1920 prepared the way for the Ecumenical Church Convention in Stockholm in 1925, and made possible the World Conference on Faith and Order at Lausanne in 1927. In America a number of organic church unions took place.

A powerful nationalistic spirit has swept over practically all foreign mission fields since the World War. "Africa for the Africans," "India for the Indians," etc., have become popular slogans. This spirit has created a desire to organize native independent national churches. There is much to be said in favor of this idea, but it involves the special danger of a possible religious syncretism, that is, the mixture of Christianity with animism and other non-Christian elements.

The Third International has carried on a world-wide campaign against established governments and against established churches during the last two decades. In Russian dominions this propaganda has resulted in the greatest persecution of Christians in history.[15] Rykoff's position with reference to world communism is this: (a) We can secure communism in one country only by introducing it in all countries. (b) We can introduce it in the other countries only if we can induce revolution. (c) We can insure the success of revolution only by disarming the governments and so far as possible training and arming the revolutionaries. (d) We will use this period of pacifications for a "breathing spell," during which we will every minute strengthen our own red army and give all possible military training to our comrades in all countries. Ancient and modern instances of communism have been short-lived. It remains to be seen whether or not the world-wide communistic organization of to-day will produce any permanent results.

54. REVIEW QUESTIONS

1. What characterized the Protestant church life of 1830-70?
2. How did Liberalism affect the church life of this age?
3. What is historical or "higher" criticism?
4. Discuss the German Lutheran contribution to the inner mission movement.
5. Outline the socialistic program of Karl Marx.
6. Why did the Reformed world organize so many free churches?
7. Account for the existence of the low-church, the high-church, and the broad-church parties in England after 1830.
8. Discuss the characteristics of the three leading dissenter groups in England, the Congregational-Baptists, the Methodist, and the Apocalyptic-Pentecostal.
9. Characterize Protestant church life between 1870 and 1914.
10. What special problems have confronted the Protestant church during the last two decades?
11. Account for the world-wide movement in favor of greater Protestant solidarity.

TOPICS FOR SPECIAL STUDY

1. The "Tübingen School" of theology.
2. Foreign missions in the nineteenth and twentieth centuries.
3. Inner missions in the nineteenth and twentieth centuries.
4. The present-day anti-Christian world propaganda and its consequences.

A SELECTED BIBLIOGRAPHY FOR CHAPTER XX

1. Lichtenberger: *History of German Theology in the Nineteenth Century.*
2. Pfleiderer: *The Development of Theology since Kant and Its Progress in Great Britain since 1825.*
3. Selbie: *Schleiermacher: A Critical and Historical Study.*
4. Mackintosh: *Albrecht Ritschl and His School.*

[15] Oscar Schabert: *Baltisches Martyrerbuch.*

5. Warneck: *Outline of the History of Protestant Missions.*
6. Atkins: *Modern Religious Cults and Movements.*
7. Machen: *Christianity and Liberalism.*
8. Rauschenbusch: *Christianity and the Social Crisis.*
9. Overton: *The Anglican Revival.*

THE CHURCH IN THE "NEW" WORLD

CHAPTER XXI

THE COLONIAL ERA, 1492-1763

I. The Significance of American Colonization.—The heroic discovery of the "new" world leads to interesting considerations. First, there was the extension of man's geographical knowledge; next, there was the significance of the discovery and the settlement of the new world for mankind in general and for the Christian church in particular.

Man's geographical knowledge was very limited about 800 A.D. The early civilization which had centered so much around the great river valleys had shifted to the Mediterranean and to a small part of the Atlantic. Few ships dared to enter the forbidden waters beyond the Pillars of Hercules (the Strait of Gibraltar). But a world-movement of geographical discovery and European expansion soon made the Atlantic and the Pacific highways of the world's intercourse and commerce.

It was no mere accident that the modern world was to be controlled by Western or Teutonic-Latin civilization. Oriental civilization had made repeated attempts to gain world supremacy, but Western civilization had always proved its superiority. From the first serious clash of the Persian Wars to the battle of Vienna in 1529 Western civilization always turned back the Orient.

The amazing possibilities of the new world were hidden through many millenniums until the fullness of time had come. Civilized man was not permitted to enter into the new world before he was prepared to control it. The Norse discovery of North America ("Vinland") and the later missions from Greenland and Iceland did not eventuate in permanent settlements. If they had, North America might well have duplicated the history of South America. As it was, all attempts to begin a Christian civilization in America proved futile until a revived Christianity could be transplanted. The beginning of Protestantism and the beginning of American colonization were contemporaneous events.

The discovery and colonization of America was, perhaps, as significant as the development of the Roman Empire.[1] The transplanting of European culture and religion resulted in unique contributions to world progress. The colonies established independent democratic governments which embraced peoples of diverse nationalities and different religious faiths. Thirteen independent and autonomous States united into a single federated nation without destroying the independence of the States. The Federal Constitution declared for religious freedom and refused to give preference to any special creed. All religions were permitted and·none was favored by law. No religious test was required as a prerequisite to holding any office. Complete separation of Church and State

POLITICAL MAP OF PRESENT SOUTH AMERICA

threw the American churches upon their own resources and left them free to develop according to inherent tendencies. Religious liberty laid the foundations upon which the American system of free, public schools have been built up.

II. The Spanish Settlements.—The first modern colonial empires were founded by Spain and by Portugal. France and the Netherlands came in for a fair share of colonial expansion, while England was more than a century behind Spain.

Early Portuguese explorations had led to the establishment of a great Portuguese commercial empire including the coasts of Africa and Asia, the Moluccas and other islands of the Pacific archipelago. These regions were dotted with fortresses, factories, and Roman Catholic missions.

[1] See pages 8-14.

Upon the return of Columbus, King Ferdinand at once requested Pope Alexander VI to confirm his title to the land discovered. The pontiff accordingly issued a bull wherein he drew from pole to pole a line of demarcation through the Atlantic one hundred leagues west from the Azores or Cape Verde. All unclaimed heathen lands lying east of this line were confirmed to Portugal, while Spain was entitled to the lands lying west. This line was later moved two hundred and seventy leagues further west. The Portuguese were prohibited from sailing any of the seas under the dominion of Spain or from visiting as traders any of her lands, and the Spaniards were barred from waters or lands granted to the Portuguese. This arrangement did not hinder Spain, however, from gaining possession of the Philippine Islands. The Portuguese established a colony in Brazil.[2]

This papal bull contemplated conquests for Christianity and gains for the Church as well as territory and revenues for the kings. Every Spanish expedition of discovery, invasion, and colonization was accompanied by priests, as chaplains to the Spaniards and missionaries to the Indians. Spanish missions were first established on the West Indies and in Mexico. A bishopric was established at Santo Domingo in 1512; another at Santiago de Cuba in 1522; and another at the city of Mexico in 1530. The University of Mexico was established in 1551, almost eighty years before the founding of Harvard, and the University of Lima was founded in 1557. From Mexico and the West Indies Spanish missionaries found their way to South America. In 1535 Peru was conquered, and by 1553 the Spaniards had extended their empire to Chile. Argentina was the next field of invasion, and in 1580 the first Spanish settlement was made at Buenos Aires. Brazil was settled by the Portuguese, beginning in 1510. All of South America was gradually conquered and Roman Catholicism was established as the official religion.[3]

Within the United States, Spanish missions were first estab-

---

[2] See map on page 414.
[3] Venezuela (or "Little Venice") was discovered by Columbus on August 1, 1498, on his third voyage. In consideration of a loan, Charles V permitted the Welsers, famous bankers and traders of Augsburg, Germany, to occupy Venezuela from 1526 to 1556, and the region was renamed Welserland. German Lutherans arrived in Venezuela (Welserland) in 1526, and by 1532 the entire colony is said to have accepted the Lutheran faith. Very little is known of these Lutherans in Venezuela. To-day there are about five Lutheran congregations and two Lutheran schools in Venezuela, according to Dr. J. N. Lenker.

The Lutheran World Almanac, 1931-33, gives the following figures for the Lutheran population in other South American provinces: Argentina has 30,000; Bolivia has 800; Brazil has 800,000; Chile has 45,000; Colombia has 2,500; Ecuador has 1,500; British Guiana has 1,000; Dutch Guiana has 4,000; Paraguay has 4,000; Peru has 2,000; Uruguay has 4,000; and Venezuela has 1,000. The total number of Lutherans in South America is estimated at 1,000,000.

lished in Florida. Ponce de Leon, Governor of Porto Rico, had been told by the Indians that to the north lay an island where gold was abundant and where there was a river whose waters would restore youth to the aged. He set out in search of this island in 1513 and discovered Florida (Flowerland), which he took possession of. All attempts to colonize Florida failed until September, 1565, when the foundations of St. Augustine, the oldest city in the United States, were laid. During the one hundred and fifteen years Spain had exclusive possession of Florida, the Spanish missionaries made some imposing gains in that region, but their mission work was sustained by Spanish arms and by subsidies from the Spanish treasury. When Florida was transferred to the British crown in 1763 the Spanish missions in that territory collapsed.

Spanish missions were also established in New Mexico and in California. In New Mexico the missions prospered until a disastrous native revolt destroyed all churches and convents and killed all Spaniards north of El Paso. Spanish rule was restored in 1700, but the missions never recovered from this stunning blow. In California the beginnings of Spanish settlement and missions[4] date from 1769. The three most northern missions, San Juan Capistrano, Santa Clara, and San Francisco, were founded between 1775 and 1777. But Spanish missions were dependent on military protection and conversion was in too many instances by coercion. When California was annexed to the United States, the Spanish missions in the province deteriorated.

III. The French in North America.—French explorers, traders, and missionaries opened up the northern part of North America. The first permanent French colony was established in Quebec in 1608.

With the founding of Quebec the French began to evolve their plan to found a splendid French empire. Men like LaSalle and Champlain, inspired by French royalty, planned a gradual spiritual and secular conquest of the entire continent. The French government sent shiploads of emigrants every year at the expense of the crown. French colonies enjoyed royal patronage, endowment, and protection. The French claims in North America included Canada, Louisiana,[5] half of New York, half of Maine, and half of Vermont.[6] Everywhere, the French colonists were accompanied by Jesuit priests who established Roman Catholic missionary stations

[4] See map on page 417.   [5] See map on page 417.   [6] See map on page 433.

and built churches, convents, and schools. It appeared that North America was to have a uniform Roman Catholic population.

But the dream vanished as in a mist. Many causes contributed to this sudden collapse. The king subordinated colonial interests to his ambitious European policies. Strict governmental control from distant France smothered all worthy individual aspiration and enterprise. French colonies were closed against all save Catholic immigrants. New France was too mucn concerned with trade and too little concerned with settlement and self-supporting agriculture. The French could not, like the English, found colonies

NORTH AMERICA IN 1783
(The dotted region indicates U. S. territory)

basically European in stock. They lacked French men and women. French colonists, like the Spanish, frequently intermarried with barbarous tribes, tending to lower rather than to elevate the standard. The close friendship of the French with the Hurons aroused the opposition of the fierce Iroquois. This tribe not only annihilated the Hurons, but checked the French advance southward. At the close of the Seven Years' War (1756-1763) Canada and all French possessions in North America east of the Mississippi save New Orleans and a little adjoining land, were ceded to England, and Louisiana west of the Mississippi River was ceded to. Spain. France, accordingly, lost every foot of land she had in North America excepting only two little islands, Miquelon and St. Pierre, in the Gulf of St. Lawrence, upon which she retained fishing rights. The French Catholic Church was almost completely removed from North America, save in eastern Canada, in parts of Maine, and in certain Western regions.

IV. The English and the Dutch Colonization of North America.—The attempts of Spain and France to establish magnificent colonial empires ended in dismal failure. Would England fare any better in her empire building and colonization? The disconnected colonies along the Atlantic seaboard, with different languages and divers creeds, unsustained by governmental arms or treasuries, did not offer much promise of success; and yet these very colonies became the nucleus of a new English state.

Various reasons may be given for England's colonial success. The destruction of the Spanish Armada in 1588 left England the mistress of the seas. The English colonies in America were able to supply people of their own stock. The settlers were concerned, not merely with trade and the search for gold, but also with the development of industry and self-supporting agriculture. Huguenots and English colonists—women as well as men—were particularly skilled. English representative institutions, Lords and Commons, trained the colonists in selecting their own rulers and successfully governing themselves. Practically all early settlers were Protestants who came to America in search of religious freedom.

1. *Episcopalianism transplanted to Virginia, 1607.*—Henry VII of England had asked John Cabot and sons to make explorations in the western and northern seas. In 1497 the Cabots sighted land in the vicinity of Newfoundland, and took possession of it in the name of the King of England. A later expedition explored the American coast from Labrador to the capes off North Carolina. On the basis of these and other alleged discoveries the English based their claim to the American coast from Labrador to Florida.

Sir Walter Raleigh explored the central coast of North America and named it Virginia in honor of the virgin queen, Elizabeth. His glowing accounts of the beauty and richness of this land led to the establishment of the first permanent colony at Jamestown, Virginia, in 1607. The settlement, named in honor of James I of England, was largely a commercial venture although not lacking a religious character. The settlers were English cavaliers, all members of the Established Church of England. This church remained established by law in Virginia till 1776, and clerical appointments were made by the bishop of London. The William and Mary College was founded in 1693 for the purpose of training a native ministry. But the influence of plantation life, the failure to provide an adequate supply of native clergy, and the lack of direct Episcopal oversight, reacted against the growth of vigorous church life.

The history of the Church of England in the other southern colonies runs parallel. North and South Carolina established the Church of England by law. Maryland, established as a Roman Catholic colony, was transferred to the crown of England in 1691, and the following year the Anglican church was established by law. Many Anglican congregations were also found among the early settlers in Georgia, New York, and New Jersey.

2. *Congregationalism established at New Plymouth in 1620.*— The history of the Plymouth colony goes back to England and to Holland. John Robinson (d. 1625), a Fellow at Cambridge, had been suspended because of his separatist tendencies. He joined a separatist congregation at Gainsborough and followed this group to the Netherlands. At Leyden he organized a congregation of several hundred English refugees, mostly industrial workers and farmers, in 1609. Two years later Henry Jacob (d. 1624), the founder of the English Independents,[7] joined the group. Jacob's congregational theory may be stated as follows: (1) The Church shall be a national church, consisting of the old, established congregations which shall be supported by the State. All separatist tendencies are to be opposed. (2) Each local congregation shall be independent in its external and internal affairs. Bishops, presbyters, or synods have no authority over the local churches. Resolutions and decisions of synods are merely advisory. (3) Within the local church, the predestined shall by a "Covenant" create its own organization. The official pastor shall perform all ministerial acts, but this special organization has a right to call its own evangelists, to hold special divine services, and to have communion for the elect only. Jacob organized a congregation in London according to these principles in 1606. Robert Browne had organized a congregation at Norwich in 1580 much according to the same principles. For this reason the early Independents were frequently called Brownists.

A large constituency of the Robinson congregation at Leyden desired to return to English soil; and yet the group did not wish to conform to the laws of the Anglican church. Finally some land was secured in Virginia, and the group embarked in two vessels, the *Mayflower* and the *Speedwell*, to sail for America by way of England. The *Speedwell* was found unseaworthy and did not cross the Atlantic. The "Pilgrim Fathers" crowded into the *Mayflower* and from Plymouth, England, the ship set sail in 1620. Storms drove it far off its course. The ship finally landed, not in Virginia, but at Cape Cod on November 9, 1620. The following

7 cf. p. 326.

month the Pilgrims moved to the western side of the Massachusetts Bay where they founded a town, calling it Plymouth from the last place they had seen in the old world. Before the Pilgrims left their vessel they signed a compact which is an epoch-making document in the history of civil governments.

Between 1620 and 1638 the Congregational colonies of Plymouth, Massachusetts, Connecticut, and New Haven established Congregationalism by law. In Connecticut this law remained effective till 1818, and in Massachusetts till 1833. Harvard College was founded in 1636 and Yale College was established in 1701. John Eliot (1604-1690), "Apostle to the Indians," started the mission work which led to the formation of the Society for the Propagation of the Gospel in New England in 1649. Eliot translated the Bible into the language of his Indian tribes.

3. *The arrival of the Dutch Reformed in 1623.*—Henry Hudson, an Englishman in the service of the Dutch East India Company,[8] explored the Hudson River from Manhattan to Albany in 1609 and took possession of the territory, named the New Netherlands, in the name of the Dutch Republic. A few straggling traders established their posts along the river but no permanent Dutch settlement was established before 1623, when New Amsterdam was founded at Manhattan.[9] Unlike other colonial founders, the Dutch did not at first profess any religious motives; yet the Dutch colonists naturally favored the Reformed Church of Holland. The first Dutch Reformed church was organized in 1628 at New Amsterdam, and this congregation became the earliest representative of the Presbyterian policy in America. But New Amsterdam soon developed a cosmopolitan character. Huguenots, Lutherans, English Puritans, Mennonites, Quakers, and others found their way there. The colonial authorities made more or less futile attempts to prevent any other form of worship. Governor Peter Stuyvesant was particularly harsh in his enforcement of religious conformity. The colony was taken by the English in 1664, and New Amsterdam was changed to New York. Efforts made by English governors to enforce conformity to the Established Church of England did not meet with success. New York retained its cosmopolitan character.

55. REVIEW QUESTIONS

1. What significance had American colonization?
2. Discuss the early Spanish settlements in America.

[8] The Dutch West India Company was chartered in 1621.
[9] Peter Minuit, who became director-general of the New Amsterdam colony in 1626, bought the Manhattan Island from the Indians for twenty-four dollars.

3. Compare the French and the Spanish attempts to build colonial empires. Why did both fail?
4. Why did the English colonies succeed?
5. Why were practically all the early permanent settlers Protestants?
6. In what ways was this spread of Protestantism similar to the spread of Christianity from ancient Judea?
7. Why was the earliest church history a chapter from European church history?
8. Discuss the establishment of the Anglican Church in Virginia and in other colonies. What special difficulties retarded the development of a vigorous church life?
9. Discuss the history of the Plymouth colony. Why did it establish Congregationalism by law?
10. What provisions did the English colonies make for the education of a native clergy?
11. How was Presbyterianism first established?

TOPICS FOR SPECIAL STUDY

1. The establishment of churches and schools in Virginia.
2. Mission work among the Indians as conducted by the Spanish, the French, and the English.
3. Motives for exploration and colonization.
4. The Puritans in New England.
5. Early colonial leaders in Virginia and in New England.

4. *Lutheranism transplanted to New Netherlands in 1623.*[10]— The first permanent group of Lutherans came from Holland, and settled in New Netherlands in 1623 and 1625. Wealthy Dutch Lutherans co-operated with their countrymen in the establishment of Dutch American colonies, and some of these Lutherans came with the early settlers. One group settled near Fort Orange (Albany) and another group settled in New Amsterdam (New York). The Lutheran group in New Amsterdam grew steadily and became very cosmopolitan in its make-up, for it included Norwegians, Swedes, Danes, Germans, and Dutch. Jonas Bronck, an influential Lutheran, has his name perpetuated in the Bronx Borough, New York City. But the Dutch colonial authorities prohibited the Lutherans, not only from organizing a congregation, but also from holding public or private Lutheran worship. The Lutherans had to attend the Reformed services, and children had to be baptized and instructed in the Reformed faith. In 1653 the Lutheran group in New York, numbering at this time fifty families, petitioned the Dutch authorities for liberty of worship and permission to send for a Lutheran pastor, but the petition was denied.[11] The Lutherans persisted, however, and four years later the first Lutheran pastor, John Ernest Gutwasser, came to New

[10] Study diagram on page 470.
[11] Governor Stuyvesant imposed a penalty of one hundred pounds on any one preaching at a Lutheran service, and twenty-five pounds for attending one. Several Lutherans were even imprisoned.

Amsterdam. But the Reformed pastors prevented him from performing any ministerial acts, and less than two years later, Gutwasser was deported. A Lutheran student, Abelius Zetskorn, who came to the colony in 1662, did not fare any better. Governor Stuyvesant sent him to the Dutch settlement of New Amstel on the Delaware where he was ordained as a Lutheran pastor by Rev. Lock, the Swedish pastor. After the Dutch surrender of the colony in 1664, the English authorities granted religious liberty to the Lutheran as well as to the Reformed colonists. A Lutheran congregation was organized at Albany and another at New Amsterdam or New York. The Lutheran congregation in New York, formed in 1648 and chartered in 1664, has had a continued history in the St. Mathew's Lutheran Church, New York City.

Meanwhile a large Swedish Lutheran group had settled on the Delaware. Gustavus Adolphus, King of Sweden, planned a colonizing project through the medium of a commercial company which he chartered in 1626; but his participation in the Thirty Years' War delayed sending out Swedish colonists. The first group landed in 1638 near the present site of Wilmington, Delaware. Land was purchased from the Indians—although the land was already claimed by the Dutch—and a colony called New Sweden was established. The first Lutheran congregation assembled in Fort Christina in 1638. This colony issued the first edict against slavery in 1638, and the first edict of religious toleration[12] in 1642. The first regular Lutheran minister, Reverend Reorus Torkillus,[13] came with the second Swedish expedition in 1639. He died in 1643 and was succeeded by Reverend John Campanius, famed for his work among the Indians. Seventeen years after its establishment, this flourishing colony fell into the hands of the Dutch. Nine years later, in 1664, it was ceded to the English.

5. *Roman Catholicism established in Maryland in 1634.*— George Calvert, first Lord of Baltimore and founder of Maryland, was anxious to establish a place of refuge for Roman Catholics and to build up a semi-feudal estate for his family. Having long enjoyed royal favor, he was able to obtain from Charles I a tract of land which included the present Maryland and parts of Pennsylvania, West Virginia, and Delaware. Over this domain the first

---

[12] Full religious liberty was practiced in the Rhode Island Colony from its beginning, in 1638, but the royal charter of the colony dates from 1647. The Maryland Assembly proclaimed religious liberty in that colony in 1649.
[13] The Danish clergyman, Rev. Rasmus Jensen, was very likely the first Lutheran pastor to conduct a Lutheran divine service in North America. He was with the Danish expedition of Jens Munk who tried in 1619-20 to find the northwest passage. Most of the members of the expedition, including Rev. Jensen, died at Hudson Bay in 1620.

Lord Baltimore was to exercise almost regal powers. He died before the charter was granted, and his eldest son, Cecelius, became the proprietor of Maryland. Actual settlement started in 1634 when Leonard Calvert, a brother of Cecelius, founded St. Marys near the mouth of the Potomac River.

The most important feature of early Maryland history was the religious toleration practiced. Cecelius Calvert wished Maryland to be a place where English Catholics might find refuge from persecution, but he could not establish Catholicism as a state religion, and he would not permit an established church of any other faith. Furthermore, a Catholic majority could not be maintained in the assembly of freemen because the majority of the settlers were Protestants. Calvert proposed, therefore, a law which would provide for religious toleration, which led to the adoption of the famous "Toleration Act" in 1649.

When James II of England was dethroned in 1689, the Protestants of Maryland used the opportunity to rid themselves of Roman Catholic rule. Maryland became a royal colony in 1692 and the Church of England was established as the state church.

6. *The Baptist denomination transplanted to Providence, Rhode Island, in 1639.*—In 1631 a learned Anglican clergyman, Roger Williams (1600-83), was cordially welcomed to the Salem colony in Massachusetts. After serving as pastor of several churches he came into serious conflict with the colonial authorities because he denied the validity of the charter of the colony, asserting that the true owners of the land were the Indians and not the English sovereign. He asserted that the oath should not be administered to the unregenerate; he taught that the state should have nothing to do with religion. Williams was banished from Massachusetts. After much suffering he found his way to the Narragansett Bay and established a colony at Providence, Rhode Island. He organized a Baptist church in 1639. Another Baptist church was organized at Newport by Dr. John Clark. Baptist churches were gradually established in other places, such as Boston, 1665, Charleston, South Carolina, 1693, and Philadelphia, 1698. Henry Dunster, first president of Harvard College, resigned his office in 1654 because of his Baptist views. Brown University, founded in 1765, was the earliest Baptist institution of learning.

The Baptists held to the Congregational principle and recognized no higher office than pastor. Each congregation was independent of every other congregation, but there was an official intercommunion of Baptist churches for missionary and educational purposes. The

Baptists rejected infant baptism, advocated the separation of Church and State, and insisted on spiritual qualification for church membership. They depended on the Bible rather than on religious creeds for their doctrine. The Baptists divided into Particular Baptists or those who held Calvinistic views, and General Baptists or those who held Arminian views, and Seventh Day Baptists or those who observed the seventh day as the day of rest. In America the Northern and Southern Baptists divided on the question of slavery in 1845.

7. *Scotch-Irish Presbyterians*[14] *organized at Long Island in 1640.*—Settlers from Scotland and from the Scotch-Irish colony of Ulster in North Ireland were quick to find their way to the new world. Reverend Alexander Whitaker, a man of Presbyterian views, settled in Virginia in 1611 as pastor of a Puritan congregation. Persecution soon drove these Virginian Puritans out of the colony and many settled in Maryland and North Carolina between 1642 and 1649. Reverend Richard Denton, who also held Presbyterian views, located with a congregation in the Massachusetts colony in 1630; but the unfriendly attitude of the coloniel authorities caused him and his friends to move to New Amsterdam. The first permanent Presbyterian church of English origin was the noted Southold church, established on Long Island in 1640. Another Presbyterian church was founded at Jamaica, Long Island, in 1656. Presbyterian churches were established in New Jersey at the following points: Newark in 1667, Elizabeth in 1668, Woodbridge in 1680, and Fairfield in 1680. A Welsh Presbyterian church was founded at Great Valley, Pennsylvania, in 1685, and another English Presbyterian church was founded at Philadelphia in 1698. By 1760 the entire region from New England to South Carolina was dotted with Scotch-Irish Presbyterian churches.

Reverend Francis Makemie became the apostle of American Presbyterianism. The presbytery of Laggan, Ireland, sent him to America in 1683 at the request of a member of the council of the colony of Maryland. Makemie set himself to the task of bringing into organic unity the scattered Presbyterian churches. He organized the first Presbytery at Philadelphia in 1705. The first synod, composed of three presbyteries, was organized in 1716. The Westminster Confession[15] was adopted as the standard of doctrine and polity in 1729.

8. *Organization of the American Quakers in 1660.*—George Fox was early in favor of making Quakerism an expanding force in

---

[14] See page 352.   [15] See page 353.

America. Quakers arrived in 1656 in Massachusetts, Virginia, and New York. Severe laws were immediately enacted against them. They were finally banished from Massachusetts and Virginia, and death penalty was fixed for those who returned. Massachusetts executed four Quakers in 1659, namely William Robinson, Marmaduke Stevenson, Mary Dyer, and William Leddra. Governor Stuyvesant persecuted the Quakers in New York. But the Quakers continued to come, and gradually the sentiment against them became less severe. At the end of two decades the laws against the Quakers were suspended. Meanwhile Monthly Meetings had been organized at Scituate and Sandwich, Massachusetts, before 1660. A Yearly Meeting was established in New England in 1661. These Monthly and Yearly Quaker Meetings are the oldest organizations of their kind in America. George Fox visited America in 1672.

New Jersey, Delaware, and Pennsylvania were the early centers of Quaker activity in America. In New Jersey a Monthly Meeting was organized in 1678, a Quarterly Meeting was established in 1680, and a Yearly Meeting in 1681. William Penn (1644-1718) helped to send more than eight hundred Quakers to New Jersey between 1677 and 1678. In 1681 Penn was granted the lands now constituting the states of Pennsylvania and Delaware in consideration of a debt due him from the government. That same year he founded the colony of Pennsylvania as a "holy experiment," consisting of the establishment of freedom and equality of rights in religion. Religious freedom was widely advertised. Large numbers of emigrants were attracted.

9. *The Mennonites organized at Germantown, Pennsylvania, in 1688.*—Dutch Mennonites appeared in America as early as in 1638. By 1644 a number lived in the New Amsterdam colony, but they did not organize any congregation. In 1683, shortly after the founding of Pennsylvania colony, thirteen Mennonite families from Crefeld, Germany, settled in Germantown,[16] ten miles north of Philadelphia. This was the first German settlement. Some of these early settlers joined the Quaker church but a Mennonite congregation was organized in 1688, after a number of co-religionists had arrived from the Palatinate and from Crefeld. The first Mennonite church was erected in 1708. A large number of Swiss, German, and Dutch immigrants, during the eighteenth century, settled in Pennsylvania. The "Pennsylvania Dutch" Mennonites, with their

---

[16] Germantown (Germanopolis), now a part of Philadelphia, was laid out in 1685, and incorporated in 1689.

Anglicized Rhenish German dialect, were mostly of Swiss descent. It is estimated that about 2,000 Mennonite families were living in America at the end of the Colonial Period.

10. *Organization of the first German Lutheran Synod in America, 1735.*—The German Lutheran immigration to New York, Pennsylvania, Delaware, and Maryland started in a small way during the last quarter of the seventeenth century. Some of these pioneers formed loosely organized congregations, but they did not have any regular pastors. A group of 51 Palatines came to New York in 1708 under the leadership of Rev. Joshua Kocherthal. Within the next two years nearly four thousand Lutheran refugees came, and they were soon followed by large bodies of South German Lutherans. The majority of these immigrants settled in New York, Pennsylvania, and North and South Carolina.

The first Lutheran synod in America was formed on August 20-21, 1735, at the old mountain church on the Raritan, by Rev. William Christopher Berkenmeyer, Rev. Michael Christian Knoll, and Rev. Johann Augustus Wolf, together with eleven laymen representing at least sixteen organized congregations in the Raritan Valley, New Jersey, and in New York. The synodical constitution[17] adopted conformed to a strict confessional standard.

The first permanent German Lutheran congregation in Pennsylvania was organized at New Hannover, or Falckner's Swamp, in 1703 by Rev. Daniel Falckner, and this congregation built the first German Lutheran church that same year. Rev. Falckner served the New Hannover congregation until 1708. His brother, Justus Falckner, was ordained in 1703 to serve the large parish of New York and vicinity.[18] Other early German Lutheran pastors were Anthony Jacob Henkel, John Casper Stoever, Sr., and John Casper Stoever, Jr. (father and son), and John Christian Schultz.

Meanwhile General James Oglethorpe projected the colony of Georgia as an asylum for religious refugees. Georgia was founded in 1733, and the following year a large number of Lutherans from the province of Salzburg in Austria settled there. The Salzburgers formed a settlement 23 miles northwest of Savannah and called it Ebenezer.[19] The settlement was ably served by three Lutheran

[17] A translation in MSS form is on file in the office of the National Lutheran Council, New York City.
[18] Falckner's church records show that at this early period there were even Negro Lutherans in America. The original ordination certificate of Justus Falckner was found in 1925 in a drawer in the office of St. James Church at Madison Avenue and 73rd Street, New York City.
[19] The Lutheran Saltzburgers in Georgia established the first orphanage in America in 1736.

pastors, John Martin Bolzius and Israel Christian Gronau, who had been instructors at the Franckean[20] Institutions at Halle, Germany, and Christian Rabenhorst, John and Charles Wesley, Whitefield[21] and Bishop Nitschmann of the Moravian church[22] visited this flourishing colony. The Lutherans in Georgia were later augmented by immigrants from Wurttemburg.

The Germans were soon more numerous than any other non-English group in the colonies, but they were widely scattered, often without pastors, and without any organic church connection. England was at this time ruled by a German king, George II (1727-60), whose court chaplain, Dr. Ziegenhagen, was a Lutheran pastor. German Lutherans in America naturally appealed to him and to Dr. Gotthelf August Francke of the University of Halle for pastors and for other help. In response, Rev. Henry Melchior Mühlenberg was sent, in 1742.

Mühlenberg was pastor of the Lutheran congregations at Philadelphia, New Providence, and New Hannover, but his influence soon extended over all Lutherans in America. He saw it as his task, not merely to serve these congregations, but to bring order into the chaotic condition of the scattered Lutherans and to lay the foundation for organized Lutheranism. For this great task he was admirably well qualified. He was strong in body and richly endowed in heart and mind. Dignified and magnetic in his personal appearance, endowed with unusual tact and adaptability, pleasant and cordial in his relations with men, capable of speaking Latin, Dutch, and English fluently besides his native German, trained in the school of German Pietism[23] in its best days, a scholarly theologian and a firm Lutheran, and possessed with remarkable powers of organization and administration—these characteristics made Mühlenberg the "Patriarch of the Lutheran Church in America." He brought the pioneer congregations into order, secured worthy pastors, and founded schools for the education of the young. On August 26, 1748, on the occasion of the dedication of the St. Michael's Church in Philadelphia, he organized the *second* Lutheran synod, called the Evangelical Lutheran Ministerium of Pennsylvania and Adjacent States. This is now a constituent synod in the United Lutheran Church. Mühlenberg's motto was: *Ecclesia Plantanda,* "the Church must be planted."

[20] See page 365.
[21] See pages 368-71.
[22] See page 367.
[23] See pages 363-66.

11. *Establishment of the first German Reformed Synod in America, 1747.*—The Germans were late in coming. A few scattered pioneers appeared during the seventeenth century, but there was no German settlement save that of Germantown, Pennsylvania. German immigration started during the first four decades of the eighteenth century and assumed enormous proportions. By 1776 the Germans numbered[24] at least 200,000. About 1709 a large number of Reformed Germans from the Palatinate settled in the South, in New York, and in Pennsylvania. Nearly all were poor, and many of them forced their way into the interior where they maintained their separate language, press, and religion. They were eager to make provisions for churches and parochial schools, although comparatively few pastors and qualified teachers attended them. The first German Reformed minister, Samuel Guldin, preached at Germantown in 1718, and John Philip Boehm[25] held the first recorded Reformed communion service at Falckner's Swamp in October, 1725. The first German Reformed church was built at Germantown in 1719. By 1725 three German Reformed congregations[26] had been established at Falckner's Swamp, Skippack, and White Marsh. Additional congregations were organized, and several German Reformed ministers came to serve the colonists. But the great majority of the Reformed people in the colonies were without ministers, and the general condition of the churches was deplorable.

Conscious of their inability to do much for these churches, the ecclesiastical authorities of the Palatinate appealed to the officials of the Dutch Reformed Church at Amsterdam, Holland. In consequence, Michael Schlatter, a native of St. Gall in Switzerland, was sent in 1746 as a missionary evangelist. His chief work was to organize the congregations into a coetus or synod, which was accomplished in 1747. The first meeting of the German Reformed synod was held in Philadelphia in September, 1747. For the next twenty-six years this synod stood in a subordinate relation to the Church of Holland, but in 1793 the German Reformed Church became an independent synod. In 1869 the official name was changed to "The Reformed Church in the United States."

12. *Organization of the Moravian Church in America in 1742.*—The first group of Moravians arrived in Georgia in 1735 under

---

[24] Beard: *The Rise of American Civilization,* I, p. 84.
[25] U. S. Religious Census of 1926, II, p. 1231.
[26] Sweet: *The Story of Religions in America,* p. 161.

the leadership of Spangenberg.[27] Additional colonists arrived the following year. But sickness and death among the Moravian settlers and friction with the colonial authorities because of their refusal to bear arms in the war with Spain, caused them to relinquish that field, and in 1740 the group moved to Pennsylvania and established Moravian settlements at Bethlehem, Nazareth, and Lititz. Another colony was subsequently established at Salem, North Carolina. In 1741 Count Zinzendorf[28] came to America, and during his brief stay of thirteen months he visited all the Moravian settlements. He first tried to unite all German settlers in Pennsylvania into one religious organization, but failed. His next endeavor was to organize the Moravian Church in America under the episcopate of Bishop David Nitschmann. This charter organization included nine Moravian congregations and four schools. Zinzendorf also promoted mission work among the Indians.

13. *The arrival of Whitefield, the first Methodist Preacher in America, 1739.*—Wesleyan immigrants came to Virginia in the early 'thirties of the eighteenth century. They adhered, like co-religionists in England, to the established Church, but instituted an order of lay preachers. This cordial relation between the Wesleyans and the Virginia officials made possible the invitation of Whitefield who preached in the colony in 1739 and 1740. A Methodist preacher, Robert Strawbridge, began to preach in Maryland in 1664 and founded a society near Pipe Creek. Philip Embury began to preach in New York in 1766 and soon founded another Methodist society. Captain Thomas Webb of the British army was another capable Methodist preacher after 1760. John Wesley sent two of his evangelists, Boardman and Pilmoor, in 1769, and Francis Asbury came in 1771. The Methodist church grew rapidly, soon outstripping the other denominations in membership. By 1773 the first American Methodist "Conference" was held in Philadelphia. The Methodist Episcopal Church in America was organized in Baltimore in 1784.

14. *The establishment of other Protestant groups in America in colonial times.*—Many additional Protestant groups were established in the colonial period. German Baptist Brethren, or Dunkers,[29] 1719-23, settled in Germantown, Pennsylvania. A group of Schwenkenfelder[30] settled near Philadelphia in 1734. Swiss immigrants transplanted the Brethren in Christ denomination to Lancaster, Pennsylvania, in 1752. This denomination was later called the

[27] See page 368.   [28] See pages 367-68.
[29] Dunkers from the German word *tunken*: "to dip."   [30] See page 330.

River Brethren because they lived by and baptized in a river. The Society of Believers, commonly called Shakers because of their physical excitement in their meetings, was established by a small group of English immigrants in New York in 1774. John Murray and his fellow-laborers built the first Universalist church at Gloucester, Massachusetts, in 1779. In 1785 the first Episcopal church in New England was re-organized as the first Unitarian church in America, under the leadership of James Freeman. The Society of Universal Baptists was organized in 1785 by Elhanan Winchester, a Calvinistic Baptist minister in Philadelphia. In 1789, when George Washington was inaugurated, twenty-eight[31] distinct Protestant denominations existed in the new republic.

V. Four Groups of English Colonies.—The early population in the colonies presented anything but a homogeneous society. The settlers were nearly all European Protestants and yet they reflected the social, political, and religious peculiarities of the various geographical regions of Europe. On the basis of the various attitudes towards problems of religious liberty and the relation of the church to the state, the English colonies in North America may be classified into four general groups. One group subordinated the church to the state. Another group subordinated the state to the church. A third group maintained that church and state should be strictly separated. Finally, a fourth group declared for religious freedom and refused to give preference to any special creed.

In Virginia and North and South Carolina the Church of England was declared "the established religion." This church enjoyed material advantages in other colonies because of governmental support. The church was in reality a department of the state, and all forms of dissent were suppressed because they constituted religious as well as civil disorder.

Massachusetts, Plymouth, New Haven, Connecticut, and New Hampshire set up a theocratic state, something on the order of Calvin's city-state of Geneva[32] and after the ideal of Augustine's "City of God."[33] Quakers and other "heretics" were forcefully kept out. During the last third of the seventeenth century a strong group representing the second generation in New England demanded the establishment of *birthright* church membership, which was granted through the so-called Half-way Covenant adopted by

[31] Bass: *Protestantism in the United States,* page 22.   [33] See pages 125-26.
[32] See pages 268-74.

a synod at Boston. This arrangement caused much strife and division.

Rhode Island, Pennsylvania, and Delaware protested from their beginnings against the principle of union of church and state. Rhode Island, under the influence of Roger Williams,[34] was most emphatic. Pennsylvania, while favoring the separation of church and state, restricted its civic privileges to those who believed in the existence of God.

Maryland and Georgia began by declaring freedom of worship, but later royal decrees established the Church of England. The Swedish colony issued the first edict of religious toleration[35] in America in 1642. Rhode Island practiced universal toleration from its beginning in 1638, though its royal charter dates from 1644; but the colony denied Roman Catholics civil rights and liberties in 1663. Pennsylvania granted liberty in religious matters from the beginning. Theoretically, a person of atheistic opinion could not enjoy civic privileges, but there is no record that this was ever enforced. In New York and New Jersey the non-conformists were at first much harassed by Dutch and English officials; but a proclamation by King James II of England in 1674 gave the broadest kind of religious liberty. Each group was permitted to worship according to its own views, provided it did not disturb the public peace, or did not molest other groups in free exercise of their religion.

VI. The First Great Awakening, 1734-1744.—The Great Awakening in America was somewhat analogous to, and practically contemporaneous with, the Pietist movement in Germany[36] and the Methodist revival in England.[37] This far-reaching movement is not to be confused with the Great Revival from 1796 to 1805.

There was a large number of unchurched people. Religion played, of course, a very prominent part in the American settlement, but the initial religious interest was soon subordinated to the all-absorbing issue of subjugating a new continent. Lack of organized churches and schools, shortage of worthy pastors, the rough frontier life, and constant border warfare,[38] had a demoralizing influence on colonial society. Something had to be done to make the colonists more interested in religion. The new technique evolved for this purpose was frontier revivalism, with its camp-meetings.

[34] See page 423.
[35] See footnote 12 on page 418.
[36] See pages 363-66.
[37] See pages 368-71.
[38] The hundred years' struggle between France and England for the Mississippi Valley included King William's War (1689-97), Queen Anne's War (1702-13), King George's War (1740-48), and the French and Indian War (1755-63).

The Great Awakening was first noticed among German Mennonites, Dunkers, and Moravians in Pennsylvania. Next came the revivalistic preaching of Theodore J. Frelinghuysen, a German Pietist minister to the Dutch Reformed of northern New Jersey (the Raritan Valley). By 1726 his preaching had resulted in numerous conversions and the ingathering of many new members. The revival movement spread, about 1728, to the English and Scotch Presbyterians through the medium of Gilbert Tennent, a young Presbyterian minister of New Brunswick, New Jersey. Tennent had been influenced, not only by Frelinghuysen, but also by his training in the Log College built by his father, William Tennent, for the education of evangelical ministers.

In 1734 a great awakening started among the people of Northampton, Massachusetts, under the ministry of Jonathan Edwards. Being alarmed by the growing tendency toward Arminianism,[39] Edwards preached a series of sermons on justification by faith alone. The result was an absorbing interest in personal religion, by young and old, in the Northampton community. Within a year more than three hundred persons, nearly all the people in town above sixteen years of age, professed conversion. From Northampton the revival spread down the river and along the coast, thence to the Middle and Southern Colonies. In Virginia it had greatest progress among the Baptists, through the activities of two Baptist preachers, Shubal Stearns and Daniel Marshall. From the Baptists it spread to the Methodists. The Swedish Lutherans on the Delaware, adhering to the official attitude of the Church of Sweden toward Pietism,[40] took a rather conservative attitude toward the Great Awakening, while the German Lutherans, on the other hand, were strongly influenced, especially through the activities of Mühlenberg. The Episcopal Church took an attitude of opposition.

The high tide of the Great Awakening came in 1740-41 during George Whitefield's second visit. His incomparable eloquence drew thousands of people to his meetings, and many were truly converted. His itinerant preaching and his visits to Gilbert Tennent, Frelinghuysen, Edwards, and other revival speakers, brought in a sense the movements in the various colonies together. Edwards and other New England ministers joined for a time the itinerant evangelistic work. The great appeal was to fear. This motive was particularly prominent in Edward's famous sermon "Sinners in the Hands of an Angry God," preached at Enfield, Connecticut,

[39] See page 348.   [40] See page 365.

in July 1741. After this date the revival lost much force and popularity because of extravagances of action and speech, including groans, outcries, convulsions, fainting, visions, ecstasies, and unbridled denunciation of all who did not agree with the revivalists.

But many important results were registered. There was a general quickening of the religious life, a revival of personal religion, a large increase in church membership, and a higher general standard of morality. The awakening promoted missionary work and benevolent enterprises in the colonies, such as the Indian Christianization and the Bethesda Orphan House which Whitefield built

THE FRONTIER LINE OF THE ENGLISH COLONIES IN 1740
(The ...... line indicates the western edge of the fully settled areas)

in Georgia. The educational influence was particularly significant. Many denominational colleges and religious schools were founded. While the revival deepened church divisions, it also aroused a general consciousness of a national religious unity. In this way it prepared for the birth of the American nation. Whitefield impressed the character of Methodism upon American church life for more than a century.

VII. Education and Theology.—The school everywhere arose as a child of the Church. European educational ideas, schools and types of instruction were transplanted by the various groups of immigrants. Gradually, three types of educational practice prevailed. New England developed a system of state-supported common schools, English Latin grammar schools, and several colleges, for both religious and civic ends. The Middle Colonies developed a parochial school system which placed the schools under the direct church control of each denomination. Such schools were dominated only by church purposes. A third type was introduced by the well-to-do planters of Virginia and other colonies. Children of the upper and middle classes attended small private pay-schools, or, they were sent to England to get their education. Colonial society was under no obligation to provide an education for children of the poorer classes. Elementary education for them was left to philanthropic and religious effort.

Massachusetts founded Harvard College in 1636, and Connecticut founded Yale College in 1702 to perpetuate learning and to insure an educated ministry for the Congregational church. William and Mary College was founded in Virginia in 1693 for the purpose of educating Anglican ministers. Several Latin grammar schools were established to prepare students for entrance requirement to college, but the attendance in all these schools was small in colonial days. Under the hard pioneer conditions, many communities even neglected the proper religious education of the children. Interest in religion frequently declined almost to the vanishing point. But the Great Awakening furnished a new stimulus. Six additional colleges were founded, Princeton as a Presbyterian institution in 1746, the Academy and College (University) of Pennsylvania in 1753-55 on a non-denominational basis, King's College (Columbia University) in 1754 as an Anglican institution, Rhode Island College (Brown University) by the Baptists in 1764, Rutgers College, New Jersey, by the Dutch Reformed in 1766, and by the Congregationalists Dartmouth College, New Hampshire, in 1769. Numerous parochial schools were established, the common school was put on a better working basis, and the English Latin grammar school was gradually replaced by the American Academy with its more practical studies.

Calvinism and Lutheranism were the leading forms of theology. The New England Calvinists had some capable theologians in John Cotton (1585-1652), Thomas Hooker (1585-1647), Richard Mather (1596-1669), Increase Mather (1639-1723), Cotton

Mather (1663-1728), Jonathan Dickinson (1688-1747), and Jonathan Edwards (1703-58). The learned Roger Williams was also a Calvinist in doctrine, though a Baptist in practice. The Irish-Scotch Presbyterians had Francis Makemie (1658-1708), and William Tennent (1673-1746), the founder of the Log College. The Dutch Reformed had Theodore Jacobus Frelinghuysen (1691-1747) and Michael Schlatter (1716-1790). The Moravians had August Gottlieb Spangenberg (1704-92), and David Nitschmann. The Lutherans had Justus Falckner, Charles Magnus Wrangel, and the brilliant and learned Henry Melchior Mühlenberg. But the all-absorbing interest in practical affairs prevented all these men, save Jonathan Edwards, from producing any creative thinking or speculative theology.

Jonathan Edwards became the founder of a school of New England theology which dominated the New England churches for more than a century. He established a middle course between Calvinism and Arminianism by asserting, in his *Freedom of the Will* and other writings, that man has some responsibility for his salvation because of his ability to make a choice of action. Edwards recharged the barren Calvinistic orthodoxy of his day with warm-hearted mysticism and intellectual life. He conceived of the church as the society of the elect.

A striking phenomenon of the church was the witch mania which gripped the New England colonies between 1688 and 1693. A number of women were brought to trial, convicted, and condemned as witches. Such beliefs were quite common also in Europe at the time. Another feature was the division into ways of thinking. The New England Congregationalists were divided into New Lights, who favored the revival, and Old Lights, who disliked it. Many left the Congregational church and joined the Baptists. The Presbyterians in the middle colonies likewise divided into New Side and Old Side, but this schism was quickly healed.

56. REVIEW QUESTIONS

1. How was Lutheranism first established?
2. Discuss the characteristics of the Rhode Island Colony and its founder.
3. When and where were the Scotch-Irish Presbyterians first organized? Why is Francis Makemie called the apostle of American Presbyterianism?
4. Discuss the origin of Quakerism. Which is the "Quaker State"? Why?
5. Who were "the Pennsylvania Dutch"?
6. What special service did Michael Schlatter render to the Dutch Reformed Church?
7. What qualifications did Mühlenberg have for organizing the first German Lutheran synod? What importance is attached to this organization?

8. Who organized the Moravian church and who was the first bishop?
9. How were the Methodists established, and why did this church soon outstrip the other denominations in membership?
10. What divided the colonies into four general groups? What colonies belonged to each group? Why?
11. Discuss the Great Awakening. Who were the prominent leaders?
12. What provisions did colonial North America make for education?
13. Why did colonial America produce so little speculative or creative theology?

TOPICS FOR SPECIAL STUDY

1. The contribution of the Swedish Lutheran colony on the Delaware to colonial America.
2. The preparations made in colonial America for universal religious liberty and complete separation of church and state.
3. The attitude of the various colonial churches toward the American Revolution of 1763-75.
4. Religious education in colonial America.
5. Frontier revivalism and its by-products.
6. Jonathan Edwards and his school of theology.

A SELECTED BIBLIOGRAPHY FOR CHAPTER XXI

1. Bacon: *History of American Christianity*, pp. 1-207. (Vol. XIII of the "American Church History Series.")
2. Sweet: *The Story of Religions in America*, pp. 1-249.
3. Rowe: *History of Religion in the United States.*
4. Bacon: *Genesis of the New England Churches.*
5. Walker: *History of the Congregationalists in the United States.*
6. Perry: *The History of the American Episcopal Church*, 1587-1883 (2 Vols.).
7. Dubbs: *A History of the Reformed Church.* (Vol. VIII of American Church History Series.)
8. Jacobs: *Lutherans* (Vol. IV of the American Church History Series).
9. Newman: *A History of the Baptist Churches in the United States* (Vol. II of American Church History Series).
10. Hanna: *The Scotch-Irish or the Scot in North Britain, North Ireland and North America* (2 Vols.).
11. Thompson: *A History of the Presbyterian Churches in the United States* (Vol. VI of American Church History Series).
12. Braithwaite: *History of the Quakers.*
13. Smith: *The Mennonites.*
14. Hamilton: *A History of the Church Known as the Moravian Church or the Unitas Fratrum.*
15. Townsend, Workman and Eyres: *New History of Methodism.*
16. O'Gorman: *A History of the Roman Catholic Church in the United States.*
17. Tracy: *The Great Awakening.*
18. Maxson: *The Great Awakening in the Middle Colonies.*

CHAPTER XXII

The Establishment of the American Nation

I. General Consequences for the Church.—The Revolutionary War resulted in the establishment of a new nation, the United States of America.[1]

The Declaration of Independence proclaimed the principles of equality, popular sovereignty, and nationality. The colonies demanded civic and religious liberty, freedom of thought and speech, personal liberty and security. Of most significance to national and international life was the American proclamation of religious liberty. This proclamation came at a time when tolerance in religion was little known to the Old World. Here the principle of religious liberty[2] and equality started its world-wide conquest.

After the Revolutionary War the Anglican and the Methodist churches in America could not well continue as subordinate divisions of the mother churches. Independent American organizations adapted to the American needs had to be established. Consequently there was organized the *Protestant Episcopal Church* in 1789, with a predominantly Anglican liturgy, but with a more democratic form of government. The needs of Methodism caused John Wesley, who up to 1784 had control, to send itinerant lay preachers, and in 1772 he commissioned Francis Asbury to superintend the work in America. Special American pastors were ordained in 1784. In the same year Dr. Thomas Coke was commissioned to superintend the Methodist work, as colleague of Francis Asbury, and the Methodists were organized into the *Methodist Episcopal Church*. The final and permanent organization of this Church was a peculiar combination of monarchical and democratic principles. The superintendents or bishops were given more administrative power than bishops of England enjoyed, but the legislative power was vested in regular Conferences which were soon almost completely controlled by the lay people, a new system which did not fit any previous theory of church government. The Methodist Episcopal Church soon became the largest Protestant church.

[1] See page 414.
[2] The demand for religious liberty was, of course, inherent in the spirit of the Protestant Reformation; but it took centuries before this idea had free course among the Christian nations.

The Constitutional Convention had to solve the problem of the relation of church and state, for the young nation was composed of peoples of diverse nationalities and of different religious faiths. No single group could claim a dominant majority to entitle that group to be considered the national church. Consequently, the Constitutional Convention refused to give preference to any creed, but incorporated into the Federal Constitution the following principles: federal neutrality in all confessional matters; federal guarantee of the free exercise of religious faith to all; complete separation of state and church. Each state was to arrange its own church affairs, but no state religion was ever to be established. This did not mean, however, that the United States became a state without religion. Official adherence to the Christian faith had, and still has, a prominent place in Congress and in the proclamations of the President.

Gradually, the various states especially in consequence of Baptist and Catholic agitation incorporated into their constitutions these federal principles and provided for the disestablishment of existing state churches, the last states to provide for disestablishment being New Hampshire in 1817, Connecticut in 1818, and Massachusetts in 1833. This arrangement threw all churches upon their own resources and left them free to develop according to their own strength and tendencies. It fostered the development of religious "denominations," each with equal rights before the law. It substituted the principle of voluntary church membership for the Old World principle of authority, unity, and church membership as a qualification for citizenship.

II. Conditions leading up to the Revolutionary War.— The eighteenth century marked a new epoch in human thinking and progress.[3] Revolutionary discoveries in the natural sciences, the humanistic idea of the dignity of man, and the changes wrought in philosophy by Bacon's inductive method and Descartes' "hypothetical doubt" gave rise to a spirit less conscious of God but more conscious of man. Man centered his interest on life here, rather than hereafter. A rising tide of individualism was the inevitable result. Old religious doctrines began to lose their hold on the people.

Colonial America experienced a change in religious thinking and a gradual estrangement from England almost immediately after the Great Awakening. These changes were caused by rude frontier conditions, the decline of the old religious fervor and intolerance, the rising interest in shipping and trade, the gradual breakdown of aristocratic traditions and customs, the rising tide of individualism, the displacement of the old religious town government and the original religious town school by a civil town government and the secular district school, and the new state theory of education which embodied the idea that schools were essentially for the promotion of the everyday interests of society and the welfare of the state. Public interest centered in political discussion rather than in religious controversy. Colonial newspapers frequently attacked both Church and State. The old religious solidarity was broken, and the life of Colonial America was rapidly secularized.

Practically all the early settlers in the thirteen colonies were Protestants, many of whom came *in search of religious freedom.* According to the first Federal census of 1790, the names indicated a national origin as follows:

Pure English origin	83.5%
Scotch origin	6.7%
German origin	5.6%
Dutch origin	2.0%
Irish origin	1.6%
French origin	0.5%
Other nationalities	0.1%

In the New England States 98.5 to 99.8 per cent of the names were British; in Pennsylvania, on the other hand, about sixty per cent of the population was German.

The settlers were all imbued with the Protestant idea[4] of an active participation of all citizens in government and religion. It asserted the divine right of the common people as against the divine right of kings.[5] English traditions of representative government and liberty[6] formed the foundation on which self-government in America was built.[7]

[4] See pages 286-87.   [5] See page 351.   [6] See page 205.

[7] The Lutherans also had a large share in the laying of the foundation stones of America. Two months prior to the Declaration of Independence, Thomas Jefferson is said to have visited Dr. J. F. Schmidt, pastor of St. Michael's Church in Philadelphia, from 4 o'clock of one afternoon until noon the next day. Jefferson spent the evening and the morning in Dr. Schmidt's office where he examined the *Articles* of the Ministerium of Pennsylvania and books which contained the fundamental principles enunciated by Martin Luther in his *Liberty of the Christian Man.* It is difficult to say how much this visit influenced Jefferson as he drafted the Declaration of Independence. Neither he nor the committee responsible, John Adams, Franklin, Sherman, and Livingston, ever claimed any originality for its principles. Daniel Webster said that the origin of American Liberty dated from the Reformation.

John Conrad Weiser, Jr., a German Lutheran, did more than any other single individual of that era, to prevent the Mohawk-Iroquois-Indian tribe from joining the British in order to destroy the colonies as they were about to declare their independence. (cf. *Lutheran World Almanac,* 1924-26, pp. 57-58).

Woodrow Wilson said: "However mortifying it may be to them or us, America did not come out of the South, and it did not come out of New England. The characteristic part of America originated in the states of Pennsylvania, New Jersey and New York, because there, from the first was the mixture of racial stocks, that mixture of antecedents, which is the singular and distinguishing mark of the United States" (*Lutheran World Almanac,* 1924-26, p. 58).

But the colonists soon displayed a love of religious and political liberty and independence to which even Englishmen were scarcely accustomed. The spirit of independence in the colonies became very pronounced, and colonial recognition of the supremacy of the British Parliament became increasingly difficult. It was evident that the colonists and the English were rapidly drifting apart.

Serious opposition was first caused by agitation for the establishment of an Anglican bishop in America, which came at a most inopportune time, for the colonists would no longer endure British domination. They knew that the appointment of an Anglican bishop would involve British supremacy in ecclesiastical matters in the colonies, and the exercise of vast political power. Opposition was especially strong among the Congregationalists and the Presbyterians of New England and the middle colonies. John Adams said, "The objection was not only to the office of a bishop, though that was dreaded, but to the authority of Parliament on which it must be founded. The reasoning was this: There is no power less than Parliament which can create bishops in America. But if Parliament can erect dioceses and appoint bishops, they may introduce the whole hierarchy, establish tithes, establish religion, forbid dissenters, make schism heresy, impose penalties extending to life and limb as well as to liberty and property."

Van Tyne[8] and others have pointed out that the more the evidences for the remote and immediate causes of the American Revolution are brought to light and studied, the more does the religious, sectarian, or ecclesiastical cause force itself to the front. Charles Evans[9] states that in its controversial phases, "the struggle for civil liberty in the American Colonies assumes something of the nature of religious warfare, in which the dissenting churches are opposed by the Established Church of England." Evans also points out that from 1700-50, two-thirds of the books and pamphlets published in the colonies were on the religious questions, and from 1750 to 1775, at least one half of the Colonial literature dealt with the religious aspect of the Revolution.

The real struggle between England and America started, however, when the English government tried to make the colonists pay some of the expenses of the Seven Years' War (1755-63), and some of the expenses of colonial administration. In order to increase the colonial revenue, the English government undertook, in 1764, to enforce the Sugar Act of 1733. For similar purposes the

[8] Van Tyne: *Influence of the Clergy and of Religious and Sectarian Forces on the American Revolution*, in the *American Historical Review*, vol. XIX, p. 44.
[9] Charles Evans: *American Bibliography*, vol. V, p. 9.

Stamp Act of 1765, and the Paint, Glass, and Paper Act of 1767 were passed by Parliament. These acts raised the question whether or not there should be taxation without representation.

This issue gradually brought about a division of sentiment among the people in the colonies, and by 1770 two parties were in the process of formation. The Loyalist or Tory party took the side of England in the taxation controversy, while the American or Patriot party cared little for England and was intensely loyal to America. The Tory party included many wealthy men and the more important colonial officials. The Patriot Party included chiefly the middle and lower classes, but also a few men of wealth, such as George Washington, Thomas Jefferson, Benjamin Franklin, Alexander Hamilton, John Dickinson, and John Adams. The Congregational ministers and the Scotch-Irish Presbyterians were almost unanimously of the Patriot party; the German Reformed and the German and Swedish Lutheran churches were decidedly patriotic. The Baptists joined the cause enthusiastically because they had suffered much at the hands of the Anglicans. The Methodists were much misunderstood because of their supposed Toryism. The Catholics of Maryland and Pennsylvania gave almost unanimous support. The Quakers, Mennonites, and Moravians, "conscientious objectors" to active resistance, were evidently patriotic at heart. The Established Church was much divided, with a probable loyalist majority.

The Patriot party asserted that taxation without representation was tyranny, and refused to pay the taxes assessed. The Boston Massacre of 1770; the burning of the *Gaspee*, a British revenue vessel, in 1772; the organization of the Committees of Correspondences in 1773; the Boston Tea Party of 1773; the passing of four intolerable acts by Parliament in 1774 against Massachusetts; the Quebec Act of 1774; the Declaration of Rights adopted by the colonies in 1765 and in 1774, and forwarded to the King; the formation of a Union of Colonies by the First Continental Congress in 1774—all these show how the colonists and the British thought and felt towards each other. War was inevitable.

III. The American Churches and the Revolutionary War. —The churches in Colonial America must not be considered as foreign or imported. They became charter members of the American Republic by right of creation. The American Revolution was not only a political, it was also a religious revolution. Churches were active in arousing and informing public opinion, in stirring the people to united action; and when the war actually started, the churches willingly gave their lifeblood and their means to help rear the Temple of Liberty.

The *Established Church* was handicapped because the colonists looked upon it as the Church which had oppressed their fathers. Furthermore, its ministry had come from England and its congregations were largely sympathetic with the mother country. This was particularly true of the Anglicans in New England. In the middle colonies the lay sentiment was more divided, while in the southern colonies it was largely pro-American. George Washington, James Madison, John Marshall, Patrick Henry, and Alexander Hamilton were members of the Established Church; Bishop Perry claims[10] that two-thirds of the signers of the Declaration of Independence were members.

This Church had been too closely identified with aristocratic society to be a notable factor in the spiritual uplift of colonial life. In Virginia three-fourths of the people were outside the Established Church. Its failure to adapt itself to the new evangelical Christianity, rather than its political connections, caused this Church to approach extinction toward the close of the war. A drastic readjustment was essential. Two prominent members, William White and Samuel Seabury, Jr., took the lead, and by 1789 the Established Church had been completely re-organized, independent of state and of English church control, and with representative bodies composed of both clergy and laymen. The new organization, the Protestant Episcopal Church in the United States, was also infused with a more aggressive evangelical spirit.

The *Congregational* church was more influential than any other denomination. This was partly because the Puritan (Congregational and Presbyterian) clergy had been entrusted with political leadership as well as with moral and spiritual guidance. The pulpit reached the masses, informing and influencing public opinion, more than any other single agency in colonial times. Numerous Puritan sermons were published in pamphlet form by act of legislature, and distributed through the colonies.

After 1750, Puritan sermons were used for political instruction.[11] Standing squarely on their rights as Englishmen, the Puritan ministers defended the rights of resistance, urging their flocks to refuse submission to royal power when arbitrarily exerted. Following the doctrines of political liberty of Sidney, Milton, Locke,

[10] Sweet: *The Story of Religions in America*, p. 256.
[11] Politics and religion were not separated.

and Hoadly, the Puritan clergy developed the whole political philosophy of the American Revolution, as set forth in the preamble to the Declaration of Independence.

"We hold these truths to be self-evident—that all men are created equal; that they are endowed by their Creator with certain unalienable rights; that among these are life, liberty, and the pursuit of happiness. That, to secure these rights, governments are instituted among men, deriving their just powers from the consent of the governed; that, whenever any form of government becomes destructive of these ends, it is the right of the people to alter or abolish it, and to institute a new government, laying its foundation on such principles, and organizing its powers in such form, as to them shall seem most likely to effect their safety and happiness."

Due credit must be given to the dominant influence of Jonathan Edwards on public opinion regarding the questions of religious liberty and the separation of church and state. Imbued with Augustine's ideal of the *City of God*,[12] he asserted that the church was greater than the state, and in an entirely different sphere. State control over religion was impossible. Edwards, more than any other man, paved the way for the complete separation of church and state.[13] His influence, exerted indirectly, induced the colonists to oppose the encroachments of the Church of England upon their religious rights. Dr. Jonathan Mayhew, another Congregational minister, exerted a lesser but similar influence.

When war broke out, many Congregational ministers became "fighting parsons." Others enlisted volunteers and pecuniary and material support. The Congregationalists proved staunch friends of the colonies.

A similar testimony must be given to the *Presbyterians*. This group included all colonists of Presbyterian descent, the Huguenots, the Dutch Reformed, and the Scotch-Irish. The Presbyterians in New York, Virginia, and South Carolina had carried on a determined struggle with the Church of England and the Tory governors, a continuation of the Presbyterian-Episcopalian conflict carried on in the mother country since Oliver Cromwell.[13a] The Scotch-Irish Presbyterians of Virginia and North Carolina formulated a declaration of independence as early as Jan. 20, 1775.

[12] See pages 125-26.
[13] Credit must also be given to the Palatine Germans of New York and Pennsylvania, who eventually had much to say in getting the first amendment to the Constitution accepted under Muhlenberg, the first speaker of the House.
[13a] See pages 351-55.

Walpole made this characteristic statement in English Parliament, "Cousin America has run off with a Presbyterian parson."

The most influential Presbyterian leader was John Witherspoon (1722-1794), a well-known Scotch preacher who became the president of the College of New Jersey in 1768. He early won recognition as an educational and religious leader and as a man of public affairs. In 1776 he was elected a member of the Continental Congress, the only clergyman among the signers of the Declaration of Independence. He also signed the Articles of Confederation. William Livingston, the distinguished lawyer in New Jersey, was also a Presbyterian.

Presbyterian ministers and elders took an active part in the struggle. George Duffield, John Rodgers, James Caldwell, Alexander McWhorter, James F. Armstrong, Adam Boyd, and Daniel McCall were chaplains in the American army. Jacob Green, Henry Patillo, William Tennent, and John Murray were members of congress from New Jersey, North Carolina, South Carolina, and Massachusetts respectively. Prominent Presbyterian elders were General Morgan, General Pickens, Colonel Campbell, Colonel James Williams, Colonel Cleaveland, Colonel Shelby, Colonel Sevier, Colonel Bratton, Colonel Sumpter, and Major Dickson.

A slight pro-British sentiment was evidenced only among the German Reformed. Two ministers, John Michael Kern and John Joachim Zubly, and a few of their followers, were prominent loyalists.

The *American Lutherans* gave almost unanimous support to the cause. The ministers privately sounded the notes of freedom and fired their audiences to political and patriotic excitement. John Peter Gabriel Muhlenberg, a son of Henry Melchior Muhlenberg, is typical of the general attitude of the Lutheran clergy. Reverend Muhlenberg, who had formed a close friendship with George Washington, Richard Henry Lee, and Patrick Henry, was appointed colonel of the Eighth Virginia Regiment in December, 1775. In the middle of January, 1776, he preached his farewell sermon, concluding, "In the language of Holy Writ, there is a time for all things. There is a time to preach and a time to fight; and now is the time to fight." He pronounced the benediction; then, throwing back his clerical robe, he stood before them in the uniform of a continental officer. He then ordered the drums to beat at the church door for recruits. The next day he was off for war with three hundred of his frontier parishioners.

Muhlenberg's association with the dragoons during his three years study in Germany had aroused a militaristic spirit inherited from his grandfather, John Conrad Weiser. He showed military talent. General Lee said of his troops, "Muhlenberg's regiment was not only the most complete in the province, but, I believe, of the whole continent. It was not only the most complete in numbers, but the best armed, clothed and equipped for immediate service. His soldiers were alert, zealous, and spirited." In recognition of his services[14] he was elevated to the rank of Brigadier General in 1777, and in 1783 he was made a Major General. He never returned to the ministrations of the altar. At the close of the war he took up statesmanship, serving in several positions of honor.

His brother, Frederick Augustus Conrad Muhlenberg, also left the pulpit for service in the halls of legislation. He had had to leave his congregation in New York when the British came. He took a prominent part in affairs of state and nation, and had the distinction of being the first speaker of the lower house in the National Congress.[15]

The example of the Patriarch Muhlenberg and his sons did much to enlist the whole-hearted support of the Germans for the American cause. "In 1775 the vestries of the German Lutheran churches in Philadelphia sent a pamphlet of 40 pages to the Germans of New York and North Carolina stating that the Germans in and near Philadelphia and the remote parts of Pennsylvania had formed not only militia companies but a select corps of sharpshooters ready to march wherever they were required. Those who could not do military service were willing to contribute according to their abilities. . . . The Lutheran German newspaper, *Staatsbote,* printed by Henry Miller, later printer of Congress, March 19, 1776, printed an appeal to the Germans: 'Remember that your forefathers immigrated to America to escape bondage and to enjoy liberty.' In the convention held in Philadelphia, June and July, 1774, and January, 1775, Michael Hillegas, later the first treasurer of the United States, and Christopher Ludwig, were members of the Continental Congress."[16]

[14] Calvin Coolidge said in 1924: "Muhlenberg and his men from Pennsylvania and the Lutheran soldiers from Western Maryland, the Shenandoah Valley of Virginia, western North Carolina and South Carolina made glorious history for the patriot cause during the Revolutionary War."

[15] John Adams said of the Muhlenberg brothers, "These two Germans who had been long in public affairs and in high office, were the great leaders and oracles of the whole German interests in Pennsylvania and the neighboring states. The Muhlenbergs turned the whole body of Germans, great bodies of the Irish and many English, and in this manner introduced the total change that followed in both houses of the legislature and in all the executive departments of national Government" (*Lutheran World Almanac,* 1924-26, p. 7).

[16] *Lutheran World Almanac,* 1924-26, p. 57.

Among the officers under Washington were the Lutherans, Baron von Steuben,[17] the drill master and inspector general; Lutterloh, the quarter-master; Dr. Bodo Otto, from Old Trinity, Reading, the sergeant general; Christopher Ludwig, the baker general from Old Zion, Philadelphia; and Henry Venderslice, wagon-master of all teamsters and wagons of the continental army. Among the Lutheran officers were Kichlein, Shimer, Kiefer, Edelman, Righter, Eckert, Hain, Young, Wenrich, Spyker, Miller, Ernst, Lechner, Lesher, Weiser, Livingood, Zerbe, Seltzer, Brown, Knopp, and Boyer.[18] The German Fusiliers of Charleston and the German regiment of the Valley of Virginia were mainly Lutherans. The Lutheran Salzburgers organized three companies for active service. Christian Streit was one of the several Lutheran pastors who served as chaplain. The most prominent Lutheran layman was, perhaps, John Adams Treutlen, elected Governor of Georgia in 1777. As Governor, he successfully thwarted the encroachments of the British and the approaches of the loyalists in that region.

Only one Lutheran minister, Reverend Bernard Michael Hausihl (Hauseal), is known to have lined up with the British. He had succeeded Rev. J. A. Weygand as pastor of the Raritan congregations in New Jersey. His church was destroyed by fire in 1776, but the British Commander gave him permission to use the Presbyterian church. His services were attended by the Hessian troops, and when peace was concluded, he went to Nova Scotia where he joined the Episcopal church and served as chaplain in the garrison. The only regions where there was a slight pro-British sentiment were among Lutherans in Georgia and in a small Lutheran settlement in Maine.

The great majority of the American *Roman Catholics* ranged themselves on the side of the colonies. Wholehearted Catholic aid was given by the comparatively small body of Catholics residing in the colonies, by the Catholic Indians of Maine and of the old Northwest, by Catholic Canadian volunteers, and by French and Spanish allies.[19]

Numerous Catholic Volunteers joined the Army and the Navy. Pennsylvania sent Colonel Moylan and Captain Barry of the Navy, Colonel Doyle, and Captain Michael McGuire. Maryland contributed Neales, Boarmans, Brents, Semmers, Mattinglys, Brookes,

---

[17] The Steuben Society in New York keeps alive the memory of this good Lutheran.
[18] *Lutheran World Almanac*, 1924-26, p. 58.
[19] Guilday, *The Life and Times of John Carroll*, p.73.

and Kiltys.[20] Among the signers of the Declaration of Independence, the Articles of Confederation, or the Constitution, were three Catholics, Thomas Fitzsimmons, Daniel Carroll, and Charles Carroll of Carrollton.

But there were also, as the Catholic historian Peter Guilday has pointed out,[21] a number of Catholic Tories. "The Roman Catholic Regiment, recruited in Philadelphia, in 1777-1778, while General Howe and his officers occupied that city, was in command of Lieutenant Colonel Alfred Clinton, then a member of St. Mary's parish."[22] The Catholics were divided, as some of the Protestant groups were.

The French Alliance of 1778 and the friendly attitude of Spain brought numerous Catholic officers from Europe. "Catholic army officers like Lafayette, Kosciusko, du Portail, Gimat, Mottin de la Balme, Pulaski, Tronson du Coudray, navy officers like Dourville and Pierre Landais, were already in America aiding by their skill and experience the brave but untrained levies of the Continental Congress."[23] In 1780 the Catholic bishops and priests of France gave six million dollars to the new Republic.[24]

At the close of the Revolution the total number of Catholics in the United States was between nineteen and twenty-four thousand. Maryland had 15,000; Pennsylvania, 7,000; Virginia, 200; New York, 1,500; and the Mississippi Valley, an unascertainable number. There were only twenty-four Catholic priests in the entire land. These American Catholics had been under the jurisdiction of the Vicar Apostolic of London; but after the establishment of the American Independence, this was impracticable. A movement was therefore started to form an American Roman Catholic organization. The Reverend John Carroll was appointed Prefect Apostolic over the new organization in June, 1784, and dependency on British jurisdiction terminated. This was superseded by the appointment of Rev. Carroll as the first Roman Catholic Bishop, in 1789. Bishop Carroll, in charge of all Catholic interests, selected Baltimore as the first American See.

The American *Baptists* were strong supporters because they felt that failure would mean the failure of the struggle for religious freedom and separation of church and state. Numerous Baptist volunteers joined the army, while prominent Baptist leaders at home kept up a continual fight. The Warren Association, made up

[20] McSherry. *History of Maryland*, p. 379 f.
[21] Guilday, *The Life and Times of John Carroll*, p. 81.   [22] Guilday, *op. cit.*, p. 83.
[23] Shea, *Life and Times of the Most Rev. John Carroll*, Vol. II, p. 165.
[24] Guilday, *The Life and Times of John Carroll*, p. 84.

of Baptist churches in New England, was organized by Isaac Backus, President Manning of Rhode Island College, John Gano, Morgan Edwards, and other Baptist leaders. This organization presented the Baptist grievances to the First Continental Congress at Philadelphia, and to the provincial congress of Massachusetts. Prominent Baptist leaders in Virginia, John Leland, David Barrow, Lewis Connor, and others, organized a General Committee of Baptists in 1784 which was made up of not more than four delegates from each district association. This Committee exerted a powerful influence, and was partly responsible for the abolishment of religious inequalities. It was through this Committee that the Baptists sent an address to the newly elected President Washington, and his reply was an address to all Baptists in the United States.

The American *Methodists* were under constant suspicion during the early years of war, because they were still a part of the Church of England and, consequently, identified with the Tory Cause. Wesley stirred up a lot of hard feeling by issuing a *Calm Address to the American Colonies*, counselling submission to the King. But when the war began, he instructed the Methodist preachers in America to observe strict neutrality. All of his English-born preachers returned to England, save Francis Asbury who believed America would become a free and independent nation. All the native Methodist preachers, including Philip Gatch, Freeborn Garrettson, and William Watters, were in sympathy with the cause of liberty, although non-combatants from principle. Methodism recovered rapidly on the close of the war, and was one of the first religious groups to form a national organization.[25]

The *Quakers*, the *Mennonites*, and the *Moravians* were "conscientious objectors" or non-combatants from principle. These groups were much misunderstood because they were not only against war, but also seemingly against the new government. Consequently, these non-resistant groups suffered heavily. Opposition to a defensive war was not, however, unanimous among Quakers and Mennonites. Many Quakers and Mennonites were at least willing to pay the war tax, while a considerable number of Quakers actually joined the army. In consequence, all who had performed military duties were expelled from the regular Quaker Society. These "disowned" members organized a society known as Free Quakers.

IV. Decline in Moral and Religious Life.—In the years immediately after the Revolutionary War, moral and religious life

* See page 437.

touched its lowest ebb-tide. The various denominations had suffered severely. Churches had been destroyed, ministers and parishioners had been slain, congregations had been scattered, vital religion had been neglected and very few new ministers had been trained. Civil warfare between Patriots and Tories had fostered the growth of crime and immorality. Excessive debts threatened to wreck the Ship of State.

But the most paralyzing influence came from the wave of English Deism, French naturalism and atheism which swept over the entire world,[26] spreading hatred against the church, the ministers of the Gospel, and Christian institutions. Voltaire (1694-1778) had as his motto: "Crush the infamous thing," that is, the Church. Rousseau (d. 1778) maintained that the right to govern came not from God but from the people.

The alliance with France brought the spirit of the French Revolutionaries to America. Jacobin clubs and societies of "Illuminism" or Illuminati were organized throughout the land for the purpose of destroying Christianity. Infidelity and atheism became fashionable, especially among the American students and educated men. Princeton had only two students who professed to be Christians in 1782. Bowdoin had one. The Yale College church had but five such in 1783. William and Mary College was a hotbed of infidelity and scepticism. Among the middle and lower classes of the people an appalling religious and moral indifference prevailed. Atheistic literature circulated freely.

This serious religious and moral depression was soon followed, however, by a remarkable spiritual awakening. The "Second Awakening" started in the eastern states in 1797, and the "Great Revival" commenced west of the Alleghanies during the opening years of the nineteenth century.

57. REVIEW QUESTIONS

1. In what ways did the birth of the American Nation affect the principle of universal religious liberty? the relation between European and American churches? the relation between church and state?
2. Discuss the national origin of the colonists. Why were the English colonists so willing to sever relations with the mother country? And why would some "foreigners" advocate submission?
3. What was at the bottom of the struggle between England and America, commercialism, or religious liberty?
4. In what sense were the various denominations charter members of the United States?

[26] See pages 371-75, and diagram on page 356.

5. Discuss the status of the Established Church in the American colonies. Why was a re-organization necessary?
6. What influence did the Congregational and Presbyterian ministers exert?
7. What part did the American Lutherans play? Did they make it a religious issue? Explain.
8. Discuss the Roman Catholic support. Why did American Catholics form a national organization?
9. Why did the American Baptists give such wholehearted support?
10. What special difficulties confronted the American Methodists, the Quakers, the Mennonites, and the Moravians?
11. What readjustments followed the close of the war?

TOPICS FOR SPECIAL STUDY

1. The right of armed resistance, or, The Right of Defensive War.
2. Protestantism and democracy.
3. The difference in background of the European free churches and the American denominations.
4. The American Republic and universal religious liberty.
5. The use of the pulpit for political questions.

A SELECTED BIBLIOGRAPHY FOR CHAPTER XXII

1. Weigle: *American Idealism*, Vol. X, Chap. V.
2. Van Tyne: *The Causes of the War of Independence*, Vol. I.
3. Humphrey: *Nationalism and Religion in America, 1774-1789*.
4. Thornton: *The Pulpit and the American Revolution*.
5. Adams: *Revolutionary New England, 1691-1776*.
6. Baldwin: *The New England Clergy and the American Revolution*.
7. Cross: *The Anglican Episcopate and the American Colonies*.
8. Briggs: *American Presbyterianism, its Origin and Early History*.
9. Tucker: *Influence of Presbyterian Polity on Civil and Religious Liberty in Virginia*.
10. Wentz: *The Lutheran Church in American History*, Chaps. VI and VII.
11. Wentz, Sandt, Fortenbaugh, Horine & Kieffer: *Lutherans in Colonial Days*.
12. Shea: *History of the Catholic Church in the United States*, Vol. II, 1763-1815.
13. Guilday: *The Life and Times of John Carroll*.
14. Cathcart: *The Baptists and the American Revolution*.
15. Asbury: *Journal*, Vol. I, 1771-1778; Vol. II, 1179-1780.
16. Jones: *The Quakers in the American Colonies*.
17. Smith: *The Mennonites*.
18. Hamilton: *The Moravians*.
19. Jameson: *The American Revolution Considered as a Social Movement*.

CHAPTER XXIII

The Catholic Church in the National Era, 1789-1935

I. General Conditions.—The first sixty years of national American life were essentially a formative period. Not only were basic national policies formulated, but the nation expanded geographically to nearly four times its original size,[1] while population increased in like proportion.

Growth in Population in the United States of America.

1790	3,929,214
1800	5,308,483
1810	7,239,881
1820	9,638,453
1830	12,866,020
1840	17,069,453
1850	23,191,876
1860	31,443,321
1870	38,558,371
1880	50,155,783
1890	62,947,714
1900	75,994,575
1910	91,972,266
1920	105,710,620
1930	122,775,046

Agriculture was the chief livelihood in this period. The opening up of an almost inexhaustible supply of public land made the Americans a nation of landowners. In 1820, there were only thirteen cities of 8,000 inhabitants or over, and they contained but 4.9 per cent of the total population. Large numbers moved westward, while a steady stream of European immigrants landed yearly. The Frontier Line gradually extended from the Mississippi River westward, until it reached the Pacific Ocean.

With the return of good times in the East about 1820, the Westward Movement slowed up. The nation turned its attention to commerce and industry. Villages and towns sprang up, frequently proving the nuclei for future cities. By 1825 the plain life of the people was rapidly being colored by the more complex life of established urban society.

These rapid changes opened up tremendous possibilities for the American churches. The churches which best understood how to meet the needs of a rapidly changing society were destined to become the leading religious bodies.

[1] See map on page 452.

II. The Age of Trusteeism, 1789-1829.—The Roman Catholic membership has had phenomenal growth. From a mere handful in 1789—between 19,000 and 24,000—it had, in 1807, grown to 150,000, with 70 parishes and 80 churches; in 1820 the number

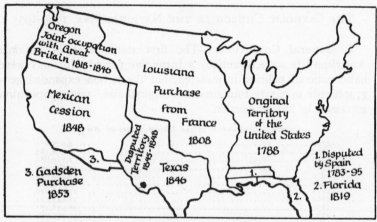

TERRITORIAL GROWTH OF CONTINENTAL U. S. A.
(Colonies listed below do not show on this map.)

1. Alaska	1867		5. Hawaiian Islands	1898
2. Philippine Islands	1898		6. Samoan Islands	1899
3. Guam Island	1898		7. Wake Island	1899
4. Porto Rico	1898			

had reached 244,500. John Gilmary Shea, Catholic church historian, shows the growth as follows:

1820	244,500	1860	3,000,000
1830	361,000	1870	4,685,000
1840	1,000,000	1880	7,067,000
1850	1,726,000	1890	10,627,000

In 1906, the Catholics numbered 12,079,142; and in 1929, the total was 20,112,758.

This rapid growth was due to immigration and superior church leadership. In earlier years the Irish and the Germans furnished the main quota of Catholic immigrants, but in later years the French-Canadians, the Poles, the Italians, the Mexicans, and various Southern Slavs, have added considerably to the number. Due credit must also be given to the remarkable vision and the capable leadership of the Catholic hierarchy in America. The quick adjustment of the Catholic Church to the growth of population may be seen from the dates of erection, and of elevation to metropolitan rank, of the seventeen archiepiscopal sees of the United States of America.

Baltimore became	a see in	1789,	an archdiocese in	1808
New Orleans "	" " "	1793	" " "	1850
New York "	" " "	1808	" " "	1850
Boston "	" " "	1808	" " "	1875
Philadelphia "	" " "	1808	" " "	1875
Cincinnati "	" " "	1821	" " "	1851
St. Louis "	" " "	1826	" " "	1847
Dubuque "	" " "	1837	" " "	1893
Chicago "	" " "	1843	" " "	1880
Milwaukee "	" " "	1843	" " "	1875
Oregon City "	" " "	1846	" " "	1850
St. Paul "	" " "	1850	" " "	1888
Santa Fé "	" " "	1850	" " "	1875
San Francisco "	" " "	1853	" " "	1853
San Antonio "	" " "	1874	" " "	1926

1. *The Episcopate of Carroll, 1790-1815.*—Much of the early success of Roman Catholicism was due to the wise, consecrated leadership of John Carroll, a native American and a member of the well-known Maryland Carrolls. Prior to this appointment as Bishop, the French hierarchy made a determined effort to subordinate the American Church to the French. This involved subjection to a French bishop residing in France, and the establishment of a French seminary to train priests for service in America.[2] The scheme failed because the American Congress refused to act in a matter of religion. Carroll, though not a candidate, was appointed Prefect Apostolic of the Catholic Church in 1784. He was consecrated in 1790, and appointed archbishop in 1808. Independent of the Old World, save the spiritual union with the Holy See, the Catholic Church of the United States inaugurated its organized life with a native American as its chief shepherd. This was significant because Carroll "saw America with American eyes and spoke of America in terms understood by the American people."[3]

a. *"Trusteeism."*—A problem engaging the attention of Carroll during his entire administration was the so-called Trustee System, which involved the spiritual authority of the bishop over the pastorates within his diocese, and also the method of holding Catholic church property. The trustees of certain Catholic congregations insisted that they had the right to choose and dismiss their own priests without interference by the bishop, and that they also could hold title to church property. The System, which originated in New York City in 1785, caused much disturbance also in Philadelphia, Baltimore, Norfolk and Charleston, S. C.

Carroll set himself resolutely against "trusteeism." He wrote to the Catholic congregation of the Barclay Street church in New

[2] Even Benjamin Franklin, American commissioner to France, favored this plan.
[3] Guilday: *The Life and Times of John Carroll*, p. 393.

York City, "If ever such principles should become predominant, the unity and catholicity of our Church would be at an end; and it would be formed into distinct and independent societies, nearly in the same manner as the Congregational Presbyterians. . . . I cannot tell what assistance the laws might give you; but allow me to say that you can make no step so fatal to that responsibility in which as a religious society you wish to stand, or more prejudicial to the Catholic cause."[4]

In 1798 Bishop Carroll won an important lawsuit, the Fromm Case, in a Pennsylvania court, receiving a verdict that every Catholic congregation was subject to his inspection, and without authority from the Bishop of Baltimore, no Catholic priest could exercise any pastoral functions over any congregation, nor enjoy the benefits of any church estates.[5]

Several churches, nevertheless, firmly resisted the authority of the bishops. The trustees of the congregations at Norfolk and Charleston, S. C., even thought of recurring to the Jansenistic bishops of Holland to effect their independence of Baltimore. Pope Pius VII condemned "trusteeism" as a pernicious and thoroughly un-Catholic system, but it took half a century before the Trustee System was completely vanquished and the present "corporation sole" system uniformly adopted. Under this system the entire property is held under the title of "The Roman Catholic (Arch) Bishop of ——." Roman Catholic church property in America is held officially, not personally, and passes automatically to the successors in the see.

The final defeat of "trusteeism" was largely due to the uncompromising stand of Archbishop Francis Patrick Kenrick of Philadelphia (1830-63), and Archbishop John Hughes of New York (1838-64).

b. *"Nationalism."*—Another problem confronting Carroll was "nationalism," or the attempt to divide the Catholic Church into independent groups based upon language and previous nationality. Carroll tried to avoid antagonisms occasioned by different nationalities, languages, and training, by incorporating the non-English speaking Catholics in the same churches with those thoroughly American. But foreign interference in American Catholic affairs, and rapidly increasing immigration soon threatened a division of his authority and jurisdiction.

The first organized effort to encroach upon his authority came

[4] O'Gorman: *A History of the Roman Catholic Church in the United States,* pp. 269-70.
[5] Shea, *The Life and Times of Archbishop Carroll,* Vol. II, p. 450.

from a group of *French colonists* in Ohio. They petitioned the Papal Nuncio in Paris to appoint a French bishop for their colony. In response, Dom Didier, a Benedictine monk of St. Maur, was appointed vicar general for seven years. Dom Didier settled in Gallipolis, and determined efforts were made to have Gallipolis established as a French Catholic bishopric. The scheme failed when it was discovered that the territory was within the jurisdiction of Bishop Carroll.

A similar Franco-American ecclesiastical scheme was the attempt to establish a French bishopric among the Oneida Indians in New York. The appellants asked for the elevation of Father Tonnelier de Coulonges as bishop. The Papal Nuncio would not, however, place the supplication before the Pope unless it was evident that the Oneida Indians were not within the Diocese of Baltimore or that of Quebec. The project was consequently dropped.

Irish intermeddling in the government of the Catholic Church in the United States caused Bishop Carroll considerable embarrassment. During the first quarter of the nineteenth century the Irish hierarchy succeeded in nominating, independently of Carroll and the American clergy, a number of Irish candidates for vacancies in various American bishoprics. Bishop Carroll kept up his determined and lifelong fight, however, for the independence of the American church from all "foreign entanglements" save the spiritual union with the Holy See, but he did not live to see the final outcome of the struggle. A plea to grant the American hierarchy the right to recommend suitable persons for vacancies in the episcopate received Papal sanction in 1821 during the administration of Ambrose Marechal, Archbishop of Baltimore.

Bishop Carroll determined to make the Catholic Church in America throb with American life; but the rapidly increasing immigration caused him, however, to deviate slightly from the general policy of extending the use of the English language as much as possible in the Catholic churches in the United States. In certain urgent cases he appointed clergy native to the various countries and familiar with the languages and customs of the groups concerned. The Germans in Philadelphia were among the first (1789) to benefit by this policy; but similar privileges were soon extended to the Irish, the French, and the Slavs.

c. *Educational Establishments.*—The American War of Independence had a disastrous effect on all types of schools in America. When the Diocese of Baltimore was formed, there were practically no opportunities for a higher education of Catholic young men in the United States, and no provisions had been made for the training of a native clergy in place of the older missionaries from Europe, mostly Jesuits, who were fast passing away. Bishop Carroll had included the establishment of a *Catholic college* which might at the same time be a seminary for future clergymen, in his *Plan of Organization* of 1782, but the plan did not materialize until 1791, when Georgetown College was founded. This school, which is the oldest and the greatest of all Catholic educational institutions in the United States, passed into the possession of the Jesuits in 1806. It was raised to the rank of a university in 1815.

As soon as Georgetown College had become a certainty, Bishop Carroll turned his attention to the problem of clerical training. The immediate difficulty was solved in a measure by the coming in 1791 of four priests of the Sulpician Congregation,[6] which had been disrupted by the French Revolution. Bishop Carroll induced these priests to found the St. Mary's Seminary at Baltimore in 1791. Thirty priests were ordained at this seminary during the episcopate of Carroll.

Among the other Catholic schools in existence in the United States during the episcopate of Carroll were (1) St. Rose's Dominican Seminary in Kentucky; (2) St. Mary's College at Baltimore, replaced by Loyola College in 1852; (3) Mount St. Mary's College at Emmitsburg, Maryland; (4) St. Thomas College in Kentucky; (5) The Ursuline Academy which is the oldest institution for the education of Catholic girls in the United States; (6) St. Joseph's Academy at Emmitsburg, directed by Mother Seton; (7) An orphan asylum for Catholic children was incorporated at Philadelphia in 1808; (8) Several private Catholic schools existed in the main centers of population.

Mother Elizabeth Ann Seton (1774-1821) may justly be said to have organized the Catholic *parochial school training* in the United States.[7] Born of non-Catholic parents, she was received into the Catholic Church in 1805. Her primary interest was in the care and education of children. With the approval of Archbishop Carroll, she organized the first teaching sisterhood in the United States, known as the Sisters of Charity. At the time of her death, more than twenty communities of this religious order had charge of free schools, orphanages, boarding-schools, and hospitals in various states.

[6] The Society of St. Sulpice was founded in France in 1642 for the single purpose of training young ecclesiastics in the seminaries in accordance with the decrees of the Council of Trent.
[7] Guilday, *The Life and Times of John Carroll*, p. 497.

Archbishop Carroll and other Catholic leaders of his time succeeded, therefore, in laying firmly and well the foundations of a school development which has been called "the greatest religious factor in the United States today," and is one of the main factors in retaining Catholic church membership.

d. *Division of the Diocese of Baltimore in 1808.*—When John Carroll took possession of the See of Baltimore in 1790, the exact geographical limits of his vast diocese were a bit uncertain, because the Bull concerned did not state definitely whether his jurisdiction comprised the Thirteen Original States only, or the whole territory claimed by the United States. The question was naturally referred to Rome for settlement, and a papal decree of 1791 made the Diocese of Baltimore coterminous with the United States of America.

The rapid Catholic growth soon made it imperative for Bishop Carroll to divide his episcopal labors with a younger man. He preferred a coadjutor-bishop and the consequent creation of a second episcopal see, but the Holy See favored the appointment of a coadjutor only because this arrangement might better preserve the unity of the Church. The matter was accordingly settled by the election of the first American coadjutor in 1793.

Geographical expansion of the United States and increased Catholic immigration soon made a division of the Diocese of Baltimore desirable. At the recommendation of Bishop Carroll and the American Catholic clergy, four new Catholic Episcopal Sees were created in the United States by a papal decree of 1808, and Baltimore was elevated to the first Metropolitan see in the new Republic. The four new bishoprics were New York, Philadelphia, Boston, and Bardstown (Kentucky). Prior to this event, in 1805, the Holy See had made Bishop Carroll Administrator Apostolic of Louisiana and the Floridas.

The four new bishops were consecrated in 1810, two years after their appointment, because of an unavoidable delay in the forwarding of the necessary documents from Rome. Archbishop Carroll was invested with the pallium on August 18, 1811. The bishops remained for several weeks after the consecration ceremony in 1810, in consultation with Archbishop Carroll, and together they drew up uniform rules of Catholic discipline in the United States. The resulting document, together with the rules and regulations adopted by the first diocesan synod in the United States as held in Bishop Carroll's house in Baltimore in 1791, forms the earliest code of canon law in the American Catholic Church.

e. *Establishment of Religious Orders.*—Religious Orders, Congregations, and Institutes are generally recognized as an integral part of Roman Catholicism. The primary purpose of these religious organizations is personal sanctification, but the members of the various religious Orders also seek to promote the moral and intellectual interests of humanity by taking a leading part in the extensively organized work of Christian charity, education and missions.

No Catholic religious Orders existed within the territory of what was then the United States, when John Carroll became Bishop of Baltimore in 1790. He was, of course, anxious to establish this important branch of Catholic life in the United States, but realized that the harsh conditions of American life of that epoch hardly warranted the successful founding of religious houses. Four Teaching Sisterhoods were founded, nevertheless, during his episcopate: the Ursulines, the Sisters of Charity in the United States, the Sisters of Charity of Nazareth, and the Sisters of Loreto at the Foot of the Cross. Religious Orders of women grew with giant strides once they had taken root in American soil. To-day there are nearly two hundred different congregations of nuns engaged in benevolent and educational work throughout the United States of America.

The attempts to establish religious Orders for men did not meet with much success during the episcopate of Carroll. Only two or three communities were able to continue. It was well toward the middle of the eighteenth century before the various religious houses for men enjoyed any marked development in the United States. To-day most of the Catholic secondary schools, colleges, and universities are conducted by the religious orders. Among the larger congregations of priests engaged in missionary and educational work are the Benedictines, the Dominicans, the Franciscans, the Jesuits, the Redemptorists, and the Vincentians. Among the smaller congregations are the Augustinians, the Carmelites, the Holy Cross Fathers, the Holy Ghost Fathers, the Josephites, the Oblates, the Marists, the Passionists, the Paulists, the Precious Blood Fathers, and the Premonstratensians.

A most important event in the history of American Catholicism was the restoration of the Society of Jesus in the United States in 1806. Eight years later, on August 7, 1814, the Jesuit Order was restored in full canonical form throughout the world by Pope Pius VII. Archbishop Carroll was himself a member of the Society of Jesus, and so was his successor, Archbishop Leonard Neale.

The Jesuits have made some remarkable conquests for Roman Catholicism since their restoration.

In concluding this discussion of the episcopate of John Carroll, it may be stated that his quarter of a century of leadership is related to the succeeding generations of American Catholics much the same as the Church in the age of the Apostles is to the Christian development in all succeeding centuries. He molded the divers elements in the United States into an organized church which became a faithful prototype of the American Catholic church of later generations. This fact justifies the rather copious space given to American Catholicism of 1789-1815 in the present chapter.

2. *The Province of Baltimore, 1815-29.*—a. *Leonard Neale, Second Archbishop of Baltimore, 1815-17.*—

Archbishop Carroll was succeeded by Leonard Neale, a native of Maryland. Though nearly seventy years old and precarious in health, he was remarkably firm, vigorous, and active in his mental powers. He established canonically a community of the Order of the Visitation of the Blessed Virgin Mary at Georgetown in 1817. The Trustee system caused him considerable trouble at Norfolk, Charleston, New York, and Baltimore, but he opposed the system with manly courage and constantly rejected it. He died in June, 1817.

b. *Ambrose Maréchal, Third Archbishop of Baltimore, 1817-28.*—

Ambrose Maréchal was a member of the Company of St. Sulpice. He was born in France, but came to America in 1792. During his administration the Diocese of Baltimore was strangely divided by authority of the Holy See, resulting in the creation of two new bishoprics, Richmond and Charleston. Furthermore, certain schismatic priests and Irish intermeddlers succeeded in having bishops appointed to Richmond, Charleston, New York, and Philadelphia without Archbishop Maréchal's knowledge or consent. These bishops were not only foreign to the country and strangers to the American clergy, but they were also bound by oath of allegiance to England, then at variance with the United States. While at Rome in 1821, the Archbishop finally obtained for the provincial bishops the right to recommend candidates for vacant bishoprics. In that same year the Cathedral which had been begun under Archbishop Carroll in 1806 was completed. In 1822 the first Catholic newspaper in the United States, "The United States Catholic Miscellany," was founded by Bishop John England. Archbishop Maréchal died in January, 1828.

c. *The First Provincial Council[8] of Baltimore in 1829.*—The year 1829 is generally accepted as a turning-point, not only in the history of American Catholicism, but also in the history of the United States. In that year the First Provincial Council of Balti-

[8] A provincial council includes all the bishops within the territory of an archbishop. A plenary or national council is an assembly of all the bishops of a country.

more was held, with Archbishop James Whitfield as the presiding officer. This council, which was attended by one archbishop and four suffragan bishops, had a unique importance for the Catholic Church in the United States because it legislated for practically the whole territory of the Republic, and furnished the norm for all succeeding provincial councils in America.

III. **From the First Provincial Council of Baltimore to the Establishment of the Apostolic Delegation, 1829-93.**— This was an epoch of rapid material growth and institutional expansion. How eager the American hierarchy was to adjust the existing church organization to the actual needs of the times may be inferred from the lists of provincial and plenary councils given below.

Provincial Councils held at Baltimore.

The First held in	1829.	Attended by	1	archbishop and	4	bishops				
The Second " "	1833.	"	"	1	"	"	9	"		
The Third " "	1837.	"	"	1	"	"	8	"		
The Fourth " "	1840.	"	"	1	"	"	12	"		
The Fifth " "	1843.	"	"	1	"	"	16	"		
The Sixth " "	1846.	"	"	1	"	"	22	"		
The Seventh " "	1849.	"	"	2	archbishops	"	23	"		
The Eighth " "	1855.	"	"	1	archbishop	"	7	"		
The Ninth " "	1858.	"	"	1	"	"	7	"		
The Tenth " "	1869.	"	"	1	"	"	12	"		

Plenary Councils held at Baltimore.

The First held in	1852.	Attended by	6	archbishops and	35	suffragan bishops.		
The Second " "	1866.	"	"	7	"	"	39	"
The Third " "	1884.	"	"	14	"	"	61	"

1. *The Period of Native Americanism, 1829-52.*—The growing strength of Roman Catholicism during the second quarter of the nineteenth century gave rise to strong counteracting tendencies which, in their organized form, became known as the Native American or Know-Nothing[9] movement. The advocates of Native Americanism accused the Catholics of being not only un-American but also anti-American, and urged "resistance to the aggressive policy and corrupting tendencies of the Roman Catholic Church." The Native American Party began in 1837 primarily as a crusade against unlimited immigration and lax naturalization laws. The party demanded that a residence of twenty-one years be made a condition for obtaining citizenship for all immigrants. In 1845 the party claimed a membership of 100,000. In 1850 it became a secret organization, "The Supreme Order of the Star-Spangled Banner," which later came to be known as the Know-Nothing party. This anti-Catholic movement resulted in a number of serious riots in various cities. The warlike preparations of Bishop John

Their common answer to inquiries was "I don't know."

Hughes of New York averted a general conflagration in that city. The movement was finally checked, and the excitement was brought to an end by the Civil War.

a. *James Whitfield, Fourth Archbishop of Baltimore, 1828-34.*—

The fourth Archbishop of Baltimore was an Englishman by birth. He was consecrated archbishop in May, 1828, and received the pallium on October 4, 1829, the day the First Provincial Council of Baltimore was opened. Being keenly aware of the practical needs of the Roman Catholic church under the rapidly changing conditions, Archbishop Whitfield called a synod in 1831 for the purpose of carrying out the Council's decrees. Two years later he called the Second Provincial Council of Baltimore. During his administration the dioceses of Mobile (1829), Detroit (1833), and Indianapolis (1834) were created. He died in September, 1834, and was succeeded by Samuel Eccleston.

b. *Samuel Eccleston, Fifth Archbishop of Baltimore, 1834-51.*—

Archbishop Eccleston was American born, being a native of Maryland and a member of the Order of St. Sulpice. Five provincial councils were held during his administration, and the following dioceses were created: Dubuque, Nashville, and Natchez in 1837; Chicago, Hartford, Little Rock, Milwaukee, and Pittsburgh in 1843; Oregon City in 1846; Albany, Buffalo, Cleveland, and Galveston in 1847; St. Paul, Santa Fé, Monterey, Los Angeles, Nesqually (Seattle), Savannah, and Wheeling in 1850. St. Louis became an archdiocese in 1847, and New York, New Orleans, and Oregon City were elevated into provinces in 1850. Cincinnati became an archdiocese in 1851. During Archbishop Eccleston's time a precedent was established by Rev. John Hickey by refusing to testify in court concerning stolen property restored through a penitent. Archbishop Eccleston died in April, 1851. He was succeeded by Francis Patrick Kenrick.

Prominent among the Catholic churchmen of this age were: Bishop Louis de Cheverus (1808-36), Bishop Benedict Joseph Flaget (1810-50), Bishop John England (1820-42), Bishop Joseph Rosati (1827-43), Bishop Pierre Loras (1837-58), Bishop Joseph Cretin (1851-57), Bishop Frederic Baraga (1853-68), Bishop John Neumann (1852-60), Archbishop Francis P. Kenrick (1830-63), Archbishop John Hughes (1838-64), Archbishop John B. Purcell (1833-83), Archbishop Martin J. Spalding (1850-72), and John Cardinal McCloskey (1844-85). During his twenty-five years of service as bishop and archbishop of New York, Dr. Hughes organized and built more than a hundred churches. He won the final victory over "trusteeism." He also founded St. Joseph's College and St. Joseph's Seminary at Fordham in 1841, and began the erection of St. Patrick's Cathedral in 1858.

c. *The First Plenary Council of Baltimore in 1852.*—An important event in the history of American Catholicism was the convening of the First Plenary Council at Baltimore in 1852. It was attended by six archbishops and thirty-five suffragan bishops. Archbishop Francis Patrick Kenrick of Baltimore presided as Apostolic Delegate. The assembled bishops "declared enactments of the seven Provincial Councils obligatory for all dioceses of the country, prescribed the Roman Ritual and the Baltimore Ceremonial,

and adopted various measures for parochial and diocesan government."

2. *From the First to the Second Plenary Council of Baltimore, 1852-66.*—a. *Francis Patrick Kenrick, Sixth Archbishop of Baltimore, 1851-63.*—

Francis Patrick Kenrick, a native of Ireland, was made Bishop of Philadelphia in 1830, and Archbishop of Baltimore in 1851. He presided over the First Plenary Council and over the Eighth and the Ninth Provincial Councils of Baltimore. At the request of the Ninth Provincial Council, held in 1858, the Holy See granted the primary rank in the American hierarchy to the incumbent of the metropolitan see of Baltimore. San Francisco became an archiepiscopal see in 1853. It fell to Archbishop Kenrick's lot to govern the Roman Catholic Church during the troubled days of the Civil War. He died in July, 1863.

b. *Martin John Spalding, Seventh Archbishop of Baltimore, 1864-72.*—

The seventh Archbishop of Baltimore was a native American. He became Bishop of Louisville in 1850, and Archbishop of Baltimore in 1864. Two years later he presided at the Second Plenary Council of Baltimore. The principal motives for holding this council were (1) to present to the country and to the world a striking proof of the strong bond of unity which held the Catholic Church together at a time when other religious groups suffered division; (2) to adjust the Catholic Church organization to the new phase of national life which the result of the Civil War had inaugurated; (3) to promote uniformity in church discipline; and (4) to discuss the future status of the Negro.

Archbishop Spalding also presided over the Tenth Provincial Council of Baltimore in 1869. He exhorted the bishops to establish missions and schools for Negroes of their dioceses. He was among the founders of the Catholic Publication Society, and among one of the first prelates to suggest the establishment of a Catholic university. At the Vatican Council[10] he favored the policy of defining the dogma of Papal Infallibility implicitly, rather than explicitly. He died in February, 1872.

3. *Preparations for the Establishment of the Apostolic Delegation, 1866-93.*—American Catholicism enjoyed a marvellous increase and a phenomenal progress during these twenty-seven years. In 1866, at the Second Plenary Council of Baltimore, there were but seven archiepiscopal sees and provinces, namely Baltimore, St. Louis, Oregon, Cincinnati, San Francisco, New Orleans, and New York. In 1893 the number had increased to fourteen. The dioceses of Philadelphia, Santa Fé, Boston, and Milwaukee became archdioceses in 1875. Chicago was raised to archiepiscopal dignity in 1880, St. Paul in 1888, and Dubuque in 1893. In this same period the dioceses increased from thirty-eight to seventy-three.

a. *James Roosevelt Bayley, Eighth Archbishop of Baltimore, 1872-77.*—

[10] See page 379.

Archbishop Bayley was a native of New York and a convert from the Protestant Episcopal Church. He was made Bishop of Newark in 1853, and Archbishop of Baltimore in 1872. A number of new sees were created during his administration, and a Catholic Bureau was established in Washington, D. C., to look after the interests of Catholic Indians. As Apostolic Delegate, he imposed the cardinal's biretta on Archbishop McCloskey of New York in 1875. Thus Archbishop McCloskey became the first American cardinal. Archbishop Bayley died in October, 1877.

b. *James Gibbons, Ninth Archbishop of Baltimore, 1877-1921.*—

Cardinal Gibbons, ninth Archbishop of Baltimore, is generally recognized as the greatest leader of the Roman Catholic Church in America. During his sixty years of clerical life, 1861-1921, he witnessed a tenfold increase in the membership of his church. He was the youngest bishop in attendance at the Vatican Council in 1870. The Knights of Columbus, a fraternal benefit society for Catholic men, was founded at New Haven, Conn., in 1882, by his sanction. Four years later he successfully defended the cause of the Knights of Labor, an organized labor association, which had been condemned by a Canadian cardinal. Cardinal Gibbons defended the organization by arguments so well conceived and unanswerable, that he assured the Catholic Church's official recognition of the right of labor to organize for the protection of its interests. He fought and defeated the so-called "Cahensly[11] movement" which sought to maintain distinct national groups among the foreign-born Catholics in America.

It fell to his lot, as Archbishop of Baltimore and as Apostolic Delegate, to prepare and preside over the Third Plenary Council, 1884. Its decrees, which were divided into twelve titles, were so comprehensive and practical, that they have ever since served as a regulative norm for the work of the Catholic Church in America. Much attention was given to the problems of educational policy. Plans were devised for the adequate training of candidates for the priesthood, and for the founding of a Catholic university. Title VI made obligatory upon priests and the people the establishment and maintenance of parochial schools for the education of Catholic children. A commission was appointed to prepare a catechism (*The Baltimore Catechism*) for general use.

The Catholic University of America was instituted in 1887, and the Archbishop of Baltimore was named, ex officio, the Chancellor. The Catholic University opened at Washington, D. C., in 1889. Three years prior to this event, in 1886, Archbishop Gibbons was raised to the Cardinalate. He thus became the second American cardinal.

c. *The Establishment of the Apostolic Delegation in 1893.*—The labors of the Third Plenary Council of Baltimore were crowned in 1893 by the establishment of an Apostolic delegation at Washington, D. C. This meant that the Pope sent a personal representative to the United States to provide for the unity of faith and for ecclesiastical discipline. By this act, the Catholic hierarchy in the United States was raised to the equality of that of any coun-

---

[11] This movement, which was led by Peter Cahensly, was particularly strong among the Germans.

try in the world.[12] From the beginning, all the incumbents of this office have been elevated to the cardinalate. Monsignor Francesco Satolli was the first Apostolic delegate to the United States. He was promoted to the cardinalate in 1895.

IV. From the Establishment of the Apostolic Delegation to the End of the World War, 1893-1918.—The Roman Catholic church kept well abreast with the developments in the United States during this epoch. Only a summary account of principal events will here be attempted.

1. *The American Protective Association.*—Henry T. Bowers founded a secret, proscriptive society in 1887, known as the American Protective Association (A.P.A.). Its members were bound by oath "at all times to endeavor to place the political positions of this government in the hands of Protestants." Lectures were arranged by "ex-priests" and much anti-Catholic literature was circulated. The movement reached its high tide in 1894, when seventy A.P.A. weeklies were in existence. Twenty members of the Fifty-fourth Congress (1895-97) were members of the order. Expressions of disapproval evoked from prominent men in public life caused the movement to lose its national influence by 1900 or shortly after.

2. *"Americanism."*—Toward the close of the nineteenth century a movement arose which sought to make converts for Catholicism by yielding to tendencies at variance with Catholic doctrine and practice. This movement, which was known as "Americanism," was condemned by Pope Leo XIII in 1899. He would not tolerate a Church in America different from that which was in the rest of the world.

3. *Formation of Catholic Societies and Associations.*—The American Federation of Catholic Societies was organized in Cincinnati in 1901. The Apostolic Mission House was founded in 1902. Its object is to prepare priests for mission work among Catholics and non-Catholics in city and rural parishes. The *Catholic Education Association* was organized at St. Louis in 1904 for the purpose of advancing the general interests of Catholic education. The *Catholic Church Extension Society* and its organ, the "Extension Magazine," were founded in 1905. The *Central Verein*, a German-American Catholic organization, established a Central Bureau in St. Louis in 1908, and started the publication of the *Centralblatt and Social Justice*, a sociological monthly in German and English. The *Holy Name Society* established National Head-

12 Up to this time it had been classed as missionary territory.

quarters in New York City in 1909. Nearly two million men are affiliated with this society. The *Jesuits* founded a national Catholic weekly review, *America*, in 1909. The *Catholic Foreign Mission Society* was founded in 1911. *Our Sunday Visitor*, a Catholic weekly, was founded in 1912.

4. *Prominent Churchmen.*—Besides Cardinal Gibbons, the following prelates came into national and international prominence: William O'Connell, who was made Bishop of Portland in 1905, Archbishop of Boston in 1908, and was created cardinal in 1911; George Mundelein, who was made Bishop of Brooklyn in 1909, Archbishop of Chicago in 1915, and cardinal in 1924; Patrick Hayes, who was Catholic chaplain bishop for the U. S. army and navy during the World War, Archbishop of New York since 1919, and cardinal since 1924; and John Farley who was made Archbishop of New York in 1902, and was elevated to the College of Cardinals in 1911.

5. *Activities during the World War.*—When the United States became involved in the World War, in the spring of 1917, the problem arose of caring for the moral and spiritual welfare of the Catholics enlisted in the army and the navy. The Chaplain's Aid Association was formed in New York in April, 1917, under the patronage of Cardinal Farley; and the Pope appointed Bishop, now Cardinal, Hayes as Chaplain Bishop of the United States forces.

The National Catholic War Council was organized in August, 1917, for the purpose of directing Catholic welfare work. The Council, which consisted of the fourteen Catholic archbishops of the United States, functioned through an Administrative Committee of four bishops. Under this Administrative Committee served two subordinate bodies, the Knights of Columbus and the Committee on Special War Activities.

V. American Catholicism Since the World War, 1918-33. —The events since the World War are too near for history. An attempt is here merely made to chronicle some of the more important happenings.

1. *The National Catholic Welfare Council.*—The work of the National Catholic War Council was perpetuated by an organization known as the National Catholic Welfare Council, formed in 1919. The name was changed in 1923 to the National Catholic Welfare Conference. This organization includes six departments, with a bishop at the head of each: the Executive Department, the Department of Education, the Press Department, the Social Action Department, the Legal Department, and the Department of Lay Or-

ganization, which is composed of two co-ordinate branches, the National Council of Catholic Men, and the National Council of Catholic Women. Eight different bureaus operate under the Executive Department. The Press Department supplies most of the Catholic newspapers in the United States and abroad with current news through its News Service. Pope Pius XI has praised the National Catholic Welfare Conference for its excellent service to Roman Catholicism.

2. *The International Eucharistic Congress in Chicago in 1926.* —The Twenty-eighth International Eucharistic Congress at Chicago, June 20-24, 1926, surpassed all its predecessors as a public demonstration of faith. It was the greatest religious gathering in point of attendance and splendor ever held in America. Its purpose was to glorify the Holy Eucharist. The Procession of the Blessed Eucharist, on the grounds of St. Mary of the Lakes Seminary at Mundelein, marked the climax of the Congress. Ozora S. Davis, a Protestant minister of Chicago, wrote: "The Roman Catholic church has been for centuries the incomparable mistress of pageantry and ceremonial; and every resource was drawn upon to the full to make the Congress the most splendid event possible. . . . In color, in symbolism, in stately march, in the timing of events, in dramatic effect realized by great groups acting in concert, it dwarfed any civic ceremony that ever had been seen by the hundreds of thousands of spectators. One was swept off his feet by the overwhelming effect of procession, song, and stately ritual which were charged with the deepest and most sacred symbolism. The spectator might not assent at all to the dogmatic implications of the scenes; but he could not remain unmoved by the artistic beauty of the spectacle."[13]

3. *San Antonio, Texas, becomes an Archdiocese in 1926.*—From 1893 to 1926 the Roman Catholic Church in the United States had fourteen archbishops. The elevation of San Antonio, Texas, to an archdiocese in 1926 raised the number to fifteen. The present organization of the American Catholic Church includes an Apostolic Delegate, fifteen archbishops, of whom four are cardinals, ninety-nine bishops, and 25,000 priests.

4. *The Sixth National Eucharistic Congress of 1930.*—This Congress, which was held September 23-25, 1930, at Omaha, Nebraska, was attended by delegates from every state in the Union. The Apostolic Delegate, Monsignor Fumasoni-Biondi presided.

[13] *The Outlook*, July 7, 1926.

Twenty-five thousand men, women, and children took part in the closing ceremonies.

5. *Recent Messages from Pope Pius XI.*—His *Encyclical on Christian Marriage,* issued on January 8, 1930, aroused universal interest. He addressed himself, not only to Roman Catholics, but to the whole human race.

On the occasion of the ninth anniversary of his coronation, February 12, 1931, Pope Pius XI inaugurated the Vatican City Radio Station HVJ (Holy See-Vatican-Jesus), by delivering a radio message to the world. He spoke in Latin for fifteen minutes, and the address was relayed by the greatest number of stations all over the world ever assembled for a single event.

His Encyclical of May 23, 1931, explained the official Roman Catholic attitude toward social and economic reform, and upheld the rights of organized labor. "It is absolutely necessary to reconstruct the whole economic system by bringing it back to the requirements of social justice, so as to insure a more equitable distribution of the united proceeds of capital and labor." He censures Socialism and Communism most severely.

On Christmas Day, 1931, Pope Pius XI issued the Encyclical called *Lux Veritatis,* "The Light of Truth," in which he made a plea for the reunion of Christendom. On October 2, 1931, he invited "all men of good will to unite in holy crusade of love and succor, in order to alleviate the terrible consequences of the economic crisis." The Pope issued a second appeal on May 18, 1932.

In conformity with a recent campaign for the reform of church observances in Rome, and for the simplicity of lives in church institutions, Pope Pius XI issued a ban on all fanatical mysticism, on November 2, 1932. The Pope has determined that the Church shall be a healthy vehicle of Christian operation in the world, and that the old idea of fanaticism and isolation shall be put aside.

On January 6, the epiphany of our Lord, in the year 1933, a papal bull called *Quod Nuper* set aside the twelve months beginning April 2 as a holy year of prayer, penance, and pilgrimage to Rome and Palestine. Declaring that the "plenary indulgence be obtained in this jubilee year only in Rome," the document urged pilgrims to "come in very large numbers." The Quod Nuper declares in part: "To all the faithful of both sexes who during this holy year, having confessed and communicated, either on the same day or on different days and in whatsoever order visit piously three times the basilica of St. John Lateran, St. Peter in Vatican, St.

Paul on Via Ostiense and St. Mary Major on the Esquiline hill, and pray according to our intention, we concede and impart mercifully in the Lord a plenary indulgence for all the punishment they must suffer for their sins of which these faithful shall have first obtained the remission and pardon. And we hereby notify the faithful that as soon as they have left the basilica after their holy visit they can immediately enter anew the same basilica to fulfil the second and third visit. This we establish to render the fulfillment of this condition more convenient.

"We further decree that this jubilee indulgence can apply both to one's self and for benefit of the defunct faithful each time that the prescribed works are faithfully executed." Then follows some interesting and detailed instructions to the pilgrims. The bull is issued according to canon 923.

Mexico has been the scene of considerable anti-Catholic propaganda in recent years. The establishment of the Republic of Mexico in 1810 in complete independence from Spain, furnished an opportunity for an anti-Catholic party to gain control over the government of the new Republic. The Constitution of 1857 decreed separation of church and state, and placed severe restrictions on the church. These laws, which were not strictly enforced, were revived in the new Constitution of 1917, and additional drastic measures were sanctioned by the Mexican Government. Places of public worship were declared the property of the state, and federal and state authorities were given powers to regulate the affairs of the church. President Calles put these laws in force in 1927, and much disturbance resulted. Emilio Portes Gil, successor of Calles, allowed certain modifications of these anti-Catholic laws in an agreement secured by the Apostolic Delegate in July, 1929. Due credit must also be given to the late Dwight Morrow, U. S. Ambassador to Mexico, for the termination of the Mexican persecution.

58. REVIEW QUESTIONS

1. What privileges and responsibilities did the powerful Westward Movement furnish the American churches during the first five decades of the National Period?
2. Why does the Roman Catholic Church constitute the largest religious group in America to-day?
3. Why should a history of American Catholicism take so much account of the episcopate of John Carroll?
4. How do you account for the intermeddling of the French and the Irish in the affairs of the national Catholic Church in America?
5. What is meant by "trusteeism"? Why was this system suppressed? By whom?

6. Explain the problem of "nationalism" in the Catholic Church. Why was this movement suppressed?
7. Discuss the early Catholic educational establishments. Who organized the Catholic parochial school training in the United States?
8. What causes promoted a division of the Diocese of Baltimore in 1808?
9. Under what circumstances was the earliest code of canon law formed in the American Catholic Church?
10. Why was Archbishop Carroll so anxious to establish religious Orders, Congregations, and Institutes in the United States?
11. What unique importance did the early provincial councils of Baltimore have for the Catholic Church in the United States?
12. What is meant by Native Americanism or Know-Nothingism?
13. Discuss the First Plenary Council of Baltimore. What place does such a council have in Roman Catholic church affairs?
14. How do you account for the phenomenal growth of the Catholic Church in America from 1866-1893?
15. What attitude did Cardinal Gibbons cause the Catholic Church to take toward the rights of organized labor?
16. Discuss the significance of the establishment of the Apostolic Delegation at Washington, D. C. What are the precise functions of this office?
17. What specified opposition did the Roman Catholic Church in the United States meet with toward the close of the nineteenth century?
18. Discuss some of the outstanding events in the history of American Catholicism since the World War. What is the present organization of the American Catholic Church?

TOPICS FOR SPECIAL STUDY

1. The Catholic School System in the United States of America.
2. The Society of Jesus in North America.
3. The Archbishops of Baltimore.
4. Religious Orders, Congregations, and Institutes in the United States.
5. Roman Catholics and Organized Labor.
6. Mother Elizabeth Ann Seton and the Catholic Parochial School.

A SELECTED BIBLIOGRAPHY FOR CHAPTER XXIII

1. Guilday: *The Life and Times of John Carroll.*
2. O'Gorman: *A History of the Roman Catholic Church in the United States.*
3. Gibbons: *A Retrospect of Fifty Years.*
4. *Catholic Builders of the Nation* (5 vols.).
5. Burns: *The Catholic School System in the United States.*
6. Hughes: *History of the Society of Jesus in North America, Colonial and Federal.*
7. Clarke: *Lives of Deceased Bishops of the Catholic Church in the United States.*
8. Griffin: *American Catholic Historical Researches* (29 vols.).
9. McMaster: *History of the People of the United States.*
10. *Official Catholic Year Book* for 1928.
11. Garrison: *Catholicism and the American Mind.*
12. Moehiman: *The Catholic-Protestant Mind.*
13. Shaughnessy: *Has the Immigrant Lost the Faith?*
14. Kinsman: *Americanism and Catholicism.*
15. McNamara: *American Democracy and Catholic Doctrine.*
16. Shuster: *The Catholic Spirit in America.*
17. Ryan: *The Catholic Church and the Citizen.*

CHAPTER XXIV

GENERAL SURVEY OF AMERICAN PROTESTANTISM[1]

The history of American churches should be studied, not only in connection with their European backgrounds, but also in their relation to American Protestantism as a whole. The European background has already been presented. An attempt will now be made to give a brief survey of American Protestantism in the National Era, including the general epochs of its history, its general lines of development, and its general characteristics.

After this survey has been made, the history of the individual Protestant denominations will be given in the same order as that of the corresponding groups in Europe.

I. Four Main Periods.—American Protestantism after 1789 may conveniently be divided into four periods coinciding with

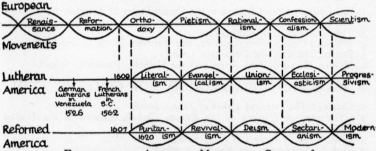

EUROPEAN AND AMERICAN MOVEMENTS COMPARED[2]

European church history, although some American movements occur a little later than the European.

In the period from 1789 to 1830 American churches experienced a general religious awakening which brought fresh life and checked the current infidelity. The "Second Awakening," and the "Great Revival," stimulated missionary effort, and led to the founding of Christian academies, colleges, and theological seminaries.

The next period, 1830-70, terminated in the Civil War and the split of the larger Protestant churches into northern and southern

---

[1] This survey of American Protestantism, including the general periods of its history, its general lines of development, and its general characteristics, may be omitted from the assignment, if the class is pressed for time.

[2] Suggested in part by Dr. O. M. Norlie. Cf. diagram on p. 356. For information regarding Lutherans in Venezuela, see footnote on page 415.

bodies. The Methodists divided in 1844, the Baptists in 1845, the New School Presbyterians in 1858, the Old School Presbyterians in 1861, and the Lutherans in 1863.

Many efforts were made during the next period, 1870-1918, to restore the relations between North and South interrupted by the Civil War. Church life became less revivalistic and individualistic, and more churchly and confessional. The churches founded their organizations on creeds, rather than on institutions. Materialism gained considerable ground.

The most important contribution since the World War has been the generous material relief given to poverty-stricken countries throughout the world. This relief work led to greater inter-denominational co-operation which has often led to organic church unity. People have come to see the need of making existing church organizations more solid and comprehensive. Efforts have been made to make church services more impressive and appealing by developing a greater wealth of forms with more fullness of ceremonial beauty. A controversy between "Fundamentalists" and "Modernists" has been in progress since 1921-22, but the main current of religious and theological thinking has followed a mediary course.

II. General Lines of Development.—American Protestantism has followed five main lines of development which will now be briefly considered.

The Revivalistic School.—The basic element in Anglo-American religious life has been, and is perhaps still, Calvinistic Puritanism as formulated and presented by Jonathan Edwards (1703-58) and his nephew, Timothy Dwight (1752-1817), President of Yale University. From Edwards, Whitefield, and Dwight, this type was reproduced and perpetuated in true Methodistic fashion by successive waves of revival that have swept through the land at intervals almost down to the present time. The Moody-Sankey revival in the 'seventies is, perhaps the greatest in the history of the Christian Church.

Charles Finney introduced the method of bringing all troubled souls up to the "anxious bench."[3] His method was later copied by the Salvation Army. Finney and his associates, Asa Maham and Thomas Upham, inaugurated the great *American Holiness Movement* which has exerted a considerable influence here, as well as in Europe. The essentials of this movement are a definite conversion preceded by severe spiritual struggles, a baptism with the Holy

---

[3] Also called the "mourner's bench" and the penitential bench.

Spirit, and the attainableness of complete holiness and Christian perfection in the present life.

The Liberal School.—In marked contrast to the American Holiness Movement and its "twice-born" adherents is the Modernistic Movement and its "once-born" adherents. The former asserts the depravity of human nature and the need of a new spiritual birth; the latter asserts that human nature is essentially good and that salvation is insured by developing the good in man. The Liberals, with the Unitarians as their main representatives, have exerted a considerable influence, especially since they gained possession of Harvard University. Among the prominent leaders were William Channing (1780-1842), Theodore Parker (1810-60), Ralph Waldo Emerson (1803-82), Henry Wadsworth Longfellow (1807-82), Charles W. Eliot (1834-1926), and William H. Taft, President of the United States, 1908-12.

The Broad-churchly School.—The effort to combine the best elements in the two schools of theological thinking, and the endeavor to smooth out differences without surrender to either group, resulted in the American Broad-church Movement. Its leading advocate was Horace Bushnell (1802-76), who was strongly influenced by Schleiermacher[4] and Coleridge. Bushnell endeavored to combine personal religion with freedom and culture. He strongly criticized the non-liturgical churches for reliance upon the emotional experience of conversion. As a warm friend of Finney, he sanctioned revivals, but only as an accidental form. The family and the church should rather insist on a systematic Christian education of the young. Let the child "grow up a Christian and never know himself as being otherwise."

Phillips Brooks (1835-93), rector of Trinity Church of Boston, and Protestant Episcopal Bishop of Massachusetts from 1891, was the other great representative. His central message was that *all men are the children of God.* Man is a child of God on which the devil has laid his hand, and not a child of the devil that God tries to steal. Brooks was the successor of Henry Ward Beecher as the first among American preachers. He described the work of preaching as "the bringing of truth through personality." His church in Boston took a leading part in the Movement for Christian Unity.

The Conservative-Evangelical School.—Strong emphasis on the historic creeds of the Protestant Reformation, coupled with a deep spirituality and an attempt to develop out of the Scriptures a new confessional theology, resulted in a strong conservative-Evangelical

---

[4] See pages 390-92.

school of religious and theological thinking. This school has been imbued with that same conviction of sin and grace, and that same submission to the authority of Scriptures that characterized the Protestant Reformers. Adherents believe in the "twice-born" nature of the Christian and in the consequent need of spiritual regeneration. Much attention is given to a quiet, systematic Christian education of the young. The conservative-evangelical group has generally resisted the prevailing spirit of confessional indifference and the growing feeling that one type of Christianity is as valid and as true as another.

Prominent leaders were Henry M. Muhlenberg and Carl F. W. Walther. Muhlenberg was trained in the school of German Pietism in its best days. He counteracted Zinzendorf's spirit of confessional indifferentism[5] and organized the Lutheran Church on a strictly confessional basis. Walther, the great leader of the Missouri Synod, laid great stress on "pure doctrine" and required strict adherence, not only to the Augsburg Confession, but also to the other symbolical books associated with it, as "the pure and uncorrupted explanation and statement of the Divine Word." He urged all affiliated congregations to establish parochial schools.

The Apocalyptic-Spiritualistic School.—The Napoleonic wars greatly stimulated religious speculations concerning "the last things" and the unseen world. These speculations, coupled with American frontier conditions, gave rise to a sensational type of religion that still exerts a considerable influence. People living lonely, monotonous lives welcomed the excitement, the thrills, and the social contacts furnished by the camp-meetings. Untutored and naive minds showed great receptivity for the strange, the bizarre, and the abnormal in religion.

William Miller (1782-1849) intiated the Apocalyptic or Adventist Movement by his prophecies concerning the end of the world. Miller, a veteran of the War of 1812, was a Baptist. In 1831 he began to lecture on the Second Coming of the Lord, predicting "that Christ would appear a second time in the clouds of heaven some time between 1843 and 1844." The meteoric shower[6] of November 13, 1833, and the great comet of March and April, 1843, led many to become converts. He endeavored to gather all his followers into an inter-denominational association without renounc-

---

[5] See page 429.
[6] Professor Olmsted of Yale University describes this meteoric shower as "probably the greatest display of celestial fireworks that has ever been seen within the annals covered by the pages of history."

ing their church membership, but his converts were soon expelled from the Baptist group and from other denominations because of their harsh judgment of those who did not sanction their views. The expelled Millerites organized what are commonly known as Adventists. They have adopted many apocalyptic ideas. One group, the Seventh Day Adventists, rests on Saturday and abstains from flesh, tobacco, and alcohol.

Charles Russel, an American business man, took great interest in apocalyptic speculations about 1870. He later organized what is known as Russelism,[7] which represents Adventism in caricature. He predicted that the overthrow of Christendom and all present governments would take place in 1914. Russel died in 1916 and was succeeded by Judge Rutherford. Russelism holds the following opinions: (1) Every organized civil government is "Satan's[8] organization." (2) The doctrine of Holy Trinity is "horrid[9] blasphemy." (3) Jesus was not begotten of the Father from eternity; he was merely the highest of God's "creation." (4) Before he was born of Mary he existed as the angel Michael, and when he was born, he gave up his spirit being and became nothing but a human being, "a perfect man, nothing more, nothing less." (5) The body of Christ was not raised from the grave. "The man Jesus must remain dead forever." But out of non-existence God raised up a new Christ, a "spirit being," who is neither God nor man. (6) Christ is not our advocate with the Father, and to worship Christ is pure idolatry.[10]

Alexander Campbell (1788-1866), a Presbyterian minister, advocated a simple literal Biblicism. While waiting for the Second Coming of the Lord, he endeavored to rally certain groups around the Word of God, adult baptism, and faith in Jesus Christ, without subscribing to any particular creed. His aim was to rid Christendom of sects and divisive creeds, but succeeded only in establishing an additional denomination known as the Disciples of Christ. This group, having since supressed the apocalyptic element, has yielded

[7] The organization has also been known as "Tower Publishing Company," later "The Watch Tower Bible and Tract Society," and lately as "The International Bible Students' Association."

[8] The word "world" in 2 Cor. 4:3-4 is wrongly interpreted to mean "organized government." Rutherford in his book *Deliverance*, pages 43 and 200, states: "Within the meaning of the Scriptures the word "world" signifies the people of this earth organized into forms of government under the supervision of their overlord, Satan the enemy."

[9] Russel called this doctrine "Trinitarian nonsense," and Rutherford in his book *Reconciliation*, page 101, says: "Never was there a more deceptive doctrine advanced than that of the Trinity. It could have originated only in one mind, and that the mind of Satan the Devil."

[10] In his book *Reconciliation*, page 92, Rutherford states: "The theory taught by some of the clergy that Jesus Christ, the Son of God, has been appealing to the Father for mercy and forbearance is entirely wrong."

to a rationalistic tendency. It is now the sixth largest Protestant body.

The Apocalyptic-Spiritualistic Movement also led to the formation of sects distinctly outside the ordinary limits of the Christian religion. Among these are the Mormons (or the Church of Jesus Christ of Latter-Day Saints), the Christian Scientists, the Spiritists, and certain groups of theosophists.

III. Characteristics of American Christianity.—The early development of the Americas was largely a transplantation of European culture and religion, but American life was more than a mere reproduction. In the unconventional atmosphere of the New World, European culture and religion generated new life, new forms, and new ideals for the enrichment of mankind. The final religious product was an Americanized form of Christianity with its own characteristic forms.

What are the characteristics of American Christianity? To the casual observer it may seem almost hopelessly divided. Not only have the religious tendencies, antagonisms, and prejudices of Europe been transplanted to America, but the United States has also proved a fertile field for additional religious divisions. Closer examination shows that this extraordinary variety of religious life has taken on certain characteristics more or less common to all denominations.

Americanization.—The institutions of the Western World have passed through the process of becoming Americanized. Among the formative elements are the unconventional atmosphere, full religious freedom, and separation of Church and State. Unhampered by the limitations of a standardizing tradition, and unhindered by dictation or opposition from the State, the self-governing and self-supporting churches have been free to develop all of their inner strength. There has developed a democratic form of church organization and an intensely practical, business-like way of doing church-work. This practical tendency, clearly reflected in religious and theological literature, has resulted in the so-called American pragmatism,[11] and the study of Religious Psychology as introduced by William James of Harvard University. A remarkable optimism, expressed in the *never give up* slogan, has characterized American Christianity. The American churches have given much attention to social service.

The Voluntary Principle.—Americans, unlike Europeans, have no legal disabilities attached to lack of church connection. American

---

[11] Pragmatism is the doctrine that personal experience is the sole test of truth.

church-membership is based on the voluntary principle, and all churches concerned must hold their members by their own strength. America has, therefore, a smaller percentage of nominal Christians than any other Christian country. About fifty-five per cent of the people are not church members.[12]

The Democratic Principle.—There is usually, in any country, a close relation between the political and the religious forms of government, and the United States is no exception. Practically all churches have modelled their organizations after the American form of government. American lay people have been given an opportunity to take a direct part in the government of their particular denomination, as well as in the government of the local congregation. The democratic atmosphere has tended to produce non-liturgical church services; and the American pastor has, in true democratic fashion, become the *primus inter pares*, or the first among equals.

Protestant Individualism.—Practically all the early settlers were imbued with the Protestant ideal of individual judgment and individual responsibility for salvation, as opposed to the Roman Catholic theory of collective judgment and collective responsibility. The authority of the Bible replaced the Catholic authority of the Church. This individualism resulted in the founding of the American church-organizations—not on institutions—but on creeds, in a thoroughly denominationalized Protestantism. Religious factions within a single state-church in Europe were usually prepetuated in America as separate denominations. All of the forty-two denominations transplanted from Europe persisted as distinct divisions in America, and became the parent stems from which branched all the denominations in America, save the Mormons and the Christian Scientists.

Tendencies Toward Religious Uniformity.—America has, strange though it seems, become a land of religious unification as well as a land of many religious divisions. The lines between some denominations are so vague that Christians find it comparatively easy to pass from one church to another. A persistent levelling process has resulted in the formation of an American type of Christianity that differs from the historic forms of Protestantism. This levelling process is characterized by a spirit of confessional indifference, an extensive inter-denominational co-operation, and a general effort to adjust existing church-organizations to correspond to American ideas.

[12] The population of the United States is 122,775,046, according to the 1930 census. The number of church members is 54,576,346, according to the 1926 census of Religious bodies. Hence 68,198,700 are not members of any church. In one generation, from 1900-1933, the total church membership in the United States has gained 82.8 per cent, while the increase in the total population in the same period has been only 65.8 per cent.

The Practical Tendency.—The conquest of the American Continent had so much to do with the material side of existence that the pioneers became intensely practical in their methods of propaganda and promotion. Interest in practical life proved so absorbing that little attention could be given to theoretical and intellectual problems or progressive thought.

IV. The Larger Religious Bodies in the United States in 1934.[13]

Name	Total Population	Adult Population (over 13 years)
Catholics, Western (3 bodies).......	20,398,509	14,646,129
Baptists (18 bodies)...............	10,027,929	9,381,129
Methodists (19 bodies).............	8,976,492	8,100,208
Lutherans (17 bodies).............	4,482,212	3,211,225
Jewish Congregations[14]............	4,081,242	2,930,332
Presbyterians (9 bodies)............	2,696,639	2,558,365
Protestant Episcopal Church........	1,898,549	1,401,129
Disciples of Christ.................	1,596,054	1,482,734
Congr. and Christian Churches......	1,020,894	993,330
Catholics, Eastern (9 bodies)........	988,440	788,364
Evangelical and Reformed..........	914,377	689,945
Latter-day Saints (2 bodies)........	747,320	591,143
Churches of Christ.................	433,714	433,714
United Brethren (3 bodies).........	424,839	386,456
Reformed (3 bodies)...............	284,481	242,632
Evangelical (2 bodies).............	256,533	235,307
Salvation Army....................	252,100	103,623
Intl. Church of Four Square Gospel..	250,000	212,423
Church of Christ, Scientist.........	202,098	202,098
Church of God in Christ...........	200,470	190,470
Brethren (5 bodies)................	190,617	178,064
Adventists (5 bodies)..............	183,992	182,777
Assemblies of God.................	158,908	142,540
Polish Natl. Catholic Church.......	150,000	103,500
Church of the Nazarene............	119,907	113,672
Mennonites (16 bodies plus)........	109,919	107,935
Friends (4 bodies).................	107,476	90,396
Church of Armenia in America......	100,000	91,000

59. REVIEW QUESTIONS

1. Why should the history of each of the American churches be studied, not only in connection with their European background, but also in their relation to American Protestantism as a whole?
2. How would you characterize American Protestantism before 1789?
3. What characterized the four periods: (a) 1789-1830; (b) 1830-70; (c) 1870-1918; (d) 1918-35?
4. Why the Fundamentalist-Modernist Controversy?
5. What lines of development has American Protestantism generally followed?

[13] Based on the *Christian Herald* for July, 1934.
[14] The Jewish Congregations are not, of course, numbered among Protestant churches.

6. What characterized the Revivalistic School and the American Holiness Movement?
7. In what ways does the Liberal School differ from the Revivalistic?
8. What does the Broad-churchly School stand for?
9. What characterized the Conservative-Evangelistic School?
10. What groups belong to the Apocalyptic-Spiritualistic School? Why?
11. What are the characteristics of American Christianity?
12. Can you name *in order* the religious bodies in the U. S. A. that each has an adult membership of 100,000 or over?

TOPICS FOR SPECIAL STUDY

1. Calvinistic Puritanism in American Life.
2. Lutheranism in American Life.
3. Liberal forces in American church life.
4. Apocalyptic-Spritualistic movements in America.
5. American sects outside the ordinary limits of Christianity.

A SELECTIVE BIBLOGRAPHY FOR CHAPTER XXIV

1. Beard: *The Rise of American Civilization.*
2. Sweet: *Our American Churches.*
3. Hargraves: *Community Religion and the Denominational Heritage.*
4. Phelan: *The New Handbook of All Denominations.* (6th ed.)
5. Frey: *The United States Looks at Its Churches.*
6. Weigle: *American Idealism.*
7. Sweet: *The Story of Religions in America.*
8. Cheyney: *European Background of American History, 1300-1600.*
9. Hall: *The Religious Background of American Culture.*
10. Thompson: *The Religious Foundations of America.*
11. Eggleston: *Beginnings of a Nation.*
12. Parrington: *The Colonial Mind.*
13. Wertenbaker: *The First Americans, 1609-1690.*
14. Schneider: *The Puritan Mind.*
15. Roosevelt: *The Winning of the West.* (4 vols.)
16. Elsbree: *The Rise of the Missionary Spirit in America, 1790-1815.*

CHAPTER XXV

The Lutheran Church in the National Era, 1789-1936

I. Nationalization of the American Lutheran Church, 1789-1830.—American Lutheran history before 1830 is almost entirely a history of German Lutheran congregations and synods. Quickened by the general religious awakening, the Lutherans kept pace with the growth of the country up to 1830, while in the next generation, 1830-1870, the Lutheran population increased three times as rapidly as the general population of the country. Influenced by the Prussian Union[1] of 1817, the Lutherans tried to unite their independent synods into a national synod (General Synod), but unexpected opposition caused the most influential groups to withdraw from the General Synod[2] for a number of years. Certain differences resulted in the formation of three Lutheran groups which respectively promoted (a) rigid confessionalism, (b) conservative Lutheranism, and (c) Lutheran solidarity. Provisions had been made, by the end of this period, for leadership by the establishment of four Lutheran theological seminaries.

1. *Territorial Expansion and Numerical Increase.*—One significant feature was the great movement of population westward. The Ordinance of 1787 providing a government for the Northwest Territory induced large numbers of people to move there. The purchase of Louisiana opened up millions of acres of good tillable land that the national government sold to the settlers at a nominal price. Settlement was so rapid that four Territories and eleven States[3] were admitted to the Union before 1830. In the first forty years, 1790-1830, population increased from 3,929,214 to 12,866,020.

In the cosmopolitan West a new race—the typical American—was first developed by the blending of the colonial types with immigrants from Europe. National consciousness was developed much earlier than in the older parts, partly because the immigrants were peculiarly appreciative of the glories of their new fatherland.

---

[1] See page 396.
[2] The Ministerium of Pennsylvania withdrew. In 1820 this group numbered 74 pastors, 276 congregations, and 24,794 members, while all other groups together had 61 pastors, and a total of 9,407 members.
[3] See map on page 480.

The West was progressive, presenting many political, social, and religious problems for solution.

A vital problem was the future of religion in America. Churches found it difficult to meet adequately the religious needs of the rapidly growing nation. Many new settlements neglected the need

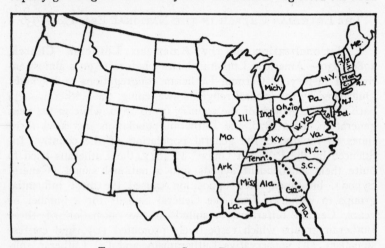

TERRITORIES AND STATES PRIOR TO 1830.
(The parallel dots indicate the Frontier Line of 1800.)

of spiritual life because they had no pastors and no teachers. How the Lutheran Church tried to fill this need may be seen by a study of its growth.

Estimated Growth of the American Lutheran Population

Year	Ministers	Congregations	Communicants
1780	70	300	
1814	85	380	40,000
1823	175	600	45,000
1833	300	680	57,000

2. *Nationalization.*—The new spirit of nationality profoundly influenced contemporary American church life. Unity of interests tended, not only to break down the barriers between states and denominations, but also to develop a spirit of religious independence from Old World standards. The new Nation insisted on doing its work in its own way. Lutheran congregations and synods put themselves in harmony with the new spirit by adjusting their organized life and work to the needs of America. This adaptation involved

⁴ Wolf, *The Lutherans in America*, p. 524.

language, organization, and the preservation of a vast Lutheran heritage.

(a) *The Language Question.*—An essential feature was, of course, a common language. But the polyglot character of the people, with the inherent conservatism of the immigrants, made assimilation slow and painful, slowing up progress.

Early Lutheran leaders encouraged the churches to cultivate the English tongue. But a party in the next generation, contrary to the spirit of Luther, resisted the introduction of English by retaining German as the official language of the Church. It jealously opposed any attempt to sever the linguistic ties binding it to Germany, preferring to lose some young people and even some of their congregations rather than to permit preaching in English.[5] This delayed transition in language caused many Lutherans to transfer their allegiance to English-speaking denominations, especially to the Episcopalians, the Presbyterians, and the Methodists.

Adherence to the German language was so strong in Pennsylvania that the word "German" was introduced into the title of that synod in 1792, and in 1805 the same synod decided that it "must remain a German-speaking ministerium," prohibiting any language but German in synodical sessions. In 1806 the question reached a critical stage in Philadelphia. The English-speaking group, under the leadership of General Peter Muhlenberg, seceded from the mother-church to found a new English Lutheran congregation. Friction was experienced by many other congregations, resulting at times in a sad loss in membership. The failure of the authorities in Sweden to recognize the demand for English services in the Swedish churches on the Delaware was largely responsible for the loss of these churches to the Episcopalians.[6]

In the South and in New York, the anglicizing process was much more rapid. Under the leadership of Dr. J. C. Kunze, Muhlenberg's son-in-law, English became the official language of the New York Ministerium after 1807.

(b) *Organization.*—From 1748 to 1786 the Lutherans had but one synodical organization, the Evangelical Lutheran Ministerium of Pennsylvania.[7] This synod was, up to the time of the War of

---

[5] "Unser Gott ist ein Deutscher Gott," that is, "our God is a German God," is the classical expression of this spirit.

[6] The official relation between the Swedish crown and the Swedish Lutheran churches on the Delaware was severed in 1789, and the congregations concerned were united, one after another, with the Episcopalians. The Lutheran name disappeared from the last charter in 1846.

[7] The organization was first known as "The United Congregations" or "The United Pastors."

Independence, under the supervision of the Francke Institute at Halle[8] and of Dr. Frederick Michael Ziegenhagen in London. Henry Melchior Muhlenberg and other pastors had been commissioned by the authorities at Halle, and to them they were responsible. Great Britain and Hanover had the same ruler, George II (1727-60), and the only two recognized churches in England were the Episcopalians and the Lutherans. Muhlenberg was a subject of Hanover, and some of the Lutherans he was to serve came from that province. Before leaving for America he was approved by the consistorium of Hanover, which meant that he was endorsed by King George II. As pastor of the Royal Chapel in London from 1722-76, Dr. Ziegenhagen became an important royal representative, in a strategic position to promote the welfare of Lutheran emigrants to America. It was through his influence that Muhlenberg was called to America.

The Evangelical Lutheran Ministerium of Pennsylvania embraced at first but ten congregations out of the seventy in Pennsylvania and adjacent states. Several pastors, including Stoever, Streit, Andreae, and Wagner had not been invited to participate in the synodical organization,[9] but the synod grew rapidly, especially after 1760.

No formulated constitution was at first adopted. The *Synodical Constitution* was developed gradually in unwritten form; later being committed to writing it was formally adopted in 1781. It, a prototype for many later synodical organizations, contained the following confessional obligation: "Every minister professes that he holds the Word of God and our symbolical books in doctrine and life." The revised Constitution of 1792 made the lay delegates full members of the synod, with decisions and resolutions of the synodical assembly and of the ministerium binding on the congregations.

A model liturgy or order of church service prepared by Muhlenberg was adopted by the synod in 1754. This liturgy was revised in 1786. An American hymn-book was prepared in 1782 under Muhlenberg's guidance.

In 1762 a model church constitution was prepared for the St.

---

[8] See page 365.

[9] The record of the synod has the following explanation. "1. They, without reason, decry us (the members of the synod) as Pietists; 2. are not sent and have neither an internal nor an external call; 3. are unwilling to observe a uniform order of service with us, each following the ceremonies of his country; 4. an experience of six years had taught Muhlenberg that their object was nothing but bread; 5. they were subject to no consistory and gave no account of the exercise of their office."

Michael's Church at Philadelphia by Muhlenberg, with the co-operation of Dr. Wrangel. This constitution, the prototype of similar constitutions, embodied the following principles: (1) the pastor was pledged to "preach the Word of God according to the foundation of the apostles and prophets and in conformity with the Unaltered Augsburg Confession;" (2) the local congregation was invested with the perpetual right to elect its pastor and officers; (3) the government of the local congregation was not direct, but through the *council*, which consisted of the elected pastor and officers; (4) synodical advice was provided for in case a pastor was to be called or deposed.

Several new synods were formed prior to 1830. The organization of the General Synod in 1820 marked a new era. Of the same faith, culture, traditions, and blood, the Lutherans desired to form a federal organization of the various synods to promote fellowship and co-operation, especially in regard to ministerial education, church literature, home mission work, and the education of the young. Politically, thirteen independent States had been united into a single federated nation without destroying the independence of the States. Could not this federal principle be successfully applied to religious organizations?

Carefully guarding the principle of the sovereignty of the individual congregation,[10] the fathers[11] of the General Synod formulated and adopted a *Constitution* modeled, partly after the constitution of the Presbyterian General Assembly, and partly after the Congregational system. The General Synod had the right to select books for public use in the churches,[12] to make emendations in the liturgy, to give advice or opinion concerning doctrine or discipline,[13] and to exercise a certain discipline over churches connected with the organizations.[14] Plans were also made for the establish-

[10] "The Lutheran Church recognizes in no form of Church government any divine right beyond that of the sovereignty of the individual congregation, which includes the office of preaching the Gospel and administering the sacraments" (Wolf, *The Lutherans in America*, p. 325).

[11] These were: Dr. J. D. Kurtz, first President; Dr. H. A. Muhlenberg, first Secretary; Dr. J. G. Schmucker; Dr. D. F. Schaeffer; Dr. George Lochman; Dr. F. W. Geissenhainer; Dr. Christian Endress; Dr. P. F. Mayer; Dr. F. C. Schaeffer; Rev. G. Schober; and Rev. P. Schmucker.

[12] The Constitution specified that "the General Synod has the exclusive right, with the consent of a majority of the special synods, to introduce new books for general public use of the churches, as well as to make emendations in the liturgy."

[13] According to Article III, Section 5, "the General Synod may give advice or opinion when complaints shall be brought before them by whole synods, or congregations, or individual ministers concerning doctrine and discipline."

[14] The revised Constitution of 1829 stipulated that "if a congregation heretofore connected with a Synod should refuse to obey the resolutions of that Synod or the precepts of this formula, it shall be excluded from the connection with that synod as long as its disobedience lasts, and without special permission from the president, neither any other synod nor a Lutheran pastor or candidate shall serve her."

ment of a theological seminary and a missionary institution, and to provide aid for poor ministers and ministers' widows and orphans.

As stated in the preamble, the Constitution was at first proposed to four synods: The Ministerium of Pennsylvania; The Ministerium of New York; The Synod of North Carolina; and The Maryland and Virginia Synod. The Ohio Synod stood aloof because a number of pastors objected to the rule of majorities; the Tennessee Synod opposed it because it did not mention tne Bible and the Augsburg Confession. Unexpected opposition developed within the General Synod itself. New York sent no delegates from 1821 to 1837. Pennsylvania withdrew in 1823 because of opposition from the churches in the rural districts,[15] and did not formally return till 1853. From 1825 to 1829 the General Synod embraced but three small synods: The Synod of North Carolina; The Maryland and Virginia Synod; and The Synod of West Pennsylvania; but the organization grew rapidly from 1831 to 1864. When the Civil War broke out, the General Synod embraced twenty-three district synods, with more than two-thirds of the Lutheran communicants in the land.

The formation of the General Synod was fraught with great importance for future progress. The General Synod gave the Lutheran Church a standing and recognition that she had not enjoyed before, and strengthened Lutheran consciousness. It diminished the danger of an organic union with the Reformed in Pennsylvania, and with the Episcopalians and the Presbyterians in North Carolina. It acted as a check on the inroads of Socinianism (Unitarianism) by inserting the confession of "Jesus Christ as the Son of God and ground of our faith and hope." It organized educational, missionary, and charitable work. The sending of a delegation abroad "in order to receive contributions in moneys and in books for the use of the seminary," created considerable interest abroad, and aroused energies at home.

(c) *The Establishment of Lutheran Schools.*—Organized work involved the establishment of appropriate educational institutions.

[15] This withdrawal was not caused by any doctrinal dissensions or by a disagreement among the leaders, but by certain agitators outside the Lutheran Church who led the people in the rural districts to believe that the General Synod would be nothing less than "an aristocratic spiritual congress" which would develop into an instrument of ecclesiastical tyranny. The leaders in the Pennsylvania Ministerium decided, therefore, to withdraw from the General Synod "until such time in the future as the congregations themselves shall see their mistake of our true intention, and shall call for a reconsideration of these resolutions."

Laudable efforts were made by practically all early Lutheran settlers to establish parish schools. Many settlers were poor and ignorant, but they were possessed with a great desire to learn something and to secure an education for their children. The greatest hindrance to a healthy educational development was the lack of well-trained and capable teachers. Lutheran pastors frequently took charge of the parish schools.[16]

There was also a demand for a well-trained native Lutheran clergy. Sensing this need, Muhlenberg secured in 1749 forty-nine acres of land in Philadelphia as a campus for a school, a seminary,[17] and a home for the aged. But war interfered and the project was dropped. Meanwhile Muhlenberg, Provost Wrangel, J. C. Kunze, and J. H. Ch. Helmuth trained theological candidates in their respective parsonages. A considerable number of students attended seminaries of other denominations, with a special preference for Princeton. Franklin College, at Lancaster, Pa., in 1787, furnished a few candidates for the Lutheran ministry, including H. A. Muhlenberg, and Ben. Keller. Two Lutheran professors at the University of Pennsylvania, Dr. Kunze and his successor, Dr. Helmuth, prepared young men for the ministry. But it was evident that the way to secure spiritual leaders from the native ranks was to establish Lutheran seminaries.

A small beginning was made in 1797 when Hartwick Seminary[18] was founded. This institution consisted for a number of years of a preparatory department located near Cooperstown, Otsego County, N. Y., a college at Albany, N. Y., and an embryo theological seminary in New York City. Each department had one teacher.[19] These departments were later consolidated, and the first seminary building was erected in 1815 near Cooperstown, the school being formally opened in 1816.

[16] Muhlenberg wrote in 1743: "Because there is a great ignorance among the youth of this land and good school-teachers are so very rare, I shall be compelled to take hold of the work myself. Those who possibly could teach the youth to read are lazy and drunken, compile a sermon from all manner of books, run about, preach, and administer the Lord's Supper for hard cash. Miserable and disgusting indeed! I announced to the people to send first their oldest children for instruction, as I intended to remain with the congregation eight days at a time. On Monday some of the parents brought their children. It certainly looks depressing when children of seventeen, eighteen, nineteen, twenty years come with the Abc-Book. Yet I am delighted that they are possessed of so great a desire to learn something."

[17] Shortly before the war, Muhlenberg and Wrangel planned a seminary to train ministers for the German and the Swedish Lutherans.

[18] This seminary was named after Rev. John Christopher Hartwig, who left his estate valued at $16,000, to found an institution for the training of missionaries to the Indians and ministers of the Gospel.

[19] Rev. J. F. Ernst was the teacher in the preparatory department; Rev. A. T. Braun, a former Roman Catholic missionary to the Indians, was in charge of the classical instruction at Albany, and Dr. Kunze was the constituted theological professor.

Training Schools for a Native Lutheran Ministry

Name	Location	Founded
1. Hartwick Seminary[20]	near Cooperstown, N. Y.	1816
2. Gettysburg Seminary	Gettysburg, Pa.	1826
3. Columbia Seminary[21]	Mount Pleasant, S. C.	1830
4. Ev. Luth. Seminary	Canton, Ohio	1830

The Theological Seminary of the General Synod of the Evangelical Lutheran Church in the United States was founded in 1826 at Gettysburg, Pennsylvania. The Synod of Ohio and Adjacent States founded the Evangelical Lutheran Seminary in Canton, Ohio, in 1830. A couple of years later this seminary was moved to Columbus, Ohio, and is now a part of Capital University. The Synod of South Carolina founded Mount Pleasant Seminary (now Columbia Seminary) in 1830 at Charleston, S. C., as a classical and theological institute to provide ministers. The Lutheran synods were at last in position to secure spiritual leaders, although the number of students was, as yet, lamentably small.

(d) *Confessional Development.*—The pioneer synods were not well united in faith and practice. They were exclusive and, in some cases, antagonistic to one another. By 1830 they had formed three general groups, each of which tried, in its own way, to preserve the historical Lutheran Church.

William Christopher Berkenmeyer and the pastors in the Tennessee Synod advocated a rigid confessionalism coupled with a deep spiritual life. The Synod declared in 1822: "Forasmuch as the Holy Bible is the only rule of matters respecting faith and church-discipline, and because the Augsburg Confession of faith is a pure emanation from the Bible, and comprises the most important doctrines of faith and discipline, hence it must always remain valid. Therefore our Synod can neither be governed by a majority nor a minority, now nor ever hereafter, with respect to doctrine and discipline." Firmly convinced that the rest of the Lutheran synods had drifted from their moorings, this group squared its doctrinal position by refusing altar and pulpit fellowship with the General Synod and the Ministerium of Pennsylvania. In the interest of doctrinal clarity and Christian unity, the Synod even felt justified in probing the orthodoxy of other synods, particularly the Ministerium of Pennsylvania and the Synod of Ohio and Adjacent States. Jacobs[22] rightly says of this group: "Many of their attempts may be criticized as ill-advised, as also their

[20] Moved to Brooklyn, N. Y., in 1932.
[21] Formerly called Mount Pleasant Seminary.
[22] Jacobs, *Lutherans*, p. 393.

earlier literature falls beneath the tests of even a moderate standard of excellence. But time has vindicated their sincerity, earnestness, and the correctness of their judgment on not a few points upon which they were greeted with opposition and ridicule."

Henry Melchior Muhlenberg and the Ministerium of Pennsylvania stood for a conservative Lutheranism. They accepted the standards of the Lutheran Church of the sixteenth century[23] without reservation, perpetuating a traditional Lutheranism in worship, in observance of the church-year and its festivals, in the use of the Gospel- and Epistle-lessons, the rite of Confirmation, and the preparatory service for the Lord's Supper connected with the confession of sins and absolution. Muhlenberg introduced a warm-hearted, devout, practical Lutheranism with a tendency toward unionism. He cultivated fraternal intercourse and intimate fellowship with other Lutherans, and even with the Episcopalians and the Reformed. Muhlenberg, on several occasions, exchanged pulpits with non-Lutheran pastors, and Whitefield preached in his church in 1763.

The General Synod stood for Lutheran solidarity. The primary object of its organization was not confessional but practical. The Constitution was drafted "only for purposes of government and discipline." Hence no mention was made of the Bible or the Augsburg Confession. A positive faith was taken for granted, but the contents of this faith were not specifically determined. The preliminary constitutional draft of 1819 declared that "the General Synod has no power to make or demand any changes whatever in the doctrine of faith adopted heretofore among us." The professors in the Theological Seminary of the General Synod were bound by oath to the Augsburg Confession and the Cathechisms of Luther "as a summary and just exhibition of the fundamental doctrines of the Word of God." Dr. Schmucker at his installation as professor was solemnly charged "to establish all students confided to your care, in the faith which distinguishes our Church from others." But the English character of the General Synod, and its manifested generosity toward other denominations, promoted a fellow-feeling with non-Lutheran churches and a special affinity for American Puritanism. This "Lutheranism modified by the Puritan element" is usually spoken of as "American Lutheranism." Having

---

[23] Muhlenberg said, "I defy Satan and every lying spirit to lay at my door anything which contradicts the teaching of our apostles or the Symbolical Books. I have often said and written that I have found neither error, nor mistake, nor any defect in our Evangelical doctrine, based, as it is, on the apostles and prophets, and exhibited in our Symbolical Books."

no English literature that properly breathed the spirit of Luther, the English-speaking Lutherans used a devotional literature that was filled with Puritanic and Methodistic suggestions.

3. *Rationalism.*—Attempts were made to spread German Rationalism among Lutherans in America. Ministers that came from Halle were trained in this school of theology. Dr. F. H. Quitman of Rhinebeck, N. Y., a thoroughgoing Rationalist, was for twenty-one years the president of the New York Ministerium. The rationalistic influence tended to shatter confessional convictions by pushing into the background the differences between Lutheran and Reforméd Protestantism. Fortunately, the rationalistic movement was soon checked.

60. REVIEW QUESTIONS

1. Why is it desirable to study the history of the Lutheran Church in America in connection with its European background, and in its general relation to American Protestantism?
2. Why were the years 1789-1830 a period of geographic expansion and numerical increase for the Lutherans?
3. In what specific ways did the Lutherans seek to keep abreast with the needs of a rapidly changing society?
4. How did the transition in language affect life and progress?
5. What characterized the first Lutheran synodical organization?
6. What Lutheran synods were organized before 1830?
7. Explain the purpose of the General Synod. Explain its influence on future progress.
8. What provisions were made for educational needs?
9. Account for the division into three general groups.
10. Why the exclusive attitude of Berkenmeyer and the Tennessee Synod?
11. Did Muhlenberg's generosity of mind, heart, and spirit toward other denominations involve doctrine and practice? Explain.
12. Why can the historic Lutheran Church exist only on a confessional basis?

TOPICS FOR SPECIAL STUDY

1. "American Lutheranism."
2. Lutheranism and American Revivalism.
3. Confessional Development among the Lutherans before 1830.
4. American Lutheran Literature before 1830.
5. The Constitution for the Ministerium of Pennsylvania.
6. The Fathers of the General Synod.
7. The course of the Lutheran theological seminaries.

II. The Age of Sectionalism, 1830-70.—Church life of 1830-70 reflected all the characteristics of the national life. Politically, the period was one of internal discord as well as of great material gain. The cotton-producing South, the grain- and wool-producing West, and the manufacturing East became increasingly conscious of their own peculiar political and economic needs. The spirit of nationalism and "good feeling" gave way to a spirit of sectionalism and "hard feeling" culminating in the Civil War. Religiously, the life of the Nation was characterized by internal discords, divisions, and strife. The problem of slavery divided all the larger Protestant churches into Northern and Southern bodies, with each denomination emphasizing its own peculiar interest. The situation was further complicated by the transplanting of the complex Protestant church life of Germany.[24]

Lutheran America enjoyed a great increase through German and Scandinavian immigration. While the general population increased three-fold, the Lutherans increased nine-fold, making the Lutheran Church third among the Protestant Churches. An effort was made to reach all newcomers. An outstanding missionary leader was Rev. William Loehe of Neuendettelsau in Bavaria, who was instrumental in sending about sixty trained workers into the new settlements. In addition, he sent about fifty students to the seminary of the newly organized Missouri Synod. Many new synods were formed, each adapted to the peculiar condition of language, previous church relation, or geographic location. These synods, representing various shades of Lutheranism, better prepared the church to gather the incoming millions into the general fold.

1. *Progress among Lutherans of German Descent.*—There was a sharp conflict between "American Lutheranism" and historic Lutheranism. Representatives of the former advocated an Anglicized form which breathed the atmosphere of doctrinal indifferentism, while representatives of the latter maintained that historic Lutheranism can exist only on a confessional basis.

(a) *"American Lutheranism."*[25]—Dr. S. S. Schmucker was the most ardent advocate of "American Lutheranism," ably seconded by Dr. C. P. Krauth, J. G. Morris, H. J. Schmidt, H. N. Pohlman, partly by B. Kurtz. All belonged to the General Synod. Dr. Schmucker had started out as a conservative, but his liberal leanings had gradually led him toward confessional indifferentism.[26] Desiring a reunion of all Evangelical churches, Schmucker issued an appeal, in 1838, for an "Apostolic Protestant Union." He was

---

[24] See page 399.
[25] By "American Lutheranism" is meant a Lutheranism that had been greatly modified by American Puritanism and American Methodism.
[26] Meanwhile there was an ever-growing group of men within the General Synod, including C. P. Krauth, Jr., Morris, Brown, and Schmucker's own son, Beale Melanchthon Schmucker, who desired to stand on the old confessional ground.

one of the founders[27] of the "Evangelical Alliance" in 1846. In 1845 he stated in a letter forwarded by the General Synod to the Church in Germany: "In most of our church principles we stand on common ground with the United Church of Germany. The distinctive doctrines which separate the Lutheran and the Reformed churches we do not consider essential. The tendency of the so-called old Lutheran party seems to be behind the times. Luther's peculiar views concerning the presence of the Lord's body in the communion have long since been abandoned by the majority of our ministers."[28] His extreme position was finally reflected in an anonymous pamphlet which he and B. Kurtz issued in 1855 entitled the "Definite Synodical Platform." In it, he claimed to have found many errors in the Augsburg Confession and urged the synods concerned to adopt the confessional standard presented by him and make it the confessional basis for the General Synod. But Schmucker's influence declined steadily because the conservative wing had by this time become the larger party.

(b) *Conservative Lutheranism.*—"American Lutheranism" was soon checked by the great wave of German immigration. New streams brought along, not only their Old World conservatism, but also some of their own pastors. A part filled the German-speaking churches in the East, while another part moved to Ohio, Illinois, Indiana, and the West. Many came by way of the Gulf of Mexico and settled along the Missouri Valley. Several new conservative synods were formed, including the Missouri Synod, the Buffalo Synod, and the Iowa Synod.

In 1839 a group of intensely pious and strictly orthodox Lutherans from Saxony settled in and about St. Louis, Missouri, to establish an ideal Church. The leadership soon passed from Rev. Martin Stephan to Rev. Carl F. W. Walther, under whose leadership, assisted by Rev. F. C. D. Wyneken and the men sent by Loehe, the Missouri Synod was organized in 1846 on the basis of a rather extreme form of congregationalism. The Synod had no authority over the congregations, the Synod being merely an advisory body. Strict adherence was required, not only to the Augsburg Confession, but to the whole body of symbolical books associated with it as "the pure and uncorrupted explanation and statement of the Divine Word." The Synod, which soon became the largest and most aggressive Lutheran synod, has held its position to the present day. In 1918 it was surpassed numerically by

[27] Dr. King of Ireland called Dr. Schmucker the father of the Alliance at the time he attended the first meeting of the organization in London in 1846.
[28] Spaeth, *C. P. Krauth*, Vol. I, p. 333.

the newly organized United Lutheran Church in America,[29] and also in 1930 by the organization of the American Lutheran Conference.

The Buffalo Synod was organized in 1845 by a group of "Old Lutherans" who had separated from the United Church in Prussia. Emigrating to America they settled near Buffalo, N. Y., and in Wisconsin. Rev. John A. A. Grabau was the founder. The Buffalo and the Missouri groups had so much in common that a union might have been expected, but the leaders soon got entangled in a long and bitter controversy regarding the doctrine of the Church, the doctrine of the ministerial office, and the doctrine concerning the office of the keys.[30] A number of ministers and congregations left the Buffalo Synod to join the Missouri Synod in 1866.

A *via media* course between the hierarchical tendencies of the Buffalo Synod and the rather extreme congregationalism of the Missouri Synod was taken by the founders of the Iowa Synod of 1854. These founders were pupils of Rev. William Loehe who had done so much for the scattered Lutherans in the "West." They had entered the service of the Missouri Synod, but left again when they were accused of holding divergent views similar to those of the Buffalo Synod. The Iowa and the Missouri groups were on different sides of various questions, including (a) the doctrine of the Church and the ministry,[31] (b) Chiliasm,[32] (c) the conversion of Israel, (d) Anti-Christ, (e) "open questions," (f) usury and universal justification, (g) predestination and conversion, (h) what unity was necessary for church union, and the like. The Iowa Synod grew slowly at first, but under two brothers, Sigmund and Gottfried Fritschel, professors in Wartburg Seminary, it later grew rapidly.

(c) *Organization of the General Council in 1867.*—The bold attack on the Augsburg Confession by the *Definite Synodical Platform* of 1855 intensified the conflict between the Lutheran and the un-Lutheran elements in the General Synod. An open rupture was

[29] Missouri Synod required renunciation of all mingling of churches and faiths; the use of church- and school-books prescribed by the synodical authorities; the regular call of pastors; and the use of the German language in all synodical sessions.

[30] Grabau insisted that the Church is essentially *visible*, while Walther held that the Church, as an invisible communion of saints, is essentially *invisible*. Grabau said regarding the ministerial office that this office is limited to duly ordained ministers only, and that the Lord's Supper administered by others is mere bread and wine. Walther said: "Every Christian as a priest of God has: (a) the office of the Word, (b) to baptize, (c) to bless and consecrate the holy bread and wine, (d) to retain sins and remit them, (e) to offer sacrifice, (f) to pray for others, (g) to pass judgment on doctrines." But because God wills it, the ministerial office must be transferred from the individual spiritual priests to certain qualified individuals, namely the pastors. In regard to the office of the office of the keys Grabau insisted that the pastor alone has a right to excommunicate, while Walther held that this right inhered in the congregation.

[31] For the Missouri view, see the previous footnote.

[32] For a brief discussion of Chiliasm, see page 108.

avoided for the time being,[33] but it was evident to many that a crisis was near. The reception into the General Synod of the liberal Melanchthon Synod[34] in 1869 caused the Norwegians and the Swedes to leave the Synod of Northern Illinois, a district synod of the General Synod, in 1860. A second exodus occurred in 1863 when the district synods of North Carolina, South Carolina, Virginia, and West Virginia formed an independent organization, later re-organized as the United Synod of the South. But the real crisis came in 1864 when the Franckean Synod, which had never formally adopted the Augsburg Confession,[35] was received into the General Synod.[36] The Ministerium of Pennsylvania protested against this reception as unconstitutional, and issued a call[37] to all synods and congregations in the United States and Canada which adhered to the Augsburg Confession to unite in the formation of a new general body "on a truly Lutheran basis." In response, thirteen synods sent representatives to a convention at Reading, Pennsylvania, in 1866, to adopt a new general plan of organization of all confessional synods. The first convention of this body, the General Council, was held at Fort Wayne, Indiana, in 1867. These disruptions deprived the General Synod of nearly half its membership.

2. *Progress among Lutherans of Scandinavian Descent.*—The great tide of Scandinavian immigration began toward the middle of the nineteenth century. The first shipload of Norwegian immigrants arrived in 1825; immigration from Sweden started in the 'thirties; and the first considerable immigration from Denmark began about 1864.

(a) *The Norwegians.*—The early Norwegian immigrants were vitally influenced by two religious awakenings in Norway. The first, brought about by the pietistic revival preaching[38] of Hans Nielsen Hauge (1771-1824), had its course among the laity. The second emanating from the national university through the theological professors Gisle Christian Johnson (1822-94) and Carl Paul C. Caspari (1814-92), had its course among the clergy. The Haugean revival, very *subjective* in character, strongly emphasized the need of lay preaching. The Johnson-Caspari movement, more

[33] C. P. Krauth, Jr. made some proposals by which the "Definite Synodical Platform" was practically repudiated.
[34] The Melanchthon Synod had openly repudiated the distinctive Lutheran doctrines and had adopted the "Definite Synodical Platform."
[35] The Franckean Synod had been declared in civil court action as not entitled to the name "Lutheran."
[36] The Franckean Synod was received on condition that it should, at its next convention, adopt the Augsburg Confession as its doctrinal basis.
[37] This call was issued after the delegates from the Ministerium of Pennsylvania had been refused seats in the 1866 convention of the General Synod.
[38] See page 398.

objective in character, opposed *organized* lay preaching. Johnson maintained, on the basis of Article XIV of the Augsburg Confession, that only duly called and ordained pastors should teach publicly in the Church. No organization had a right to send out lay preachers. He believed, however, that, in order to satisfy crying spiritual needs, qualified laymen with an *inner* call might preach the Gospel, if they did so on their own responsibility, without financial or moral backing.

These differences caused mutual suspicions between the Haugean and the state church parties. Hauge and his followers had broken with the established church by introducing lay preaching. The state church party had in turn provoked the Haugeans by unkind treatment of them. This gave rise to division, which was reflected in the Norwegian immigrants.

The Evangelical Lutheran Church of America (Eielsen Synod) was organized[39] in 1846, largely on the initiative of Elling Eielsen,[40] a staunch follower of Hans Nielsen Hauge. Its chief aim was to unite the "awakened," to work more effectively for the salvation of souls. Its growth was slow, partly because of its insistence upon proof of conversion for admission to membership. This Donatistic clause in the synodical constitution caused Rev. P. A. Rasmusen and his followers to leave the synod in 1856. A more serious rupture occurred in 1876 when a majority revised the old constitution to form a new synod called Hauge's Norwegian Evangelical Lutheran Synod.

In 1853 the pietistic element of the more objective type organized the Synod of the Norwegian Evangelical Lutheran Church of America (Norwegian Synod) at East Koshkonong, Wisconsin. Early leaders, Rev. C. L. Clausen,[41] Rev. J. W. Dietrichson, Rev. A. C. Preus, Rev. H. A. Preus, Rev. U. V. Koren, Rev. J. A. Otteson, Rev. H. A. Stub, and Prof. Laur. Larsen, insisted upon an educated, regularly called, and ordained ministry.[42] The Synod enjoyed a rapid growth and was, until 1890, the largest body of Norwegian Lutheran congregations. It was affiliated with the Synodical Conference, with its ministers educated at St. Louis, Missouri, until the Synod founded its own theological seminary.

A few Norwegian immigrants joined the Franckean Synod;

[39] The organization took place at Jefferson Prairie, Rock County, Wisconsin.
[40] Eielsen came to America in 1839 and was ordained in October, 1843, by a German Lutheran pastor, Rev. F. A. Hoffman.
[41] It was Loehe who induced Norwegian mission friends who visited him, to send Clausen, a Dane, to America to minister to the spiritual needs of his Norwegian brethren. Clausen came without ordination, as he had not finished the whole customary university course. He was ordained by Rev. Krause of the Buffalo Synod.
[42] Not all of the leaders in the Norwegian Synod had had any direct contact with the Johnson-Caspari awakening, but some of them held religious views similar to Prof. Johnson.

some joined the Synod of Northern Illinois. The Scandinavian element in the latter withdrew in 1860 to form the Scandinavian Augustana Synod. Ten years later the Norwegians and the Swedes separated, mainly for linguistic reasons, with mutual good-will. The Norwegian group again divided into two groups in 1870: the minority formed the Norwegian Augustana Synod while the majority organized the Norwegian-Danish Evangelical Lutheran Conference. This last named took a mediary position between the Eielsen Synod and the Norwegian Synod, which *via media* tendency was later perpetuated in the United Norwegian Lutheran Church of America, organized in 1890.

The predestinarian controversy in the Synodical Conference caused a split in the Norwegian Synod in 1886 when a group withdrew to form the Anti-Missourian Brotherhood. This group merged in 1890 with the Norwegian Augustana Synod and the Norwegian-Danish Evangelical Lutheran Conference to form the United Norwegian Lutheran Church of America. Three years later a small group known as the Augsburg Friends seceded from the United Norwegian Lutheran Church because of a controversy regarding the ownership of Augsburg Seminary, and because of differences in the emphasis on the local congregation and the education of pastors. These Augsburg Friends organized in 1897 as the Lutheran Free Church. In 1900 a small group which insisted upon proof of conversion for admission to membership, seceded from the Lutheran Free Church and from the United Norwegian Lutheran Church, and organized as the Lutheran Brethren.

(b) *The Swedes.*—Sweden experienced several religious awakenings during the nineteenth century.[43] The Schartau revival had much in common with the Caspari-Johnson movement, particularly in the attitude taken toward lay preaching; and the revival started by Rosenius was much like the Haugean movement.[44] Differences between Schartau and Rosenius divided the more objective from the more subjective pietistic element in Sweden, which differences were represented among the early Swedish immigrants.

The first Swedish Lutheran congregation of nineteenth century America was organized in 1850 at Andover, Illinois, by Rev. L. P. Esbjorn. The following year Rev. Esbjorn, together with two Norwegian Lutheran pastors, participated in the organization of the Synod of Northern Illinois. Rev. T. N. Hasselquist, one of the founders of the Augustana Synod, arrived in 1852.

[43] See page 397.
[44] The association of Rosenius with George Scott, an English Methodist revival preacher who operated in Sweden from 1830 to 1842, injected schismatic tendencies which resulted in serious losses to the Swedish Church in America.

The Scandinavian element in the Synod of Northern Illinois withdrew in 1860 to form the Scandinavian Augustana Synod. When the Norwegians withdrew ten years later, the Swedish group took as its new name the Evangelical Lutheran Augustana Synod in North America (Augustana Synod). Rev. Hasselquist exerted a compelling influence on early policies.

Some early pastors in the Augustana Synod were adherents of the Schartau school, thoroughly orthodox and conservative. Hence the Augustana Synod failed to appeal to some of the more subjective pietists. A number found their way into the Swedish Evangelical Mission Covenant of America, and into the Swedish Evangelical Free Mission. These two have not in recent years been classified among the Lutheran synods by the U. S. Census of *Religious Bodies* (for 1906, 1916, 1926). A number of Swedish immigrants also joined the Methodists, the Episcopalians and the Baptists.

(c) *The Danes.*—The two synodical organizations of Danish Lutherans in America are based on certain religious tendencies which developed within the Church of Denmark. The Grundtvigian[45] view is perpetuated in the Danish Evangelical Lutheran Church of America, and the so-called "Inner Mission" tendency is perpetuated in the United Danish Evangelical Lutheran Church in America. The Grundtvigian movement, which led to the establishment of the well-known Danish Folk High Schools, stresses the educational factor; while the Inner Mission movement is more revivalistic. Again, the Grundtvigians declare the Apostle's Creed and the Lord's Prayer to be the living Word and the rest of the Bible is placed on a lower level; the Inner Mission Friends consider all of the Holy Scripture as the true norm for life and faith.

Some early Danish immigrants affiliated with the Norwegian-Danish Conference, founded in 1870. In 1872 a group of Danish pastors of the Grundtvigian tendency organized the Danish Evangelical Lutheran Church in America. A visit to America a few years later by a son of Grundtvig furnished a pretence for some writers to publish in the synodical paper derogatory remarks about the Holy Scripture. This was strongly resented by a number of pastors who did not hold Grundtvigian views. After heated controversy, these pastors and their followers withdrew in 1894.

In 1884 a group of Danish pastors, predominantly Inner Mission Friends, left the Norwegian-Danish Conference to organize the Danish Evangelical Lutheran Church Association of America. The

[45] See page 397. The Rev. Wilhelm Beck was the "Inner Mission" leader.

synod united with the group that had left the Grundtvigians in 1896 to form the United Danish Evangelical Lutheran Church in America.

III. The Age of Industrialism, 1870-1918.—Large cities sprang into existence; much wealth accumulated in a few hands; large masses suffered from extreme poverty. These changes called for drastic re-adjustments in American churches. America, becoming industrialized, no longer thought in terms of agriculture. The Church, to be of service, had to move with the people to the cities. A number of new Lutheran synods were formed during these years.

1. *Organization of the Synodical Conference.*—Several synods felt that the General Council had not gone far enough in its return to a "truly Lutheran basis." The so-called "four points" regarding (1) Chiliasm, (2) pulpit fellowship, (3) mixed communion, and (4) secret societies, caused much debate and agitation finally leading to several German synods withdrawing from the General Council. In 1872 a number of these more "strict" Lutherans, namely Missouri, Wisconsin, Minnesota, Illinois, Norwegian and Ohio Synods organized the Synodical Conference on the basis of the Formula of Concord of 1580. The Synodical Conference was, until 1918, the largest body. The organization is not very compact because of its strictly congregational polity, its main object being "to express, preserve, and promote the unity of faith in doctrine and practice."

The Synodical Conference took a rather extreme position in regard to pulpit and altar fellowship.[46] The General Synod, on the other hand, went to the other extreme in stressing a common fellowship with churches of other communions. The General Council took a *via media* course.

2. *The Predestinarian Controversy.*[47]—At the meeting of the Wisconsin District in 1868, Rev. Huegli proposed that God's election is the cause of man's salvation and faith. He stamped the old Lutheran doctrine of the *Intuiti fidei finalis* unto glorification as Pelagian[48] and synergistic.[49] This predestinarian view, ably seconded by Dr. Walther, provoked a violent controversy finally leading to several synods severing relations with the Synodical Conference. The Ohio Synod left in 1881, and the Norwegian Synod withdrew in 1884 to avoid disruption within its own ranks. The

---

[46] The Synodical Conference soon developed its own type of Lutheranism which was not identical, but closely related to the orthodox Lutheranism of the seventeenth century.

[47] For references to this controversy, see Keyser, *Election and Conversion;* Pieper, *Conversion and Election;* Tressel, *The Error of Modern Missouri;* Schuette, *Testimonies in Furtherance of a Union and Peace in Truth;* Zorn, *Bekehrung und Gnadenwahl.*

[48] See pages 124-25.   [49] See page 283.

rupture occurred, however, in 1886 when a group known as the Anti-Missourian Brotherhood left the Norwegian Synod. A similar disruption occurred within the ranks of the Michigan Synod.

3. *Tendencies toward Lutheran Solidarity.*—It is quite beyond the scope of this book to present even a brief history of individual synods.[50] An attempt will be made, however, to show how various small synods of the same race, faith, and tradition began to cultivate fraternal relations which, in most instances, led to organic church union.

In 1890 three Norwegian synods united as the United Norwegian Lutheran Church of America. The Danes followed suit in 1896 when they organized the United Danish Evangelical Lutheran Church in North America. In 1917 the Norwegian Synod, the Hauge Synod, and the United Norwegian Lutheran Church merged as the Norwegian Lutheran Church of America. In 1918 the greatest merger took place by the union of the General Synod, the General Council, and the United Synod of the South, into the United Lutheran Church in America. Shortly before this merger, the Augustana Synod withdrew from the General Council. The Joint Evangelical Lutheran Synod of Wisconsin and Other States was organized between 1917 and 1919 by a merger of the Wisconsin, Minnesota, Michigan, and District of Nebraska Synods.

4. *The Lutherans and the World War.*—In the recent World War about *six* per cent of the membership of the Lutheran congregations enlisted, as against only *four* per cent of the total population.

(a) *The National Lutheran Commission for Soldiers' and Sailors' Welfare*[51] was organized in 1917 to co-ordinate Lutheran efforts to serve the men "with the colors." Thirteen separate Lutheran synods co-operated through the agency of a general executive committee. One hundred and fifty camp pastors[52] were sent where Lutheran soldier and sailor boys were located. It equipped seventy-eight army chaplains and eleven navy chaplains. It co-operated closely with the French Lutheran Church in ministering to the sick and dying, and rendered a great variety of service to

[50] Your school library containing, of course, much material dealing with the history of your particular synod. See the bibliography at the end of this chapter. Special assignments in synodical history should be made, if time permits.

[51] The Lutheran Brotherhood of America, organized Sept. 13, 1917, at Des Moines, Iowa, soon joined its forces with this Commission. The motto of the Lutheran Brotherhood is: Loyalty to Home, Church and Country. "It aims to foster an 'esprit de corps' among the Lutheran men of our land that has heretofore been lacking, and in the future will base its efforts on the establishing of a real unity among Lutherans of our country."

[52] The Synodical Conference is not a constituent member of the National Lutheran Council.

individuals, families, and organizations. The Commission was dissolved when the emergency was over.

(b) *The National Lutheran Council.*[53]—In order to perform the emergency work made necessary by war and reconstruction, a number of Lutheran synods organized the National Lutheran Council as a co-operative agency for Lutheran world service.[54] Its activities are governed by the following regulations:

Division A. Regular Work

1. To witness for the Lutheran Church and give publicity to its utterances on all matters which require an expression of the common conviction and sentiment of the Church.

2. To represent Lutheran interests before

(a) National and state governments whenever needed. This is not to exclude direct approach to the governments which any General Body may wish to make.

(b) Organized bodies and movements outside of the Lutheran Church that may require common action. This is to be undertaken only after consultation with the authorities of the General Bodies.

3. To bring to the attention of the Church all such matters as require common utterance or action.

4. To further the work and coordination of the activities and agencies of the Church in the solution of common problems affecting the religious life and consciousness of the people, e.g., social, economic and educational problems.

5. To foster true Christian loyalty to the State, and to labor for the maintenance of a right relation between Church and State as distinct, divine institutions.

6. To publish information about, and to promote the gathering and publication of, accurate and uniform statistics of the Lutheran Church.

7. To undertake additional work with the specific consent of the participating Bodies.

Division B. Emergency Work

1. To take the necessary steps to meet emergencies requiring common action, with special reference to the welfare and protection of the foreign missions and distressed Lutheran constituencies.

---

[53] This organization was the direct outgrowth of the National Commission for Soldiers' and Sailors' Welfare.

[54] The National Lutheran Council was originally organized for home service (cf. "Regulations" in *Lutheran World Almanac* for 1921, pp. 493-94), but the organization soon centered its energies also on European Relief and Reconstruction and Foreign Missions.

2. Each participating Body shall determine the extent of its co-operation in emergency work.

IV. The Age of Lutheran Solidarity, 1918-33.—Outstanding characteristics of Lutheranism during the last two decades have been the extensive co-operation of Lutheran synods, and the increasing consciousness of Lutheran solidarity. A number of notable mergers have taken place, while several federations have been formed, including the Lutheran Foreign Missions Conference of America (1919), the American Lutheran Home Mission Council (1931), the National Lutheran Inner Mission Conference (1922), the National Lutheran Educational Conference (1910), the National Lutheran Education Association (1917), the Lutheran Student Association of America (1923), the Lutheran Publishing House Managers' Association (1914), the National Lutheran Editorial Association (1913), the American Lutheran Publicity Bureau (1914), the American Lutheran Statistical Association (1917), the American Federation of Lutheran Brotherhoods (1927), the Lutheran Federation of Charities (1931), the Lutheran Youth Conference (1930), and the Radio Broadcasting Commission (1930).

1. *The Lutheran World Convention.*—The work of the National Lutheran Council assumed a universal character finding visible expression in the Lutheran World Convention. Conscious as never before of the ecumenicity of Lutheranism, its unity of spirit and inner life, Lutherans from various parts of the world sent one hundred and sixty delegates and representatives to the first meeting, held at Eisenach, Germany, August 19-26, 1923. At the Second Lutheran World Convention, at Copenhagen, June 26 to July 4, 1929, the following Confessional Declaration was unanimously adopted:

"The Second Lutheran World Convention's confessional declaration can only contain a statement which clearly and emphatically expresses the Convention's unconditional and unchanged adherence to the Holy Scriptures and the confession given by our Lutheran fathers before God and before the entire world.

"This expression of firm and unchanging adherence to the faith of our fathers must not be diluted with modifications and admonitions which are motivated by present conditions but which would divert attention from the confessional content itself.

"The Convention's statement must be expressed so clearly that it cannot be misunderstood but also so briefly that it will indelibly imprint itself on mind and conscience.

"The Eisenach Convention expressed this adherence to Scripture and confession in such a way. Therefore we recommend the re-enactment of that Confessional Declaration as follows:

"'The Lutheran World Convention acknowledges the Holy

Scriptures of the Old and New Testaments as the only source and infallible norm of all church doctrine and practice, and sees in the Confessions of the Lutheran Church, especially in the Unaltered Augsburg Confessions and Luther's Small Catechism, a pure exposition of the Word of God.'"

Through its Executive Committee, the Lutheran World Convention tends to become "a world service station for the Evangelical Lutheran Churches throughout the earth." At its meeting in Hanover, Germany, in 1933, the Executive Committee recommended very strongly the participation of the cooperating Evangelical Lutheran Churches in the joint exercise of brotherly love freely on the basis of their unity of faith for continued constructive relief,

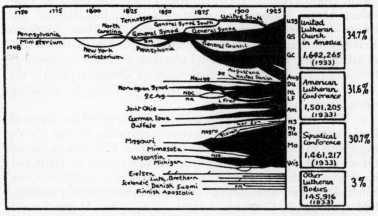

LUTHERAN CHURCH BODIES WITH HEADQUARTERS IN THE U. S. A.[65]
(From the "L. W. A. 1931-33" by permission of the
National Lutheran Council.)

particularly "(a) for the relief of the suffering Lutheran Church of Russia in the maintenance of the Seminary in Leningrad, for the relief and aid of indigent pastors and their families, and for administration of physical relief to the famine-stricken in South Russia; (b) for the support of the Lutheran work among the Ukrainians in Poland where twenty Ukrainian Lutheran congregations have been organized already and are ministered to by Ukrainian Lutheran pastors; (c) the relief and assistance of hard-pressed Lutheran churches in the smaller countries of eastern and

[65] The 1933 figures are given by Dr. G. L. Kieffer in a letter of June 1, 1933. They include the United States, Canada, Possessions and Territories of the U. S., and other countries and foreign missions.

southeastern Europe; (d) the aid in cases of extraordinary merit and need of young Lutheran churches on foreign mission fields, in cases where the supporting home boards have been shorn by the economic depression of the power of maintaining their own work."

The third Lutheran World Convention was held in October, 1935, in Paris, France.

2. *The American Lutheran Church* was organized on August 11, 1930, at Toledo, Ohio, through the merger of the Lutheran Synod of Buffalo (1845), the Evangelical Lutheran Synod of Iowa and Other States (1854), and the Evangelical Lutheran Joint Synod of Ohio and Other States (1818). Certain doctrinal differences had kept them apart, but these were gradually ironed out, so the merger was based on real unity in faith, doctrine, and practice.

3. *The American Lutheran Conference* was organized on October 29-31, 1930, at Central Lutheran Church, Minneapolis, Minn., "for the purpose of giving testimony to the unity in the faith of the participating church bodies." This organization is not a merger into a general church body, but is a federation of synods which seek to "co-operate in matters of common interest and responsibility." The constituent synods, all retaining individual identities, include (1) the Augustana Synod, (2) the Norwegian Lutheran Church, (3) the Lutheran Free Church, (4) the American Lutheran Church, and (5) the United Danish Lutheran Church.

Lutherans maintain 37 theological seminaries, 33 senior colleges, and 87 junior colleges and academies. Much attention is also given to elementary Christian education. The Church carries on extensive work in foreign, home, and inner mission fields.

61. REVIEW QUESTIONS

1. Why were the years 1830-70 an age of sectionalism?
2. Explain the formation of so many Lutheran Synods. Was this apparent division good or bad?
3. How did "American Lutheranism" influence the development of the Lutheran church life?
4. Why did conservative Lutheranism gain the upper hand against "American Lutheranism"?
5. What differences separated the Missouri, the Buffalo, and the Iowa groups?
6. Why the organization of the General Council in 1867?
7. Discuss the "four points" and the part they played in the formation of the Synodical Conference of 1872.
8. In what ways did the transition from an agricultural to an industrial society affect Lutheran synods?
9. How did the Lutheran Church meet its responsibilities during the World War?
10. Is there any difference between Lutheran solidarity and Lutheran unity?

TOPICS FOR SPECIAL STUDY

1. A brief outline of the history of your particular synod.
2. Lutheran educational institutions in America.
3. Lutheran Missions, at home and in foreign fields.
4. Lutheranism and social service.
5. Prominent Lutheran leaders of German descent.
6. Prominent Lutheran leaders of Scandinavian descent. (See Roseland, *American Lutheran Biographies*.)
7. Prominent Lutheran leaders of Icelandic, Finnish, or Polish descent.

A SELECTED BIBLIOGRAPHY FOR CHAPTER XXV

Jacobs: *Lutherans* (Vol. IV of the American Lutheran Church History Series).
Neve: *A Brief History of the Lutheran Church in America* (2nd ed.).
Wentz: *The Lutheran Church in American History.*
Hazelius: *History of the American Lutheran Church.*
Norlie and Kieffer: *The Lutheran World Almanac* (7 vols., 1921-33).
Jacobs: *Lutheran Cyclopedia.*
Nicum: *Geschichte des New York Ministeriums.*
Proceedings of the One Hundredth Annual Convention of the Synod of New York.
Wentz: *Centennial History of Gettysburg Theological Seminary.*
Sheatsley: *History of the Joint Synod of Ohio.*
Bernheim & Cox: *History of the Evangelical Lutheran Synod of North Carolina.*
Henkel: *History of the Evangelical Lutheran Synod of Tennessee.*
Dau: *Reviews of the Work of the Missouri Synod.*
Graebner: *Geschichte der Missouri-Synode.*
Wentz: *History of the Evangelical Lutheran Synod of Maryland.*
Strobel: *Memorial Volume to Commemorate the Semi-Centennial Anniversary of the Hartwick Lutheran Synod.*
Fritschel: *Dokumente und Quellen zu Geschichte der Iowa Synode.*
Deindoerfer: *Geschichte der Iowa-Synode.*
Burgess: *History of the Pittsburg Synod.*
Mgebroff: *Gesch. der Synode von Texas* (continued by Krausse).
Hinman: *History of Northern Illinois Synod.*
Koehler: *Geschichte der Wisconsin Synode* (Vol. I).
Haase, et al.: *Geschichte der Minnesota Synode.*
Heathcote: *The Lutheran Church and the Civil War.*
Rohne: *Norwegian-American Lutheranism up to 1872.*
Norlie: *History of the Norwegian People in America* (revised).
Blegen: *Norwegian Migration to America*, Vol. I.
Stephenson: *The Background of the Beginnings of Swedish Immigration, 1850-1875.*
Forsander and Delen: *History of the Augustana Synod.*
Vig: *Danish Evangelical Lutheran Church in America.*
Ilmonen: *History of the American Finns.*
Trabert: *English Lutheranism in the Northwest.*
Knubel and Sherer: *Our Church.*
Nothstein: *Lutheran Makers of America.*
Wentz: *The Second Lutheran World Convention.*
Fortenbaugh: *The Development of the Synodical Polity of the Lutheran Church in America, to 1829.*
Ochsenford: *Documentary History of the General Council of the Evangelical Lutheran Church in North America.*

CHAPTER XXVI

The Protestant Episcopal Church, 1789-1936

The Church of England ceased to exist in America when England recognized the independence of the American Colonies. Its successor was the Protestant Episcopal Church, organized in 1789. This body perpetuated the faith, the liturgy, and the spiritual traditions of the mother church, but its organization was carefully adjusted to American needs. The advantage of its American freedom is its government by convention instead of by bishops. The General Convention is composed of the House of Bishops and the House of Clergy and Lay Deputies. Lay representation has since been adopted by branches of the Anglican Communion in some of the self-governing English colonies.

I. Organization of the Protestant Episcopal Church.— When the Revolution was over, the Anglican parishes were outside the jurisdiction of the English episcopate. Disestablishment in the southern colonies deprived them of property and accustomed revenues. The remnants were left without a head (bishop), without reputation, in a condition of incipient bankruptcy. There was no association of Anglican parishes; there were wide differences between the Anglicans of the North and of the South as to how the new church body was to be organized. It was no easy task to bring these groups into a national, vigorous American Episcopal Church, but America had the men equal to the task. Prominent was Bishop William White who has been called the Patriarch of the Protestant Episcopal Church.

1. *Various Plans of Organization.*—Anglicans had, to begin with, no unity of plan for organization. One group refused to organize until a bishop had been secured. Another group proposed a nation-wide church body, and then to apply for the episcopate. It was evident that different motives and purposes dominated.

(a) *The Maryland-Virginia Plan.*—In Maryland and Virginia the first motive was interest in the temporal welfare of the individual churches. Organization was necessary to hold the property and the endowments formerly belonging to the Church of England. Dr. William Smith took the initiative, calling a conference of clergymen and laymen of Maryland, for November 9, 1780. In order to appear an ecclesiastical organization with legal standing before the new government, a name was requisite, so the name proposed and adopted by the conference was the "Protestant Episcopal Church."[1] A petition was sent to the General Assembly of Maryland for an act empowering the vestries and the wardens to raise money by pew rents and other means in order to repair the churches now rapidly falling into ruin. When the war was over, Dr. Smith yielded to the general demand for a complete church organization by calling a second conference in August, 1783, at Annapolis, Maryland. The Annapolis Convention adopted a "Declaration of Certain Fundamental Rights and Liberties" in which the Protestant Episcopal Church of Maryland claimed a distinct independence of the Episcopal churches in other states. The Episcopalians of Maryland had as yet apparently no thought of one Protestant Episcopal Church. Dr. Smith was chosen Bishop of Maryland, but no steps were taken toward consecration. In Virginia the process was much like Maryland.

(b) *The New England Plan.*—In New England the dominant purpose was the desire to preserve and perpetuate the spiritual ideals and traditions of the Church of England. Dr. William White had proposed in 1782 that the churches, as a temporary expedient, organize an American Episcopal Church without a bishop. His plan was strongly opposed by the New England clergy who took the position that a church without a bishop is no church.[2] Greatly stirred by Dr. White's proposal, the Connecticut clergy held a secret meeting on March 15, 1783, at Woodbury, Connecticut, selecting two men, either of whom was to go to England to secure Episcopal consecration. Rev. Jeremiah Leaming declined because of his age. The other candidate, Dr. Samuel Seabury, accepted and went to England to be consecrated Bishop of Connecticut. Political conditions made it impossible, however, for the English bishops to consecrate Dr. Seabury, and the English Parliament was as yet unwilling to make the needed exception in its ruling regarding the required oaths of allegiance to the crown. After waiting more than a year in London, Dr. Seabury went to Aberdeen where he, on November 14, 1784, secured consecration from the non-juring[3] bishops of Scotland.

---

[1] This name, which was evidently proposed by Dr. Smith, was later accepted by the national body of Episcopalian churches. The term "Protestant" set it apart from the Roman Catholic Communion, and the term "Episcopal" distinguished it from the Presbyterian and the Congregational Communions.

[2] This view was clearly stated by Dr. Abraham Jarvis.

[3] The non-juring bishops were the descendants of the Scotch bishops who, in 1688, had refused to disown James II or to take the oath of allegiance to William III, and hence were called "non-jurors."

(c) *The National Plan.*—In the two plans there was little or no recognition of churches of different states. Dr. White inaugurated a movement to organize an Episcopal Church for the whole of the United States. In his pamphlet, "The Case of the Episcopal Churches in the United States Considered," published in 1782, he proposed that the Episcopal churches in each state should first organize. These organizations should again unite into a nation-wide church, and then application should be made for the episcopate. With tact, consecration, and much patience Dr. White arranged for a series of informal meetings, but the churches were slow to respond. At the convention held in September, 1785, at Philadelphia, only seven out of the thirteen states were represented. This Convention prepared and adopted the "Ecclesiastical Constitution of the Protestant Episcopal Church in the United States of America," and urged the State conventions to elect bishops. A petition was addressed to the English bishops, that they ordain bishops elected by the various American state conventions, and expressing the desire to be connected with the Church of England rather than Scotland. John Adams presented the petition to the Archbishop of Canterbury and soon an Act of Parliament authorized the consecration of the American bishops. Dr. White of Pennsylvania and Dr. Samuel Provoost of New York were consecrated in London on February 4, 1787, and Dr. James Madison of Virginia was consecrated on September 19, 1790. The Protestant Episcopal Church was now equipped to perpetuate its own episcopate. Any objection to the Scottish office was thus obviated. The two lines combined when Dr. Seabury assisted the other three American bishops in consecrating Dr. Thomas John Claggett Bishop of Maryland on September 17, 1792. The distinctive American Episcopate had been inaugurated.[4]

2. *The General Convention of 1789.*—The Protestant Episcopal Church was organized the same year as the United States of America, and partly by the same men. The General Convention of 1789 united all the Episcopal groups into one national organization. A Constitution was adopted, along with the Prayer Book. In the preface to the American Prayer Book of 1789 fellowship with the Anglican Communion was expressed in the following words, "This Church is far from intending to depart from the Church of England in any essential point of doctrine, discipline or worship; or further than local circumstances require." The Thirty-Nine

---

[4] This episcopate includes the threefold historic ministry of unbroken Catholic custom: bishops, priests, and deacons.

Articles were accepted with some revision in 1801, resulting in the omission of the Athanasian Creed in Article VIII, the omission of Article XXI, and the recasting of Article XXXVII. The Church broke traditions governing Episcopacy for about a thousand years by giving laymen seats in the councils.

II. Adjustment and Slow Growth, 1789-1830.—1. *Difficult Years.*—The Protestant Episcopal Church had been organized, but conditions facing her made it difficult to function effectively. The men of 1789, reared in the environment of the old order, found it difficult to adjust themselves to the new régime. The idea of propagandism, prevailing in other churches, was hardly present in the minds of this group because the State idea still controlled. The identity of the Protestant Episcopal Church with the Church of England, made it widely unpopular and distrusted as being an English institution. To the people, formality of the Episcopal worship made little or no appeal. America was dominated by French infidelity and French manners. The French had abolished God by decree, and many thought the days of Christianity were numbered. The Episcopalian bishops prior to 1811 were often slack and neglectful. They were all rectors of parishes, with the exception of Bishop Madison who was President of William and Mary College, so they gave slight attention to their duties as bishops. The loss of the Methodistic element deprived the organization of some strength; the hostilities preceding the War of 1812 did not improve the situation. It was a chaotic time for the Church, and at times it seemed that the work of the founders was to be fruitless.

2. *New and Aggressive Leadership.*—A change for the better came after twenty-two years of hard struggle. Under the aggressive leadership of four new bishops, John Henry Hobart of New York (1811), Alexander V. Griswold of New England (1811), Richard Channing Moore of Virginia (1814), and Philander Chase of Ohio and Illinois (1819), a new spirit seemed to fill the church. These energetic, progressive, and alert bishops made diligent and regular visitations and promoted interest in the Sunday School movement. New parishes were organized in newly settled sections, especially in the West, and diocesan organizations replaced State organizations. The General Convention Journal for 1820 indicates that the Church enjoyed steady progress. The General Theological Seminary was founded in New York in 1819, and the Virginia Theological Seminary was founded at Alexandria in 1823. The special convention of 1821 organized the Domestic and Foreign Missionary

Society. The Protestant Episcopal Church began to take its place in the Nation.

III. Years of Rivalry and Debate, 1830-70.—1. *The Propaganda Policy of 1835.*—At the General Convention of 1835, much attention was given to the fact that the numerical growth of the Church was not keeping pace with the increase in population. New methods were necessary if the Church was to win in the Nation. In consequence the General Convention of 1835 made a departure by resolving that the Church itself is a missionary society and that all members are missionaries by virtue of their baptism. The result was revolutionary. The Church enjoyed a remarkable growth only coming to a pause with the outbreak of the Civil War. Through its missionary bishops, it became fully organized in the Territories as well. Bishop Jackson Kemper did active pioneer work from 1835 to his death in 1870. Bishop Henry Benjamin Whipple, active in new settlements from 1859 to 1901, has often been called "Apostle to the Indians." The same title has also been given to Bishop William Hobart Hare who worked so successfully among the Indians of South Dakota from 1873 to 1909.

Growth was not merely along lines of geographical expansion and numerical increase. An enlarged hymnary came into general use, the church ritual was enriched, and church architecture was improved. Dr. William A. Muhlenberg, one of the most remarkable men in the history of the Church, founded a system of church schools;[5] established the principle of free churches, open to all without renting of pew; developed the first order of Evangelical Sisterhoods in America;[6] founded St. Luke's Hospital, the first church hospital; and encouraged the use of a choir of men and boys.[7] W. A. Muhlenberg exerted a powerful influence on the Church through religious statesmanship, prophetic vision, and measureless devotion.

2. Party Rivalry and Friction.—All important movements of thought in the Church of England found representation here. Low Church Evangelism[8] had its great champions in Bishop White of Pennsylvania and Bishop Meade of Virginia, its center of learning in the Theological Seminary at Alexandria, Va. Rigid High Churchmanship had its stronghold in Connecticut where Episcopalians had been obliged to fight for their existence against Con-

---

[5] Muhlenberg's school for boys in his own parish became the model for the private secondary schools of the Protestant Episcopal Church.
[6] Muhlenberg calls the order *The Sisterhood of the Holy Communion*, founded in 1852.
[7] St. Michael's Parish, Charleston, S. C., had a vested choir with boy choristers at the close of the 18th century. Muhlenberg's choir was not vested (cf. Coleman, p. 63).
[8] See pages 394 and 404-405.

gregationalism. The Broad Church group was generally identified with New York and Massachusetts. Of the three groups, the American High Churchmen differed, perhaps, most widely from the corresponding group in England. American High Churchmen were interested in the Church's present life rather than in past history. They addressed themselves to practical rather than to theoretical problems.

One-sided emphasis on party interests produced much internal discord. It was an era of "hard feeling" also for the Episcopalians. The main conflict was between the Evangelical party and the aggressive High Church party. A division of labor was defined in 1835 when it was understood that the Evangelicals should work for foreign missions and the High Churchmen should have charge of the inner mission field. This unhappy state lasted till 1877 when the two organizations became auxiliary. The ordination in 1842 of Arthur Carey, a staunch defender of Tractarianism,[9] resulted in much heated controversy. It culminated in 1853 when the General Convention deposed Bishop Ives of North Carolina, who had declared his submission to the Roman Catholic Church.

3. *The Muhlenberg Memorial of 1853.*—A notable victory for reconciliation was wrought through the Memorial which a group of ministers, headed by William A. Muhlenberg, presented to the General Convention of 1853. The Memorial urged "a broader and more comprehensive ecclesiastical system," with more "freedom in opinion, discipline, and worship." Both parties had a legitimate place within the Church. The Memorial was generally accepted, and the reconciliation became an accomplished fact.

4. *Results of the Civil War.*—The Church suffered only a temporary division by the Civil War, and this division was caused, not by slavery, but by civil relations. During the years of conflict, the Southern dioceses functioned independently under the name of the Protestant Episcopal Church in the Confederate States of America. In the North this division was regarded only as a temporary necessity, since bishops and delegates of the Southern dioceses were prevented from attending the General Convention of 1862. At the General Convention of 1865 several Southern dioceses were represented, and the Convention joined in the consecration of Bishop Quintard of Tennessee, completing the reunion of the two sections.

IV. An Era of Vigorous Growth, 1870-1918.—1. *The Reformed Episcopal Secession of 1873.*—The Church enjoyed an un-

[9] See pages 404-405.

precedented growth during the next fifty years. Its membership grew steadily from a proportion of one communicant in 400 of population in 1830 to one communicant in 107 in 1900. Only one incident marred progress. The ritualistic movement[10] made a number of Evangelicals suspect that the Church was becoming seriously "Romanized." This culminated in 1873 when a small group withdrew to organize the Reformed Episcopal Church. Its leader was G. D. Cummins, Assistant Bishop of Kentucky. He soon secured the able assistance of Dr. C. E. Cheney.

2. *The Broad Church Movement.*—The Church had many adherents who were dissatisfied, not only with Evangelicalism, but also with High Churchmanship. Their awakened sense of the catholicity of the Church and their desire to make this Communion as comprehensive as possible, to make it the Church of the Nation, caused this group to turn to Broad Churchmanship.[11] They accepted the traditional Broad Church view of the fatherhood of God, the sonship of man, and the blessed hope for the future of all men. They manifested an interest in social reforms. The early recognized leaders of the American Broad Church group were Edward A. Washburn of New York, Phillips Brooks of Boston, Dr. Edwin Harwood of New Haven, John Cotton Smith, Bishop Clark of Rhode Island, and Alexander H. Vinton of Boston.

3. *Movements toward Church Union.*—When the American Episcopal Church awoke to a consciousness of her catholicity, she immediately began to seek ecclesiastical fellowship by reaching out with a sympathetic heart toward the Catholic Communion on the one side, and to Protestant groups on the other.

(a) *Negotiations with the Russian Church.*—In 1868 the General Convention was requested "to take into immediate and prayerful consideration the question whether it is not alike your duty and your privilege to at once open up formal negotiations with authorities of the Russian Church, and if it seems good to you, with the other orthodox Churches of the East." Negotiations were started, but results were rather unpromising. Since the war, however, a new impulse has been given, owing to the formal recognition of the validity of Anglican Orders announced by the patriarchs of Constantinople and Alexandria, and by the presence of a large delegation of Orthodox churchmen at the last Lambeth Conference in 1930.

(b) *Interest in the "Italian Reform Movement."*—When the

[10] This movement centered the interest, not only in the use of ritual and vestments, but also in the doctrinal implications involved in the terms "Catholic" and "Protestant."
[11] See pages 404-405.

dogma of Papal Infallibility was promulgated in 1870, some refused to accept the decree and organized as the Old Catholics. The Protestant Episcopal Church expressed its sympathy and sought to enter into fraternal relations. The response, however, was at first not great. Following the Lambeth Conference[12] of 1920, there was a great revival of interest, and further negotiations, approved by the Lambeth Conference of 1930, have now resulted in a formal concordat of union between the Old Catholics and the Anglican Church.

(c) *Negotiations with the "New Christian Church in Mexico."* —After the overthrow of Santa Anna in Mexico, 1855, seventy-four Catholic priests signed a protest and a memorial against the abuses of the Roman Catholic Church. Although the resulting reform was carefully suppressed, a loose organization was maintained under the name of the "New Christian Church in Mexico." In 1866 its members asked the American Episcopal Church to consecrate the presbyter Rafael Diaz Martinez as bishop. The investigations following disclosed that there was no national organization which could be called a Mexican Church. The Protestant Episcopal Church finally established a "Missionary District" in Mexico, and in 1931 a Suffragan Mexican Bishop was consecrated.

(d) *The Episcopalian Plan of 1886.*—A vigorous movement for the corporate reunion of all Christendom had its beginning at the General Convention in Chicago in 1886. The basic platform included (1) the Holy Scriptures of the Old and New Testament as the revealed word of God, (2) the Nicene Creed as a sufficient statement of the Christian faith, (3) the two Sacraments, baptism and the Supper of the Lord, ministered with unfailing use of Christ's words and of the elements ordained by Him, and (4) the historic episcopate, adapted in its administration to the varying needs of nations and peoples. This platform was endorsed by the Lambeth Conference[13] of 1888.

(e) *The Commission of 1910.*—The General Convention of 1910 appointed a "Commission on Faith and Order." The Commission invited representatives of a considerable number of churches, including the Roman Catholic and the Eastern Orthodox Churches. After seventeen years of preparation, the first[14] meeting of the World Conference on Faith and Order was held in August, 1927, at Lausanne, Switzerland, under the presidency of Bishop Brent. A

---

[12] The Lambeth Conference of 1920 was attended by 252 Anglican bishops.
[13] The Lambeth Conference is an assembly of all bishops of the Anglican Communion, meeting in London once in ten years at the call of the Archbishop of Canterbury.
[14] A preliminary conference was held in Geneva, Switzerland, in 1920.

continuation committee is now carrying on for the corporate re-union of all Christendom.

(f) *Negotiations with Presbyterians and Congregationalists.* The Presbyterians had conferences with the Episcopalians after the Plan of 1886 had been adopted, but after several years the appointed committees came to a deadlock when the Episcopalians refused to acknowledge the validity of Presbyterian orders. Nego-tiations with the Congregationalists have resulted in a Concordat which the Episcopalians ratified at their General Convention in 1919. Both Communions continue, however, as separate and inde-pendent organizations.

4. *The Episcopalians and the World War.*—The Protestant Episcopal Church made valuable contributions through her leader-ship, her war-time relief, and the war loans. The chief chaplain for the American Expeditionary Forces during the war was a bishop of the American Episcopal Church. The Episcopalians also organ-ized a special commission which served the spiritual interests of soldiers and sailors.

V. Post-War Developments, 1918-36.—1. *Organization of the National Council in 1919.*—In the Protestant Episcopal Church the highest ecclesiastical authority is the General Conven-tion which meets every third year. As a body with authority to act between conventions, the National Council[15] was organized in 1919, with a presiding bishop at its head. The National Council organized into six departments, including (1) Department of Mis-sions and Church Extension, (2) Department of Religious Edu-cation, (3) Department of Christian Social Service, (4) Depart-ment of Finance, (5) Department of Publicity, and (6) Field Department. The Woman's Auxiliary, formed in 1872, was re-organized to support these several activities.

2. *Church Activities.*—The Church finds expression in a great number of societies and organizations. Work is carried on in eight-een continental domestic missionary districts, and in eight foreign field missionary jurisdictions. The American Episcopal Church has fourteen theological institutions and five distinct church colleges, besides a large number of secondary schools.

3. *Corporate versus Individual Religion.*—The impulse toward world unity, toward a world organized for common effort and com-mon accomplishment, has ushered in an age of corporations. Indi-vidual ownership has gradually yielded to incorporated companies;

[15] The name was adopted in 1922.

individual laborers have combined in labor unions; and individual development has been subordinated to organized efficiency. Personal religion and individual responsibility for salvation have been superseded by corporate religion and institutional responsibility for salvation.

This transition has brought about a change in the conception of the function of the Church as well as the office of the Pastor. Organized social activities have multiplied, and Parish Houses have become their headquarters. The Pastor's influence is no longer exerted primarily from the pulpit, but rather as General Manager of a complicated organization. His essential functions are no longer confined to the traditional teaching, preaching, and pastoral activities, but his task is rather to supervise efficiently a certain round of Christian social service. It is self-evident that this has produced a corresponding change in equipment and the method of pastoral training.

4. *General Influence of the Protestant Episcopal Church.*—The special contribution of the Church has been along the lines of theological and religious moderation and comprehension, coupled with institutional strength.[16] The conception of the Church as an "Institute of Righteousness" has centered the interest on right living and on practical problems. Doctrine and emotional religious experiences have been subordinated to the development of character. Divine worship has a wealth of forms and a fullness of ceremonial beauty not ordinarily found in other Protestant churches.

62. REVIEW QUESTIONS

1. What is the relation between the Protestant Episcopal Church and the Church of England?
2. In what ways did the Maryland-Virginia Plan, the Ecclesiastical Plan of Connecticut, and the Federal Plan affect the final organization of the American Episcopal Church?
3. What special difficulties faced the Episcopal Church during its first twenty years of organized existence?
4. How did the idea of the universal priesthood of believers affect the composition of the General Convention?
5. Discuss Hobart, Griswold, Moore, and Chase as representatives of a new type of bishop.
6. Why were the Episcopalians so slow to introduce the propaganda policy into their church work?
7. Of what importance in the religious history of the New World was the establishment of the Protestant Episcopate?
8. In what ways did party rivalry and friction influence the progress of the Church during the years 1835-73?
9. Why the Muhlenberg Memorial of 1853?
10. Why the American Broad Church movement?

[16] See pages 287-88.

11. Explain the inherent urge of the Protestant Episcopal Church toward Church Union?
12. Why the National Council of 1919?
13. In what ways has the corporate idea of religion influenced the life of the American Episcopal Church?
14. What are the special contributions of the Episcopalian Communion?

TOPICS FOR SPECIAL STUDY

1. The essentials of the "historic episcopate."
2. The episcopate as factor in corporate church union.
3. Bishop William White, Patriarch of the Protestant Episcopal Church.
4. Bishop John Henry Hobart as a church leader.
5. Phillips Brooks.
6. Bishop Brent and the World Conference on Faith and Order.
7. Corporate versus individual religion.
8. Missionary activities of the American Episcopal Church.
9. "The Free Church System" in the Episcopal Church.
10. Episcopalianism and the new social conscience.

A SELECTED BIBLIOGRAPHY FOR CHAPTER XXVI

1. Tiffany: *A History of the Protestant Episcopal Church.*
2. McConnell: *History of the American Episcopal Church* (tenth edition).
3. Perry: *The History of the American Episcopal Church, 1587-1883* (2 vols.).
4. Hawkes: *Contributions to the Ecclesiastical History of the United States of America* (2 vols.).
5. Coleman: *The Church in America.*
6. Anderson: *The History of the Church of England in the Colonies.*
7. White: *Memoirs of the Protestant Episcopal Church in the United States.*
8. Perry: *Historical Collections Relating to the American Colonial Church.*
9. *The Living Church Annual.*
10. Cross: *The Anglican Episcopate and the American Colonies.*
11. Cheshire: *The Church in the Confederate States; A History of the Protestant Episcopal Church in the Confederate States.*
12. *Anglican Theological Review.* Evanston, Ill. 1919.
13. Bolton: *Colonization of North America, 1492-1783.*
14. Doyle: *English Colonies in America.* (5 vols.)
15. Beardsley: *History of the Episcopal Church in Connecticut from 1635 to 1865.* (2 vols.)
16. Greenwood: *A History of King's Chapel in Boston, the First Episcopal Church in New England.*
17. Goodwin: *The Colonial Church in Virginia.*
18. Jarratt: *Life of Devereux Jarratt.*
19. Meade: *Old Churches, Ministers and Families of Virginia.* (2 vols.)
20. Emory: *A Century of Endeavor 1821-1921. A Record of the First Hundred Years of the Domestic and Foreign Missionary Society of the Protestant Episcopal Church in the U. S. A.*
21. Ellwood: *The Reconstruction in Religion: A Sociological View.*
22. Barker: *The Social Gospel and the New Era.*
23. Slosser: *Christian Unity: Its History and Challenge in All Communions, in All Lands.*
24. Briggs: *Church Unity: Studies of Its Most Important Problems.*
25. Manross: *A History of the American Episcopal Church.*

CHAPTER XXVII

The Congregational Church in the National Era, 1789-1936

The Congregational and the Presbyterian Churches enjoyed a special prestige at the beginning of the National Era, because the population was essentially English[1] in origin, in political and religious conceptions, and because Calvinistic Puritanism was as yet the basic religious element. As descendants of the Pilgrim Fathers, the Congregationalists enjoyed a special popular esteem. They not only inherited the powerful initiative of the old English Independents, but they also maintained a high standard of culture. They took the first great initiative in the promotion of world missions by the organization of the American Board for Foreign Missions in 1810. They took an early lead in founding seminaries for the education of ministers, and in founding schools and colleges. They furnished a large number of religious leaders, and made valuable contributions to theological literature and religious journalism. But "a curious modesty" and a lack of the propaganda spirit, prevented a normal growth of Congregationalism prior to the Albany Convention of 1852. The denomination suffered heavy losses during the Unitarian controversy at the opening of the nineteenth century, while the "Plan of Union" of 1801 caused a large element to merge in Presbyterianism. Congregationalism enjoyed a powerful renaissance after the Civil War. At present the Congregationalists constitute the seventh largest Protestant denomination.[2]

I. Conflict, Awakening, and Slow Growth, 1789-1830.—
1. *Disestablishment of New England Congregationalism.*—The early New England settlers were not all Independents. The Boston and the Salem colonists were Puritans[3] who adhered to the Church of England, although they desired certain reforms from within, including a Presbyterian form of church government. But these early tendencies were soon checked,[4] and New England Puritanism

---

[1] Consult table on page 439.
[2] For a numerical order of the denominations, see page 477.
[3] For a distinction of Independents and Puritans, see page 326.
[4] This victory for Congregationalism was largely due to the influence of Dr. Samuel Fuller, a deacon of the Pilgrim church, who gave medical aid to the Salem people during a serious illness. He persuaded the Salem Puritans that the Plymouth Separatism was not so dangerous as they had supposed.

merged in Congregationalism.[5] Between 1638 and 1655 the colonies of Massachusetts Bay, Connecticut, and New Haven made all Congregational worship a matter of public taxation, which state support continued after the colonial governments became state governments. Vigorous protests from the Baptists finally caused Connecticut to sanction disestablishment in 1818, New Hampshire in 1817, and Massachusetts in 1833.

To the close of the 18th century Congregationalism was practically confined to New England. Strong emphasis on autonomy of the local congregation prevented the churches from uniting effectively during the great national expansion. Nathaniel Emmons opposed state associations on the ground that "Association leads to Consociation; Consociation leads to Presbyterianism; Presbyterianism leads to Episcopacy; Episcopacy leads to Roman Catholicism; and Roman Catholicism is an ultimate fact." This decentralizing tendency caused the Congregationalists to lose considerable ground in the subsequent westward New England emigration.

2. The Unitarian Controversy.—Unitarianism developed within Congregationalism, but its separate denominational life was begun by an Episcopal church[6] which in 1787 publicly renounced belief in the deity of Christ, withdrawing from the Episcopal communion. This rupture stimulated a controversy which had been in progress among Congregationalists since the "Great Revival." Disagreement over the theology of Jonathan Edwards and the value of revivals had caused them to divide into two theological groups, developing considerable party friction even before 1776. The cleavage increased during the revivals during the 1790's. The anti-Trinitarians registered vigorous protests, not only against the deity of Christ, but also against the rigid Calvinism. The ensuing controversy divided a large number of churches in eastern Massachusetts, and a few went over bodily to Unitarianism. The Old Pilgrim Church at Plymouth, the first Congregational church in America, became Unitarian in 1801.

At that time all Congregational churches had a double organization, the "church" and the "society." The latter was the legal corporation, and Chief Justice Parker ruled that it had the right to decide whether the church should be Congregational or Unitarian.

---

[5] John Robinson, the early Congregational leader in England, had predicted that once outside the reach of the Established Church, Puritan and Separatist would no longer be distinguishable.

[6] This Episcopal church was King's Chapel, Boston, and its rector was James Freeman.

Through skilful management the Unitarians gained control of the "societies" so that about 1300 Unitarians dispossessed 3900 orthodox Congregationalists of property to the value of more than $600,000.[7] Eighty-one congregations in Massachusetts lost their church property.

The Unitarian controversy reached a climax in 1805 when the Liberals succeeded in electing Dr. Henry Ware to the professorship of theology in Harvard University. The loss of Harvard was the immediate cause of the establishment of Andover Seminary in 1808 and of the founding of Amherst College in 1821. The real Unitarian separation came in 1820, but the Unitarian Association was not formally organized till 1825. Under the leadership of Ralph Waldo Emerson, Unitarianism was later modified by Transcendentalism.

3. *The "Plan of Union" of 1801.*—When the great Westward Movement in the 1790's began, the Congregationalists and the Presbyterians were intimate friends of long standing. Before the end of the 18th century, delegates with full power to vote were interchanged between the Presbyterian General Assembly and the Congregational state associations of Connecticut, Massachusetts, Vermont, and New Hampshire. This arrangement continued until the Presbyterians divided in 1837. In 1801 the two denominations formed a "Plan of Union" allowing Congregationalists and Presbyterians to work together in founding new churches. Each union church was to conduct its discipline according to the majority of the church members. This arrangement was followed for about half a century, 1801-52. The Old School Presbyterians abrogated the "Plan of Union" in 1837 because they felt their group was being infected by "New Haven theology" and undermined by Congregational principles. The Congregationalists withdrew from the New School Presbyterians 15 years later because the majority of the union churches became Presbyterian.

The general results of the "Plan of Union" were a minimum of duplication of church work, the practical elimination of Presbyterianism from New England, the loss in new communities to the West of about 2000 Congregational churches, and a stimulation of Congregational missionary movement.

4. *Missions and Schools.*—The Great Revival resulted in a remarkable development of missionary evangelization and religious education. In 1798 the General Association of Connecticut or-

[7] Dexter's Congregationalism as seen in its literature, p. 616; quoted by Huntington, Outlines of Congregational History, p. 119.

ganized itself as the Connecticut Missionary Society "to Christianize the heathen in North America and to support and promote Christian knowledge within the new settlements of the United States." Similar missionary societies were organized throughout New England before 1812. The American Tract Society was organized in 1814; the American Education Society in 1816; the Massachusetts Sunday School Union in 1825; and the American Home Missionary Society in 1826. In 1829 a group of Yale students organized the "Illinois Band" of home missionaries. Illinois College at Jacksonville is a part of their monument.

In 1810 the missionary movement culminated in the organization of the American Board of Commissioners for Foreign Missions. Its birth-place was the "Haystack Prayer Meeting" of 1806, attended by students from Williams College. Seeking shelter during a violent thunderstorm, they pledged themselves to devote their lives to missionary service. On graduating from Williams, they entered Andover Theological Seminary where graduates from other colleges joined them. They wanted to go to Asia, but there was no missionary society to which to appeal. Four of them, Adoniram Judson, Samuel Nott, Samuel Mills, and Samuel Newell, presented a memorial, June 27, 1810, to the General Association of Massachusetts, asking "their advice, direction, and prayers." In response the American Board of Commissioners for Foreign Missions was organized, and two years later, February 6, 1812, Gordon Hall, Adoniram Judson, Samuel Newell, Samuel Nott, and Luther Rice were ordained as missionaries. Mills remained in America to arouse interest in foreign missions. On the way to India, Judson and Rice turned Baptists, and through their influence the Baptist denomination organized its foreign board in 1814. Other off-shoots of the American Board were the foreign missionary societies of the Presbyterians and the Dutch Reformed. At present the American Board maintains educational, medical, and evangelistic missions in Africa, Turkey, India, China, Japan, and the Islands of the Pacific.

The Congregationalists founded numerous schools and colleges as they extended westward.[8] The following Congregational schools were established between 1789 and 1830: Williams College in 1793; Bowdoin College in 1794; Andover Theological Seminary in 1808; Bangor Theological Seminary in 1816; Amherst College in 1821; and Yale Divinity School in 1822.

[8] At present 42 colleges and universities, and 10 theological seminaries are the progeny of the Congregational influence.

II. A New Era of Congregationalism, 1830-70.—1. *Nettleton and Finney.*—The Congregational Church experienced many powerful evangelistic revivals before 1850. Prominent among early revivalists were Asahel Nettleton and Charles G. Finney.[9] Nettleton's wonderful evangelistic career, begun in 1812, resulted in large accessions to the Church. Even more remarkable was the revivalistic career of Finney, who started to preach in 1824, continuing with few interruptions until 1860. For some years he gave the whole of his time to revivalistic campaigns. He also exerted a powerful influence, first as professor of theology at Oberlin College, later as its president.

2. *Improved Organization on the Frontier.*—At first the New England churches feared that the Congregational polity would not work in the newer settlements in the West. In consequence the fruits of their labor were largely appropriated by others. This theory of limited adaptability was finally repudiated by the successful organization of Congregational churches on the frontier, and by the 'formation of these churches into State associations.[10] With organization came strength and progress. The Congregationalists began to develop in the new communities. Congregational organizations like the "Iowa Band,"[11] the "Andover-Kansas Band," and the "Yale-Dakota Band" founded permanent Congregational churches and schools. Before the Civil War, Congregationalism had been established in practically all States, save in the South.

3. *National Conventions.*—There came an increasing denominational consciousness and a demand for some form of national church organization. A national convention was called in 1852 at Albany, New York, which was the first general meeting of Congregationalists since the Cambridge Synod of 1646-48. The deliberations resulted in the abrogation of the "Plan of Union," gifts of $61,891 as a fund to aid in building western churches, establishment of the "Congregational Church Building Society,"[12] inauguration of a denominational literature and the organization of the "Congregational Library Association,"[13] approval of the

[9] Moody was converted in a Congregational church, but during his evangelistic career he belonged to the independent Chicago Avenue Church.

[10] Rev. John D. Pierce, home missionary to Michigan, organized many Congregational churches in that State, and was largely responsible for the formation of the General Association of Michigan in 1844.

[11] The idea of the "Iowa Band" was, "If each of us can only plant one good and permanent church and all together build a college, what a work that would be" (Pilgrim Deeds and Duties, p. 60).

[12] The society was organized in 1853 as the "American Congregational Union," but this rather indefinite name was exchanged for the present in 1892.

[13] Organized in 1853. The name was changed in 1864 to the "American Congregational Association."

"American Home Mission Society,"[14] and a change in the whole atmosphere of Congregationalism.

Consolidation was greatly extended by the Boston Council in 1865. This gathering gave an unprecedented impulse to home-missionary work in the South and in the West. It drew up a statement of polity, and also a statement of doctrine known as the "Burial Hill Declaration."[15] Another national gathering, the Pilgrim Convention, was held in 1870 in Chicago, Ill., to commemorate the two hundred and fiftieth anniversary of Congregationalism in America. These national gatherings proved so advantageous that a permanent triennial organization, known as the National Council of the Congregational Churches in the United States, was effected in 1871 at Oberlin, Ohio. The Council has met biennially since 1913.

4. *Intellectual Readjustment.*—Horace Bushnell,[16] Lyman Beecher, and Henry Ward Beecher ushered in a new era of intellectual exploration and a wide readjustment of thought. Bushnell (1802-76) was a prominent exponent of Schleiermacher and Coleridge. Lyman Beecher (1775-1863) was a conservative leader in the Unitarian controversy, but later he was charged with holding heretical views on the atonement. He was tried and acquitted in 1835. His agitation against slavery and intemperance aroused public opinion against those evils. The famous *Uncle Tom's Cabin* was published by his daughter, Mrs. Harriet Beecher Stowe, in 1851. Henry Ward Beecher (1813-87), fourth son of Lyman Beecher, is generally considered one of the greatest pulpit orators America has produced. He was intensely opposed to slavery, and in a series of addresses in the cities of England, he helped to change English sentiment toward the United States and to prevent recognition of the Southern Confederacy by the British. In 1882 he withdrew, with his church, from the Congregational Association to which he belonged, because of his liberal views.

American Congregationalism has had a number of eminent preachers, theologians, and educators. Not mentioning those who

[14] This society had been formed in 1846 as a protest against slavery.
[15] During one of the sessions held at Burial Hill, Plymouth, the Boston Council of 1865 adopted a statement of faith which is usually referred to as the "Burial Hill Declaration." It substantially embodied the confessions and platforms of the Cambridge Synod of 1648 and the "Confession of 1680." But word "Calvinism" was omitted. (The Cambridge Synod of 1648 was attended by New England churches which, on that occasion, formally approved of the doctrinal portion of the Westminster Confession. But English Congregationalists gathered at the "Savoy," London, in 1658 modified the Westminster Confession and its publication has since been known as the "Savoy Declaration." This Savoy revision of the Westminster Confession was adopted by the Boston Synod in 1680, on behalf of the Massachusetts churches; and by the Saybrook Synod in 1708, on behalf of the Connecticut Colony.)
[16] See pages 392 and 472.

are still living, the list includes Richard Salter Storrs, George A. Gordon, Frank W. Gunsaulus, Edwards A. Park, Mark Hopkins, William J. Tucker, George B. Fisher, William DeWitt Hyde, Washington Gladden, Amory H. Bradford, Bushnell and Beecher, Jonathan Edwards, Thomas Hooker, and others mentioned elsewhere in this chapter.

III. In the Years of "Big Business," 1870-1918.—About 1870 the United States entered upon a period of phenomenal economic growth. Machines and mass production, the great increase in population, the rapid growth of cities and the consequent changes in home life, the new situation created by "big business" with its almost unlimited opportunities for political corruption, the comprehensive organization of labor and its struggle against capitalism, the rise of natural and historic sciences, the various technical discoveries,—all added to the complexity of American society, presenting many new problems for the churches. In the attempt to solve these problems, several denominations gave a new social emphasis to the principles of Christianity. The Gospel had a real message of salvation for society as well as for the individual. A "saved man in a saved society" was the new ideal, finding expression in phrases such as "the social gospel," and "the institutional church." Awakened social consciousness demanded that the churches take an active part in much-needed political and social reforms, moulding communities and nations according to the life of Christ.

1. *Congregationalism and the New Social Order.*—Congregationalism took a very active part. Josiah Strong, Samuel B. Capen, William Hayes Ward, Charles M. Sheldon, Washington Gladden, Lyman Abbott, Graham Taylor, Edward A. Steiner, Owen Lovejoy, Raymond Robbins, Robert A. Wood, Jane Addams, and others felt that the Church was responsible for right relationships between men. This is strikingly expressed in the Burial Hill Declaration, "It was the grand peculiarity of our Puritan fathers that they held this gospel, not merely as the ground of their personal salvation, but as declaring the worth of man by the incarnation and sacrifice of the Son of God; and therefore applied its principles to elevate society, to regulate education, to civilize humanity, to purify law, to reform the church and the state, and to assert and defend liberty; in short, to mould and redeem, by its all-transforming energy, everything that belongs to man in his individual and social relations." In the new Creed of 1913 it is declared to be the business of the Christian Church to "labor for the promotion of

justice, the reign of peace and the realization of human brotherhood . . . to work and pray for the transformation of the world into the Kingdom of God."

2. *Organization of the Young People's Society of Christian Endeavor.*—During the "Prayer-meeting Revival" of 1857-58, weekly prayer meetings of young people were inaugurated in various churches. As the movement grew, there arose a demand for a more permanent form of organization. Accordingly, Francis E. Clark, pastor of Williston Congregational Church in Portland, Maine, organized the Young People's Society of Christian Endeavor in 1881.[17] It was an "out-and-out" religious society whose activities centered around the weekly prayer meeting. Each member pledged himself to "take some part aside from singing." The plan proved so successful that Christian Endeavor societies were organized by other denominations in America and abroad. "Father Endeavor" Clark, as the founder was fondly called, resigned his pastorate in 1885 to devote all his time to the Society. The success of the Christian Endeavor Society stimulated the organization of other strictly denominational agencies for young people, including the Young Men's Hebrew Association, The Epworth League, the Baptist Young People's Union, and the Young People's Christian Union of the United Presbyterians.

3. *Increased Denominational Unity.*—In order to be of larger service, the Congregationalists found it necessary to perfect a closer denominational organization. A step was taken by Rev. Dr. Amory H. Bradford when, as Moderator of the National Council for the term 1901-04, he devoted much time to speaking and writing in the interest of the churches. Many feared that his larger service would infringe upon the rights of the local church and its independence of ecclesiastical control, but Dr. Bradford's successful ministry-at-large so disarmed criticism that the incoming moderator in 1904 was asked to continue the practice.

The Council of 1913 marked "the definite recognition of the Congregational churches as an organized religious body with specific purposes and definite methods." Without modifying the essential autonomy of the individual church,[18] the new Platform of

[17] Fourteen years earlier, or in 1867, Rev. Theodore L. Cuyler of the Lafayette Avenue Presbyterian Church in Brooklyn, had organized the young people of his church into a Young People's Association which aimed at "the conversion of souls, the development of Christian character, and the training of new convert in religious work." But this organization was purely local.

[18] A number of independent and autonomous States had been united into a single federation without destroying the independence of the States. Why could not this federal principle be applied to the Congregational churches?

1913 associated more fully than ever before all Congregational churches in "an organic unity based upon a fundamental union in faith, common purpose in action, and mutual fellowship." A Council Secretary was chosen to represent the churches of the nation in their relation to smaller Congregational organizations, other denominations, and international relationships.[19] Missionary and general educational activities were more closely integrated with the National Council, five classes of organization resulting: foreign missions; church extension at home; education of backward or exceptional populations; religious education and publication; and ministerial pensions and relief. Additional plans of national organization were adopted by the National Councils of 1925 and 1927. Nine commissions have been established to secure a better coordination of denominational activities. These commissions are on missions, on social relations, on evangelism, on international relations, on inter-church relations, on law enforcement, on men's work, on recruiting for Christian work, and on interracial relations. All services of the National Council are rendered without assuming any rights of judicature.

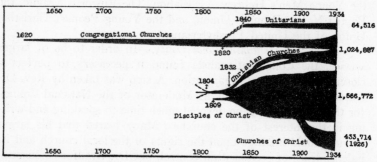

DISCIPLES OF CHRIST, CHURCHES OF CHRIST, CONGREGATIONAL AND
CHRISTIAN CHURCHES, AND UNITARIANS.

IV. American Congregationalism Since the World War.

—1. *Recent Events.*—The celebration of the Tercentenary of Congregationalism in America was held in 1920. In 1925 the Evangelical Protestant Church of North America[20] was received into the National Council of Congregational Churches. In the same year the Congregationalists, the Methodists, and the Presbyterians of Canada merged into the United Church of Canada.[21] On June 27,

---

[19] Before this three International Congregational Councils had been held, the first in London in 1891; the second in Boston in 1899; and the third in Edinburgh in 1908.

[20] This was a body of independent and congregationally administered churches.

[21] The statement of faith of the United Church of Canada is purely declaratory and is not to be made an imposition upon any.

1931, the National Council of Congregational Churches of the United States and the General Convention of the Christian Church were merged at Seattle, Washington. The new organization was called the General Council of the Congregational and Christian Churches. Congregationalism has taken a prominent part in the Federal Council of Churches in Christ, and in problems connected with Faith and Order.[22]

2. *General Influence of Congregationalism.*—Congregationalism has always maintained that it can best serve the cause of God's Kingdom on earth by being loyal to its own ideals. These Congregational ideals or central convictions have been stated[23] as follows:

"1. The Supreme Place of the Person and Message of Jesus Christ as Revealed in the Scriptures and the Continuous Leadership of the Holy Spirit.
2. The Missionary Obligation which Summons every Christian and Organization of Christians to Labor for the Kingdom of God Throughout the World.
3. The Duty of Making the Church of Christ a place of Wide Liberty.
4. The Obligation of Shaping All the Life of the Church on the Democratic Model.
5. The Privilege and Duty of Close Fellowship between Christians.
6. Emphasis upon Personal and Social Righteousness as the Practical End for which the Church Exists.
7. A Confident Conviction of the Value of All Knowledge.'

Congregationalism looks upon Christianity as a way of life rather than as a system of doctrine. Hence all shades of theological opinions are represented among its clergy and laity. Their deepest sense of unity is the bond of common worship and a common program of service.

63. REVIEW QUESTIONS

1. Why did Congregationalism enjoy a special prestige at the beginning of the National Era?
2. What causes resulted in the "disestablishment" of Congregationalism in New England?
3. Why did the Congregationalists lose heavily during the Unitarian controversy?
4. Explain the lack of denominational aggressiveness in early Congregationalism.
5. Discuss the "Plan of Union."
6. When and how was the American Board founded?
7. Discuss the founding of important educational institutions of the Congregational order and of the beginnings of Home Missions.

[22] Congregationalism has taken a prominent part in all union movements such as the American Bible Society, the Y. M. C. A., the Y. W. C. A., the Student Volunteer Movement, the Missionary Education Movement, and the Laymen's Missionary Movement.
[23] *Pilgrim Deeds and Duties,* p. 89.

8. What factors promoted a closer church organization on the frontier?
9. How did Congregationalism express itself against slavery?
10. How has increased denominational consciousness expressed itself in recent Congregationalism?
11. What attitude has Congregationalism taken toward the natural and the historical sciences?
12. How has Congregationalism been related to the social awakening?
13. Discuss the origin and the influence of the Christian Endeavor movement.
14. What attitude does Congregationalism take toward movements for church unity? toward cooperation with other denominations?
15. Discuss the place and responsibility of Congregationalism as indicated by the seven central convictions for which Congregationalism stands.

TOPICS FOR SPECIAL STUDY

1. Contributions of Congregationalism to education and theology.
2. Congregationalism and its present relation to Calvinism.
3. Congregationalism and Christian Socialism.
4. The place of Bushnell, Lyman Beecher, and Henry Ward Beecher in the history of American Christianity.
5. Nettleton and Finney and their influence on Congregationalism.
6. Congregationalism and the "Social Gospel."
7. Congregational church organization.
8. The Christian Endeavor Movement.

A SELECTED BIBLIOGRAPHY FOR CHAPTER XXVII

1. Walker, *History of the Congregational Churches in the United States.*
2. Dunning, *Congregationalists in America.*
3. Hood, *The National Council of the Congregational Churches of the United States.*
4. Bacon, *The Congregationalists.*
5. Noble, *The Pilgrims.*
6. *Pilgrim Deeds and Duties,* prepared by direction of Tercentenary Commission.
7. Huntington, *Outlines of Congregational History.*
8. Walker, *The Creeds and Platforms of Congregationalism.*
9. Boardman, *A History of New England Theology.*
10. Foster, *Genetic History of New England Theology.*
11. Cheney, *Life and Letters of Horace Bushnell.*
12. Heermance, *Democracy in the Church.*
13. Nash, *Congregational Administration.*
14. Barton, *The Law of Congregational Usage.*
15. *Year Book of American Churches for 1933.*

CHAPTER XXVIII

THE PRESBYTERIAN CHURCH IN THE NATIONAL ERA, 1789-1936

Distinguished ancestry, history, and culture gave the early American Presbyterians much prestige. They were better organized than the Congregationalists and more assertive in their denominational spirit. Vital interest in industry and commerce rewarded them with great wealth.[1] The capital gained was used, not for luxury and easy living, but as an investment in additional undertakings, and also as a means of promoting higher education. The intelligent, thrifty, and cultural character of its constituency soon made Presbyterianism a most powerful influence. Numerically, the Presbyterians at present are the fourth largest Protestant group. There are nine distinctively Presbyterian churches. Five of these[2] are directly connected with the Secession and Relief movements of the Kirk of Scotland. Three Presbyterian churches[3] owe their origin to English, Welsh, French (Huguenot), Scotch, and Scotch-Irish elements; and one[4] is composed of colored people. Four Reformed churches[5] also use the Presbyterian form of church government and the Calvinistic confessional standards. These churches differ from the Presbyterian in the names of the church offices and certain other details. Instead of a session they have a consistory, a classis instead of a presbytery, and a general synod instead of a general assembly.

I. Keeping Abreast of the New Era, 1789-1830.—1. *Organization of the General Assembly, 1788.*—The Church soon rallied from the crippled condition of the Revolutionary War. Broken walls were restored; waste places were built up; scattered members were again brought into the fold; and adjustments were made

---

[1] For a discussion of Calvinism as a nursery for capitalism and modern industry, see page 273.

[2] The five churches of distinctively Scotch origin are: the Synod of the Reformed Presbyterian Church of North America; the General Synod of the Reformed Presbyterian Church; the Associate Reformed Presbyterian Church; the United Presbyterian Church of North America; and the Associate Synod of North America (also known as the Associate Presbyterian Church).

[3] The three churches are: the Presbyterian Church in the United States ("Southern"); the Presbyterian Church in the United States of America ("Northern"); and the Cumberland Presbyterian Church.

[4] This is the Colored Cumberland Presbyterian Church.

[5] These Reformed churches are: the (Dutch) Reformed Church in America; the Christian Reformed Church; the (German) Reformed Church in the United States;. and the Free Magyar Reformed Church in America.

in polity and organization to enable Presbyterianism to meet worthily pressing demands.

American Presbyterianism had no General Assembly[6] at the close of Revolution. The highest court was the Synod of New York and Philadelphia, and this was not a delegated body. Hard times and wide areas over which the Presbyterian churches were spread, made it increasingly difficult for ministers and churches to attend a general synod. The synod of 1786 accordingly resolved that, "considering the number and extent of the churches under our care, and the inconveniences of the present mode of govern-

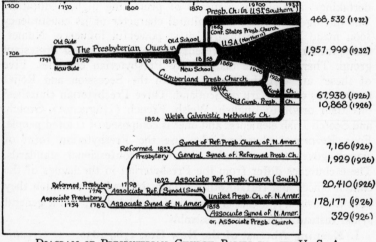

DIAGRAM OF PRESBYTERIAN CHURCH BODIES IN THE U. S. A.

ment by one synod, this synod will establish out of its own body three or more subordinate synods, out of which shall be composed a General Assembly, synod or council, agreeable to a system hereafter to be adopted." The General Assembly was formally organized in 1788. The following year the whole Church met for the first time in General Assembly. The synod of 1788 also adopted the Westminster Confession, the Larger and Smaller Catechisms, and a constitution consisting of a form of government, a book of discipline, and a directory for worship. Preserving sacred the principles inherited, the synod of 1788 found it necessary, nevertheless, to adjust the Westminster Confession, and the Directory to Ameri-

---

[6] The General Assembly is a delegated body representative of the whole American Presbyterian Church.

can conditions of church and state. Thus organized and equipped, the Church wsa prepared to enter upon an independent existence.[7]

2. *Widening of the Frontier.*—From its very beginning, the Church had been a zealous missionary society which had requested its ministers "to supply neighboring and destitute places." Presbyterianism had consequently spread rapidly from its main fountain in Maryland and Pennsylvania, over a large territory extending from New York to Georgia. As population moved westward, the Church kept bravely abreast. The General Assembly of 1789 adopted measures to furnish both missionaries and means for the establishment of churches on the frontier. Steps were also taken by the same assembly to aid in the publication and distribution of an American edition of the Bible. Later assemblies pushed the work of the Church vigorously forward. The General Assembly of 1800 adopted the following plans for the spread of the Gospel, (a) evangelistic work among the Indians;[8] (b) "instruction of the negroes, the poor and those who are destitute of the means of grace in various parts of this extensive country"; (c) distribution of the Bible and religious books; (d) support of candidates for the ministry; and (e) securing "professors of theology."

In view of conditions, this aggressive work was truly remarkable.

Churches in Western Pennsylvania experienced a quickening during the years 1781-87. In Virginia the movement started with a prayer meeting of four students hidden in the deep recesses of the woods at Prince Edward, about a mile from Hampden-Sidney College. The revival spread rapidly. Presbyterian ministers frequently went forth two by two through the neglected regions, preaching the Gospel to the settlers with great power. Under the leadership of James McGready[9] and William McGee, Presbyterian, and John McGee, Methodist, the "Great Revival" assumed its largest proportions in Kentucky and Tennessee during the years 1799-1801. Thousands came from far and near, bringing with them provisions and conveniences for camping over the week-end. This was the origin of camp meetings. The camps at Red River, Gaspar River,

[7] Presbyterians in America had always been ecclesiastically independent of European or British churches of like faith, but adjustments to American conditions produced a distinctively American type of Presbyterianism.

[8] This was not the beginning of Presbyterian missions among Indians. The Synod of New York had established missions among the Indians as early as in 1756.

[9] In 1796 Rev. James McGready organized a "praying band," the members of which entered into the following covenant: "We bind ourselves to observe the third Saturday in each month for one year as a day of fasting and prayer for the conversion of sinners in Logan County and throughout the world. We engage to spend half an hour every Saturday evening, beginning with set of sun, and half an hour every Sabbath morning at the rising of the sun, in pleading with God to revive his work."

and Muddy River in 1800, and at Concord and Cane Ridge in 1801, were particularly notable.

The Great Revival brought a great increase to the Church [10] A remarkable band of missionaries went forth to establish missions, churches, and schools along the frontier; and an equally devoted group of ministers continued the work in the East. During the decade 1802-12 practically every presbytery brought cheering reports of victory of grace over infidelity. The churches also rejoiced in the fact that the educated mind of the young republic was turning more and more to the Gospel of Christ.

3. *The Cumberland Presbyterian Church.*—This created a demand for preaching which the few available ministers were unable to meet. Meanwhile laymen, and even children, begat a desire to preach, and they were heard eagerly. The call for ministers in Kentucky led the Cumberland Presbytery, which in 1802 had been set off from the Presbytery of Transylvania, to license seven and to ordain four pastors who had not received the required classical and theological training. Some of these men were unable to subscribe to all of the Westminster Confession. Having been licensed and ordained contrary to the rules and traditions of the Presbyterian Church, the Synod of Kentucky requested these men, through a commission appointed in 1805, to present themselves to be reexamined. Refusing to appear, the synod suspended them from the ministry in 1806 and dissolved the Cumberland Presbytery. [11]

Not being convinced of wrong, [12] the suspended members sought redress from the General Assembly. Twice the assembly expressed a kindly concern declaring a willingness to give them a hearing, if they would seek redress in the manner prescribed by the Rules of Discipline. When they failed to do this, the General Assembly of 1809 endorsed the action of the Synod of Kentucky.

Three ministers were necessary to the constitution of a new presbytery, but only two of the aggrieved brethren were willing to go forward. Securing the support of the aged Rev. Samuel McAdow, [13] they organized a new Cumberland Presbytery on Feb-

[10] Advantages to Presbyterians from the Plan of Union of 1801 were mentioned in the previous chapter.

[11] The unseemly bodily exercises, which accompanied the Great Revival to a larger extent than any other such movement, produced a division of sentiment among the Presbyterians, resulting in a revival and an antirevival party. The involuntary bodily exercises, such as weeping, falling to the ground, muscular jerking, loss of consciousness, shouting, barking, singing, leaping, and dancing, caused many to feel, with the venerable Rev. Rice, "father of Kentucky Presbyterians," that the revival was "sadly mismanaged, dashed down and broken to pieces."

[12] They maintained that the great need for preachers growing out of the revival, and the impossibility of meeting this need by securing duly trained ministers of the Gospel, justified their procedure.

[13] Rev. McAdow was an earnest promoter of the revival. When asked by Finis Ewing and Samuel King if he would help them furnish the requisite number for a new pres-

ruary 4, 1810. It grew with amazing rapidity. In 1813 the Cumberland Synod was formed, and in 1829 this synod became the General Assembly of the Cumberland Presbyterian Church, with sixteen presbyteries. It held to Presbyterian standards, but rejected what was considered "fatalism" in the Westminster Confession. This church was largely a revival church which produced many prominent men and several institutions of learning.

4. *Missions and Schools.*—Organizing power, missionary zeal, learning and wealth, made Presbyterianism a powerful agency for the spread of the Gospel and for the establishment of institutions of learning. The earliest organized foreign mission work was carried on together with Congregational churches through the American Board of Commissioners for Foreign Missions. In 1831 the Western Foreign Missionary Society was organized as a distinctively denominational agency, and the Presbyterian Board of Foreign Missions was organized in 1837. Systematic home mission work was formally inaugurated in 1802 when the General Assembly appointed the first Standing Committee of Missions. In 1816 the work of this Committee was transferred to a Board of Home Missions, later known as the Board of Domestic Missions. The Board of Education was established in 1819.

Organized educational work had been carried on by the Presbyterians ever since the founding of Tennent's "Log College" in 1726 on the banks of the Neshaminy. Similar schools had been established during the Colonial Era.[14] A number of theological seminaries were founded: Princeton Theological Seminary, 1812; Auburn Theological Seminary, 1819; Union Theological Seminary in Virginia, 1824; Western Theological Seminary, 1827; Presbyterian Theological Seminary at Columbia, S. C., 1828; Lane Theological Seminary, 1829; McCormick Theological Seminary,[15] 1829; and Union Theological Seminary in New York, 1836. Princeton gained much fame as an institution of learning and as a stronghold of Calvinism.

II. **Growth, Division, and Reunion, 1830-70.**—Between 1790

bytery, he asked them to wait for an answer until next day. He spent the night in prayer, and answered in the affirmative.
[14] Other schools of the "Log College" type were those of Blair at Fagg's Manor, Pa.; of Finley at Nottingham, Md.; of Thaddeus Dod on Ten-Mile Creek, Pa.; of Joseph Smith at Upper Buffalo; of Dr. McMillan on the banks of the Chartiers (the later Jefferson College); of Patillo at Granville, N. C.; of Dr. Hall at Snow Creek, N. C.; of McGready at his own house; of Wallis at New Providence; of McCorkle at Salisbury, N. C.; of McCaule at Centre, N. C.; etc.
[15] McCormick Theological Seminary was founded at Hanover, Indiana, in 1829. In 1840 it was moved to New Albany, Indiana, and renamed the New Albany Theological Seminary. It was later moved to Chicago and the name was changed to McCormick Theological Seminary of the Presbyterian Church.

and 1837 Presbyterianism increased its membership from 18,000 to 220,557. This was due, partly to the large Scotch-Irish immigration, and partly to a revival of religion. But certain workings of the Plan of Union soon threatened disruption.

1. *Causes leading up to the Old and New School Schism.*—The Plan of Union, operated mainly in the region north of the Ohio River, gained large, influential New England groups.[16] With their Congregational background and their uniform adherence to "New Haven theology,"[17] these groups gradually imparted a dual character to Presbyterianism, including two sets of agencies for work, two sets of church order, and two types of doctrine.[18] This development being strongly resented by the rigid Scotch-Irish element, friction developed between the old and the new, giving rise to the Old and New School.

The Old School party demanded that missionary and evangelistic work be placed under separate denominational control. This propaganda started about the year 1825. In 1828 Dr. Nathaniel W. Taylor of Yale Divinity School delivered a commencement address in which he was particularly severe on the doctrine of original sin. The following year, a brilliant Presbyterian minister, Albert Barnes of Morristown, New Jersey, declared himself in sympathy. The next year, as pastor of the First Presbyterian Church of Philadelphia, he became the storm center of the Church. Charges of heresy were lodged, and ecclesiastical trials were instituted, not only against him, but against Lyman Beecher of Lane Seminary, Edward Beecher, J. M. Sturtevant, William Kirby of Illinois College, and George Duffield. The controversy was intensified in 1836 when the New School party founded the Union Theological Seminary in New York, independent of the control of the General Assembly. This event drove Princeton from its moderate position over to the Old School party.

2. *The Schism and Its Consequences.*—The controversy reached its culmination in 1837 when the Old School men in the General Assembly abolished the Plan of Union, and expelled four synods—Western Reserve, Utica, Geneva, and Genesee, numbering 536 churches—known to be New School in sentiment. At the General Assembly of 1838, delegates were refused admission. This led to the formation of a General Assembly of the New School group.

[16] It was said that "Congregationalism is a river rising in New England and emptying south and west in Presbyterianism."

[17] Nathaniel W. Taylor, who organized the Yale Divinity School in 1822, was the creator of the "New Haven theology." He modified the traditional Calvinistic theology by making the freedom of the will the real working theory of theology and practice.

[18] This was a direct result of the Plan of Union.

One hundred and forty commissioners and 126,000 communicants remained with the Old School, while 136 commissioners and 106,000 communicants went with the New School.

For more than thirty years the two church bodies claimed the same name, held the same doctrinal standards, observed the same ritual, followed the same discipline, and occupied much the same territory. Yet, they allowed bitterness to keep them apart, losing much ground to the Methodists and the Baptists. During the first third of the century, Presbyterianism increased sixfold; during the second third of the century it scarcely doubled. Of the two churches, the Old School group enjoyed the largest increase.

3. *Schisms caused by Slavery.*—The subject of slavery produced earnest discussion and deep, widespread agitation in both branches of the Church. The New School Assembly developed an intolerant antislavery sentiment which caused its six Southern synods to withdraw in 1858 to form the United Synod of the Presbyterian Church.

When the Civil War broke out, the Old School Church also divided. The passage of the "Spring Resolutions"[19] by the General Assembly (Old School) in 1861, caused the churches of the Southern Confederacy to withdraw, and to organize the Presbyterian Church of the Confederate States of America. This organization united in 1863 with the Southern New School body, to form the Presbyterian Church in the United States ("Southern"). In 1869 the Synod of Kentucky joined this Southern church, and the Synod of Missouri was received in 1874.

4. *Reunion of Old and New School in the North.*—The Old and the New School in the North rapidly came together. Interchange of delegates, proposed in 1862, was started in 1863. Three years later, committees were appointed to consider a plan of union. Joint meetings were held, and differences were explained. Formal reunion came in 1869 on "the doctrinal and ecclesiastical basis of our common standards." In May, 1870, the reunited General Assembly of the Presbyterian Church in the United States of America voted to raise a memorial fund of five million dollars. The Church responded by raising $7,883,983.

III. Presbyterianism in the New Industrial and Progressive Era, 1870-1918.—Presbyterians in the North united just in

---

[19] So called because they were introduced by Dr. Gardner Spring of New York. These resolutions professed loyalty to the Federal Government. It must be borne in mind that when the General (Old School) Assembly met in May, 1861, eight of the Southern States had seceded from the Federal Union, and war had been in progress for about a month. Dr. Charles Hodge, who favored the Federal Government, opposed the "Spring Resolutions" on the ground that the General Assembly had no right to determine questions of civil allegiance.

time to meet the many new demands of the nation. Aggressiveness, activity, and expansion characterized the reunited Church. The Scotch-Irish common-sense, with its peculiar appeal to the practical mind of America,[20] upheld traditional Christianity against materialism; and enthusiastic evangelistic propaganda served as a bulwark against liberalizing forces.

1. *Relations with the Southern Assembly.*—Efforts made in 1870 and in 1874 for closer relations between the Northern and the Southern Assemblies proved unsuccessful, evidently because of the "obnoxious things said and done in time of great excitement," during the Civil War. Fraternal relations were definitely established, however, in 1882, making possible a joint celebration in 1888 of the centenary of the adoption of the constitution of the Church, and another joint celebration in 1897, of the two hundred and fiftieth anniversary of the Westminster Assembly. Closer cooperation has been effected in foreign missions, in publication, and in education. Reunion is the prayer of earnest souls in both church bodies, but so far, all efforts to unite the two groups have been without success.

2. *Years of Steady Progress.*—With commendable wisdom Presbyterianism has kept pace with ever-enlarging demands at home and abroad, making steady progress along all lines. Better organized Sunday-schools have added much to the efficiency of local churches. A Woman's Executive Committee of Home Missions[21] was organized in 1878. Other organizations were the Board of Temperance and Moral Welfare, 1880; the Board of Aid for Colleges, 1883; the Permanent Committee of Sabbath Observance, 1888; the Department of University Work, 1900; the Committee on Evangelism, 1901; the Sustentation Department in 1906; the Permanent Committee on Men's Work, 1912; the Committee on Army and Navy Chaplains, 1915; and the New Era Expansion Movement,[22] about 1918. Great advance was made in contributions. In 1908 an executive commission (General Council) was established to carry on the work between the meetings of the General Assembly. A committee was appointed by the General Assembly of 1903 "to consider the whole subject of co-operation, confederation

[20] The Scotch-Irish Realism has been called "the typical American philosophy."
[21] This organization became the Woman's Board of Home Missions in 1897.
[22] Precursors of this movement were: the "Every Member" idea, pioneered by Dr. W. H. Hubbard; the "Forward Movement," pioneered by David McConaughy; and the "Every Member Plan Committee." The New Era Movement, which seeks to co-ordinate all the work of "local congregations, presbyteries, synods, boards, and other agencies of our Church with special reference to family religion, evangelism education, missions, social service, and stewardship," has the following program: (a) visualizing the whole task, (b) unifying the program, (c) organizing the Church, (d) setting the goals, (e) grouping the members, (f) providing the capital, (g) cultivating the sense of solidarity in our united calling in Christ, and (h) nurturing of the spiritual life of the Church.

and consolidation with other churches." This committee identified the Presbyterian Church with the movement for interdenominational fellowship;[23] it also effected the reunion of the Cumberland Presbyterian Church in 1906; and the merger with the Welsh Calvinistic Methodist Church in 1920.

The heresy trials of Dr. David Swing in 1874, of Dr. Charles A. Briggs in 1893, of Dr. Henry Preserved Smith in 1894, and of Dr. A. C. McGiffert in 1899 threatened for a time to disturb the peace. Dr. Swing was accused of denying the divinity of Christ. Drs. Briggs and Smith differed from the traditional teachings regarding the authority of religion and the credibility of the Bible. Dr. McGiffert had adopted the methods and accepted some of the radical findings of higher criticism. The determined stand of the Church indicated that organized Presbyterianism was zealously adhering to its orthodox faith.

3. *Revision of the Standards.*—In response to many pastors for a brief statement in modern language of what the Presbyterian Church believes and teaches, the General Assembly of 1902 adopted a "Brief Statement of the Reformed Faith," consisting of sixteen articles. This Statement forms no part of the standards of the Church, but merely interprets the Confession in untechnical language.

The revision of the Confession of Faith was successfully completed in 1903. To the original thirty-three chapters of the Westminster Confession were added two more; one on the Holy Spirit, and one on "missions and the love of God for all men." A Declaratory Statement was also added to explain certain statements in Chapters III and X. As the General Assembly of 1904 declared that this revision did not impair the system of doctrine contained in the Westminster Confession, it appears that the Presbyterian Church is as genuinely Calvinistic as ever. In 1906 a Book of Common Worship was approved by the General Assembly for optional use.

4. *The Merger of 1906.*—The revision of the Confession of Faith was the basis for a "Plan of Union," approved by the General Assemblies of the Presbyterian Church in the United States of America and the Cumberland Presbyterian Church in 1904. Formal reunion came about in 1906. A minority in the Cumberland Presbyterian Church refused to join, since continuing the name and the organization of their church.

[23] The Presbyterians took an active part in the organization of the Federal Council of the Churches of Christ in America, in 1908. Presbyterians are also represented on the Advisory Committee of the World Conference on Questions of Faith and Order.

IV. American Presbyterianism since the World War.—Presbyterians gave hearty support to the United States Government during the recent war.[24] When the war was over, the various agencies were readjusted to post-war conditions for continued world-wide evangelization.

1. *Consolidation of Organized Activities.*—A notable feature is consolidation of organized denominational work. During the years 1923-1925, the office of the General Assembly was organized into five departments, administration, publicity, vacancy and supply, church cooperation and union, and historical research and conservation. The executive committee of 1908 was changed to a General Council; and the boards of the General Assembly were reduced to the original four, namely, the Board of National Missions, the Board of Foreign Missions, the Board of Christian Education, and the Board of Ministerial Relief and Sustentation, later called Board of Pensions.

In 1925-27 a Special Commission was elected to study the causes of unrest in the Church.

2. *A National, not a Sectional Church.*—It is no longer correct to think of the Presbyterian Church in the United States of America as a "Northern" Church, because it has churches in every State. Several races are represented. Four synods consist of colored ministers and churches; one synod is German; six synods are Welsh (Calvinistic); two presbyteries are Bohemian. But the great majority is American-born.

3. *Educational Work.*—Presbyterianism has always placed great emphasis on education. The various groups own a large number of institutions of higher learning, including 39 colleges and universities and 12 theological seminaries. Fourteen additional colleges and universities are controlled by the Church. The Presbyterian Church in the United States (South) owns 29 colleges and universities and five theological seminaries. The United Presbyterian Church of North America has six colleges and one theological seminary.

4. *Fundamentalism.*—In 1910 "Fundamentalism" started as a protest against the rising tide of "Modernism." Fostered by the Moody Bible Institute in Chicago and by the Bible Institute of Los Angeles, California, it advocated the following five test-points

[24] The various Christian churches in America have always tried to promote the welfare of the American Republic. Devotion to freedom and love for everything truly American have been prominent characteristics of the Presbyterians. Walpole said in the English Parliament during the Revolutionary War, "Cousin America has run off with a Presbyterian parson."

of true Christianity: (a) the Virgin Birth of Christ, (b) the physical resurrection, (c) the inerrancy of Scriptures in every respect, (d) the substitutionary theory of the Atonement, and (e) the imminent, physical Second Coming of Christ. It caused much controversy, particularly among Baptists, Presbyterians, and the Disciples of Christ. In the Presbyterian Church, the attempted heresy trial[25] of Harry Emerson Fosdick in 1924, and the breach in the Princeton Theological Seminary ranks[26] in 1929, are notable illustrations.

5. *Presbyterian Contributions.*—Presbyterianism, as a typical representative of Calvinism, has been a great force.[27] Presbyterians have made a particular contribution to church organization.

There are several radically different theories on church government. (1) Erastianism maintains that the Church is only one form of the State. (2) Quakerism does not provide for the external organization of the Church. (3) The papal theory assumes that the pope is Christ's Vicar on earth, that the apostleship is perpetuated in the order of prelates, and that the people must be subject to their infallible control. (4) The episcopal theory assumes a three-fold order in the ministry—deacons, elders, and bishops—and that Christians are subject to the apostle-bishops. (5) The Congregational theory assumes (a) the governing and executive power of the entire Church as a brotherhood, and (b) the autonomy of the local congregation. (6) The Presbyterian theory assumes that the ministers are the representatives of Christ and the ruling elders are the representatives of the people. Presbyterianism occupies an intermediary position between episcopacy and congregationalism. In episcopacy the ecclesiastical unit is the diocese; in congregationalism it is the single congregation; in presbyterianism it is the presbytery composed of pastors and elders representing all congregations within a specified district. In episcopacy authority is vested in the bishop; in congregationalism it is vested in the people; in presbyterianism it is vested in representatives chosen by the people.

[25] Harry Emerson Fosdick is a Baptist minister who became professor of practical theology in Union Theological Seminary in 1915. He also accepted the invitation to be permanent preacher for the First Presbyterian Church of New York. The Presbytery of Philadelphia tried to bring him to trial for heresy, because of his outspoken "modernistic" views. The General Assembly of 1924 did not pass judgment upon his views, but invited him to enter the ministry of the Presbyterian Church or to vacate his pulpit. He chose the latter alternative, and has since founded a new independent church in New York.

[26] The controversy regarding Princeton Theological Seminary resulted in the withdrawal of some of the conservative members of the faculty, and the formation of a new school, the Westminster Theological Seminary of Philadelphia, in 1929.

[27] For contributions of Calvinism, see pages 285-88.

64. REVIEW QUESTIONS

1. Why was Presbyterianism a dominant force in the early life of the American Republic?
2. In what ways did the Presbyterians adjust themselves to national life?
3. What part did the Presbyterians have in the "Great Revival"?
4. Account for the Cumberland schism.
5. How did the "Plan of Union" influence the course of Presbyterianism?
6. Explain the Presbyterian schism of 1837.
7. How did the Southern Church come into being?
8. How and when did the Old and the New School in the North reunite?
9. Discuss the relations of the Northern and the Southern General Assemblies.
10. Why has Scotch-Irish Realism made such an appeal?
11. What part has Presbyterianism played in industrial life?
12. What inferences do you draw from the heresy trials?
13. Why does the Presbyterian Church interest itself in Christian education?
14. What is meant by the New Era Movement?
15. What contributions have the Presbyterians made to Western civilization?

TOPICS FOR SPECIAL STUDY

1. The influence of the Fundamentalist-Modernist controversy on the Presbyterian Church.
2. Presbyterianism and higher education.
3. Scotch-Irish Realism, "the typical American philosophy."
4. Presbyterian organization.
5. Presbyterianism and slavery.

A SELECTED BIBLIOGRAPHY FOR CHAPTER XXVIII

1. Reed: *History of the Presbyterian Churches of the World.*
2. Baron: *History of American Christianity.*
3. Gillett: *History of the Presbyterian Church in the United States* (2 vols.).
4. Thompson: *A History of the Presbyterian Churches in the United States.*
5. Hanna: *The Scotch-Irish or the Scot in North Britain, North Ireland and North America* (2 vols.).
6. Green: *The Foundations of American Nationality.*
7. Hodge: *The Constitutional History of the Presbyterian Church in the United States of America.*
8. Davidson: *History of the Presbyterian Church in the State of Kentucky.*
9. Paxon: *History of the American Frontier, 1763-1893.*
10. Smith: *Old Redstone, or Historical Sketches of Western Presbyterianism.*
11. Cleveland: *The Great Revival in the West, 1797-1805.*
12. Speer: *The Great Revival of 1800.*
13. McDonnald: *History of the Cumberland Presbyterian Church.*
14. Green: *Presbyterian Missions.*
15. Barber: *The Slavery Controversy and the Presbyterians.*
16. Glasgow: *History of the Reformed Presbyterian Church in America.*

CHAPTER XXIX

THE METHODIST EPISCOPAL CHURCH, 1784-1936

Methodists and Baptists enjoyed almost equal popularity in America. Both took a prominent part in pioneer church work, and both enjoyed a remarkable ingathering.[1] By 1830 the Methodists had become one of the largest Protestant denominations in the New World.[2] Their organization, doctrine,[3] and discipline proved to be particularly well suited to the new democracy. Methodism, as "an Anglo-Saxon translation of Lutheranism,"[4] or rather—as a mediary between Lutheranism, Anglicanism, and Calvinism—has made an important contribution to religion; and its rigid, militaristic church discipline has made it a great moral force.

I. The Methodist Circuit System at Its Best, 1784-1830.— A distinguishing feature of early Methodism was its organization of itinerant preachers under the direction of bishops and presiding elders.[5] The circuit system was admirably suited to propaganda. Methodist circuit riders kept pace with the frontier. They followed almost every wagon-train of pioneers, and frequently "got on the ground" with the first settlers. It was a merciless calling, but it brought marvellous results.

1. *Organization of the Methodist Episcopal Church.*—John Wesley intended Methodism to be merely a movement, not a church. His lay preachers in England did not seek ordination or settled pastorates, nor did they presume to offer the sacraments. Methodist societies were organized for Christian fellowship and the development of spiritual life, and itinerant lay preachers were directed to minister to them. It was this systematized movement— not an organized church—that Wesley transplanted to America.

---

[1] Both were popular in spite of their differences. The Methodists had a solid organization, a militaristic regime; while the Baptists had, perhaps, the least compact organization among the larger Protestant churches. The Methodists were schooled in Wesley's discipline of absolute obedience; the Baptists left much room for individualism. The Methodists emphasized the need of culture and education more than did the Baptists. Both made a powerful appeal to the American people through their simple, direct Gospel message.

[2] The Methodists still constitute the second largest Protestant denomination.

[3] The Methodists emphasized free grace, free will, and individual responsibility for salvation. This personal, experiential note made a peculiar appeal. In theology the Church is, of course, Arminian.

[4] Holmquist, Kirkehistorie, Vol. III, p. 89.

[5] Other outstanding characteristics of early Methodism were its enthusiastic singing and its extemporaneous and emotional preaching.

It was soon evident, however, that an ordained Wesleyan ministry was essential. The Methodists now numbered about 15,000, including 83 itinerant preachers and several hundred local preachers. These preachers were not ordained, and hence could not baptize, officiate at marriage ceremonies, or administer the communion. For such services the Methodists had to look to the Episcopalian clergy, at this time sadly disorganized.[6]

Wesley asked bishops of the Church of England to ordain Methodist preachers for America. Failing in this, he himself took the authority to ordain ministers. Convinced that presbyters and bishops are of the same order,[7] with the same right to ordain, he ordained Richard Whatcoat and Thomas Vasey as deacons,[8] on September 1, 1784. The next day they were ordained presbyters or elders for America. Dr. Thomas Coke was ordained as "superintendent" of the brethren in America. These three were instructed to ordain Francis Asbury as joint superintendent of North America. Wesley said, "As our American brethren are now totally disentangled, both from the state and the English hierarchy, we dare not entangle them again, either with the one or the other. They are now at full liberty, simply to follow the Scriptures and the primitive church. And we judge it best that they should stand fast in the liberty wherewith God has so strangely made them free."

When the three men arrived, a Methodist Conference was called on December 24, 1784, at Baltimore. This so-called Christmas Conference[9] adopted the Order of Worship and the Articles of Religion[10] prepared by Wesley, and approved the name "Methodist Episcopal" for the new organization. Asbury would not accept office merely by appointment of Wesley. The Conference elected him, therefore, by unanimous vote. On successive days he was or-

[6] The Methodist situation was so intolerable that a serious schism was barely avoided in 1779. The Southern Methodists were especially impatient with the cautious attitude of Wesley. Two Methodist conferences were held that year. At the Conference at Fluvanna, several Methodist preachers were actually ordained. Asbury succeeded, however, in averting a schism, assuring his people that Wesley would act in due time.

[7] Wesley had held this view for nearly fifty years. He wrote in 1756, "I still believe the episcopal form of church government to agree with the practice and writings of the apostles; but that it is prescribed in Scripture I do not believe. This opinion, which I once zealously espoused, I have been heartily ashamed of ever since I read Bishop Stillingfleet's 'Irenicon.' I think he has unanswerably proved that neither Christ nor his apostles prescribed any particular form of church government; and that the plea of divine right for diocesan episcopacy was never heard in the primitive church."

[8] The Church of England has a threefold ministry, namely, deacons, presbyters, and bishops.

[9] The Christmas Conference was held in Lovely Lane Chapel, lasting from December 24, 1784 to January 2, 1785.

[10] Wesley had reduced the Thirty-Nine Articles of the Church of England to Twenty-Five, striking out everything of a sectarian nature, and all references to allegiance to the British Government. He endeavored to form the Articles of Religion in such a way that they could be subscribed to by almost any evangelical Christian. The Christmas Conference added another article which declared Methodist allegiance to the United States Government.

dained deacon, elder, and superintendent.[11] The Methodist Episcopal Church was now fully organized.

2. *How Early American Methodism was Organized.*—Methodism retained the peculiar features of English Methodism. The smallest unit was the "class" of twelve or more members, supervised by a class leader.[12] Several classes made up a "society" or

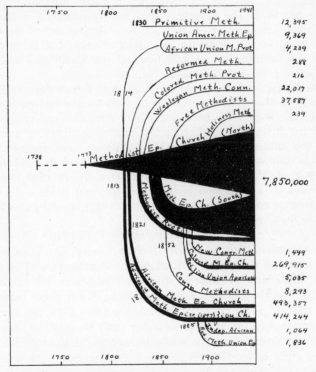

DIAGRAM OF AMERICAN METHODIST CHURCH BODIES

a local group of Methodists. Next came the "circuit," or several societies under one preacher.[13] Several circuits were again united

[11] Asbury had been appointed Wesley's "general assistant in America" in 1772, with power over all Methodist preachers and societies in the land. But Thomas Rankin had superseded him the following year. Rankin returned to England at the outbreak of the Revolutionary War, while Asbury chose to remain. Meanwhile he functioned as the generally recognized supervisor until formally appointed by Wesley and elected by the Conference.

[12] At the "class meeting" the members came together for prayer, instruction, and mutual edification. It was the duty of the leader to watch over the souls and to give spiritual counsel.

[13] The circuit preacher was so faithful in his itineracy that it became a proverbial saying, on a bitterly cold winter day, "There is nothing out today but crows and Methodist preachers."

in a "district" under a presiding elder. Above all were the itinerant —not diocesan—superintendents or bishops, with absolute control over the entire denomination.

The ministry was of two orders, deacon and elder. Appointments of itinerant preachers were changed, at first every six months, then every year, and then every two years. These circuit riders were assisted by local preachers from whose ranks itinerant preachers were recruited. The preachers were poorly educated in the sense Abraham Lincoln was poorly educated. They preached the Gospel with great fervor, designing to convict of sin and to bring repentance and faith in God for salvation and sanctification. There was a probation period of six months for new converts.

Methodism differed from the English in the conference system. Quarterly conferences were held by each society and each district under the care of a presiding elder. Annual Conferences were held for itinerant preachers, and General Conferences were held for the entire denomination for legislative, administrative, and judicial purposes. The General Conference held its first meeting in 1792, and has since convened quadrennially. In 1808 it was established as a delegated body,[14] and the first delegated General Conference convened in 1812. Prior to 1872, lay delegates had no seat in the General Conference.

3. *Asbury's Episcopal Administration, 1784-1816.*—Most of the administrative work was under Bishop Asbury. Dr. Coke was absent a part of every year in England,[15] and after Wesley's death in 1791, he became a leader of English Methodism. He labored incessantly in the cause of foreign missions.[16] For these reasons he was relieved from his office in America after 1808, but his name was retained on the *Minutes* as bishop until his death in 1814.

Asbury's administration was arbitrary and despotic.[17] Ministers had a right to express their wishes, but the power to determine rested with him, and he used this power fearlessly in the discharge of his duty. He was witty, shrewd, far-sighted, and a good organizer. He knew the spirit of America, and while he governed the ministers and the lay members, he studied how to be governed

[14] Up to this time the General Conference had been composed of all travelling preachers. Consequently, the region nearest the place where the Conference was held had the largest representation. After 1808 only one out of every five members of each Annual Conference could be chosen delegate to the General Conference. This reduced the General Conference to a more desirable size, and insured representation from all districts.
[15] Dr. Coke crossed the Atlantic eighteen times.
[16] He was the head of the first Methodist missionary committee in England in 1790, and president of the reorganized society of 1804.
[17] Next to the Roman Catholic Church, the early Methodist Episcopal Church was the most clerically organized denomination in America.

by them. He did not tolerate his preachers going into winter quarters in the city churches. Theirs was a saddlebag ministry. He demanded that they be alert, brave, consecrated, and ready to obey orders by bringing the Gospel message to the most remote settlements. And Asbury never asked more of his preachers than he was willing to do himself. He travelled continually, from Maine to Georgia, and from the Atlantic coast to the frontier settlements in Kentucky and Tennessee.

Knowing that the title "superintendent" meant in fact "bishop,"[18] he made the change in 1787. Wesley reprimanded him, saying, "How can you, how dare you suffer yourself to be called Bishop? I shudder, I start, at the very thought! Men may call me a knave or a fool, a rascal, a scoundrel, and I am content: but they shall never by my consent call me a bishop! For my sake, for God's sake, for Christ's sake put a full end to this!" But the majority of the preachers approved.

Bishop Asbury divided the country into districts with an academy in each. This plan was adopted by the General Conference of 1796, and provisions were made for six Annual Conferences, one for each district. Because of the frequent absence of Dr. Coke, Wesley requested in 1787 that Richard Whatcoat be ordained joint superintendent.[19] Whatcoat was not elected bishop, however, till 1800. He died in 1806 and was succeeded two years later by William McKendree, a native American. Bishop McKendree later became Bishop Asbury's successor.[20]

4. *The Circuit Preacher.*—As the circuit embraced a whole group of communities, it usually took from two to six weeks to make the round. He rode to his task and preached wherever opportunity offered. In his preaching he emphasized personal experience of God's saving grace, victory over all sin, and a buoyant, triumphant life. He preached with a tremendous earnestness and a rustic rudeness that made a peculiarly strong appeal to the frontiersman. And he not only preached and lived this Gospel, but he sang it, and made his audiences sing it, through Charles Wesley's hymns, so expressive of true and personal religious experiences. The Methodist Book Concern, established in 1789, arranged for suit-

---

[18] That is, bishop in the older sense, or shepherd-bishop.

[19] American Methodists answered Wesley that they were not ready *now* to obey his command.

[20] Mention might be made of two peculiar schemes developed by the two early leaders. Bishop Asbury proposed to form a "Council" composed of the bishops and the presiding elders. This Council was to take the place of the more democratic General Conference as the chief authority. The plan was strongly opposed, especially by Dr. Coke, and had to be given up. Dr. Coke also developed a purely personal plan of bringing about a union of Methodists and Episcopalians, but the matter was not brought to attention.

able religious literature, and it was the duty of every circuit preacher to keep his people supplied with books. Few preachers were married because the circuits could not support a married preacher; and none of the bishops prior to 1816 were married. A large number of early preachers died before they were thirty years old because of strenuous work.

Theodore Roosevelt said, "The whole country is under a debt of gratitude to the Methodist circuit riders, the Methodist pioneer preachers, whose movement westward kept pace with the movement of the frontier, who shared all the hardships in the life of the frontiersman, while at the same time ministering to that frontiersman's spiritual needs and seeing that his pressing material cares and the hard and grinding poverty of his life did not wholly extinguish the divine fire within his soul." Typical were Bishop Asbury, Freeborn Garrettson, Jesse Lee, Peter Cartwright, and Bishop McKendree.

5. *Frontier Revivalism.*—The early Church was a revival church. It made the greatest contribution to frontier revivalism, and it also enjoyed the largest ingathering. As a result of the "Great Revival," lasting about eighty years, membership in the Western circuits more than doubled.

Revivalism was most successfully conducted through camp meetings. Originating with the Presbyterians, they developed as a Methodist institution. The early meetings were attended by many extravagances,[21] and yet these meetings were peculiarly adapted to the circumstances. Something strong was needed to stir the frontiersman.

Among the largest camp meetings was the sacramental meeting at Cane Ridge, Kentucky, in August, 1801, where about twenty-five thousand people were in attendance, including the Governor. Seven stands were erected so that seven ministers could preach at the same time. Presbyterian, Methodist, and Baptist ministers preached, and "they were of one mind and soul," according to Barton W. Stone, Presbyterian minister at Cane Ridge. This meeting lasted about seven days and nights.

---

[21] Peter Cartwright, who did not approve of the peculiar bodily commotions of those who attended, described the "jerks" as follows, "They would be taken under a warm song or sermon, and seized with a convulsive jerking all over, which they could not by any possibility avoid, and the more they resisted, the more they jerked. . . . Most usually persons taken with the jerks, to obtain relief, as they said, would rise up and dance. Some would run, but could not get away. . . . To see these proud young gentlemen and young ladies, dressed in their silks, jewelry and prunella, from top to toe, take the jerks, would often excite my risibilities. The first jerk or so, you would see their fine bonnets, caps and combs fly. . . . It was, on all occasions, my practice to recommend fervent prayer as a remedy, and it almost universally proved an effectual antidote."

6. *McKendree's Episcopal Administration, 1808-1834.*—William McKendree was Presiding Elder over the Western Conference for eight years before he was elected bishop. The Western Conference included all circuits beyond the Alleghanies, from Central Ohio to the borders of Georgia. The "Great Revival" tended to obliterate denominational lines. Presbyterian, Methodist, and Baptist ministers labored together, and Bishop Asbury cordially approved this co-operative work. But William McKendree and some of his brethren differed. McKendree said, "The union meetinghouses have been no blessing to us, but a great injury. For two years I was stationed in a union church; from ever being stationed in another, good Lord, deliver me."

McKendree's election as bishop in 1808 marked a turning-point in American Methodism. He was a great preacher and a very capable administrator. But his outstanding service was the change from the one-man autocracy of Asbury to a constitutional and settled legal order.

7. *Missions and Schools.*—The organization of the Missionary Society in 1819 marked the beginning of Methodist missions.[22] From 1819 to 1907 this society included both home and foreign work. Many auxiliary societies were formed to contribute to the funds of the general society, and also for carrying on other work. Prior to 1830, missions were largely confined to the Indians.

Educational interests centered in primary and secondary schools. Bishop Asbury established at least one strong academy in each district, and he made several attempts to establish a college.[23] He was of the opinion, however, that "the Lord called not Mr. Whitefield or the Methodists to build colleges." Very few preachers before 1840 had a college education or a regular theological training. There was a strong prejudice against educated preachers because study and learning, it was thought, might interfere with soul-saving.

But this apparent antagonism toward higher education was not inherent. The Holy Club, formed in a famous university, combined evangelistic passion with genuine zeal for education. This found expression in America after 1820. By 1840 the Church had sixteen colleges and twenty-six secondary schools. The first theo-

[22] The actual beginning of mission work was made by John Stewart, a humble mulatto, who preached the Gospel to the Wyandot Indians in 1815.
[23] Cokesbury College was founded in Abingdon, Maryland, in 1785. The name was a combination of the names of the two bishops—Coke and Asbury. The college building was destroyed by fire in 1795. Cokesbury College was then moved to Baltimore, but the new college building was destroyed by fire in 1796, and the college was given up. In 1816 another attempt was made to establish a Methodist school—Asbury College—in Baltimore. This school was also short-lived.

logical seminaries[24] were The Methodist General Biblical Institute at Concord, New Hampshire, in 1847; and Garrett Biblical Institute, established in 1855. Drew Theological Seminary was opened in 1867.

8. *Early Methodist Schisms.*—Conflict between autocratic and democratic tendencies led to several schisms. The first occurred in 1792. Objecting to the large authority and life-tenure of the superintendents, Rev. James O'Kelley of Virginia asked the General Conference of 1792 to amend the *Discipline* so that a preacher dissatisfied with his appointment could appeal to the Conference, and if the Conference concurred, the bishop should give him another appointment. He had many sympathizers, but the Conference opposed. He withdrew, with a considerable number of preachers and church members, later organizing the Republican Methodist Church. But the new organization did not prove permanent. Some returned to the Methodist Episcopal Church, while others joined the Christian Church.

The first permanent schism[25] came in 1830. A party insisted that there be more democracy in government. It favored (a) election—not appointment—of presiding elders, (b) lay representation in Annual and General Conferences, and (c) representation of local preachers in the General Conferences. The General Conference of 1828 was formally petitioned to concede to lay representation in all conferences, but the petition was rejected. Convinced that conciliation was impossible, the party organized the Methodist Protestant Church, on November 2, 1830, at Baltimore. The new organization grew rapidly.

II. **Change from Circuit to Station System, 1830-1870.**—The outstanding features from 1830 to 1870 were the gradual transition from circuit to station system, the great schism caused by slavery, the attempts at reconstruction after the Civil War, and the establishment of the Board of Education of the Methodist Episcopal Church in 1868.

1. *Why the station system was adopted.*—By 1834, the camp meeting and the circuit rider had established Methodism to the Mississippi and beyond. The Methodists kept pace with the Western movement, but would they be able to hold their ground?

Conditions were rapidly changing. There was a growing stability, a more elevated level of society, and an increasing denomina-

---

[24] Some theological training was also given in certain secondary schools.
[25] There was a small secession of Reformed Methodists in 1814.

tional rivalry. The circuit preacher making his round every two to six weeks could no longer adequately serve. Influenced by other denominations, the local church—often a single congregation—demanded a stationary pastor who could give his entire time to that church. The circuit preacher was gradually replaced.[26]

2. *Slavery.*—Two factors brought the slavery situation to a crisis. *First,* the invention of spinning and weaving machinery and the rise of a new cotton market in England made cotton the most important American product. Southern agriculture was revolutionized between 1790 and 1830, and the slave was needed more than ever. *Second,* while slavery was acquiring an increasing importance, abolitionism was being fervently proclaimed in the North, especially in New England. A conflict was inevitable.

Methodism had taken a strong stand against slavery,[27] but exigencies in slave territory led to an abandonment of the old ground. Attempts were made to avoid complicity in the institution on the one hand, and to repress abolition agitation on the other. Opposers of slavery would not yield, however, and the result was the formation of the Wesleyan Methodist Church, in 1843.

The great schism which came in 1844-45, began with Bishop James O. Andrew of Georgia, who by marriage had become a nominal slaveholder. According to law, neither he nor his wife could free their slaves. At the General Conference of 1844, the Northern delegates forced a resolution which advised Bishop Andrew to "desist from the exercise of office" so long as he continued to hold slaves. The resolution was adopted by a vote of 110 to 68. The Southern delegates refused to allow Bishop Andrew to resign, so the Conference adopted a provisional plan of separation, to become effective whenever the Southern conferences should deem it necessary. They approved the separation and on May 17, 1845, the Methodist Episcopal Church, South, was organized.[28]

3. *Reconstruction after the Civil War.*—The churches suffered much from the Civil War, but they recovered quickly and began to reconstruct their religious institutions. The Methodist Episcopal Church, South, made several important changes at the General Conference of 1866. Lay representation was admitted in Annual·

[26] The transition from circuit to station system came to a close about 1890. The title "presiding elder" was changed to that of "district superintendent" in 1908.

[27] Wesley called slavery "the sum of all villainies." In Rule Forty-two of the "Discipline" of 1784, the American Methodists had formulated an elaborate plan "to extirpate the abomination of slavery."

[28] The General Conference of 1848, North, declared the "plan" of separation null and void. Consequently, the provisions for an equitable division of the Book Concern accounts, stock, funds, etc., were also declared null and void. Law suits resulted, 1849-54, culminating in an appeal to the Supreme Court of the United States. This court ordered a pro rata division of the Book Concern properties.

and General Conferences;[29] the probationary period for church membership was abolished; and the term of pastoral appointment was lengthened to four years. Contributions to home and foreign missions increased considerably, and churches and schools were erected.

In the North, the Centenary Celebration of the introduction of Methodism, 1766-1866, produced a strong propaganda movement to build churches and schools and to carry on aggressive home and foreign mission work. A Sunday School Children's Fund of $65,000 was created, and two years later the Methodists inaugurated an annual observance of Children's Day. The Church Extension Society was organized in 1864, and the Woman's Foreign Missionary Society was formed in 1869. The Methodist Episcopal Church, North, also carried on aggressive mission work in the South, among the colored people, particularly in localities from which the Southern Methodists had fled before Union armies. This policy was highly resented by the Southern church.

4. *Establishment of the Board of Education.*—Important to Northern Methodists was the establishment of the Board of Education in 1868. More than two hundred Methodist schools had been founded before the Civil War. Lack of denominational control had resulted in wasteful duplication and low standards, so control over all schools necessarily led to the Board of Education.

III. **Methodism and the New Social, Educational, and Economic Order, 1870-1918.**—Democracy had developed a sturdy lay type of religion with prominent lay activities. There was a growing insistence upon organization and efficiency.

1. *Admission of Laymen to the General Conference.*—As a result, lay delegates were admitted in 1868 to the General Conference.[30] They sat in the General Conference for the first time in 1872.[31] Women delegates were admitted in 1904, but only two lay delegates from each Annual Conference could be admitted. Equal lay representation was granted by the General Conference of 1932.

2. *The Moody-Sankey Revival.*—One of the greatest revivals of the Christian Church came through the efforts of Dwight Lyman Moody (1837-1899) and Ira David Sankey (1840-1908). Starting their joint revival work in 1871, they worked together for more

---

[29] Laymen took their seats as delegates in the General Conference for the first time in 1870. There is equal representation of laymen in the General Conference.

[30] It is a thoroughly Protestant and American principle that the clergy has no "divine right" to control the affairs of the Church. The Methodists were slow in adopting this principle.

[31] The Methodist Episcopal Church, South, seated lay delegates in the General Conference in 1870.

than twenty years, in the large cities of Great Britain and America. During a four months' visit in London, they held two hundred and eighty-five meetings, attended by two million five hundred and thirty thousand people. Moody was converted in a Congregational church in Boston, but his later church connection was in the inde pendent Chicago Avenue Church, in the city of Chicago. Sankey was a Methodist lay evangelist. He assisted Moody by his simple but soul-stirring singing, by conducting the singing of the vast audiences, and by rendering assistance in the inquiry-meetings. But the Moody-Sankey activities belonged to the Church universal.

3. *International Uniform Sunday-school Lessons.*—The first great interdenominational movement was the Sunday-school movement, started about 1870. Recognizing the many advantages of a uniform lesson for all Sunday-schools, Benjamin Franklin Jacobs —Baptist, and John H. Vincent—Methodist, induced the Fifth National Sunday School Convention, held in 1872, to adopt Uniform Sunday-school Lessons and to appoint an International Sunday-school Lesson Committee. Dr. John H. Vincent, the first chairman, held this post for twenty-four years. The lessons ran in a seven-year cycle. They were uniform in that all teachers and pupils, in all schools, studied the same passage of Scripture at the same time. They were international because they were used in Canada and in Great Britain. A system of graded lessons was adopted by the International Sunday School Convention in 1908.[32]

4. *The Chautauqua Institution.*—In 1874 Dr. John H. Vincent and Lewis Miller assembled a group of Sunday-school teachers to a fortnight's meeting at Chautauqua Lake, New York, to study methods of Sunday-school teaching, and to plan how the Sunday-school might be more intimately connected with other agencies. The Chautauqua plan proved so successful that it was adopted by other organizations, practically all over the country. The Chautauqua idea is seen in summer schools and in summer assemblies of religious and secular groups. Theodore Roosevelt said, "Chautauqua is the most American thing in America."

5. *Organization of the Epworth League.*—The interest of Methodism in her young people was demonstrated in the young people's societies. These societies, beginning to appear about 1870, were organized as the Epworth League in 1889 by Northern Methodists, and in 1890 by the Southern. The Epworth League was or-

[32] In 1867 Lewis Miller of Akron, Ohio, devised plans for special Sunday-school buildings. Class rooms were arranged in a semi-circle so that all groups could be seen from the superintendent's desk, but the classes were separate for the teaching of the lesson. Many churches erected Sunday-school buildings modeled on this plan.

ganized under four departments, Spiritual Work, Mercy and Help, Literary, and Social Work.

6. *The Holiness Movement.*—Between 1880 and 1900 complaints were lodged that the Church was becoming too formal, that "heart religion" was disappearing, that the Wesleyan doctrine of entire sanctification was being suppressed, and that certain leaders were accepting modernistic views. Parties emphasizing the doctrine of holiness were formed in the Church, both North and South. Three steps were considered necessary in order to attain to holiness, namely, justification, cleansing, and baptism of the Spirit, or, "second blessing." Some of the holiness people also believed in divine healing, the speaking in tongues, and the premillennial return of the Lord.

The holiness movement reached a crisis between 1890 and 1894. Numerous groups broke away, and more than twenty-five different bodies were organized, the largest being the Church of the Nazarene, formed in 1894.[33] The holiness movement was interdenominational in scope—with Charles Finney, Asa Maham, Thomas Upham,[34] Dwight L. Moody, Robert Pearsal Smith, and R. A. Torrey[35] as representatives—but the largest membership and the main leadership came from the Methodists. Many of the churches are in doctrine and polity patterned after the Methodist Church, modified, of course, by the emphasis on holiness and a wider democracy. After 1900, the movement issued largely in the pentecostal movement.

7. *Struggle for a Christian Social Order.*—Prior to 1870, the chief emphasis of American churches was on the salvation of the individual. After 1870, a new social order developed. The churches began to pay attention, not merely to the individual, but to society as well. Must not the principles of Christianity apply to all institutions? Should not the churches make the whole social order Christian?[36]

The Methodists played an important role in the social awakening. They took a leading part in the temperance movement and in the fight for the abolition of child labor. The General Conference of 1908 adopted a Social Creed, which was later adopted in

---

[33] The better known holiness bodies include the Church of God, the Christian and Missionary Alliance, the General Council of the Assemblies of God, Volunteers of America, American Rescue Workers, Reformed Methodist Church, Wesleyan Methodist Connection, Free Methodist Church, and Pilgrim Holiness Church.
[34] Finney, Maham, and Upham were all connected with Oberlin College.
[35] Dr. Torrey was a Baptist.
[36] In this new emphasis on a "social gospel," several groups went so far that they failed to emphasize individual salvation. Hence some of the opposition to the new social emphasis was justifiable.

slightly modified form, by the Federal Council of the Churches of Christ in America as the Social Creed of the Churches. The Social Ideals of the Churches, as revised and adopted at Indianapolis, December 7, 1932, are as follows:

1. Practical application of the Christian principle of social well-being to the acquisition and use of wealth; subordination of speculation and the profit motive to the creative and co-operative spirit.
2. Social planning and control of the credit and monetary systems and the economic process for the common good.
3. The right of all to the opportunity for self-maintenance; a wider and fairer distribution of wealth; a living wage, as a minimum, and above this a just share for the worker in the product of industry and agriculture.
4. Safeguarding of all workers, urban and rural, against harmful conditions of labor and occupational injury and disease.
5. Social insurance against sickness, accident, want in old age and unemployment.
6. Reduction of hours of labor as the general productivity of industry increases; release from employment at least one day in seven, with a shorter working week in prospect.
7. Such special regulation of the conditions of work of women as shall safeguard their welfare and that of the family and the community.
8. The right of employes and employers alike to organize for collective bargaining and social action; protection of both in the exercise of this right; the obligation of both to work for the public good; encouragement of co-operatives and other organizations among farmers and other groups.
9. Abolition of child labor; adequate provision for the protection, education, spiritual nurture and wholesome recreation of every child.
10. Protection of the family by the single standard of purity; educational preparation for marriage, home-making and parenthood.
11. Economic justice for the farmer in legislation, financing of agriculture, transportation and the price of farm products as compared with the cost of machinery and other commodities which he must buy.
12. Extension of the primary cultural opportunities and social services now enjoyed by urban populations to the farm family.
13. Protection of the individual and society from the social, economic, and moral waste of any traffic in intoxicants and habit-forming drugs.
14. Application of the Christian principle of redemption to the treatment of offenders; reform of penal and correctional methods and institutions, and of criminal court procedure.
15. Justice, opportunity and equal rights for all; mutual good-will and co-operation among racial, economic and religious groups.
16. Repudiation of war, drastic reduction of armaments, participation in international agencies for the peaceable settlement of all controversies; the building of a co-operative world order.
17. Recognition and maintenance of the rights and responsibilities of free speech, free assembly, and a free press; the encouragement of free communication of mind with mind as essential to the discovery of truth.

8. *Adoption of the Area System.*—The General Conference of 1912 adopted the "area system" dividing the Church into episcopal

areas for residential supervision. The purpose was more continuity of administration and more effective leadership. The General Conference of 1924 decreed that no bishop remain in an area more than eight years. He must retire at the General Conference nearest his seventieth birthday, according to a law of 1932.[37] The limit of pastoral service in one station was removed in 1900.

9. *Methodism and the World War.*—In the World War, the Methodists supported the Government and took care of their soldiers and sailors to the full extent of their resources. The National War Council of the Methodist Episcopal Church was organized, with four departments, visiting clergymen, activities near camp, war industry work, and chaplains. About 325 chaplains came from Methodist ranks.

IV. The Centenary of Methodist Missions, 1819-1919.— After the war, Methodism inaugurated a new forward movement. This program was formulated largely during the centenary anniversary of the beginning of Methodist missions.

A committee of one hundred recommended that (1) Methodists now take a full share in the evangelization of the world, (2) that eight million dollars a year be raised for five years for missions, (3) that the Centenary Commission conduct a joint campaign under the auspices of Boards of Foreign and Home Missions, (4) that they conduct a church-wide educational campaign, by means of press, picture, and pulpit, (5) that the entire Church, from the smallest to the largest organized units, be a vital missionary organization, (6) that the local congregation be made dominantly evangelistic at home and missionary in its outreach, (7) that teaching of stewardship of life, character, and material possessions be taught as fundamental to Christianity, (8) that the Church be zealous in its cultivation of prayer life, (9) that a denomination-wide celebration be held on the State Fair Grounds at Columbus, Ohio, in June, 1919, as the culmination of the Centenary, and (10) that when this program has been approved by the Board of Bishops and the Boards of Foreign and Home Missions, the authorities of the Methodist Episcopal Church, South, be asked to co-operate.

This program was given hearty support. The war had taught people to think of religious enterprise in terms of world service. The financial end proved so successful that other denominations launched similar campaigns.

---

[37] The General Conference of 1912 had decided that the bishop must retire from active service at the General Conference nearest his seventy-third birthday.

1. *Doctrinal Controversies.*—Methodism has been quite free from rigid doctrinal tests. Wesley himself said, "They do not impose, in order to their admission, any opinions whatsoever. Let them hold particular or general redemption, absolute or conditional decrees; let them be Churchmen or Dissenters, Presbyterians or Independents, it is no obstacle. Let them choose one mode of baptism or another, it is no bar to their admission. The Presbyterian may be Presbyterian still; the Independents and Anabaptists use their own mode of worship. So may the Quaker; and none will contend with him about it. They think and let think."

Yet the Methodists had three doctrinal conflicts. The first arose between 1895 and 1905 in connection with Dr. H. G. Mitchell of Boston University. He was accused of having gone too far in accepting higher criticism. His colleague, Professor Borden P. Browne, was also accused of heresy in 1904. Both were acquitted. The third was the Fundamentalist-Modernist controversy. Conservatives organized a Methodist League for Faith and Life, in 1925, "to reaffirm the vital and eternal truths of the Christian religion, such as the inspiration of the Scriptures, the deity of Jesus, his virgin birth," etc. The Fundamentalist movement has apparently been on the decline since 1927.

2. *Unification of American Methodism.*—Many and persistent efforts to unify American Methodism have finally culminated in success. On April 26, 1939, the opening session was held of a Uniting Conference, where the Methodist Episcopal Church, South and North, and the Methodist Protestant Church merged in organic union, with a combined membership of about 7,850,000, about 25,000 clergymen, and nearly 40 bishops. *No new legislation* was allowed in the union. The new united church remains loyal to John Wesley. Negro Methodist churches are excluded.

3. *Methodist Promotion of Christian Unity.*—Wesley nourished the hope that Methodism would be the nucleus of a reunited Christendom, a hope not forgotten by his American followers. They have long been prominently identified with church federation. Dr. Stephen Olin, President of Wesleyan University, was a most influential delegate to the organization meeting of the Evangelical Alliance in London in 1846. Bishop Matthew Simpson and Dr. John McClintock were delegates to the World Evangelical Alliance meeting in Berlin, in 1857. Methodists were influential in establishing a branch of this Alliance in America in 1867. They took a prominent part in the formation of the Federal Council of the

Churches of Christ in America, organized in 1908; and Bishop E. R. Hendrix, of the Methodist Episcopal Church, South, was the first president of the Federal Council. Methodists were prominently represented at the World Conference on Faith and Order, at Lausanne, Switzerland, in 1927.

65. REVIEW QUESTIONS

1. What was Wesley's original intention regarding Methodism?
2. What factors aided the organization of the Church?
3. Did Wesley's ordination of preachers conflict with the theory of "apostolic succession"?
4. How was the Church organized?
5. Compare the episcopal administration of Bishops Asbury and McKendree.
6. Describe the calling of the circuit preacher.
7. What part did the Methodists take in frontier revivalism?
8. Explain the antagonism toward college-bred preachers among the early Methodists.
9. Why the Methodist schisms of 1892, of 1830 and of 1845?
10. Why the gradual change from circuit to station system?
11. What characterized reconstruction work after the Civil War?
12. How did the Methodists adjust themselves to the new social order, after 1870?
13. What is meant by (a) the International Uniform Sunday School Lessons? (b) the Chautauqua Institution? (3) the Epworth League? (d) the Holiness movement? (e) a Christian Social Order?
14. Why was the area system adopted in 1912?
15. How did the Centenary of Methodist missions influence progress?

TOPICS FOR SPECIAL STUDY

1. The circuit rider as a home missionary type.
2. The Methodist Holiness movement.
3. Methodism and the "Social Gospel."
4. Wesley's ideal of a re-united Christendom through Methodism.
5. The Methodist Episcopal Church and Education.

A SELECTED BIBLIOGRAPHY FOR CHAPTER XXIX

1. Sweet: *Methodism in American History.*
2. Simon: *John Wesley, the Master Builder.*
3. Wakeley: *Lost Chapters Recovered from the Early History of American Methodism.*
4. Watters: *First American Itinerant of Methodism, William Watters.*
5. Stevens: *A History of the Methodist Episcopal Church in the United States* (4 vols.).
5. Hurst: *The History of Methodism* (7 vols.).
7. Tigert: *Constitutional History of American Episcopal Methodism.*
8. Sweet: *The Rise of Methodism in the West.*
9. Swaney: *Episcopal Methodism and Slavery.*
10. Faulkner: *The Quest of Social Justice, 1898-1914.*
11. Mathews: *The Church and the Changing Order.*
12. Diffendorfer: *The World Service of the Methodist Episcopal Church.*
13. Duvall: *The Methodist Episcopal Church and Education up to 1869.*
14. Simpson and Matthew: *Cyclopedia of Methodism.*
15. Garber: *The Methodists Are One People.*

CHAPTER XXX

The Baptist Church in the National Era, 1789-1936

American Baptists, organized in 18 distinct bodies, constitute the largest Protestant denomination in the United States. While these bodies differ considerably on certain matters, they all hold to the three cardinal Protestant principles as well as to the following Baptist views, (1) conversion as a condition[1] of church membership, (2) individual responsibility[2] to God, (3) separation[3] of Church and State, (4) congregational[4] church government, and (5) immersion in water as the only Scriptural mode of baptism.[5] Starting as a comparatively small group, the Baptists aimed at nothing less than a spiritual conquest of the Continent for God; and they pursued this aim with a remarkable singleness of purpose, always proclaiming the elemental facts of sin and grace. Up to about 1890 the Baptists took pride in calling themselves the poor man's church, and they still make a powerful appeal to the common people.

I. Baptist Expansion through Local and State Conventions, 1789-1832.—Emphasis on the independence of the local church prevented the Baptists from organizing their home mission work on a national basis prior to 1832. But their vision of the great new need, coupled with a strong propaganda spirit, caused them to combine strength in associational organization as an effective means of meeting frontier needs.

1. *Status of the Baptists at the Beginning of the National Era.* —In colonial times the Baptists consisted of small, persecuted groups made up largely of poor and uneducated people. But their

---

[1] Baptists do not believe in hereditary church membership, or in infant baptism. A church is a body of regenerate people who have been baptized on profession of personal faith in Christ. People who die before they have attained to the years of discretion are saved, though they have not been baptized.

[2] Protestant individualism is very marked among Baptists.

[3] Baptists deserve much honor as pioneers of religious toleration and as advocates of the separation of Church and State. Largely through Baptist influence, the State of Virginia became the first government in the world to establish an absolute separation of Church and State, in 1785.

[4] Baptist churches are independent in their local affairs, and guard most carefully against centralization of power.

[5] Baptism, according to the Baptists, does not accomplish regeneration. It is merely a mark of obedience, symbolizing the regeneration that has already taken place. Likewise is the Lord's Supper considered as a symbol of Christian life continued, sustained, and nourished.

553

long and determined struggle for civil and religious liberty, and their almost unanimous support of the patriot cause in the War of Independence, changed their status. They gained many influential and wealthy members, with considerable popularity. During the first decade they more than doubled their membership, and gradually outgrew all Protestant denominations numerically, the Methodists being the closest rivals.

2. *Various Baptist Groups.*—The Baptists did not move toward the western frontier as a unified body. They were divided into

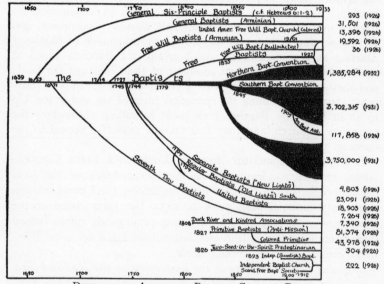

DIAGRAM OF AMERICAN BAPTIST CHURCH BODIES
(The 3,750,000 group is the National Baptist Convention, Colored)

several groups, representing various shades of Baptist opinion and practice, which situation made them all the better prepared to gather the people into the Baptist fold.

General Six Principle Baptists[6] differed from other Baptists mainly in requiring the laying on of hands after baptism as a symbol of receiving the Holy Spirit. This ordinance was equally obligatory with the Lord's Supper.

[6] They were called "General" because the adherents usually held Arminian views, that is, that Christ died and atoned for the sins of all, and not merely for the elect. They were called "Six Principle" because they took as their standard the six principles summarized in Hebr. 6:1-2, namely, repentance, faith, baptism, laying on of hands, resurrection of the dead, and eternal judgment.

Seventh Day Baptists considered it essential to observe the Jewish Sabbath as the day of rest. In other respects they belonged to the Calvinistic group of Baptists. Some claim that the Seventh Day Baptists are but a continuation of earlier sects, known as Nazarenes,[7] Cerinthians,[8] and certain communities of Albigenses and Waldenses.[9]

General and Free Will Baptists were Arminian in doctrine, while practically all other Baptist groups were Calvinistic. The Free Will Baptists[10] practiced foot-washing, anointed the sick with oil, and restricted the ministerial office to men. General and Free Will Baptists uniformly practiced open communion after 1830.

Separate and Regular Baptists issued from the Great Awakening, 1734-44. This revival caused sharp discussion among Baptists. The Separates or "New Lights" withdrew from the churches which did not support the awakening, while those who did not separate were known as Regulars. The Separates were bitterly opposed to lay preachers and to church members who had not experienced conversion. They were also distinguished from the Regulars by a milder Calvinism.

Primitive Baptists[11] were ultra-Calvinist in doctrine and declined fellowship with any churches which supported "human institutions" such as missionary, Bible, tract, Sunday school, or temperance societies, or advocated State conventions or theological schools. They maintained that such agencies did not exist in the Apostolic Era, and that God in his sovereign power did not need human agencies to prepare his ministers to preach or to bring the elect to repentance. Man could not interfere with God's decrees. The elect would eventually be saved, and the non-elect would be lost in spite of all the preaching in the world.

Two-Seed-in-the-Spirit Predestinarian Baptists derived their name from a doctrine expounded by Daniel Parker in 1826. God created Adam and Eve and infused into them particles of himself, which is the good seed. God also decreed that Eve and her daughters should bring forth a definite number of good offspring. After the fall of man there was also planted in Eve and in all her daughters the "seed of the serpent." Neither seed was capable of any change in character, but reproduced after its kind. Hence some children born were of divine seed, and some were of the

[7] See page 73.　　　[8] See page 53.　　　[9] See page 182.
[10] These Free Will Baptists, which at times were called Original Free Will Baptists, are not to be identified with the Bullockites.
[11] Primitive Baptists were called by a variety of names, such as "Old School," "Anti-Mission," "Regular," and "Hard Shell."

seed of the devil. The Atonement was for the elect only, and it was extreme folly to bring the Gospel to the non-elect who of necessity would return to their father, the devil. In recent years, this absolute fatalism has been toned down considerably.

3. *Formation of Baptist Associations.*—All Baptists, save the Primitive and the Two-Seed-in-the-Spirit, were imbued with a strong missionary spirit. As the young Nation expanded, they immediately strengthened their home base and then addressed themselves to the task of planting the Gospel and the church in new regions. Their chief competitors were the Methodists, whose marked Wesleyan Arminianism caused Arminian Baptists to move toward the moderate Calvinistic ranks.[12]

The first Baptist home mission work was done by local pastors who believed they were commissioned by the Lord to preach also to those who lived beyond their parishes. These pastors-at-large travelled at their own expense, preaching the Gospel and organizing small churches. This work was sporadic, and yet it was surprisingly effective.

Baptists, like Congregationalists, were rather reluctant in forming associations.[13] But vision of the new need on the frontier, coupled with fiery evangelistic enthusiasm, led them to form cooperative associations for more effective home mission work. The first organization was the Philadelphia Association, formed in 1707. Baptists in other regions soon formed similar associations in newer sections. These Associations met frontier problems effectively. They helped to establish new churches, and to organize associations. Each association adopted a constitution and a profession of faith, elected two officials—Moderator and Clerk—and held quarterly meetings. At these meetings the "messengers"[14] discussed questions of doctrine, discipline, administration, and current problems.

Being essentially revivalistic, the Baptists enjoyed a great increase in membership during the revival movements. The Baptist ingathering was particularly large in Kentucky and Tennessee. In 1820 the Baptists in Kentucky had twenty-five associations, 491 churches, and nearly 32,000 members.

4. *Baptist Missions and Schools.*—The organization of a foreign missionary society in England in 1792, and the sending of

[12] Separate and Regular Baptists in Virginia united in 1794 and in Kentucky in 1804. The Elkhorn and South Kentucky Associations united in October, 1801, the terms of union being a compromise between Arminian and Calvinistic views.

[13] According to Baptist and Congregational principles, each church must be strictly independent of other churches.

[14] Members elected to attend Baptist Associational meetings were never thought of as regular delegates, since a Baptist church cannot theoretically be represented by an individual member. The chosen members were called "messengers."

William Carey to India, stimulated interest among American Baptists. The conversion of Adoniram Judson and Luther Rice[15] to Baptist views in 1812, and their desire to serve as Baptist missionaries in India, awakened Baptists again to their foreign responsibility. Two years later the General Missionary Convention of the Baptist Denomination in the United States of America for Foreign Missions was formed, representing eleven states.

At the second meeting of the Convention, in 1817, it was decided that "the Board shall have power at its discretion to appropriate a portion of its funds to domestic missionary purposes in such parts of this country where the seed of the Word may be advantageously cast, and which Mission Societies, on a small scale, do not effectively reach." The Convention chose John M. Peck and James E. Walch as its first missionaries to the far West, and voted them one thousand dollars for their salaries and travelling expenses. But the strong anti-mission sentiment among Baptists on the frontier caused the Convention in 1820 to withdraw its support and to give all its attention to foreign missions. From 1820 to 1832 most home mission work was carried on by local and state associations. A publication and tract society was formed in 1824 to provide suitable literature. This organization was renamed the American Baptist Publication Society in 1840.

Pioneer Baptists were prejudiced against an educated and salaried ministry, favoring the farmer-preachers who worked six days and preached on Sundays and at week-day meetings and funerals without pay. There were two types of frontier preachers. The "licensed" performed services similar to those of "local" or "lay" preachers among the Methodists. The "ordained" had charge of the congregations.

Although the average lay member failed to see the need of supporting denominational schools, prominent leaders made evangelism and education outstanding features of Baptist home missionary work. By 1830 the following Baptist schools had been founded:

Brown University .... 1764 in Rhode Island
Hamilton Institute .... 1819 in New York
Waterville College .... 1820 in Maine
Columbian College .... 1821 in District of Columbia
Newton Theological Institute .... 1825 in Massachusetts
Furman Institution .... 1825 in South Carolina
New Hampton Literary and Theological Institution .... 1826 in New Hampshire

[15] These men were on their way to India as missionaries for the American Board of Commissioners for Foreign Missions. Knowing that they would meet Baptists in India, they made a special study of their doctrine and came to the conclusion that the Baptists had the Scriptural mode of baptism.

5. *The Baptist Anti-Mission Movement.*—The Triennial Convention aroused considerable "denominational consciousness" by combining the strength of local units in co-operative undertakings. But these centralizing tendencies were powerfully counter-acted by a strong and persistent emphasis on the absolute independence of the local church. Thousands of anti-mission Baptists opposed every new scheme for the extension of Christianity, finally gathering into separate churches.

How is this essentially *Baptist* anti-mission movement to be explained? The views of the Primitive and the Two-Seed-in-the-Spirit Baptists furnish a partial explanation. Arguments formulated in part by John Taylor,[16] Daniel Parker,[17] and Alexander Campbell[18] must also be considered. Anti-mission agitators made the following claims: (1) No authority can be found in the New Testament for missionary societies or Sunday schools. Such societies are man-made and contrary to Scripture; (2) Missionary associations usurp the authority of Christ over his Church. He alone can call men to preach, and he alone can assign them fields of labor; (3) Missionary associations violate the independence of the local church by centralizing authority in field secretaries and other officials; (4) A paid ministry is like a modern Tetzel, or like the money changers whom Christ drove out of the Temple; (5) The better educated ministers overshadow the less educated and unpaid preachers; (6) Mission societies and schools are schemes of Arminianism, prompted by desire for money and fame.

For a number of years this anti-mission propaganda hindered progress, but gradually the conflicting groups came to a parting of the ways. Two-Seed-in-the-Spirit Predestinarians organized in 1826, the Primitive Baptists in 1827, and the "Campbellites" or Disciples of Christ had their first formation between 1830 and 1832.

[16] John Taylor published his anti-mission views in 1819 in a pamphlet called *Thoughts on Missions.* He is said to have changed his views on missions in his late years, and to have repented his attack upon Baptist mission friends.

[17] Daniel Parker, founder of the Two-Seed-in-the-Spirit Predestinarian Baptists, was the arch enemy of missions on the frontier. John M. Peck wrote in 1841: "Mr. Parker is one of those singular beings whom Divine providence permits to arise as a scourge to his church, and as a stumbling block in the way of religious effort. Raised on the frontiers of Georgia, without education, uncouth in manners, slovenly in dress, diminutive in person, unprepossessing in appearance, with shrivelled features and small piercing eyes, few men, for a series of years, have exerted a wider influence on the lower and less educated class of frontier people. With a zeal and enthusiasm bordering on insanity, firmness that amounted to obstinacy, and perseverance that would have done honor to a good cause, Daniel Parker exerted himself to the utmost to induce the churches within his range to declare non-fellowship with all Baptists who united with any missionary or other benevolent (or as he called them, newfangled) societies."

[18] Alexander Campbell was a Baptist from 1812 to 1830. He published his anti-mission views in a periodical called the *Christian Baptist,* and later the *Millennial Harbinger.* Campbell's followers were at first called *Reformers.*

II. Baptist Expansion through National Conventions, 1832-1907.—Development of foreign missions was the first significant movement. Development of a national Baptist literature came next, resulting in the formation of the American Baptist Publication Society in 1824. Development of home missions followed, leading to the formation of the American Baptist Home Mission Society in 1832. Controversy regarding slavery resulted in the formation of three Baptist conventions—northern, southern, and national.

1. *Organization of the American Baptist Home Mission Society.*—John M. Peck was for a number of years the most eminent Baptist missionary preacher in the central West. He travelled extensively and helped to organize churches in Illinois and Missouri. In 1827 he established a school, the present Shurtleff College. He founded, edited, and published *The Pioneer*, the first religious newspaper in the western states. His *Emigrant's Guide* (1832) and *Gazetteer of Illinois* (1834) were widely circulated. Finally, he appealed to Massachusetts for a better organized home mission work. In response, Rev. Jonathan Going of Worcester, Mass., visited the Mississippi Valley in 1831. A conference revealed that the two men saw exactly alike concerning a national home mission society. In April, 1832, a convention was called in New York, and the American Baptist Home Mission Society was organized. Dr. Going was its first secretary, and Dr. Peck was its chief Western representative. The whole body of churches thus united in a national organization for Christianizing the West. It was to meet once in three years, and at the same time and place as the Triennial Convention.

The significance of the Society for the advancement of home mission work can hardly be overestimated. During its first year, the Society had 50 home missionaries in its service; the second year it had 80; the third it had 96; the fourth it had 150. After fifty years of service, it had established churches in every State and Territory beyond the Mississippi. It is largely through this Society and its sister organization in the South,[19] that the Baptists have become numerically the largest Protestant denomination.

2. *The Slavery Controversy.*—Slavery was a subject of bitter debate. The difference in sentiment was characteristically expressed in the controversy between Francis Wayland and Richard Fuller.

[19] With the organization of the Southern Baptist Convention in 1845, Southern Baptists organized their own Home Mission Board, which aimed to do for the people in the South what the American Baptist Home Mission Society was doing for the people in the North.

Matters were brought to a crisis in 1844 when the Executive Board of the Triennial Convention declared that under no circumstances would they appoint a missionary who held slaves. This was considered a technical violation of constitutional rights, or a denial of the equal rights of the Southern churches.

Realizing that no compromise was workable, the Southern churches met at Augusta, Ga., in May, 1845, and organized the Southern Baptist Convention. It was not a new denomination, but simply a new organization to carry on its own home and foreign missionary work through separate boards and meetings. In other respects Northern and Southern Baptists enjoyed perfect fellowship with each other.

3. *The Southern Baptist Convention.*—The Southern Baptist Convention was compact, flexible, and effective. Common missionary enterprises were carried on by the Convention through various boards responsible to it. There was *one* central organization where Northern Baptists had *three*.[20] Prior to the Civil War, the Southern Baptist Convention met biennially. Since that time it has usually met annually.

Up to 1918, work was carried on through *three* boards, in charge respectively of home missions, foreign missions, and Sunday School activities. The Board of Ministerial Relief and Annuity was established in 1918, and the Board of Education in 1920. In 1928 the name of the latter board was changed to the Southern Baptist Education Commission. These *five* boards enjoy the cooperation of the Women's Missionary Union, organized in 1888.

The Board of Home Missions works through several departments, including evangelism, church extension, and publicity. The Foreign Mission Board conducts evangelistic, educational, and medical mission work in a number of countries. The Sunday School Board[21] works through nine departments, as well as through cooperative work with the other boards and agencies. The Board of Ministerial Relief and Annuity cares for superannuated ministers, widows, and dependent children. The Southern Baptist Education Association has advisory supervision of the 112 Baptist educational institutions. Of these the three theological seminaries are under the auspices of the Convention. In doctrine the Southern

[20] The three entirely independent central organizations of Northern Baptists were, the American Baptist Missionary Union, the American Baptist Home Mission Society, and the American Baptist Publication Society. The Northern Baptist Convention was not organized until 1907.
[21] The Sunday School Board of the Southern Baptist Convention was organized in 1863. Ten years later its work was taken over by the Home Mission Board because of financial difficulties. The present Sunday School Board was established in 1891.

Baptists are generally considered more strictly Calvinistic than their Northern brethren.

4. *The Northern Baptist Convention.*—After the division in 1845, the three natic..al Baptist organizations, the General Missionary Convention of the Baptist Denomination in the United States of America for Foreign Missions (1814), the American Baptist Publication Society (1824), and the American Baptist Home Mission Society (1832), continued as independent denominational organizations supported almost entirely by Northern Baptists.[22] In 1846 the lengthy name of the foreign missionary society was changed to the American Baptist Union, and in 1910 it was changed again to the American Baptist Foreign Missionary Society.

Having three central organizations, instead of one, resulted in duplication of work. Efficiency and economy demanded a more centralized administration. As organic union of the societies was beset with legal difficulties, some other method had to be found whereby the churches could secure the desired unity and control. The outcome was the formation of the Northern Baptist Convention in 1907 as a strictly delegated body from Baptist churches of the North and West. The Northern Baptist Convention elects officers of the three societies, supervises their work, and controls their expenditures.[23] Other societies—including the Woman's American Baptist Home Mission Society, and the Woman's American Baptist Foreign Mission Society—have placed themselves under the direction of the Convention. This arrangement secures consolidation of Baptist agencies, eliminates useless expenditures, and prevents overlapping.

5. *The National Baptist Convention.*—This organization includes only Baptist churches whose members, officers, and pastors are of the Negro race. As Negro Baptists multiplied, it seemed best to have their own churches which in time were organized in associations, State conventions, and finally in a national body. The first association—the Providence Association—was formed in Ohio in 1836; the first State convention was organized in North Carolina in 1866; and the American National Baptist Convention was formed in 1886. The National Education Convention, organized in 1893, and the Foreign Missionary Baptist Convention, organized in 1880, became constituent parts of the American National

---

[22] The American Baptist Publication Society retained its distinctly national character and continued its work in the various States.

[23] The Northern Baptist Convention prepares an annual budget which is to provide duly for the needs of each society concerned. The adopted budget is then apportioned to State conventions, thence to associations, and finally to every Baptist church.

562 A HISTORY OF THE CHRISTIAN CHURCH

Baptist Conventions. Its object was to unite all Negro Baptists for the promotion of home and foreign mission work and education. The organization was incorporated in the District of Columbia in 1915 as the National Baptist Convention, U. S. A.

In 1897 a group withdrew[24] to form the Lott-Carey Convention for Foreign Missions. For several years it co-operated with the American Baptist Union (white), but in 1905 it became a co-operative body with the National Baptist Convention. In 1915 another group withdrew[25] to form the National Baptist Convention, Unincorporated. The Lott-Carey Convention, which retains its autonomy, entered into co-operation with the National Baptist Convention, Unincorporated, in 1924.

The National Baptist Convention, U. S. A., the Lott-Carey Convention, and the National Baptist Convention, Unincorporated, carry on an extensive work for home and foreign missions and education. The best known school is, perhaps, the Tuskegee Normal and Industrial Institute, Tuskegee, Ala., headed for many years by Booker T. Washington (1859-1915).

6. *Bible Controversies.*—The American Bible Society was formed in 1816 to supply Protestant groups with the Bible. At the expense of the Society, a Baptist translation of the New Testament was published in 1835 in which the Greek word *baptizein* was rendered by the English *immersion* or an equivalent. Regarding this as a sectarian version, the Society indicated that it would henceforth "encourage only such versions as conform in the principle of their translation to the common English version." Taking offense, the Baptists formed the American and Foreign Bible Society in 1837.

Differences then arose amongst Baptists as to the expediency of making a new translation of the entire Bible. Those favoring the project organized the American Bible Union in 1850. The Baptists now had two Bible societies while some support was also given to the American Bible Society. The situation was intolerable. It was remedied by the Saratoga Convention of 1883 which decided to discontinue the two Baptist Bible societies and to have the circulation of Scriptures on the home mission field in charge of the American Baptist Publication Society, and on the foreign field by the Missionary Union.

7. *The Baptist Young People's Union of America.*—The great

[24] The differences arose concerning the production of literature. One group favored the production and control of literature by members of the Negro race. The other group did not think this feasible.
[25] The division arose regarding the National Baptist Publication Board.

increase in young people's work, stimulated by the Christian Endeavor movement, developed a desire for a distinctively denominational young people's organization. The Northern Baptists organized the Baptist Young People's Union of America in 1891 for the purpose of promoting Christian activity, intelligence, and denominational spirit among Baptist young people. In its organ, *Service,* Christian Culture Courses are published, including study on the Bible, missions, and Baptist teachings and history. Southern Baptists formed a similar young people's organization in 1896. In the 1926 Census, the Southern organization reports 19,773 societies, with a membership of 498,386. The Northern organization reports approximately 5,000 societies, with 130,000 members, and 1,800 Christian Endeavor Societies with 65,000 members.

III. **Recent Developments among American Baptists, 1907-1936.**—There has been a great advance in home and foreign missions in recent years. Next to home missionary societies, the Sunday school is the key to Baptist progress.

1. *A Nation-Wide Plan of Evangelism.*—While evangelism has always been prominent, Baptists were rather slow to establish any co-operative denominational evangelism. This was finally accomplished in 1906 through the efforts of Cornelius Woelfkin and James A. Francis. In 1915 the American Baptist Home Mission Society adopted a nation-wide plan. The country was divided into several divisions, each with a general evangelist. In 1919 Dr. Herbert F. Stilwell was appointed superintendent of evangelism. His successor, Benjamin T. Livingston, introduced a type of lay service known as Friendly Visitation Evangelism. Earle D. Sims has since 1919 served as "church invigorator" under the supervision of State convention secretaries. He visits pastorless churches, puts the meeting-house in good physical condition, preaches the Gospel, and conducts a campaign resulting in the calling of a regular minister. Rev. Sims stays long enough to install the new pastor, and then proceeds to another pastorless church.

2. *The Department of Architecture.*—The Northern Baptist Convention, in 1919, suggested the employment of a competent church architect to devote his time to help small churches to secure adequate plants. The result was the creation of a Bureau of Architecture, in 1920, with George Earnest Merrill, nationally known architect, as secretary. The Bureau of Architecture makes a preliminary study on any particular project, prepares drawings and plans, and continues as adviser until the church building is

completed. The Department also acts as a clearing house of information, through conference, correspondence, books, leaflets, and other literature.

3. *The New World Movement.*—The Northern Baptist Convention of 1915 authorized a Five-Year Program to stimulate greater interest in education, evangelism, and missions. The program was really inaugurated in 1918, when the Convention elected the National Committee of Laymen, and voted to raise six million dollars to meet educational and missionary needs. The six million dollars were paid the following year. The National Laymen's Committee then decided, upon suggestion of F. W. Padelford, to raise one hundred million dollars in five years. Although but a little more than one half was actually paid, this movement created general interest and a "denominational consciousness."

4. *The Confessional Movement.*—During the years 1925-1928 there was agitation to adopt a confession or creed as binding on all churches. This was partly a result of the Fundamentalist-Modernist controversy, partly a result of the post-war movement to make existing church-organizations more solid. The confessional movement was overwhelmingly defeated, however, because it was regarded as contrary to Baptist polity. Baptists consider the New Testament (not excluding the Old) as the only sufficient rule for Christian life and faith. Creeds are not obligatory standards, but rather manifestos of prevailing doctrine.

5. *Inter-Church Relations.*—Baptists have taken a prominent part in the various inter-denominational movements. Southern Baptists have declined to join the Federal Council of Churches in Christ in America, but Northern Baptists are affiliated. They are also represented on the Advisory Committee on a World Conference on Questions of Faith and Order.

66. REVIEW QUESTIONS

1. Name the general and specific Baptist principles. In what ways do these principles distinguish Baptists from other denominations?
2. Why were the Baptists comparatively slow in organizing on a national basis?
3. Account for the rapid growth of the Baptists.
4. Explain the differences in the eighteen Baptist bodies.
5. In what ways did Baptist Associations promote work on the frontier?
6. Account for the Baptist anti-mission movement.
7. Name some of the denominations that have branched out from the Baptists. Why did they not remain in the Baptist fold?
8. What part has the American Baptist Home Mission Society, and its sister organization in the South, played in the development of Baptist life? Why?

9. Who were the following: John M. Peck; Jonathan Going; Booker T. Washington; and F. W. Padelford?
10. Why did Northern and Southern Baptists separate in 1845?
11. How are Northern, Southern, and Negro Baptists organized?
12. Explain the Baptist Bible controversies.
13. What do the Baptists do for the young?
14. Discuss recent developments among the Baptists. What attitude do they take toward inter-denominational movements?

TOPICS FOR SPECIAL STUDY

1. Baptists as pioneers of civil and religious liberty.
2. Baptist church organization as compared with the Congregational.
3. The eighteen Baptist bodies, their unity and their differences.
4. Baptist revivalism and evangelism.
5. Baptist home missions.
6. Baptist foreign missions.
7. The Baptist Sunday school movement.
8. The educational work of the Baptist Young People's Union.
9. Baptists as promoters of general and higher education.
10. Why Baptists are numerically the strongest Protestant denomination in America.
11. The Baptist New World Movement.
12. The Baptist confessional movement.
13. Baptists as promoters of Christian world unity.
14. Outstanding Baptist leaders.

A SELECTED BIBLIOGRAPHY FOR CHAPTER XXX

1. White: *A Century of Faith.*
2. Sweet: *Religion on the American Frontier: The Baptists, 1783-1830.*
3. Vedder: *Baptist History.*
4. Merriam: *History of American Baptist Missions.*
5. Newman: *History of the Baptist Churches in the United States* (American Church History Series, Vol. II).
6. Christian: *History of the Baptists.*
7. Newman: *A Century of Baptist Achievement.*
8. Horr: *The Baptist Heritage.*
9. Wright: *Missionary Work of the Southern Baptist Convention.*
10. *Baptist Encyclopedia.*
11. Carroll: *Genesis of American Anti-Missionism.*
12. Cleveland: *The Great Revival in the West.*
13. Fisher: *History of Negro Baptists* (MSS).
14. Hart: *Slavery and Abolition.*
15. Leonard: *One Hundred Years of Missions.*
16. Locke: *Anti-Slavery in America.*
17. Roosevelt: *The Winning of the West* (4 vols.).
18. Gates: *The Early Relation and Separation of Baptists and Disciples.*
19. *American Baptist Year Book.*
20. *The Baptist World Alliance, Second Congress* (1911).
21. *The Baptist World Alliance* (1923).
22. Carey, S. P.: *William Carey.*
23. Easton: *Roger Williams, Prophet and Pioneer.*
24. Cathcart: *The Baptists and the American Revolution.*
25. Thom: *The Struggle for Religious Freedom in Virginia; The Baptists.*
26. Mode: *The Frontier Spirit in American Christianity.*
27. McCoy: *History of Baptist Indian Missions.*
28. Vail: *The Morning Hour of American Baptist Missions.*
29. Loud: *Evangelized America.*

CHAPTER XXXI

THE DISCIPLES OF CHRIST[1]

Early in the 19th century a group of pastors from various denominations began to plead for a re-union of all Christendom on the basis of the New Testament teaching. They rejected all creeds and denominational organizations as detrimental to the cause of re-union. In 1809 the movement took on the form of a voluntary Christian Association which, about 1830-32, developed into a separate communion popularly known as the Disciples of Christ. This organization constitutes at present the sixth largest Protestant body in the United States, with a total membership of 1,566,772, as reported in 1934.

I. Beginning of the "Restoration Movement."—Decline in moral and religious life at the close of the 18th and the beginning of the 19th century caused a number of men in America and abroad to locate the source of the trouble in the *divided condition of Christendom*. As a remedy they proposed to go back of all creeds and councils, of all denominations and schools, and return to what they understood to be the doctrines, ordinances, and practices of primitive Christianity. They aimed to be restorers and not reformers. Two brothers, James and Robert Haldane, together with John Glas and Robert Sandeman, were the early leaders of this restoration movement in the British Isles. Among the early American leaders were James O'Kelly who operated in Virginia and North Carolina; Abner Jones and Elias Smith in the New England States; Barton W. Stone in Kentucky; Walter Scott in Ohio; and Thomas and Alexander Campbell, father and son, in West Virginia and vicinity.

Starting in widely separated localities and nearly simultaneously, three American restoration groups led by James O'Kelly, Barton W. Stone, and Elias Smith came together without negotiation or formal organic action. They were known as "Christians" and made Christian character their only test of fellowship or membership. This was the beginning of the "Christian Church"[2] which united with the Congregationalists in 1930; but it was also the beginning of the "Disciples of Christ" because Barton W. Stone and many

---

[1] Consult diagram on page 522.   [2] Consult diagram on page 522.

other "Christians" later joined the movement headed by Thomas and Alexander Campbell.

Thomas Campbell, a Presbyterian minister of Irish birth, came to America in 1807. The Seceder Synod of Philadelphia, with which he became associated, assigned him to a territory connected with the presbytery of Chartiers in western Pennsylvania. His indifference to ecclesiastical rules, and his pleadings on behalf of Christian liberty and fellowship brought upon him the censure of the presbytery and he withdrew in 1808. The following year he formed the Christian Association of Washington and issued his famous *Declaration and Address*. The one rule to govern himself and his associates was, "Where the Scriptures speak, we speak; and where the Scriptures are silent, we are silent." That same year his son, Alexander Campbell, broke with the Seceder Presbyterian Church in Glasgow and came to America. He cordially endorsed the principles of his father's *address* and began to advocate them publicly in 1811.

In 1810 Thomas Campbell made overture "to be taken into Christian and ministerial communion" of the Pittsburgh Synod of the Presbyterian Church, but his application was refused because the movement he represented was considered "destructive to the whole interest of religion." His next move was to reorganize the Christian Association as a Church, in 1811. The first congregation was established at Brush Run with twenty-nine charter members. Here Alexander Campbell was ordained to the ministry in January, 1812. Later that same year the Campbells began to practice baptism by immersion. At this time Thomas Campbell conceded to his son, Alexander, the leadership of the movement he had originated.

Adoption by immersion led to a union with the Baptists which lasted, with increasing tension, for seventeen years. The Brush Run Church united with the Redstone Baptist Association in 1813 and with the Mahoning Baptist Association in 1823. There was general agreement between Campbell's group and the Baptists regarding the action of baptism and the organization of the church, but they differed in the following: (1) administering baptism upon a simple confession of faith versus Baptist insistence on religious experience; (2) baptism leads to forgiveness of sins versus Baptist insistence that forgiveness of sins precedes baptism; (3) man's death in "trespasses and sin" did not destroy his power of choice versus Baptist insistence of "total depravity"; (4) though the Old Testament is the Word of God it has no binding authority on Christians versus Baptist insistence of the equally binding authority of the Old and the New Testament; (5) observance of the Lord's Supper weekly versus Baptist quarterly observance; (6) minimizing the need of ordination and the distinction between clergy and laity versus Baptist regard for the ministerial office and status; (7) faith as "belief of testimony" versus Baptist insistence that "faith is an effect of almighty power and regenerating grace." These views, which received wide publicity through the *Christian Baptist* and a series of public debates, caused a final separation from the Baptists in 1827, but the separation process was not complete until 1830.

Meanwhile Walter Scott identified himself with the restoration movement and through the combined efforts of Scott and Campbell, many new churches were organized. Scott put into practice what the Campbells had been talking and writing about. His "plan of salvation" was put into the simple form of a five-finger exercise: (1) faith, upon proof; (2) repentance, motivated by promises; (3) baptism, in obedience to command; (4) remission of sins; and (5) the gift of the Holy Spirit. This definiteness of presentation, combined with force, sincerity, rationality, and authoritativism, made a powerful appeal to the people on the frontier. Scott's evangelistic activity became a crusade, and converts were won, not only from the un-churched, but also from Baptist, Presbyterian, Methodist, and "Christian" camps.

A most important gain was made in January, 1832, when Barton W. Stone and about ten thousand followers united with Campbell and his group. This flowing together of two like-minded groups brought to the restoration movement resources of great value, including more than fifty churches and a number of able preachers. From this time on the movement took on the form of a separate communion, with Alexander Campbell as the recognized leader.

II. Independence and Growth.—The combined restoration movement spread rapidly over a number of states and soon gathered to itself a large body of adherents. Agencies used in promoting the movement were evangelism, journalism, propaganda pamphlets, schools, district and other general meetings for fellowship, and organization for missionary purposes. Campbell's *Christian System*, published in 1836, may also be included. This book contained a system of doctrine which the author claimed to be the infallible revealed truth as given authoritatively and unmistakably in the New Testament; yet it was not a creed because nobody was asked to subscribe to it as a condition of membership. The *Christian System* had great value because it expressed the common faith and practice of the Disciples. The *Millennial Harbinger*, edited by

Campbell from 1830 till his death in 1866, was the outstanding religious journal among the early disciples.

Emergence as a distinct communion forced upon the Disciples the issue of functioning as a denomination. This distinctly new phase of the restoration movement placed the leaders in a delicate position. Claiming that there was no Scriptural authority for the existence of associations and synods, they had severely denounced the societies and organizations through which the denominations carried on much of their work. Campbell had been particularly severe with the professional clergy and in his condemnation of the tendency to legislate, as seen in conventions, synods, and associations. Now he had to sanction some sort of machinery for co-operation as supplementary devices and "expedients." His cherished system of a "plurality of elders" had to yield gradually to the "one-man-system" of professionally trained ministers. These adjustments were made slowly and cautiously, and Campbell took great care in explaining that co-operative organizations claimed no authority over the churches.

The new communion was quite successful in the establishment of educational institutions, in systematizing the Sunday-school work, and in co-operative evangelism, though some of the members protested this "aping the sects." The early conventions, held to device means of co-operation, functioned so much like camp-meetings that they gave no cause for dissent. But when the first National Convention of Disciples was held in 1849, many questioned the legitimacy of such gatherings and of the proposed missionary organizations; to which Campbell gave the characteristic reply, "In all things pertaining to public interest, not of Christian faith, piety, or morality, the church of Jesus Christ in its aggregate character is left free and unshackled by any apostolic authority." The two issues were settled as follows: (1) the national conventions became mass meetings and not meetings of delegates; (2) the conservative anti-missionary-society churches achieved statistical independence in 1906 under the name of "Churches of Christ" which, in 1934, had a reported membership of 433,714.

Other issues of importance were: the slavery question; open or closed communion; heresy trials; government support; training of pastors; music in the churches; architectural respectability in the planning and building of churches and schools; dancing, card playing, reading of novels, and the like. But these controversial issues gradually passed out of the focus of attention for the main body of Disciples, and the communion enjoyed a rapid increase.

III. New Adjustments.—After 1870 the Disciples began to

emerge slowly from their general cultural and intellectual isolation. By 1890 there was a beginning stream of young men going to Eastern universities for graduate study in further preparation for the ministry or for teaching. The founding of the Disciples Divinity House at the University of Chicago in 1894 was another step in the direction of a better educated ministry. Some of these university trained men promoted a movement among the Disciples toward "liberalism" and "open membership" which in time divided the communion into two large camps: a "restoration" group which was averse to federation, higher criticism, and every form of "modernism"; and a progressive group which demanded greater freedom of intellectual action and whose professed aim it was to unite Christians in doing the work of Christ rather than to create a correct but exclusive fellowship.

The original and animating principle of the restoration movement was a passionate longing for a re-union of the people of God on the basis of "Christ and his simple word." In consequence, the Disciples made many efforts to promote Christian union. Their reply to the overtures made by the House of Bishops of the Protestant Episcopal Church in 1887 was *negative* because they rejected all creeds as well as the *historic episcopate* as essential to union. By 1900 there was a decided revival of interest among the Disciples in Christian union which led to an active participation in the organization of the Federal Council of Churches in 1908. An Association for the Promotion of Christian Union was formed in 1910. Its first activity was the calling, in 1911, of a conference of Congregationalists, Disciples, Episcopalians, and Presbyterians for the purpose of cultivating a better acquaintance and the practice of closer cooperation. Negotiations for a closer co-operation between Baptists and Disciples culminated in 1929, but did not lead to organic union. At present there is a significant movement among the Disciples to bring the communion into more cordial relations with other denominations, and to place less emphasis on the restoration of a particular pattern of church organization and procedure.

Having no tribunal to exercise authority over local congregations and no form of centralized clerical control, the Disciples have always been so much given to following editorial leadership that some found occasion to talk about "newspapers popes." The most influential journals have been the *Millennial Harbinger*, published by Alexander Campbell from 1830 to 1866, and discontinued in 1870; the *Christian Standard*, made famous through the editorship of Isaac Errett; the *Christian-Evangelist*, which gained much prestige through its distinguished editor, J. H. Garrison; and the *Christian Century* which soon gained national prominence.

At present the Disciples have as their rallying center the annual International Convention. Their important organizations include the United Christian Missionary Society; the Board of Education; the Association for the Promotion of Christian Unity; the Board of Temperance and Social Welfare; the Pension Fund; the Board of Church Extension; the National Benevolent Association; and the Christian Board of Publication.

67. REVIEW QUESTIONS

1. What was the original and animating principle of the Restoration Movement?
2. Why did this movement make such powerful appeal to the people on the frontier?
3. How did the leaders of the movement differ from Presbyterians, Baptists, Congregationalists, and Methodists?
4. What contribution did Walter Scott make to the movement?
5. When and why did Barton W. Stone join forces with Alexander Campbell?
6. What contributions did Thomas and Alexander Campbell make to the movement?
7. Why was Alexander Campbell forced to modify his original program?
8. Why did not the Disciples split on the slavery question?
9. In what ways did currents of modern scholarship and culture influence the Disciples after 1890?
10. What obstacles have the Disciples met with in their efforts to promote Christian union?
11. What contribution has the Disciples made to religious journalism?
12. What is the present status of the Disciples of Christ?

TOPICS FOR SPECIAL STUDY

1. The program of Christian union as conceived of by the Disciples of Christ.
2. The Disciples' conception of the "New Testament order" in theory and practice.
3. Lessons learned from the Restoration Movement.
4. Alexander Campbell as a leader.

A SELECTED BIBLIOGRAPHY FOR CHAPTER XXXI

1. Tyler: *History of the Disciples of Christ.*
2. Garrison: *Religion Follows the Frontier.*
3. Welshimer: *Concerning the Disciples.*
4. Ainslie: *The Message of the Disciples of Christ for the Union of the Church.*
5. Davis: *How the Disciples Began and Grew.*
6. Jennings: *Origin and Early History of the Disciples of Christ.*
7. Errett: *Our Position.*
8. Richardson: *Memoirs of Alexander Campbell.*
9. Rogers: *Biography of Barton Warren Stone.*
10. Ware: *A History of the Disciples of Christ in North Carolina.*

CHAPTER XXXII

REFORMED AND EVANGELICAL CHURCHES

The *Reformed* communion[1] includes all churches that trace their origin directly or indirectly to the activities of Zwingli and Calvin. However, only four of these churches[2] came to be known by the name *Reformed*. In France the followers of Calvin were called Huguenots; in Scotland they were called Presbyterians; in England they were called Puritans and Independents; and in Bohemia and Hungary they preserved their national names.

Several denominations—generally classified as Evangelical churches—arose as a result of the revival movements of the first third of the nineteenth century.

I. The (Dutch) Reformed Church in America.—This is a daughter of the Church of Holland. The name *Dutch*, which still clings to it, designates its origin. Its first congregation,[3] formed in 1628 at New Amsterdam (New York), was the earliest in the New World organized on Presbyterian principles. Thirteen additional Dutch Reformed congregations were organized before the surrender of the colony to the English in 1664. The Dutch West India Company[4] had placed these churches under the supervision of the Church of Holland, or more directly, under the Classis of Amsterdam.

The change of sovereignty threw them on their own resources; yet they continued—for a century and a half—their organic connection with the Mother church. Meanwhile, as a number of other congregations were organized, the necessity of more ministers was felt. Few ministers were willing to leave Holland for America, and few American candidates could afford the expense of going to Holland to receive authority to preach. Eventually, an American organization had to be established with authority to ordain its own ministers.

[1] The Protestant Reformation produced three main types of communions or confessions, the Lutheran, the Reformed, and the Anglican.
[2] These four churches are, the Dutch Reformed Church of Holland; the (Dutch) Reformed Church in America; the Christian Reformed Church; and the (German) Reformed Church in the United States.
[3] This church, which was first known as the "church in the fort," is now known as the Collegiate Church of New York City. It was organized by Rev. Jonas Michaelius with 50 communicants.
[4] The Dutch West Indian Company was organized in 1621. A part of its task was to conquer and to colonize the western shores of the Atlantic, from the Strait of Magellan to the North Pole.

Rev. Theodore J. Frelingheusen initiated the first formal move, in 1737, to organize an Assembly or a Coetus. A plan of organization was sent to the Classis of Amsterdam for approval. Definite answer was delayed several years because the Classis tried to unite the Dutch, the Reformed Germans of Pennsylvania, and the Presbyterians in one general organization. Failing, permission was given in 1747 to the Dutch of New York and New Jersey to organize a Coetus. This organization was so restricted, however, that it could neither license candidates, nor ordain licentiates, without per-

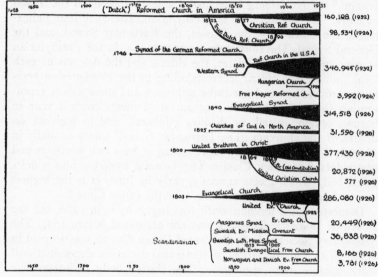

DIAGRAM OF REFORMED AND EVANGELICAL CHURCH BODIES

mission from the Classis of Amsterdam. Furthermore, appeals from disciplinary cases could be carried to Holland.

In 1754 an assembly of eleven ministers changed the Coetus into a constitutional Classis, assuming all the powers of a self-governing body. This action was opposed by five conservative members, partly because they questioned independent church authority in America, and partly because they wanted to secure educational advantages from King's College (Columbia), an Episcopalian school. A split resulted, lasting seventeen years. The seceders, styling themselves a Conferentie, organized formally in 1764 into an "Assembly Subordinate to the Classis of Amsterdam." Two years later the Classis secured a charter for Queens College (later Rutgers).

Through the efforts of Dr. John Henry Livingston (1746-1825), the Classis and the Conferentie were united in 1771. A formal constitution[5] was adopted in 1792, and in 1794 a General Synod with complete autonomy was organized. The organization was incorporated in 1819 as "The Reformed Protestant Dutch Church." This name was changed in 1867 to "The Reformed Church in America."

The doctrinal standards of this church body are, the Belgic Confession,[6] the Heidelberg Catechism,[7] and the Canons of the Synod of Dort.[8] The organization is Presbyterian. There are four judicatories, the Consistory, the Classis, the Particular Synod, and the General Synod. The *consistory*, corresponding to the Presbyterian *session*, includes the minister, the elders, and the deacons of each local church. The *classis*, corresponding to the Presbyterian *presbytery*, must have at least three ministers and three elders representing three churches. This organization meets twice a year to license, ordain, install, or dismiss ministers, and to legislate on affairs of the churches. The Particular Synod[9] meets annually in May. It is a delegated body representing at least two ministers and two elders from each Classis. The General Synod is also a delegated body which meets annually, early in June. It is the highest court of appeal, with jurisdiction over the entire Church.

Domestic home mission work was begun by it in 1786, but the Board of Domestic Missions was not organized before 1831. The Missionary Society of the Reformed Dutch Church was formed in 1828. With the formation of these two societies, denominational work became more aggressive. The church body maintains five secondary schools, two colleges, and two theological seminaries, supervised by a Board of Education. The Board of Publication and Bible School Work supplies denominational literature, with the American Bible Society as a recognized agency. A progress committee was organized in 1918 to co-ordinate and unify denominational activities. In 1923 this committee was succeeded by the Progress Council.

[5] The 84 articles of the Synod of Dort were enlarged by adopting 73 explanatory articles. The Constitution omitted, of course, all that belonged in government to a state church.

[6] See page 312.

[7] The Heidelberg Catechism was compiled in 1563 under Frederick III, Elector of the Palatinate, by Zacharias Ursinus, a pupil of Melanchthon, and Caspar Olevaanus, a pupil of Calvin.

[8] See page 351.

[9] The Reformed Church in America has five Particular Synods: New York, Albany, Chicago, New Brunswick, and Iowa.

The Church is a member of the Federal Council of the Churches of Christ in America, and of the Alliance of Reformed Churches throughout the World holding the Presbyterian system.[10] A close relation is maintained with the Mother Church of Holland.

II. The Christian Reformed Church.—This body is composed of three constituent parts, the True Reformed Dutch Church (1822), a group of immigrants from the Christian Reformed Church of Holland (1857), and a group of seceders from the Reformed Church in America (1890).

The True Reformed Dutch Church was formed in 1822 by six ministers who seceded because of alleged "errors in doctrine and looseness of discipline." By 1830 the organization embraced thirty congregations and ten ministers. The organization decreased, and the feeble remnant finally joined the Christian Reformed Church in 1890.

A group of Dutch immigrants who settled in Michigan in 1846-47 made up the next oldest element. They joined the Reformed Church in America in 1849 with the understanding that later they might "bid a fraternal adieu and be by themselves." They withdrew in 1857 to form the "Holland Reformed Church." Since 1904 the official denominational title has been the "Christian Reformed Church."[11]

The third element was a secession from the Reformed Church in America in 1882. This group withdrew because the parent church refused to condemn freemasonry, and to reject from Christian fellowship members of secret societies.

In doctrine and polity, this body is so much like the Reformed Church in America that no separate treatment is necessary. Its chief educational institution is Calvin College at Grand Rapids, Mich., and a theological seminary connected with it.

III. The (German) Reformed Church in the United States. —This is a German Calvinistic denomination which traces its origin to German immigration in the eighteenth century. Its early history was given in Chapter XXI. Dependence upon the Classis of Amsterdam[12] made development of this body similar to its sister organization, the (Dutch) Reformed Church in America. The

---

[10] This organization had, at its meeting in Cardiff in Wales in 1925, five hundred delegates representing one hundred Reformed churches in various parts of the world.

[11] The first title, "Holland Reformed Church," was changed in 1861 to "True Dutch Reformed Church." In 1880 the name was changed to "Holland Christian Reformed Church in America." The word "Holland" was dropped in 1890, and the words "in America" were eliminated in 1904.

[12] As the Reformed authorities of the Palatinate were unable to do much for the German Reformed churches in America, they requested the help of the Classis of Amsterdam and commissioned Michael Schlatter as missionary evangelist to the American churches.

Synod or Coetus organized by Michael Schlatter in 1747 had no authority to license candidates or to ordain licentiates. Finally, the necessity for more preachers became so urgent that the Synod decided, in 1772, to ordain its own ministers. This was virtually a declaration of independence, although a nominal subordination was continued until 1791, when the Coetus passed the following resolution: "Resolved, that the Coetus has the right at all times to examine and to ordain those who offer themselves as candidates for the ministry, without asking, or waiting for permission to do so from the fathers of Holland." A synodical constitution was adopted the following year, and the synod held its first meeting in 1793.

Unsuccessful attempts were made to unite the German and the Dutch Reformed churches in America before they formed independent synodical organizations. The one great hindrance was the unwillingness of the Germans to subscribe to more than *one* doctrinal standard, the Heidelberg Catechism, while the Dutch Reformed insisted on *three*, adding the Belgic Confession and the Canons of Dort.

The Reformed Church in the United States grew rapidly after it became an independent church body. Provisions were made for the education of ministers; vacant charges were supplied; new churches were formed, in turn organized into classes or presbyteries. Due to difficulties of communication, the western classes asked the synod for permission to ordain its own ministers. The request being refused, the formation of an independent Ohio Synod resulted. Fortunately, a permanent division was avoided. Delegates from the two bodies met in triennial conventions after 1844, and in 1863, on the occasion of the celebration of the three hundredth anniversary of the formation and adoption of the Heidelberg Catechism, the two synods were united into a General Synod, meeting every three years.

Developments of synodical activities were rapid after 1863. Aggressive home and foreign mission work was carried on. New District Synods were added to the General Synod. Between 1844 and 1881 the denomination was disturbed[13] by the so-called Mercersburg controversy centering around two theological professors, J. W. Nevin, and Philip Schaff. These men were co-workers in the Theo-

---

[13] An earlier controversy, which led to the formation of the United Brethren in Christ, will be discussed in the following Section. A schism over the establishment of a theological seminary occurred in 1822, resulting in the formation of the "Synod of the Free German Reformed Congregations of Pennsylvania." This secession, which later adopted the name of the "German Reformed Synod of Pennsylvania and Adjacent States," returned to its parent synod in 1837.

logical Seminary at Mercersburg. Dr. Schaff's inaugural address provoked a heresy trial. He was acquitted, but opposition of the conservative element was thoroughly aroused. Dr. Nevin, serving on a committee to revise the liturgy of the church, also aroused opposition because of his inclination toward an "altar liturgy." A schism was skilfully averted by a "Peace Commission" which harmonized the various views in a "Directory of Worship" published in 1881. Peace and harmony were gradually restored.

A "Forward Movement" was organized and brought to a successful conclusion by the church body between 1920 and 1925. More than five million dollars were raised and appropriated for various denominational agencies.

The Reformed Church in the United States has a Presbyterian form of government. It is a member of the Alliance of Reformed Churches throughout the World holding the Presbyterian System, and of the Federal Council of the Churches of Christ in America.

IV. The Free Magyar Reformed Church.—In 1904 the Hungarian Reformed Church in America was organized under the supervision of the Reformed Church in Hungary. Relations were interrupted during the World War, and plans were made to have the daughter church affiliate with some kindred organization in America. According to the "Tiffin Agreement"—made at Tiffin, Ohio—the Hungarian Reformed Church in America was to be transferred, in 1924, to the Reformed Church in the United States. Some of the congregations refused to accept, and organized under the name "Free Magyar Reformed Church in America." This church body follows the mother church in Hungary in doctrine and organization. Its church government occupies a middle position between presbyterianism and episcopalianism.

V. The United Brethren in Christ.—During the last quarter of the eighteenth century, the Germans of Pennsylvania, Maryland, and Virginia experienced a revival under the leadership of Philip William Otterbein (1726-1813), a German Reformed minister,[14] and Martin Boehm (1725-1812), a Mennonite.[15] They had no intention of forming a new denomination, but converts multiplied rapidly and provision had to be made for their spiritual care. At the suggestion of Francis Asbury, leader of the Methodists, Otter-

[14] Otterbein had been brought over from Germany by Michael Schlatter in 1752. In his first pastorate at Lancaster, Pa., he had a profound personal religious experience which prompted him to conduct evangelistic meetings in the German settlements of Pennsylvania, Maryland, and Virginia.
[15] Boehm had passed through a religious experience similar to that of Otterbein. The two men conducted evangelistic meetings for more than fifteen years, usually holding "great meetings" which lasted for two days.

bein and Boehm organized their followers into Reformed church societies of a Wesleyan type for the promotion of personal piety. Some of the best qualified members were licensed to preach. In 1789 the evangelistic preachers held a formal conference at Baltimore.

These Reformed church societies were drawn together by common interests, so in 1800, at a conference near Frederick City, Maryland, a new denomination was organized. The name "United Brethren in Christ" was based on an utterance of Otterbein when he, at the conclusion of a stirring sermon by Boehm, grasped his hand and said, "We are brethren."

The new body was organized along Methodist lines, with episcopal government and Arminian theology. Otterbein and Boehm were elected bishops, and successive elections kept them in office until their death. The first delegated General Conference, held in 1815 at Mount Pleasant, Pa., adopted a confession of faith, rules of order, and a book of discipline. A revision of 1889 admitted women to the ministry on the same terms as men. Objecting to this, a group withdrew to form a new body, known as the United Brethren (Old Constitution).

Denominational work is conducted through three agencies, known as conference missions, the Home Mission and Church Erection Society, and the Foreign Mission Society. The church body has seven colleges and one seminary. Emphasis is placed upon personal work of the individual members. The denomination is a member of the Federal Council of the Churches of Christ in America.

VI. The Evangelical Church.—This church originated as a result of the evangelistic labors of Jacob Albright (1759-1808), born and confirmed a Lutheran. Later he came under the influence of a Reformed minister, but he joined the Methodists and became a licensed Methodist exhorter. Starting about 1790 as an itinerant preacher among Germans in eastern Pennsylvania, he soon gained a large following. He had no intention of founding a new denomination, but he was compelled to organize because the Methodists did not wish to engage in distinctively German work. In 1803 a general assembly elected and ordained Albright as presiding elder or chief pastor. At the first annual conference, in Kleinfeltersville, Pa., Albright was elected bishop. The conference authorized him to compile a Scriptural creed and a plan of organization, but he died before the work was completed. The creed and the constitution were completed by George Miller, John Walter and John Dreisbach. At the first delegated General Conference, held in 1816, the name "The Evangelical Association" was adopted. This name was retained until the union with the United Evangelical Church in 1922, when the present name was adopted.[16]

In doctrine the Evangelical Church is Arminian; in policy it is modeled after the Methodist.[17] The governing bodies are, the Quarterly Conference, the Annual Conference, and the General Conference.[18] Denominational work is carried on through the Board of Home Missions, the Woman's Missionary Society, the Board of Missions, the Board of Church Extension, and the Board of Education. A large number of young people's societies are enrolled in the Evangelical League of Christian Endeavor.

VII. The Evangelical Synod of North America.—In 1840 six ministers organized a synod representing a union of Lutheran and Reformed churches. A number of similar synods were formed, including the Evangelical Synod of the North West, the German Evangelical Society of Ohio, and the United Evangelical Society of the East. These synods organized as a denomination in 1877, under the name of the Evangelical Synod of North America. This church subscribes—strangely enough—to the symbolic books of both Lutheran and Reformed churches. Liberty of conscience is allowed in doctrine concerning the Lord's Supper and similar problems.

The Evangelical Synod of North America is divided into twenty districts, each district in charge of a district president. The church meets in a General Conference once every four years. It is a constituent member of the Federal Council of the Churches of Christ in America. This synod merged with the Reformed Church in the United States in June, 1934.

VIII. The Churches of God in North America.—John Winebrenner, a minister of the German Reformed Church, promoted a revival among Germans in Pennsylvania which finally led to the formation of an independent church, in 1825, of Baptist principles and Methodist organization under the name "Church of God." Similar churches were formed in surrounding communities,

---

[16] The Evangelical Association was divided in 1891, due to a "division brought about by an unwarranted assumption of power exercised by those in official position, in that they refused to submit to the findings of duly constituted trial conferences, assumed to expel ministers and members without trial, and refused to arbitrate the differences existing between the parties in the controversy." After lengthy negotiations, this group was re-united with the parent organization in 1922.

[17] The Evangelical Church is episcopal in government, and connectional in organization. The General Conference elects bishops for a four year term, but they are not consecrated as such. They are eligible for re-election.

[18] The General Conference meets once in every four years.

and these organized as the "General Eldership of the Church of God" in 1830. By 1845 three elderships had been formed, which organized the "General Eldership of the Church of God in North America." In 1896 the name was changed to the "General Eldership of the Churches of God in North America." The doctrine of this church is Arminian.[19] Three ordinances are obligatory—baptism, the Lord's Supper, and the religious washing of the feet of the saints.

IX. Scandinavian Evangelical Bodies.—The three church bodies listed below are offshoots of the evangelical free-church movement in Scandinavia. None of these groups subscribe to any particular creed, but they accept the Bible as the word of God and as the only infallible guide in faith, doctrine, and practice. The two Swedish groups were formerly tinged with the doctrinal views of Paul Peter Waldenström.[20]

1. *The Swedish Evangelical Mission Covenant of America.*—The evangelistic movement started by Carl Olof Rosenius[21] and perpetuated by P. P. Waldenström, led to the formation of two national societies known as the National Evangelical Foundation,[22] founded in 1856, and the Swedish Mission Covenant,[23] founded in 1878. Swedish immigrants transplanted this movement to America, where they founded two church organizations, the Swedish Lutheran Mission Synod (1873), and the Swedish Lutheran Ansgarius Synod (1874). The two bodies united under the present name in 1885.

2. *The Swedish Evangelical Free Church of the United States of America.*—A number of congregations which failed to unite with the Swedish Evangelical Mission Covenant of America, formed an organization known as the Swedish Evangelical Free Mission. This church body was incorporated in 1908 under the laws of Minnesota as the Swedish Evangelical Free Church. The polity is congregational, while the Mission Covenant occupies a middle position between Congregationalism and Presbyterianism.

3. *The Norwegian and Danish Evangelical Free Church.*—This body was formed by immigrants who were Separatists from the

---

[19] They have no written creed. The Word of God is accepted as their only rule for faith and practice.

[20] Waldenström differed from contemporary Lutherans in his emphasis on the Atonement. He claimed that "the reconciliation through Christ is of us to God, not of God to us: not through grace on account of Christ, but on account of grace through Christ. The subject is God, the Father of Christ; the source is the love of God; the object is the whole world; the mediator is Christ, the only begotten God . . . the Son of God; the end is the restitution of men to God, not the reconciliation of God to men."—(Dr. J. O. Evjen.)

[21] See page 397.

[22] The Swedish name is *Evangeliska Fosterlandsstiftelsen.*

[23] The Swedish name is *Svenska Missionsförbundet.*

state churches of Norway and Denmark. Toward the latter part of the nineteenth century a number of congregations organized into two associations, one for the Eastern States, and one for the Middle West. In 1910 these associations organized as the Norwegian and Danish Evangelical Free Church Association of North America. This church body is evangelical in doctrine and Congregational in polity. A part of its home mission work is affiliated with the Congregationalists.

68. REVIEW QUESTIONS

1. What is meant by the Reformed communion? By Evangelical churches?
2. Account for the comparatively slow growth of the (Dutch) Reformed Church in America.
3. Why the Christian Reformed Church?
4. Why have the Dutch and the German Reformed in America failed to unite?
5. How was the Free Magyar Reformed Church organized?
6. What conditions promoted the formation of the United Brethren in Christ?
7. Was the organization of the Evangelical Church necessary? Explain.
8. What characterizes the Evangelical Synod of North America?
9. Why did not John Winebrenner affiliate with some church body already in existence?
10. What characteristics do the three Scandinavian Evangelical Bodies have in common? Why are they not listed as Lutheran church bodies?
11. Account for the fact that so many Swedish immigrants to America have organized their religious life outside the Lutheran denomination.
12. Why the Norwegian and Danish Evangelical Free Church?

TOPICS FOR SPECIAL STUDY

1. What part has personal ambition played in the formation of American church bodies?
2. Could American Protestantism reasonably simplify its manifold organization? If so, along what practicable lines?
3. Chart the main American denominations as to (a) doctrine, (b) organization, (c) minor characteristics. What is your conclusion?

A SELECTED BIBLIOGRAPHY FOR CHAPTER XXXII

1. Reed: *History of the Presbyterian Churches in the World.*
2. Demarest: *The Reformed Church in America.*
3. Demarest: *Centennial Discourses on the Reformed Church.*
4. Corwin: *The Manual of the Reformed Church in America* (4th ed.).
5. Corwin: *Digest of Constitutional and Synodical Legislation of the Reformed Church in America.*
6. Good: *History of the Reformed Church in the United States.*
7. Good: *Historical Handbook.*
8. Berger: *History of the Church of the United Brethren.*
9. Shuey: *Handbook of the United Brethren in Christ.*
10. Drury: *Life of Philip William Otterbein.*
11. Orwig: *History of the Evangelical Association.*
12. Stapleton: *Annals of the Evangelical Association of North America and History of the United Evangelical Church.*

CHAPTER XXXIII

THE CHRISTIAN CHURCHES IN CANADA

The Dominion of Canada has one of the largest areas, and at the same time one of the lowest densities of population of any country in the world. The area is divided into nine provinces and several territories which together form a federation under the British Crown. Canada is the only country in the world to recognize by law two official languages: English and French. How Christian congregations and denominations were founded and developed in this vast portion of the "New World" will be briefly outlined in the present chapter. Newfoundland, though not an integral part of Canada, will be included in this dicussion.

I. **The French Canadian Era, 1534-1759.**—Scandinavian adventurers discovered North America about the year 1000, but they founded no permanent settlements. In 1497 John Cabot made an expedition in search of the North-West Passage and discovered Labrador and Newfoundland. The following year his brother, Sebastian Cabot, sailed up Davis Strait. Fisheries were formed along the coast of Newfoundland, and an effort was made in 1610 to establish a regular settlement, but the attempt failed, and the center of interest shifted to the St. Lawrence Valley.

In 1534 the Frenchman Jacques Cartier explored the St. Lawrence with a view of reaching the Pacific. He took possession of Labrador in the name of his sovereign, Francis I, and in 1535-36 he ascended the St. Lawrence as far as Montreal. The first permanent settlement in Canada was established in 1608 in Quebec under the lead of Samuel Champlain, the "father of French colonization in Canada." The increase in French colonists was slow, however, and the stream of immigrants flowed westward toward the Mississippi. The plan of a French colonial empire in North America and why it did not materialize has been discussed in pages 416-17.

French colonists were usually followed by Roman Catholic priests who established mission stations and built convents and schools. Three Recollect (Franciscan) priests settled in 1615 in Quebec and formed the first regular religious establishment in Canada. These priests laid a splendid foundation for successful missionary activity among the Indians. Jesuit priests arrived in 1625. They not only usurped the place held so worthily by the Recollect priests, but brought pressure to bear in France to prevent further emigration of Recollects to Canada. In consequence, Quebec was but a little more than a Jesuit mission by the middle of the seventeenth century.

The French settlements were generally closed against all save Roman Catholic immigrants. Admiral Coligny, wishing to establish a Protestant French empire in North America, procured a concession from Charles IX, and in 1564 planted a colony of Huguenots in Florida, on the banks of the May River, near St. John's Bluff. But in Canada the Huguenots were not allowed to settle after 1627. The Edict of Nantes, published in 1598 and revoked in 1685, gave the Huguenots of France freedom of conscience and practical freedom of worship, but Huguenots in *New France* derived no benefit from this religious toleration in the homeland after 1627.

Jesuit leaders promoted a strong ecclesiastical control which, during the French regime, reached its zenith about 1672. Jesuit influence was increased by the policy of appointing government officials for the colony who were acceptable to the Society of Jesus. But the struggle in France between the Gallican or National party and the Ultramontane or Papal party also affected the affairs in Quebec. Gallican influence gradually limited the ecclesiastical control so that the colonial government, instead of being a handmaid of the Church, gradually became the master. Transfer to British control in 1763 was therefore not altogether unwelcome by certain French-Canadian church leaders.

Francois Xavier de Laval-Montmorency was appointed vicar apostolic of New France in 1657. His nomination by the pope, and not by the king, was a triumph for papacy. Protests from the Archbishop of Rouen and from the parliaments of Rouen and Paris at this exclusion of Canada from the Concordat, proved ineffective. Upon his arrival in Canada, Laval succeeded in ousting the Sulpician Vicar-general, Queylus, appointee of the Archbishop of Rouen.

Laval was determined to uphold papacy at the expense of the Gallican church. He turned his attention to the establishment of a bishopric at Quebec, and he influenced Louis XIV to send the proper petition to the pope. The king sent the petition in 1664, but he insisted that the new diocese should be dependent upon the Archbishop of Rouen, while the Propaganda insisted it should be an immediate dependency of Rome. A compromise was finally reached, and on October 1, 1674, the Papal Court established the See of Quebec. The right of nomination was vested in the king, and the bishopric became directly dependent upon Rome. The episcopal authority vested in the new office, helped the Church to meet the growing power of the State. Laval not only organized the church system, but he unified the ecclesiastical factions by the transfer of control from Gallican France to Ultramontane Rome.

The charter of the Company of New France was cancelled in 1663, and New France became a royal province. At this time French Canada had five settlements: Quebec (1608), Three Rivers (1634), Sillery (1637), Montreal (1642), and Fort Richelieu (1642), and a total population of less than.2500 consisting largely of priests, officials, and fur traders. Progress under the rule of the Company of New France had been slow because the company had neglected colonization in favor of fur trade. But during the first ten years of direct royal control the population nearly trebled, and by 1673 Canada had a population of about 7000 colonists. In 1759, the year of conquest by the English, the total population of New France was approximately 65,000, or about one-twentieth of the estimated population of the thirteen British colonies.

From 1672 till the end of the French regime, the influence of the church in New France was more and more confined to the spiritual sphere. The royal representatives naturally followed the Gallican principle that the king and not the pope was the head of the church in matters affecting the king's temporal dominion. The influence of the hierarchy in the Sovereign Council of Quebec was curbed, and the state interfered actively in matters of tithes, establishment of religious houses, church discipline, excommunication, and the public ministry of the church. Nevertheless, the church was well organized and prosperous at the time of the transfer to British rule. About one-fourth, or 25.6 per cent of all land granted in Canada by the French king belonged to the church and to religious orders.

Canada was conquered by England in 1759, and in the Treaty of Paris, 1763, France ceded to Great Britain all of Canada and all her claims in North America east of the Mississippi River. This defeat of the French proved to be a victory for Roman Catholicism. The Quebec Act of 1774[1] and the Constitutional Act of 1791[2] in-

---

[1] The Quebec Act of 1774 has been called "the Magna Charta of the French-Canadian race." It stipulated "free exercise of Religion of the Church of Rome, subject to the King's Supremacy."

[2] The Constitutional Act of 1791 recognized the fact that there were two separate

vested the Roman Catholic Church in Canada with a control which is without a parallel in Roman Catholicism.

Joseph Octave Plessis, Bishop of Quebec from 1806, became the first Canadian archbishop in 1819. An Apostolic Delegation was established in Canada in 1899, and from 1910 the title has been the Apostolic Delegation for Canada and Newfoundland. The provinces include:

Halifax	became a diocese in 1842,	an archdiocese in 1852
Kingston	" " " " 1826,	" " " 1889
Montreal	" " " " 1836,	" " " 1886
Ottawa	" " " " 1847,	" " " 1886
Quebec	" " " " 1674,	" " " 1844
St. Boniface	" " " " 1847,	" " " 1871
Toronto	" " " " 1841,	" " " 1870
Regina	" " " " 1910,	" " " 1915
Vancouver (New Westminster)	" " " " 1890,	" " " 1908

Winnipeg became immediately subject to the Holy See in 1915
Edmonton (St. Albert) became a diocese in 1871, an archdiocese in 1912
St. John, Newfoundland, became a diocese in 1847, a metropolitan see in 1904

The French Canadian is of a traditionalistic and conservative type of mind. The French language, controlled by the church, has proved an effective weapon of isolation, and a warding off of modernism in every form. French literature has been carefully censored so that only ideas in complete harmony with the church have been allowed to come to the reading French-Canadian public. The use of two official languages, English and French, has proved a barrier to spiritual understanding and sympathy and has given rise to a difficult educational problem in communities where instruction is desired in both languages.

II. The British Era, 1759 to Present.—The conquest by the English in 1759, and the Treaty of Paris of 1763, opened up Canada for Protestant immigration. The nature of this immigration was somewhat different, however, from that of the earlier migration to the Thirteen Colonies. Puritan migration to New England was prompted by religious motives, or by the desire for "freedom to worship God," while the early immigration to Canada was largely economic and political. The 60,000 Loyalists, who migrated to Canada after the American Revolutionary War, came because they preferred to remain under British rule; and other early Protestant settlers came to Canada rather than to the United States because they preferred the British connection and Monarchical government. As a general consequence, Protestant Canadian character became rooted in traditionalism and conservatism, while

races or nations in Canada which could not at first unite. Provisions were consequently made for a division of Canada into Upper and Lower Canada, each with a separate government. Lower Canada became subject to French-Canadian rule.

American character became more rooted in idealism and progressivism.[3]

Sir Humphrey Gilbert paved the way for British colonization of Canada in 1583 when he took formal possession of Newfoundland in the name of the King of England. All during the French-Canadian era, Newfoundland remained nominally under British control. Nova Scotia or Arcadia, "with all its ancient boundaries," was ceded to England by the Treaty of Utrecht in 1713, but little provision was made for an early Protestant setlement of either Newfoundland or Nova Scotia. The first permanent Protestant settlement in Canada was made when Lord Cornwallis founded Halifax in 1749. Four years later Halifax had a population of approximately 5000 people.

Most of these settlers came from New England. After 1763, many New Englanders also found their way to Montreal. A considerable number of Loyalists came immediately after the American Revolutionary War and settled in Nova Scotia and in Ontario. German Mennonites and Lutherans migrated from Pennsylvania to Welland, Waterloo, and York counties in Ontario. Other Protestant settlers in Canada before 1900 came mainly from England. Of the early Scottish immigrants, some were Protestant and some were Catholic. They settled largely in Prince Edward Island, in Glengarry County in Ontario, and in certain parts of Nova Scotia. The majority of Irish immigrants were Protestants, coming from North Ireland. The more dominant Irish-Canadian group is therefore Protestant, and "Orangeism" (Loyal Orange Order) is said to have as much of a stronghold in Toronto as in Belfast. On the other hand, many of the Scotch-Canadians are strong and influential Catholics. A small but influential group of Lutheran Icelanders settled around Lake Winnipeg after 1872.

The Protestant immigrants to Canada were, as has already been indicated, of a mixed religious inheritance. A brief account will now be given of the progress of each of the major Protestant groups in Canada, including Anglicans, Methodists, Presbyterians, Congregationalists, Baptists, Lutherans, and Mennonites.

1. *The Church of England in Canada.*—While England gave the French-Canadians freedom of worship according to the Roman Catholic faith "so far as the laws of England do permit," His Majesty's Council also planned to establish Protestantism in Canada. Two Protestant churches were organized in Halifax in

---

[3] Protestant Canadians are very cautious in their espousal of new causes, and generally turn to the lessons contained in the pages of British history for a norm and corrective. The Canadians deal with situations rather than with theories.

1749, one for the Established Church, and one for dissenters. In 1758 the first legislative assembly of Nova Scotia made provisions for the establishment of the Church of England in the colony. The Crown was to appoint the clergymen, and these were to be under the jurisdiction of the Bishop of London. Settlers from New England became so alarmed by this legislation that the Governor found it necessary the following year to issue a proclamation, declaring that Nova Scotia would grant full religious toleration to all groups.

Governor Murray was appointed Captain-General and Governor-in-Chief of the Province of Quebec in December, 1763. He received instructions to survey the land, to fix the parish boundaries, to maintain a Protestant ministry and Protestant schoolmasters, and to arrange for Divine Service on Sundays and holidays according to the Book of Common Prayer. No Protestant minister was to be appointed to any ecclesiastical benefit unless he had a certificate from the Bishop of London. The English policy was evidently to make the Church of England the particular recipient of Protestant governmental favors in Canada.[4]

Early progress of the Angelican communion in Canada was, however, very slow. To begin with the Anglicans in Quebec and Montreal had no church building of their own, the first metropolitan church being built in Quebec in 1796. In the absence of a sufficient number of Anglican clergymen, foreign Protestant ministers were appointed as curates in Quebec, Montreal, and Three Rivers. Effective oversight was lacking until colonial bishops were appointed. Charles Inglis was appointed by the English Crown in 1787 as Bishop of Nova Scotia, and Jacob Mountain was appointed Bishop of Quebec in 1793.

The Constitutional Act of 1791 provided for the support of the Anglican clergy by the setting aside of approximately one-seventh of all land thrown open for settlement, as Clergy Reserves. This special endowment of a state church in Upper Canada, and the later attempts to establish colleges and universities under the jurisdiction of the Anglican bishops, but supported by public funds, proved a source of great irritation, not only for all dissenting Protestant bodies, but also for ministers of the Church of Scotland.[5] The prob-

[4] The Anglicans practically monopolized education in Upper Canada during the first century of British rule, and pastors for "dissenter sects" could not perform legal marriages until in 1831.

[5] By the terms of the Union of England and Scotland in 1707, the (Presbyterian) Church of Scotland was recognized by law as the Established Church of Scotland. Nothing was stated, however, as to the arrangement in new colonies; but Canadian Presbyterian ministers naturally claimed a right to a share of the Clergy Reserves.

lem was finally settled in 1853 by the secularization of all undivided Clergy Reserves. Seignorial tenure was abolished the same year.

New dioceses were created as occasion demanded: Toronto in 1839; Fredericton, N. B., in 1845; Rupert's Land in 1849; and Montreal in 1850. But the Church of England in Canada had not, as yet, a constitutional or synodical form of government. Bishops were appointed by the Crown and consecrated in England. The Anglican church establishment in Canada was financed mainly by the Crown, and partly by the Society for the Propagation of the Gospel. Realizing that this reliance upon outside help did not promote the best interests of an indigenous Anglican-Canadian Church, and being confronted with an economic crisis due to the secularization of the Clergy Reserves in 1853, the Bishops of Quebec, Toronto, Newfoundland, Fredericton, and Montreal took steps to establish a synodical and constitutional government. Plans were made for a synodical government in each diocese, where the laity should have representation. Provisions were also made for a synod of the Province of Canada, to be presided over by a Provincial Metropolitan. Negotiations with the Archbishop of Canterbury were finally completed, and the Church of England in Canada was formally launched in 1861.

As the settlement of Northwest Canada grew, it was expedient to establish a new ecclesiastical province under the Bishop of Rupert's Land. The existence of two ecclesiastical provinces again gave occasion for the formation of a general synod, organized in 1893, for the purpose of governing the whole Anglican communion in Canada. At present the Church of England in Canada is governed by a general synod, presided over by a Primate; four provincial synods, each presided over by a Metropolitan; and twenty-six dioceses, each presided over by the Bishop of the Diocese. The primacy is peripatetic and is usually awarded on the basis of seniority. This arrangement is not entirely satisfactory, since the Primate of the Dominion is also the Metropolitan of a province and the bishop of a diocese. In the near future, the Church of England in Canada may find it necessary to establish a primatial see.

By 1902 the Church of England in Canada had enough inner strength and consolidation to launch an aggressive missionary and church-planting campaign in the West. But the unity of the Church has also suffered by the influence of the Oxford movement which has tended to divide the Anglicans in Canada into two party camps: the one with strong Evangelical emphasis, and the other with leanings toward Rome. The controversy has resulted in the establishment of two rival theological seminaries: Wycliffe and Trinity in Toronto.

The Church of England in Canada has taken a broad and cordial attitude toward negotiations for a National Protestant Church of Canada. But insistence upon the acceptance of the historic episcopate as a basic requirement for organic church union, made a corporate union with the United Church of Canada in 1925 impossible.

69. REVIEW QUESTIONS

1. What are some of the conditions peculiar to Canada?
2. What efforts were made to establish European settlements in Canada prior to 1608?
3. What influence did the Edict of Nantes have on the early course of events in the French-Canadian settlements? Explain.
4. Why was Jesuit influence so strong in Quebec, and why was there a transfer of church control from Gallican France to Ultramontane Rome?
5. In what respects did the French-Canadian settlements differ from those of the English in the Thirteen Colonies?
6. Why did the Roman Catholicism in Quebec secure such unparalleled control?
7. How is the Roman Catholic Church in Canada organized?
8. In what ways did the Protestant immigrants to Canada differ from Protestant immigrants to the Thirteen Colonies?
9. What efforts and events paved the way for Protestant settlement of Canada?
10. Where and by whom was the first permanent Protestant settlement in Canada founded?
11. In what ways did the Protestant settlers in Canada differ as to religious and national inheritance?
12. Why was the Church of England established by law in Canada?

TOPICS FOR SPECIAL STUDY

1. Canada and the United States of America compared and contrasted.
2. The rise of ecclesiastical control in Quebec.
3. Jesuits in Canada.
4. Gallicanism versus Ultramontanism in Canada.
5. Why the French colonial empire in North America failed.
6. Differences between Protestant Canadian and Protestant American character.
7. The establishment of the Church of England in Canada.

2. Canadian Congregationalism before the Union of 1925.— Although Congregationalism was the first dissenting group to take foothold in Canada, it always remained a very small body, being only 0.63 per cent of the total population in 1871, and 0.35 per cent of the total population in 1921. Congregationalism in the West touched only a few of the major centers of population, and in the East it was in some cases smothered through the organization of

competitive churches. A brief explanation of this anomalous position will now be made.

The first dissenter church in Canada, established in Halifax in
1749, was a *union church* composed mainly of Congregationalists
from New England and of some Presbyterians. New England Congregationalists made the first extensive settlements in Nova Scotia,
but many of these settlers returned to the United States before and
after the outbreak of the American Revolutionary War. Those who
remained were invaded by New Light Congregationalism which
broke up several congregations, and these New Light churches
later formed the nucleus of the first Baptist Convention in Nova
Scotia. Only four of the original Congregational churches continued as organized, and these, together with sister churches organized later, became a part of the United Church of Canada in 1925.

Congregationalists in Quebec were first organized into a congregation in 1801, but this church soon turned Presbyterian. The first
congregation in Ontario was organized in 1819 in Elgin County
under the name of The Congregational-Presbyterian Prince of
Peace Society. A minor portion of the membership of this church
was Presbyterian. Congregational churches in Canada were, however, comparatively few and far between. Canadian Congregationalism benefited very little by English immigration, since it was predominantly Methodist or Anglican. Immigration from Scotland
and North Ireland was, of course, Presbyterian. Little help came
from the United States, since the American Revolutionary War
greatly impaired the Congregational connection with New England.
Furthermore, the early Canadian Congregationalism lacked the
strong church organization and the aggressive spirit of the Presbyterian and the Methodist communions.

Canadian Congregationalism was extended considerably between
1827 and 1832 through the efforts of the Home Missionary Society, organized in 1827 by Canadian Baptists, Congregationalists,
and a few Presbyterians. Henry Wilkes, the first secretary of the
society, helped to establish many new Congregational churches in
Canada.

The Congregational Union of England and Wales in 1831 led
to the sending of a fraternal delegation to convey greetings to
Congregationalists in North America. Upon the return of this delegation, the Colonial Missionary Society was formed in 1836 for
the purpose of establishing Congregational churches in all British
colonies. This society helped Canada for over seventy years.

Though Canadian Congregationalism was numerically small, it

succeeded well in inner consolidation. The churches of Nova Scotia and New Brunswick formed a union in 1846. The churches of Ontario and Quebec amalgamated in 1853. These two united bodies came together in 1906 to form the Congregational Union of Canada. The fourth Congregational union was with the United Brethren in Christ in 1907. This body numbered only 1,400 members, and the Congregational membership at the time of union in 1925 was 12,586.

3. *Canadian Presbyterianism before the Union of 1925.*—Presbyterianism constituted the second largest Protestant body in British North America prior to the Church Union of 1925. Its history is like that of a river with many tributaries from Scotch, Irish, English and American sources. Scotch and Irish ecclesiastical differences, which had no real pertinence to colonial life, were transplanted to Canada by Presbyterian immigrants, and the early Presbyterian organizations represented a wide variety of outlook, tradition, and customs. But gradually, as the diagram indicates, these groups were drawn together, and by 1875 they constituted one organic unit, adjusted to meet the exacting needs of the growing West. These adjustments to colonial conditions were made with spiritual tact, elasticity of spirit, and great missionary zeal for the promotion and extension of the Kingdom of God on earth, at home and abroad.

Tracing the many broken threads of Scotch and Irish Presbyterianism, as transplanted to British North America, and weaving these together into one cord, is not an easy task. Matters are made more complicated because the territory under consideration includes not only Canada proper, but also the Maritime Provinces. Perhaps the problem may be simplified by starting with the four groups that united in 1875, tracing each group back to the sources. Following the arrangement in the diagram, top to bottom, the groups will be discussed in the following order, (1) The Synod of Maritime Provinces, 1868 (Church of Scotland); (2) The Presbyterian Church of the Lower Provinces; B.N.A., 1866; (3) The Canadian Presbyterian Church, 1861; and (4) The Presbyterian Church of Canada, 1840 (Church of Scotland).

a. *The Synod of the Maritime Provinces, 1868-75.*—This organization had two tributaries and one secession. The Synod of New Brunswick had its beginning in 1817 through the efforts of ministers from the Church of Scotland. The presbytery was formed in 1833, and the synod in 1835 with the presbyteries of St. John and Miriamichi. The Disruption in Scotland in 1843 caused a division

A HISTORY OF THE CHRISTIAN CHURCH

NOTES ON CHURCH UNION IN CANADA

The Northwest Territories comprise the districts of Assiniboia, Athabasca, Keewatin, Yukon, Mackenzie, Ungava, and Franklin. According to the census of 1931 population for Canada was 2.96 persons per square mile, as compared with 35.5 persons in U. S. A.

Congregationalists fought consistently, but without success, for simplification of the articles on doctrine.

The policy was to effect union with as little disturbance of local congregations as possible.

The Presbytery of the United Church also has some of the District Meetings in Methodism, and the Association in Congregationalism. As to the charges formed subsequent to the union, the Session, referred to above, was to have oversight over the spiritual interests of the pastoral charge; the Committee of Stewards was to manage the temporal and financial affairs of the charge; and the Official Board, consisting of the Session and Committee of Stewards, was to meet for the consideration of matters of joint interest.

The General Council in the United Church was to be similar to the General Conference in Methodism, the General Assembly in Presbyterianism, and the Union of Congregationalism.

After the union in 1925, the United Church of Canada prepared a lengthy statement that "the existing ministry of the United Church of Canada is a true ministry of the Church of God," and that "those ordained by The United Church of Canada have a true ministry in the Church of God." It may be remembered that John Wesley rejected Apostolic Succession, as did John Knox, the Presbyterians, and the Congregationalists.

*These figures exclude membership of Newfoundland and Bermuda.

**These figures exclude Newfoundland and Bermuda. Furthermore, less than seventy per cent of the Presbyterian membership was carried into the United Church of Canada in 1925. The remaining thirty per cent continued as the Presbyterian Church of Canada, with a total membership in 1931 of 180,956.

THE CHRISTIAN CHURCHES IN CANADA

NOTES ON CHURCH UNION IN CANADA

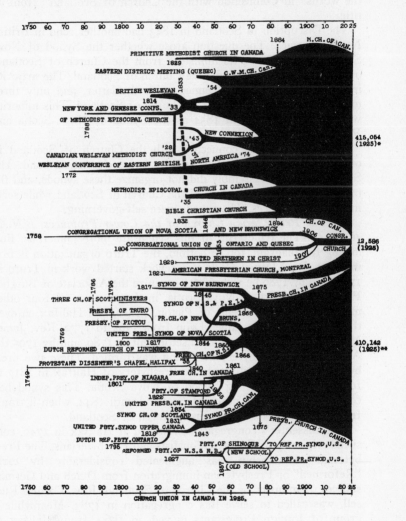

of the Synod of New Brunswick in 1845. The secession group signified its adherence to the Free Church of Scotland by dropping the words "in Connection with the Church of Scotland" from its title.

The Disruption in Scotland in 1843 had another echo in British North America. The question arose whether the Synod of Nova Scotia should receive its ministers from the Church of Scotland, or from the newly formed Free Church of Scotland. The majority in the synod decided to connect with the latter, and only three ministers remained loyal to the Church of Scotland. This minority was able to organize in 1854 as the Synod of Nova Scotia and Prince Edward Island.

Both synods were connected with the Church of Scotland in origin and sympathy, rather than by any ecclesiastical bond. The Scottish General Assembly did not organize these synods, and the ministers were not ministers of the Church of Scotland while serving in the provinces. The synods were self-governing.

b. *The Presbyterian Church of the Lower Provinces, B.N.A., 1866-75.*—The tributaries of this synod are more numerous. Following the diagram, top to bottom, the Truro organization is first in order. Rev. Daniel Cock of Grenock started work in Truro in 1770, and by 1786 he was able to organize the Associate or Burgher Presbytery of Truro, Nova Scotia, in the presence of four other ministers. The settlements of Pictou, Truro, and Halifax enjoyed the services of Rev. James Lyon from 1764 to 1772. Rev. James MacGregor came to the Pictou settlement in 1786, and by 1795 the Anti-Burgher Presbytery of Pictou was formed. These two presbyteries joined heartily with the Presbytery of Halifax in 1817 to form the self-governing Synod of Nova Scotia. This synod had connection with the Church of Scotland until 1844, when it transferred its allegiance to the Free Church of Scotland.

The Dissenter's congregation, founded at Halifax in 1749, consisted originally of Congregationalists and Presbyterians. The Presbyterian membership was augmented considerably by early "Reformed" or Presbyterian immigration from Dutch and German sources. A minister of the Church of Scotland, Rev. Thomas Russell, was called to serve this congregation in 1783. Meanwhile a group of foreign Protestants moved, in 1769, from Halifax to Lunenberg where they built a small Dutch Reformed church, and called as their first pastor Rev. Bruin Romcas of Comingo.

Friction developed in the Maritimes between representatives of the Church of Scotland and representatives of the Glasgow Colonial

Society, organized in 1825 by Evangelicals of the National Church. This led to the formation of the Free Church of Nova Scotia in 1833. Seven years later, in 1840, this new synod was joined by the Dissenter's Church (St. Mathew's Church) of Halifax, and by the Dutch Reformed Church at Lunenberg. Twenty years later, in 1860, the Free Church of Nova Scotia and the United Presbyterian Synod of Nova Scotia united to form The Synod of the Presbyterian Church of the Lower Provinces of British North America.

c. *The Canadian Presbyterian Church, 1861-70.*—American Presbyterian ministers, mostly of the Associate or Secession Synod organized at Philadelphia in 1753, operated in the Niagara Peninsula as early as 1791. Prominent among these pioneers was Rev. Daniel Ward Eastman. The Presbytery of Niagara was formed in 1833, but it remained independent of any synod until 1850, when it joined the Synod of the Free Church of Canada.

Ministers sent by the Associate Reformed Church of the United States started work in the Stamford region in 1822. By 1836 they were able to organize the Presbytery of Stamford. Most of the churches of this presbytery joined the Synod of the Free Church of Canada in 1850, but the mother church at Stamford still retains its connection with the United Presbyterian Church, U. S. A.

Twenty-three ministers, in sympathy with the newly formed Free Church of Scotland, seceded from the Synod of the Presbyterian Church of Canada in 1843 and formed, in the following year, the Free Church of Canada. This synod received the Presbytery of Niagara in 1850, and the Presbytery of Stamford in 1855.

The Missionary Presbytery was organized in Canada by ministers of the reunited Secession Church of Scotland. Rev. William Proudfoot was one of the founders of this presbytery. It was transformed into a synod in 1843, and in 1847 it took the name of the United Presbyterian Church in Canada. In 1861 it united with the Synod of the Free Presbyterian Church in Canada to form the Synod of the Canada Presbyterian Church.

d. *The Synod of the Presbyterian Church of Canada, 1840-75.* —The American Dutch Reformed Church sent, through its classis at Albany, Rev. John Ludwig Broeffle in 1795, and Rev. Robert McDowall in 1798, as missionaries to Ontaria. By 1819 a dozen charges had been formed, but the War of 1812 caused some of the ministers to withdraw from the Classis at Albany, and to join the Presbytery of the Canadas, formed in 1818. This presbytery consisted mainly of Secessionist ministers who had organized churches in the settlements concerned. It was transformed into a synod in

1820, but failing in its operation, it was later reorganized as the United Presbytery of Upper Canada.

In June, 1831, a number of ministers organized the Synod of the Presbyterian Church of Canada in Connection with the Church of Scotland. This synod had presbyteries at Quebec, Glengarry, Bathurst, and York (Toronto). In 1840 the synod united with the United Synod of Upper Canada to form The Synod of the Presbyterian Church of Canada in Connection with the Church of Scotland.

e. *The Presbyterian Church in Canada, 1875-1925.*—After 1861 British North America had but two important types of Presbyterianism: one that was connected with the Established Church of Scotland, and one that was not. The general trend was toward union, and the union movement was possibly accelerated by the Confederation of the Canadian Provinces in 1867. The question in the minds of many leaders was whether or not complete union could best be reached by two stages on a territorial basis, or by one. At the initiative of Dr. William Ormiston of Hamilton, a definite plan was proposed for the negotiation of a union of all four synods. A Joint Committee, composed of three ministers and three laymen from each synod, was elected and held its first meeting in September, 1870. It declared its conviction that there was "no obstacle in principle to said Union," and the proceeded to draft a Basis of Union. The union of the four synods was formally consummated on June 15, 1875.

Canadian Presbyterianism was merged and could present a united front in meeting the unprecedented challenge to keep pace with the stream of immigration and the shift of population from the Maritime Provinces to the western regions. Presbyterianism grew rapidly, and the intelligent, thrifty and cultural character of its constituency made it a most powerful influence in Canadian life. Educational institutions were established in the great educational and university centers, in Halifax, Montreal, Kingston, Toronto, Winnipeg and Vancouver. Home and foreign mission work was carried on with characteristic aggressiveness. The Twentieth Century Fund Campaign, projected in 1898, and the Forward Movement, started at the close of the World War, brought needed help to missions, education, and benevolences. Canadian Presbyterianism has also endeavored to adjust itself to the great movements of modern thought.

4. *Canadian Methodism before the Union of 1925.*—Methodism constituted the largest Protestant body in British North America

at the time of the Union of 1925. Canadian Methodism benefited greatly by British immigration; and Methodist organization, doctrine, discipline and aggressiveness made it particularly well suited to the colonial life in the New World.

Methodism in Canada had a number of tributaries and streams, as indicated in the diagram. How these started, developed and merged into one great body will now be briefly explained. Following the diagram, top to bottom, each of the four groups which united in 1884 will be traced back to their sources. The groups will be discussed in the following order: (1) The Primitive Methodist Church in Canada; (2) The Methodist Church of Canada; (3) The Methodist Episcopal Church in Canada; and (4) The Bible Christian Church.

a. *The Primitive Methodist Church in Canada, 1829-84.*—This church body had its beginning in the Primitive Methodist Connexion, which was started in Stafford County, England, about 1808 by two Methodist preachers, Hugh Bourne and William Clowes. Influenced by the eccentric American minister, Lorenzo Dow, who then visited England, they began to hold field meetings, contrary to the decision of the Church courts. They were promptly expelled from the Wesleyan Methodist Church, and a little later the Superintendent minister of the Burslem Circuit refused to accept about ten of their converts unless they promised to have no connection with the two expelled preachers. This marked the beginning of a separate Methodist church. The official name was taken in 1812.

One of the members of this church body, Mr. William Lawson, came to Toronto in 1829 and began to preach. He was joined by two other laymen, Mr. Robert Walker who had been in Mr. Lawson's employment in England, and Mr. Thompson who had been a member of the Primitive Methodist Society at Duffield, Yorkshire, England. A class meeting was organized, and as the converts increased in number, the leaders decided to send for a pastor. In response to their request, Mr. R. Watkins arrived in 1830. From that time on the organization enjoyed a steady progress, and at the time of union in 1884, the Primitive Methodist Church in Canada had a membership of 8,090 and 98 travelling and 214 local preachers, 231 churches, and 58 other places of worship.

b. *The Methodist Church of Canada, 1874-84.*—This church was formed by the merging in 1874 of three bodies, the Conference of the Wesleyan Methodist Church in Canada, the Canada Conference of the Methodist New Connexion, and the Wesleyan

Conference of Eastern British North America. These three bodies had again a number of tributaries, as indicated on the diagram.

The Conference of the Wesleyan Methodist Church in Canada had its beginning in 1788 when a class was formed in Augusta by Paul and Barbara Heck, their three sons, John Lawrence, some of the Emburys, and others. Prior to this date, two Methodist army officers had done some preaching in Canada. One of them, Major George Neal, organized a class at Stamford in 1790. The first regular, Methodist itinerant in Canada was William Losee who came in 1790. By 1791 he had organized three classes and the Kingston Circuit. Two additional circuits, Oswegotchie and Cataraqui, were soon formed, and on September 15, 1792, the first quarterly meeting was held in Ernestown. On that occasion the Lord's Supper was administered for the first time in Canada from the hands of a Methodist preacher.

William Losee was soon joined by other Methodist preachers. A visit by Bishop Asbury in 1811 stimulated much promotional interest. In 1812 the Upper and the Lower Canada Districts had 18 preachers and total membership of 2,845. This organized Methodism was an intimate and recognized part of the New York and Genesee Conferences, and as such it formed a part of the Methodist Episcopal Church in the United States.

This American connection was greatly disturbed by the war of 1812-15. The Genesee Conference resumed its work in Canada in 1815, but in that same year the Missionary Committee in London began to send British Wesleyan missionaries to the Canadas proper. In consequence, Canadian Methodism was soon troubled by the problem of British or American affiliation. Contentions and divisions arose on all sides. Through the negotiations of Rev. John Emory, an agreement was reached in 1820 by which American Methodists should continue to occupy Upper Canada, and British Methodists should occupy Lower Canada. But the churches of Upper Canada were formed into a separate conference in 1824, and four years later, in 1828, this conference was declared an autonomous communion and took the name of the Episcopal Methodist Church in Canada.

In consequence of this change, British Methodists considered themselves released from the agreement of 1820. British missionaries entered Upper Canada under the pretense that many British immigrants had settled there and that the newly formed Episcopal Methodist Church in Canada was unable to take proper care of them. Work was now carried on by American and British missionaries until the two groups united in 1833; the British Wesleyan Conference merged with the Methodist Episcopal Church in Canada, and the President of the Upper Conference became Chairman of the Lower Canada District. The new organization was called the Canada Methodist Episcopal Church.

This church suffered a temporary division, 1840-47, because of differences with respect to the "Clergy Reserves." Canadian Methodists, under the leadership of Adolphus Egerton Ryerson, fought for the recognition of the rights of the "dissenters" to share in the income of these reserves, while the conservative, old-world, English Methodists in Canada looked upon this campaign as "political intermeddling." At the same time, however, these same British Methodists accepted certain grants from the Crown out of the Casual and Territorial Revenue. The factions were re-united in 1847, and Wesleyan Methodism was further consolidated in 1854, when the Eastern District Meeting (Quebec) merged with the Canadian Methodist Episcopal Church to form the Conference of the Wesleyan Methodist Church in Canada. Twenty years later, in 1874, it become a part of the Methodist Church of Canada.

The Canada Conference of the Methodist New Connexion started in 1828 when Henry Ryan and a few followers refused to join the proposed Episcopal Methodist Church in Canada. These so-called "Ryanites" formed the Canadian Wesleyan Church in 1829. Through the negotiations of Rev. John Addyman a New Connexion missionary from England, the Canadian Wesleyan Church united with the New Connexion group in 1841 to form the Canada Conference of the Methodist New Connexion. A little later the church was augmented by a small group of Protestant Methodists in eastern Canada. The membership at the time of the union in 1874 was approximately 8,312.

The Wesleyan Conference of Eastern British North America had its beginning in 1772 when a party of immigrants, mostly Methodist, came from Yorkshire and settled in Cumberland County. Laurence Coughlin preached in Newfoundland in 1775, but the "Apostle of Methodism in the Eastern Provinces" was William Black, who started his evangelistic labors in the Eastern Provinces in 1781. His work benefited greatly by the immigration of the United Empire Loyalists who came after the American Revolutionary War. Methodism grew, especially in New Brunswick, where some help was received from the Methodist Episcopal churches in the United States. Methodism in Nova Scotia, on the other hand, retained its connection with British Wesleyanism.

In response to an eloquent appeal from William Black, the "Christmas Conference" of 1784, held at Baltimore, sent Freeborn Garrettson and James O. Cromwell as missionaries to Nova Scotia and New Brunswick. Freeborn Garrettson was charged with the oversight of the work. The first Methodist conference was held in Halifax in 1786. Mr. Garrettson was recalled to the United States in 1787, and two years later Mr. Black was appointed to the superintendency in Nova Scotia and Newfoundland. The work prospered in Nova Scotia, New Brunswick, Prince Edward Island, and Newfoundland. The churches concerned were organized into an affiliated conference in 1855, and numbered a little more than 20,000 when it entered the Methodist Church of Canada in 1874.

A general desire to unify the Methodist forces in Canada led to negotiations for organic union of the churches concerned, involving lay delegation. The Methodist Episcopal, the Primitive Methodist, and the Bible Christian Churches withdrew from the movement, while the three remaining bodies continued negotiations. A Basis of Union, prepared by the committees of the Wesleyan and the New Connexion bodies, was formally adopted by the New Connexion Conference at Dunnville, England, in 1873, and by the Wesleyan Conference, held in London, England, that same year. Organic union, involving lay representation in the General Conference, was consummated in 1874. The new organization, called the Methodist Church of Canada, enjoyed a gratifying spiritual and material progress during its ten years of existence. At the time of union in 1884 it had 1,216 ministers, 128,644 members, and 2,202 churches.

c. *The Methodist Episcopal Church in Canada, 1835-74.*—The merging in 1833 of the British Wesleyan Conference and the Methodist Episcopal Church in Canada into the Canada Methodist Episcopal Church was greeted with mixed emotions by some of the members concerned. A dissatisfied group seceded in 1835 to form a new body which retained the former name of the Methodist Episcopal Church in Canada. This church enjoyed a distinguished career, and at the time of union in 1884, it had 228 ministers and 25,671 members. Belleville Seminary was founded by this church in 1857, and in 1860 it became affiliated with Toronto University as Belleville College.

d. *The Bible Christian Church, 1832-84.*—William O'Bryan, a Wesleyan Methodist local preacher, started successful evangelistic work in the County of Devon, England, in 1815. The work grew, societies were formed, and the first Conference of the group was held in 1819. Two years later the Bible Christian Missionary Society was formed. This organization sent two missionaries to North America in 1831. One of these, John Glass, got discouraged and returned. The other, Francis Metherall, settled on Prince Edward Island in 1832. He began to preach, and by the end of the year he had sixty members. Other missionaries were sent from England, of which Mr. and Mrs. John Hicks Eynon are among the best remembered. Mrs. Eynon, the former Elizabeth Dart, was the first of the fourteen female preachers the first Bible Conference sent out. Mr. and Mrs. Eynon settled in Cobourg, Upper Canada, and this became the cradle of the Bible Christian Church in Canada. The first Missionary Meeting of this group was held at Cobourg in 1845, and in 1854 the parent Conference in England decided to grant a separate Canadian Conference with full control over provincial affairs. At the time of the union in 1884, this church had 80 ministers and a membership of 7,400 and about 30,000 adherents.

e. *The Methodist Church of Canada, 1884-1925.*—Methodism in Canada was divided into four groups in 1874, namely, the Methodist Church in Canada, formed in 1874, the Methodist Episcopal Church in Canada, the Primitive Methodist Church in Canada, and the Bible Christian Church. These bodies merged in the Methodist Church of Canada in 1884 with a combined full membership of 157,752. The Basis of Union included two principles: *first,* the episcopate was abandoned and the general superintendency was adopted; *secondly,* laymen were given a large representation in the work of the church and also in its courts. These principles helped pave the way for the union in 1925 with Presbyterians and Congregationalists.

To begin with, united Methodism in Canada showed great aggressiveness along all lines of endeavor, including home and foreign missions, education, and benevolences. The peak in point of membership was reached in 1891 when it constituted 17.54 per cent of the total population. Ten years later, in 1901, it had dropped to 17.07 per cent, and by 1921 it was down to 13.19 per cent of the total population. These losses may have been due, partly to the discarding of the revivalistic emphasis, and partly to the shift of population from East to West.

Among Methodist connectional educational institutions in Canada, mention may be made of Victoria University, Toronto; Mount Allison University, Sackville, N. B.; Wesleyan Theological College, Montreal; Wesley College, Winnipeg; Albert College, Belleville, Ont.; Alma College, St. Thomas; Methodist College, St.

Johns, Newfoundland; Columbian College, New Westminster, British Columbia; Ontario Ladies' College, Whitby; and Stanstead Wesleyan College, Stanstead, Quebec.

70. REVIEW QUESTIONS

1. How do you explain the fact that Congregationalism remained a comparatively small body in Canada?
2. How was the Congregationalism established in British North America?
3. In what ways did Congregationalism in Canada consolidate its strength?
4. Why did Presbyterianism in Canada have so many tributaries?
5. Why did Presbyterianism in Canada unite in 1875?
6. How did each of the four uniting bodies originate and develop prior to the union of 1875?
7. What characterized Canadian Presbyterianism from its consolidation in 1875 until its participation in the church union of 1925?
8. Why was Methodism in Canada the largest Protestant body prior to the union of 1925?
9. How did the principal Methodist bodies in British North America originate and develop prior to the union of 1884?
10. In what ways did this union pave the way for the church union of 1925?
11. What part did Methodism take in the educational work in British North America?
12. Why did Methodism in British North America decrease after the turn of the century?

5. *The Church Union in Canada in 1925.*—National, economic and religious conditions in Canada gradually brought to the fore the issue of consolidating the Protestant forces concerned. By the turn of the twentieth century, Canadian life had developed remarkable approximations in temper and organization, resulting in a new consciousness of Canadian nationalism. Sound economy and sanctified common sense demanded that unseemly religious rivalry and the wasteful overlapping of church work in the sparsely settled communities cease, and that the surplus energy be translated into more useful types of Christian service. Furthermore, some of the ecclesiastical differences transplanted by the Canadian immigrants had no real pertinence to colonial life, and consequently some of the Protestant churches were drawn together more and more in the great, common task of ministering to the spiritual needs of people that were so widely scattered over such an immense territory. But what form of approximation would best meet the existing needs: cooperation, or federation, or organic union?

Cooperative efforts were made along the lines of Bible and Tract Societies, Sunday School work, Missions to French Canadians, Indian Missions, Temperance movements, Y.M.C.A., and Y.W.C.A. activities, the Evangelical Alliance, Anti-Catholic organizations, Moral and Social Reforms, Social Welfare, Home and Foreign

Missions, the Student Volunteer Movements, and Christian education. But church leaders felt that no adequate or final settlement could be reached by these more or less temporary measures of expediency, and that it would be more useful and practical to bring the churches concerned together in organic union. As a matter of fact, Canada in 1901 already had 267 union churches and 554 union Sunday Schools.

The federal idea also had its advocates. The Methodists proposed a federation of churches in Canada in 1894, but they met with little response from the groups concerned. A few voices favoring federation were also raised during the negotiations for organic church union, but they received practically no hearing. Canada did not evolve a Federal Council of Churches, as in the United States. Popular attention centered more and more in the subject of organic church union.

Efforts to promote organic church union were first made by the Anglicans at the Provincial Synod of Canada, in 1885. Negotiations proved fruitless, however, because the groups approached would not subscribe to the fourth clause in Lambeth Quadrilateral, with reference to the Historic Episcopate. Canadian church union was henceforth limited to non-episcopal churches.

New efforts toward church union were made in 1892 when the Presbyterian General Assembly sent fraternal delegates to the Congregational Union, where they "held out the hand of fellowship and invited closer cooperation and even corporate union." Next year the General Assembly appointed a Committee on Union which was instructed "to hold themselves ready to confer with any similar body or bodies which may be appointed by any other Church or Churches, should the way be clearly opened for such conference." Some friendly gestures were made, and considerable discussion followed, but the only tangible results were, *first,* "anent cooperation of different Christian bodies in thinly settled districts of the country, for the joint management of weak congregations and stations, by agreement with other Christian denominations"; *secondly,* the formation of the Canadian Society of Christian Union in 1898.

The great Canadian church union enterprise was formally launched in 1902, when the Methodist General Conference, held at Winnipeg that year, made overtures to the Presbyterian and Congregational communions with a view to organic church union. The overtures were favorably received by the bodies concerned; committees were appointed; and the first parley was held in Toronto,

April 21, 1904. The Joint Committee resolved that organic union was both "desirable and practicable." A joint meeting was then called together at Knox Church, Toronto, on December 21, 1904, for the purpose of preparing a basis of union.

After spending the first three days in general discussion, the joint meeting found the way clear for further progress, and five subcommittees on Doctrine, Polity, the Ministry, Administration, and Law, were elected and set to work. Five years passed before the draft of the Basis of Union was completed.

Meanwhile invitations had been sent out, in 1906, to Baptists and to Anglicans to attend the conferences of the Joint Committee. The Church of England referred to the above mentioned clause in the Lambeth Quadrilateral as a required basis of negotiation for union; and the Baptists courteously but firmly replied that they refused organic relation with churches that used creeds and offered membership to children in baptism.

The major problems involved in the preparation of the Basis of Union may be briefly set forth under the same headings as those assumed by the five subcommittees:

1. *Doctrine.* The task of the Committee on Doctrine was not to formulate a new creed, but to find a sufficient number of doctrinal points on which the churches concerned could agree and unite. The dominant school of philosophy at that time was the Kantian-Hegelian, and theological thinking was somewhat influenced by that school of thought. While the Committee could not find a suitable re-definition of the Gospel, it did agree that the living church had a right to re-interpret the Gospel and to adjust its doctrine in relation to the modern world. In this general attitude of mind, the Committee prepared twenty articles on doctrine, so formulated that the distinctive doctrinal emphases of the uniting bodies would be recognized.[6] The twenty articles were a composite of the Brief Statement of the Reformed Faith, prepared and published by authority of the General Assembly of the Presbyterian Church, U. S. A. in 1902; and the Articles of Faith of the Presbyterian

---

[6] At the first meeting of the Committee, the Rev. Dr. Potts of the Methodist Church stated that there never could be any reconciliation between Calvinism and Arminianism. The Rev. Dr. DuVal replied: "Thank God we do not have to reconcile Calvin and Arminius. Read the Apostle Paul in I Cor. 3:3-13, as he said, 'Who is Paul, and who is Apollos but ministers whom ye believe.' So I say, who is Calvin and who is Arminius but servants whom some believe. It is our business as in the 11th verse to get back to the foundation which is Jesus Christ. It seems to me, Sir, that Dr. Potts and many others think that Calvin was a Presbyterian and Arminius a Methodist. Why, they were both Presbyterians. . . . That old struggle reaching beyond the mind of men through 'Pre' and 'Inter' Sublapsarianism (better known as Supra and Infralapsarianism), was rightly judged by the Supreme Court of Holland to 'have no bearing on the main points pertaining to salvation.' We were then, not to fight over the metaphysical theories of men, but to go back to the plainer teachings of Christ."

Church in England, formulated in 1890. Article XII, however, was taken almost verbatim from the Congregational Statement of 1886.

2. *Polity.*—The Committee first prepared a summary of the polities of the three negotiating bodies in order to get an exact survey of existing similarities and differences. The next task was to prepare a form of church government which would observe two great principles: liberty and efficient cooperation. In addressing itself to this difficult task, the Committee decided to proceed from the local unit to the central body, and not vice versa. The unit of organization in the United Church was to be the Pastoral Charge, which may consist of more than one local church. The higher governing bodies were to be the Presbytery, the Conference and the General Council. At least four distinct types of local church polity were permitted. Congregational, Presbyterian and Methodist churches existing previous to the church union were entitled to continue the organization and the practices enjoyed by them at the time of union, though "subject in general affairs to the legislation, principles and discipline of the United Church;" while churches formed after the union were to adopt the new basis, including a Session, a Committee of Stewards, and an Official Board. The Presbytery was to be similar to the Presbytery in the Presbyterian Church, but the final right of ordination and settlement was to rest with the next higher court, the Conference and its Settlement Committee. The Conference was to be similar to the Annual Conference in Methodism, and to the Synod in Presbyterianism. The General Council, meeting every other year, was to have "full power to legislate on matters respecting the doctrine, worship, membership and government of the church, subject to the condition that, before any rule or law relating to these matters can become a permanent law, it must receive the approval of the majority of the Presbyteries and, if advisable, of pastoral charges."

3. *The Ministry.*—Three major problems were involved; *first,* the pastoral office, including term of service; *secondly,* training for the ministry; *thirdly,* the relation of the minister to the doctrines of the church. As to the first problem, the Committee did not define the nature of the ministry. The term of office was to be, "as far as possible, a pastorate without interruption." The local congregation or pastorate or circuit had a right to call a new minister, but the right of appointment was to be vested in the Settlement Committee of the Conference. In reference to training for the ministry, the Committee recommended that the candidate should have a B.A.

degree, followed by three years of study of theology, and twelve months of preaching and pastoral work prior to ordination. As to the third problem, the Committee recommended that "these candidates shall be examined on the Statement of Doctrine of The United Church, and shall, before ordination, satisfy the examining body that they are in essential agreement therewith, and that as ministers of the Church they accept the statement as in substance agreeable to the teaching of the Holy Scriptures."

4. *Administration.*—In the field of Missions, two departments were recommended: Home and Foreign. Recognition was given to the value of the Women's Missionary Societies. The General Council of the United Church was to determine to what extent publications issued by the negotiating bodies were to be amalgamated. The colleges connected with the three church groups were to continue their educational activities, unless the Supreme Court of the United Church should decide otherwise. A General Board of Education was to be elected for the purpose of having a general oversight of the educational interests of the United Church. As to Annuity and Benevolent Funds, the Committee recommended that the status of ministers duly connected with any of the negotiating churches should not be affected by the union in respect to pension funds; but "all ministers received into or ordained in the United Church after union, shall be required at the time of their reception or ordination to become members of and contributors to the proposed fund."

5. *Law.*—Careful preparations were made to secure enabling legislation, to have the United Church of Canada incorporated by a Special Act of the Parliament of Canada. Many legal obstacles had to be overcome. The three negotiating church bodies held property in a variety of ways. Furthermore, it was necessary to consider, not only the Dominion Parliament, but also the Provincial Legislatures. Another problem was the question as to what exent the United Church should assume the debts of the uniting churches. Various colleges had constitutions which stipulated that the teaching in said colleges should be in accordance with Westminster Standards, or with the Notes of John Wesley. But worst of all, the Anti-Unionists made every effort to prevent legislation. The difficulties were, however, overcome, and Provincial Legislatures passed the enabling act in the following order: Manitoba, March 13, 1924; Saskatchewan, March 25, 1924; Alberta, April 12, 1924; New Brunswick, April 17, 1924; Nova Scotia, May 9, 1924; British

Columbia, December 19, 1924; Prince Edward Island, April 9, 1925; Ontario, April 9, 1925; Quebec, March 24, 1926. After one of the greatest struggles in Canadian history, the Dominion Parliament passed the enabling act, and it was to come in force on June 10, 1925.

The lengthy negotiations for church union created very little internal disturbance in either Congregational or Methodist churches, but practically one-fourth of the Presbyterian churches failed to enter the union in 1925. These churches are continuing the Presbyterian Church in Canada. The formal inauguration of the United Church of Canada, was held on June 10, 1925, in the Arena, the largest building in Toronto, Ontario.

6. *The United Church of Canada, 1925-36.*—Much of the energy of the United Church of Canada has been used in adjusting itself to the new situation. There has been a steady increase in membership, from 609,729 in 1925 to 671,443 in 1931. A "Hymnary" was published in 1931, and a "Book of Orders" in 1933. The church-union movement has also promoted the erection of many new churches, and also a growing respect for the more ancient traditions in church architecture.

The dominant tendencies in the United Church of Canada are apparently toward inclusiveness, emphasis of the supremacy of Christian experience over creedal statements, theological latitudinarianism, and a marked trend toward ritualism in worship.

Besides the steady increase in membership, the United Church had, by 1931, been able to build up a Sunday School enrollment of 653,315, approximating the total membership of the entire church, and exceeding the resident membership which, in 1931, was given as 615,751.

Church union in Canada is more than a method of procedure; it is a goal. The United Church works towards a national church, and openly accepts responsibility for groups of people in the Dominion not already served by some other church. While its progress has been somewhat hampered by the bitterness and friction caused by local majorities and minorities and their adjustments, the United Church is peculiarly fitted to cope with the religious situation in Canada, and its churches at present dot most of the rural areas, and practically every district in the cities of Canada. In 1931 the United Church constituted 19.44 per cent of the entire population; the Anglican had 15.76 per cent; the Roman Catholic had 39.48 per cent; and the Lutheran had 3.80 per cent.

71. REVIEW QUESTIONS

1. What general and what specific causes promoted the church union in Canada in 1925?
2. Can you see why the proposed cooperation and federation did not succeed in Canada? Explain.
3. Why did not the Anglicans and the Baptists enter the church union of 1925?
4. When was the Canadian church union movement formally launched; and when did it terminate in organic union?
5. What major problems confronted the Joint Committee?
6. On what basis did the Committee on Doctrine prepare its recommendations?
7. What type of church government did the United Church adopt, and why?
8. What recommendations were made with reference to the Christian ministry?
9. How did the United Church decide to solve its administrative problems?
10. What legal obstacles had to be overcome in order to secure enabling legislation?
11. How did the lengthy negotiations influence the internal situation in the Congregational, the Presbyterian, and the Methodist churches? Can you see why?
12. In what general ways has the United Church of Canada demonstrated its usefulness and its possibilities of future growth?

TOPICS FOR SPECIAL STUDY

1. Is the historic episcopate essential as a basis of church union?
2. Racial, traditional, temperamental, economic and geographic elements as factors for or against church union.
3. The relative merits of church federation and church union.
4. The right or wrong of re-interpreting and re-formulating doctrinal standards.
5. Standards for the Christian ministry.

7. *The Presbyterian Church in Canada (Continued)*.—Approximately 30 per cent of the Presbyterian membership failed to enter the United Church of Canada in 1925. This non-concurrent membership, which represented in a fairly general way the large and self-supporting Presbyterian congregations, continued as the Presbyterian Church of Canada. In 1931 this religious body constituted 8.39 per cent of the entire population. The two leading Presbyterian theological institutions, Knox College, Toronto, and Presbyterian College, Montreal, became the property of this non-concurrent group.

The Presbyterian Church in Canada is a rather uniform and compact religious body which stands for pure Presbyterianism in doctrine and in practice. The refusal of this group to enter into the union has hastened considerably the fusion of Methodists, Presbyterians and Congregationalists in the United Church of Canada, because these were forced to stand together for the cause of union on various fronts, including the fight for enabling legislation. As it is, the United Church of Canada and the Presbyterian Church in Canada continue to work, at home and abroad, according to inherent strength and possibilities.

8. *The Baptists.*—Baptist membership in Canada has not kept pace with the increase in total population. In 1871 they had 6.87 per cent, and in 1931 that had only 4.27 per cent of the entire population. In Canada proper they rank among the smaller denominations, while in the Maritime provinces they constitute one of the most vigorous and important bodies. In 1921 they held a numerical superiority over both Presbyterians and Methodists in the three provinces of Nova Scotia, New Brunswick, and Prince Edward Island.

a. The Maritimes.—Baptists were among the early permanent settlers in Nova Scotia. Some of the German immigrants in 1750 were Anabaptists, and other early Baptist settlers came from New England. Henry Alline, though he died a Congregationalist, is generally considered the father of the Baptist churches in Nova Scotia, because most of the New Light churches formed as a result of his preaching, later became Baptist. Andres, a Dutch Baptist, is said to have settled in Lunenberg in 1752. Ebenezer Moulton, who came from Massachusetts, organized a Congregational-Baptist church in Horton, Nova Scotia, which soon became wholly Baptist. Many New England Baptist loyalists immigrated before and after the American Revolutionary War to Nova Scotia, New Brunswick and Prince Edward Island.

For a number of years, the Baptist communion in the Maritime provinces were divided into Free Baptists (Arminian) and Regular Baptists (Calvinistic). Nova Scotia and New Brunswick each organized a close communion Baptist Convention, and these united in 1846 to form the Regular Baptists Convention of the Maritimes. Meanwhile some of the Free Baptists had organized in 1837 as Free Christian Baptists, while others had formed the Free Baptist Conference of Nova Scotia. These two organizations united in 1866 to form the Free Baptist Conference of Nova Scotia. The Baptist communion was again reduced to two groups. But a division occurred in 1879 in the Free Baptist ranks, and the new group took the name of Primitive Baptists. Another seccession came in 1886 with reference to the "Holiness" question, and the secessionists took the name of Reformed Baptists. The various Free Baptist groups, except the Reformed Baptists, united in 1898 to form the

Free Baptist General Conference. This organization again united in 1906 with the Regular Baptists, to form the Maritime Convention. The Reformed Baptists continue to be unrelated to this large and influential organization.

b. *Ontario and Quebec.*—A small group of Baptist loyalists were among the early settlers in Quebec and Ontario. By 1800 about six congregations had been organized in widely separated localities. They were served by missionaries from the United States, and their membership was augmented by further immigration from America and from Scotland and England. Additional Baptist churches were organized, but there was, for many years, practically no cooperation between Baptists of what was then called Upper and Lower Canada. Baptists in Lower Canada were generally advocates of open communion, while Baptists in Upper Canada promoted a restricted communion. Baptists in England formed a society in 1836 for the purpose of fostering Baptist work in Canada, but as this work was under open communion auspices, the Baptists of Upper Canada refused to cooperate.

The formation of the Regular Baptist Missionary Convention of Canada West, in 1851, and the organization of a similar convention for Quebec and the Ottawa Valley in 1858, marked a new era in Baptist proximation and cooperation. The two organizations were united in 1888 into the present Baptist Convention of Ontario and Quebec.

Central educational institutions for Baptists in Ontario and Quebec are the Canadian Literary and Theological Institute at Woodstock, and the McMaster University at Toronto.

c. *The West.*—Baptists in Canada did not consolidate their forces, as did their brethren in the United States, in order to keep pace with trek to the West to conquer the Continent. In consequence, the Baptist work in western Canada has been rather sporadic and casual. The Baptist Convention of Manitoba was formed in 1884, and the Baptist Convention of British Columbia was organized in 1897. In 1907 these two conventions united to form the Baptist Union of Western Canada.

From this it will be seen that British North America has no central convention of Baptist churches: but it has three territorial conventions, including the Maritime provinces, Ontario and Quebec and Western Canada respectively. These three conventions are served by a common foreign missionary society, organized in 1911; but there are still three separate home missionary societies.

The trend among Canadian Baptists is undoubtedly toward greater consolidation of Baptist forces. The Fundamentalist-Modernist issue has caused a considerable stir among Baptists in Canada. The controversy started in connection with teaching at McMaster University.

9. *The Lutherans.*—Lutheranism has enjoyed a steady and rapid progress in Canada. In 1871 it constituted only 1.09 per cent of the entire population. In 1881 it was 1.06 per cent; in 1891, 1.32 per cent; in 1901, 1.72 per cent; in 1911, 3.19 per cent; in 1921, 3.26 per cent; and in 1931, 3.80 per cent of the entire population in the land.

LUTHERAN POPULATION IN CANADA BY PROVINCES, 1931

Prince Edward Island	76
Nova Scotia	7,949
New Brunswick	969
Quebec	8,261
Ontario	97,022
Manitoba	46,892
Saskatchewan	113,676
Alberta	82,411
British Columbia	36,635
Yukon	239
Northwest Territories	64
Total	393,194

The first permanent Lutheran settlers in British North America were some of the Germans who came to Halifax, Nova Scotia, in 1750. Three years later a group of 1453 of these pioneers moved from Halifax to Lunenberg and vicinity. Descendants of these Lunenberg pioneers form the nucleus of the present Lutheran Synod of Nova Scotia. The members are settled in but three counties of the province. From 1876 to 1903 they formed a conference of the Pittsburgh Synod of the United Lutheran Church of America, and then a separate synod was organized. In 1932 this synod had 8 pastors, 31 congregations, and 5,498 souls.

German Lutherans migrated from Pennsylvania and from the Mohawk and Schoharie valleys, New York, to Welland, Waterloo and York counties, Ontario, immediately after the American Revolutionary War. These Lutherans were aided by individual synods from the United States, particularly by the Pittsburgh Synod, now a constituent synod of the United Lutheran Church of America. Home mission parishes were organized and a Canada Conference of the Pittsburgh Synod was formed in 1859. Two years later, in 1861, this conference was organized as the Evangelical Lutheran Synod of Canada. The English congregations of this synod withdrew in 1901 and affiliated with the Synod of New York and New

England; but in 1909 they formed an independent organization called the Synod of Central Canada; and this synod united with the Evangelical Lutheran Synod of Canada in 1925 to form the Synod of Canada. This synod had 85 pastors, 96 congregations and 28,041 souls in 1932.

Icelandic Lutherans who settled around Lake Winnipeg were first served by two Icelandic ministers, Jon Bjarnason and Paul Thorlaksson. They also served Icelanders who had settled in Wisconsin, North Dakota and Minnesota. In 1885 they organized an international synod called the Icelandic Evangelical Lutheran Synod in North America. The growth of this religious body has been somewhat limited by immigration. In 1927 it numbered 18 pastors and 56 congregations, 14 of these congregations being located in the United States.

George Gehrke of the Evangelical Lutheran Joint Synod of Ohio and Other States did pioneer work for his synod in Canada. The Canada Conference of the Minnesota District was organized in the fall of 1906. Two years later this conference became the Canada District of said synod. It has enjoyed a remarkable growth.

Other American synods have followed the Lutheran immigrants to Canada. A Canada District has been organized by each of the following Lutheran bodies: the Norwegian Lutheran Church of America, the Evangelical Lutheran Augustana Synod of North America, the Lutheran Free Church, and the United Danish Evangelical Lutheran Church in America. The most extensive Lutheran work in Canada is carried on by the United Lutheran Church of America, through the following constituent synods: the Synod of Canada; the Synod of Nova Scotia; the Pacific Synod-Prince Rupert (English); the Pacific Synod-Vancouver (English); the Pacific Synod-Vancouver (Finnish); the Northwest-Winnipeg (English); the Michigan-Windsor (English); and the Pittsburgh-Windsor (Siebenburger). The international character of some of these synods will largely disappear as soon as the Canadian groups are ready to form independent synods.

Lutherans in Canada have established a number of educational institutions, including academies and junior and senior colleges. They also have two theological seminaries: Lutheran Theological Seminary, Waterloo, Ontario, and Saskatoon Seminary, Saskatoon, Saskatchewan.

10. Other Religious Groups.—Other church groups in Canada are very small and constitute, according to the census, a rather insignificant percentage of the entire population. In 1931 the Greek

Catholic had 1.80 per cent; the Greek Orthodox, 0.98 per cent; the Jews, 1.50 per cent; the Mennonites, 0.86 per cent; the Salvation Army, 0.30 per cent; the Pentecostal, 0.25 per cent; the Evangelical, 0.21 per cent; the Mormons, 0.21 per cent; the Adventists, 0.15 per cent of the entire population. It is also interesting to notice that 0.23 per cent are Confucian, and 0.15 per cent are Buddhist. The Society of Friends (Quakers) constituted but 0.02 per cent of the entire population in 1931. It is beyond the scope of the present volume to trace the beginning and the development of each of these small groups.

72. REVIEW QUESTIONS

1. How would you characterize the present Presbyterian Church in Canada?
2. In what ways may this religious body have influenced the constituency and the progress of the United Church of Canada?
3. What has characterized the Baptist churches of Canada?
4. What is the present status of these churches?
5. How do you account for the rapid growth of Lutheranism in Canada?
6. In what Canadian provinces are most Lutherans found?
7. What portion of the Lutheran population in Canada is rural? what portion is urban?
8. What nationalities are numerically strongest among Lutherans in Canada?
9. When and where did the Lutherans form the first permanent settlement in British North America?
10. What is briefly the history of Lutherans in Nova Scotia?
11. What is the history of the Synod of Canada (1925)?
12. What other Lutheran synods are represented in Canada?

TOPICS FOR SPECIAL STUDY

1. Prominent Presbyterian leaders in Canada.
2. The social, political and economic status of Presbyterians in Canada.
3. Prominent Baptist leaders in Canada.
4. The social, political and economic status of Baptists in Canada.
5. The Canadian Lutheran population by racial origins.

A SELECTED BIBLIOGRAPHY FOR CHAPTER XXXIII

1. Audet, *Canadian Historical Dates and Events, 1492-1915.*
2. Eastman, *Church and State in Early Canada.*
3. Wittke, *A History of Canada.*
4. Thwaites, *Jesuit Relations and Allied Documents, 1610-1791.* (73 vols.)
5. Kenton, *Jesuit Relations and Allied Documents, Selected and Edited.*
6. Gosselin, *L'èglise du Canada dèpuis Monseigneur de Laval jusqu' à la conquête.* (3 vols.)
7. Lindsey, *Rome in Canada: the Ultramontane Struggle for Supremacy over the Civil Authority.*
8. Riddell, *The Rise of Ecclesiastical Control in Quebec.*

CHAPTER XXXIV

CHRISTIAN MISSIONS

The term *Christian missions* designates those forces and activities which aim to preserve, promote, and extend the Kingdom of God on earth. They illustrate in a most positive way the fundamental laws of self-preservation and self-extension. Christ told his followers not merely to guard carefully what they had received through him, but to share these values with all the rest of mankind. He prepared them carefully for this world wide mission and issued a definite command to them, just before his ascension, to spread the Gospel to all nations.

In the course of time the Christian Church has come to distinguish between various types of Christian missionary activities. *Foreign* missions designates the spread of Christianity among non-Christian tribes and nations including pagans, Jews, and Mohammedans. *Home* missions includes the promotional work done by various religious bodies in mission territories in the home land and among emigrants in the colonies. *Inner* missions is the collective name for a variety of institutions of mercy established, not merely as humanitarian agencies for the relief of need and distress, but as evidences of Christian "faith that worketh by love." They include rescue missions, orphanages, homes for wayward boys and girls, homes for aged, distribution of religious tracts and papers, organized Christian relief work, and the like.

There are three great missionary periods: the spread of the Gospel among Jews, Greeks, Romans, and barbarians by the apostles and by other early Christians; the conversion of the barbarian tribes in Europe during the middle ages; and modern missions in all parts of the world. Each of these periods will be presented in bird's eye perspective.

I. Missions in the Ancient World.—The small beginning of the spread of the Gospel from Jerusalem may truly be likened to the insignificant grain of mustard seed. One hundred and twenty men and women from the ordinary walks of life were gathered in the "upper chamber" praying and waiting for the Holy Spirit. What could these few disciples do in a great world that was diametrically opposed to almost everything Christianity stood for?

Spiritual darkness covered the earth, and gross darkness the peoples. Would these simple folks succeed as merchants of the new spiritual light?

"Not by might, nor by power, but by my Spirit," was the answer. God sent the Holy Spirit on the day of Pentecost, and immediately the timid disciples became witnesses for the crucified and risen Lord Jesus Christ. About 3,000 souls were added that day, and soon the number increased to more than 10,000. Additional multitudes were added, both of men and women; "and the number of the disciples multiplied in Jerusalem exceedingly; and a great company of priests were obedient to the faith."

Some of these Christians were, no doubt, visitors and travelling merchants who returned and became the nuclei of Christian congregations in their home lands. The persecution recorded in the eighth chapter of Acts, scattered large numbers of Christians throughout Judea and regions outside of Palestine, including Cyrene, Phoenecia, Antioch, Cyprus, and Damascus. For some time they tried to preach the Gospel to "none save Jews only," and yet it was soon brought to Ethiopia, and to the half-Gentile Samaritans, and a number of Greeks in Antioch, and Paul was selected as the great "Apostle to the Gentiles."

While Christianity was spread successfully by means of Christian migrations, its most active agents were the apostles and the early evangelists who travelled in all portions of the then civilized world, preaching the Gospel and establishing Christian congregations. Eusebius in his *Ecclesiastical History*, III, 1, states that shortly after the ascension of Christ, the apostles divided the field so that each had his portion assigned in advance. While there may be an element of truth in this, the statement can hardly be taken at its face value. Paul's missionary record is fairly complete. For traditions concerning the other apostles and early evangelists, see pages 47-48.

By the end of the Apostolica Era, about 100 A.D., the Gospel had spread to all important eastern, southern, and western portions of the Roman Empire, and also to extensive outside regions toward India, the Sea of Aral, the Caspian Sea, and in Africa. By 300 A.D, according to conservative estimates, about one-fifth of the entire population in the Roman Empire was Christian. These important victories for Christianity were won amidst great persecutions and difficulties, as related elsewhere in this volume.

What happened in these three centuries may be thought of in the terms of people travelling by aeroplane over dark country by night. Suddenly they are cheered by an exceedingly intense and pleasing light emanating from a large city. Little by little they see similar, but much smaller, lights in other portions of the land. The lights increase in size and intensity. They spread to new centers. They soon cover the entire country like a network. Darkness must gradually yield to a cheerful, invigorating, and renovating light.

Missionary methods centered in the office of preaching the Gospel and in administering the two Sacraments. The large centers of population were usually selected as starting points, and from these the Gospel spread to surrounding territories. While the main emphasis was on evangelistic work, the educational, the medical, and the charitable activities were not lacking.

II. Missions in the Medieval World.—As soon as Christianity had been firmly established in the Graeco-Roman world, the invisible hand of God opened up the *Great Human Gateway* between the Caspian Sea and the Ural Mountains, and a deluge of Barbarian tribes from the north and east poured over the Roman Empire. The "fullness of time" had come for these tribes, and the Church was charged with the tremendous task of bringing them the Gospel. How this challenge was met has been discussed elsewhere in this volume. Mention may here be made of the outstanding missionaries of each century: Ulfilas among the Visigoths in the fourth; Patrick in Ireland in the fifth; Columba in the Scottish islands in the sixth; Augustine in England late in the sixth and early in the seventh; Willibrord among the Frisians in the seventh; Boniface among the Germans in the eighth; and Ansgar in the North in the ninth century.

Christian missions in the middle ages differed from that of the ancient period in several important respects: *first,* it centered increasingly in papal authority and in the Roman form of organization and worship; *secondly,* the Church in the middle ages met the invading people with a superior culture; *thirdly,* political influence became a dominant factor in winning tribes and nations nominally for Christianity. King Clovis accepted Christianity and forced his army to be baptized. Charlemagne compelled the Saxons, after bloody crusades (772-804), to accept Christianity. King Vladimir of Russia received Christian baptism in 992 and compelled his subjects to do the same. By 1300 all of Europe had been nominally Christianized except a few tribes in Lapland to the far north.

While the theater of medieval missions was limited almost entirely to the Occident, more particularly to Spain, Gaul, Great

Britain, and Germany, the Christian Church did not forget altogether her missionary obligations to Asia and Africa. Olupun, a missionary of the Nestorian Church in Syria, brought Christianity to the interior of China, to Singanfu in the Shensi Province, in 631. The famous *Inscription of Singanfu,* set up in 781 and discovered in 1625, attests to the reality of the almost unprecedented success of the Christian faith in the Chinese Empire. Some time later, about the year 1000, appears the remarkable legend concerning the "Priest-King" John, who is said to have worked in Tartary, north of China, where more than 200,000 are said to have been baptized. Unfortunately, the frequent clashes between Nestorian and Roman missionaries proved detrimental to the progress of Christianity in China.

The best known Roman missionary to China in the middle ages was John of Monte Corvino (1246-1330?), a Franciscan monk from Italy, who first worked as a missionary in Persia and India and later moved to China. Amidst constant friction with Nestorian missionaries, he won 6,000 souls in Peking alone, translated the New Testament, built an impressive church and bought 150 pagan children for the purpose of bringing them up in the Christian faith. The pope appointed him Archbishop of Cambalu (Peking). The time seemed ripe for the permanent establishment of Christianity in China, but Rome did not, or could not enter heartily through the opened door, and a generation later the Mongol supremacy in China was lost. Buddhism began to spread rapidly, and the connection with Europe was soon cut off completely.

Mission work among Mohammedans was largely neglected during the middle ages, and the little work that was done came mainly through private initiative. Christian Europe spent much time and energy in crusading against the Moslem infidels, but very few gave any thought to the value of Moslem souls. Francis of Assisi went to Egypt in 1219 in order to win the Sultan and his subjects for Christianity, but he met with very little success. He was followed later by missionaries of the Franciscan and the Dominican orders. The Trinitarian Order was founded in 1198 for the purpose of purchasing Christian slaves from the Moslems and converting the "infidels." Raymond Lully (1236-1314), the greatest missionary in the late middle ages, wrote several books in Arabic in the interest of Christianity, and educated a number of missionaries, and went himself three times as a missionary to Africa. But none of these missionary efforts among Mohammedans brought any lasting results.

Mongol invasions in the thirteenth century brought as overwhelming calamity to Russia as the later conquests by the Ottoman Turks brought to the lands of southern Europe. Pope Innocent IV (1243-54) sent a legation to the Mongols, and through this official relation which lasted for about one hundred years, the name of Jesus Christ was also mentioned in that distant region of Europe and Asia.

But medieval missions was, after all, quite well limited to southern and western Europe, and the Church spent most of her energies in assimilating and Christianizing the nominally Christian tribes within her boundaries. When this task had been reasonably well accomplished, and a new Teutonic-Latin civilization had been developed, the Occident was ready for the transition from medieval to modern times.

III. Missions in the Modern World.—The intellectual and religious awakenings which ushered in the modern period were accompanied by an era of great geographical discoveries and a corresponding colonial expansion. The theater of world history expanded tremendously, and a part of the new scene was the European contact with a large number of primitive tribes in the various colonies. This situation was in turn bound to influence the course of Christian missions.

Division of modern Europe into Protestant and Roman Catholic camps was also destined to influence the basis, history, and results of modern missions. According to the Protestant conception, the missionary task consisted in Christianizing the non-Christians; while Roman Catholicism conceived of it as the Catholicizing of non-Catholic peoples. Protestant missions insisted upon personal Christianity and submission to the authority of Scriptures; Catholic missions emphasized the submission of the pagan masses to the external authority of the Roman hierarchy. This difference in conception resulted in a corresponding difference as to missionary methods and lasting results.

1. *Roman Catholic Missions.*—The first modern colonial empires were founded by Roman Catholic nations: Spain, Portugal, and France. Hence the Roman Catholic Church enjoyed the priority in bringing the Gospel to the heathen populations in these colonies. Dominican, Franciscan, and Jesuit missionaries followed the colonizers to the new fields which soon were dotted with fortresses, factories, and Roman Catholic missions. Many imposing gains were made for the Roman Church, but conversion was in many instances by coercion, and the missions usually depended upon military pro-

tection and government support. Hence the downfall of political power usually meant a rapid decline or a complete collapse of the missions concerned.

The organization and mobilization of the Catholic forces during the Counter-Reformation era gave new impetus to foreign missions. Zealous missionaries have since planted stations and churches and schools in nearly every known portion of the world. The central agency for this great work is the Congregation for the Propogation of Faith, organized in 1622 with the pope as the chief leader. There are also a number of missionary societies in different Roman Catholic countries, and a number of missionary seminaries have been established for the purpose of training missionaries.

Excessive Jesuit leniency toward pagan culture and customs gave cause for much comment and criticism. Roberto de Nobili, for instance, renounced all fellowship with simpler Christians in India and lived as a Brahman in order to win the Brahmans for the Church. Brito, another Jesuit missionary tried to gain the confidence of the Hindus by saying he had found "the fifth Veda." In China the Jesuit missionaries tried to accommodate Chinese ancestor worship to Catholic saint worship. Complaints registered by Dominican and Franciscan missionaries resulted in papal condemnation of these Jesuit practices.

Catholic mission history sparkles with names of prominent and self-sacrificing missionaries and martyrs. Greatest among these is perhaps Francis Xavier (1506-1552), "Apostle to India and Japan." Most prominent among Catholic missionaries to the West Indies and Central and South America is Bartholomé de las Casas (1474-1566), who is wrongly accused by some as being the instigator of negro slavery. Other outstanding missionaries have been referred to in other portions of this volume.

2. *Protestant Missions.*—For a brief survey of Protestant missions, study pages 392-94. Repetition of that material in the present chapter is superfluous.

The great era of discovery and conquest which preceded and accompanied the Reformation did not immediately inspire Protestantism to extended mission work in the new fields. About 200-300 years passed before the Protestants fully recognized their missionary obligation. Several reasons may be given for this surprisingly slow development. *First,* the early discoveries and conquests were principally made by Roman Catholic powers; hence early Protestantism lacked any direct contact with the new mission fields; and if Protestant missionaries had entered those fields, Spain, Portugal, and France would certainly have been hostile. *Secondly,* the missionary idea was generally lacking among the Reformers. Zwingli, Calvin, Butzer, and Beza did not recognize continuous mission work as the duty of the Church. Luther, in his later years, had plans for foreign missions which were to be detached, both from specific colonial interests and from promotion of ecclesiastical power. But contemporary Protestant struggle against papal and imperial aggression, and the necessity of being thoroughly established and built up from within, made Luther's plans impracticable. *Thirdly,* representatives of Lutheran and Reformed orthodoxy in the seventeenth century decidedly denied the continuous missionary duty of the Church on the grounds that the apostles, they claimed, had already preached the Gospel throughout the whole world and, that the missionary vocation of the Church ceased with the apostles. *Fourthly,* while new colonies were opened by military conquest, the natives concerned were not immediately ready to receive and assimiliate the Gospel as preached by Protestant missionaries. They were, however, in this preparatory stage, more responsive to Catholic missionary methods.

How the Protestant Churches were gradually aroused, and how they responded to the challenge of a world wide need of foreign missions, may be seen in pages 392-94. It is beyond the scope of the present volume to enumerate all Protestant missionary societies and to outline the history and accomplishment of each. Suffice it to say that at present, Protestant mission stations, schools, and institutions of mercy dot almost every known portion of the inhabited world; and the time is rapidly approaching when the Gospel shall have been preached "in the whole world for a testimony unto all nations."

The older generation of Protestant missionaries addressed themselves mainly to the twofold task of bringing the heathen into a personal, living relation with Jesus Christ, and to gather these converts into congregations. In recent years this conception of the missionary task has broadened so as to include the aim of founding self-supporting and self-governing churches, independent of organization in the home land. This threefold aim naturally defines, and to some extent unifies, the Protestant missionary methods. For the general results of Protestant missions, see pages 392-94 and 399-402.

Considering the "great cloud of witnesses" of Protestant missionaries, a number of names and faces stand out more prominently than others. But ours is not the task of classifying these

missionaries into great, mediocre, and small. Among the recent
world known mission leaders are Gustav Warneck, Robert P.
Wilder, and John R. Mott.

73. REVIEW QUESTIONS

1. What does the term "Christian Missions" signify?
2. Why, do you think, did Christ issue the command recorded in Matth. 28:19-20?
3. How do you distinguish between foreign, home, and inner missions?
4. Which are the great missionary periods? Why?
5. What characterized Christian missions in the ancient world?
6. In what ways did Christian missions in the middle ages differ from that of the ancient period? Can you see why?
7. Why was the field of Christian missions so limited in the middle ages?
8. In what ways did modern Christian missions differ from that of the middle ages and the ancient period?
9. How would you characterize the basis, history, and results of modern Roman Catholic missions?
10. Why were the Protestant churches so slow to recognize their missionary obligation?
11. What is the threefold aim of modern Protestant missions?
12. How do you estimate the results of Protestant foreign missions?

TOPICS FOR SPECIAL STUDY

1. The historical interpretation of Matthew 28:19-20.
2. Recent trends in foreign missions.
3. Inner missions and social service.
4. Early missionary methods.
5. Medieval missionary methods.
6. Modern missionary methods.

A SELECTED BIBLIOGRAPHY FOR CHAPTER XXXIII

1. Schlunk: *Die Weltmission des Christentums: Ein Gang durch neunzehn Jahrhunderte.*
2. Barnes: *Two Thousand Years of Missions Before Carey.*
3. Ussing: *Evangeliets Seiersgang ud over Jorden* (3d ed.).
4. Robinson: *History of Christian Missions.*
5. *Encylopedia of Missions.*
6. Schmiedlin: *Katholische Missionsgeschichte.*
7. Arens: *Handbuch der katholischen Missionen.*
8. *Missiones catholicae.*
9. Streit: *Die Weltmission der katholischen Kirche.*
10. Warneck: *Outline History of Protestant Missions from the Reformation to the Present Time.*

CHAPTER XXXV

Church Unity

I. The Nature of Church Unity.—The Bible has much to say about the nature of the kingdom of God on earth with reference to church unity. In the Old Testament the progress of God's kingdom is likened to the growth of a tree;[1] and in the New Testament the founder of the Christian Church said that "the kingdom of heaven is like unto a grain of mustard seed, which a man took, and sowed in his field: which is less than all seeds; but when it is grown, it is greater than the herbs, and becometh a tree, so that the birds of the heaven come and lodge in the branches thereof."[2] He also used the vine and its branches to illustrate certain organic relations in the kingdom of God; and in his high priestly prayer he prayed for his disciples, "holy Father, keep them in thy name which thou hast given me, that they may be one, even as we are." Paul sets forth the unity of the Church under the image of a human body of which Christ is the head.

How is the Christian Church to express this spiritual unity in visible form? *One* answer may be found in the Biblical analogy of the tree. It is a biological unit as over against other trees, as the Church is a religious unit as over against other religions. Furthermore, as the tree has normally several main branches as well as a multitude of smaller branches and twigs, so also has the Christian Church, in the course of twenty centuries, come to consist of several main bodies as well as of a host of smaller bodies and groups. Note the apt comparison of the numerous present day denominations with the mustard tree which, when fullgrown, has an extraordinary wealth of branches and twigs where birds like to congregate.

Historically, the first great Church division came in 1054 with the permanent parting into Greek and Roman Catholic branches.

---

[1] Ezek. 17:22-24; Psalm 80:8; cf. worldly kingdoms, Dan. 4:10-12; Ezek. 31:3-9.

[2] Matth. 13:31-32. Christ does not merely speak of an herb, but of an herb "that becometh a tree." For an interpretation, see pp. 2-3. Bishop Lightfoot states in his *Horae Hebraicae* that in hot countries like Judea, the mustard tree attains to a size which is never seen in colder latitudes. Sometimes it will allow a man to climb into its branches; and a traveller in Chile states that he rode on horseback under them; cf. Trench: *Notes on the Parables*, p. 92. This parable does not refer to the leaven of the Pharisees, but to "the kingdom of heaven."

Centuries later the Roman branch was permanently parted into Protestant and Roman Catholic branches. The Protestant branch was in turn permanently divided into Lutheran, Reformed, and Anglican branches. All these main branches have in turn produced smaller branches and twigs, making for symmetry similar to that of the natural tree. Due recognition must be given to this historic development of Christianity.

The Christian Church has, therefore, a most intimate organic unity, but it is *a unity in diversity,* where each main branch is permitted to grow and develop according to inherent characteristics. Great violence would be done to a natural tree if its main branches were to be bent or grafted together to form the appearance of a single branch, or a mere trunk. Similar violence would be done to the church tree if its main branches were to be brought together into one single, visible organization. And what would be gained by such procedure? A tree reduced to a mere trunk, or to a trunk and a single branch, would possibly make the same peculiar impression as a church tree shorn of its great, historic branches.

A great lesson from the past appears to be that no single church branch or denomination has been big enough to minister to the fullness of Christ's message to the entire world. In consequence, God has permitted the Greek, the Roman, the Lutheran, the Reformed, and the Anglican branches to develop in various directions. Each branch has performed, and is still performing its characteristic duty, and who can fail to see the beautiful symmetry of it all?[3]

Unity and strength in the Christian Church is consequently best promoted, not by obliteration of the past, and not by coercion into one great outward organization, but by the cultivation of mutual recognition and good will. This appears to be in harmony with all true progress. To illustrate: individual progress does not destroy but it develops inherent and latent characteristics and possibilities. Likewise, civilized society does not destroy but it preserves and develops the family unit. And true internationalism does not obliterate but it preserves and promotes national interests and characteristics. The historic branches of the Christian Church are not to be obliterated, nor are they to be viewed with anxiety

[3] The symmetry and harmony of the Kingdom of God on earth may also be thought of in terms of a harp, an organ, a symphony orchestra, or some singing organization. Playing or singing but one part makes for monotony; but the blending of various notes and parts make for greater harmony and has the inherent possibility of almost unlimited development.

or hostility. These branches are with us to perform their God-given tasks to the best of their several abilities.

But the main branches of a tree need pruning or grafting from time to time, and this is also true of the historic branches of Christendom. Records indicate that certain main church branches have produced such a superabundance of smaller branches and twigs that these have actually retarded the normal growth of the main branch. Much has already been done, and more will likely be done in the immediate future to remedy this situation. Church leaders will do their share, and the *Husbandman* will cleanse and unify each branch in order that it may bear more fruit.

II. Growth of Christian Co-operation.—It is interesting to notice the very close analogy there usually is, and has been, between the political form of government and the form of church government in practically every country concerned. This applies also to the United States of America. The formation of a number of independent and autonomous States into a single federated nation without destroying the independence of those States, has had far-reaching consequences, not only for the political realm, but also for the development of religious federations and other co-operative movements. The church groups concerned have become fairly well convinced that the only sure way to greater unity in ecclesiastical life is through federated service.

1. *Foreign Missions.*—Increasing general interest in the whole cause of foreign missions has in recent years called into being a number of significant missionary conferences and continuation committees through which interdenominational co-operation and endeavor may have found a most useful expression.

The first great missionary gathering of the present century was the Ecumenical Missionary Conference which was held in Carnegie Hall, New York, from April 21st to May 1st, 1900. This conference has never been surpassed with reference to numbers present and enthusiasm shown. Fifteen hundred delegates from America and Canada; two hundred delegates from British and Continental Societies; and six hundred foreign missionaries were present.

Two years later, in 1902, the Missionary Education Movement was founded in the United States for the purpose of promoting interdenominational co-operation in preparing and disseminating missionary information.

A most significant by-product of the Student Volunteer Movement was the Laymen's Missionary Movement, organized in the

United States in 1906. The many conventions held under its auspices in strategic cities stimulated great interest in interdenominational co-operation for foreign mission endeavor.

The World Missionary Conference, held in Edinburgh in 1910, proved to be the most important conference of its kind in modern Christendom. The eleven hundred delegates present represented all mission fields in the world except South America. The conference, which was consultative, deliberate, and educational rather than demonstrative, based its work on the exact and extensive information gathered by eight Commissions as follows: 1) Carrying the Gospel to All the Non-Christian World; 2) The Church in the Mission Field; 3) Education in Relation to the Christianization of National Life; 4) The Missionary Message in Relation to Non-Christian Religions; 5) The Preparation of Missionaries; 6) The Home Base of Missions; 7) Missions and Governments; and 8) Co-operation and the Promotion of Unity. The published report of the last named Commission is very valuable as a study of Christian co-operation and unity. It was largely through the influence of this last Commission that the Edinburgh Conference Continuation Committee was appointed, with Dr. John R. Mott as its Chairman. The essential purpose of the Continuation Committee was to continue and extend the movements of co-operation and the promotion of unity on the mission fields and in the home lands.

At the meetings of the Continuation Committee in 1911 and 1912 and 1913, groups of missionary leaders in Europe, Great Britain, and North America gathered and discussed the most urgent problems that had arisen out of the Edinburgh Conference. Among the outstanding achievements of these conferences were the launching of *The International Review of Missions,* and the arrangement for financial co-operation amongst the foreign mission boards.

During the fall of 1912 and the early part of 1913 Dr. John R. Mott conducted twenty-one conferences in Asia. Six regional conferences were held in China in 1913, and in April that year the Japanese National Conference convened at Tokyo. Among the first concrete results of these conferences were the formation of the National Missionary Council in India, the China Continuation Committee, and the Continuation Committee in Japan.

Follow-up work of the Edinburgh Conference was continued also in the home lands. The first international post-war missionary conference was held in June, 1920, at the chateau of Crans, on the shores of Lake Geneva, and at this conference the International Missionary Council was proposed. This Council was approved by the Churches, and its organization was completed at Lake Mohonk, New York, in October, 1921.

Among the many other missionary conferences held in recent years, mention must be made of the Jerusalem Conference of the International Missionary Council, held at Jerusalem from March 24th to April 8th, 1928. This significant conference was attended by about two hundred and fifty representatives. At that time the Constitution of the International Missionary Council was revised to the effect that the Council is hereafter to be composed of the national missionary organizations or Church Councils in the mission fields.

2. *Church Federations.*—There has been an increasingly strong conviction among Evangelical Christians in recent years that the various church groups should federate as churches for the furtherance of God's kingdom in all matters which do not involve transgression upon their own doctrines or the compromise of conscience. This conviction has found concrete expression in the formation of church federations.

The Evangelical Alliance, formed in England in 1846, and the American Evangelical Alliance, formed in New York in 1876 (1873), came as real expressions of the hitherto unexpressed unity in the British and the American churches. These organizations were forerunners of the Federal Council of Churches of Christ in America, formed in 1908; and of the Federal Council of the Free Churches of England, formed in 1917. The Federal Council of Churches of Christ in America is the most powerful and efficient federation of churches with reference to universality of representation, comprehensiveness of work, and the power it has to speak for its constituent bodies. Its chief headquarters are in New York City, with branch offices in Washington, D. C.; Chicago, Ill.; Berne, Switzerland; and Athens, Greece.

German Evangelicals organized the German Evangelical Church Federation in September, 1921, with a constituent membership of twenty-eight national churches, and with the German Association of Moravian Brethren as an affiliated member. The *Reformirte Bund*, which is a branch of this German federation, seeks to preserve the Calvinist tradition as associated with the Heidelberg Catechism. The Methodist, the Baptists, the Evangelical Association, and the Association of Free Evangelical parishes in Germany have organized a federation for the promotion of their common cause.

In 1920 all Cantonal Churches of Switzerland, the Free Churches of the Free Section, the Association of the Diaspora, the Methodist Churches, and a few congregations outside Switzerland, formed themselves into the Swiss Church Federation. This federation sponsored the International Church Congress for Investigating the Situation of Protestantism in Europe, held in Copenhagen in August, 1922. This was the first officially representative gathering of Evangelical Churches in Europe.

A Federation of the Protestant Churches of France was formed in 1907. Final adoption of the Constitution took place at a national gathering in 1909 with the following constituent membership: the National Union of the Evangelical Reformed Churches; the National Union of Reformed Churches; the Evangelical Lutheran Churches; the Evangelical Free Churches; the Evangelical Methodist Churches; the Federation of the Evangelical Baptist Churches; the Reformed and Lutheran Churches of Alsace and Lorraine; and the Society Centrale Evangelique. A similar but much smaller federation of Evangelical and Reformed Churches in Spain was formed in 1923.

The Churches of Scotland, except the Roman Catholic and the Synod of the Free Presbyterian Church, formed a federal union in 1925. Mention should also be made of the Conference on Christian Politics, Economics, and Citizenship, held in England in April, 1924; the Universal Christian Conference on Life and Work at Stockholm, Sweden, in 1925; and the Lausanne World Conference on Faith and Order, held in Switzerland in 1927.

Attention should also be called to the Ecumenical Methodist Conferences of 1901, 1911, and 1921; the Baptist World Alliance which met in 1905, 1911, and 1923; the Lutheran World Conventions of 1923, 1929, and 1935; the American Lutheran Conference, formed in 1930; the International Congregational Council, with sessions in 1891, 1899, 1908, and 1920; the International Congress of Religious Liberals which met in 1900 and in 1927; and the Meetings of the World Alliance of the Reformed Churches Holding the Presbyterian System, with sessions in 1896, 1899, 1904, 1909, 1913, 1921, and 1925. Mention may also be made of such undenominational organizations as the Y.M.C.A.; the Y.W.C.A.; the Christian Endeavor Society; the Student Volunteer Movement; and the like.

3. *Organic Church Unions.*—Efforts to promote organic church

unions have met with culminative success only within certain denominational families, that is, Reformed have united with
Reformed; Lutherans with Lutherans; Presbyterians with Presbyterians; Baptists with Baptists; and Methodists with Methodists.

Two significant unions took place in 1905 among the Reformed
churches of France, namely, the Union of the Reformed Churches,
and the Union of the Reformed Evangelical Churches.

Three significant unions have recently taken place among Lutherans in America, namely, the formation of the Norwegian Lutheran Church of America in 1917; and of the United Lutheran
Church of America in 1918; and of the American Lutheran
Church in 1930.

Two mergers have taken place among Presbyterians in America
in recent years, namely, the merging of a part of the Cumberland Presbyterian Church with the Presbyterian Church in U. S.
A., in 1906; and the merging into the same body of the Welsh
Calvinistic Methodist Church in 1920. Presbyterian participation
in the Church Union of Canada in 1925 has been discussed in
another chapter. Another significant Presbyterian merger took
place in 1929 when the Church of Scotland united with the Free
Church of Scotland. Eight years before this union the participating
bodies had secured from the Imperial Parliament the famous
Declaratory Act, 1921, which acknowledged on the part of Parliament the complete spiritual independence of the church.

In 1931 the National Council of Congregational Churches of the
United States and the General Convention of the Christian Church
merged, and the new body was called the General Council of the
Congregational and Christian Churches.

4. *Steps toward Organic Union.*—Numerous negotiations have
been carried on in recent years with a view to organic church
union. The Anglican and Eastern Orthodox Churches Union was
formed in 1906 for the purpose of promoting church union; and
the Fifth Lambeth Conference, 1908, created an important committee on the subject of re-union and intercommunion. The
Protestant Episcopal Church in America prepared a *Proposed
Concordat* in 1920 as a basis for the restoration of corporate
unity and intercommunion with the Eastern Orthodox and the Old
Catholic Churches. In January, 1921, the Ecumenical Patriarchate
of Constantinople issued an Encyclical Letter "Unto All the
Churches of Christ Wheresoever They Be," with a general invitation to Christian re-union. These negotiations found a fitting cli-

max in the celebration of a Solemn Eucharist in Westminster Abbey, June 29, 1925. The Malines Conversations, held in 1921, in March 1923, in November 1923, in 1925, and in 1926, were arranged by Lord Halifax of the Anglican Communion with Cardinal Mercier, with the knowledge of the Holy See and the semi-official co-operation on the part of the Archbishop of Canterbury; but an *Encyclical Letter on Fostering True Religious Union,* issued by Pope Pius XI on January 6, 1928, put an end to these negotiations. He commanded the *faithful* to have no part in unity movements and ideals which do not lead directly to an entering of the Roman fold. The Lausanne World Conference on Faith and Order, 1927, promoted church unity and union.

Encouraging negotiations are at present carried on between the Methodist Episcopal Churches in America, North and South; and a re-union of these two great bodies seems imminent. Plans for organic union of Presbyterian Churches in America have been discussed and formulated through the American Council on Organic Union, organized in 1918. The Anglican Church has made cautious overtures to Scottish Presbyterianism and to certain Nonconformist Churches in England. Protestant Churches in Australia have carried on negotiations very similar to those which led to the Church Union in Canada in 1925. In the famous Concordat of 1919, the Protestant Episcopal Church in America made proposals for an approach towards organic union with the Congregational Churches.

III. Obstacles to be Overcome.—From the previous discussion it is evident that there has been a marked progress in the movement for church unity. Brief consideration will now be given to some of the difficulties this movement has to encounter.

1. It is difficult to formulate proposals that everybody can understand and that everybody concerned will work for. People are not aroused until they can visualize the movement. They like to know beforehand how the new Church is to be organized; what form it will take in the local community; what the larger program will be; what advantages and disadvantages the new organization will bring; and the like. Advocates of federation have the advantage over advocates of organic union because they can put a more definite and appealing plan before the churches.

2. Church members at large are usually well satisfied with things as they are. Advocates of church union are consequently looked upon by many as disturbers of peace and are placed in the same category as socialists and labor agitators.

3. Advocates of church union have frequently been in danger of antagonizing the popular mind by the stress of small and inferior motives, including that of financial economy. Any crusade for greater church union must be based on great spiritual and divine motives.

4. Organic church union frequently means, figuratively speaking, the moving together of several households, the discarding of certain pieces of furniture, and the consolidation of certain jobs. In other words, church union involves consolidation of institutions and churches and offices, and the consequent loss of salary by a number of teachers, clergymen, and officials. Unwillingness to take this loss is a real obstacle to church union.

5. Differences in traditions and tastes are prominent obstacles to church union. Difference in race, language, territory, economic interests, culture, religious background, political tradition, and political unity account to a large extent for our highly and deeply divided Christendom.

6. Denominations are usually based on real and deep-seated convictions, and denominational loyalty and consciousness demand that the members abide by these convictions. How would the convictions of a Baptist and an Anglican fare, if both were to be united in one organic church?

7. The question of orders presents an obstacle which seems insuperable. Rome does not recognize the validity of orders of Protestant ministers. The Anglican or Episcopalian communion does not recognize the order of Protestant ministers outside the historic episcopate. The other Protestant communions recognize the orders of ministers in all other denominations as valid. And there is very little evidence that any of these three groups will change their views.

8. Finally, there is a fixed gulf between the Evangelicals and the extreme Sacerdotalists which few, if any, see any means of bridging. This was clearly revealed at the Lausanne Conference in 1927. These two groups are so far apart that it seems, sometimes, as if they hold two different religions. The Evangelicals believe that the Gospel is the seat of authority in religion; that salvation is through personal faith in Christ as Savior; and that the Church has no divine authority. The Sacerdotalists believe that the Church, rather than the Bible, is the seat of divine authority; that salvation is through the Church; and that the Church is the voice of God on earth. These widely divergent views naturally involve divergence in all forms of worship and practice.

IV. Conclusion.—A careful study of the record of the Christian Church seems to indicate, *first,* that schisms based on selfishness, prejudice, hate, or error should be done away with; *secondly,* that elimination of the main historic branches of Christendom is neither desirable nor feasable; *thirdly,* that Christians should look upon the Church Tree and its branches and beautiful symmetry with love, admiration, and reverence; *fourthly,* that additional consolidations and unions should take place within the various denominational families.

74. REVIEW QUESTIONS

1. What does the Bible say about church unity?
2. How is this spiritual unity to be expressed in visible form?
3. What attitude shall a Christian take toward the great, historic branches of Christendom? Why?
4. Along what lines may church unity be best promoted? Why?
5. How has work for foreign missions influenced the church unity movement?
6. How do you explain the remarkable progress of church federations?
7. How would you characterize the recent church unions?
8. What steps have been taken recently toward comprehensive church union?
9. What are some of the obstacles to church union?
10. What are some of the advantages of comprehensive church union?
11. Why does the historic episcopate present an obstacle to church union?
12. What are your conclusions with reference to church unity and church union?

TOPICS FOR SPECIAL STUDY

1. The meaning of John 17:11.
2. The world wide revival of nationalism and its bearing on church unity and union.
3. America as a racial, national, and religious melting pot.
4. The desirability of more extensive denominational church unions.
5. The historic episcopate and church union.
6. The gulf between Evangelicals and extreme Sacerdotalists.

A SELECTED BIBLIOGRAPHY FOR CHAPTER XXXIV

1. Slosser: *Christian Unity: Its History and Challenge in All Communions, in All Lands.*
2. Briggs: *Church Unity.*
3. Lynch: *The Christian Unity in America.*
4. Schaff: *Creeds of Christendom.*
5. Schmucker: *The True Unity of Christ's Church.*
6. Sanford: *The History of the Federal Council of Churches, U. S. A.*
7. Lee: *Essays on the Re-union of Christendom.*
8. Mackenzie: *The Confusion of the Churches.*
9. Parker: *The Church of England and the Eastern Patriarchates.*
10. Thomas: *The Five Lambeth Conferences.*
11. Dollinger: *Re-union of the Churches.*
12. Gairdner: *Edinburgh Conference, 1910.*

INDEX

Abbot, Lyman, 520
Abelard, Peter, 179-80
Aberdeen, University of, 312
Abraham, 7
Absolution, 173, 200, 215
Abyssinia, 120, 385, 392
Act in Restraint of Appeals, 321
Act of Submission of Clergy, 321
Act of Supremacy, 321, 322, 325
Act of Uniformity, 325
Actio catholica, 382
Acts, Book of, 37, 43
Adalbert, Archbishop, 168
Addams, Jane, 520
Addyman, John, 597
Adiaphore, 282
Adoptionists, 107
Adoration of martyrs and saints, 113
Adventist movement, 473-74
Agricola, John, 282
Agricola, Michael, 299
Aix-la-Chapelle, Synod of, 149
Albert of Brandenburg, 232
Albertus Magnus, 180
Albigenses, 182
Albright, Jacob, 578
Alcibiades of Apamea, Book of Elchesai, 74
Alcuin, 149
Alexander II, 168
Alexander III, 182
Alexander V, 190, 192
Alexander VI, 415
Alexander of Hales, 180
Alexander the Great, 9, 22
Alexandria, school of, 83
Alliance of Reformed Churches, 577
Alline, Henry, 607
Altar Book of 1811, 397
Ambrose, Bishop of Milan, 125
America, periodical, 465
American Baptist Foreign Missionary Society, 561
American Baptist Home Mission Society, 559
American Baptist Publication Society, 557, 560
American Baptist Union, 562
American Bible Society, 393, 562
American Board, missions, 393, 517, 529
American Broad-church movement, 472
American Catholicism, 459, 466
American Christianity, 475-77
American Education Society, 517
American Episcopate, 505
American Federation of Catholic Societies, 464
American Federation of Lutheran Brotherhoods, 499
American Holiness Movement, 471
American Home Missionary Society, 517
American Lutheran Church, 501
American Lutheran Conference, 491, 501
American Lutheran Home Mission Council, 499
American Lutheran Publicity Bureau, 499

American Lutheran Statistical Association, 499
American Methodist Conference, first, 429
American National Baptist Convention, 561
American Protective Association, 464
American theologians, early, 435
American Tract Society, 517
Ammonius Saccas of Alexandria, 105
Amsdorf, 282
Amurath I, 208
Anabaptism, 311, 328, 331, 332, 359
Anabaptists, 248, 250, 258, 259, 276, 301, 304, 311, 328 329, 331, 332, 333, 358; Catechism, 329; teachings, 328-29; types, 329; controversy, 106-107
Andover-Kansas Band, 518
Andover Theological Seminary, 516-17
Andreae, Jacob, 284
Andreae, Johann Valentine, 362
Andreae, Laurentius, 296-97
Andrew, Bishop, 545
Angels, worship of, 131
Anglican Catholicism, 325
Anglican Church, 318, 325, 368
Anglican Confession, 287-88, 307, 325
Anglican high-churchism, 394-95
Anglican liturgy, 318, 353
Anglicanism, 268, 287-88, 352, 354, 503
Anglo-Catholic Church, 287-88
Anglo-Catholicism, 405
Anglo-Saxon missionaries, 141
Angouleme, 264
Annapolis Convention, 504
Annates, 188
Anselm of Canterbury, 179-80
Ansgar, missionary, 144
Anti-mission agitators, claims, 558
Anti-Missourian Brotherhood, 494, 497
Anti-Romanism, 308
Anti-Trinitarian, 334, 515
Antinomistic controversy, 282
Antioch in Syria, 37, 43-45, 383, 385; Gentile Christianity, 43-49; first congregation, 44
Antonin, Bishop, 386
Antonius, 109
Antonius Pius, persecutions, 85
Apocalyptic-Pentecostal movement, 406
Apocalyptic-Spiritualistic School, 473
Apocrypha, 25; controversy, 394
Apollinaris, 83
Apollonius of Tyana, 82
Apologists, 71, 83
Apology, Augsburg Confession, 249, 277, 284
Apostasy, 19th century, 409
Apostles, 34-35, 40, 48, 63
Apostles' Creed, 78, 89
Apostolate, 35-36, 40, 63
Apostolic Christianity, characteristics, 40-42, 67-69
Apostolic Constitutions, 110, 112
Apostolic Council, 45
Apostolic Delegation, Washington, 463
Apostolic Fathers, writings of, 71
Apostolic Mission House, 464